KU-721-675

Argentina
Handbook

Charlie Nurse

Latin America series editor: Ben Box

Footprint Handbooks

*"A man must carry knowledge with him,
if he would bring home knowledge."*
Samuel Johnson

Footprint Handbooks

®

6 Riverside Court, Lower Bristol Road
Bath BA2 3DZ England
T 01225 469141 F 01225 469461
E mail handbooks@footprint.cix.co.uk

ISBN 1 900949 10 5   ISSN 1369-1406
CIP DATA: A catalogue record for this book is
available from the British Library

In North America, published by

PASSPORT BOOKS
NTC/Contemporary Publishing Group

4255 West Touhy Avenue, Lincolnwood
(Chicago), Illinois 60646-1975, USA
T 847 679 5500 F 847 679 2494
E mail NTCPUB2@AOL.COM

ISBN 0-8442-4946-7
Library of Congress Catalog Card
Number: 97-78491
Passport Books and colophon are registered
trademarks of NTC/Contemporary Publishing
Company

©Footprint Handbooks Limited
May 1998

® Footprint Handbooks and the Footprint mark
are a registered trademark of Footprint
Handbooks Ltd

**Every effort has been made to ensure that
the facts in this Handbook are accurate.
However travellers should still obtain
advice from consulates, airlines etc about
current travel and visa requirements and
conditions before travelling. The editors
and publishers cannot accept responsibilty
for any loss, injury or inconvenience,
however caused.**

**Maps - the black and white text maps are
not intended to have any political
significance.**

Cover design by Newell and Sorrell;
photography by South American Pictures and
John Wright Photography

Production: Design by Mytton Williams;
Typesetting by Jo Morgan, Ann Griffiths
and Alex Nott; Maps by Sebastian Ballard,
Kevin Feeney and Aldous George; Proofread
by Rod Gray.

Printed and bound in Great Britain by
Antony Rowe, Chippenham

Contents

6

4 Information for travellers

5 Rounding up

We try as hard as we can to make each Footprint Handbook as up-to-date and accurate as possible but, of course, things always change. Many people write to us with new information, amendments or simply comments. Please do get in touch. In return we will send you details of our special guidebook offer.

See page 518 for more information.

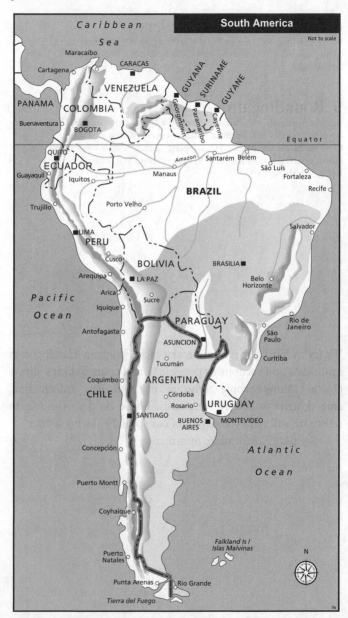

The Editors

Charlie Nurse

After studying and working in Spain, Ecuador and Nicaragua, Charlie Nurse first visited Argentina in 1990. Since then he has returned several times, travelling the length and breadth of the country and becoming, in the process, responsible for the Argentina chapter of the *South American Handbook*.

Ben Box

A doctorate in medieval Spanish and Portuguese studies provided few job prospects for Ben Box, but a fascination for all things Latin. He switched his attention to contemporary Iberian and Latin American affairs in 1980 when he became a freelance writer. While contributing regularly to national newspapers and learned tomes, he became increasingly involved with the *South American Handbook*, becoming editor in 1989. To seek diversion from a household immersed in Latin America, Ben plays village cricket in summer and is discovering more about his corner of Suffolk with the help of the family's new dog.

The Team

For substantial advice and contributions to the text the Editor would like to thank:

Federico Kirbus, author of many travel books on Argentina and a long-time contributor to the *South American Handbook*. Federico researched and wrote the section on offroading as well as several of the boxes; he provided maps and diagrams, and his faxes from Buenos Aires were a constant source of information and inspiration. The text of several chapters benefitted from Federico's corrections to the first draft.

Santiago de la Vega, one of Federico's co-authors, who drew on his extensive knowledge of Argentine wildlife to write the sections on fauna and flora.

Brad Krupsaw and **Gilda Bona**, Buenos Aires correspondents of the *South American Handbook*, researched and wrote boxes on the city, checked the first drafts of the corresponding chapter and provided valuable insights on life in the capital.

Specialist Contributors

Sarah Cameron for the economy; Dereck Foster (*Buenos Aires Herald*) for food and wine; Nigel Gallop for music and dance; John King (University of Warwick) for cinema and literature; Jane Norwich for flora; Gabriel Pérez Barrero (University of Essex) for fine art and sculpture; Philip Horton for horseracing and polo; Peter Pollard for geology and landscape; Chita van der Sande (*Flyer Viajes y Turismo*, Buenos Aires) for *estancias*; Dr David Snashall for Health; Eric Weil (*Buenos Aires Herald*) for sport; Gustavo R Carrizo for the drawings of fauna and flora.

Acknowledgements

Much additional help has been received during the preparation of this edition. All contributions are gratefully acknowledged on page 489.

Argentina

ALTHOUGH ARGENTINA is one of the best known countries in South America, its attractions to the traveller are less familiar than those of most of its neighbours. The worldwide release of Alan Parker's film *'Evita'* with Madonna in the title-role probably reinforced many of the old stereotypes: of beef, tango and football, all being enjoyed by the population of a large European-style city. Great for beef-eating, tango-mad footballers but what about the rest of us?

Buenos Aires, a vibrant, dynamic and exciting city, attracts many thousands of foreign travellers every year. With its museums, fashionable shops and nightlife, it has a feel completely different from that of any other South American capital; neither is it European in character, despite superficial resemblances. When you tire of it, there are launch trips on the Paraná delta and visits to *estancias* while the beautiful colonial city of Colonia del Sacramento in neighbouring Uruguay lies a short boat trip away.

Few countries in the world, however, deserve to be judged by their capital cities and this is particularly true of Argentina. Far away from the capital, west across the pampas, the Andes rise to some of the highest mountain peaks on the American continent. There are ski-resorts, lakes and great trekking country, much of it in a series of national parks along the frontier with Chile. The rivers offer great fishing and watersports such as rafting, little heard of a few years ago, are growing rapidly. Further north, around Salta, you can travel on one of the most spectacular railway lines on the continent. Away from the Andes, in the far northeast is one of the natural wonders of South America, the giant Iguazú falls, set in a region of subtropical rainforest. Patagonia, the great empty southern expanse in the south, attracts visitors to see the sea-mammals which breed along its coasts, and, inland, its glaciers, mountains and lakes.

All of these are, of course, only part of the attraction of any country. Many countries in South America and elsewhere can boast mountains, rivers and forests. Part of what makes Argentina different lies back in Buenos Aires and the other big cities nearby. One of the great things about travelling in Argentina is that Argentines themselves travel; you will usually find yourself travelling with Argentines rather than exclusively with other foreigners. Even if you do not speak Spanish (and we strongly recommend that you learn at least a few words) this alone will often add to your enjoyment. You may even meet some beef eating, football-mad tango artists.

Argentina, the South Atlantic and Antarctica

The Argentine government considers the republic to exist in three regions (see map opposite). First is the South American portion, the frontiers of which are virtually undisputed. Second is the 'Islas del Atlántico Sur' which covers the Falkland Islands/Islas Malvinas, Shag and Black Rocks, South Georgia and the South Sandwich Islands; these are in dispute with Britain which led to a small war in 1982. Third is 'Antártida Argentina', a sector of the Antarctic and some islands, defined in 1943 and extended in 1947; this is under the aegis of the Antarctic Treaty (1959) of which Argentina is one of the original signatories. Sovereign claims in this portion are therefore in abeyance regardless of the overlap with the British Antarctic Territory (1908) and the Territorio Antártico Chileno (1940).

All maps of Argentina promulgated within the country are legally obliged to indicate these three portions of the republic. This book, however, concerns itself with South America only.

In accordance with the practice suggested by the United Nations, this book uses both British and Argentine names for the Falkland Islands/Islas Malvinas.

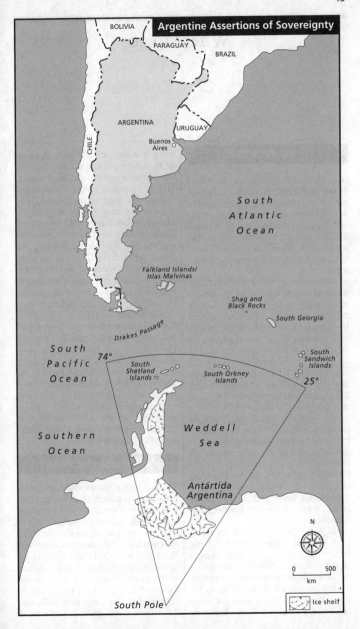

Argentine Assertions of Sovereignty

Where to go

In common with the practice established by the *South American Handbook* this book makes no attempt to be prescriptive. Tastes in travel, as in everything else, differ and Argentina's attractions are so varied that the country has something to offer most visitors. Several destinations, however, stand out for their popularity with travellers.

Many travellers visit South America in search of its wild natural beauty. Any list of attractions in Argentina has to include two great natural sights: the magnificent Iguazú falls, which straddle the frontier with Brazil in the far north east, and the Perito Moreno glacier in Patagonia. The city of Salta in the northwest is a popular destination; apart from the justly famous *Tren a las Nubes* (Railway to the Clouds), it is an ideal base for exploring the mountain valleys of this region. Further south is the Argentine lake district, with its string of beautiful lakes and mountains protected by three major national parks. Bariloche is the most popular base for this region which offers great opportunities for walking, climbing, skiing, fishing and other activities. The sea mammal colonies around Trelew and Puerto Madryn on the Patagonian coast are another major attraction.

Argentina is, however, much richer than this list suggests. Buenos Aires, home of the tango, is one of the great cities of South America. With its European-inspired architecture and atmosphere of *fin de siecle* decadence, it should be on the itinerary of all but the most hardened city-hater. Though other large Argentine cities lack the capital's cultural attractions, they are often much friendlier and offer the observant traveller great insights into the lifestyle of ordinary Argentines.

Less visited alternatives abound. Two areas just opening up to tourism are the Sierras de San Luis, a wild area almost unknown even to Argentine travellers, and the Fitz Roy area, a trekking and climbing paradise at the north end of the great Parque Nacional de los Glaciares in Patagonia. Visit these now if you want to beat the rush. The far northwestern province of Jujuy has wilder and more spectacular scenery than nearby Salta, but is less visited except by day trippers on coach tours. Most of Argentina's National Parks receive few travellers from overseas. Special mention should, perhaps, be made of three little known parks in the north, El Rey, Calilegua and Baritú; though access is difficult, they offer spectacularly varied fauna and flora. Though most areas of the country are rich in birdlife, bird lovers should head northeast to the Argentine Chaco.

The three main factors which determine possible itineraries in Argentina are 1) the time at your disposal; 2) how and where you enter the country; 3) the time of year.

It goes without saying that the more time you have, the more you can see and that if you have the luxury of unlimited time you can visit all parts of the country at leisure. For those with more limited time and money, several routes can be suggested. If your entry point is Buenos Aires, there are two obvious routes; north

Argentina: Mainland

1 Buenos Aires &
the Río de la Plata
2 The Pampas
3 The Central Sierras
4 The West
5 The Northwest
6 The Northeast
7 The Lake District
8 Patagonia
9 Chilean Patagonia
10 Tierra del Fuego

0   400
km

or south. In summer the northeast is very hot and humid, while summer is also the rainy season in the northwest, which may make unpaved roads impassable. In winter the southern areas are cold; the further south you go, the greater the chance that transport will not operate or will be disrupted and that hotels, tours and sights will be closed.

There are many other entry points from neighbouring Bolivia, Chile and Paraguay. The main ones are as follows: in the West by road or air from Santiago (Chile) to Mendoza; in the Northwest by road from Villazón (Bolivia) to Jujuy and Salta; in the Northeast by road from Asunción (Paraguay) to Resistencia, from Encarnación (Paraguay) to Posadas and from Foz do Iguazú (Brazil) to Puerto Iguazú; in the Lake District by boat and bus from Puerto Montt (Chile) to Bariloche; in Patagonia by road from Puerto Natales (Chile) to Calafate or by road and ferry crossings from Tierra del Fuego to Río Gallegos and Calafate. There are also three road crossings from Uruguay via bridges over the Río Uruguay as well several ferry crossings, the most important of which are from Montevideo and Colonia de Sacramento to Buenos Aires. Entering via any of these will affect your choice of routes within the country.

The following suggestions are intended merely to give a rough idea of how long you could spend in a particular region. They do not allow for the detailed exploration which some travellers will prefer.

1.   Buenos Aires and the Río de la Plata From a few days to 2 weeks, allowing for excursions to nearby areas including the Uruguayan city of Colonia de Sacramento and depending on how much you enjoy the city's nightlife and other attractions.

2.   The Pampas A few days unless you are particularly fond of the coastal resorts (warmer months only) or *estancias*.

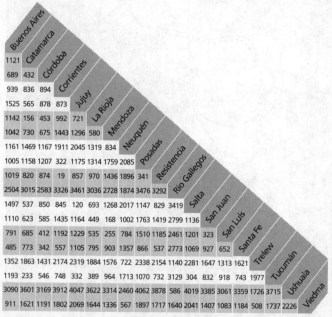

	Buenos Aires	Catamarca	Córdoba	Corrientes	Jujuy	La Rioja	Mendoza	Neuquén	Posadas	Resistencia	Río Gallegos	Salta	San Juan	San Luis	Santa Fe	Trelew	Tucumán	Ushuaia
Catamarca	1121																	
Córdoba	689	432																
Corrientes	939	836	894															
Jujuy	1525	565	878	873														
La Rioja	1142	156	453	992	721													
Mendoza	1042	730	675	1443	1296	580												
Neuquén	1161	1469	1167	1911	2045	1319	834											
Posadas	1005	1158	1207	322	1175	1314	1759	2085										
Resistencia	1019	820	874	19	857	970	1436	1896	341									
Río Gallegos	2504	3015	2583	3326	3461	3036	2728	1874	3476	3292								
Salta	1497	537	850	845	120	693	1268	2017	1147	829	3419							
San Juan	1110	623	585	1435	1164	449	168	1002	1763	1419	2799	1136						
San Luis	791	685	412	1192	1229	535	255	784	1510	1185	2461	1201	323					
Santa Fe	485	773	342	557	1105	795	903	1357	866	537	2773	1069	927	652				
Trelew	1352	1863	1431	2174	2319	1884	1576	722	2338	2154	1140	2281	1647	1313	1621			
Tucumán	1193	233	546	748	332	389	964	1713	1070	732	3129	304	832	918	743	1977		
Ushuaia	3090	3601	3169	3912	4047	3622	3314	2460	4062	3878	586	4019	3385	3061	3359	1726	3715	
Viedma	911	1621	1191	1802	2069	1644	1336	567	1897	1717	1640	2041	1407	1083	1184	508	1737	2226

Argentina: distance chart (km)

3. The Central Sierras Córdoba can be seen in 1-2 days, while the nearby Sierras can be visited as day-trips from Córdoba and San Luis or on longer visits.

4. The West Allow 2 days for Mendoza with its vineyards. The cities of San Juan and La Rioja can be explored in half a day, but visits to the more distant valleys in these provinces will probably require more than a day-trip. To these add as many days as required for skiing, climbing and other activities, especially around Malargüe.

5. The Northwest The city of Salta can be explored in a day, but add several days for excursions. Careful planning and advance booking are advised if you wish to travel on the *Tren a las Nubes*. Those with more time could spend up to 10 days exploring the remote parts of Jujuy or a few days in Catamarca.

6. The Northeast Suggesting time schedules becomes more difficult here. Travellers should award the Iguazú falls at least 2 days of their lives and side-trips can be made into Brazil and Paraguay. San Ignacio Miní is a good base for a few relaxing days walking. Further south in this region, the cities attract few travellers, but there are several good options for 2-day stopovers, including Santa Fe and the neighbouring city of Paraná. Day-trips and longer excursions to the Chaco can be arranged from Resistencia and Formosa.

7. The Lake District Bariloche is the main centre for excursions and boat trips and many travellers pass two or 3 days here. Those with more time may wish to base themselves elsewhere, perhaps on one of the smaller lakes, especially if camping.

8. Patagonia Planning a trip in Patagonia requires careful planning as distances are large and transport needs to be booked in advance especially in high summer. The main attractions are: Puerto Madryn, with the nearby Valdés Peninsula (allow 2 days) and the great Parque Nacional Los Glaciares: the Perito Moreno glacier, in the park, is usually visited on a day trip from Calafate and, although there is little else to do in Calafate, a further 3 or 4 days could be added for exploring the Fitz Roy region at the north end of the park.

9. Chilean Patagonia The Parque Nacional Torres del Paine is a must. This requires at least an overnight stay, but to make the most of the hiking opportunities in this stunning region allow 5-6 days. A further 2 days could be added for visiting Punta Arenas.

10. Tierra del Fuego Due to heavy demand in the high season journeys to and from Tierra del Fuego require careful planning and advance booking. The main centre is Ushuaia; with excursions and boat trips allow 2-3 days.

TOURISM IN ARGENTINA

Argentina's climatic and geographical diversity is so great that most tourist activities are available somewhere in the country. Most outdoor activities are covered in detail below. Travellers interested in the arts will find much to attract them in the cultural life of Buenos Aires. For wine lovers Mendoza provides opportunities to visit vineyards and *bodegas*; similar tours are also available elswhere in the Andean foothills, notably in San Juan and Cafayate. Those interested in wildlife will be attracted by Argentina's network of national parks.

Although Argentina is no longer cheap to visit, many of these types of tourism can be enjoyed by budget travellers, especially if they avoid the most popular destinations and travel off-season.

ESTANCIA TOURISM

The word *estancia* has a wide range of meanings, covering cattle ranches, farms, plantations, villas or country houses. In recent years many *estancias* have opened their gates to guests. Although in most cases this is merely a way of earning extra income, on some *estancias* it is fast becoming their main activity; some have added swimming pools, tennis courts and large restaurants. Visiting an *estancia*, whether for an afternoon or for several days, offers not only the opportunity to relax in the countryside, but also insights into important aspects of the culture and economy of Argentina.

Though *estancias* are found throughout rural Argentina, they vary enormously in climate, landscape and activities. In the province of Buenos Aires you will find *estancias* covering thousands of hectares of flat grassland with large herds of cattle and windpumps to extract water; in Patagonia there are giant sheep *estancias* overlooking glaciers, mountains and lakes; in Mendoza, San Juan and La Rioja *estancias* have vineyards and in the northeast, in the swamps between the Ríos Uruguay and Paraná, you will find *estancias* where the horses readily swim through the swamps, with or without a rider. Many *estancias* concentrate more on arable farming, growing cereals, rice, fruit and other crops.

The *estancia* itself, the owner's house with its surrounding buildings, also varies in style: many older *estancias* are built in so-called "colonial style", introduced by settlers from Europe in the late 19th century. Some of the larger ones have their own little school for the workers' children and a chapel for mass and local weddings. Some, especially in Patagonia, have their own landing strip for small planes, reducing the isolation of *estancias* which may be well over 100 km apart.

Argentine landowners used to live in the large cities, especially in Buenos Aires, leaving a *capataz* (foreman) to oversee their *estancia*, which they visited for holidays or at weekends or to entertain friends. Nowadays many *dueños* (owners) live on the *estancia*, doing the job of the *capataz*, while their wives stay in town for much of the year to look after the children's education. Perhaps one of the most interesting features of a stay at an *estancia* is eating with the *dueño* and listening to his stories of daily life.

Estancia workers, usually referred to as *gauchos*, can still be seen on horseback, whether on the *estancia* itself or along the roads and in neighbouring villages. Typical gaucho clothing today includes *bombachas* (baggy trousers which are very comfortable for spending hours on horseback), a wide leather belt with silver clasps and a knife, a *poncho*, a *pañuelo* or neckerchief, a beret and on the feet *alpargatas* (espadrilles). Regional variations include the flat-topped felt hat worn on sunny days.

Not surprisingly a visit to an *estancia* offers great opportunities for riding horses. Argentines have their own style of horseriding, quite distinct from the European style which is known as *estilo inglés*: using one hand only, the rider is meant to be as comfortable as possible for the long distances involved. The other activities available on *estancias* vary, often depending on the season: birdwatching, canoeing, fishing and walking are very common, while an *asado* (barbeque) is part of any visit. Often there are also opportunities to watch the work of the *estancia*.

Combining a visit to an *estancia* with some of the other highlights of Argentina is not difficult. The *Estancia Mercedes*, situated in the subtropical forests of Misiones, for example, can be visited fairly easily by travellers to the Iguazú falls. At the other extreme is the *Estancia Monte Dinero*, south of Río Gallegos, which can be combined with a trip to see the colony of Magellanic penguins at Cabo Vírgenes. Further details of these, and other *estancias* can be found in the text. Accommodation prices given are usually full board per person in a shared room. Some *estancias* do not have private bathrooms. Advanced booking is strongly advised, either by contacting the *estancia* itself or through travel agencies which specialize in this area.

FISHING

The three main areas for fishing are the Northern Zone, around Junín de los Andes, extending south to Bariloche; the Central Zone around Esquel; the Southern Zone around Río Gallegos in Patagonia and Río Grande in Tierra del Fuego. The first two of these areas are in the Lake District. In the Northern Zone some of the best fishing can be found in the lakes of the Parque Nacional Lanín, notably Meliquina, Falkner, Villarino, Nuevo, Lacar, Lolog, Curruhué, Chico, Huechulafquen, Paimún, Epulafquen and Tromen. The Río Limay has good trout fishing, as do the rivers further north, the Quilquihue, Malle, Chimehuín, Collón-Curá, Hermoso, Meliquina and Caleufú. All these rivers are 'catch and release'. The Central Zone includes Lagos Gutiérrez and Mascardi, and, further south, Lago Futalaufquen in the Parque Nacional Los Alerces. In the far south Lago Argentino is good for trout and salmon and there is good sea trout fishing along the southern Patagonian coast.

Fishing can also be found in other parts of the country and is offered by many *estancias*. *Pejerrey*, *corvina* and *pescadilla* can be found in large quantities along the coast of Buenos Aires province. Many of the reservoirs of the Central Sierras, the West and Northwest are well stocked.

The season runs from early November to the end of March, but the best time is at the beginning of the season. To fish anywhere in Argentina you need a permit, which costs US$10 per day, US$30 per week, US$100 per year. In the Northern Zone forestry commission inspectors are very diligent. For tours arranged from the UK, contact Sport Elite (JA Valdes-Scott), Woodwalls House, Corscombe, Dorchester, Dorset, DT2 0NT.

BIRDWATCHING

An increasing number of foreign visitors are birdwatchers. At least 980 of the 2,926 species of birds registered in South America exist in Argentina, in places with easy access. Enthusiasts head for Península Valdés, Patagonia, the subtropical forests in the northwest, or the Chaco savannah in the northeast. Specialist tours led by expert guides can be arranged. For further details contact the Asociación Ornitológica del Plata (address under **Buenos Aires**).

ADVENTURE TOURISM

Though Argentina may lag behind Chile in this respect, adventure tourism is growing rapidly and an increasing number of agencies specialize in this area. The main adventure tourism regions are well away from the capital and include Mendoza, Salta and the Lake District, as well as the Fitz Roy Area in Patagonia. In the Lake District San Martín de los Andes is rapidly growing as an adventure tourism centre, while the small town of Malargüe in southern Mendoza, which somewhat grandly styles itself the 'national capital of adventure tourism', is a fairly good base, though there are surprisingly few agencies.

CLIMBING

The Andes offer great climbing opportunities. Among the most popular peaks are Aconcagua, in Mendoza province (see under The West), Pissis in Catamarca (see under The Northwest) and Lanín and Tronador (see under The Lake District). The northern part of the Parque Nacional Los Glaciares around Fitz Roy (see under Patagonia) offers some very difficult climbing. There are climbing clubs (known as *Clubs Andino*) in Bariloche, Esquel, Junín de los Andes, Mendoza, Ushuaia and a number of other cities. Further details and equipment hire are given in the text.

WATERSPORTS

Surfing, windsurfing and waterskiing are practised along the Atlantic coast south of Buenos Aires. White water rafting and other watersports are growing in popularity. Rafting is found in Mendoza province, both near the provincial capital and further south near San Rafael and Malargüe, as well as in the Lanín, Nahuel Huapi and Los Alerces National Parks in the Lake District.

SKIING

The skiing season runs from May to the end of October, but dates vary between resorts. Las Leñas, south of Mendoza, is a major international ski resort with varied accommodation. There are three other major resorts, all of them in the Lake District, Cerro Catedral and Cerro Otto, both near Bariloche, and Chapelco near San Martín de los Andes. Smaller resorts include Los Penitentes, Vallecitos and Manantiales, all near Mendoza, and Caviahue, Cerro Bayo and La Hoya, all in the Lake District. In the far south there are small resorts near Río Turbio in Patagonia and near Ushuaia in Tierra del Fuego. Smaller resorts are cheaper but have fewer facilities. Details of all of these resorts are given in the text.

TREKKING

The best areas for trekking are in the west of the country: in the West around Mendoza and further south near Malargüe, as well further north around San Juan and La Rioja; in the Lake District in the Lanín, Nahuel Huapi and Los Alerces National Parks; in the valleys around Salta in the Northwest; and in the Fitz Roy area of the Glaciares National Park in Patagonia.

On the basis of treks made with Sr Ramón Ossa of Barreal, Sr Herbert Levi of Buenos Aires recommends the following additions to the organizer's list of recommendations for equipment on any Andean trip: plastic drinking mugs, metal containers to prevent tubes of toothpaste etc emptying themselves in mule packs, long underpants to protect against chafing, woollen cap, insect repellent, sunburn cream, laxatives, soap, nylon groundsheet for sleeping bag (depending on weather), tent for privacy, and fishing gear for those who prefer catching their own meals (No 3 spoons are best for Andean streams).

OFFROADING

Large areas of Argentina are ideal for offroading. Across wide expanses of flat land or gently rolling hills there are no woods to obstruct you, nor snow or ice; the vegetation is sparse and there are few animals and hardly any people. Patagonia in particular, with its endless steppes interrupted only by rivers, gorges and gullies, is recommended but some of the Andean valleys of the West and Northwest are worth exploring in this way. Three of the rougher roads in the Andes are especially recommended: the route from San Antonio de los Andes to Catamarca via Antofagasta de la Sierra; the route from Catamarca to Chile via Paso San Francisco and the Laguna Brava area in La Rioja.

Though 4WD vehicles are difficult to hire in Buenos Aires, they can be hired from hire companies such as Localiza and Hertz in some major cities of the interior, notably Mendoza, Tucumán, Bariloche and Ushuaia, as well as from Marina Servicios in Salta. Prices are high, from US$2,000 for 15 days, US$3,500 for 1 month, plus fuel, but if you divide this between 4 adults it becomes more reasonable. Buy road maps in advance from the **Automóvil Club Argentino** (ACA) in Buenos Aires. Before setting out you should obtain as much information as possible; employees in the provincial tourist information offices are unlikely to be able to answer your questions, so it is more important to ask them for names of local guides (*baqueanos*). It is important to avoid the coldest and the wettest months of the year; spring (October and November) and autumn (April and May) are the best seasons.

How to go

WHEN TO GO

Ideal visiting seasons depend on the geographical location and climate. The Northeast is best visited in winter when it is cooler and drier. Winter is also a good time to visit the Northwest, but routes to Chile across the Andes may be closed by snow at this time and spring and autumn may be better: summer rains, especially in Jujuy, can make roads impassable. Spring and autumn are best for Buenos Aires; summer is unpleasantly hot and humid and the city is half-closed in late December and early January as many people escape on holiday. Spring and autumn are the best seasons for visiting the Lake District, as many services are closed off season. Ideally Patagonia should be visited in December or February/March, avoiding the winter months when the weather is cold and many services are closed. January is best avoided if you can as this is the Argentine summer holiday period and some destinations, notably in Patagonia, are very crowded. There are also school

holidays in July and some facilities such as youth hostels may be heavily booked in this period. Note that Bariloche is a very popular destination for school groups in July and December/early January.

HOW TO GET THERE

There are international flights from Europe, North America, Australasia, South Africa and from other parts of Latin America; for details see **Information for Travellers**. Most international flights land at Ezeiza international airport in Buenos Aires.

There are also international bus services from Brazil, Bolivia, Chile, Paraguay, Peru and Uruguay. Boat services also operate across the Río de la Plata from Uruguay to Buenos Aires. Tourists can take into the country their own cars and vehicles hired in neighbouring countries for up to 8 months under international documentation. Officially a written undertaking is required that the car will be exported after a given period, but in practice you are usually only required to show the title document. No specific papers are usually required to take a Brazilian registered car into Argentina.

Few nationalities require more than a valid passport to enter the country. Permission to stay up to 90 days is usually given. Full details of entry requirements are given in **Information for travellers**.

PRACTICALITIES

INFORMATION

Tourist information is provided by provincial tourist offices which are situated in provincial capitals. Most other towns are served by municipal tourist offices, often located in the *municipalidad* (town hall). All provinces maintain offices (*casas de turismo*) in Buenos Aires, where there are also national and municipal tourist

Changing phone numbers

In 1997/1998 changes will be made to all phone numbers in Argentina. An initial '4' will be added to all numbers. Thus in Buenos Aires 820-5656 will become 4820-5656. Phone codes will also be altered by adding an initial '1' for Buenos Aires, and initial '2' for the South of the country and an initial '3' for the North. Thus the code for Buenos Aires will change from 01 to 011, for La Plata from 021 to 0221 and for Córdoba from 051 to 0351. Confusingly for travellers and residents alike, these changes will be phased in gradually.

offices. Leaflets and maps are readily available, though the quality of these is variable.

MONEY

The Argentine currency, the *peso*, is equal in value to the US dollar and dollars are readily accepted in cities and major tourist destinations. Travellers cheques are often difficult to change especially in small towns and at weekends. ATMs are available in Buenos Aires and a few other cities. There is no point in taking your spending money in any currency other than dollars. Some provinces issue bonds which circulate as currency within the province but are not accepted outside. For further details see **Information for travellers**.

COMMUNICATIONS

The official language is Spanish, though Quechua and other languages are used by indigenous peoples especially in rural areas in the north. Although English is understood and often spoken in tourist offices, banks etc especially in major cities and you may meet people who speak German, French or Italian, you should try to learn some Spanish before setting out; as in most countries people tend to respect you more if you make the effort.

International communications by post, phone and fax are generally good especially from major cities and communication via the Internet is expanding.

ACCOMMODATION AND RESTAURANTS

Good hotels can be found in most parts of the country and, as Argentines travel a lot within their own country, there is no shortage of places to stay outside the cities and resorts. In some places, such as beach resorts, a lot of the accommodation caters for families. Cheap accommodation can be difficult to find, especially in Patagonia and Tierra del Fuego, but you can often negotiate a discount off season especially if staying for several nights. Cheaper dormitory-style accommodation is becoming more widely available, especially in tourist areas. There is a good network of campsites and a more variable range of youth hostels.

Though standards of hygiene in restaurants vary, eating out is not usually beset with the kind of health hazards common in some parts of South America. Beef and pasta are staples, but salads are more widely available than in the past and there is a small but increasing number of vegetarian restaurants.

Lunch, often the main meal of the day, is eaten between 1230 and 1430. Around 1700, many people go to a *confitería* for tea, sandwiches and cakes. Dinner often begins at 2200 or 2230; it is, in the main, a repetition of lunch. Eating out is expensive: the cheapest option is to have the set lunch as a main meal of the day and then find cheap, wholesome snacks for breakfast and supper. Budget travellers should note that especially in Buenos Aires a number of cheaper restaurants are advertised as *tenedor libre* – eat all you want for a fixed price. Those wishing to prepare their own food will find supermarkets fairly cheap for basics.

GETTING AROUND

Internal air services are good. Aerolíneas Argentinas, the national airline, and/or Austral, its domestic subsidiary, offer services between Buenos Aires and many

Route 40

Route 40 is to Argentina what the Trans-Alaskan Highway is to North America or the (now largely disused) Trans-Amazon Highway to Brazil. Route 40 is a trunk road which runs along the eastern edge of the Andes, virtually from the frontier with Bolivia in the north almost to Tierra del Fuego in the south.

Almost 5,000 km long, one third paved, the rest *ripio* or dirt, it runs through practically every type of climate from boiling hot to freezing cold and through all kinds of surroundings, ancient and modern, indigenous societies and modern cities. At the Abra del Acay (4,895m) it even climbs to an altitude higher than Mont Blanc. And, on top of this, it provides access to several national parks and other wonders such as Mount Aconcagua and the great glaciers of the southern lakes.

In recent years the idea of driving along this magnificent route has become a great attraction to Argentines. Now an increasing number of foreigners is beginning to head towards it, whether by ordinary car or by a vehicle with 4WD, for which Route 40 is ideal. 5,000 km, which becomes 10,000 if you add on the distance to get there at each end, obviously demands adequate time. Allow yourself time and then start to consider the idea once you are in Argentina.

Federico Kirbus

destinations, as does the private airline LAPA which is often cheaper. Regional airlines, operating smaller aircraft, offer flights between regional centres. The military airline, LADE (Líneas Aereas del Estado), serves many destinations in the south; though their flights are often heavily booked ahead, they are cheaper than other airlines. It is important to reconfirm all bookings and check for rescheduled times as all flights are subject to change and cancellation at short notice.

Argentina is served by about 215,578 km of road, but only 29% are paved and a further 17% improved. The 30,059 km (1992) of railway line, owned mostly by British companies until they were taken over by the State in 1948, used to carry less than 10% of passengers and freight, until privatization in the early 1990s caused an even greater reduction in rail's share of national transportation. There are now very few trains outside the Buenos Aires area but the country is served by an extensive network of bus services. Long-distance buses usually offer coffee and juice and some services offer snacks and/or meals as well as video. There are often different types of interurban buses; those offering a direct service are usually more expensive but much quicker than those advertised as *servicio común* which stop frequently. Local services are often more interesting, even if perhaps less reliable. There are often special fare reductions, especially off season. For travelling by car, motorcycle and bicycle see under **Information for travellers**.

NB To prevent the spread of pests no fresh fruit, vegetables or cold meats may be taken into the provinces of Mendoza, San Juan, Río Negro, San Luis or Neuquén.

HEALTH

Although Argentina is generally a healthy country to visit, health is a key consideration for anyone travelling overseas. There are general rules to follow when travelling in Latin America; these should help you stay as healthy as at home. They are dealt with in full detail in **Health in Latin America** on page 493.

STAYING HEALTHY IN ARGENTINA

Make sure the medical insurance you have is adequate. Smallpox vaccination is no longer required to enter the country. If intending to visit the low-lying tropical areas, it is advisable to take precautions against malaria. Chagas' disease (see

---

Street names

Argentine street names, in common with those in most countries, are often named after historical characters, events and dates. To foreigners, unaware of their significance, this practice can be confusing.

Independence is the major historical event marked in this way. San Martín's name is found on the main streets of most Argentine towns, closely followed by Belgrano. Other independence figures remembered include Bernardino Rivadavia and, in Salta, the local leader Martín Güemes. 25 May, anniversary of the establishment of the revolutionary junta in 1810, is recorded with an important street in Buenos Aires. The declaration of independence by the Tucumán Congress on 9 July 1816 is marked by the capital's widest avenue. Second to independence is perhaps the fall of the dictator Rosas, widely marked with the date 3 de Febrero, marking his defeat at the Battle of Caseros (1852). Urquiza's rising against Rosas, is commemorated in the main square of Paraná, capital of his home province, by the date 1 de Mayo.

Not surprisingly, most 19th century presidents are remembered in street names, the most common, apart from Urquiza, being Sarmiento and Mitre. This honour has been accorded to few of their 20th century successors. Roque Sáenz Peña, under whom universal male suffrage was granted, is recalled in Buenos Aires and elsewhere, as is his successor, the Radical Hipolito Yrigoyen. Surprisingly few street names remember Perón or Evita or the dates in their careers: the great demonstration on 17 October which rescued Perón from gaol and launched his bid for the presidency is however marked by a street in San Luis, one of the staunchest Peronist provinces.

Health in Latin America) is found in the Northwest. Cholera presents no problem except in some remote villages on the Bermejo and Pilcomayo rivers in the tropical lowlands of the Salta and Jujuy provinces, where the Mataco and Toba tribes have been affected by the disease. If travelling through this region, use bottled water and take your own food.

NB In Patagonia, in 1997, a disease known locally as "hantavirus" was affecting many areas and caused major disruption to tourism. It is spread by rats and campers are most at risk. Seek local advice because the virus is fatal.

In some provinces, like Neuquén and Salta, medical assistance, including operations, X-ray and medication, is free in provincial hospitals, even for foreigners. Sometimes, though, a charge is made pay for materials. All private clinics, on the other hand, charge. Medicines are more expensive than in Europe (eg US$8.20 for Paracetamol drops for children).

FOOD AND DRINK RISKS

The commonest affliction to visitors in most of South America is travellers' diarrhoea. Although this is less of a problem in Argentina than elsewhere there are certain rules to follow (see **Health in Latin America**). Certain shellfish from the Atlantic coast are affected once or twice a year by red tide '(*Marea roja*), at which time the public is warned not to eat them. Buy seafood, if self-catering, from fishmongers with fridges or freezers. To be certain, soak fish for 30 minutes in water with a little vinegar.

ALTITUDE AND CLIMATE

Altitude sickness (*soroche*) is a particular problem in the Northwest. It by no means affects everyone, but to counter its effects you should slow down, avoid heavy meals and excess alcohol. The local remedy is coca leaves either chewed gently over a long period or consumed as a herbal tea (*te de coca* or *maté de coca*): the use of coca is legal, its trade is not. The Northeast can be very hot and humid: keep up your fluid intake. In the south take plenty of sunscreen to prevent burning owing to the thinning of the ozone layer. If travelling at altitude or in the south remember to take plenty of warm clothing.

RETURNING HOME

Report any symptoms to your doctor and say exactly where you have been.

Horizons

THE LAND

Argentina is the second largest country in South America in area, extending across the continent some 1,580 km from east to west and 3,460 km from north to south. Its northernmost point is at latitude 22°S, ie just within the tropics; at Tierra del Fuego and Isla de los Estados it extends south of 54°S, the latitude of Scotland or Labrador. The coast of this territory, extending over 2,000 km, runs wholly along the Atlantic apart from the north coast of the Beagle Channel which links the Atlantic and the Pacific. The western frontier with Chile follows the crest of the Andes, but below 46°S, the drainage is complex and border disputes have arisen ever since the Treaty of 1881 between the two countries established the principle that the frontier should follow the watershed.

GEOLOGY AND LANDSCAPE

Together with Brazil, Paraguay and Uruguay, Argentina is the visible part of the South American Plate which has been moving for the past 125 million years away from its former union with Africa. The submerged part of this plate forms a broad continental shelf under the Atlantic Ocean; in the south this extends over 1,000 km east and includes the Falkland Islands/Islas Malvinas. Since the 'break' between the plates, there have been numerous invasions and withdrawals of the sea over this part of the South American continent, but the Andean mountain building from the end of the Cretaceous (65 million years ago) to the present day dominates the surface geology. Of the many climatic fluctuations, the Pleistocene Ice Age up to 10000 BC has done most to mould the current landscape. At its maximum, ice covered all the land over 2,000m and most of Patagonia. In the mountains, ice created virtually all the present day lakes and moraine deposits can be found everywhere. However, the special feature of the heartland of Argentina is the fine soil of the Pampas, the result of ice and water erosion and the unique wind systems of the southern cone of the continent.

The Northwest

Northern and western Argentina are dominated by the satellite ranges of the Andes. Between the mountains of the far northwest is the *puna*, a high plateau rising to 3,400-4,000m, on which are situated saltflats or *salares*, some of which are of interest for their wildlife. East of this is the *pre-puna*, the gorges and slopes ranging in altitude from 1,700m to 3,400m which connect the *puna* with the plains. On the fringe of the Andes are a string of important settlements, including Salta, Tucumán and Mendoza. Though the climate of this region is hot and dry, there is sufficient water to support maize and pasture and a thriving wine industry, mostly relying on irrigation. East of the Andes lie several ranges of hills, the most important of which are the Sierras de Córdoba and the Sierras de San Luis. These are mostly of ancient Pre-Cambrian rocks.

The Paraná Basin

The vast Paraná basin stretches from the borders with Brazil and Paraguay to the Atlantic at Buenos Aires. In the northeast it mainly consists of geologically recent deposits. The easternmost part of this basin, between the Ríos Paraná and Uruguay, is the wettest part of the country. Known as Mesopotamia and consisting of the provinces of Entre Ríos, Corrientes and Misiones, it is structurally part of the Brazilian plateau of old crystalline rocks, the 'heart' of the South American Plate. Here there are undulating grassy hills and marshy or forested lowlands, among them the Esteros del Iberá, an extensive area of flooded forest similar to the Pantanal in Brazil. The horizontal strata of the rocks in this area is dramatically evident in the river gorges to the north and the spectacular Iguazú falls shared with Brazil.

The Chaco

Northwest of Mesopotamia and stretching from the Paraná and Paraguay rivers west to the Andean foothills and north into Paraguay and Bolivia, lies the Gran Chaco, a vast plain which covers the provinces of Formosa, Chaco and Santiago del Estero, as well as parts of Entre Ríos and Corrientes. It is crossed from west to east by three rivers, the Teuco-Bermejo, the Salado and the Pilcomayo. Annual rainfall ranges from 400 mm in the western or Dry Chaco, a semi-desert mainly used for cattle ranching, to 800-1,200 mm in the eastern or Wet Chaco, where periodic floods alternate with long periods of drought.

The Pampas

South of 33°S, the latitude of Mendoza and Rosario, is a great flat plain, known as the Pampas. Extending almost 1,000 km from north to south and a similar distance from east to west, the Pampas cover some 650,000 sq km, including most of Buenos Aires province, southern Córdoba, Santa Fe and Entre Ríos, northwestern La Pampa and a small part of San Luís. This area is crossed by meandering rivers and streams and there are many lakes, lagoons and marshes. Geologically the Pampas are similar to the Chaco, basic crystalline and granite rocks almost completely overlain with recent deposits, often hundreds of metres thick. Prevailing winds from the southeast and southwest help to create the fine loess type soils which make this one of the richest farming areas in the world, ideal for grasslands and cattle ranching. Being comparatively close to the ocean, extremes of temperature are rare, another favourable feature.

A distinction is often made between the 'wet' *Pampa* and the 'dry' *Pampa*. The former, inland from Rosario and Buenos Aires is the centre of wheat, maize and other cereal production and the latter, west of 64°W, is where cattle ranching predominates.

The Patagonian Steppe

Patagonia extends from the Río Colorado (39°S) south to the Magellan Straits and covers some 780,000 sq km. Most of this area consists of a series of tablelands and terraces which drop in altitude from west to east. The basic rocks are ancient, some classified as Pre-Cambrian, but the surface has been subjected to endless erosion. Rainfall is lighter and the winds stronger than in the Pampas frequently stripping the surface of cover and filling the air with dust. Only where rivers have scored deep valleys in the rock base can soil accumulate, allowing more than extensive sheep farming.

From the Straits of Magellan north to Lago Argentino (46°N) and beyond, a geological depression separates the edge of the South American Plate from the Andes. Most of Patagonia was under ice during the Quaternary Ice Age, and has been rising since the ice receded. This area was presumably the last to be uncovered. However, considerable volcanic activity associated with the uplift of the Andes has taken place along the depression which is transversely divided into basins by lava flows. Alluvial and glacial deposits have created relatively fertile soils in some areas, useful for sheep and producing attractive wooded landscapes in the lake regions in contrast to the general desolation of Patagonia.

The Andes

Geographically the Isla de los Estados forms the southernmost extent of the Andes, which then swing north to become the border between Chile and Argentina just north of the Paine mountains. The 350 km section north of Paine is one of the most dramatic stretches of the Andes. The crest lies under the Southern Patagonian Ice-cap, with glaciers reaching down to the valleys on both the Argentine and Chilean sides. On the Argentine side this has created the spectacular range of glaciers found in the *Parque Nacional Los Glaciares*, the most famous of which, the Perito Moreno Glacier, is one of the highlights for many travellers to Argentina. The northern end of this section is Cerro Fitz Roy, which, along with the Torres del Paine (in Chile) at the southern end, is among the most spectacular hiking and climbing centres in South America.

Further north between 46°S and 47°S there is another icecap, the North Patagonian Icecap, centred on Monte San Valentín on the Chilean side of the frontier. North of this lie 1,500 km of mountain ranges rarely exceeding 4,000m; on the east side of these are a series of attractive lakes, formed by a mixture of glacial and volcanic activity. The high section of the Andes begins at 35°S and includes Aconcagua, 6,960m, the highest peak outside the Himalayas. For a further 1,000 km northwards, the ranges continue to the border with Bolivia with many peaks over 6,000m, the Argentine side becoming progressively drier and more inhospitable.

RIVERS

The most important river system in the country is the Río de la Plata; fed by the Paraná and Uruguay rivers. With their major tributaries, the Bermejo-Teuco, the Pilcomayo, the Paraguay and the Salado del Norte, the Ríos Paraná and Uruguay, drain the northeast and northwest of the country as well as Uruguay, Paraguay and large parts of southern Brazil. Western Argentina is drained by the Ríos Mendoza and San Juan, which form the Desaguadero, which flows into a series of lakes in the Pampas and thence via the Colorado into the Atlantic south of Bahía Blanca. The Río Negro, formed by the Ríos Neuquén and Limay, drains most of the Lake District, flowing into the Atlantic at Viedma. Further south the Chubut flows eastwards to reach the sea near Trelew.

CLIMATE

Climate ranges from sub-tropical in the north east to cold temperate in Tierra del Fuego, but is temperate and quite healthy for much of the year in the densely populated central zone. Between December and the end of February Buenos Aires can be oppressively hot and humid. The Andes have a dramatic effect on the climate of the south: although on the Chilean side of the mountains there is adequate rainfall from Santiago southwards, very little of this moisture reaches the Argentine side. Furthermore, the prevailing winds in Patagonia are southeast to northwest from the South Atlantic. The result is a temperate climate with some mist and fog near the coast, but not much rain. Further inland, the westerlies, having deposited their moisture on the Andes, add strength to the southerly airstream, creating the strong dry wind (*El Pampero*) characteristic of the Pampas. Only when these systems meet humid maritime air in the northeast of the country does rainfall significantly increase, often through violent thunderstorms, with the heaviest precipitation in Mesopotamia where August and September are particularly wet.

The highest temperatures are found in the northeast where the distance from the sea and the continuous daytime sunshine produce the only frequently recorded air temperatures over 45°C anywhere in South America. The northwest is cooler due to the effects of altitude, rainfall here occurring largely in the summer months. Further details are given in the text.

FLORA AND FAUNA

Few countries offer as wide a range of natural environments as Argentina; its varied vegetation supports equally diverse fauna. The main types of vegetation are described below. Details of some of the animals to be seen are given where

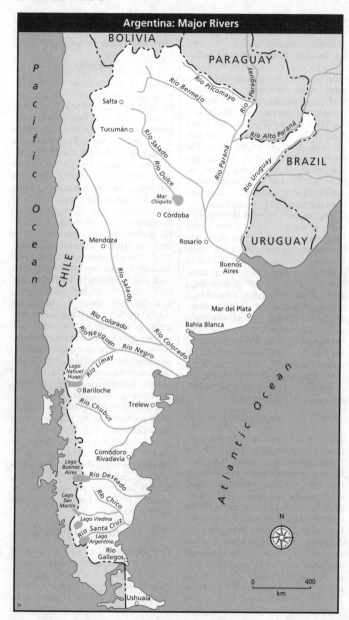

The Ceibo

(*Erythrina cristagalli*) This is the national flower and national tree of both Argentina and Uruguay. Though it is the most common tree found in the Plata estuary, it rarely grows above 5m in this area, whereas in the northern provinces it can reach twice this height. It is a member of the bean (*Leguminosae*) family and in Spring has racemes of deep scarlet waxy flowers which are the reason for its alternative names of Coral tree or Coxcomb tree. Its fruits are insignificant. Its grey/green leaves reach 10 cm in length and are trifoliate.

Ceibo

Jane Norwich

appropriate in the text; to avoid repetition they are not described here. The ten main vegetation types are as follows:

Llanura Pampeana

Extensive cattle grazing and arable farming have altered the original vegetation of the Pampas, notably through the introduction of tree species, such as the eucalyptus for shelter. The least altered areas of the pampas are the coastal lowlands, the Paraná delta and the southern sierras. The sandy soils of the coastal lowlands, including marshes and estuaries, are home to pampas-grass or *cortadera*. In the marshy parts of the Paraná delta there are tall grasses, with *espinillo* and *ñandubay* (prosopis) woods in the higher areas. Willows and alisos grow along the river banks while the ceibo, the national flower of Argentina, grows in the nearby woodlands.

Espinal

These are open woodlands and savannas which extend in an arc around the pampas covering southern Corrientes, northern Entre Ríos, central Santa Fe, large parts of Córdoba and San Luis and the centre-west of La Pampa. In these areas xerophitic and thorny woods of prosopis and acacia predominate. The major prosopis species are the *ñandubay*; the white algarrobo; the black algarrobo and the caldén. The *ñandubay* is found in Entre Ríos and parts of Corrientes, along with the white *quebracho*, *tala*, *espinillo*

and, on sandy soils, *yatay* palms. The white algarrobo and black algarrobo are found in areas of Santa Fe, Córdoba and San Luis which have been heavily affected by farming. The caldén appears across large areas of La Pampa, southern San Luis and southern Buenos Aires, along with bushes such as the alpataco and the creosote bush (*larrea*).

Monte

Bushy steppe with few patches of trees, in areas with rainfall from 80 mm to 250 mm. Covering large areas of San Juan, Mendoza, La Pampa and Río Negro, it can be found as far north as Salta and as far south as Chubut. Vegetation includes different species of the creosote bush, which have small resinous leaves and yellow flowers, as well as thorny bushes from the cacti family and bushes such as *brea*, *retamo* and *jume*. In the northern

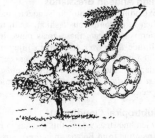
Caldén

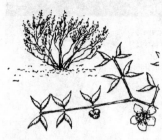

Creosote bush

areas of *monte* the white algarrobo and sweet algarrobo can be found, while the native willow grows along the riverbanks as far south as the Río Chubut.

Puna and Prepuna

Low rainfall, intense radiation and poor soils inhibit vegetation in the *puna*, the major species being adapted by having deep root systems and small leaves; many plants have thorny leaves to deter herbivors. These include species of cacti, which store water in their tissue, and the *yacreta*, a cushion-shaped plant, which has been overexploited for firewood, as well as the *tolilla*, the *chijua* and the *tola*. The *queñoa*, which grows to over 5m high in the sheltered gorges and valleys of the *prepuna*, is the highest growing tree in Argentina. These valleys also support bushes from the *leguminosae* family such as the *churqui*, and species of cacti, such as the cardoon and the *airampu*, with its colourful blossom.

High Andean Grasslands

Extending from Jujuy to Neuquén, and then in discontinuous fashion, south to Tierra del Fuego, these areas range in altitude from over 4,2000m in Jujuy to 500m in Tierra del Fuego. Main grasses, adapted to the cold and winds include *iroa*, *poa* and *stipa* as well as some endemic species.

Subtropical Cloudforest

Often known as *yungas*, this extends into Argentina from Bolivia and covers parts of the sub-Andean sierras; it is found in eastern Jujuy, central Salta and Tucuman and eastern Catamarca. Its eastern sides receive the humidity of the winds which cross the Chaco from the Atlantic. Winters are dry but temperature, rainfall and humidity vary with changes in latitude and altitude. These forests are important regulators of the water cycle, preventing erosion and floods. It is best visited in three national parks: Baritú, Calilegua and El Rey.

Vegetation changes with altitude. Along the edge of the Chaco at the foot of the hills and rising to 500m, where annual rainfall up to 1,000m, is a transition zone with mainly deciduous trees such as the *palo blanco*, the *lapacho rosado* and *lapacho amarillo* (pink and yellow tabebuia); the *palo borracho* (chorisia bottle tree), the *tipa blanca* and the huge *timbo colorado* or black eared tree. Higher and reaching from 500 to 800m in altitude, where there is greater humidity, are montane or laurel forests. Predominant tree species here are the laurel, the jacaranda and the *tipa;* epiphytes (orchids, bromeliads, ferns, lichens, mosses) and climbers are abundant. Above 800m and rising to 1,300-1,700m annual rainfall reaches some 3,000 mm, concentrated between November and March. Here myrtle forest predominates, with a great diversity of species, including great trees such as the *horco molle*, a wide range of epiphytes, and, in some areas such as Baritu, tree ferns. Higher still the evergreen trees are replaced by deciduous species, including the mountain pine (podocarpus), the only conifer native to the northwest, the walnut and the alder. Above these are clumps of *queñoa* and, higher still, mountain meadow grasslands.

The Chaco

The eastern or Wet Chaco is covered by marshlands and ponds with savanna and caranday palm groves, as well as the characteristic red quebracho, a hardwood tree overexploited in the past for tannin. The dry Chaco, further west, is the land of the white quebracho as well as cacti such as the quimil (*opuntia*) and

Epiphytes

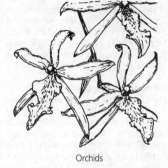

Orchids

the palo borracho (*chorisia*). Similar climatic conditions and vegetation to those in the Dry Chaco are also found in northern San Luis, Córdoba and Santa Fe and eastern Tucumán, Catamarca, Salta, Jujuy, La Rioja and San Juan.

Subtropical Rainforest

This is found mainly in Misiones, extending southwards along the banks of the Ríos Paraná and Uruguay. The wet climate, with annual rainfall up to 2,000 mm, and high temperatures produce rapid decomposition of organic material. The red soils of this area contain a thin fertile soil layer which is easily eroded.

This area offers the widest variety of flora in Argentina. There of over 2,000 known species of vascular plants, about 10% of which are trees. Forest vegetation rises to different strata: the giant trees such as the *palo rosa*, the Misiones cedar, *incienso* and the *guatambú* rise to over 30m high. The forest canopy includes species such as strangler figs and the pindo palm, while the intermediate strata includes the fast growing *ambay* (*cecropia*), tree-ferns, the *yerba maté* and bamboos. Llianas, vines and epiphytes such as orchids and bromeliads as well as ferns and even cacti compete in the struggle for sunlight.

In the hills of northwestern Misiones there are remnants of forests of Paraná pine (*araucaria angustifolia*).

Sub-Antarctic Forest

This grows along the eastern edges of the southern Andes, from Neuquén in the north to Tierra del Fuego and Isla de los Estados in the south. These are cool temperate forests including evergreen and deciduous trees. Species of *nothofagus* predominate, the most common being *lenga* (low deciduous beech), *ñire* (high deciduous beech), *coihue* and *guindo*. The *Pehuen* or Monkey puzzle tree (*araucaria araucana*), is found in northwestern and northcentral Neuquén. The fungus *llao llao* and the hemiparasitic *misodendron* are also frequent. Flowering bushes include the *notro* (firebush), the *calafate* (burberis boxifolis) and the *chaura* (prickly heath).

Areas of the lake district with annual rainfall of over 1,500 mm are covered by Valdivian forest, with a wider range of species. The *coihue* (southern beech) is the predominant species of *nothogagus*, reaching as far south as Lago Buenos Aires. Below colihue canes form a dense undergrowth; flowers include the *amancay* (alstromeria), mutisias, and near streams, the fuschia. Arrayán trees also grow near water, while the Andean Cypress and the *Maiten* grow in the transition zone with the Patagonian steppe.

In areas where annual rainfall reaches over 3,000 mm, there is a wider range of trees, as well as epyphites, climbers, ferns, and lichens such as Old Man's Beard. The *alerce* (larch) is the giant of these forests, rising to over 60m and, in some cases over 3,000 years old.

Magallanic forest, found from Lago Buenos Aires south to Tierra del Fuego, is dominated by the *guindo* (evergreen beech) as well as the *lenga*, the *ñire* and the *canelo* (winter bark). There are also large areas of peatbog with *sphagnum* mosses, and even the carnivorous *drossera uniflora*.

Patagonian Steppe

Plantlife in this area has adapted to severe climatic conditions: strong westerly winds, heavy winter snowfall, high evaporation in summer, low annual rainfall and sandy soils with a thin fertile layer on top. The northwest of this area is covered by bushy scrublands: species include the *quilembai*, *molle*, the *algarrobo patagónico*, the *colpiche*, as well as *coiron* grasses. Further south are shrubs such as the *mata negra* and species of *calafate*. Nearer the mountain ranges the climate is less severe and the soil more fertile: here there is a herbaceous steppe which includes *coiron blanco* and shrubs such as the *neneo*. Overgrazing by sheep has produced serious desertification in many parts of the Patagonian steppe.

Dinosaurs in Argentina

Few countries can equal Argentina in importance for students of dinosaurs; the relative abundance of fossils near the surface has made the country one of the most significant for the study of dinosaur evolution. The main Argentine examples of dinosaurs from the Triassic period (225-180 million years ago) can be found in the Ischigualasto and Talampaya National Parks in San Juan and La Rioja respectively. Among them is the small *Eoraptor lunensis*, 220 million years old, considered one of the oldest discovered anywhere in the world.

Outstanding examples of Jurassic dinosaurs (180-135 million years old) have been discovered in Patagonia. Cerro Cóndor, in Chubut, is the only site of Middle Jurassic dinosaurs found in the Americas, and is therefore of great importance for understanding the evolutionary stages between the Upper and Lower Jurassic periods. At least five examples of *patagosaurus fariasi* have been found here, indicating that these dinosaurs at least were social creatures, possibly for purposes of mutual defence. In Santa Cruz traces of dinosaurs from the Upper Jurassic period have been found in rocks which indicate that at that time the climate was arid and desert-like. This also demonstrates that dinosaurs could live and reproduce in such adverse conditions.

Important discoveries of dinosaurs from the Cretacic period (135 to 70 million years ago) have been made in Neuquén and Chubut. Dating from the period of the separation of the continents of South America and Africa, these provide evidence of the way in which dinosaurs began to evolve in different ways due to their geographical isolation. One example of this is *carnotaurus sastrei*, which has horns and very small hands. One of the interesting features is the greater size of Patagonian dinosaurs: the *Argentinosaurus huiculensis* is one of the largest herbivorous dinosaurs found on earth while the carnivorous *Gigantosaurus carolinii* was larger than the better known *Tyranosaurus Rex* discovered in North America.

Santiago de la Vega

Carnotaurus Sastrei

Argentina: National Parks and Protected Areas

BOLIVIA

PARAGUAY

Monumento Natural
Laguna de
los Pozuelos

Jujuy

Parque
Nacional
Baritú

Parque
Nacional
Calilegua

Parque
Nacional
El Rey

Salta

Reserva
Natural
Formosa

Formosa

Parque
Nacional
Pilcomayo

Parque
Nacional
Iguazú

Reserva
Natural
San
Antonio

Tucumán

Reserva Natural
Colonia Benítez

Chaco

Misiones

Reserva
Natural
Laguna
Brava

Catamarca

Santiago
Del
Estero

Parque
Nacional
Chaco

Corrientes

BRAZIL

La Rioja

Reserva
Provincial
Talampaya

Reserva
Natural
Ibera

San Juan

Santa Fe

Parque
Nacional
El Palmar

Reserva
Nacional
Ischigualasto

Córdoba

Entre Ríos

URUGUAY

Parque
Nacional
Las Quijadas

Parque
Nacional
Diamante

Reserva Natural
Otamendi

Buenos
Aires

Mendoza

San
Luis

Buenos Aires

La Pampa

Parque
Nacional
Lihue Calel

Parque
Nacional
Laguna
Blanca

Parque
Nacional
Lanín

Neuquén

Río Negro

Parque
Nacional Los
Arrayanes

Parque Nacional
Nahuel Huapi

Reserva Natural
Península Valdés

Parque Nacional
Lago Puelo

Parque Nacional
Los Alerces

Chubut

Monumento
Natural Bosques
Petrificados

Parque Nacional
Perito Moreno

Santa Cruz

Parque
Nacional
Glaciares

Tierra Del Fuego

Parque Nacional
Tierra del Fuego

P a c i f i c   O c e a n

C H I L E

A t l a n t i c   O c e a n

N

0   400
km

Argentina has an extensive network of parks and protected areas, the most important of which are designated as National Parks. The history of Argentine national parks is a long one, dating from the donation by Francisco 'Perito' Moreno of 7,500 hectares of land in the Lake District to the state. This grant formed the basis for the establishment of the first National Park, Nahuel Huapi, in 1934.

There are 19 National Parks, stretching from Parque Nacional Baritú, on the northern frontier with Bolivia to Parque Nacional Tierra del Fuego in the far south. Additional areas have been designated as Natural Monuments and Natural Reserves and there are also Provincial Parks and Reserves. The largest National Parks are all in western Argentina; these include a string of eight parks in the Andean foothills in the Lake District and Patagonia. The main National Parks and other protected areas are shown on the map and further details of all of these are given in the text.

The main administration office of the Argentine National Parks authority is at Santa Fe 680, near the Plaza San Martín in central Buenos Aires. Leaflets are available on some of the parks. Further details are given under Buenos Aires.

History

ARCHAEOLOGY AND PREHISTORY

Earliest origins

Some 30,000 years ago the first peoples crossed the temporary land bridge spanning Asia and America and the Bering Straits, and began a long migration southwards, reaching South America about 20,000 BC and Tierra del Fuego by 9,000 BC. Hunters and foragers, they followed in the path of huge herds of now extinct animals such as mammoths, giant ground sloths, mastodons and wild horses which became extinct due to climate change. In some areas, as along the Chilean coasts, these early inhabitants switched to fishing; in others they began to plant crops and domesticate animals, adopting in the process a more sedentary lifestyle.

Northwestern Argentina

The most important archaeological sites in Argentina are situated in the Northwest and West which were the areas of the most highly developed cultures south of the Central Andes. This region became a meeting place for people already settled there with peoples and influences from northern Chile, the Central Andes, the Chaco and the hunter-gatherers of the south. Three distinct periods can be identified in the cultural development of the region: the Early period (500 BC to 650 AD), the Middle period (650-850 AD) and the Later period (850-1480 AD). The early period witnessed the beginnings of agriculture as well as pottery and metalworking. The Middle period was marked by the influence of the great culture of Tiahuanaco in present-day Bolivia. Fine metal objects, some of them of gold and silver, were made and new plant varieties were introduced. The later period featured the influence of the cultures of Santa María and Belén, notable for their giant, polychrome funerary urns.

In general the peoples of the northwest lived in chiefdoms led by one or more leaders. Practicing intensive agriculture and successfully domesticating animals, they produced food surpluses. A special house was used as a temple, but they left little architecture. Two of the most important of these cultures were the Tafi of Tafi del Valle and the Condorhuasi in the western valleys of La Rioja and San Juan. Both produced fine metal objects from gold, copper and copper alloy. Ceramics and stone sculptures produced by both show feline-related figures, while Condorhuasi artefacts often show males and females as crawling figures. The Tafi are famous for their stone pillars and

Town planning in the 16th century

Perhaps the most obvious influence of Spanish settlement for the traveller is the characteristic street plan of towns and cities. Colonial cities were founded by means of an official ceremony which included the tracing of the central square and the holding of a mass. A series of Royal Ordinances issued in Madrid in 1573 laid down the rules of town planning. The four corners of the main *plaza* were to face the four points of the compass "because thus the streets diverging from the plaza will not be directly exposed to the four principal winds, which would cause much inconvenience." The *plaza* and the main streets were to have arcades which were seen as "a great convenience for those who resort thither for trade." Away from the *plaza* the streets were to be traced out "by means of measuring by cord and ruler" in the now-familiar grid-pattern. Once this was done building lots were to be distributed, those near the *plaza* being allocated by "lottery to those of the settlers who are entitled to build around the main plaza".

The Ordinances specified the principles underlying the distribution of the major public buildings: "In inland towns the church is not to be in the centre of the plaza but at a distance from it in a situation where it can stand by itself, separate from other buildings so that it can be seen from all sides. It can thus be made more beautiful and it will inspire more respect. It should be built on high ground so that in order to reach its entrance people will have to ascend a flight of steps. Nearby the *cabildo* and the customs house are to be erected in order to increase its impressiveness but without instructing it in any way. The hospital of the poor who are ill with non-contagious diseases shall be built facing the N and so planned that it will enjoy a southern exposure."

The Ordinances also advised settlers on how to deal with hostility from the indigenous population: "If the natives should wish to oppose the establishment of a settlement they are to be given to understand that the settlers desire to build a town there not in order to deprive them of their property but for the purpose of being on friendly terms with them; of teaching them to live in a civilized way; of teaching them to know God and His Law ... While the new town is being built the settlers ... shall try to avoid communication and intercourse with the Indians. Nor are the Indians to enter the circuit of the settlement until the latter is complete and in condition for defence and the houses built, so that when the Indians see them they will be filled with wonder and will realize that the Spaniards are settling there permanently and not temporarily."

"Royal Ordinances Governing the Laying Out of New Towns" by Zelia Nuttall, Hispanic American Historical Review, May 1922, pages 249-254.

monoliths, often used to form enclosures or placed as the focus of a stone enclosure. A third centre of cultural development occurred further north, in the Humahuaca valley, where the Middle and Later periods saw the building of small villages of rectangular stone houses, which gradually, as at Tilcara, grew into small urban settlements in good defensive sites and with fortifications. Metal working was fully developed and tools made of bones were also used. Unlike the Tafi and Condorhuasi, the Humahuaca cultures also used hallucinogenic substances characteristic of San Pedro de Atacama (Chile) and the Central Andes. Later sites in the valley have the bodies of adults placed face down inside houses or in stone-lined tombs. Ceramics imported from Bolivian cultures and Pacific shells have been found in these tombs.

By the end of the Later period, the peoples of the Northwest had been drawn into informal links with the Inca empire: highways linking their communities with the empire were built and trade with the Incas is indicated by their clothing, music, handicrafts and fortifications.

Central and Southern Argentina

Away from the northwestern highlands were other peoples who have left less archaeological evidence. Among them were the Comechingones, who inhabited what are now the provinces of Córdoba and San Luis. Living in settlements of pit-dwellings, the bottom half of which were built underground, they used irrigation to produce a range of crops. In the far northeast on the eastern edge of the Chaco were the Guaraní; organized into loose confederations, they lived in rudimentary villages and practised slash-and-burn agriculture to grow maize, sweet potatoes, manioc and beans. They also produced textiles and ceramics.

Further south the Pampas and Patagonia were much more sparsely populated than the Northwest and most groups were nomadic until long after the arrival of the Spanish. One of the most important of these were the Querandí, who eked out a living by hunting guanaco and rheas. Patagonia was inhabited by scattered nomadic groups, including the Pampa, the Chonik and the Kaingang. Most of these managed to avoid contact with white settlers until the 19th century. In the steppes of southern Patagonia the Tehuelche and Puelche lived as nomadic hunters living off guanaco, foxes and game.

In the far south, in southern Patagonia and Tierra del Fuego, there were four indigenous peoples, two of them land-based and two sea-based. All lived as hunter-gatherers. Considering the inhospitable climate all wore very little clothing: capes, waterproof moccasins, feather headdresses and jewelry. The sea based peoples, Yaghanes and Alacaluf, had canoes, paddles, bailers and mooring rope, but lacked fishhooks, catching fish with spears or by hand. Seals were their main food, but they also ate sea-birds and fish. The land-based Ona and Haush gathered plants and hunted guanaco and foxes for food and for their hides. They also hunted sea-mammals from the shore.

EUROPEAN EXPLORATION AND SETTLEMENT

At the time of the arrival of the first Europeans the territories which today make up Argentina were sparsely populated. About two-thirds of the indigenous population lived in the northwest of the territory, the present-day provinces of Córdoba, Santiago del Estero, Tucumán, Catamarca, La Rioja, Salta and Jujuy. European exploration began in the Plata estuary. In 1516 Juan de Solís, a Portuguese navigator employed by the Spanish crown, landed on the shore of the estuary, but his men were killed by Querandí Indians. Four years later he was followed by Magellan who explored the Plata, before turning south to make his way into the Pacific. In 1527 both Sebastian Cabot and his rival Diego García sailed into the estuary and up the Ríos Paraná and the Paraguay. Cabot founded a small fort, Sancti Spiritus, not far from the modern city of Rosario, but it was wiped out by the Indians about 2 years later. Despite these difficulties Cabot took back to Spain stories of a great Indian kingdom beyond the Plata estuary, rich in precious metals. A Portuguese expedition to the estuary, led by Affonso de Souza, returned with similar tales and this led to a race between the two Iberian powers. In 1535, Pedro de Mendoza, set out with 16 ships and a well-equipped force of 1,600 men and founded a settlement at Buenos Aires; the natives soon made life too difficult; the settlement was abandoned and Mendoza returned home, but not before sending Juan de Ayolas with a small force up the Río Paraná in search of the fabled Indian kingdom. In 1537 this force founded Asunción, in Paraguay, where the natives were friendly.

After 1535 the attention of the Spanish crown switched to Peru, where Pizarro was engaged on the conquest of the Inca empire, and the small settlement at Asunción remained an isolated outpost. It was not until 1573 that a force from Asunción travelled south to establish Santa Fe. Seven years later Juan de Garay refounded Buenos Aires but it was only under his successor, Hernando Arias de Saavedra (1592-1614), that the new settlement became secure.

By the time of Mendoza's expedition to the Plata estuary, Spanish expeditions were already exploring northern parts of present-day Argentina. In 1535 Diego de Almagro led a party from Peru which crossed the northwest. In the latter half of the 16th century expeditions from Chile and Peru led to the foundation at the eastern foot of the Andes of the oldest towns in Argentina: Santiago del Estero, Tucumán, Córdoba, Salta, La

The British invasions of Buenos Aires, 1806-7

The history of southern Latin America would be very different if British attempts to displace Spain as the dominant power in the region in 1806 and 1807 had succeeded. These attacks, at a time when Spain was France's ally in the Napoleonic Wars against Britain, involved 25,000 men, including over 14,000 troops. The first invasion was the brainchild of naval captain Sir Home Popham. Having captured Cape Town from the Dutch early in 1806, Popham decided, without British government authorisation, to launch an attack on Buenos Aires, anticipating support from London in the event of success. On 25 June 1806 Popham's force of 1,571 men, under the command of General Beresford, landed near Buenos Aires, forcing the city of 50,000 inhabitants to surrender within a few days and seizing nearly US$1.5 million in bullion and specie.

Once the *porteños* realized that Beresford's occupation was unauthorised and that he could not guarantee British support against Spain if they opted for independence, they began to plan to drive the invaders out. After 47 days of British rule Beresford's small army was attacked in the centre of the city by a larger force and, on 12 August, he was forced to surrender, he and his men being interned in the interior. Meanwhile the British government had decided to send troops under General Whitelocke to reinforce the British toe-hold in South America. After a short seige, Montevideo surrendered to the British in February 1807 and became the forward base for the attack on Buenos Aires. On the morning of 5 July 1807 6,000 British troops stormed the city, but as they advanced through the narrow streets they were raked with artillery and musket fire and assaulted by missiles hurled from the rooftops. With British casualties reaching 50%, Whitelocke surrendered and agreed to evacuate the Río de la Plata altogether on condition that all British prisoners would be released. The dream of establishing a British presence in Spanish Southern America had received a major setback.

Peter Pyne

Rioja, Jujuy, San Juan, Mendoza, and San Luis. The aims of the Spanish was to create better trading links between the Chilean heartland and Peru (avoiding the Atacama desert) and to find new sources of Indian labour. A total of 25 cities were founded in present-day Argentina in the 16th century, 15 of which survived, at a time when the total Spanish population was under 2,000.

Colonial rule

Throughout the colonial period the Argentine territories were an outlying part of the Spanish empire and of minor importance. Spanish colonial settlement and government was based in Peru, which was endowed with the vast mineral wealth of Potosi in Alto Peru (present-day Bolivia) and large supplies of Indian labour. In the Argentine lands, by contrast, there were no great mineral deposits and the Indian population was sparse. The nomadic nature of many Indian groups made any attempt at control difficult, again in contrast to Peru where Spanish rule could be superimposed on the centralized administration of the defeated Incas.

From 1543 all the Spanish territories in South America were governed from Lima, the Vice-Regal capital and trade with Spain was routed via Lima, Panama and the Caribbean, thus preventing Buenos Aires from becoming an important port. Its slow growth after 1680 was partly due to the establishment of a Portuguese base at Colonia del Sacramento on the opposite bank of the estuary in 1683: the need to confront the Portuguese led Spain to strengthen her presence, while the Tigre delta north of the city provided ample opportunities

'The Caligula of the River Plate'

Juan Manuel de Rosas, is the most controversial figure in 19th century Argentine history. Born in 1793 into a landholding family, Rosas rose to dominate Buenos Aires province and the Río de la Plata for over two decades. After building a fortune in the meat-salting business and acquiring large estates in the south of the province, he allied with the Federalists against the Unitarists, defeating the Unitarist leader Lavalle and becoming provincial governor in 1829. Though he gave up office in 1832, he returned in 1835 and remained governor until his defeat at the battle of Caseros in 1852.

Though Rosas opposed the Unitarists and claimed to be a Federalist, he was no supporter of the rights of the other provinces. He opposed the Unitarists because they stood for European ideas and 'progress'; he used his control over Buenos Aires to dominate the other provinces, but resisted plans to link them formally under a constitution. Arguing for territorial expansion at the expense of the Indians, he based his power on the support of other *estancieros*, who were rewarded with sales and gifts of conquered land, and on the *gauchos* whose following he cultivated and to whom he appealed as a proven military leader and horseman. Arguing, on becoming governor, that the only alternative was chaos, he demanded and received 'extraordinary powers' which simply legalised his brutal methods. Ruling by decree, he replaced the bureaucracy with his own supporters and built a standing army of 20,000 men, paid from the proceeds of *estancias* confiscated from his opponents. In many cases 'justice' was administered personally, Rosas reading the police reports and simply writing the sentence on the files.

In government Rosas's reliance on propaganda, conformity and terror draw parallels with 20th century dictatorships: terror was in the hands of the *Mazorca*, death squads which answered directly to the Dictator; all citizens were forced to wear red, the Federalist colour; newspapers, official documents and even private

for smuggling British and Portuguese goods into Buenos Aires. By 1776 the city's population was only 24,000, though this was double the size of any of the cities of the interior. Although in that year when Spain reorganized its colonial administration and created the Viceroyalty of Río de la Plata, with Buenos Aires as capital, the city's control of the *cabildos* (town councils) in distant towns was very tenuous.

The Wars of Independence

As in the rest of Spanish America, independence was partly a response to events in Europe, where Spain was initially allied to Napoleonic France. In 1806 and 1807 the British, at war with Napoleon, made two attempts to seize Buenos Aires but were defeated. In 1808 Napoleon invaded Spain, deposing King Ferdinand VII, and provoking widespread resistance from Spanish guerrilla armies. Throughout Spanish America the colonial elites debated where their loyalties lay: to Napoleon's brother Joseph, now officially King? to Ferdinand, now in a French prison? to the Viceroy? to the Spanish resistance parliament in Cadiz?

On 25 May 1810, the *cabildo* of Buenos Aires deposed the viceroy and established a *junta* to govern on behalf of King Ferdinand VII. This move provoked resistance in outlying areas of the viceroyalty, Paraguay, Uruguay and Upper Peru (Bolivia) breaking away from the rule of Buenos Aires. Factional rivalry within the *junta* between supporters of independence and their opponents added to the confusion and instability. Six years later, in July 1816, when Buenos Aires was threatened by invasion

correspondence had to begin with the slogan 'Long live the Federation and Death to the Unitarist Savages'. Opponents fled to Montevideo from where they plotted his overthrown and Rosas responded by blockading the Uruguayan capital.

Controlling the other provinces was more difficult. Allying himself to provincial *caudillos* such as Quiroga in La Rioja, Rosas overthrew opponents or weakened them by blockading the Río Paraná. It was this that led to his downfall. His treatment of French merchants led to a French blockade of Buenos Aires in 1838-40 and a dispute over access to the Río Paraná led to an Anglo-French blockade in 1845-1848. His policy over the Paraná also annoyed the Brazilian government, which wanted access to Mato Grosso, and provoked unrest in the Argentine province of Entre Ríos, governed by his ally Urquiza. In 1852 Urquiza challenged Rosas and, supported by Brazilian and Uruguayan forces as well as Unitarists from Montevideo and British and French finance, defeated the dictator at Caseros, just outside Buenos Aires. Rosas rode from the battlefield to the house of the British Consul, took refuge on a British ship and left to spend the remaining 25 years of his life farming quietly in Hampshire, where, according to John Lynch, he treated the farm workers in much the same way as he had treated the *gauchos* of the pampas.

Controversy still surrounds Rosas's career. Sarmiento and others saw him as the epitome of barbarism, opposing their mission to 'civilize' the pampas by bringing education, European ideas and European settlers. Later generations have sometimes portrayed him as a nationalist hero, focussing on his imposition of unity and his resistance to British and French pressure. Before his election as president Carlos Menem praised Rosas and grew long sideburns in imitation of the dictator. The recent use of his portrait on the 20 peso note is just one of the latest moves in the continuing debate over the man labelled by his opponents the "Caligula of the River Plate".

from Peru and blockaded by a Spanish fleet in the Río de la Plata, a national congress held at Tucumán declared independence. The declaration was given reality by the genius and devotion of José de San Martín, who boldly marched an Argentine army across the Andes to free Chile, and (with the help of Lord Cochrane, commander of the Chilean Navy), embarked his forces for Peru, where he captured Lima, the first step in the liberation of Peru.

SINCE INDEPENDENCE

THE 19TH CENTURY

The achievement of independence brought neither stability nor unity. For over 40 years conflict centred around disputes between Unitarists and Federalists. The former, found mainly in the city of Buenos Aires, looked to Europe for their inspiration and advocated free trade, education, white immigration and

Juan Domingo and Evita

The casting of Madonna as Evita in the Alan Parker film of the same name showed yet again how divisive a figure Eva Perón remains in Argentina: the *Peronistas* were outraged at what they saw as an insult to '*Santa Evita*' while anti-Peronists were delighted by their opponents outrage. Yet if Evita is undoubtedly better known to foreigners than her former husband, the latter is perhaps more puzzling and complex than the wife who died tragically of cancer at the age of 33.

The story of Evita's early life is well known. Born in 1919 near Los Toldos in Buenos Aires province, the fifth illegitimate child of Juana Ibarguren and Juan Duarte, she was brought up in Junín, before moving at the age of 15 to Buenos Aires. Despite failing to make it as a film or theatre star, she was successful in radio soap operas. Her relationship with Perón began in 1944 and they married in October 1945. As first lady in a society in which women were denied the vote, she offended the elite by the key role she played in government. As president of the Eva Perón Foundation, a social welfare organization, she distributed help to the needy who queued for hours to see her. The Foundation, funded by 'voluntary' donations from the trade unions and taxes on lottery tickets and entry to casinos and horseracing, built hospitals, low-income housing and schools. In 1948 she toured France, Italy and Spain, receiving film star attention in weary post-war Europe. In 1951, when Perón ran for reelection, her nomination as his vice-presidential running mate aroused so much hostility among the armed forces that she was forced to withdraw. Her death in 1952 transformed her into a myth so powerful that after Perón's overthrow, the military had her embalmed corpse smuggled from the country and buried in a secret grave in Italy to prevent it falling into the hands of the Peronist masses.

Although he was to dominate Argentine politics for 30 years, Perón was unknown to most Argentines until 1943 when he was aged 48. Brought up on a Patagonian *estancia* where his father was manager, he was sent to a boarding school before attending the military academy. He rose slowly in the army, becoming, in 1931, an instructor at the military academy, where he wrote books advocating the need for strong political leadership and a state-regulated economy. After periods as military attaché in Chile and Italy, he was one of the organizers of the Grupo de Oficiales Unidos, a secret society of junior officers which sympathized with the Axis cause in the Second World War. After a military coup in June 1943, Perón, though initially only a junior minister, soon emerged as the leading member of the government: as Under-Secretary of War, he put his supporters into key positions; as Secretary of Labour he encouraged the formation of trade unions, winning the

strong central government. The Federalists, backed by the provincial elites and many of the great *estancieros* of Buenos Aires province, resisted, defending local autonomy and traditional values. Behind the struggle were also economic interests: Buenos Aires and the coastal areas benefitted from trade with Europe; the interior provinces did not. As the conflict raged the territory, known officially as the United Provinces of the Río de la Plata, had none of the features of a modern state:

there was neither central government, army, capital city nor constitution.

Order, of a sort, was established after 1829 by Juan Manuel de Rosas, Governor of Buenos Aires. His overthrow in 1852 unleashed another round in the battles between Unitarists and Federalists and between Buenos Aires and the provinces. In 1853 a constitution establishing a federal system of government was finally drafted. Buenos Aires province refused to join the new Argentine Confederation,

support of their members by approving pay increases and benefits. His rise provoked hostility among fellow officers and the Argentine elite; in October 1945 he was dismissed and arrested, but massive workers demonstrations on 17 October led to his release and historic appearance on the balcony of the Casa Rosada.

Elected president in February 1946, he was re-elected in 1951 after altering the constitution to permit his candidacy. Perón aimed to create what he called the 'organized community': all important social and economic groups were forced to join an organization linked to the Peronist party. The regime's power-base was the labour movement which Perón, hailed as 'Argentina's No 1 Worker', had organized; workers received increased wages and a range of welfare benefits. An attempt was made to force industrialization, financed by a state monopoly over foreign trade.

After his overthrow in 1955 Perón spent 17 years in exile in Paraguay, Panama, Venezuela, the Dominican Republic and Spain. From exile he controlled the Peronist party and its trade unions through a network of agents. His return, in 1973 was dramatic, his plane being diverted from Ezeiza airport after rival left and right wing Peronists opened fire on each other. This incident heralded the final showdown of his career. Elected president in October 1973, he was faced by hyperinflation and the struggle between incompatible groups of left and right wing supporters in the Peronist movement. The young revolutionary Peronists, whose support he had encouraged in exile, were soon disillusioned and resumed their violence. By the time of his death, in July 1974, Argentina was on the threshold of a new and more terrifying round of conflict.

The continuing controversy over Perón's place in Argentine history mirrors the contradictory nature of his regime. An army officer for over 30 years, he was ejected by the army in 1955, an institution which then prevented his return until 1973. Descendent of a bourgeois family, he drew his support from the urban workers and rural poor and was hated by the Buenos Aires middle classes. Most recently, his role after 1945 in the sale of passports to escaping war criminals from the Fascist powers has been the subject of considerable discussion, both in Argentina and abroad.

From Guerrilla War to 'Dirty War'

🐛 The 'Dirty War', unleashed by the armed forces after 1976 in response to the guerrilla attacks of the early 1970s, is one of the most violent incidents in modern South American history. While Argentine society is understandably chastened by the experience, hardly a month goes by without this grim episode provoking further controversy.

Guerrilla groups began operating in most Latin American countries in the 1960s, usually with little success. From 1969 several groups emerged in Argentina, among them the *Montoneros* and the People's Revolutionary Army (*Ejército Revolucionario del Pueblo* or ERP). The former, inspired by a curious mixture of Peronism, Catholicism and Marxism, proclaimed allegiance to the exiled Perón. Often middle and upper-middle class by background and wanting to liberate the working classes from the evils of capitalism, they idealized Perón and the 'social justice' of his government of 1946-1955, which most of them were too young to remember. Since the urban working classes were mainly Peronist, these youthful idealists assumed that Perón was a revolutionary leader and that his return would be the prelude to revolution. The ERP, by contrast drawing their inspiration from Trotsky and Che Guevara, argued that political violence would push the military government towards increased repression which would ignite working class opposition and lead to civil war and socialist revolution.

If Peronists and non-Peronists disagreed over their aims, their methods were similar: kidnappings and bank robberies raised money and gained publicity; army and police officers were assassinated along with right wing Peronists. Wealthy Argentine families and multinational companies were forced to distribute food and other goods to the poor to obtain the release of kidnap victims. Perhaps the most spectacular of these episodes was carried out by the Montoneros: in 1970 they kidnapped and later 'executed' General Pedro Aramburu, a former president.

Called upon to denounce the guerrillas which operated in his name, Perón from

which had its capital at Paraná. Conflict between the two states erupted over the attempt by Buenos Aires to control and tax commerce on the Río Paraná. The victory of Buenos Aires at Pavón (1861) opened the way to a solution: the city became the seat of the federal government; Bartolomé Mitre, former governor of Buenos Aires became the first president of Argentina. There was another political flare-up of the old quarrel in 1880, ending in the humiliation of the city of Buenos Aires, which was separated from its province and made into a special federal territory.

Although there was resistance to the new constitution from some of the western provinces, the institutions of a modern state were created in the two decades after 1861: a national bank, bureaucracy,

postal service and army were all established, but perhaps it was the building of railways across the pampas which did most to create national unity, breaking the power of the provincial leaders (*caudillos*) by enabling the federal government to send in troops quickly. The new army was quickly employed to defeat Francisco Solano López of Paraguay in the War of the Triple Alliance (1865-1870) and then to conquer all the Indian tribes of the pampas and the south in the 'Conquest of the Wilderness' (1879-1880).

In the last quarter of the 19th century Argentina was transformed: the newly acquired stability encouraged foreign investment; the pampas were fenced, ploughed up and turned over to commercial export agriculture; railways and port facilities were built; and widespread

his exile in Madrid, refused. With the return to civilian rule the Montoneros ended their violence and worked to elect their hero. Now operating semi-openly, the movement gained many supporters, especially students and young people. In May 1974, months before his death, Perón, denounced his leftist supporters and after his death they resumed their violence, this time under the slogan "If Evita were alive, she would be a Montonera". In 1974 they kidnapped Jorge and Juan Born, heirs and managers of the giant Bunge y Born grain exporting company, and ransomed them for US$64 million.

Long before Perón's return, right wing groups linked to the army and police had begun to take action against suspected guerrillas. By 1974 suspected leftists were regularly disappearing at the hands of the Argentine Anticommunist Alliance (known as the 'Triple A') which was linked to José López Rega, Minister of Social Welfare and closest advisor to Isabel Perón who became president after her husband's death. The 'Dirty War', launched by the military government which seized power in 1976 was, in a sense, a continuation of this: all three armed services operated their own death squads and camps in a campaign of indiscriminate violence. By 1978/79 both the ERP and the Montoneros had ceased to function. In the process thousands of people disappeared: although an official report produced after the return to civilian rule put their number at 8,960, some 15,000 cases have now been documented and human rights groups now estimate the total at some 30,000. They are remembered still by the **Mothers of the Plaza de Mayo**, a human rights group made up of relatives, who march anti-clockwise around the Plaza de Mayo in central Buenos Aires every Thursday at 1530 with photos of their 'disappeared' loved ones pinned to their chests. Their continued protests highlight one of the most controversial aspects of the restoration of civilian rule: the laws passed in 1986/7 which shielded junior officers from prosecution on the grounds that they were obeying orders.

immigration from Europe transformed the character of Buenos Aires and other cities around the Plata estuary. Political power, however, remained in the hands of a small group of large landowners and their urban allies. Few Argentines had the vote and the opposition Unión Cívica Radical, excluded from power, conspired with dissidents in the army in attempts to overthrow the government.

THE 20TH CENTURY

One of the landmarks of modern Argentine history was the 1912 Sáenz Peña law which established universal manhood suffrage. Sáenz Peña, president between 1910 and 1916, sought to bring the middle and working classes into politics, gambling that the Conservatives could reorganize themselves and attract their votes. The gamble failed: the Conservatives failed to gain a mass following and the Radicals came to power. Radical presidents Hipólito Yrigoyen (1916-1922 and 1928-1930) and Marcelo T de Alvear (1922-1928) found themselves trapped between the demands of an increasingly militant urban labour movement and the opposition of the Conservatives, still powerful in the provinces and with allies in the armed forces.

The military coup which overthrew Yrigoyen in 1930 was a turning point: the armed forces returned to government for the first time in over 50 years and were to continue to play a major political role until 1983. Through the 1930s a series of military backed governments, dominated by the Conservatives, held power; the Radicals were outlawed and elections were so fraudulent that in Avellaneda in 1938 more people voted than were on the register. Yet the armed forces themselves were disunited: while most officers supported the Conservatives and the landholding elites, a minority of ultra-nationalist officers, inspired by developments in Europe, supported industrialization and the creation of a one-party dictatorship along fascist lines. The outbreak of war in Europe increased these tensions and a series of military coups in 1943-1944 led to the rise of Colonel Juan Domingo Perón. When the military allowed a return to civilian rule in 1946 Perón swept into power winning Presidential elections. His government is chiefly remembered by many Argentines for improving the living conditions of the workers, through the introduction of paid holidays and welfare measures. Especially in its early years the government was strongly nationalistic, taking control over the British-owned railways in 1948. Opposition parties were harassed and independent newspapers taken over. Although Perón was easily re-elected in 1951, his government soon ran into trouble: economic problems led to the introduction of a wage freeze which upset the labour unions which were the

The Anglo-Argentine War of 1982

Though the dispute between Britain and Argentina over the Falkland Islands/Islas Malvinas led to armed conflict in 1982, its historical roots can be traced to before Argentine independence. Records of early European voyages in the area are ambiguous but the Dutch sailor Sebald de Weert made the first generally acknowledged sighting of the islands in 1598. When the English navigator John Strong landed in 1690 he named the Falkland Sound after Lord Falkland; this name was later applied to the island group. The Spanish name Islas Malvinas is derived from the French *Iles Malouines*, the appellation given by sailors from the French port of St Malo who also visited in the 17th century.

In 1764 France established a small colony on the islands at Port Louis. At about the same time the British built an outpost at Saunders Island. In 1766 the French government sold Port Louis to Spain which turned it into a military garrison and penal colony and, in 1770, expelled the British from Saunders Island. Although Madrid, under threat of war, permitted the reestablishment of the British post the following year, it was withdrawn in 1774.

In 1811, following the outbreak of the Wars of Independence in South America, Spain also withdrew her forces from the islands. In 1820 they were claimed by an expedition from Buenos Aires, which raised a flag at Port Louis (renamed Soledad). In 1831 a United States warship destroyed a promising colonisation project under the auspices of a German-born merchant from Buenos Aires who had arrested United States sealers operating in the area. After British warships expelled a force from Buenos Aires in 1833, the islands came under British rule.

During his first administration (1946-1955) Perón focused on the disputed status of the islands as part of an appeal to Argentine nationalism and linked the issue to Argentina's claim over parts of the Antarctic and his plan to create a 'Greater Argentina'. In 1965 the United Nations called on the two states to resolve their differences peacefully. Talks over the islands took place but were complicated by the hostility of the islanders themselves towards any change in their status.

Though contingency plans for an Argentine invasion had existed for many years, in 1982 the Argentine military regime calculated that the opportune moment had arrived. The decision by the British government to reduce its military commitment in the area and withdraw the patrol ship HMS *Endurance* suggested London was losing

heart of Peronist support; the death of Evita in 1952 was another blow; a dispute with the church in 1954-1955 added to Perón's problems. In September 1955 a military coup unseated Perón who went into exile, in Paraguay, Panama, Venezuela, the Dominican Republic and, from 1961 to 1973, in Spain.

Perón's legacy dominated Argentina for the next two decades. No attempt was made to destroy his social and economic reforms, but the armed forces determined to exclude the Peronists from power. Argentine society was bitterly divided between Peronists and anti-Peronists and the economy struggled, partly as a result of Perón's measures against the economic elite and in favour of the workers. Between 1955 and 1966 there was an uneasy alternation of military and civilian regimes. The military officers who seized power in 1966 announced their intention to carry out a Nationalist Revolution, but were quickly discredited by a deteriorating economic situation. The Cordobazo, a student and workers insurrection in Córdoba in 1969, was followed by the emergence of several guerrilla groups and the growth of political violence. As Argentina became

interest. Severe economic problems in Argentina threatened the military's hold on power and the regime calculated that a successful invasion would unite the population behind it. An incident on the island of South Georgia, also claimed by Argentina though not part of the Falklands/Malvinas group, provided the opportunity.

The Argentine force of 5,000 men which landed on 2 April 1982 quickly overwhelmed the small British garrison without loss of life. The British military and civilian authorities were expelled and the 1,700 inhabitants placed under an Argentine military governor. Though most Latin American states sympathized with Buenos Aires over the sovereignty issue, many were unhappy with the use of force. Backed by a United Nations resolution and the crucial logistical support of the United States, the British government launched a naval force to regain the islands. On 25 April, as this fleet approached the area, a British force recaptured South Georgia. Over the following three weeks the war was fought in the air and on the seas around the Falklands/Malvinas: the Argentines lost numerous aircraft, the cruiser *General Belgrano*, and several other vessels. The British lost two destroyers, two frigates and a landing vessel. After the sinking of the *General Belgrano*, the Argentine navy stayed in port or close to shore, leaving the airforce and army to carry on the battle.

The British reoccupation of the islands began with an amphibious landing under heavy fire at San Carlos on 21 May. From here British troops marched across the island and attacked ineffective Argentine defensive positions around the capital. Though some Argentine army and marine units resisted, most of the Argentine troops were poorly trained and equipped conscripts who were no match for British regular forces. On 14 June Argentine forces surrendered.

Casualties in the war outnumbered the small island population. Argentine losses were 746 killed, over 300 on the *General Belgrano*, and 1,336 wounded; the British lost 256 killed and 777 wounded. Three islanders were killed on the final assault on the capital.

The consequences of the war for Argentina were wide-ranging. The military government was, perhaps, discredited less by defeat than by its obvious misjudgement of the situation, by its blatant misleading of the public during the conflict and by the accounts given by returning troops of incompetent leadership and lack of supplies. General Galtieri was replaced as President and preparations were made for a return to civilian rule.

more ungovernable Perón, from his exile, refused to denounce those guerrilla groups which called themselves Peronist.

In 1971 General Alejandro Lanusse seized power, promising a return to civilian rule and calculating that the only way to control the situation was to allow Perón to return. When the military bowed out in 1973, elections were won by the Peronist candidate, Hector Campora. Perón returned from exile in Madrid to resume as President in October 1973, but died on 1 July 1974, leaving the Presidency to his widow, Vice-President María Estela Martínez de Perón, his third wife, known as 'Isabelita'. Perón's death unleashed chaos: hyper-inflation, resumed guerrilla warfare and the operation of right wing death squads who abducted people suspected of left-wing sympathies. In March 1976, to nobody's surprise, the military overthrew Isabelita and replaced her with a *junta* led by Gen Jorge Videla.

The new government closed Congress, outlawed political parties, placed trade unions and universities under military control and unleashed the so-called 'dirty war', a brutal assault on the guerrilla groups and other displays of opposition. Gen Videla was appointed President in 1978 by the military; his nominated successor, Gen Roberto Viola took over for 3 years in March 1981 but was overthrown by Gen Leopoldo Galtieri in December 1981. The latter was in turn replaced in June 1982 by Gen Reynaldo Bignone, following military defeat in the South Atlantic.

Confidence in the military ebbed when their economic policies began to go sour in 1980. In 1982-1983 pressure for a return to civilian rule grew, particularly after the South Atlantic conflict with Great Britain in 1982. Discredited by the stories of returning conscripts, the armed forces withdrew to barracks. Elections in October 1983 were won by Raúl Alfonsín and his Unión Cívica Radical (UCR). During 1985 Generals Videla, Viola and Galtieri were sentenced to long terms of imprisonment for their parts in the 'dirty war'. While Alfonsín's government struggled to deal with the legacy of the past, it was overwhelmed by continuing economic problems, the most obvious of which was hyperinflation. When the Radicals were defeated by Carlos Menem, the Peronist (*Justicialist*) presidential candidate, Alfonsín stepped down early because of economic instability. Strained relations between the Peronist Government and the military led to several rebellions, which Menem attempted to appease by pardoning the imprisoned Generals. His popularity among civilians declined, but in 1991-92 the Economy Minister, Domingo Cavallo, succeeded in restoring confidence in the economy and the Government as a whole. The symbol of this stability was the introduction of a new currency pegged to the United States dollar. After triumphing in the October 1993 congressional elections at the expense of the UCR, the Peronists themselves lost some ground in April 1994 elections to a constituent assembly. The party to gain most, especially in Buenos Aires, was Frente Grande, a broad coalition of left wing groups and disaffected Peronists. Behind the loss of confidence of these dissident Peronists were unrestrained corruption and a pact in December 1993 between Menem and Alfonsín pledging UCR support for constitutional changes which included re-election of the president for a second term of 4 years.

By the 1995 elections, the majority of the electorate favoured stability over constitutional concerns and reelected Menem, without recourse to a second ballot. The Peronists also increased their majority in the Chamber of Deputies and gained a majority in the Senate. Menem made his priorities the reduction of joblessness and of corruption, although on neither score did he achieve immediate success. Concurrent with changes at the Finance Ministry and measures to take the economy beyond the 1995 recession (see **Economy** below), labour legislation reform was highly unpopular as it contravened some of Peronism's founding tenets. Menem further had to contend with criticisms from ex-Finance Minister Domingo Cavallo over corruption and links with crime at government level, and with the boost given to the Radicals by that party's victory in the first direct elections for mayor of Buenos Aires in July 1996.

People

The population at latest estimate (1995) was 34.6 million, the 3rd largest population in South America after Brazil and Colombia, making Argentina one of the least densely populated countries in the continent. In the Federal Capital and Province

Blacks in Argentina

Though Argentina is usually seen as a nation of white, predominantly European immigrants, Africans played an important role in its history. While slavery was by no means as important as in Brazil or the Caribbean, by the 18th century it was common in many parts of the colony, especially in towns, as most slaves were domestic servants or artisans; slavery was also important on the sugar estates of Tucumán, in the textile workshops of Catamarca and in rural areas of Mendoza and Córdoba. In Buenos Aires there were black *cofradías* (Catholic lay organizations) open to slaves and free blacks alike. One aspect of black community life which particularly disturbed the authorities was dancing: in the 1760s it was banned, but later it was tolerated within limits. In 1769 one priest complained that Africans dancing outside his church to celebrate Easter had made so much noise that he had been unable to perform the service. At independence there were probably 30,000 slaves in a total population of 400,000, while in the city of Buenos Aires 29% of the population were black or mulatto.

The creole leaders of the independence movement were ambivalent towards slavery: the slave trade was banned in 1812, though illegal trading continued for many years. Although no moves were made to abolish slavery, the new government's desperate need for troops to fight the Spanish led it to buy slaves from masters; such soldiers were promised freedom after five years if they survived. Black troops played an important role in the struggle for independence. Some 1,500 of the 5,000 troops in San Martín's Army of the Andes were black and San Martín regarded them as his best infantry.

Slavery was finally abolished 1853 when the Constitution formally outlawed it, but the decline in numbers of blacks and mulattoes in the 19th century is rarely explained by historians: massive European migration is part of the answer as well as the high mortality rate of black soldiers who formed an important part of the Argentine forces in the War of the Triple Alliance against Paraguay. However, another explanation is that as Argentine society became more self-consciously white, writers and historians ignored the black contribution, while blacks themselves dyed their hair and tried to hide their origins.

of Buenos Aires, where almost 40% of the population lives, the people are mainly of European origin. In the far northern provinces, at least half the people are *mestizos* though they form about 15% of the population of the whole country.

INDIGENOUS PEOPLES

Though Argentina is a largely white society there are 13 different indigenous minorities, totaling about 500,000 people, 3% of the total population. Most live in communities in the north, bordering Bolivia and Paraguay. The largest group, about 30% of the total, are the *Colla* in the northwest, who speak Quechua and are closely related to indigenous groups in Bolivia. The other large minorities are the *Toba* (20%), the *Wichi* or *Mataco* (10%), the *Mapuche* (10%) and the *Guarani* (10%). Several of the smaller groups are in danger of extinction: in 1987 the Minority Rights Group reported the death of the last *Ona* in Tierra del Fuego and noted that the 100 remaining *Tehuelches* were living on a reservation in southern Patagonia. A number of organizations represent indigenous interests, but any legislation, under federal law, has to be enacted separately by each province.

IMMIGRATION

The transformation of the Humid Pampa through immigration, began a process which has made Argentina into a society of predominantly European origin. White immigration was encouraged by the 1853 Constitution and the new political stablity after 1862 encouraged a great wave of settlers from Europe. Between 1857 and 1930 total immigration was over 6 million, almost all from Europe. About 55% of these were Italians, followed by Spaniards (26%), and then, far behind, groups of other Europeans and Latin Americans. British and North Americans normally came as stockbreeders, technicians and business executives. By 1895 25% of the population of 4 million were immigrants. There were also large numbers of migrant workers, known as *golondrinas* (swallows) who crossed the Atlantic each year to work on the harvest.

Over 1.3 million Italians settled in Argentina between 1876 and 1914, a majority of them from the north. Their influence can be seen in the country's food, its urban architecture and its language, especially in Buenos Aires where the local vocabulary has incorporated *Lunfardo*. Though this started out as the language of thieves, many of its expressions have become part of the city's slang. Today it is estimated that 12.8% of the population are foreign born. Although most immigrants are of European origin, there are also important communities of Syrians, Lebanese, Armenians, Japanese and Koreans.

Main indigenous minorities

Culture

ARTS AND CRAFTS

Modern South American handicrafts represent either the transformation of utilitarian objects into works of art or the continued manufacture of pieces which retain symbolic value. Some traditional handicrafts are threatened by factors such as urbanization, the loss of types of wood and plant fibres through the destruction of forests and the replacement of the horse by farm machinery. At the same time, the survival of handicrafts has been helped by new demands from city dwellers and tourists. The most important areas for arts and crafts in Argentina are in the north of the country, regions where the indigenous minorities and pre-hispanic traditions are strongest.

As the Inca empire grew in the years before the arrival of the Spanish, it inherited many of the skills and traditions of pre-Inca cultures. Although northwestern Argentina had not been brought within the Inca Empire, it had developed strong links with modern Peru and Bolivia. After the conquest Spanish trade routes which ran through the northwest towards Lima contributed towards maintaining these influences. Two of the major areas of craftwork today are in the valleys of Catamarca and western Salta.

WOODCARVING

In colonial times the most important area for woodcarving was the northeast. Though woodcarving dated back beyond the Spanish conquest, a major influence on its development was the Catholic church, and particularly the Jesuit missions or *reducciones*. In Misiones, as in Paraguay, the indigenous Guaraní were set to work to build churches and produce woodcarvings and other handicrafts to decorate them. Although the Indians were

The Gaucho in history and legend

The *gaucho*, the cowboy of the Pampas, played an important role in Argentine history though, like his North American counterpart, he has long since become a cultural and political symbol. *Gauchos* emerged as a distinct social group in the early 18th century, hunting wild cattle on the pampas and adopting aspects of the lifestyle of the Indians. The classic *gaucho* lived on horseback, dressing in a poncho, a *chiripá* (baggy trousers) which were held up by a *tirador* or broad leather belt and homemade boots with iron spurs. Armed with *boleadoras* (three stones linked by leather which when expertly thrown would wrap round the legs of an animal) and a *facón* or large knife, he roamed the pampas in a period before fencing and private property, when the herds of wild cattle and horses seemed inexhaustible. Understandably his way of life gave little time for officials who tried to extend government control over the pampas. The urban population in turn regarded the *gaucho* as a savage, almost on a par with the Indians, and governments tried to tame him with anti-vagrancy laws and military conscription.

Inevitably, perhaps, this lifestyle was doomed, brought to an end in the 19th century by fencing, railways, the campaigns against the Indians and the redistribution of land which followed them. Increasingly the term *gaucho* came to mean a ranch worker who made a living on horseback tending cattle. However, as real *gauchos* disappeared from the pampas, they became a major subject of Argentine folklore and literature.

The Buenos Aires Herald

🐾 Founded in 1876, the *Herald* was not the only English language newspaper in Argentina, or, until the 1920s the most successful: its rival, *The Standard*, founded in 1861, outsold it until the First World War and only ceased publication in 1959. Until 1913, the paper was published sporadically (daily in theory but not in practice). Though a public company since 1920, the *Herald* has been controlled since 1968 by the Evening Post Publishing Company of Charleston, South Carolina.

The newspaper's finest hour occurred during the dark days of the 1976-1983 military government; despite death threats, the *Herald* was the only Argentine paper to cover human rights abuses and its news editor, Andrew Graham-Youll, was forced to leave for Britain. The newspaper's courageous stand received international recognition; in 1978 it was awarded the Moors-Cabot prize, seen by some as the 'Oscar of journalism' for being a "still, small voice of calm" in a climate of fear and violence.

The paper's fortunes have fluctuated since the return to civilian rule in 1983; its attempt to launch a Spanish-language evening paper *El Heraldo* in 1988 failed in the hyperinflation of the period, but the return of Andrew Graham-Youll from Britain in 1994 has led to new ventures, most importantly the launch of a monthly supplement on World Trade and the publication of *The Guardian Weekly* as a free supplement on Sundays.

The *Herald* offers a highly individualistic view of the world, described by Nicholas Tozer, its former co-editor, as "a universal view of what the world looks like as seen from Buenos Aires". The paper's latest readership survey may help explain its self-identity: some 57% of readers define themselves as Argentines for, as Tozer points out "speaking English doesn't necessarily mean that you are a foreigner here ... our readers identify with Argentina. Some 13% are from the US and 9% from the UK." The paper's policy is, he adds, "to talk knowledgeably about both Argentina and the rest of the world."

The *Herald* tends therefore to be indispensable to English-speaking visitors not only as a source of international news, but also for insights into Argentine life. Since these insights also appear at times through the mirror of the particular interests and concerns of the English-speaking communities, the result can be intriguing: world news, English cricket and football results, Argentine polo, baseball from the United States, livestock prices, shipping: perhaps the particular genius of the paper is that this combination works. The Sunday edition may be of particular interest to travellers, apart from *The Guardian Weekly*, the paper carries a regular review of local political and economic developments and Dereck Foster's justly famous food column.

Nicholas Tozer, former co-editor of the Herald, was interviewed by Brad Krupsaw.

left to fend for themselves after the expulsion of the Jesuits, some of the traditional techniques survive today in the woodcarvings of this area.

Further north *palo santo* (Bulnesia sarmiento), a greenish scented wood, is used extensively in wood carving by communities who live along the Río Pilcomayo which forms the frontier with Paraguay. At Campo Durán, north of Tartagal in the lowland area of northeastern Salta, the hollow trunk of the *palo santo* tree is adapted for making wooden masks, used in traditional agricultural ceremonies. Isolated groups of Toba, Chane and Mataca Indians in this part of the province produce exquisite carvings of birds and animals, using a variety of local woods including *palo santo*, the reddish *quebracho* (Schinopsis balansae), the brown or black *guayacan* (Caesalpina Paraguariensis) and a yellow wood known locally as *mora* (Chorophora Tinctoria). Cowbones are used to make the beaks and feet, as well as an inlay to decorate spoons and other utilitarian items. *Palo santo* vessels for drinking *maté* are made, replacing the traditional gourd.

In the valleys of Catamarca and Salta in the northwest wood from the cardoon cactus is used for carving small objects and furniture, though overexploitation of the cardoon has led to restrictions on its use.

TEXTILES AND WEAVING

Woven cloth was the most highly prized possession and trading commodity in the Andes in pre-Columbian times. Some of that tradition survives in the valleys of Catamarca and Salta, where ponchos, blankets, wallhangings and rugs are woven from alpaca and lambs wool. Ponchos are produced in most of these valleys including the beautiful red and black *poncho de Güemes*, named after the local independence leader Martín Güemes. Hand-made ponchos represent at least a week's work and often much more. Perhaps the most important centre is the village of Santa María in Catamarca province but just south of Cafayate.

Further south on the pampas from colonial times through to the 19th century the most readily available source of clothing was animal hides, which were cut into strips of different widths and then used to plait clothing, saddlery and stirrups. Fine leatherwork is still produced in many parts of the pampas.

JEWELLERY AND METALWORK

While the Spanish were dazzled by the Incas' use of gold, it was the pre-Inca cultures who had mastered the art of working with metal. In the colonial period the Spanish preferred to work in silver rather than gold and great quantities of silver were mined at Potosi in Alto Peru. In Argentina silverwork is particularly associated with the gauchos of the pampas. Here as in neighbouring Uruguay all the trappings of riding: stirrups, bits, rings, halters and spurs, were often made from silver, as well as costume accessories such as engraved buttons and belts. *Maté* drinking is another tradition associated with the *gauchos*; the traditional gourd, used for drinking *maté* was also often replaced with a vessel made of silver; the *bombilla* or pipe through which it is drunk is still frequently made of silver.

Handicrafts can be purchased in Buenos Aires and in northern Argentina. Details are given under **Shopping** in the text and in **Information for travellers**. For further information see *Arts and Crafts of South America* by Lucy Davies and Mo Fini (Tumi, 1994).

CINEMA

'To enter a cinema in Calle Lavalle and find myself (not without surprise) in the Gulf of Bengal or Wabash Avenue seems preferable to entering the same cinema and finding myself (not without surprise) in Calle Lavalle.' (Jorge Luis Borges).

Borges, Argentina's greatest writer and sometime film critic, had a lifetime attachment to the movies, even when his eyesight failed him later in life. In the 1920s and 1930s, however, he could go regularly to the cinemas clustered in Calle Lavalle or in Avenida Corrientes, in central Buenos Aires. In 1922, the city had some 27 million film goers each year and 128 movie theatres, the largest, the Grand Splendid seating 1,350 people. By 1933 there were 1,608 cinemas throughout Argentina, with 199 in the capital. However, as Borges points out, the taste of the cinema going public was for Hollywood movies. Hollywood has dominated the screens in Latin America for the first hundred years of film history, averaging some 90% of viewing time in Argentina. The history of a national cinema in Latin America is, therefore, the story of men and women working under the influence of the power of Hollywood, with its control of production, distribution and exhibition.

The question of whether to reject or accept the Hollywood model is not a simple one, certainly not as simple as the radical theorists of cultural imperialism

Fernando Solanas

After an early career working in different facets of the culture industry, from advertising to journalism, Solanas began working on documentary shorts from the early sixties and became a founder member of the radical group of film makers, Cine Liberación, together with Octavio Getino, Gerardo Vallejo and others. Between 1966 and 1968 this group directed *La hora de los hornos* (The Hour of the Furnaces), a colossal four hour documentary divided into three parts which traced the nature of Argentina's neo colonial dependency on Europe and postulated revolutionary Peronism as the liberating future for Argentina. Formally complex, ideologically black and white, the film was screened in a clandestine manner throughout the military regimes of the late sixties and early seventies and went on general release with the return of Perón in 1973. It became one of the touchstones of the 'new' Latin American cinema. The film was accompanied by a seminal essay, 'Towards a Third Cinema', which looked to revolutionary Latin American cinema as an alternative to the dominance of both Hollywood and 'author' cinema.

Solanas's first work of fiction *Los hijos de Fierro* (The Sons of Martin Fierro) was started in 1972 but was not completed until 1977, by which time he had been forced into exile by the military government. This attempt to link the mythology of Peronism to the nationalist, liberationist myths surrounding the 19th century epic poem *Martín Fierro* was condemned to a circuit of international film festivals outside Argentina where its symbolism was largely misunderstood.

Solanas's exile in France was difficult: he produced only one documentary and later examined the complexities of the exile experience in *Tangos, el exilio de Gardel* (Tangos, the Exile of Gardel, 1985), a film part financed under the new democratic regime of Alfonsín in Argentina. The tone of this was very different to the earlier films, seeking to explore dreams and desires through music and choreography and hauntingly beautiful imagery. His next film, *Sur* (South, 1988) explored Argentina-under dictatorship and finding its path in the new democracy- in the same evocative blend of music, theatre, dream narrative and strong political concern. *El viaje* (The Journey, 1992), a search of a son for his father, who personifies Argentine (and Latin American) identity, drew on the strong Argentine theatrical tradition of the grotesque: it is in part a grotesque farce levelled at corrupt politicians. Solanas's uncompromising political engagement has brought him death threats and exile and has disrupted his career, but he remains irrepressibly committed to politics and to new ways of making movies that break conventions and ask us to look afresh at the world around us.

John King

in the 1960s (such as the film maker Fernando Solanas, see below) would have us believe. It is not just a matter of rejecting the dominant model and asserting a utopian free space of national cinema. Hollywood created a universal way of seeing cinema which was strongly influenced by the advanced technology itself, technology with which poorer competitors could not compete. However Hollywood also offered communities access to modernity and ways of understanding modern, urban life. Argentine culture has always developed through dialogue between cultures; receiving and understanding the lessons of Hollywood as well as its powerful limitations is an integral part of the cultural process. Hollywood stimulates debates and adds a dynamic element in the development of artistic creation. Argentine cinema must therefore be seen within this broader global framework.

The earliest pioneers of Argentine cinema concentrated on documentaries because this was a niche in which international competitors were not greatly concerned. Documentaries on regional topics, football competitions, civic ceremonies and military parades reflected society's self image, especially that of Argentina's ruling elite: its fashions, its power, its ease and comfort in modern cities and in a spectacular rural landscape. The most successful fictional film maker of the silent era (and beyond), José ('El negro') Ferreyra (1889-1943) used the structures of melodrama, embodied in the lyrics of tango, to express a society in transition. The tango protagonist is often stranded in the world of modernity ('*Anclado en París*' or anchored in Paris) dreaming and singing nostalgically of his mother, friends, the lovers' nest (*bulín*) and the neighbourhood (*barrio*). In contrast, an *ingenu(e)* is propelled into the world of modernity, prostitutes have hearts of gold and the *barrio* offers the site for homespun wisdom. The trauma of the new in these early movies is both desire and threat. Ferreyra could sometimes count on Argentine band leaders such as Roberto Firpo to give his silent films live backing. Remarkably, in a world of solitary small-scale production,

María Luisa Bemberg, 1922-1995

Born into one of Argentina's wealthiest families, María Luisa Bemberg had a conventional aristocratic education, taught by a succession of British nannies. She would later explore the advantages and limitations of this background in one of her most personal films, *Miss Mary* (1986) starring Julie Christie as an Irish nanny sent out to Argentina in the 1930s to tutor the three children of a complex upper class family. Schooling-mainly in languages: she spoke fluent French and English- was followed by marriage to an architect and the raising of four children. It was after her divorce that she began working in theatre and cinema, becoming a scriptwriter at the age of 48. She would fulfil her ambition to direct movies a decade later, rapidly achieving the deserved status of being one of the finest and most respected film-makers in Latin America.

Her first two features, *Momentos* (Moments, 1981) and *Señora de nadie* (Nobody's Wife, 1982) were produced under the military dictatorship and caused controversy in her depiction of women caught in, and trying to escape from, the restrictions of loveless marriages and comfortable, cloying, middle class existence. They became successful at the box office and, remarkably for a film maker in Latin America, showed a profit, as would all her later films. She had a genuinely popular appeal. She gained widespread national and international recognition with *Camila* (1984), based on the story of Camila O'Gorman, a young aristocratic woman who, during the mid-19th century dictatorship of Rosas, fell in love and eloped with a Catholic priest and was punished for her transgression by execution. This beautifully constructed melodrama became a huge box office success, striking a chord in Argentine society still healing the scars of a more recent dictatorship. After *Miss Mary* (1986) she explored in *Yo, la peor de todas* (I, the Worst of All, 1990) the life of one of Latin America's most famous women of letters, the 17th century Mexican poet and nun, Sor Juana Inés de la Cruz. This was followed in 1992 with *De eso no se habla* (We Don't Want to Talk About It), another study in female constraint and transgression, this time from the point of view of an enigmatic and beautiful dwarf. María Luisa Bemberg completed a final screenplay at the time of her death through cancer, working to the end in the profession that she had so enriched.

John King

the first animated feature film in the world was produced in Argentina – *El apóstol* (The Apostle, 1917), animated by Quirino Cristiani and produced by Federico Valle. Most films, however, did not reveal such technical virtuosity and Argentine movies could only be seen sporadically among the foreign imports.

The coming of sound in the late 1920s created a new, complex situation in Latin America. Many shared the optimism that talkies would call a halt to the dominance of Hollywood: if the image could be understood everywhere, surely language and music were particular to specific cultures. These optimists could surely have been right, but they were wrong: for a number of years, the expense and complexity of the new technologies were too daunting for poorer countries, while Hollywood soon got over its hesitancies about dubbing and subtitling to remain the world market leader. But sound did give an opportunity for certain countries- in particular Argentina, Brazil and Mexico- to develop national industries. In Argentina two major studios were opened, Lumitón and Argentina Sono Film, which began production in 1933 to exploit the potential of tango-led national cinema. Ferreyra continued his work from the silent era, while a new director, Manuel Romero (1891-1954) made formulaic movies in rapid succession and to great popular acclaim: titles such as *Mujeres que trabajan* (Working Women, 1938) and *Los muchachos de antes no usaban gomina* (Back Then, Boys Didn't Use Hair Cream, 1937), which starred Mireya, the tart with the heart, oblivious to the advances of rich men about town. The great tango singer Carlos Gardel (1890-1935) made his movies as part of Hollywood's Hispanic film drive in the early 1930s, when the studios were afraid of losing regional markets and remade versions of Hollywood films in different languages. But the question of whether he might have stayed in the Hollywood system as a singing star in English, or return to Argentina to help develop the national industry, remained unanswered with his early death in a plane crash in 1935. Other

stars, but with nothing like the national or indeed international resonance of Gardel, Latin America's first cultural superstar, were actress Niní Marshall (1913-), the comic Luis Sandrini (1905-1980) and the singer Libertad Lamarque (1908-).

Other directors began to learn the language as well as the successful formulae of film making. A growing sophistication can be seen in the work of Leopoldo Torres Ríos (1899-1960) in his realist urban dramas, Mario Soffici (1900-1977), in particular the memorable *Prisioneros de la tierra* (Prisoners of the Land, 1939), which had a favourable review even from Borges, and Luis Savlavsky (1908-1995). A fleeting attempt was made to create an epic Argentine western (a southern?) with Lucas Demare's (1910-1981) *La guerra gaucha* (The Gaucho War, 1942) and *Pampa bárbara* (Barbarous Pampa, 1945), but the gauchesque tradition, outlined in the section on literature, never achieved even a fraction of the same mythic significance in film as the cowboy in the western.

By the late 1940s the formulae were becoming somewhat weary and repetitive and state protection for national cinema, introduced by the Peronist regime, could not halt this decline. International companies could soon bully the government into lifting credit restrictions, exhibitors could flaunt the screen quotas and production money tended to be channelled into safe, non innovative productions. It was time for a change. From the mid to late fifties, the changes could be perceived in several different countries and were given the name, by critics and the film makers themselves, of 'new cinema'.

New cinema had both aesthetic and highly charged political meanings. Film clubs and journals created a climate of awareness of film as an art form and the tenets of Italian neo-realism and the '*politique des auteurs*' of *Cahiers du Cinema* provided alternatives to the studio based Hollywood system. In Argentina, Leopoldo Torre Nilsson (1924-1978) and Fernando Birri (1925-)

showed the different tendencies within new cinema. Torre Nilsson was an 'author' who explored aristocratic decadence and his early film *La casa del ángel* (The House of the Angel, 1957) was greeted with praise all over the world. Influenced by Bergman, French New Wave and its British contemporaries, Karel Reisz and Lindsay Anderson and in close collaboration with his wife, the writer Beatriz Guido, he explored the contradictions and decline of Argentine upper class and genteel bourgeois society. Birri, a student of Zavattini and neo realism, sought to use neo realist principles to explore the hidden realities of Argentina. His film school in Santa Fé made an important documentary about young shanty town children, *Tire dié* (Throw us a dime, 1957) and helped pioneer a more flexible, socially committed, cinema, 'with a camera in hand and an idea in the head' in the famous phase of Brazilian director Glauber Rocha.

Younger film makers of the sixties like Manuel Antín (1926-), David Kohon (1929-) and Leonardo Favio (1938-) initially followed Torre Nilsson's and their Parisian counterparts' example in exploring, often through literary adaptations, middle-class anomie and alienation or the sexual rights of passage of the young, set in the cafés and streets of Buenos Aires. Meanwhile, the growing climate of revolutionary sentiment of the late 1960s was reflected in Solanas's *La hora de los hornos* (The Hour of the Furnaces, 1966-8), a key text of populist radicalism.

After a brief spell of radical optimism in the late 1960s and early 1970s, reflected in a number of other nationalist-populist movies, the dream of the second coming of Perón turned into the nightmare that led to the brutal military takeover in March 1976. Strict censorship was imposed on cinema, with only the lightest comedies and thrillers escaping total ban or cuts. Film makers such as Solanas, who went into exile, found it difficult to adapt to the new conditions and remained in a cultural wilderness, unlike the Chilean refugee Diaspora, which made many important films in exile.

Within Argentina, the tight military control began to slacken in the early 1980s and some important films were made, including María Luisa Bemberg's (1922-1995) *Señora de nadie* (Nobody's Woman, 1982) which was premiered the day before the invasion of the Falklands/Malvinas.

With the return to civilian rule in 1983, the Radical government abolished censorship and put two well known film makers in charge of the National Film Institute, Manuel Antín and Ricardo Wullicher (1948-). Antín's granting of credits to young and established directors and his internationalist strategy had an immediate effect. For several years there was a great flowering of talent, a development that would only be halted temporarily by the economic difficulties of the late 1980s. The trade paper *Variety* (25 March 1987) commented on this new effervescence: 'Never before has there been such a mass of tangible approval as in the years since democratic rule returned at the end of 1983. In 1986, the Hollywood Academy sealed the trend with its first Oscar for and Argentine picture, "The Official Version".' The first massive box office success of these years was Bemberg's *Camila,* which commented by analogy on the recent traumas of Argentine society, a topic taken up directly in Luis Puenzo's (1946-) *La historia oficial* (The Official Version, 1986) and Solanas's two films about exile and the return to democracy: *Tangos, el exilio de Gardel* (Tangos the Exile of Gardel, 1985) and *Sur* (South, 1988). Puenzo, Bemberg and Solanas remained the most visible directors in the 1980s and 1990s, but dozens of other directors made movies in a range of different styles. Eliseo Subiela (1944-) directed several poetic, highly personal, movies, while Lita Stantic, made perhaps the most complex film about the 'dirty war' of the military regime, *Un muro de silencio* (A Wall of Silence, 1993). This was a success with the critics, but was ignored by the public, which preferred to view politics and repression through a gauze of melodrama and rock music, as in Marcelo Piñeyro's *Tango feroz* (1993).

Since 1989 the Menem government has introduced credits and a percentage of box office and video sales to the film industry and there is currently buoyancy and optimism in the industry. How this will be sustained in times of economic decline and with the increasing globalization of cinema remains the open question for the next century.

LITERATURE

'Hard to imagine that Buenos Aires had any beginning/ I consider it as eternal as air and water', wrote Jorge Luis Borges in a homage to the city of his birth in 1923. By the 1920s, Buenos Aires was a thriving metropolitan centre, but its beginnings were altogether more modest.

The isolation of the Río de la Plata region and the low priority attributed to it by the Spanish during the colonial period were reflected in the underdevelopment of intellectual life: in 1776 there were only four primary schools and two secondary schools in Buenos Aires, all church run, to serve a city of some 25,000 people. Yet Enlightenment ideas, Romanticism and the economic tenets of free trade were introduced into this ever more complex society from Europe and North America. The works of Smith, Locke, Voltaire, Rousseau amongst others influenced the small literate elite of young intellectuals such as Mariano Moreno (1778-1811), one of the architects of the Independence movement. The way in which European forms could be adapted to American realities became one of the constant themes of Argentine intellectual and literary production, first in the form of political tracts and later in early nationalist poetry. Outside the cities, popular culture did not rest on strong cultural survival among the scattered and impoverished indigenous groups or in any developed African Argentine presence, but rather in the oral tradition of storytelling and music of the gauchos, Argentina's cowboys, the itinerant inhabitants of the pampas. Gaucho poets, like Medieval troubadours, would travel from settlement to settlement, to country fairs and cattle roundups, singing of the events of the day and of the encroaching political constraints that would soon bring restrictions to their traditional way of life.

The 19th century

The earliest literary forms of Argentina in its struggle for independence between 1810 and 1820 were patriotic poems written by Bartolomé Hidalgo (1788-1822) and Hilario Ascasubi (1807-71), amongst others, which gave an urban, stylized form to the oral culture of the gaucho and put literature at the service of political struggle. As the attempt to consolidate the nation state in the aftermath of independence would be fought out for a further 30 years, writers such as Esteban Echeverría (1805-51) would play a leading role in these debates through literary salons, in poetry and in short fiction. Perhaps the most important tract of the generation, which was to become one of the vertebral texts of Argentine cultural history, was published in 1845 by an exile politician, Domingo Faustino Sarmiento (1811-88): *Facundo: Civilization and Barbarism*. Other memorable protest literature against the Rosas regime included Echeverría's 'El matadero' ('The Slaughterhouse', published posthumously in 1871) and José Mármol's melodramatic novel of star crossed lovers battling against the cut-throat hordes of Rosas: *Amalia* (1855).

The consolidation of Argentina along the lines advocated by Sarmiento and the growth of the export economy in alliance with British capital and technology may have benefitted the great landowners of the Littoral provinces, but those who did not fit into this dream of modernity- in particular the gaucho groups, turned off the land and forced to work as rural labourers- found their protest articulated by a provincial landowner, José Hernández (1834-1886), who wrote the famous gaucho epic poems *El gaucho Martín Fierro* (1872) and its sequel, *La vuelta de Martín Fierro* (The Return of Martín Fierro), 1879. The first part of *Martín Fierro* (the second part was an

Jorge Luis Borges, 1899-1986

Borges always talked of the two lineages that made up his family history: the Argentine and the British. Born in Buenos Aires, he observed a tension between the world 'outside', the city in the process of great demographic change, and the world 'inside' his father's library 'of unlimited English books'. Throughout his life he was obsessed by both the myths and realities of Argentina and its culture and also by the heterodox space of readings from universal literature. His original blending of these different concerns and sources has made him the most widely cited and influential figure in Argentine literature, with a world-wide reputation that transcends national boundaries.

In 1914, at the age of fifteen, Borges travelled with his family to Europe, only returning to Buenos Aires in 1921. He lived in Switzerland and Spain, he learned Latin, French and German, became acquainted with the modernist movements in Europe and began to write. He was thus well equipped to become an active member of the literary avant garde which emerged in Buenos Aires in the 1920s: a decade in which he was frantically busy, contributing to every little magazine and publishing seven books of poetry and essays. Although in later life he called these works naive, they reveal his dominant obsessions: a sideways view of life and literature, perceived from 'las orillas' (the outskirts, the margins) and a philosophical and literary reappraisal of authorship and individual consciousness.

From the 1930s he worked as a librarian and a literary journalist, producing his first book of short stories, *Historia universal de la infamia* (A Universal History of Infamy) in 1935. From the late 1930s, he moved quietly onto the offensive, publishing in quick succession a series of significant essays, book prologues and short stories, the latter comprising what is arguably the most important collection of stories in the history of Latin American literature, the magisterial *Ficciones* (Fictions, 1944). In this volume, he turned inside out the received conventions of literary nationalism, realism and authorship, in stories that explored the nature of literature itself, philosophy and metaphysics. *Ficciones* was followed by *El Aleph* in 1949 and his most important book of essays, *Otras inquisiciones* (Other Inquisitions, 1952). A masterful story-teller, he never wrote more than a few pages and was never tempted by the novel form, insisting that more could be explored in a few elliptical, highly suggestive and poetic lines than in hundred of pages of dull realist prose.

The late forties brought almost total blindness and a running dispute with the demagoguery of Perón, who, for Borges, was the embodiment of a populist nationalism that he considered the worst aspect of Argentine identity. Borges's opposition to a figure who, in the forties and from the late sixties, embodied the hopes of so many, led a whole generation of Argentine critics to ignore the truly radical propositions of his own writing. His rise to international prominence occurred in the sixties in Europe and the United States, at a time when his own work was mainly confined to poetry, a form which, with the onset of blindness, he could compose and restructure in his head. But it was perhaps the world-wide attention to his fictions which brought him, late in life, to publish two further books of stories, *El informe de Brodie* (Dr Brodie's Report, 1970) and *El libro de arena* (The Book of Sand, 1975), works that he claimed to be 'realist' but which are just as ironic and subversive as his earlier work. In his final years he kept up publishing essays and poems, and travelled the world with his constant companion María Kodama, whom he married. He died in Geneva in June 1986, the city where, as an adolescent, he had learned new languages and developed his heterodox readings.

John King

accommodation to political power interests) is a genuine shout of rage against the march of progress and modernity that disrupts local communities and traditional ways of life. Framed as a gauchesque song, chanted by the dispossessed outlaw, it became one of the most popular works of literature and Martín Fierro came to symbolize the spirit of the Argentine nation.

Yet this was an isolated cry of protest. As a small group of families led the great export boom, the 'gentleman' politicians of the 'Generation of 1880' wrote their memoirs, none better than Sarmiento's *Recuerdo de Provincia* (Memoirs of Provincial Life, 1850.). Also among this group are Lucio Victoria Mansilla (1831-1913) and Miguel Cané (1852-1905). But, as Buenos Aires grew into a dynamic modern city, the gentleman memorialist soon gave way to the professional writer: professional not in the sense of the possibility of writers making a living through writing - difficult today, impossible then - but rather in the writers' perceptions of themselves as writers. The key poet in this respect was the Nicaraguan Rubén Darío (1867-1916), who lived for an important period of his creative life in Buenos Aires and led a movement called *modernismo* which asserted the separateness of poetry as a craft, removed from the dictates of national panegyric or political necessity. It was Darío who would give inspiration to the poet Leopoldo Lugones (1874-1938), famous also for his prose writings on nationalist, gauchesque themes. Lugones's evocation of the gaucho as a national symbol would be developed in the novel *Don Segundo Sombra*, by Ricardo Guiraldes (1886-1927), the story of a boy taught the skills for life by a gaucho mentor.

The early 20th century

The complex urban societies evolving in Argentina by the turn of the century created a rich cultural life. In the 1920s a strong vanguard movement developed which questioned the dominant literary orthodoxies of the day. Little magazines such as *Martín Fierro* (another appropriation of the ubiquitous national symbol) proclaimed novelty in poetry and attacked the dull social realist writings of their rivals the Boedo group. Argentina's most famous writer, Jorge Luis Borges (1899-1986) began his literary life as an avant garde poet, in the company of writers such as Oliverio Girondo (1891-1967) and Norah Lange (1906-1972). Many of these poets were interested in expressing the dynamism and changing shape of their urban landscape, Buenos Aires, this Paris on the periphery. Roberto Arlt also caught the dreams and nightmares of the urban underclasses in novels such as *El juguete rabioso* (The Rabid Toy, 1926) and *Los siete locos* (The Seven Madmen, 1929).

Much of the most interesting literature of the 1930 and 1940s was first published in the literary journal *Sur*, founded by the aristocratic writer, Victoria Ocampo. By far the most important group to publish in its pages were Borges and his close friends Silvina Ocampo (1903?-1993), Victoria's sister, and Silvina's husband, Adolfo Bioy Casares (1914-) who, from the late 1930s, in a series of short fictions and essays, transformed the literary world. They had recurrent concerns: an indirect style, a rejection of realism and nationalist symbols, the use of the purified motifs and techniques of detective fiction and fantastic literature, the quest for knowledge to be found in elusive books, the acknowledgement of literary criticism as the purest form of detective fiction and the emphasis on the importance of the reader rather than the writer.

Peronism and Literature

The 10-year period of Perón's first two presidencies, 1946-1955, can be seen as a deliberate assault on the aristocratic, liberal values which had guided Argentina since the Generation of 1880. Claiming to be a new synthesis of democracy, nationalism, anti-imperialism and industrial development, Peronism attacked the undemocratic, dependent Argentine oligarchy (personified in such literary figures as Victoria Ocampo or Adolfo Bioy Casares). The period 1946-1955 was seen by most intellectuals and writers as an era of cultural obscurantism and some writers such as Julio Cortázar (1914-1984) – in the 1940s and 1950s a writer of elegant fantastic and realist stories- chose voluntary exile to remaining in Perón's Argentina. The novelist, Ernesto Sábato (1911-) set his best novel *Sobre héroes y tumbas* (On Heroes and Tombs, 1961) partly in the final moments of the Peronist regime, when the tensions of the populist alliance were beginning to become manifest. But Perón was not much interested in the small circulation of literature and concentrated his attention on mass forms of communication such as radio and cinema. This period saw further mature work from the poets Enrique Molina (1910-), Olga Orozco (1922-) and Alberto Girri (1919-1991), whose austere, introspective verse was an antidote to the populist abuse of language in the public sphere. The literary field was to be further stimulated, after the downfall of Perón, with the development of publishing houses and the 'boom' of Latin American literature of the 1960s.

The 1960s

In Argentina the sixties was a decade of great literary and cultural effervescence. The novel to capture this mood was Cortázar's *Rayuela* (Hopscotch, 1963), which served as a Baedeker of the new, with its comments on literature, philosophy, new sexual freedoms and its open, experimental structure. It was promoted in a weekly journal *Primera Plana*, which also acted as a guide to expansive modernity. Thousands of copies of *Rayuela* were sold to an expanded middle class readership in Argentina and throughout Latin America. Other novelists and writers benefited from these conditions, the most significant being the Colombian Gabriel García Márquez who published what would later become one of the best selling novels of the 20th century, *Cien años de soledad* (One Hundred Years of Solitude, 1967) with an Argentine publishing house. Significant numbers of women writers helped to break the male monopoly of literary production, including the novelists Beatriz Guido and Marta Lynch

and the poet Alejandra Pizarnik (1936-1972), with her intense exploration of the inner self.

Literature under the Military Dictatorships

The 'swinging' sixties were curtailed by a military coup in 1966. As, in the years which followed, Argentine political life descended into anarchy, violence and repression, virtually all forms of cultural activity were silenced and well known writers including Haroldo Conti and Rodolfo Walsh 'disappeared'. Many more had to seek exile including the poet Juan Gelman, whose son and daughter in law counted among the disappeared.

Understandably this nightmare world provided the dominant themes of the literary output of these years. The return in old age of Perón, claimed by all shades of the political spectrum, was savagely lampooned in Osvaldo Soriano's (1943-) novel *No habrá más penas ni olvido* (A Funny, Dirty Little War, 1982, but completed in 1975). The world of the sombre designs of the ultra right wing López Rega, Isabel Perón's Minister of Social Welfare, is portrayed in Luisa Valenzuela's (1938-) terrifying, grotesque novel *Cola de lagartija* (The Lizard's Tail, 1983). Of the narrative accounts of those black years, none is more harrowing than Miguel Bonasso's (1940-) fictional documentary of the treatment of the Montoneros guerrilla group in prison and in exile: *Recuerdo de la muerte* (Memory of Death, 1984). Other writers in exile chose more indirect ways of dealing with the terror and dislocation of those years. Daniel Moyano (1928-1992), in exile for many years in Spain, wrote elegant allegories such as *El vuelo del tigre* (The Flight of the Tiger, 1981), which tells of the military style takeover of an Andean village by a group of percussionists who bring cacophony.

Within Argentina critical discussion was kept alive in literary journals such as *Punto de Vista* (1978-) and certain novels alluded to the current political climate within densely structured narratives: Ricardo Piglia's (1941-) *Respiración artificial*

(Artificial Respiration, 1980) has disappearance and exile as central themes, alongside bravura discussions of the links between fiction and history and between Argentina and Europe.

The Return to Civilian Rule

Following Alfonsín's election victory in 1983, the whole intellectual and cultural field responded to the new freedoms. Certain narratives depicted in harsh realism the brutalities of the 'dirty war' waged by the military and it was the novelist, Ernesto Sábato, who headed the Commission set up to investigate the disappearances. He wrote in the a prologue to the Commission's report *Nunca más* (Never

Manuel Puig, 1932-1990

Argentina's most talented postmodernist writer, Puig was brought up in a small town in the Argentine pampas, some fourteen hours by train from the capital. A survival instinct, he often said, made him construct another point of reference to that of everyday provincial life: the town cinema, which, from early childhood, became a daily pilgrimage. He tried to pursue this abiding love of the movies in professional terms, leaving Argentina in the mid fifties for Italy to study in the heart of Cinecittà at the famous *Centro Sperimentale di Cinema*. However, he was not impressed by its dominant orthodoxy of neo-realist social protest, which did not conform to what he called his 'hybrid pampa-MGM' view of the world.

He began writing film scripts but found his métier when a script based on his own personal experiences turned into a novel. He set the story in an Argentine laundry room, with his aunt gossiping about everyday life. She was supposed to have only a few lines of dialogue, but ended up talking for over thirty pages, the opening of Puig's first novel, *La Traición de Rita Hayworth* (Betrayed by Rita Hayworth, 1968).

It was Puig's particular genius to turn banality into a form of art, expressing the desires and hopes and frustrations of ordinary people: hopes which were structured, in the main, by the culture industry through serial novels, women's magazines and advertisements, radio soaps, the lyrics of tango, film melodrama, film stars. These cultural forms allowed one to dream alternative dreams for a while but made the awakening all the more difficult: in the end, living in a small town in Argentina in the thirties or forties, one would always be betrayed by Rita Hayworth. In his best novels, *Rita Hayworth, Boquitas Pintadas* (Heartbreak Tango, 1969) and the book (turned into a film) that brought him international recognition, *El beso de la Mujer Araña* (Kiss of the Spider Woman, 1976), he shows the attractions and entrapments of the spider woman's web of mass culture. These novels also reveal his abiding interest in the way that gender roles are constructed and reproduced in society (often through mass culture) and his sympathy for women and homosexual men.

It was the radical proposition of *Kiss* - a dialogue and a developing love affair in prison between a lower middle class homosexual and an upper middle class revolutionary - that caused some of Puig's novels to be banned in Argentina under the dictatorship and forced him into exile from the mid seventies in New York and later in Brazil. Four novels followed, together with several published plays and film scripts, all structurally complex but effortlessly fluid in their narration, exploring the gaps between illusion and reality and exploring the survival strategies, against the odds, of his sympathetically drawn characters. His early death from a treatable illness, at the age of 57, seemed, like his life, to be drawn from one of his novels: optimistic, futile and ultimately courageous.

John King

Again, 1984): "We are convinced that the recent military dictatorship brought about the greatest and most savage tragedy in the history of Argentina".

Current literature echoes the famous lines by Borges in the essay 'The Argentine Writer and Tradition': "I believe that we Argentines ... can handle all European themes, handle them without superstition, with an irreverence which can have, and already does have, fortunate consequences." While many of the writers that first brought modernity to Argentine letters have died – Borges, Victoria and Silvina Ocampo, Girri, Cortázar, Puig – the later generations have assimilated their lessons. Juan Carlos Martini writes stylish thrillers, blending high and low culture. Juan José Saer (1937-), from his self imposed exile in Paris, recreates his fictional world, Colastiné, in the city of Santa Fé, in narratives that are complex, poetic discussions on memory and language. The most successful novel of recent years is Tomás Eloy Martínez's (1934-) *Santa Evita* (1995) which tells/reinvents the macabre story of what happened to Evita's embalmed body between 1952 and the mid 1970s. The narrative skilfully discusses themes that are at the heart of all writing and critical activity. The critic, like the embalmer of Evita's body, 'seeks to fix a life or a body in the pose that eternity should remember it by'. But what this critic, like the narrator of Eloy Martínez's novel, realizes is that a corpus of literature cannot be fixed in that way, for literature escapes such neat pigeon holes. Instead, glossing Oscar Wilde, the narrator states that 'that the only duty that we have to history is to rewrite it'. The ending of the novel makes the point about the impossibility of endings: "Since then, I have rowed with words, carrying Santa Evita in my boat, from one shore of the blind world to the other. I don't know where in the story I am. In the middle, I believe. I've been here in the middle for a long time. Now I must write again". (*Santa Evita*, New York and London, 1996, page 369.)

FINE ART AND SCULPTURE

Pre-Conquest and Colonial Art

Argentina (along with neighbouring Uruguay) is arguably the most European of Latin American cultures. Mass immigration and the 19th century extermination of the few remaining Indians have made a culture which defines itself largely in relation to Europe. The partial exception to this is in the north of the country, where proximity to the great Andean civilizations had some effect on local production, but on a much smaller scale than in neighbouring countries.

As the region which is now Argentina was of little importance to the Spanish, there is very little colonial art or architecture in most of Argentina. In the Northern regions of Salta, Jujuy and Misiones, there are some impressive colonial buildings, and some good examples of colonial painting, especially the remarkable portraits of archangels in military uniform in the churches at Uquía and Casabindo, but nothing on the scale of neighbouring Peru or Bolivia.

The 19th century

In the 19th century, as Argentina gained Independence and consolidated itself as a modern nation, the ruling elite of the country were determined to make Argentine culture as close to Europe as possible, against what they saw as the 'barbarism' of native customs. The prosperous Buenos Aires bourgeoisie commissioned European architects to build their mansions and collected European fine and decorative arts to decorate them. Rich Argentines travelled to Europe to buy paintings, and gradually began to demand that European painters come to Argentina to depict the wealth and elegance of the ruling class through portraits and landscapes. The most famous of these foreign artists was Carlos Enrique Pellegrini, whose fine society portraits can be seen in the Museo Nacional de Bellas Artes in Buenos Aires. While painters like Pellegrini came to work in Buenos Aires, another type of artist came to South America on scientific expeditions to register topography or flora and fauna. Many of these 'traveller artists' provided an image of the country which was to influence local artists: a familiar case of Europeans providing Argentina with an image of itself rather than vice-versa. Most famous of these traveller artists were the Englishman Emeric Essex Vidal and the German Johann Moritz Rugendas.

By the middle of the century, as Argentina became more politically stable, a new generation of Argentine-trained artists appeared in Buenos Aires. They absorbed some of the techniques and interests of the European artists who were the first to depict their country, but they also discovered a new interest in Romanticism and Realism. Most famous in this period was Prilidiano Pueyrredón (1823-70), who Argentines consider to be their first national painter. Of more obvious appeal is the rather eccentric Cándido López (1839-1902) whose work has only recently been reevaluated. López followed the Argentine army to the north of the country during the wars with Paraguay and Uruguay. There he began to depict the great battles in a characteristic naive style. López left behind a remarkable series of paintings, which are often displayed in their own room in the Museo Nacional de Bellas Artes in Buenos Aires.

By the end of the century, there were a considerable number of artists working in Argentina, many of whom had been through the National Art School. Generally speaking, they absorbed European movements such as Impressionism, Realism or Expressionism several decades after they appeared in their original forms. Some, such as Martin Malharro, Fernando Fader or Benito Quinquela Martin, were quite talented. Their often melancholic works can be seen in the Bellas Artes Museum or the Municipal 'Eduardo Sivori' Museum in Buenos Aires.

The 20th century

It is in the 20th century that Argentina really found its artistic expression, becoming for many decades an artistic 'superpower' in Latin America and beyond. The dynamism, size and mix of nationalities in the capital created a complex urban society in which artists and intellectuals have prospered. Some of the bohemian attraction of Buenos Aires can still be felt in its more intellectual cafes and districts. This cultural effervescence has been at the expense of the regions; the capital totally dominates the country, and most artists are forced to move there to have any chance of success.

The first avant-garde artistic movement in Buenos Aires emerged in 1924 with the formation of a groups which called itself 'Martin Fierro', in homage to the national epic poem of the same name. This group brought together a small number of high class intellectuals, the most famous of which was the writer Jorge Luis Borges. The most important visual artist was Xul Solar (1887-1963), who illustrated many of Borges's texts. Solar was one of the 20th century's most eccentric and engaging artists. He had a great interest in mysticism and the occult, and tried to create an artistic system to express his complex beliefs. Solar's works are mostly small scale water-colours in which a sometimes bizarre visionary world is depicted. Many of them are covered in inscriptions in one of the languages he created: Neo-Creole or Pan-Lengua. During the final decades of his life Solar lived in a house on the Tigre Delta, where he created a total environment in accordance with his fantastic world, even inventing a new game of chess with rules based on astrology. There is now a Xul Solar Museum in the house where he was born in Buenos Aires and where many of his water-colours and objects are displayed.

Intellectual life in the 1920s was divided into two factions, each named after districts in the city. The elegant Avenida Florida gave its name to the sophisticated Martin Fierro set, who belonged to the elite. Several blocks away, the working class Boedo district gave its name to a school of working class socialist artists who rejected the rarefied atmosphere of Florida in favour of socially critical paintings in a grim realistic style. Possibly the most important artist associated with this group was Antonio Berni (1905-81). Some of Berni's murals, together with those of his colleagues, can be seen on the roof of the Galerias Pacifico in Avenida Florida.

It was not until the 1940s, with the political crisis provoked by the Second World War, that a new avant-garde movement emerged to overtake the Martin Fierro group. In the mid 1940s, a group of young artists founded an abstract art movement called 'Madí' (a nonsense word) which attempted to combine sophisticated abstract art inspired by Russian Constructivism with a more chaotic sense of fun. Madí works are characterized by blocks of bright colours within an irregular frame, often incorporating physical movement within the structure of the work. As such, they are somewhere between painting and sculpture. For the first time in Argentina, Madí developed artistic principles (such as the irregular frame, or the use of neon gas) before the rest of the world.

Madí was a short-lived adventure, plagued by infighting amongst its members and political divisions. The cultural climate under Perón (1946-55) rejected this type of 'decadent' art in favour of a form of watered-down populism. It was not until the 1960s that cultural life regained its momentum.

The 1960s were a golden age for the arts in Argentina. As in many countries, the decade brought new freedoms and questions to young people, and the art scene responded vigorously. Artistic activity was focused around the centre of Buenos Aires between Plaza San Martin and Avenida Cordoba, an area known as the 'manzana loca' (crazy block). This area contained a huge number of galleries and cafes, and most importantly the Di Tella Institute, a privately-funded art centre which was at the cutting edge of the visual arts. Artistic movements of the time ranged from a raw expressionism called 'Nueva figuración' to very sophisticated conceptual art. The most provocative form of art during this period took the form of 'happenings', one of the most famous of which (by Marta Minujin) consisted of a replica of the Buenos Aires obelisk made in sweet bread, which was then eaten by passers-by.

After the military coup of 1966 the authorities began to question the activities of these young artists, and even tried to censor some exhibitions. The Di Tella Institute closed, leaving the 'manzana loca' without a heart, and making it more dangerous for alternative young artists to live without harassment (often for little more than having long hair). During the 'leaden years' of the military government during the 1970s, there was little space for alternative art, and many left-wing artists abandoned art in favour of direct political action. However, one space in Buenos Aires continued to show politically challenging art: the Centro de Arte y Comunicación (or CAYC), often through works which were so heavily coded that the authorities would not pick up the message.

Since the restoration of democracy in 1983, Argentina has been coming to terms with the destruction or inefficiency of many of its cultural institutions over recent decades. The last few years have seen a rebirth of activity, with improvements in the National Museum of Fine Arts and the creation of the important Centro Cultural Recoleta and more recently the Centro Cultural Borges (in the Galerias Pacifico). There are important alternative art centres, especially the Ricardo Rojas Centre and the Klemm Foundation which show some of the most interesting young artists. The art scene in Buenos Aires is now very vibrant, if somewhat confusing, with myriad conflicting and apparently contradictory styles and tendencies.

MUSIC AND DANCE

Buenos Aires contains a third of the country's population and its music is the Tango. Indeed to the outside world there is no other Argentine music. Although also sung and played, the Tango was born as a dance just before the turn of the 20th century. The exact moment of birth was

Carlos Gardel

Gardel, whose name is virutally synonymous with Tango, was born in 1890 in Toulouse, France, to Berthe Gardés and, according to his birth certificate, "an unknown father". To avoid the social stigma, his mother emigrated to Buenos Aires when her son was only 2 years old. Just as the exact origin of the Tango is itself something of a mystery, Gardel's formative years around the Abasto (or wholesale market) district of the city are obscure, at least until around 1912 when he began his artistic career in earnest, performing as one half of the Duo Gardel-Razzano, singing songs in the local traditional styles of the Estilo and Cifra. Only a year later he began his prolific career with Columbia, recording 15 traditional songs. It was not until 1917, however, that Gardel and Tango finally came together, but by the early 1920s he was singing entirely within this relatively new genre and achieving success as far afield as Madrid. The Duo Gardel-Razzano dissolved in 1925 and Gardel became a solo artist and the very epitome of the Tango both in Argentina and, following his tours to Europe, around the world. Between 1933 and 1935 he was based in New York, where he played roles in four Spanish-speaking films and one English-speaking film for Paramount. On 24 June 1935, while on a tour of South America, his plane from Bogota to Cali crashed into another on the ground while taking off from Medellín, Colombia. Gardel was killed instantly, to the immense grief of his public. The brilliance of his voice and personality, the manner in which he represented the spirit of the Río de la Plata to his fans at home combined with the universality of his appeal, the sheer volume of his recordings and the untimely nature of his dramatic death to ensure the endurance of his name.

Nigel Gallop

not recorded by any contemporary observer and continues to be a matter of debate, though the roots can be traced. The name 'Tango' predates the dance and was given to the carnivals (and dances) of the black inhabitants of the Río de la Plata in the early 19th century, elements of the black tradition being taken over by whites as the black population declined. However, the name 'Tango Americano' was also given to the Habanera (a Cuban descendent of the English Country Dance) which became the rage in Spain and bounced back into the Río de la Plata in the middle of the 19th century, not only as a fashionable dance, together with the polka, mazurka, waltz and cuadrille, but also as a song form in the very popular 'Zarzuelas', or Spanish operettas. However, the Habanera led not a double, but a triple life, by also infiltrating the lowest levels of society directly from Cuba via sailors who arrived in the ports of Montevideo and Buenos Aires. Here it encountered the Milonga, originally a Gaucho song style,

but by 1880 a dance, especially popular with the so-called 'Compadritos' and 'Orilleros', who frequented the port area and its brothels, whence the Argentine Tango emerged around the turn of the century to dazzle the populace with its brilliant, personalized footwork, which could not be accomplished without the partners staying glued together.

As a dance Tango became the rage and, as the infant recording industry grew by leaps and bounds, it also became popular as a song and an instrumental genre, with the original violins and flutes being eclipsed by the *bandoneón* button accordion, then being imported from Germany. In 1911 the new dance took Paris by storm and returned triumphant to Buenos Aires. It achieved both respectability and notoriety, becoming a global phenomenon after the First World War, with the golden voice of the Carlos Gardel giving a wholly new dimension to the music of the Tango until his death in 1935. After losing some popularity in

Argentina, it came to the forefront again in the 1940s (1920-50 is considered the real golden age). Its resurgence was assisted by Perón's decree that 50% of all music played on the radio must be Argentine, only to suffer a second, much more serious decline in the face of rock music over the following 2 decades. Fortunately, it has lately experienced a notable recovery, to the point where it is no longer difficult, as was the case until quite recently, to see the Tango and Milonga danced in Buenos Aires. Apart from Carlos Gardel, other great names connected with the Tango are Francisco Canaro (Uruguayan), Osvaldo Pugliese and Astor Piazzolla, who has modernized it by fusion with jazz styles (*nuevo tango*).

If the Tango represents the soul of Buenos Aires, this is not the case in the rest of the country. The provinces have a very rich and attractive heritage of folk dances, mainly for couples, with arms held out and fingers clicked or handkerchiefs waved, with the 'Paso Valseado' as the basic step. Descended from the Zamacueca, and therefore a cousin of the Chilean Cueca and Peruvian Marinera, is the slow and stately Zamba, where the handkerchief is used to greatest effect. Equally popular throughout most of the country are the faster Gato, Chacarera and Escondido. These were the dances of the Gaucho and their rhythm evokes that of a cantering horse. Guitar and the *bombo*

drum provide the accompaniment. Particularly spectacular is the Malambo, where the Gaucho shows off his dextrous footwork, the spurs of his boots adding a steely note to the rhythm.

Different regions of the country have their own specialities. The music of Cuyo in the west is sentimental and very similar to that of neighbouring Chile, with its Cuecas for dance and Tonadas for song. The northwest on the other hand is Andean, with its musical culture closer to that of Bolivia, particularly on the Puna, where the Indians play the *quena* and *charango* and sound mournful notes on the great long *erke*. Here the dances are Bailecitos and Carnavalitos, while the songs are Vidalitas and the extraordinary high pitched Bagualas, the very essence of primeval pain. In the northeast provinces of Corrientes and Misiones, the music shares cultural similarities with Paraguay. The Polca and Galopa are danced and the local Chamamé is sung, to the accordion or the harp, the style being sentimental. Santiago del Estero has exerted the strongest influence on Argentine folk music as a result of the work of Andres Chazarreta: it is the heartland of the Chacarera and the lyrics are often part Spanish and part Quichua, a local dialect of the Andean Quechua language. Down in the Province of Buenos Aires you are more likely to hear the Gauchos

The Zamba de Vargas

The stately and elegant Zamba, directly descended from the colonial Zamacueca and thus a first cousin to the Chilean and Bolivian Cueca and the Peruvian Marinera, is the quintessential Argentine folk dance. Of the many Zambas in the contemporary repertoire, none is finer than the justly famous Zamba de Vargas. Although first made famous by Andres Chazarreta, the words and melody are traditional and Chazarreta always claimed to have learned the song at his grandmother's knee. The words refer to an incident in the Battle of Pozo de Vargas (1867) between forces led by the rebel Felipe Varela from La Rioja and the government forces recruited in Santiago del Estero by General Antonio Taboada. According to the lyrics, Taboada's forces were at the point of being routed by Varela when their band struck up a popular zamba which so inspired them that they took new heart and crushed their foes. To my mind the most beautiful and stirring version on record is that of the Salta group, Los Chalchaleros.

Nigel Gallop

The Payadores

The *payadores*, originally Gaucho troubadors, can still, with luck, be heard at the *domas de potros* (rodeos) in the pampas. Accompanying themselves on the guitar, the *payadores* engage in musical duels (*payadas*), alternating in improvising verses and aiming to outdo each other with clever rhyming and verbal wit. The verses develop a particular theme within a strictly regulated format, relating historical or contemporary events or expressing popular morality. Similar contests are held elsewhere in Latin America: in the Brazilian Northeast, the Venezuelan Llanos and the hill country of Puerto Rico.

The most famous old-time *payador* was Santos Vega, said to have lived in the early 19th century and to have been finally defeated in a *payada* by "Juan Sin Ropa" (Naked John), though it must be added that Vega's existence is wrapped in mystery. More recently Gabino Ezeiza (1858-1916), a black *payador*, achieved a fame that has lasted to this day as the last "natural" (ie unlettered) *payador*. Alas, I have not been able to find out anything about the Englishman, A MacCarthy, "*El Inglesito de la Boca*"! Among contemporary *payadores* who have been recorded are Angle Colovini, Catino Arias, José Curbelo, Roberto Ayrala and Miguel Franco.

Nigel Gallop

singing their Milongas, Estilos and Cifras and challenging each other to a Payada or rhymed duel. Argentina experienced a great folk revival in the 50s and 60s and some of the most celebrated groups are still drawing enthusiastic audiences today. These groups include Los Chalchaleros and Los Fronterizos, the perennial virtuoso singer and guitarist, Eduardo Falú and, more recently, León Gieco from Santa Fe.

FOOD AND DRINK

FOOD

Argentine cuisine, strictly speaking, does not exist. What is eaten in Argentina is, by and large, an inherited culture; an adaption of Spanish, Italian, Arabic (Middle Eastern anyway) and other European influences. Lately a smattering of Oriental – Chinese, Japanese and Korean basically restaurants have sprung up in Buenos Aires and a few cities of the interior – Mar del Plata in particular – giving local cuisine a slightly more cosmopolitan touch. What should be the basis of Argentina cooking – the authentic and truly native dishes – is almost non-existant except in isolated pockets and regions of the country.

It is true that America has given its share of treasures to the world. Maize (corn), potatoes, cocos (chocolate), chillies, tomatoes and peanuts are but a small part of its bounty unknown to the world before Columbus landed on Santo Domingo for the first time. None of the Columbus indigenous to Argentina, although it is now a large producer of many of them, such as maize, potatoes and peanuts.

Argentina is basically beef eating country. South of the Rio Negro, where Patagonia officially commences, beef gives way to sheep, Argentina being one of the world's major producers of wool, lamb and mutton. However, only recently have Argentines come to appreciate what one lamb lover and expert, Iranian restaurateur Fereydoun Kia, calls "the best lamb in the world". The trouble is that local cooks have still to learn how to cook and present lamb, and Argentina housewives still have to throw off the idea that mutton (and lamb by inference) is solely the dogs – as it was until quite recently.

Beef is consumed in a variety of ways. The most traditional is, of course, the *parrilla* or *parrillada*, the local version of the American barbecue. (Barbecue being a derivative of the Inca word *barbacoa* –

their method of cooking meat over hot coals impaled on green branches taken from nearby bushes and trees.) Parrilla refers to the roasting method: on a grill over hot coals; parrillada is a sum of different meats and cuts – including variety meats and offal – served together. Sausages, blood sausages, sweet-breads, thin intestines, rib roast cut in strips and tenderloin are but some of the many possibilities, which also include chicken but hardly ever lamb, pork or kid. It is usual to order one parrillada for two and menus frequently specify how many people can normally eat from one order.

Lamb, pork and kid are generally roasted on a spit stuck into the ground and slightly leaning over the hot coals. This method is called al asador. One can also find an asador al speido, a mechanical spit which turns in front of an electric or gas heater. Nowadays it is usually used to roast chickens. All roasts are cooked with a touch of salt and nothing else. With the meat will be served a series of local condiments, chimichurri being very typical and usually quite spicy. It is a mixture of dried herbs, garlic, oil and (sometimes) vinegar.

Pasta is also very widespread, and if we except the new fad of hamburgers and hot dogs, represents, along with pizza, the most visible evidence of the foreign influence. Argentine pizza, at least that which is found in Buenos Aires, is considered one of the finest and most varied in the world. New Yorkers, who claim the pizza championship, frequently admit that they have found a worthy rival in Buenos Aires.

Argentines are not great vegetable eaters, and their choices seldom go much beyond potatoes, tomato, lettuce, onion and garlic. The classic ensalada mixta (mixed salad) however, has aquired a name for itself amongst visitors from abroad. A simple combination of crisp lettuce, sliced tomato, sliced onion, oil and vinegar (lemon juice is also popular) it owes its popularity to the fact that local vegetables still maintain all the flavour and characteristics which hothouse vegetables lack. Argentina still relies on nature rather than technology for its food supplies. (This explains the particular quality of local beef, Argentine steers being range bred and fed the year round.)

Eating in Buenos Aires and environs is quite different to the cuisine which is found in the rest of the country. Buenos Aires is modern and relatively sophisticated; the rest of the country, including such important cities as Rosario, Córdoba, Mendoza and Mar del Plata are another story altogether. Mendoza is a particularly curious case. Capital of Argentina's wine country and industry – one of the world's largest – it has no local cuisine to boast of and its restaurants are very poor indeed. Only Bariloche, centre of Argentina's spectacular Andean tourist country, has something resembling a regional cuisine, largely based on German, Austrian and Central European influences.

In spite of being one of the worlds last great fishery reserves, fish and seafood occupies a very small role in local eating habits. Like lamb, fish is an almost unknown quantity in Argentina and local cooks tend to overcook their dishes mercilessly. Even in Mar del Plata, centre of the fishing industry, it is hard to obtain a really good seafood meal. Centolla (King crab) in Ushuaia, Tierra del Fuego, is one of Argentina's most interesting sea products, while from rivers and lakes can be fished the prejerrey (Brasilichthys Argentinensis), a unique and extremely fine and delicate fish indeed.

One has to go to the northwestern corner of Argentina (and to a lesser extent the northeast) to discover traces of the old, authentic cuisine. A number of foods based on maize, such as the humitas and the tamales are quite common, and tasty

Noquis on the Payroll

Noquis or potato dumplings are usually only served them on the 29th of the month, when you should put a coin under your plate for luck. The term is, however, also used for employees who turn up for work once a month to collect their salary.

Beef, Argentine style

Although beef plays a less important part in the national diet than it did in the past, meat-eaters will find that knowing how to order the cut they want could make their trip just that bit more enjoyable. In some cases knowing what to avoid may be just as important.

Some of the more popular items found on menus include:

bife de lomo	loin steak
medallón de lomo, lomito	sirloin steak
asado de tira	short rib
bife de chorizo	rumpsteak
bife a caballo	steak topped with a fried egg
churrasco	a thick grilled steak
matambre	filled flank roll
parrillada mixta	mixed barbeque
chorizo	sausage
morcilla	blood sausage

Offal include:

mollejas	sweet bread
riñones	kidneys
chinchulines	small intestines
mondongo	tripe
corazón	heart
higado	liver

Further details are given in the diagram, below:

Federico Kirbus

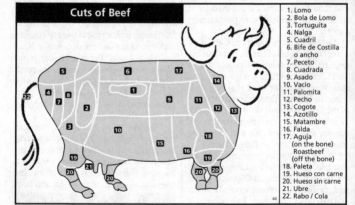

Cuts of Beef

1. Lomo
2. Bola de Lomo
3. Tortuguita
4. Nalga
5. Cuadril
6. Bife de Costilla o ancho
7. Peceto
8. Cuadrada
9. Asado
10. Vacio
11. Palomita
12. Pecho
13. Cogote
14. Azotillo
15. Matambre
16. Falda
17. Aguja (on the bone) Roastbeef (off the bone)
18. Paleta
19. Hueso con carne
20. Hueso sin carne
21. Ubre
22. Rabo / Cola

and filling stews such as *carbonada* and *locro* should not be passed up if one has the chance to taste them. And I have said nothing about the traditional *puchero* which knows no particular region or recipe. A local version of a French pot-au-feu it can be made with whatever meat and vegetable there is to hand. Tradition has

it however, that to be a true puchero it must have some sort of beef, chickpeas and corn on the cob, amongst the ingredients.

Argentines have a sweet tooth but are not very imaginative as to desserts. The local flan has nothing to do with the English version; it is a baked custard served with a caramel sauce and can also be garnished with a little whipped cream or dulce de leche. This extremely sweet and delicious confection can best be described as milk jam. It is milk boiled with plenty of sugar until it turns thick and caramel colour. Quince or sweet potato preserve with cheese (queso y dulce) is very popular, as is a true Argentine creation: *panqueque de manzana* (apple pancake, which is made by cooking thinly sliced apple in batter and caramel on both sides. Pastries and cakes are European in style and jams are faithful copies of what can be found the world over. Fresh fruit is bountiful and varied. Local apples and pears are especially fine (most are exported) and citrus fruits are abundant.

The *South American Handbook* adds: *arroz con pollo* is a delicious combination of rice, chicken, eggs, vegetables and strong sauce. *Puchero de gallina* is chicken, sausage, maize, potatoes and squash cooked together. *Milanesa de pollo* (breaded, boneless chicken) is usually good value. *Empanada* is a tasty meat pie; *empanadas de humita* are filled with a thick paste of cooked corn/maize, onions, cheese and flour. **NB** Extras such as chips, *puré* (mashed potato), etc are ordered and served separately, and are not cheap. Other popular desserts not already mentioned are *almendrado* (ice-cream rolled in crushed almonds), *postre Balcarce*, a cream and meringue cake and *alfajores*, maize-flour biscuits filled with *dulce de leche* or apricot jam (very popular). Note that *al natural* in reference to fruit means canned without sugar (fresh fruit is *al fresca*). Croissants (known as *media lunas*) come in two varieties: *de grasa* (dry) and *de mantequilla* (rich and fluffy). Sweets: the Havana brands have been particularly is recommended. Excellent Italian-style ice-cream is sold in many exotic flavours. For local recipes (in Spanish) *Las Comidas de Mi Pueblo*, by Margarita Palacios, is recommended.

WINE

Argentina has been making wine since the first Spanish settlers planted the first vines in 1554. During the present century it has consistently figured amongst the major world producers, occupying fourth or fifth ranking according to the annual harvest. Yet its wines have never, until the last 2 or 3 years, been recognized abroad, mainly because Argentines have devoted themselves to drinking what they produce. (Per capita consumption, up to the start of the 50s, was third in the world.)

Argentina's wine country extends along the length of the Andean foothills, from Salta in the north, to the Rio Negro valley in the province of the same name, in the south. Scattered vineyards can be found in the provinces of La Pampa, Neuquen, Cordoba and even Buenos Aires (exclusively a home inudustry). However, the heart of the winelands and capital of wine is Mendoza province, with over 70% of production.

It is a surprise for the first-time vistor to this part of the country to see the lush vineyards and vegetation in general emerge as if by magic out of the semi-arid desert which is a feature of most of western Argentina, which suffers from the Andean rain-shadow. Only south of San Rafael, in the southernmost part of Mendoza, does the desert begin to give way to the lush natural vegetation which is typical of western Patagonia. The answer is, of course, irrigation, the eternally snow-capped Andean range providing some of the purest and most mineral-rich water available anywhere. This system of irrigation – rainfall seldom surpasses 200 mm per year, and mostly falls in the summer when it is little needed – is one of the reasons for Argentina's rather special and characteristic wines.

Reflecting its strongly European character, with Spanish and Italian influence predominating, but with strong minor inputs, Argentine wine and drinking habits are strongly European in character. The main grape varietals are mostly of French origin. Cabernet Sauvignon, Merlot, Malbec and Syrah for red wines; Chardonnay, Chenin, Sauvignon Blanc, Riesling and Torrontés for whites.

If one can select two grapes which can be called truly Argentine, Malbec and

Yerba Maté

Originally drunk by precolombian Indians and known in the colonial period as 'Jesuit tea', *yerba maté* is a herbal tea made from the leaves of ilex paraguaiensis, a bush similar to holly. The Jesuit Missions encouraged its consumption as an alternative to alcohol and produced some of the best quality *yerba maté*; finding that Buenos Aires traders offered low prices, they set up their own marketing system. It became popular among the *gauchos* but today it is consumed widely in Argentina, Uruguay, Paraguay and southern Brazil. The main producing areas in Argentina are the provinces of Misiones and Corrientes.

Traditionally it was served in a gourd, called a *maté*, used because it preserved the temperature and flavour of the brew; alternatives to the gourd are now common, among them *palo santo* (a very hard wood), cowhorn and, less interestingly, aluminium. The container is filled to above half-capacity with leaves and hot water is added; the liquid is drunk through a *bombilla*, a metal straw with a filter at the base, with extra water and leaves being added as required. It is normally consumed without sugar, though milk is sometimes added instead of water. In summer it is drunk as *tereré*, cold with a little lemon.

Drinking maté is a great ritual and most maté-drinkers adopt their own techniques which they argue gives the best brew. It is an exceptionally social drink: *maté* is usually drunk in company and passed around the group, with one person being responsible for adding more water. It can be considered an insult to refuse when offered. If you develop a liking for it, remember that saying 'thank you' after drinking maté indicates that you do not want any more.

Torrontés are they. In Argentina the Malbec grape has found climates and soils which allow it to develop to far greater heights than it can reach in France. Argentina's finest red wines, in the opinion of such experts as Hugh Johnson and Jancis Robinson, are her Malbec varietals; superior – and different – to the far better known Cabernet Sauvignon. If Argentina is finally becoming known abroad, it is as much due to her Malbec wines as to any other.

If Malbec can be considered almost Argentine in character and nationality, Torrontés has no such limits. Its origin is somewhat doubtful, but most experts agree that it is probably a descendant of a vine originally brought over from Galicia (Spain). It is only found as a noble grape in Argentina, where it produces, according to where it is cultivated, a strongly perfumed, sweet-smelling wine which when tasted is incredibly dry but fruity. The strongest and most marked characteristics are found in the provinces of Salta and La Rioja. Those that are made in San Juan and Mendoza are of lesser interest and generally less perfumed, while that which comes from Rio Negro is a light, more delicate and extremely easy wine to drink. For first timers, it is probably best to begin with a Rio Negro Torrontés before graduating to a Salta or La Rioja version. The best brands are Canale (Rio Negro), Nacari (La Rioja) and Etchart (Salta).

With a per capita consumption of 40 litres of wine per annum, Argentines are amongst the world's leading wine consumers (third in the global league), but are now far off the all time record of nearly 91 litres registered in 1970. More than 90% of that wine was common table or jug wine. Today, while drinking less Argentines are drinking better. The drop in consumption has been all in the jug wine sector, while noble wines have increased at their expense, particularly the sparkling wine sector, which is booming. Apart from local concerns, sparkling wines are made by local affiliates of Möet & Chandon, C H Mumm and

Piper-Heidsieck. By far the most popular is that made by Chandon, who also make generic and varietal wines. Top noble wines range between the $7 and $12 per bottle range at good wine stores, while excellent medium range wines can be had from between $3 and $5. Restaurants tend to double and even triple these prices.

SPORTS

It is said that sport came to Argentina through the port of Buenos Aires, brought first by British sailors, who played football on vacant lots near the port watched by curious locals who would later make it their national passion, and later by immigrants who brought with them their own favourite sports.

Football is out on its own, both in terms of participation and as a spectator sport. Behind it in second place come two sports which attract far more fans than players: boxing and motor-racing. Although there are now few Argentine boxing champions and world title fights are rarely held here, there is a big TV audience for most title fights abroad. Despite the lack of local world class drivers, the legend of Juan Manuel Fangio is still very much alive and the Argentine Formula One Grand Prix in April is one of the events of the year in Buenos Aires, even if there are no Argentine drivers.

Though the best polo in the world is played in Argentina, it is not a major participation sport, due to its cost. Though it is played throughout the country and all year round, the top players who play all over the world return only for the high handicap season between September and November. This consists of three main tournaments, played on the outskirts of Buenos Aires, followed by the Argentine Open, which takes place in Palermo, the 'cathedral of polo'.

Golf is another popular sport which, thanks to the climate, can be played all year round in most of the country. While 33,311 players registered with the Argentine Golf Association at the last count, it is calculated that about 100,000 people

Football crazy?

Argentina's first World Cup victory in 1978 at the River Plate stadium is, for many people, a lasting memory: the streets of central Buenos Aires packed with crowds, jumping and dancing. Even today, whenever the national team wins a World Cup match, thousands dance around the obelisk in central Buenos Aires, while cars rush round them, sounding their horns as they did in 1978.

First played in an organized fashion by British residents in the late 19th century, football quickly became the passion of the people, the main talking point in bars, clubs and wherever people meet. It fills most of the sports pages in newspapers and can be seen on TV screens on most evenings. This popularity, more or less common to most of South America, has been put down to the 'Latin temperament' and the low living standards of the majority of people, who can afford little enjoyment and find something to live for through following their favourite team: at the end of an often frustrating week they give vent to their feelings in a soccer stadium. Although Argentina is one of the great exporters of players, mostly to European clubs, as soon as a leading player is sold, another young star replaces him: they seem to spring up like weeds.

The season stretches from the end of August to the end of June, with a 2-month break in the heat of the summer from Christmas to the end of February. Most matches are played on Sundays, with two games brought forward for TV screening, one to Friday evening and another to Saturday evening. Club members get into home games free. Although the Argentine Football Association has set a standard price of US$10 for standing room, clubs are free to set whatever price they wish for seating.

Eric Weil

'The hand of God'

👣 When Argentines travel abroad they are frequently asked about Diego Maradona, perhaps the only well-known Argentine in most countries. A national hero and arguably the best footballer ever (though Brazilians would counter this with the claims of Pele), Maradona's story is the kind of rags to riches tale typical of many South American football stars, more poignant, perhaps, because he reached such fame in Europe as well as in his homeland. After making his first division debut when barely 17 years old, Maradona played 91 times for his country and would have easily passed the century mark had his career not been interrupted by 15 month bans for drug-taking. Sadly, the man who, as a little boy, used to astound spectators at half time during matches and on TV with his unequalled ball juggling skills could never quite handle fame. Moreover, many would say that he has made a habit of surrounding himself with the wrong people.

The high point of Maradona's career was undoubtedly the World Cup finals of 1986, when he led Argentina to the title, scored his famous 'hand of God' goal in the 2-1 victory over England and was judged best player in the tournament. His nadir came in his fourth World Cup in 1994, when he received his second suspension for drug-taking. Nevertheless, despite his unpredictable behaviour, the Argentine love affair with Maradona continues. When he made his fifth comeback recently at the age of 36, a delirious capacity crowd at the Boca Juniors stadium greeted him with smokebombs, fireworks and ticker-tape, even though he showed few signs of his former artistry.

Eric Weil

play golf each weekend at the country's 200 plus courses. About half of these players and half the courses are in *Gran Buenos Aires*, with one right in the city at Palermo, as well as several driving ranges. Some clubs allow visitors to play in return for a green fee.

Other popular participation sports include rugby, hockey and tennis, although the latter's popularity, at its height in the 70s and 80s, has declined since the retirement of international stars like Guillermo Vilas and Gabriela Sabatini. There is, of course, nothing like international success to popularise a sport, and this has been the case with both rugby and hockey.

One typical sport which is native to Argentina is *pato* (duck), a cross between polo and basketball. Originally played between large bands of *gauchos* on horseback using a duck in a basket as a ball, it was at one point prohibited for being dangerous. Today, with proper rules, teams of four horsemen and a football with handles instead of a duck in a basket, it is one sport which is unique to Argentina.

In Buenos Aires, unlike most other cities in the country, there are numerous sports clubs where members can play a wide range of sports and, with ability and inclination, represent the club in national and international competitions. There are also large numbers of private clubs where, paying by the hour, you can rent a tennis court, play five-a-side football or practice a variety of other sports.

The Economy and Government

STRUCTURE OF PRODUCTION

Argentina is one of the more highly developed countries of the region. It has the third largest gdp in Latin America, but by far the highest per capita income. Wealth traditionally came from farming although agriculture, forestry and fishing now account for only 6% of gdp. Nevertheless, over half of export earnings are generated by farming and food processing. There has been a shift from livestock to crop production since the 1960s. The area sown to oilseeds has risen steeply, now exceeding that of wheat. Although the fertility of the pampas was once so high that fertilizers were unnecessary, overexploitation and soil erosion have made its use essential, increasing the costs of farmers also hit by rising costs, falling commodity prices and lack of cheap credit to invest in modernization. In the 1990s, 150,000-200,000 small and medium sized farms were under severe financial pressure and many faced bankruptcy, leading to a consolidation of land holdings. Cresud, the only landholding company traded on the stock market, increased its holdings from 20,000 to 348,000 ha in 1994-96. Cattle and sheep herds have been reduced because of stiff competition abroad, low wool prices and outbreaks of foot and mouth disease. A vaccination drive started in 1989 has been successful and no further outbreaks have been recorded since 1994, leading farmers to hope that beef import bans imposed by the USA, Japan and Southeast Asian countries might be lifted. Exports of about 450,000 tonnes a year, earning some US$900mn, could double if the bans are lifted. Fishing received a boost in 1993 from an agreement with Britain to share fish resources in the South Atlantic, thereby increasing by 70% Argentina's share of the illex squid catch.

Railways

🐟 Until recently building and maintaining roads was a major problem in the pampas: the soil lacks gravel or stones to surface the roads, and dirt roads become a quagmire in wet weather and a fume of dust in the dry. Railways, on the other hand, were simple and cheap to build. The system grew as need arose and capital (mostly from Britain) became available. The lines in the pampas radiated out fanwise (with intricate inter-communication) from the ports of Buenos Aires, Rosario, Santa Fe and Bahía Blanca. By the 1940s there were some 80,000 railway waggons transporting produce across the country. Argentina, unlike most other countries, had extensive railways before a road system was built.

Carlos Saul Menem

Born in 1930, the son of Syrian immigrants who settled in La Rioja province, Carlos Menem has been President of Argentina since 1989. Active in the *Partido Justicialista* (Peronist party) from his days as a student, he was elected to the La Rioja parliament in 1955, rising to be elected provincial governor in 1973. Imprisoned for five years by the military government which seized power in 1976, he was re-elected governor on the return to civilian rule in 1983.

Menem's victory over Antonio Cafiero for the Peronist nomination in 1989 came as a surprise to many observers; La Rioja is one of the smallest provinces and Menem had a reputation as a playboy with an appetite for publicity stunts such as appearing in the national football team in a friendly match. As President he has provided further surprises; while the media, especially abroad, has continued to focus on his lifestyle and marital difficulties (he was once famously locked out of the *Casa Rosada* by his then-wife) and the corrupt practices of his family and former associates, his government has stabilised the currency, virtually eliminated inflation, reduced taxes and import duties and privatised many industries, in doing so reversing many of the policies associated with his party's founder, Juan Perón. In 1993 he pursuaded the opposition Radicals to support reforms to the constitution which enabled him to stand for another term. His victory in 1995 gave him a further four years in office; despite rumours of further constitutional changes to enable him to stand again, it is likely that 1999 will see the retirement of a man who has led the most reforming government in Argentina since the first Perón administration.

Manufacturing was developed behind high import protection barriers, but these have now been swept aside. The sector accounts for 26% of gdp and is closely linked with agricultural activity, with food processing and beverages accounting for a quarter of manufacturing output. The regional customs union, Mercosur, opened up a huge market for companies established in Argentina and many food companies have been bought by multinationals. Trade with Brazil has traditionally been biased towards foodstuffs but enterprises in other areas are now growing. Several multinational motor vehicle companies are investing in new plant, many around Córdoba. All plan to sell vehicles to other Mercosur countries as well as within Argentina.

Argentina is self-sufficient in energy and has an exportable surplus of oil, natural gas and hydroelectricity. Hydroelectric potential lies on 10 main rivers: the rivers Paraná and Uruguay in the north where huge joint projects have been built with Paraguay (Yacyretá, Corpus) and Uruguay (Salto Grande), and on rivers in Río Negro and Neuquén provinces. The Government is divesting its stake in electricity generating and will offer its participation to private investors once ratification is secured from the Paraguayan and Uruguayan parliaments. More hydroelectricity generating plants are planned which will be built under concession by private contractors. Argentina has had nuclear power since 1974 when the first stage of the Atucha power station was opened using German technology. Crude oil output is around 785,000 b/d (domestic consumption 485,000 b/d, exports 300,000 b/d) and reserves are to be kept at 10 years' production with more exploration in a US$3 billion, 10-year investment programme. The country has more natural gas than oil and reserves are about 560 billion cubic metres, equivalent to about 30 years' consumption at present rates.

Mining was discouraged by previous administrations, who declared the border region a security zone and closed to foreign investment, but there are substantial mineral deposits in the foothills of the Andes. Investment is now being encouraged by new legislation introduced in 1993. The first major project will be the Bajo de la Alumbrera porphyry copper and gold deposit in Catamarca which is believed to have 752 million tonnes of ore. Mining operations will start in 1997 and production should reach 180,000 tonnes of copper and 640,000 ozs of gold a year. Another copper-gold deposit in Catamarca is Agua Rica, which could be developed into an open pit mine to rival Alumbrera. Both are being developed by Australian and Canadian companies. Lithium deposits at the Salar del Hombre Muerto dry lake bed also in Catamarca are believed to be sufficient for 70 years' production.

RECENT TRENDS

In the 1980s large fiscal deficits, monetary expansion and a high velocity of circulation caused very high inflation, which was difficult to curb because of structural imbalances in the economy, inadequate levels of investment and inefficiencies and corruption in both the public and private sectors. The Government introduced several stabilization programmes, the first of which was the Austral Plan, named after the currency it introduced, but none was successful. Output and investment contracted as confidence was eroded and the economy became increasingly dollarized. The external debt rose sharply but rescheduling agreements with commercial bank creditors backed by IMF financing facilities all collapsed as policy commitments were not met and payment arrears mounted.

The Menem administration tackled structural economic reform, which initially brought further recession and unemployment. In 1991 it passed a Convertibility Law, fixing the peso at par with the US dollar and permitting the Central Bank to print local currency only if it is fully backed by gold or hard currency. This was the key to achieving price stability; the annual average growth of consumer prices fell from 3,080% in 1989 to 3.9% in 1994 and remained in single

Argentina: fact file

Geographic
Land area	2,780,400 sq km
forested	18.6%
pastures	51.9%
cultivated	9.9%

Demographic
Population (1995)	34,995,000
annual growth rate (1990-95)	1.2%
urban	86.9%
rural	13.1%
density	12.5 per sq km
Religious affiliation	
Roman Catholic	90.9%
Birth rate per 1,000 (1995)	19.5
	(world av 25.0)

Education and Health
Life expectancy at birth,	
male	68.2 years
female	71.5 years
Infant mortality rate	
per 1,000 live births (1994)	20.3
Physicians (1992)	1 per 376 persons
Hospital beds	1 per 227 persons
Calorie intake as %	
of FAO requirement	109%
Population age 25 and over	
with no formal schooling	5.7%
Literate males (over 15)	96.2%
Literate females (over 15)	96.2%

Economic
GNP (1994)	US$275,657mn
GNP per capita	US$8,060
Public external debt (1994)	
	US$66,005mn
Tourism receipts (1994)	US$3,970mn
Inflation (1994-95)	3.3%
Radio	1 per 1.6 persons
Television	1 per 4.8 persons
Telephone	1 per 7.1 persons

Employment
Population economically active (1990)	
	12,305,346
Unemployment rate (1989)	7.3%
% of labour force in	
agriculture	12.0
mining	0.5
manufacturing	19.9
construction	10.1
Military forces	67,300

Source *Encyclopaedia Britannica*

Mainland Provinces of Argentina

Provinces of Argentina (South America only)		
Province	**Area (Sq Km)**	**Population**
Buenos Aires	307,571	12,594,974
Catamarca	102,602	264,234
Chaco	99,633	839,677
Chubut	224,686	357,189
Córdoba	165,321	2,766,683
Corrientes	88,199	795,594
Entre Ríos	78,781	1,020,257
Federal Capital	200	2,965,403
Formosa	72,066	398
Jujuy	53,219	512,329
La Pampa	143,440	259,996
La Rioja	89,680	220,729
Mendoza	148,827	1,412,481
Misiones	29,801	788,915
Neuquén	94,078	388,833
Río Negro	203,013	506,772
Salta	155,488	866,153
San Juan	89,651	528,715
San Luis	78,748	286,458
Santa Cruz	243,943	159,839
Santa Fe	133,007	2,798,422
Santiago del Estero	136,351	671,988
Tierra del Fuego	21,571	69,369
Tucumán	22,524	1,142,105

figures thereafter. Dozens of state companies were privatized, many using debt reduction techniques. Fiscal surpluses were recorded in 1992-93 and gdp growth rates averaging 7.7% a year were recorded in 1991-94. After a current account surplus in 1990, increasing deficits were recorded in following years, reaching nearly US$10bn in 1994, but these were amply financed by capital inflows and international reserves increased. Imports soared from US$3.7bn in 1990 to US$19.9bn in 1994, while gross domestic investment in the same years rose by 22% to 23% of gdp. In 1993 an agreement was signed with international banks to restructure bank debt by securitizing it into bonds, following the Mexican model of debt or debt service reduction.

Cracks began to appear in the model in the second half of 1994 when a fiscal deficit became apparent. Tax collections fell and current spending rose. The tax structure concentrates on consumption with a high rate of VAT, but the demand side of the economy had been growing only slowly, partly because of rising unemployment as a result of privatizations and streamlined payrolls. The devaluation of the Mexican peso in December 1994 created what became known as the 'tequila effect'. Loss of confidence in Mexico spread to other Latin American countries and Argentina suffered a sharp liquidity squeeze as US$8bn in bank deposits, 15% of the total, fled the country. Many banks were merged, yet at 130, there were still too many for the country's deposit base. Unemployment soared to over 18% by May 1995, consumer demand fell sharply, tax collections dwindled and a recession loomed. Riots broke out in parts of the country as provincial governments failed to pay wages for several months.

The Government turned to the IMF, which negotiated a US$7bn rescue package with multilateral lenders. In 1995 exports rose by 33%, as goods were diverted from the weak domestic market, encouraged by high commodity prices and a consumer boom in Brazil, but gdp declined by 2.5%. The recession appeared to be over by the end of the year, though, with industrial production, imports and demand picking up, and unemployment declining, while 90% of bank deposits had returned. A private pension scheme was launched to ease pressure on the bankrupt state scheme as well as raise the savings ratio, reduce dependence on foreign capital and increase investment funds for industry.

Argentina: Main Routes from Buenos Aires

In the first half of 1996 the slow rate of recovery had a negative impact on fiscal revenues and the target for the deficit was exceeded. The introduction of new and unpopular austerity measures led to the dismissal of Finance Minister Cavallo, the architect of the 1990s economic restructuring and liberalization programme, for political reasons. His successor, Roque Fernández, formerly president of the central bank, pursued similar economic policies, which provoked strikes. Nevertheless, gdp expanded by 4% in 1996, with the recovery based on investment and exports rather than domestic consumption. Fiscal revenues improved and were to be boosted in 1997 by more privatizations of state enterprises.

GOVERNMENT

The country's official name is La República Argentina (RA), the Argentine Republic. The form of government has traditionally been a representative, republican federal system. Of the two legislative houses, the Senate has 72 seats, and the Chamber of Deputies 257. Under the 1853 Constitution (amended most recently in 1994) the country is divided into a Federal Capital (the city of Buenos Aires) and 23 Provinces. Each Province has its own Governor, Senate and Chamber of Deputies. The Constitution grants the Federal Capital self government under a Mayor who is directly elected.

The location of power within this system is complex. Though the Federal government is usually seen as very powerful, this power partly depends on the President's own party having control over Congress. Moreover the Federal Capital and the provinces of Buenos Aires, Santa Fé and Córdoba, which between them contain 70% of the total population, can exercise a powerful counterweight, especially if they are controlled by the opposition.

Buenos Aires and the Río de la Plata

THE CITY of Buenos Aires with its museums, theatres, public buildings, parks and shopping, lies on the Río del la Plata. This section includes other attractions on the Argentine side of Plata estuary, including the Tigre Delta (waterways, lunch spots) and the city of La Plata, as well as excursions across the estuary into Uruguay, notably to visit the beautiful colonial city of Colonia del Sacramento.

GEOGRAPHY

The Río de la Plata (literally 'silver river') is neither silver nor a river: it is a large estuary produced by the confluence of the Paraná and Uruguay rivers. These two rivers drain an area comprising 100% of Paraguay, 80% of Uruguay, 32% of Argentina, 19% of Bolivia and 17% of Brazil. Some 300 km long, the estuary widens from an initial width of 37 km to 220 km at the point at which it enters the Atlantic. While its northern shore (in Uruguay) is relatively steep, reaching 50m in some places, its southern (or Argentine) shore is flat and in some areas consists of swampland. The estuary is muddy and shallow and the passage of ocean vessels is only made possible by continuous dredging. The tides are of little importance, for there is only a 1.2m rise and fall at spring tides. The depth of water is determined by the direction of the wind and the flow of the Ríos Paraná and Uruguay.

CLIMATE

From mid-December to the end of February the Buenos Aires area can be oppressively hot and humid, with temperatures ranging from 27°C (80°F) to 35°C (95°F) and an average humidity of 70%. Beware of the high pollen count in the pollinating season if you have allergy problems. The winter months of June, July and August are best for business visits, though spring is often very pleasant. **NB** Extreme humidity and unusual pollen conditions may affect asthma sufferers.

BUENOS AIRES

HISTORY

The first attempt to found a settlement on the Río de la Plata by Pedro de Mendoza in 1536 failed and it was not until 1580 that an expedition under Juan de Garay succeeded in founding the city which he named after the patron saint of sailors, *Santa María del Buen Aire* (Santa María of the good winds). For much of the colonial period the city, though an administrative centre, was of little importance but, by 1776, when it became capital of the Vice-Regency of Río de la Plata, it was a growing city with an economy based on trading (much of it illegal) and servicing the cattle economy of the pampas. By independence its population was some 40,000.

In 1862 following the long struggle between Buenos Aires province and the Argentine interior, the city emerged as capital of the newly united state of Argentina, but shortly afterwards it was split from its province and made into a separate federal district. The massive waves of immigration into Argentina after 1870 transformed the city; between 1869 and 1914 its population grew from 177,000 to over 1 million and by 1914 half of its residents were foreign-born. By 1914 Buenos Aires was regarded as the most important city in South America. As the city grew and prospered, urban improvements were made: gas, street lighting and better water supplies were introduced and suburban railway lines and a metro system were built. Many of the city's public buildings and major avenues date from this period, leaving very few older buildings.

During the 20th century the city has continued to grow, expanding across the boundaries of the federal territory into the province of Buenos Aires. Though immigration dropped after 1929, the city's population continued to increase as it absorbed large numbers of migrants from the poorer interior provinces. The connurbation of Gran Buenos Aires is the country's major industrial centre; by the 1980s it accounted for about half of all industrial jobs in Argentina.

Palo borracho

🦶 The name palo borracho (meaning drunken tree) is given to two related species: chorisia insignis and chorisia speciosa. The former, known as *yuchán,* comes from the Argentine Northwest and prefers a drier climate than the latter. Known in North America as the White Floss tree or Silk Floss tree, it has white or yellow flowers and likes a dry climate. It was used by the Indians for making canoes. Chorisia speciosa, known as Samohú, comes from the Northeast and has pink, red or purple flowers and can grow to 20m in height. Good examples of both species can be found in Buenos Aires, some as old as 100 years. Both varieties have palmate leaves and their green trunks turn grey with age.

Jane Norwich

Hooligans in the 1820s?

🦶 "The society of the lower class of English at Buenos Aires is very bad, and their constitutions are evidently impaired by drinking, and by the heat of the climate, while their morals and characters are much degraded. Away from the religious and moral example of their own country, and out of sight of their own friends and relations, they sink rapidly into habits of carelessness and dissipation, which are but too evident to those who come fresh from England; and it is really too true, that all the British emigrants at Buenos Aires are sickly in their appearance, dirty in their dress, and disreputable in their behaviour."

Francis Bond Head, *Journeys Across the Pampas and Among the Andes 1825-6* (Southern Illinois University Press, 1967).

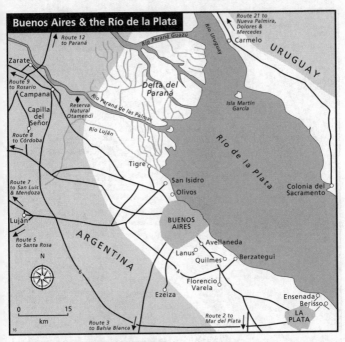

Buenos Aires & the Río de la Plata

Route 21 to Nueva Palmira, Dolores & Mercedes

Carmelo

URUGUAY

Route 12 to Paraná

Río Parana Guazu

Río Uruguay

Zarate

Route 9 to Rosario

Campana

Delta del Paraná

Isla Martín García

Capilla del Señor

Reserva Natural Otamendi

Río Paraná de las Palmas

Route 8 to Córdoba

Río Luján

Río de la Plata

Route 7 to San Luis & Mendoza

Tigre

San Isidro

Olivos

Colonia del Sacramento

Luján

BUENOS AIRES

ARGENTINA

Avellaneda

Route 5 to Santa Rosa

N

Lanus

Quilmes

Berzategui

Florencio Varela

Ezeiza

Ensenada

Berisso

LA PLATA

0 ___ 15

km

Route 3 to Bahía Blanca

Route 2 to Mar del Plata

INTRODUCTION TO THE CITY

Though the federal capital extends over some 200 sq km with a population of about 2.92 million, the conurbation of Gran Buenos Aires, which includes the suburbs in the province of Buenos Aires covers 4,326 sq km and has a population of 10.87 million. *Phone code* 01.

POINTS OF ARRIVAL

Airports

Ezeiza (officially Ministro Pistarini), the international airport, is 35 km southwest of the centre by a good dual carriageway, which links with the General Paz circular highway round the city.

Facilities include exchange (Banco de la Nación, 1.5% commission) and ATMs (Visa and Mastercard), post office (open 0800-2000) (under the stairs) a left luggage office (US$5 per piece) and a Tourist Information desk which offers a free hotel booking service with a list of competitively-priced hotels. There are no hotels nearby. A display in immigration shows choices and prices of transport into the city (see below).

Airport information, T 480-0217.

For departing travellers there is a duty free shop (expensive) and a desk marked *Devolución IVA* for return of VAT on purchases such as leather goods. Reports of pilfering from luggage; to discourage this have your bags sealed after inspection by Your Packet International SA, US$5-10 per piece (British Airways insists on, and pays for, this for backpacks).

● Airport buses

Two companies run efficient special bus services to/from the centre: *Manuel Tienda León* (office at customs exit), service to the company office at Avenida Santa Fe 790 (T/F 315-0489, F 311-3722, or airport T/F 480-0597/0374 – 24 hours), 0400, 0500, then every 30 minutes till 2030, US$14, return US$25, credit cards accepted. City centre office has check-in desk for Aerolíneas Argentinas flights. *San Martín Bus* office opposite Air France and KLM, service to company office at Santa Fe 887 (next to Secretaría Nacional de Turismo), T 314-4747/3446, Ezeiza 480-9464, 15 minutes past each hour, US$11, 10% ISIC and GO 25 discount (will also collect passengers from hotels in centre for no extra charge, book previous day).

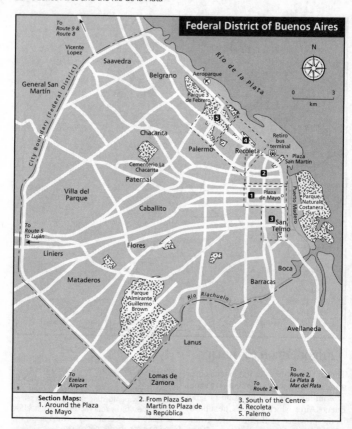

Federal District of Buenos Aires

Section Maps:
1. Around the Plaza de Mayo
2. From Plaza San Martín to Plaza de la República
3. South of the Centre
4. Recoleta
5. Palermo

Security

Buenos Aires is a fairly safe city, but, as in most cities of its size, travellers should be aware of the risk of street crime, especially in areas frequented by tourists. Be particularly careful when boarding buses and near the Retiro train and bus stations. Beware of bagsnatching gangs in parks and markets; though not violent, they are particularly skilful, often creating a disturbance to distract victims' attention. Beware of the common trick of spraying mustard, ketchup or some other substance on you and then getting an accomplice to clean you off (and remove your wallet). If you are sprayed, walk straight on. If your passport is stolen, remember to get a new 'entrada' stamp at the Dirección Nacional de Migraciones.

The Federal Police operate a helpline **T 370-5911** in Spanish and English for travellers in case of theft or attack.

● **Local buses**

86 bus (white and blue, marked 'Fournier') runs to the centre from outside the airport terminal to the right (*servicio diferencial* takes 1½ hours, US$4; *servicio común* 2¼ hours, US$1, coins only, no change given) between 0500 and 2400. To travel to Ezeiza, catch the bus at Avenida de Mayo y Perú, one block from Plaza de Mayo – make sure it has '*Aeropuerto*' sign in the window as many 86s stop short of Ezeiza. Only one bag is normally allowed and passengers with backpacks may be charged double fare.

● **Taxis**

Remise taxis charging fixed fare, can be booked from the Manuel Tienda León counter at Ezeiza, US$35 (including US$2.70 toll) payable in advance. If you take an ordinary taxi, the Policía Aeronáutica on duty notes down the car's licence and time of departure. Avoid unmarked cars no matter how attractive the fare may sound; drivers are adept at separating you from far more money than you can possibly owe them. From the centre to Ezeiza ordinary taxis charge US$30-35 depending on your bargaining skills while remises charge US$18-20. Remises will also do return trip for US$18 plus US$6 per hour waiting time and US$3 per hour parking.

● **Trains**

Local electric trains run between Ezeiza station and Buenos Aires (Constitución station) US$0.80, 40 minutes. Ezeiza station is reached from the airport by bus 502, 20 minutes, US$0.70.

● **Transfers to Aeroparque**

Manuel Tienda León operates buses between Ezeiza and Aeroparque airports, stopping in city centre, US$15. Aerolíneas Argentinas offer free transfers between the two airports to passengers whose incoming and connecting flights are both on: ask at AR desk for a voucher.

Aeroparque

Aeroparque (officially known as Jorge Newbery Airport) 4 km north of the centre near the river, T 771-2071, handles all internal flights, services to Punta del Este and Montevideo and flights from Latin American countries with an intermediate stop in Argentina.

The terminal is divided into three sections, one each for Aerolíneas Argentinas and Austral and the third, in between, for other airlines. Aerolíneas Argentinas section has duty free facilities, tourist information, *confitería*, car rental, Manuel Tienda León office (see below) and luggage deposit (US$3 per piece). Exchange: Banco de la Ciudad (Austral section) and Aeromar (between sections), also Visa ATM.

No post office or post box. Very expensive and poor quality restaurant upstairs.

● **Airport buses**

Manuel Tienda León buses to/from centre (see above for address), 0710-2110 every 30 minutes, US$5.

● **Local buses**

Bus 45 runs from outside the airport to the Retiro railway station, then follows Avenida Alem and Paseo Colón to La Boca. Bus 37C goes from Plaza del Congreso to Aeroparque but make sure it has '*Aeroparque*' sign, US$0.50.

● **Taxis**

To Congreso US$7, Plaza de Mayo US$6, Retiro US$5, La Boca US$9.

Remise taxis: are operated by Universalflet (office in Austral section, T 772-2950) and Manuel Tienda León, US$11-13 to centre, US$40 to Ezeiza.

● **Bus Terminal**

All long-distance buses arrive at the Retiro bus terminal at Ramos Mejía y Antártida Argentina. There are left-luggage lockers, tokens from kiosks, US$2.50. Luggage porters charge US$5 per load. Information desk on 1st floor. T for information 314-2323. All offices are on the east side on the ground floor.

Nearby is the Retiro railway station and entrance to Subte Line C. The passage between the bus station and Retiro is packed with market stalls and is narrow (beware pickpockets), all designed to inconvenience those with luggage (although, as one correspondent points out, this also slows down anyone trying to make a speedy escape with your belongings).

CITY TRANSPORT

● **Buses**

Colectivos (city buses) cover a very wide radius, and are clean, frequent, efficient and very fast (hang on tight). The basic fare is US$0.60, US$1 to the suburbs. Have coins ready for ticket machine as drivers do not sell tickets. **NB** The bus number is not always sufficient indication of destination, as each number has a variety of routes, but bus stops display routes of buses stopping there and little plaques are displayed in the driver's window. Two guides, *Guía T* and *Lumi*, obtainable at news stands give routes of all buses (see under Tourist information).

● **Metro ('Subte')**

There are five lines, labelled 'A' to 'E' which run under major avenues. Four of them link the outer parts of the city to the centre while the fifth, Line 'C', links Plaza Constitución with the Retiro railway station, and provides connections with all the other lines. Note that in the centre

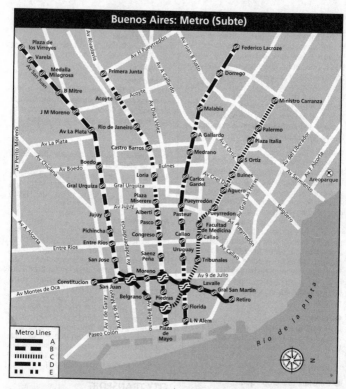

Buenos Aires: Metro (Subte)

Metro Lines
— A
— B
||||||| C
— D
▪▪ ▪▪ E

three stations, 9 de Julio (Line 'D'), Diagonal Norte (Line 'C') and Carlos Pellegrini (Line 'B') are linked by pedestrian tunnels.

Trains are run by Metrovías, T 553-0044. The fare is US$0.50 and covers any direct trip or combination between lines; tokens (fichas) must be bought at the station before boarding; buy a few in advance to save time (dollars not accepted). System operates Monday-Saturday 0500-2215 approximately, Sunday 0800-2215 approximately. Backpacks and luggage allowed. Map available free from stations and from tourist office.

● **Taxis**

Taxis are painted yellow and black, and carry *Taxi* flags. Fares are shown in pesos. The meter starts at US$1.12 when the flag goes down and US$0.14 is added for each 200m travelled; make sure it isn't running when you get in. A charge is sometimes made for each piece of hand baggage (ask first). Tips not usual. In theory fares double for journeys outside city

limits (General Paz circular highway), but you can negotiate over this.

Remise taxis operate all over the city; they are run from an office, have no meter but charge fixed prices and are often much cheaper than yellow-and-black cabs. Some remise companies do not charge extra for journeys outside the city limits. The companies are identified by signs on the pavement. Fares can be verified by phoning the office and items left in the car can easily be reclaimed. One good company is *Le Coq*, T 963-9391/2, 963-8532, US$2-3 tip expected.

For transport from Buenos Aires to other parts of Argentina and to neighbouring countries see below under **Local information**.

CITY LAYOUT

The city centre is situated just inland from the docks on the south bank of the Río de la Plata. The main public buildings are grouped around the Plaza de Mayo; from here a broad avenue,

Taxis in Buenos Aires

Taxi drivers in Buenos Aires, in common with their counterparts all over the world, are the subject of numerous complaints. Though most drivers are as honest and courteous as anywhere else, there are a number of common tricks:

- Taking you on a longer than necessary ride

- Switching low-denomination notes for higher ones proffered by the passenger (don't back down, demand to go to the police station)

- Grabbing the passenger's baggage and preventing him/her from leaving the taxi (scream for help)

- Quoting 'old' prices for new, eg 'quince' (15) for 1.50 pesos, 'veinte y seis' (26) for 2.60 pesos, etc.

All taxis are licensed: avoid unofficial taxis and unmarked cars. Worst places used to be the two airports and the Retiro bus terminal, but when you catch a taxi from these points you are now given a certificate with the cab number and contact phone number. If possible, keep your luggage with you. Make sure you know what the fare should be before the journey. If you think you have been cheated, ask to see the taxi driver's licence. T 343-5001 to complain.

Avenida de Mayo leads west 1½ km to the Congress building in the Plaza del Congreso. Halfway it crosses the wide Avenida 9 de Julio, one of the widest avenues in the world: it consists of three major carriageways, with heavy traffic, separated in some parts by wide grass borders. In the north the Avenida 9 de Julio meets the Avenida del Libertador, the principal way out of the city to the north and west.

The city's commercial and banking area is located north of the Plaza de Mayo. The traditional shopping centre, Calle Florida runs north from Avenida de Mayo to Plaza San Martín: pedestrianized, it is the popular down-town meeting place, particularly in the late afternoon and the buskers in the 500 block are worth visiting. Another shopping street is Avenida Santa Fe, which crosses Florida at Plaza San Martín; it has become as touristy and as expensive as Florida. The traditional entertainment centre, Avenida Corrientes, which runs westwards parallel to Avenida de Mayo, is a street of theatres, restaurants, cafés and night life. There are cinemas and many good and reasonable restaurants in the nearby streets; though this area is in decline as the city's main entertainment areas move out from the centre, it is still worth a visit. The main hotel areas are around Avenida de Mayo and north of it towards Plaza San Martín.

East of the centre is the Puerto Madero dock area; its 19th century warehouses have been renovated and turned into a popular nightspot, with restaurants and bars; it also provides a pleasant area for a stroll. Further east still is a stretch of marshland which forms the Parque Natural Costanera Sur, a wildlife reserve.

The remainder of the city fans out north, south and west from the central area. To the south are some of the older *barrios* (neighbourhoods); two of them, San Telmo and La Boca, attract visitors. San Telmo is an artistic centre, with plenty of cafés, antique shops and a pleasant atmosphere; and there is a regular Sunday antiques market at the Plaza Dorrego. La Boca, further south, is fairly run down, but has its own distinctive life. To the northwest are the wealthier *barrios* of Recoleta and Palermo, both of interest to visitors, the former chiefly for its museums, the latter for its parks.

Streets are organized on a grid pattern. Numbers start from the dock side rising from east to west, but north/south streets are numbered from Avenida Rivadavia, one block north of Avenida de Mayo rising in both directions. Note that some streets may be referred to by two names, notably Calle Juan D Perón which used to be called Cangallo

PLACES OF INTEREST

Opening arrangements

Most historic churches apart from the Cathedral are open 0730-1230, 1600-2000. State and municipal museums and parks are free on Wednesday. Check opening hours with Tourist Office; many close in January or February.

THE CITY CENTRE

The Plaza de Mayo

Surrounded by some of the major public buildings, this is the historic heart of the city. On its east side, in front of the famous Casa de Gobierno, is a statue to General Belgrano. Further east, behind the Casa de Gobierno, in the semicircular Parque Colón, is a large statue of Columbus.

The **Casa Rosada**, the Presidential Palace, lies on the east side. It is notable for its statuary, the rich furnishing of its halls and for its libraries. Tours Monday, Tuesday, Thursday, Friday 1000-1800, Sunday 1400-1800, T344-3804. On the east side (at the back of the palace) is the entrance to the **Museo de los Presidentes**, containing historical memorabilia of former Presidents; open Tuesday, Wednesday, Thursday 0900-1400, Friday, Sunday 1400-1800. The museum also provides access to the tunnels and warehouses built in 1854 as part of the *Aduana* (customs house).

The **Antiguo Congreso Nacional** (Old Congress Hall) on the south side of the plaza, built in 1864, was encircled and built over by the Banco Hipotecario: it now functions as a conference centre. Guided tours Thursday, 1500-1700, free.

The **Cabildo**, or town hall, opposite the Casa Rosada on the west side of the plaza, has been rebuilt several times since the original structure was put up in the 18th century, most recently in 1940. Inside is the **Museo del Cabildo y la Revolución de Mayo**, containing paintings, documents, furniture, arms, medals and maps recording the May 1810 revolution and the 1806 British attack; also Jesuit art. In the patio is La Posta del Cabildo café and stalls selling handicrafts. Tuesday-Friday 1230-1900, Sunday 1500-1900. T 334-1782 for English tours. Library, Monday-Friday, 1100-1900. Entry free.

The **Cathedral**, on the north side of the plaza, lies on the site of the first church in Buenos Aires. The current structure was built between 1758 and 1807, when funds ran out before the twin towers could be erected: the architectural proportions have suffered as a result. A frieze upon the Greek façade represents Joseph and his brethren. Inside is the imposing tomb of General José de San Martín (1880). Masses: Monday-Friday 0900,1100,1230, Saturday 1730, Sunday 1100,1200,1300. Visiting hours Monday-Friday 0800-1830, Saturday 0900-1230, 1700-1930, Sunday 0900-1400, 1600-1930.

The **Banco de la Nación**, just east of the Cathedral, is regarded as one of the great works of the architect Alejandro Bustillo. Built in 1939, its central hall is topped by a marble dome 50m in diameter. It contains the **Museo Numismático e Histórico del Banco Nacion**, entrance at B Mitre 326, 1st floor, coins and notes, furniture and historical documents, Monday-Friday 1000-1500, T 342-4041, extension 607.

La City

Just north of the Plaza de Mayo, between 25 de Mayo and the pedestrianized Calle Florida, lies the main banking district known as *La City*.

The Casa Rosada

Built 1874-1882, the Casa de Gobierno is known as the *Casa Rosada* because it is coloured pink: the result of a decision made by Sarmiento to symbolize national unity by blending the colours of the rival factions which had fought each other for much of the 19th century: the Federalists (red) and the Unitarians (white).

The palace is particularly well-known for its balcony, used in the film *Evita* as the location of Eva Perón's speech renouncing public office. Sadly, though the balcony was the scene of other Peronist triumphs, the renunciation did not take place here: Evita was offered, and turned down, the Vice-Presidential nomination on 22 August 1951 at a great rally held on the Avenida Nueve de Julio, which could accommodate larger crowds than the Plaza de Mayo.

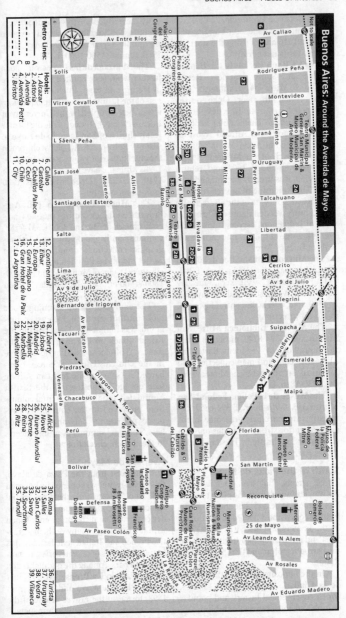

Buenos Aires: Around the Avenida de Mayo

Not to scale

Metro Lines:
- ···· A
- ···· B
- ···· C
- ···· D

Hotels:
1. Alcázar
2. Astoria
3. Avenida
4. Avenida Petit
5. Bristol
6. Callao
7. Castelar
8. Ceballos Palace
9. Cecil
10. Chile
11. City
12. Continental
13. Elbar
14. Europa
15. Gran Hispano
16. Gran Hotel de la Paix
17. La Argentina
18. Liberty
19. Lisboa
20. Madrid
21. Majestic
22. Marbella
23. Mediterraneo
24. Micki
25. Novel
26. Nuevo Mundial
27. Orense
28. Reina
29. Ritz
30. Roma
31. Salles
32. San Carlos
33. Savoy
34. Sportsman
35. Tandil
36. Turista
37. Uruguay
38. Vedra
39. Vilaseca

The **Bolsa de Comercio**, 25 de Mayo y Sarmiento, is a handsome building dating from 1916 and housing the stock exchange. Visits not permitted.

Lloyd's Bank (formerly the Bank of London and South America), Reconquista y B Mitre, has a miniature museum on its 5th floor. Open during banking hours; the building, designed by SEPRA (Santiago Sánchez Elia, Federico Peralta Ramos, and Alfredo Agostini) and completed in 1963 is worth seeing.

The Church of **La Merced**, Reconquista 207, founded 1604 and rebuilt 1760-1769, was used as a command post in 1807 by Argentine troops resisting the British invasion. One of the altars has an 18th century wooden figure of Christ, the work of indigenous carvers from Misiones. It has one of the few fine carillons of bells in Buenos Aires.

The **Museo Numismático del Banco Central**, San Martín 216, 1st floor, T 394-8411, fascinating, well kept, Tuesday 1000-1400, Wednesday and Friday tour at 1400, free, overlooks central foyer, ask guard for directions.

The **Museo y Biblioteca Mitre**, San Martín 336, T 394-8240, preserves intact the household of President Bartolomé Mitre; has coin and map collection and historical archives. Open Monday-Friday 1330-1830, US$1.

The **Museo de la Policía Federal**, San Martín 353, 8-9th floor, T 394-6857. Interesting but extremely gruesome forensic section (for strong stomachs only; no one under 15 admitted), Tuesday-Friday 1400-1800.

South of the Plaza de Mayo

Three streets, Balcarce, Defensa and Bolívar, lead south from the plaza towards San Telmo (see below). The church of **San Francisco**, Alsina y Defensa, controlled by the Franciscan Order, was built 1730-1754 and given a new façade in 1911. Note the barroque pulpit and the chapel of San Roque.

On the opposite corner is the **Museo de la Ciudad**, Alsina 412, T 343-2123, which covers social history and popular culture and houses special exhibitions on daily life in Buenos Aires (changed every 2 months) and a reference library open to the public. Open Monday-Friday 1100-1900, Sunday 1500-1900, US$1.

The **Manzana de las Luces**, one block further west, is celebrated as the centre of learning in early Buenos Aires. The seat of the Jesuits before their expulsion, it was then occupied by the University of Buenos Aires. On the corner is the former Jesuit church of **San Ignacio de Loyola**, Alsina y Bolívar 225, the oldest church in the city. Its two lofty towers date from the 1690s while the nave was rebuilt between 1710 and 1734. Open weekends 1700 (guided tours only).

The **Museo Etnográfico J B Ambrosetti**, one block south of the San Francisco church at Moreno 350, T 331-7788, contains anthropological and ethnographic collections from around the world, including Bolivian and Mapuche silverwork. Open Monday-Friday 1400-1800 (1900 on Saturday/Sunday) closed February, US$1.

The church of **Santo Domingo**, one block further south at Defensa y Belgrano, was founded in 1751. During the British attack on Buenos Aires in 1806 some of Whitelocke's soldiers took refuge in the church. The local forces bombarded it (some of the hits can still be seen on one of the towers); the British capitulated and their regimental colours were preserved in the church. The remains of General Belgrano are buried here. There are summer evening concerts in the church; check times.

Avenida de Mayo

Running west from the Plaza de Mayo, this broad avenue was opened up between 1889 and 1894 to link the Presidential Palace to the Congress building then under construction at the other end. Lined with tall buildings, many of them attractive French and Italian style facades, it is a street of hotels of all categories, restaurants and bars. Among the highlights are:

The **Palacio La Prensa**, No 575, just off the Plaza de Mayo and dating from 1898, formerly the offices of one of the country's most important newspapers.

The **Café Tortoni**, No 825, is the most famous bar in Buenos Aires, closely associated with the history of tango. The walls are decorated with posters and photos of its heyday in the 1930s and earlier. Live music is performed here in the evenings. Next door is the *Academia Nacional del Tango*.

The **Teatro Avenida**, No 1222, which opened in 1908, will take your passport and give you a ticket for your seat and a pink slip to reclaim your passport. You may stay as long as you wish, but must remain seated. Guided tours (in Spanish and English) can be taken on Monday, Tuesday and Friday at 1100 and 1700 when Congress is not sitting.

From Retiro to the Plaza de la República

10 blocks north of the Plaza de Mayo is the Plaza San Martín, with, nearby, the Retiro railway and bus terminals.

The **Plaza San Martín**, lies on a hill overlooking the Retiro stations. In the centre is an equestrian statue to San Martín, first erected in 1862. At the northern end of the plaza is a memorial with an eternal flame to those who fell in the Anglo-Argentine conflict of 1982.

Around the Plaza are several elegant mansions, among them the **Palacio La Paz**, housing the Circulo Militar (a military club) and the **Museo de Armas**, T 311-1071, which contains a collection of all kinds of weaponry related to Argentine history, including the 1982 South Atlantic conflict, plus Oriental weapons; open Tuesday-Friday 1400-1930, Saturday 1100-1700, Sunday 1300-1800, closed 15 December-15 March, US$1. The **Edificio Kavanagh**, east of the plaza, was the tallest building in South America when completed in 1935; behind it is the **Basilica del Santísimo Sacramento** (1916), favoured by wealthy *porteños*. The **Palacio San Martín**, just west of the plaza, is now occupied by the Ministry of Foreign Affairs.

The **Plaza de la Fuerza Aérea**, northeast of Plaza San Martín, was until 1982 the Plaza Británica; in the centre is a clock tower presented by British and Anglo-Argentine residents in 1916; 'a florid Victorian sentinel, royal crest upon its bosom'. Nearby, opposite the Retiro stations is the Plaza Canadá in which there is a Pacific Northwest Indian totem pole, donated by the Canadian government.

The Café Tortoni

Founded in 1858 and named after a Parisian café, the Tortoni moved to its present site in 1880, though at that time the entrance was on Avenida Rivadavia: with the opening up of Avenida de Mayo, it gained a new frontage and greater popularity. Its greatest period was between 1926 and 1943 when it was the meeting place of the famous *Peña de Tortoni*, a group of bohemian artists and writers. The Tortoni's owner, Celestino Curutchet, laid down one of the most important rules of the *peña*: "here you may talk, drink in moderation and give full expression to your opinions, but only the arts may be discussed". Despite such strictures, Curutchet arranged for the *peña* to meet in the basement to avoid offending the upper-class clientele upstairs. As the fame of the Tortoni spread, it was frequented by many important Argentine artists and in its heyday poems and tangos were written in its honour.

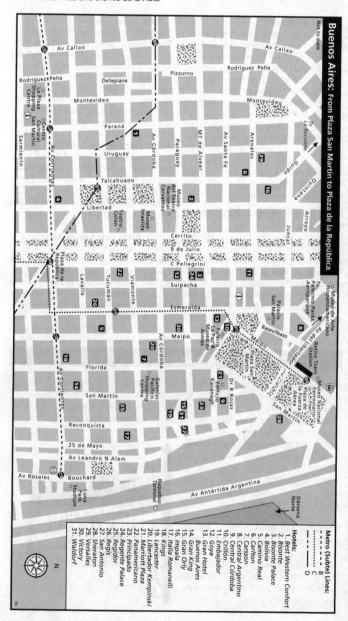

Buenos Aires: From Plaza San Martín to Plaza de la República

Metro (Subte) Lines:
- – – – B
- ——— C
- ·········· D

Hotels:
1. Best Western Comfort
2. Bisonte
3. Bisonte Palace
4. Bolivia
5. Camino Real
6. Carlton
7. Carson
8. Central Argentino
9. Central Córdoba
10. Crillón
11. Embajador
12. Goya
13. Gran Hotel Buenos Aires
14. Gran King
15. Gran Orly
16. Impala
17. Italia Romanelli
18. Kings
19. Lancaster
20. Libertador Kempinski
21. Marriott Plaza
22. Panamericano
23. Principado
24. Regente Palace
25. Regidor
26. San Antonio
27. Sheraton
28. Versailles
29. Victory
30. Victory
31. Waldorf

The **Retiro** railway station is really three separate termini; the westernmost of these, the **Mitre**, is the finest, dating from 1908; its *confitería* is worth a visit. Behind the station at Avenida del Libertador 405 is the **Museo Nacional Ferroviario**, for railway fans. It contains locomotives, machinery and documents on the history of Argentine railways. Building in very poor condition. Monday-Friday, 0900-1800.

Three blocks west of the Retiro along the Avenida del Libertador is the **Museo de Arte Hispanoamericano Isaac Fernández Blanco**, Suipacha 1422, containing an interesting and valuable collection of colonial art, especially silver, in a beautiful colonial-style mansion. Open Tuesday-Sunday, 1400-1900, entry US$2; Thursday free, closed January. For guided visits in English or French T 327-0228; guided tours in Spanish Saturday, Sunday 1600.

Avenida Santa Fe, one of the city's most expensive streets runs west from Plaza San Martín. It crosses the broad Avenida 9 de Julio, which leads south to the great **Plaza de la República**, in the centre of which is a 67m obelisk commemorating the 400th anniversary of the city's founding.

Overlooking 9 de Julio, between Calles Viamonte and Tucumán, is the **Teatro Colón**, one of the world's great opera houses, opened in 1908 on the site of an earlier theatre of the same name. The interior, seating over 4,000 people, is resplendent with red plush and gilt; the stage is huge, and salons, dressing rooms and banquet halls are equally sumptuous. The season runs from April to early December and the theatre also stages concerts, recitals and ballet. Open daily to visitors (not Sunday), guided tours Monday-Friday hourly 0900-1600, Saturday 0900-1200, in Spanish, French and English, US$5 (children US$2), from entrance at Viamonte 1180, recommended. Closed January-February, T 382-6632. Tickets, sold several days before performance, on the Calle Tucumán side of the theatre. The cheapest seat is US$6 (available even on the same day), and there are free performances most days (Tuesday-Friday) at 1730 in the Salón Dorado – check programme in the visitors' entrance. In the same building at Tucumán 1161 is the **Museo del Teatro Colón**, T 382-1430, which displays documents and objects related to the theatre. Monday-Friday 0900-1600, Saturday 0900-1200, closed in January.

Nearby are two other museums: the **Museo Israelita**, Libertad 773, with religious objects relating to Jewish presence in Argentina, Tuesday-Thursday 1600-1800; and the **Museo del Teatro Nacional Cervantes**, Córdoba y Libertad, with displays on the history of the theatre in Argentina, Monday-Friday 1430-1800, Saturday/Sunday 1000-1300, T 815-8881 in advance.

The **Centro Cultural San Martín**, four blocks west of the Plaza de la República at Avenida Corrientes 1530, houses the **Teatro Municipal San Martín** and a salon of the **Museo Municipal de Arte Moderno**, US$1, Wednesday free.

SOUTH OF THE CENTRE

San Telmo

The *barrio* of San Telmo, south of the Plaza de Mayo, built along the slope which marks the old beach of the Río de la Plata, is one of the oldest parts of the city. Though one of the few areas where buildings remain from the mid-19th century, its network of narrow streets is much older. One of the wealthiest areas of the city, it was abandoned by the rich after the great outbreak of yellow fever in 1871. It is a recognized artistic centre, with plenty of cafés, antique shops and a pleasant atmosphere.

The *barrio* centres on the **Plaza Dorrego**, 10 blocks south of the Plaza de Mayo. Here on Sundays, 1000-1700 there is one of the best, and most famous, 'antiques' markets.

Nearby on Humerto I is the church of **Nuestra Señora de Belén**, begun by the Jesuits in 1734, but only finished in 1931. Next door at Humberto I 378, is the **Museo Penitenciario Argentino**

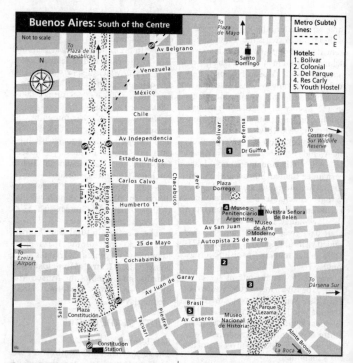

Buenos Aires: South of the Centre

Metro (Subte)
Lines:
– – – – – C
– – – – – E

Hotels:
1. Bolívar
2. Colonial
3. Del Parque
4. Res Carly
5. Youth Hostel

Antonio Ballue, the museum of the penal system; open Tuesday-Friday 1000-1200, 1400-1700, Sunday 1000-1200, 1300-1700, US$1.

The **Museo Municipal de Arte Moderno**, one block further south at San Juan 350, houses international exhibitions and a permanent collection of 20th century art; open Monday-Friday 1000-2000, Saturday and Sunday 1200-2000, US$1.50 T 361-1121. (The museum also has a salon in the Centro Cultural San Martín, Corrientes 1530.

The **Museo Internacional de Caricatura y Humorismo**, six blocks west of Plaza Dorrego at Lima 1037, houses a collection of original 20th century cartoons and caricatures, though with a very small international section. Monday, Tuesday, Thursday, Friday 1700-2000, Saturday 1200-1700, US$1.

The **Parque Lezama**, Defensa y Brasil, was originally one of the most beautiful parks in the city. According to tradition Pedro de Mendoza founded the city on this spot in 1535: there is an imposing statue to him in the centre of the park. On the west side of the park is the **Museo Nacional de Historia**, T 307-4457, containing trophies and mementoes of historical events, divided into halls depicting stages of Argentine history. Here are San Martín's uniforms, a replica of his sabre, and the original furniture and door of the house in which he died at Boulogne.

La Boca

East of the Plaza de Mayo, behind the Casa Rosada, a broad avenue, Paseo Colón, runs south towards the picturesque old port district known as La Boca, where the Riachuelo flows into the Plata.

An area of heavy Italian immigration, La Boca has its own distinctive feel. Though parts of it are becoming touristy, the area, with the adjacent industrial and meat-packing suburb of Avellaneda across the high Avellaneda bridge, is generally dirty and run down. For a tour of La Boca, start at Plaza Vuelta de Rocha, near Avenida Pedro de Mendoza, then walk up Caminito, the little pedestrian street used as a theatre and an art market.

The **Museo de Bellas Artes de la Boca**, Pedro de Mendoza 1835, T 301-1080, has many works on local life, contemporary Argentine painting, also sculptures and figureheads rescued from ships. Monday-Friday 0800-1800, Saturday/Sunday 1000-1700, entrance free.

• **Transport To La Boca**: from the centre take Bus 152 which runs along Santa Fe and Alem, or bus 29 from Plaza de Mayo, US$0.60.

ALONG THE COSTANERA SUR

East of San Telmo the spacious Avenida Costanera runs north along the far side of the docks. The Puerto Madero dock area, west of Avenida Costanera, with its 19th century warehouses has been renovated and turned into a popular nightspot, with restaurants and bars; it also provides a pleasant area for a stroll.

The **Parque Natural Costanera Sur**, east of the costanera, lies on a stretch of marshland claimed from the river by a system similar to the one used in the construction of the Dutch polders. Though drained between 1978 and 1981 to provide a site for a satellite city, the project was abandoned. More than 200 species of birds can be seen including the rare black-headed duck and the curve-billed reed hunter and there are also large numbers of *coypu* (large rodents). There are three trails ranging from 2 km to 6 km long. In summer it is very hot with little shade. For details, contact *Fundación Vida Silvestre*, Defensa 245, 6th floor. Open daily 0700-1900 in summer, 0800-1800 in winter but much can be seen from the road (binoculars useful); free, guided tours available at weekends.

• **Access** The entrance is near the southern end of the park at Avenida Tristán Achabal Rodríguez 1550 (reached by buses 4 and 2).

The **Museo de Telecomunicaciones** lies about 1 km further north along the Costanera at Avenida de los Italianos 851, T 312-5405 in a magnificent art-deco building which used to belong to Cervecería Munich. Open Friday-Sunday 1400-1800.

Further north in the docks at the northern end of Puerto Madero are two sailing ships which can be visited. The **Fragata Presidente Sarmiento**, at Avenida Dávila y Cangallo, was the Argentine flagship from 1899 to 1938, after which it served as a naval training ship until 1961. Open Monday-Friday 0900-2000, Saturday/Sunday 1000-2200, US$1. Nearby is the **Corbata Uruguay**, the sailing ship which rescued Otto Nordenskjold's Antarctic expedition in 1903. Open daily 0800-2000 all year, US$1.

NORTH OF THE CENTRE

Recoleta

Situated 1.5 km north of Plaza San Martín and built on the site of a Jesuit monastery, Recoleta became fashionable when wealthy families city moved here from the crowded city centre after the yellow fever outbreak of 1871. An area of parks and museums, at its heart is the **Plaza de la Recoleta**, with expensive *confiterías* and the famous *gran gomero*, a large rubber tree. There is a good craft market here on Saturday and Sunday (1100-1800).

The **Cementerio de la Recoleta**, just off the plaza, is the final resting place of the most famous names in Argentine history; open 0700-1800. With its streets and alleys separating family mausoleums built in every imaginable achitectural style, La Recoleta is frequently compared to a miniature city. Among the famous names from Argentine history is Evita Perón who lies in the Duarte family mausoleum: to find it from the entrance walk straight ahead to the main plaza; turn left and where this avenue meets another main avenue (about 13 'blocks'), turn right and take the third passage on the left.

The former Jesuit church of **El Pilar**, next to the cemetery, is a jewel of colonial

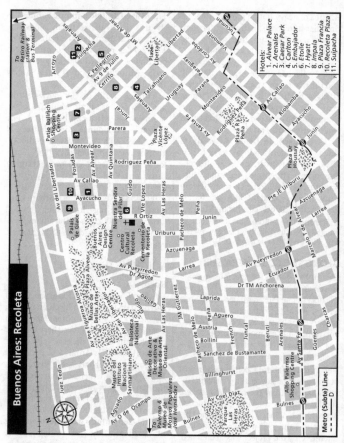

Buenos Aires: Recoleta

Hotels:
1. Alvear Palace
2. Arenales
3. Caesar Park
4. Carlton
5. Embajador
6. Etoile
7. Hyatt
8. Impala
9. Plaza Francia
10. Recoleta Plaza
11. Suipacha

Metro (Subte) Line: D

architecture dating from 1732, restored in 1930. See the colonial altarpiece, made in Alto Peru and the fine wooden image of San Pedro de Alcántara, attributed to the famous 17th century Spanish sculptor Alonso Cano, which is preserved in a side chapel on the left.

The **Centro Cultural Recoleta**, alongside the Recoleta cemetery, occupying the former monastery, specializes in contemporary local art with many free exhibitions by young artists. It includes a section of the **Museo de Arte Moderno Eduardo Sivori**, open Tuesday-Friday 1400-2100,

Saturday/Sunday 1000-2100. A passage leads from the Centre to the **Buenos Aires Design Centre**, near which there is another square, the **Plaza San Martín de Tours**, with more *gomeros* and a natural amphitheatre as well as the glass-covered **Palais de Glace**, built in the late 19th century and used as an exhibition centre.

The **Museo de Bellas Artes**, Avenida del Libertador 1473, T 801-3390, lies just north of the Recoleta cemetery. In addition to a fine collection of European works, particularly strong in the 19th century French school, there are 16th and

The Argentine way of death

The cemeteries of Buenos Aires offer fascinating insights into Argentine society. Two cemeteries are particularly interesting: La Recoleta and La Chacarita.

Although the Argentine elite, the so-called 'bovine aristocracy', was perhaps less ostentatious than some of its counterparts, the taste for displaying wealth was fairly strong. Nowhere was this more apparent than after death: an Argentine landowner, industrialist or politician was not really dead if their obituary had not been published in *La Prensa*, a newspaper with the prestige of the London Times; neither could they rest in peace if their remains did not lie in the Recoleta cemetery. To be buried here was (and still is) so important that it was said to be the most expensive plot of land in the world. It is so densely occupied that in many of the mausoleums, the caskets are piled up 8m to 10m high. In the past (and, maybe still) fictitious funerals took place in which the remains of the dead were taken to their "ultimate" resting place in the Recoleta, only to be removed quietly a few days later to a common cemetery.

La Chacarita to the west of the centre (see below) is much less socially exclusive. Here cost, rather than social acceptability, are the barriers to entry, though families unable to keep up with maintenance payments are told to move their loved ones elsewhere.

To walk through La Recoleta is, therefore, not only to pass through a forest of interesting sculptures, but also a way of revisiting Argentine history, for just as almost everyone who has played an important role in the country's past is remembered through a street or *plaza*, so they have a space in La Recoleta. Here lie the remains of Sarmiento and Mitre, of Roca and many other names from the past. Also here are their former enemies: Juan Manuel de Rosas; Facundo Quiroga, the *caudillo* demonized by Sarmiento; and Eva Perón, despised and hated in life by the Argentine elite and now lying among them in death. At least two great 20th century figures did not qualify for La Recoleta, Juan Perón and Carlos Gardel, both are buried at La Chacarita.

Federico Kirbus

17th century paintings representing the conquest of Mexico, many good Argentine works including new 19th and 20th century exhibits, and wooden carvings from the Argentine hinterland. Open Tuesday-Sunday 1230-1930, Saturday 0930-1930. Entrance US$1 (Thursday free), ISIC holders free. Warmly recommended.

● **Transport To Recoleta** buses: 110, 17; 60 (walk from corner of Las Heras y Junín, two blocks); from downtown, eg Correo Central, 61/62, 93, to Pueyrredón y Avenida del Libertador, or 130 to Facultad de Derecho.

North of Recoleta

Avenida del Libertador runs north from Recoleta towards Palermo past further parks and squares as well as several museums.

The **Biblioteca Nacional** or National Library, is now housed in a futuristic new building at Avenida del Libertador 1600 y Agüero 2502, T 806-6155, where only a fraction of its stock of about 3,500,000 volumes and 10,000 manuscripts is available. Cultural events and festivals are held here. Excellent guided tours (Spanish) Monday-Friday 1530 from main entrance, for tours in other languages contact in advance.

The **Museo Nacional de Arte Decorativo**, Avenida del Libertador 1902, contains collections of painting, furniture, porcelain, crystal, sculpture; classical music concerts Wednesday and Thursday; open daily except Tuesday 1400-1900, T 802-6606, US$2, half-price to

ISIC holders, closed January. Also in the same building is the **Museo Nacional de Arte Oriental**, containing a permanent exhibition of Chinese, Japanese, Hindu and Islamic art, open daily 1500-1900.

The **Museo del Instituto Nacional Sanmartiniano**, nearby at Gral Ramón Castillo y Avenida A M de Aguado, is a Replica of San Martín's house in exile in Grand Bourg near Paris. There is also a large library on the Liberator. Open Monday-Friday 0900-1700, T 802-3311 in advance.

The **Museo de Motivos Populares Argentinos José Hernández**, Avenida Libertador 2373, housing the widest collection of Argentine folkloric art, with rooms dedicated to prehispanic, colonial and Gaucho artefacts; handicraft sale and library. Open Wednesday-Friday 1300-1900, Saturday/Sunday 1500-1900. T 802-7294 for guided visits in English or French. Entrance US$1 (closed in February).

Palermo

Further northwest is Palermo, named after Juan Dominguez Palermo who owned these lands in the 17th century. The site of Rosas's mansion in the early 19th century, its series of great parks, established by Sarmiento and designed by Charles Thays, make it the most popular spot in the city for spending weekends.

The **Parque Tres de Febrero**, the largest park, has lakes, tennis courts, a rose garden, a Japanese garden with fish to feed (closed Monday, admission US$2)

and an Andalusian Patio. It also contains the **Planetarium**, at the entrance to which there are several large meteorites from Campo del Cielo (see page 319); open Saturday and Sunday only (1500, 1630, 1800), entry US$5. The **Museo de Arte Moderno Eduardo Sivori**, also in the park, T 774-9452, specializes on 19th and 20th century Argentine art, Tuesday-Sunday 1200-2000, US$1.

Further north is the **Hipódromo Argentino** (the Palermo race course) with seats for 45,000 (Sunday 1500, entry US$3, senior citizens free). Nearby are the Municipal Golf Club, Buenos Aires Lawn Tennis Club, riding clubs and polo field, and the *Club de Gimnasia y Esgrima* (Athletic and Fencing Club).

The **Jardín Zoológical** or zoo, west of the Japanese gardens, has been privatized and is open Tuesday-Sunday 0930-1830, guided visits available, US$4 entry for adults, children under 13 free.

The **Municipal Botanical Gardens**, west of the zoo at Santa Fe 2951, contain characteristic specimens of the world's vegetation. The trees native to the different provinces of Argentina are brought together in one section. The Gardens, closed at 1800, contain the **Museo del Jardín Botánico**, T 831-2951, whose collection of Argentine Flora is open Monday-Friday 0700-1600. The Gardens are full of stray cats, fed regularly by local residents. Entrance is from Plaza Italia (take Subte, line D).

North of the zoo are the showgrounds of the **Sociedad Rural Argentina**, where

---

Charles Thays

The main plazas of most large Argentine cities bear witness to the influence of Charles Thays. A landscape gardener born in France, Thays probably did more to change Argentine city centres in the early 20th century than any single architect. He was responsible for replacing the traditional colonial plazas, bare expanses devoid of greenery, with the gardens which adorn them today. Although his major works in Buenos Aires were the Plaza San Martín, the Parque Tres de Febrero and the Jardín Botánico, he also designed the Parque San Martín in Mendoza, the Parque Nueve de Julio in Tucumán and the Parque Sarmiento in Córdoba as well as parks in Chile and Uruguay. The Buenos Aires botanical gardens are, though, his greatest legacy: a lover of native Argentine plants, Thays travelled throughout the country in search of specimens for his collection.

Buenos Aires: Palermo

Av Leopoldo Lugones

Padre Mujica

Av Casares

Av Casares

Planetarium

Parque Jorge Newbery

J Salguero

Cavia

Parque 3 de Febrero

Paso Alcorta Shopping Centre

To Hipódromo Argentino

Av Pte Figueroa Alcorta

Gelly

Av Adolfo Berro

Castex

Av Infanta Isabel

Jardin Japones

Castex

Rosita

Museo de Motivos Populares José Hernández

Parque 3 de Febrero

Av del Libertador

R Salabini Ortiz

Saburano

Av Pte Montt

Av del Libertador

JF Segui

Cervino

Plaza Int Saebr

Tupiza

Rep Araba Sria

Cabello

Av Colombia

Rep de la India

Lafinur

JF Segui

Demaria

JM Gutierrez

French

Av Cervino

Jardin Zoológico

Juncal

Sociedad Rural Argentina

Av Gral Las Heras

Beruti

Juncal

Jardin Botánico

Arenales

Beruti

Plaza Italia

Av Santa Fe

Güemes

Metro (Subte) Line: D

0   200
Metres
(approx)

7a

in July the Annual Livestock Exhibition, known as Exposición Rural, is staged. Entrance from Plaza Italia.

The **Museo de la Asociación Evaristo Carriego**, 10 blocks south of the botanical gardens at Honduras 3784, is dedicated to tango, open Monday-Friday 1300-2000.

North of the parks on the coast is **Aeroparque** (Jorge Newbery Airport), the city's domestic airport. Next to it is the **Museo Nacional de Aeronáutica**, Avenida Costanera Rafael Obligado 4550, housing a collection of civil and military aircraft, plus displays of navigational material, documents, equipment, US$3, Tuesday-Friday 0830-1630, Sunday 1400-1900, T 773-0665.

Belgrano

Lying northwest of Palermo, this suburb is the location of several museums.

Museo Histórico Sarmiento, Cuba 2079, T 783-7555, the National Congress and presidential offices in 1880; documents and personal effects of Sarmiento; library of his work, Thursday-Sunday 1500-1900 (2000 in summer).

Museo de Arte Español Enrique Larreta, Juramento 2291 (entrance on Avenida Rafael Obligado). Saturday-Sunday 1500-1900; Monday, Tuesday, Friday 1400-1945. Closed Wednesday, Thursday and January, US$1. The home of the writer Larreta, with paintings and religious art; T 783-2640 for guided tour in language other than Spanish. Also **Biblioteca Alfonso El Sabio**, Monday-Friday, 1300-1930.

The **Museo Histórico Saavedra**, northwest of Belgrano at Crisólogo Larralde 6409, T 572-0746 (also known as the Museo Histórico de la Ciudad de Buenos Aires and not to be confused with Museo de la Ciudad) houses city history from the 18th century, furniture, arms, documents, jewellery, coins and religious art; daily guided tours. Tuesday-Friday, 0900-1800, Sunday 1400-1800, US$1, closed February.

WEST OF THE CENTRE

La Chacarita, reputedly the largest cemetery in South America, is less socially exclusive than Recoleta. The most-visited tombs here are those of Juan Perón and Carlos Gardel, the tango singer. It is reached by Subte Line B to the Federico Lacroze station.

The **Museo de Ciencias Naturales Bernardino Rivadavia**, Avenida Angel Gallardo 470, facing Parque Centenario, T 982-5243. There are palaeontological, zoological, mineralogical, botanical, archaeological and marine sections. Meteorites from Campo del Cielo are on display. Open all year, daily, 1400-1730 (closed holidays), US$0.50. Library, Monday-Friday, 1100-1700. In the same building is the **Museo de la Dirección Nacional del Antártico**, with specimens of Antarctic flora, fauna and fossils and a library of taped birdsong. Open Tuesday, Thursday and Sunday, 1400-1800.

Museo de Esculturas Luis Perlotti, Pujol 642, T 431-2825, in the former workshop of this Argentine sculptor, Tuesday-Friday 1400-1900, Saturday/Sunday 1000-1300, 1400-2000, US$1.

● **Transport** Subte Line A to Primera Junta or Buses 25, 26, 55, 76, 84, 86, 92, 96, 99.

Museo Municipal de Cine, Sarmiento 2573, T 952-4598, traces the development of Argentine cinema and contains permanent exhibitions on María Luisa Bemberg and Niní Marshall, Monday-Friday 1000-1830, US$1.

● **Transport** Subte A to Plaza Miserere or buses 5, 7, 24, 26, 41, 61.

Museo y Biblioteca Ricardo Rojas, Charcas 2837 (Tuesday-Friday 1400-1800). The famous writer Rojas lived in this beautiful colonial house for several

Ups and downs in the Subte

The Buenos Aires metro is the oldest in Latin America and one of the first in the world; only 11 cities had underground railways when the first section of Line A was built in 1913 from Plaza de Mayo to Plaza Once, a distance of 3,970m. This line still runs many of its original carriages, the oldest operating underground wagons in the world. Line B opened in 1930 with two innovations: turnstiles and the first escalators in the country. Lines C, D and E were completed in 1934, 1937 and 1944 respectively.

A further line, Line F is under construction below Avenida Entre Ríos, Avenida Callao and Avenida Las Heras; it will provide a badly needed connection between Constitución and Plaza Italia.

Many of the stations in the centre especially on Line E have fine tilework murals, the work of Argentine and Spanish artists, which depict typical national landscapes and recount popular Argentine legends.

Today there are over 44 km of track and 65 stations. Each weekday the trains travel some 80,000 kilometres and transport some 800,000 Argentines. Nevertheless the system has been dwarfed in recent decades by the rapid growth of the city. Lacking investment and strained by ever-increasing numbers of passengers, the network was near collapse when privatized in 1991.

Since privatization there have been many changes: the acquisition of 100 used Japanese carriages on Line B may be an unwelcome reminder to some passengers of the encroaching stainless-steel and glass modernity above ground, but it has meant greater travel comfort. Closed circuit television screens in many stations offer distraction, advertising and noise. More litter bins, greater frequency of service during rush hour, a few more benches and better lighting on platforms, have made the system more bearable. Nevertheless when trains break down in dark tunnels, when doors slam on passengers' limbs, when passengers are forced to climb stationary escalators or force their way as civilly as possible into overcrowded carriages during an ever-extending rush 'hour', you can hear the now customary Argentine 'privatization' groan move down the platform or carriage in waves.

Brad Krupsaw

Historic trains and trams

One of the most dynamic and enterprising cities in South America in the early years of this century, Buenos Aires was a pioneer in the development of municipal transport. Transport *aficionados* should not miss the opportunity to travel in the *Tren Histórico*, a Scottish-built 1888 Neilson steam engine pulling old wooden carriages, which runs from the Federico Lacroze station to Capilla del Señor with lunch or a folkloric show at an *estancia* (departs Sunday 0900, returns 1900). Prices: return fare US$15, return fare with lunch and show US$30, reductions for children. T 796-3618 or cellular phone 15-578-0738.

Another attraction is the old-fashioned green and white tram (street car) operated by Asociación de los Amigos del Tranvía (T 476-0476) which runs (free) from April-November on Saturdays and holidays 1600-1900 and Sunday 1000-1300, 1600-1930 (not Easter Sunday) and from December-March on Saturdays and holidays 1700-2000, Sundays 1000-1300, 1600-1900. The circular route runs along the streets of Caballito district, from Calle Emilio Mitre 500, Subte Primera Junta (Line A) or Emilio Mitre (Line E), no stops en route.

decades. It contains his library, souvenirs of his travels, and many intriguing literary and historical curios.

EXCURSIONS

The main excursions are as follows: **northwest** to Tigre and Isla Martín García (see below), Luján and San Antonio de Areco (see under **The Pampas**) and the Reserva Nacional Otamendi (see under **The Northeast**); **southeast** to La Plata (see below); and **northeast** across the Río de la Plata to the Uruguayan coastal resorts including Colonia del Sacramento (see below). For excursions to visit estancias see below under **Estancias**, page 129.

LOCAL INFORMATION

● **Accommodation**

Hotel prices

L1	over US$200	L2	US$151-200
L3	US$101-150	A1	US$81-100
A2	US$61-80	A3	US$46-60
B	US$31-45	C	US$21-30
D	US$12-20	E	US$7-11
F	US$4-6	G	up to US$3

Unless otherwise stated, all hotels in range **D** and above have private bath. Assume friendliness and cleanliness in all cases.

All hotels, guest houses, inns and camping sites are graded by the number of beds available, and the services supplied. The Dirección de Turismo fixes maximum and minimum rates for 1, 2 and 3-star hotels, guest houses and inns, but the ratings do not provide very useful guidance. 4 and 5-star hotels are free to apply any rate they wish. Hotels in the upper ranges can often be booked more cheaply through Buenos Aires Travel Agencies. Hotels can be booked through the tourist information offices at Ezeiza and Jorge Newbery airports, but this is more expensive as commission is paid.

The following list is only a selection; exclusion does not necessarily imply non-recommendation. Rates given below are generally the minimum rates. Room tax is 15% and is not always included in the price. Air conditioning is a must in high summer. Many of the cheaper hotels in the central area give large reductions on the daily rate for long stays. Hotels with red-green lights or marked *Albergue Transitorio* are hotels for homeless lovers (for stays of 1½-2 hours).

5-star hotels in our L1-2 range: *Alvear Palace*, Alvear 1891, T 804-4031, F 804-6110, older-style, near Recoleta, with roof garden, shopping gallery, elegant, extremely good; *Caesar Park*, Posadas 1232, T 814-5151, F 814-5157, pool, solarium; *Claridge*, Tucumán 535, T 314-7700, F 314-8022, highly recommended, but variable reports about its restaurant; *Etoile*, Ortiz 1835 in Recoleta, T 804-8603, outstanding location, rooftop pool, rooms with kitchenette, recommended; *Libertador Kempinski*, Córdoba y Maipú, T 322-0032, F 322-9703; *Marriott Plaza*, Florida 1005, T 318-3000, F 318-3008, good restaurant; *Panamericano/Holiday Inn Crowne Plaza*, Pellegrini 525, T 393-6017, F 348-5250; *Park Hyatt*, Posadas 1088, T 326-1234, F 326-3736; *Sheraton*, San

Martín 1225, T 318-9000, F 311-6353, good buffet breakfast.

4-star: **L3** *Best Western Confort*, Viamonte 1501, T 814-4917, with breakfast, English spoken, 50% ISIC discount; **L3** *Bisonte*, Paraguay 1207, T 394-8041, F 393-9086, air conditioning, bar, modern, central, good value; **L3** *Bisonte Palace*, MT de Alvear y Suipacha, T 328-4751, F 328-6476, very good, welcoming; **L3** *Carlton*, Libertad 1180, T/F 812-0080, with breakfast; **A1** *Bristol*, Cerrito 286, T 382-3228, F 382-3384, good breakfast; **A1** *Carsson*, Viamonte 650, T 322-3601, F 332 3551, comfortable, quiet except rooms on street (ending in 17); **L3** *Continental*, Sáenz Peña 725, with breakfast, comfortable; **L2** *Crillón*, Santa Fe 796, T 312-8181, comfortable, good breakfast; **A1** *Gran Hotel Buenos Aires*, M T de Alvear 767, T/F 312-3003, rundown but clean; **L3** *Gran King*, Lavalle 560, T 393 4012/4052, helpful, English spoken; **L3** *Lancaster*, Córdoba 405, T 312-4061, F 311-3021, includes breakfast, expensive laundry service, charming; **L3** *Principado*, Paraguay 481, T 313-3022, F 313-3952, with breakfast, central, helpful; **A3** *Regidor*, Tucumán 451, T 314-9516, F 311-7441, air conditioning, breakfast included, recommended; **L2** *Regente Palace*, Suipacha 964, T 328 6628, F 328-7460, very good, central, English spoken, buffet breakfast, sports facilities, stores luggage; **Salles**, 9 de Julio/Cerrito y J D Perón, two blocks from Obelisco, T 382-0091, F 382-0754, recommended; **A1** *Savoy*, Callao 181, T 372-5972, F 325-9589, helpful.

3-star: **L2** *Camino Real*, Maipú 572, T 322-3162, F 325-9756, pleasant, central; **A2** *City*, Bolívar 160, T 342 6481, F 342-6486, recommended; **A3** *Constitución Palace*, Lima 1697, T 305-9020, with breakfast, 30% ISIC discount; **A1** *Deauville*, Talcahuano 1253, T 813-1427, F 814-5732, air conditioning, restaurant, bar, garage, recommended; **A2** *Ecuador*, Alsina 2820, near Plaza Once, T 956-0533, F 97-9987, recommended; **A1** *Embajador*, Pellegrini 1181, T 393-9485, good; **A2** *Eibar*, Florida 328, T 325-0969, with breakfast, quiet, helpful, old fashioned; **A3** *Gran Orly*, Paraguay 474, T/F 312-5344, old fashioned, good service, good lunches, English spoken, holds mail for guests, air conditioning, good value, recommended; **A1** *Impala*, Libertad 1215, T/F 816-0430, with breakfast; **A1** *Italia Romanelli*, Reconquista 647, T/F 312-6361, comfortable, recommended; **A1** *Liberty*, Corrientes 632, T/F 325-0261, with breakfast, English spoken, luggage stored, various sized rooms; **A3** *Nuevo Mundial*, Avenida de Mayo 1298, T 383-0011, F 383-6318, good beds, comfortable; **A3** *Promenade*, M T de Alvear 444, T/F 312-5681, no charge for credit cards, helpful, stores luggage, recommended; **A2** *Regis*, Lavalle 813, T 327-2613, F 312-5681, good value, nice atmosphere, quiet at back; **A3** *San Carlos*, Suipacha 39, T 345-1022, F 345-1766; **A2** *Sarmiento Palace*, Sarmiento 1953, T 953 3404, comfortable, English spoken, recommended; **A2** *Victory*, Maipú 880, T 314-0655, F 322-8415, air conditioning, modern, heating, TV, comfortable, front rooms noisy, luggage storage unreliable; **A3** *Waldorf*, Paraguay 450, T 312-2071, F 312-2079, comfortable, rooms of varying standards, garage, air conditioning, recommended.

2-star, on Avenida de Mayo: **A2** *Castelar*, No 1152, T 383-7873, F 383-8388, elegant and attractive 1920s hotel, good value; **A3** *Gran Hotel Hispano*, No 861, T/F 342-3472, without breakfast, attractive, spacious, pleasant patio, stores luggage, helpful; **A3** *Astoria*, No 916, T/F 334-9061, without breakfast, pretty patio, nice rooms, poor beds; **B***Novel*, No 915, T 345-0507, with breakfast. **Elsewhere**: **A3** *Gran Hotel de la Paix*, Rivadavia 1187, T 383-7140, old but good, large rooms; **A3** *Goya*, Suipacha 748, T 322-9269, air conditioning, quiet;

A3 *Plaza Roma*, Lavalle 110, T/F 311-1679, includes breakfast, recommended; **A3** *San Antonio*, Paraguay 372, T 312-5381, nice atmosphere, garden, recommended; **A3** *Tres Sargentos*, Tres Sargentos 345, T 312-6081, secure, new bathrooms, good value; **A2** *Ayacucho Palace*, Ayacucho 1408, T 806-1815, F 806-4467, 10 minutes from centre bus 10, helpful, comfortable, English spoken, recommended.

1-star or below, on Avenida de Mayo near Plaza del Congreso: A3 *Chile*, No 1297, T/F 383-7877, with breakfast, also cheaper rooms, clean, friendly, noisy; **A3** *Madrid*, No 1135, T 381-9021, without breakfast; **B** *Vedra*, No 1350, T 383-0584, good value, good beds, stores luggage, recommended; **B** *Marbella*, No 1261, T/F 383-3573, modernized, quiet, breakfast pricey, fans, English spoken, highly recommended, no credit cards; **B** *Reina*, No 1120, T 381-0547, old fashioned with masses of character and large breakfast, 20% ISIC discount; **C** *Alcazar*, No 935, T 345-0926, attractive, good value; **C** *Roma*, No 1413, T 381-4921, without breakfast, also rooms without bath, old but clean, good value; **C** *Cecil*, No 1239, T 383-3511, F 383-7929, without breakfast. **Also near Plaza del Congreso: A3** *Callao*, Callao y Sarmiento, T 476-3534, noisy; **A3** *Majestic*, Libertad 121, T 351-949, good value, includes breakfast; **A3** *Orense*, Mitre 1359, T 476-3173, **C** without bath, with breakfast, fan, laundry and cooking facilities, recommended; **B** *Ceballos Palace*, Virrey Cevallos 261, T 372-7636, safe (next to police HQ); **B** *Europa*, Mitre 1294, T 381-9629, air conditioning, 10% ISIC discount **B** *Lisboa*, Mitre 1282, T 383-1141, with breakfast, central; **C** *Sportsman*, Rivadavia 1426, T 381-8021/2, old fashioned, without bath, ISIC discount; **D** *Mediterráneo*, Rodríguez Peña 149, T 476-2852, basic, central, helpful, safe, stores luggage, laundry facilities, recommended; **B** *Micki*, Talcahuano 362, T 371-2376, no air

conditioning, basic, good value; **D** *Hosp Esterlina*, Mitre 1266, old, rambling, dirty. **On Avenida de Mayo towards Plaza de Mayo: A3** *Avenida*, No 623, T 342-5664, without breakfast, modernized, bar, clean, pleasant; **B** *Turista*, No 686, T 331-2281, nice rooms, comfortable; **B** *Vilaseca*, No 776, T 340-952, basic, helpful, noisy; **B** *Avenida Petit*, No 1347, T 381-7831, without breakfast; **C** *La Argentina*, No 860, T 342-0078/9, without breakfast, run down, comedor; **C** *Tandil*, No 890, T 343-2597, without breakfast, poor beds, clean. **In San Telmo: C** *Bolívar*, Bolívar 886, T 361-5105, good; **D** *Res Carly*, Humberto 1° 464, without bath, fan, quiet, basic, kitchen facilities, good value; **D** *Colonial*, Bolívar 1357, IYHA reduction, also dormitories, good kitchen; **D** *Hotel del Parque*, Defensa 1537, basic; **E** pp *Hostal de San Telmo*, Carlos Calvo 614, T 300-6899, F 300-9028, small dormitories, kitchen and laundry facilities, clean, quiet, modern, English spoken, warmly recommended. **Elsewhere: A3** *Aguirre*, Aguirre 1041, T 773-5027, safe; **A3** *El Cabildo*, Lavalle 748, T 392-6745, without breakfast; **A3** *Central Argentino*, Avenida del Libertador 174, T 312-6742/3166, secure, near Retiro stations, noisy, overpriced; **A3** *Kings*, Corrientes 623, T 322-8161, F 393-4452, with breakfast, air conditioning, helpful, top floor rooms have balcony; **A3** *Versalles*, Arenales 1394, T 811-5214, west of Avenida 9 de Julio, basic, no breakfast, fine staircase and mirrors; **B** *Central Córdoba*, San Martín 1021, T/F 312-8524, very central, air conditioning, helpful, quiet, good value; **B** *Hispano Argentino*, Catamarca 167, T 304-5835, some rooms with bath, quiet, convenient; **B** *Juncal Palace*, Juncal 2282, T 821-2770, old fashioned, 20% ISIC discount; **B** *Maipú*, Maipú 735, T 322-5142, popular, hot water, basic, stores luggage, laundry facilities, recommended; **B** *O'Rei*, Lavalle 733, T 393-7186, **C** without bath, basic, central, dark, ask

for a balcony; **B** *Uruguay*, Tacuarí 83, T 334 3456, central, good value, no credit cards, recommended; **C** *Du Helder*, Rivadavia 857, T 345-3644, old fashioned, clean, poor beds; **C** *Bahía*, H Yrigoyen 3062, hot showers, pleasant, safe, central but noisy, recommended; **C** *Bolivia*, Corrientes 1212, T 382-1780, without bath; **C** *Frossard*, Tucumán 686, T 322-1811, heating; **C** *Metropolitan I*, Corrientes 3973, T 862-3366 and *Metropolitan II*, Boedo 449, T 932-7547, F 931-1133 (Subte Line A to Barros Arana or Line E to Boedo), with breakfast, kitchen and laundry facilities, parking, English spoken, good value; **C** *Sil*, H Yrigoyen 775, T 231-8273, nice but no heating. **D** *Res Bahía*, Corrientes 1212, T 382-1780, very central, noisy.

Two student residences, **E** pp *Hosp Encuentro*, Sarmiento 4470, T 865-5684 (Subte Line B to Gallardo) and Entre Ríos 2165, T 306-6021, with bath, also meals, social areas, reduced rates for longer stay. Longer term accommodation (minimum 2 weeks) is offered by Juan Carlos Dima, Puan 551 C, T 432-4898, F 432-7101, US$450 per month per room, kitchen faciities, English spoken.

Youth hostels: *Youth Hostel*, Brasil 675 near Constitución station, T 300-7151, **E** pp with YHA card (ISIC card accepted), includes breakfast, sheets provided, hot water 24 hours, basic, recommended, no cooking facilities, cheap meals, doors closed 1200-1800 and from 0200, women should be aware that they could attract unwelcome attention near Constitución station as prostitutes operate there; **E** pp *Del Aguila*, Espinosa 1628, T 581-6663, hot water, cooking and laundry facilities, membership not necessary (buses 24, 105, 106, 109, 146). For Youth Hostal associations see **Useful addresses** below.

Apartments: contracts are usually for at least 1 year and owners will demand a guarantor or a deposit covering at least 6 months rent (security or cash). One agent is Sr Aguilar, Florida 520, 3°-314, T 322-4074. An agency which arranges sharing apartments (often with senior citizens) is Martha Baleiron, Esmeralda 1066, 5°F, T 311-9944; US$50 fee if an apartment is found, US$10 if not. All agencies should provide contracts which should be read carefully. To rent flats on a daily basis try *Edificios Esmeralda*, M T de Alvear 842, T 311-3929, includes cleaning; facilities for up to 6 persons. Also *Edificio Suipacha*, Suipacha 1235, T/F 322-6685, and *Aspen Apartment Hotel*, Esmeralda 933, T 313-9011; *Edificio Lemonde*, San Martín 839, T 313-2032, recommended; *Res Trianon*, Callao 1869, T 812-3335.

Camping About 15 km out at Lomas de Zamora, US$3 per person per night, includes swimming pool, 24-hour security, take own drinking water; take bus 141 from Plaza Italia

or 28 from Pellegrini to Puente La Noria then No 540 to Villa Albertini which passes the entrance.

● **Places to eat**
'The Buenos Aires Herald' publishes a handy *Guide to Good Eating in Buenos Aires* (with a guide to local wines) by Dereck Foster. There is also *El Libro de los Restaurantes de Buenos Aires*, published annually, describing the city's major restaurants. Eating out in Buenos Aires is very good but is expensive. In 1997 good restaurants were charging US$30 per person and up; more modest places were charging US$20-25 per person. **NB** In many mid to upper range restaurants, lunch is far cheaper than dinner. Lunch or dinner in a normal restaurant cost US$9-12 (cutlet, salad, 1/4 of table wine, dessert); a portion at a *comidas para llevar* (take away) place cost US$2.50-3.50. Many cheaper restaurants are *tenedor libre*, eat as much as you like for a fixed price.

The following list, for reasons of space, not quality, gives only those restaurants easily accessible for people staying in the city centre. **In the banking district**, between Avenida Corrientes and Plaza de Mayo: *Clark's*, Sarmiento 645, in old English outfitter's shop (also at Junín 1777), well cooked food, very expensive, busy, fish and lamb specialities, set lunch very good value; *Bolsa de Comercio*, 25 de Mayo 359, downstairs at the Stock Exchange, good but expensive; *London Grill*, Reconquista 455, British, busy, famous for roast beef and turkey curries, open 0800-1700 only; *El Pulpo*, Tucumán 361, very good seafood (US$30 including wine); *Sabot*, 25 de Mayo 756, very good business lunches; *Brizzi*, Lavalle 445, business lunches, good and worth the price; *Blab*, Florida 325, sole, veal, pork specialities, lunchtime only; *Don Pipon*, Esmeralda 521, large portions, good value; *La Pipeta*, San Martín 498, downstairs, serving for 30 years, good, noisy, closed Sunday; *La Estancia*, Lavalle 941, popular with business people, excellent grills and service, expensive; *La Casona del Nonno*, Lavalle 827, popular, *parrilla* and pasta, not cheap; *ABC*, Lavalle 545, traditional, good value; *El Palacio de la Papa Frita*, Lavalle 735 and 954, Corrientes 1612, Laprida 1339, Maipú 431, 10% discount for ISIC and youth card holders; good value *parrillas* at *La Posada del Maipú*, Maipú 440. *Memorabilia*, Maipú 761, pizzas, bar, music, 20% discount for ISIC cards; *La Rural*, Suipacha 453, recommended for *parrillada* and *bife de lomo*, expensive or cheaper *table d'hôte*, English-speaking head waiter is excellent; *Pizzería Roma*, Lavalle 800, cheap and good quality, delicious spicy *empanadas* and *ñoquis*, good breakfast; *Los Inmortales*, Lavalle 746, specializes in pizza, good value, large selection, 10% ISIC discount. There are other locations: some serve *à la carte* dishes which are plentiful, and are open from 1500-2000 when most other restaurants are closed.

El Figón de Bonilla, rustic style, Alem 673, good, another branch at Junín 1721; *Dora*, Alem 1016, huge steaks, get there early to beat the queue; *Los Troncos*, Suipacha 732, good grills, US$18 *menú*; *Catalinas*, Reconquista 875, seafood, very expensive. **A few blocks from this district:** *El Aljibe*, at *Sheraton*, smoked salmon, tournedos Rossini, baby beef; *Dolli*, Avenida del Libertador 312, near Retiro, very good food, fairly expensive; *La Chacra*, Córdoba 941, good parrilla, expensive. La Recova, on the 1000 block of Posadas, near *Hyatt*, has several moderate to expensive restaurants, eg *El Mirasol* and *Piegari*, No 1052, US$40 per person plus wine.

In Recoleta: on the corner of Roberto M Ortiz is *La Biela* (see **Tea rooms**, etc, below), and opposite *Café de la Paix*. Turning left on Ortiz: *Lola*, No 1805, good pasta, lamb and fish but expensive; *Don Juan*, No 1827; *La Tasca de Germán*, No 1863, highly recommended, European. Cross Guido to: *Gato Dumas*, Junín 1745, expensive but has good fixed price menus; *La Bianca*, Junín 1769, very good value, lunch US$16 per person; *Harper's*, Junín 1773; *Hippopotamus*, Junín 1787, dinner expensive, good value executive lunch; *Munich Recoleta*, Junín 1871, good steaks, pleasant atmosphere, US$20 per person, no credit cards. Nearby, two blocks from Recoleta towards Avenida Callao, *Au Bec Fin*, Vicente López 1827, reservations needed, open 2000-0200 daily; *Rodi Bar*, López 1900, excellent *bife*.

In the San Telmo area: *Calle de Angeles*, Chile 318, nice setting in an old, covered street, high standards; *La Convención de San Telmo*, Carlos Calvo 375, good, but expensive; *El Repecho de San Telmo*, Carlos Calvo 242, excellent, expensive, reserve in advance (T 362-5473); *La Casa de Estebán de Luca*, Defensa 1000, very good, good wines. For ice cream, *Sumo*, Independencia y Piedras.

The Costanera Rafael Obligado along the river front (far end of Aeroparque) is lined with little eating places (take taxi, or colectivo 45 from Plaza Constitución, Plaza San Martín or Retiro to Ciudad Universitaria): *El Rancho Inn* is best, try also *Happening*, *La Marea* and *Los Años Locos*, good beef, parrilla, cold buffet. *Clo Clo*, La Pampa y Costanera, reservation required. Typical *parrilla* at *Rodizio*, Costanera Norte, opposite Balneario Coconor, self-service and waiter service, other branches, eg Callao y Juncal, good value, popular.

In Puerto Madero, across the docks from Plaza de Mayo, are *Las Lilas*, Dávila 516, excellent *parrilla*; *Cholila*, Dávila 102, chic; *Xcaret* Dávila 164; *Mirasol*, No 202, and opposite, *Bice*, Dávila 192, mostly Italian, good; *Caballerizá*, Dávila 560, overpriced; *Columbus*, popular (all about US$40 per person including wine and tip); a bit cheaper (US$30-35) are *Bahía Madero*, Dávila 430, highly recommended; branches of *Rodizio* and *Happening*.

Near the Teatro Colón: *Tomo Uno*, ellegrini 525 (*Hotel Panamericano*), expensive, trout, mignon, shrimp, mandé mata pasta, closed Sunday; *9 de Julio*, Pellegrini 587, very good value; *Posta del Gaucho*, Pellegrini 625, accepts Visa; *Edelweiss*, Libertad 431, tuna steaks, pasta, grill, expensive and famous; *Pizza Piola*, Santa Fe y Libertad, good, pricey. **By Congreso**: *Quorum*, Combate de los Pozos 61, behind Congress, popular with politicians. Also near Congress: *Plaza Mayor*, Venezuela 1399, estancia-style, very popular and, opposite, *Campo dei Fiori*, Italian, both recommended.

Boca typical Boca restaurants on Necochea, but check the hygiene. They all serve antipasto, pasta and chicken; no point in looking for beef here. All bands are loud. *La Barca*, Pedro de Mendoza, on river bank near Avellaneda bridge, seafood, recommended; also recommended for seafood and good value, *Viejo Puente*, Almirante Brown 1499. *El Pescadito*, Mendoza 1483, recommended for pasta and seafood.

Other recommendations: *Pepito*, Montevideo 381, very good; *Pippo*, Montevideo 341, large pasta house, simple food, very popular, also at Paraná 356; *Chiquilín*, Montevideo 321, pasta and meat, good value; *Los Angeles*, Uruguay 707, US$7 for salad bar, main meal and dessert, recommended; *Los Teatros*, Talcahuano 350, good (live music 2300-0100); *Nazarenas*, Reconquista 1132, good for beef, expensive, recommended; *Ostramar*, Santa Fe 3495 y Julián Alvarez (Subte station Ortiz, then walk back towards town), good quality fish; *Rivadavia*, Sanchez de Bustamante 2616, Palermo Chico, huge portions, good value; *El Salmón II*, Reconquista 1014, large portions of good food, not cheap.

Other Italian: *Broccolino*, Esmeralda 776, excellent, very popular, try *pechugitas*; *Mama Liberata*, Maipú 642, excellent; *Prosciutto*, Venezuela 1212. Three famous *pizzerías* in the centre are on Corrientes: *Banchero*, No 1298; *Las Cuartetas*, No 838, and *Los Inmortales*, No 1369, same chain as above; *Il Gatto*, Corrientes 959, popular and reasonably priced.

International Spanish: *El Imparcial*, H Yrigoyen 1204, and opposite, *El Globo*, No 1199, both recommended. **Swedish**: food at *Swedish Club*, Tacuarí 147, open to non-members. **Hungarian**: *Budapest*, 25 de Mayo 690, cheap. **British**: *The Alexandra*, San Martín

774, curries, fish and seafood, nice bar, closed in evening.

Oriental: *Nuevo Oriental*, Maipú near Lavalle, Chinese *tenedor libre*, US$6, good choice; *La China*, J D Perón y Montevideo, *tenedor libre*; *Tsuru*, ground floor of *Sheraton*, authentic Japanese, small, recommended.

Vegetarian: *Granix*, Florida 126 and 467 *tenedor libre* US$8, bland but filling, lunchtime Monday-Friday. *Ever Green* is a chain of *tenedor libre* vegetarian restaurants, branches: Paraná 746, Sarmiento 1728 and Cabildo 2979; *La Esquina de las Flores*, Córdoba 1599, excellent value, also good health-food shop; *La Huerta II*, Lavalle 895, 2nd floor, *tenedor libre*, US$7, reasonable; *Macrobiotica Universal*, Paraguay 858, highly recommended.

Fast food: *Pumper-nic* is a chain of rather pricey fast food restaurants. Many *McDonalds* in the centre. *The Embers*, Callao 1111, fast food, 10% discount for ISIC and youth card holders.

Cheap meals: several supermarkets have good, cheap restaurants: *Coto* supermarket, Viamonte y Paraná, upstairs; also *Supercoop* stores at Sarmiento 1431, Lavalle 2530, Piedras y Rivadavia and Rivadavia 5708; *Pizzalandia*, on Brasil (near Youth Hostel) serves cheap *empanadas*, *salteñas* and pizzas. Best Bolivian *salteñas* and *humitas* from El Horno, Güemes 4689, Palermo. Good snacks all day and night at Retiro and Constitución railway termini. For quick cheap snacks the markets are recommended. The snack bars in underground stations are also cheap. *DeliCity* bakeries, several branches, very fresh pastries, sweets, breads, authentic American donuts; *Biscuit House*, bakery chain, 20 branches, *media lunas*, *empanadas* and breads.

For restaurants with shows, see **Nightclubs and folklore** below.

Tea rooms, cafés and bars: *Richmond*, Florida 468 between Lavalle and Corrientes, genteel (chess played between 1200-2400); well-known are the *Confitería Suiza*, Tucumán 753, and the *Florida Garden* Florida y Paraguay. *Confitería Ideal*, Suipacha 384, old, faded, good service, cakes and snacks, recommended. Many on Avenida del Libertador in the Palermo area. *Café Querandí*, Venezuela y Chacabuco, popular with intellectuals and students, good atmosphere, well known for its Gin Fizz. The more bohemian side of the city's intellectual life is centred on Avenida Corrientes, between Cerrito and Callao, where there are many bars and coffee shops; *Bar Seddon*, 25 de Mayo, small tango bar, packed from midnight on; *Pub Bar Bar O*, Tres Sargentos 451, good music and prices. *El Molino*, Rivadavia y

Callao, popular with politicians, near Congress, Belle Epoque décor, frequent art sales, good value, self service section; *The Shamrock*, Rodriguez Peña 1220, Irish run, Guinness until 0500; *Café 1234*, Santa Fe 1234, good and reasonable; *Clásica y Moderna*, Callao y Paraguay, bookshop at back, expensive but very popular, jazz usually on Wednesday night, open 24 hours. *Freddo*, Pacheco de Melo y Callao, with another branch at Santa Fe y Callao, "the city's best ice-cream" (Brad Krupsaw). Next door (Quintana y Recoleta) is café *La Biela*, restaurant and *whiskería*, elegant. Also in Recoleta: *Café Victoria*, Ortiz 1865, whiskería/sandwichería, popular; *La Vanguardia*, Montevideo 1671, 30% discount for ISIC card; in Paseo del Pilar *Hard Rock Café*, great salads, and *Café Rix*, both with ISIC and GO 25 discount; *Henry J Bean*, Junín 1747, ISIC and GO 25 discount. On Lavalle there are *whiskerías* and *cervecerías* where you can have either coffee or exotic drinks. *Barila*, Santa Fe 2375, has excellent confectionery. *Café Tortoni*, Avenida de Mayo 825-9, delicious cakes, coffee, a haunt of artists, very elegant, over 100 years old, interesting *peña* evenings of poetry and music. On Saturday at 2315 it becomes a 'Catedral del Jazz', with Fénix Jazz Band, US$15 entrance. *Café El Verdi*, Paraguay 406, also has live music. *Parakultural New Border*, Chacabuco 1072, mostly avant-garde theatre, popular; *Die Schule*, Alsina 1760, hard rock bar with avant-garde theatre. A 'bohemian, bizarre' bar is *El Dorado*, H Yrigoyen 971. Good bars in San Telmo around Plaza Dorrego, eg *El Balcón de la Plaza*, and on Humberto I. Watch whisky prices in bars, much higher than in restaurants. Most cafés serve tea or coffee plus *facturas*, or pastries, for breakfast, US$2.50-3 (bakery shops sell 10 *facturas* for US$2).

● **Airline offices**
See **Introduction and Hints** for Argentina and Mercosur Airpasses. **Aerolíneas Argentinas**, Paseo Colón 185, T 340-7800, with 4 branches, plus airport offices, reservations T 340-7777, Monday-Friday 0945-1745; **Austral Líneas Aéreas**, Alem 1134, T 317-3600; **Líneas Aéreas del Estado** (LADE), Perú 714, T 361-7071, erratic schedules, uninformed office; **Líneas Aéreas Privadas Argentinas** (Lapa), M T de Alvear 790, T 819-5272 (reservations), or Aeroparque Puente Aéreo section, T 772-9920, cheapest fares to main tourist centres, good service; **Dinar**, Sáenz Peña 933, T 326-6374, 778-0100; **LAER**, Lavalle 347, 2nd floor B, T 394-5641; **Kaiken**, Almafuerte Travel, Avenida de Mayo 580, 6th floor, T 331-0191; **AeroPerú**, Santa Fe 840, T 311-4115; **Varig**, Carabelas 344, T 329-9200; **Lan Chile**, Paraguay 609

1st floor, T 311-5334, 312-8161 for reconfirmations; **Ecuatoriana**, T 312-2180; **United**, M T Alvear 590, T 326-9111; **Lufthansa** M T Alvear 636, reservations T 319-0600; **Air France**, Santa Fe 963, T 317-4700; **British Airways**, Córdoba 690, T 325-1059; **American**, Santa Fe 881, T 318-1111; **KLM**, Reconquista 559, 5th floor, T 480-9473.

● **Banks & money changers**
Many shops and restaurants accept US dollar bills. Most banks charge very high commission especially on travellers' cheques (as much as US$10). Banks open Monday-Friday 1000-1500, be prepared for long delays. US dollar bills are often scanned electronically for forgeries, while travellers' cheques are sometimes very difficult to change and you may be asked for proof of purchase. American Express travellers' cheques are less of a problem than Thomas Cook. Practices are constantly changing. **Lloyds Bank** (BLSA) Ltd, Reconquista y Mitre, Visa cash advances provided in both US dollars and pesos. It has 10 other branches in the city, and others in Greater Buenos Aires. **Royal Bank of Canada**, Florida y Perón, branch at Callao 291. **Citibank**, B Mitre 502, changes only Citicorp travellers' cheques, no commission, also Mastercard; branch at Florida 192. **First National Bank of Boston**, Florida 99. **Bank of America**, JD Perón y San Martín changes Bank of America travellers' cheques morning only, US$ at very high commission. **Banco Tornquist**, B Mitre 531, Crédit Lyonnais agents, advance cash on visa card. **Banco Holandés**, Florida 361; **Deutsche Bank**, B Mitre 401 (and other branches), changes Thomas Cook travellers' cheques, also Mastercard, both give cash advances. **Banco Roberts**, 25 de Mayo 258, changes Thomas Cook travellers' cheques without commission. Thomas Cook rep, **Fullers**, Esmeralda 1000 y M T Alvear. **American Express** offices are at Arenales 707 y Maipú, by Plaza San Martín, T 312-0900, where you can apply for a card, get financial services and change Amex travellers' cheques (1000-1500 only, no commission into US$ or pesos). **Client Mail** in same building, Monday-Friday 0900-1800, Saturday 0900-1300. Mastercard ATMs (look for Link-Mastercard/Cirrus) at several locations, mostly **Banco Nacional del Lavoro** including Florida 40 and Santa Fe y Esmeralda.

There are many *casas de cambio*, some of which deal in travellers' cheques. Most are concentrated around San Martín and Corrientes: *Cambio Topaz*, San Martín 1394-1400, 5% commission; *Casa Piano*, San Martín 345-347, changes travellers' cheques into pesos or US$ cash for 2-3% commission, *Cambios Trade Travel*, San Martín 967, 3% commission on

travellers' cheques; *Exprinter*, Suipacha 1107, open from Monday-Friday 1000-1600, Saturday closed; *Casa América*, Avenida de Mayo 959, accepts Thomas Cook travellers' cheques. Many *cambios* will exchange US$, travellers' cheques for US$ cash at commissions varying from 1.25 to 3%. If all *cambios* closed, try Mercadería de Remate de Aduana, Florida 8, or *Eves*, Tucumán 702, open until 1800. On Saturday, Sunday and holidays, cash may be exchanged in the *cambio* in some of the large supermarkets (eg *Carrefour*, Paseo Alcorta Shopping Center, open daily 1000-2200). There is no service charge on notes, only on cheques. Major credit cards usually accepted but check for surcharges. General **Mastercard** office at H Yrigoyen 878, open 0930-1800, T 331-1022/2502/2549; another branch at Florida 274 (open 1000-1730). **Visa**, Corrientes 1437, 2nd floor, T 954-3333/2000, for stolen cards, helpful. Other South American currencies can only be exchanged in *casas de cambio*.

● **Cultural centres**
Argentine Association of English Culture, Suipacha 1333 (library for members only); **British Chamber of Commerce**, Corrientes 457; **British Council**, M T de Alvear 590, 4th floor, T 311-9814/7519, F 311-7747 (open 1000-1200, 1430-1630); **Goethe Institut**, Corrientes 311, German library (open 1300-1900 excluding Wednesday, and 1000-1400 first Saturday of month) and newspapers, free German films shown, cultural programmes, German language courses. In the same building, upstairs, is the German Club, Corrientes 327. **Alliance Française**, Córdoba 946; **USA Chamber of Commerce**, Diagonal Sáenz Peña 567; **Instituto Cultural Argentino-Norteamericano** (ICANA), Maipú 686, T 322-3855/4557, large library, borrowing only for members; **St Andrew's Society**, Perú 352.

Clubs: **American Club**, Viamonte 1133, facing Teatro Colón, temporary membership available; **American Women's Club**, Córdoba 632, 11th floor; **English Club**, 25 de Mayo 586, T 311-9121, open for lunch only, temporary membership available to British business visitors. The American and English Clubs have reciprocal arrangements with many clubs in USA and UK. **Swedish Club**, Tacuarí 147; **Organización Hebrea Argentina Macabi**, Tucumán 3135, T 962-0947, social and sporting club for conservative Jews.

● **Embassies & consulates**
All open Monday-Friday unless stated otherwise. **Bolivian Consulate**, Belgrano 1670, 2nd floor, T 383-7038, open 0900-1400, visa while you wait, tourist bureau which gives misleading information; **Brazilian Consulate**, Carlos

Pellegrini 1363, 5th floor, open Monday-Friday, 0930-1400, visa takes 48 hours, US$24 to US passport holders, T 394-5278; **Paraguayan Consulate**, Viamonte 1851, 0900-1400, T 812-0075; **Peruvian Consulate**, San Martín 691, 6th floor, T 311-7582, 0900-1400, visa US$5, takes 1 day; **Uruguayan Consulate**, Las Heras 1907, open 1000-1800, T 807-3040, visa takes up to 1 week; **Chilean Consulate**, San Martín 439, 9th floor, T 394-6582, Monday-Thursday 0930-1330, 1530-1830, Friday 0915-1430; **Ecuadorean Embassy**, Quintana 585, 9th and 19th floors, T 804-6408.

Unless otherwise stated consulates are located in the respective embassy. **United States**, Colombia 4300, T 777-4533/7007, 0900-1730, visas 0800-1100, calls between 1500 and 1700; **Australia**, Santa Fe 846 (Swissair Building), T 312-6841, Monday-Thursday 0830-1230, 1330-1730, Friday 0830-1315; **Canada**, Tagle 2828, T 805-3032; **South Africa**, M T de Alvear 590, 7th floor, T 311-8991/7, Monday-Thursday 0900-1300, 1400-1630, Friday 0900-1330; **Israel**, Avenida de Mayo 701, 10th floor, T 342-1465; **Japan**, Paseo Colón 275, 9th and 11th floor, T 343-2561, 0900-1300, 1430-1800.

Austria, French 3671, T 802-1400, 0900-1200; **Belgium**, Defensa 113-8, T 331-0066/69, 0800-1300; **United Kingdom**, Luis Agote 2412/52 (near corner Pueyrredón y Guido), T 803-7070, open 0915-1215, 1415-1615; **Denmark**, Alem 1074, 9th floor, T 312-6901/6935, 0900-1200, 1400-1600; **Finland**, Avenida Santa Fe 846, 5th floor, T 312-0600/70, Monday-Thursday 0830-1700, Friday 0830-1200; **France**, Santa Fe 846, 3rd floor, T 312-2409, 0900-1200; **Germany**, Villanueva 1055, Belgrano, T 778-2500, 0900-1200; **Greece**, Sáenz Peña 547, 4th floor, T 342-4958, 1000-1300; **Ireland**, Suipacha 1380, 2nd floor, T 325-8588, 1000-1230; **Italy**, Billinghurst 2577 (consulate M T de Alvear 1149, T 816-6132, 0900-1300; **Netherlands**, Edificio Buenos Aires, Avenida de Mayo 701, 19th floor, T 334-3474, 0900-1200, 1300-1530; **Norway**, Esmeralda 909, 3rd floor B, T 312-1904, 0900-1430; **Spain**, Florida 943 (Consulate, Guido 1760), T 811-0070, 0900-1330, 1500-1730. **Sweden**, Corrientes 330, 3rd floor, T 311-3088/9 (Consulate, Tacuarí 147, T 342-1422), T 1000-1200; **Switzerland**, Santa Fe 846, 12th floor, T 311-6491, open 0900-1200.

● **Entertainment**

For details see *El Ocio*, US$1, and *La Maga*, US$5, both published weekly, both available from newsstands.

Cinemas: the selection of films is as good as anywhere else in the world and details are listed daily in all main newspapers. Films are shown uncensored and most foreign films are subtitled. Tickets best booked early afternoon to ensure good seats (average price US$6 in 1996, 50% discount Wednesday and for first show Monday-Friday). Tickets obtainable, sometimes cheaper, from ticket agencies (*carteleras*), such as *Vea Más*, Paseo La Plaza, Corrientes 1600, local 19 (the cheapest), *Cartelera*, Lavalle 742, T 322 9263, *Teatro Lorange*, Corrientes 1372, T 372-7386, and *Cartelera Baires*, Corrientes 1372, local 25. Many cinemas on Lavalle, around Santa Fe and Callao and in Belgrano (Avenida Cabildo and environs). Film club at *Foro Gandhi*, Montevideo 453 on Friday and Saturday evenings, showing old, foreign and 'art' films, US$1.50, open to non-members. Free films at Asociación Bancaria, Sarmiento 337/341, T 313-9306/312-5011/17, once a month (Wednesday); old films at Cine en la Cinemateca Argentina, Sarmiento 2255, T 952-2170 (half price of other cinemas, plus 20% discount for ISIC holders), and at Sarmiento 2150, T 48-2170. ISIC holders also entitled to discounts at Cine IFT Sala 1, Boulogne Sur Mer 549 (50%). On Saturday nights many central cinemas have *trasnoches*, late shows starting at 0100.

Cultural events: the *Luna Park* stadium holds pop/jazz concerts, ballet and musicals, at Bouchard 465, near Correo Central, T 311-5100, free parking at Corrientes 161. *Teatro Alvear*, Corrientes 1659, T 374-9470, has free concerts Friday at 1300, usually Orquesta de Tango de Buenos Aires. *Tango Week*, leading up to National Tango Day (11 December), has free events all over the city, details posted around the city and at tourist offices. *Teatro Municipal General San Martín*, Avenida Corrientes 1530, organizes many cultural activities of which quite a few are free of charge, including concerts Saturday and Sunday evenings, 50% ISIC and GO 25 discount; the theatre's Sala Leopoldo Lugones shows international classic films, Saturday-Sunday, US$2. Free concerts at ProMusica music shop, Florida 638; schedule in window. *Centro Cultural General San Martín*, Sarmiento 1551, and the *Centro Cultural de Recoleta*, Junín 1930, next to the Recoleta cemetery have many free activities: for details see main newspapers and *La Maga*. **NB** From mid-December to end-February most theatres and concert halls are closed.

Gay discos: *Bunker*, Anchorena 1170, Friday-Sunday, large, loud; *Experiment*, Pellegrini 1085, open nightly; *Enigma*, Suipacha 927, Friday-Saturday; *Diesel*, Argoz 2424, Friday-Sunday. Most gay discos charge US$15-20 entry on door; tickets are much cheaper if bought from bars around Santa Fe y Pueyrredón from 0100.

Jazz: *El Subsuelo*, Perón 1372, good bands featured; *Oliverio*, Paraná 328, excellent live jazz features the great Fats Fernández, Friday-Saturday 2330 and 0100; *Café Tortoni*,

Avenida de Mayo 829, T 342-4328, classic tango spot, features the Creole Jazz Band, Friday 2300, 40% ISIC and GO25 discount, also tango concert Friday-Sunday 2130, recommended.

Music: bars and restaurants in San Telmo district, with live music (usually beginning 2330-2400): *Players*, Humberto I 528 (piano bar); *Samovar de Rasputin*, Iberlucea 1251,

Caminito, T 302-3190, good blues, dinner and/or show. Cover charges between US$5 and US$20, or more.

Bailantas are music and dance halls where they play popular styles which for years have been despised as 'low class' but which are now fashionable among the upper classes. A popular place is **Terremoto Bailable**, Paraguay y Thames; **Metropolis**, Santa Fe at Plaza Italia.

Fun times in Buenos Aires

For years it was the classic Avenida Corrientes, followed by Calle Lavalle, but today both of these are considered faded and the most popular parts of town chosen by most *Porteños* for having a good time are around Palermo. Here both the Paseo de la Infanta and Los Arcos (Mitre y Cáceres), located some 500m from each other, are lined with fine bars and restaurants which, come midnight, pull in their tables, turn on the dance lights and turn into hopping discos and gathering spots for those who come to see and be seen. Age groups range from 14 to what one *Porteño* calls 'marrying age'. The most popular spots on the lips of late night weekenders include *Buenos Aires News, Puente Mitre, Tequila, Bonito Bonito, Coyote, Hanoi, Gitana* and *Fashion Café*.

Equally fashionable but only slightly less popular is the Paseo del Pilar in Recoleta, where a string of restaurants compete along an airy and well-lit promenade. Other attractions are the *Hard Rock Café*, a couple of gay bars and the *Centro Cultural Recoleta*, which offers live music and art exhibitions.

The Puerto Madero docks are quickly gaining popularity with pleasant areas for strolling along the river, restaurants bathed in soft light and an ultra-modern cinema complex. Costanera Norte also manages to whip up an active nightlife. *Pizza Banana*, a dance and mingle spot more for the middle-aged crowd and popular with couples as well as singles, receives good revues, as do *Happening, Pacha* (disco for 20s and 30s) and *El Cielo* (a disco with terrace overlooking the river).

Although traces of the Argentine passion for cinema can still be seen at weekends on Calle Lavalle and Avenida Corrientes, their glory days are long gone. Corrientes is still second to none for theatre, but the most popular cinemas are now around the intersection of Avenida Santa Fe and Avenida Callao, though this has been surpassed by a modern multiplex in Puerto Madero.

For a more unique evening the *cantinas* along Calle Necochea 1200 block, in La Boca, move to a colourful perhaps more popular rhythm with their Italian tarantellas and local, Brazilian or Caribbean live music. Non-stop noise, dancing and great portions of food mark this traditional Italian neighbourhood as a spot for those with a taste for the slightly crude and bizarre.

During the daytime *Porteños* flock to the new *Tren de la Costa* so they can get out and window-shop at the shopping-stations (San Isidro is a favourite) and restaurants. The Costanera Sur Wildlife Reserve attracts crowds for walking, sunbathing and biking (rent a cycle here) along its dirt roads in warmer weather. Tourists and locals alike roam the antique shops and weekend market in San Telmo or mix with the crowds at the Recoleta crafts market. At the rose garden in Palermo you can paddle-boat around the artificial lake or sit on a shady bench with the masses. The zoo is a social event, while the Botanical Gardens next door are that rarest of phenomena in Buenos Aires: an island of peace.

Brad Krupsaw

Tango in Buenos Aires

After years of decline, the tango scene is once again enjoying great popularity. Most neighbourhoods of the city have their own tango scene with even the kids dancing a kind of hybrid tango-rock. The best way to enjoy tango is to see it the way the *porteños* do, away from the tourist spots. In San Telmo there are several famous clubs which any hotel employee or resident will tell you are a 'must' but two of the best places are less well-known.

One of these is the *Club del Vino*, Cabrera 4347, where the repertoire is a spectacular blend of the traditional and the Piazzola-style modern. Some of the finest shows in the city feature members of the '*guardia vieja*' (old guard) who still linger on from the 1940s and 1950s, considered by many to be the best decades of Buenos Aires tango. At the *Club del Vino* on a Saturday night you can be witness to living tango history. Here Nelly Omar, who came out of the Francisco Canaro orchestra, one of the first so-called '*tipica*' groups which were all the rage in the 30s, 40s and 50s, still sings her heart out. *Tipica* groups were made up of concertina, violin, piano and bass and the *Club del Vino* still features the eminent concertinist Nestor Marconi, who performed in the first orchestra which accompanied the legendary singer Roberto Goyeneche.

Of the better known places in San Telmo, *El Viejo Almacén* has a show which features the concertinist Julian Plaza who used to arrange the famous orchestra of Aníbal 'Pichuco' Troilo, while *La Cumparsita* shines on Fridays and Saturdays with the excellent singer Roberto Ayala.

If you are looking to dance tango, then another spot off the beaten track is the *Club Almagro*, Medrano 522, T 774-7454; every evening of the week the dancing starts with a one hour class for US$6; after this warm-up the place starts dancing.

Brad Krupsaw

For salsa: *El Club*, Yerbal 1572, friendly, for all ages, not trendy, all welcome; *La Salsera*, Yatay 961, highly regarded salsa place.

Nightclubs and folklore: **Tango**: *Casablanca*, Balcarce 668, T 331-4621, very touristy, large coach parties, US$40 per person including drinks; *Michelangelo*, Balcarce 433, T 334-4321, impressive setting, concert café in an old converted monastery, various types of music including tango and folklore, Tuesday-Sunday, and *La Ventana*, Balcarce 425, Monday-Saturday shows at 2230, T 331-3648/334-1314, very touristy but very good show, US$50 for show, dinner and unlimited wine, through an agency, 20% discount for ISIC and youth card holders, from Asatej office (see **Useful addresses** below); *El Viejo Almacén*, Independencia y Balcarce, T 307-7388; *Querandí*, Perú 302, expensive but good dinner-show. Tango shows also at *La Cumparsita*, Chile 302, T 361-6880, authentic, US$50 for 2 including wine; *Club del Vino*, Cabrera 4737, T833-0050; *Bar Sur*, Estados Unidos 299, T 362-6086, and *Antigua Tasca de Cuchilleros*, Carlos Calvo 319, T 362-3811/28, pleasant surroundings, show US$20, show and dinner, US$32, both in San Telmo.

The best affordable tango bars are in La Boca, but it is difficult to find authentic tango for locals, most are tourist-oriented. Good show also at *La Veda*, Florida 1, T 331-6442, average meal with wine and other drinks US$40, Tuesday-Saturday. *Viejo Buzón*, Corrientes y Rodríguez Peña, good tango, no dinner but plenty of dancing, locals and tourists; *Café Mozart*, Esmeralda 754, tango, jazz, theatre, no dinner; *La Casa de Aníbal Troilo*, Carlos Calvo 2540, good singers and bands, for tourists; *Tango Danza*, J M Moreno 351, Friday, Saturday, Sunday, from 2200; *Salón La Argentina*, Rodríguez Peña 365, Thursday-Sunday, 2200, more modern-style tango with *bandoneon* (report that address changed). Also recommended are *Café Homero*, J A Cabrera 4946, Palermo; *Italia Unita*, Perón 2535; *Mesón Español*, Rodríguez Peña 369, T 35-0516, good folk music show and good food; *Galería Tango Argentino*, Boedo 722 y Independencia, T 93-1829/7527, Wednesday-Saturday, less touristy than others, dinner (usually), show and dancing, has dancers and tango lessons (Monday-Friday, 1800-2100), well-known bands; *Paladium*, San Martín 954, tango/bolero dance hall; *Volver*, Corrientes 837, Monday-Friday, 1800-2100. Tango lessons at **Champagne Tango**, Rio de Janeiro 387, Tuesday, Friday, Sunday.

Recommended nightclub/discos: including *Hippopotamus*, Junín 1787, Recoleta, French restaurant (lunch and dinner), fashionable nightclub; *Le Club*, small and exclusive, Quintana 111; *Morocco*, H Yrigoyen 851, exclusive, restaurants, ISIC and GO 25 discounts; *Cemento*, Estados Unidos 1238, disco with live shows, usually hard rock and heavy metal, popular with younger crowds, as are *New York City*, Alvarez Thomas y El Cano, T 552-4141, chic, and *Halley*, Corrientes 2020, heavy metal and hard rock. Some discos serve breakfast for additional charge at entry. Generally it is not worth going to discos before 0230 at weekends. Dress is usually smart.

Also recommended: *Bembe*, Niceto Vega 5510, salsa, Friday and Saturday, bar opens 2000, dancing from 0100, salsa dance class Friday 2100; *Mama Baker*, Santa Fe 2800; *Cinema*, Córdoba 4633, inside a former cinema; *El Dorado*, H Yrigoyen y 9 de Julio, interesting, different; *El Nacional*, Reconquista 915, in tunnels formerly used for smuggling; *El Angel*, Corrientes 1768 y Callao; *Cachaça Tropical*, on Brasil (one block from Plaza Constitución), big disco with Latin American music, good meeting place; *Roxy*, Rivadavia 1900 block, rock and roll, reggae, recommended.

Theatre: about 20 commercial theatres play all year round. Recommended is the *Teatro Liceo*. There are many amateur theatres. You are advised to book as early as possible for a seat at a concert, ballet, or opera. For ticket agencies, see **Cinemas**, above.

● **Hospitals & medical services**
Innoculations: *Centro Médico Rivadavia*, Bustamante 2531 y Las Heras, Monday-Friday, 0730-1900 (bus 38, 59, 60 or 102 from Plaza Constitución), or *Guardia de Sanidad del Puerto*, Monday and Thursday, 0800-1200, at Ing Huergo 690, T 334-1875, free, bus 20 from Retiro, no appointment required (typhus, cholera, Monday-Friday 0800-1200; yellow fever, Tuesday-Thursday 1400-1600, but no hepatitis, take syringe and needle, particularly for insulin and TB). Buy the vaccines in *Laboratorio Biol*, Uriburu 159, or in larger chemists. Many chemists display signs indicating that they administer innoculations. Any hospital with an infectology department will do hepatitis A.

Urgent medical service: (day and night) (**Casualty ward**: *Sala de guardia*). For free municipal ambulance service to an emergency hospital department, T 342-4001/4, 107 (SAME). In case of intoxication, T 962-6666 for information or first aid. Public Hospital: *Hospital Argerich*, Almirante Brown esquina Pi y Margall 750, T 931-5555; *British Hospital*, Perdriel 74, T 23-1081, US$14 a visit; cheap dental treatment at Caseros y Perdriel 76; *German Hospital*, Pueyrredón 1657, between Berutti and Juncal, T 821-4083. Both maintain first-aid centres (*centros asistenciales*) as do the other main hospitals. *French Hospital*, Rioja 951, T 97-1031; *Children's Hospital* (Ricardo Gutiérrez), Bustamante 1399, T 86-5500; *Centro Gallego*, Belgrano 2199, T 47-3061; *Hospital Juan A Fernández*, Cerviño y Bulnes, good medical attention. If affected by pollen, asthma sufferers can receive excellent treatment at the *Hospital de Clínicas José de San Martín*, Córdoba 2351, T 821-6041, US$6 per treatment. *Dental Hospital*, Pueyrredón 1940, T 941-5555; *Eye Hospital*, San Juan 2121, T 821-2721.

● **Language schools**
Instituto de Lengua Española para Extranjeros (ILEE), Lavalle 1619, 7th floor C, T/F 375-0730, US$19 per hour, groups US$12 per hour, recommended by individuals and organizations alike, accommodation arranged; *Bromley Institute*, Paraná 641, 1st floor A, T 371-4113/375-3229, courses in

English language teaching

👣 If English is your native tongue or you are comfortable using it as a second language, teaching English can be a relatively simple way of making a living in Buenos Aires: you need little start-up capital, demand for teachers always outstrips supply, pay is competitive and it can even give you a chance to be creative.

The best place to begin is the Sunday edition of the *Herald*, where there is usually a good handful of adverts seeking *profesores*. Though a *curriculum vitae* is not necessary, some employers may ask to see an informal summary of your background, even if it is unrelated to English language teaching, and there is always an advert or two which require no teaching background at all. Others may request a CUIT (pronounced "kweet"), a sort of social security number but most employers do not require this and you may be able to pursuade those who do to pay you a slightly lower wage in lieu of it.

Most adverts are placed by *institutos* which run classes on their own premises or send teachers to companies to teach individuals or small groups. Other adverts are placed by *coordinadores* who do the same work but from their homes. Under both systems the teacher receives about 70% of what the companies pay. In time a teacher often makes his/her own contacts through word of mouth and may eventually branch off into private classes. This is more profitable, but it can be risky, since you have no guarantee of a constant supply of students; at holiday-times, when many students leave classes for weeks, only an *instituto* or a *coordinador* can fill your timetable and guarantee you an income. Depending on your persistence and bargaining skills, pay varies from 13 to 20 pesos an hour; even if you are too shy to bargain you should have no problem finding 15 pesos an hour, while private classes can pay as much as 25 pesos. You are likely to be busiest at the beginning, middle and end of the students' working day, around 0830, 1300 and 1800.

Brad Krupsaw

Spanish, Portuguese, French, English, high standards, well-regarded, recommended. Free Spanish classes at *Escuela Presidente Roca*, Libertad 581, T 35-2488, Monday-Friday, 1945-2145 (basic level only). Spanish classes also at *Instituto del Sur*, Callao 433, 9th floor S, T/F 375-0897, individual lessons, cheap; *Encuentros*, Scalabrini Ortiz 2395 – 6th floor M, T/F 832-7794; *Estudio Buenos Aires*, San Martín 881, 4th floor, T 312-8936, owner also lets out rooms; *Link Educational Services*, Arenales 2565, 5th floor B, T 825-3017; *Universidad de Buenos Aires*, 25 de Mayo, offers cheap, coherent courses. CEDIC, Reconquista 719, 11th floor E, T/F 315-1156, US$16 per hour private tuition, US$11 per hour in groups, recommended. Graciela

Klein T 772-0918, recommended as private tutor. For other schools teaching Spanish, and for private tutors look in *Buenos Aires Herald* in the classified advertisements. Enquire also at Asatej (see **Useful addresses**).

Schools which teach English to Argentines include: *International House*, Pacheco de Melo 2555, British-owned and run; *Berlitz*, Avenida de Mayo 847; Santiago del Estero 324; *American Teachers*, Viamonte y Florida, T 393-3331. There are many others. Before being allowed to teach, you must offically have a work permit (difficult to obtain) but schools may offer casual employment without one (particularly to people searching for longer-term employment), if unsure of your papers, ask at Migraciones (address below).

● **Laundry**

Many dry cleaners and many launderettes, eg Alvear 861, in centre: Junín 15 y Rivadavia, Monday-Saturday 0800-2100; Junín 529 y Lavalle; Rivadavia 1340. *Laverap*, Paraguay 888 y Suipacha, Córdoba 466, Local 6, T 312-5460, US$6.50 per load (10% discount to ISIC and youth card holders, also at Brasil y Bolívar and Rodríguez Peña 100-200), Arenales 894, Solís near Alsina (cheaper). The laundry at Brasil 554 costs US$4 per load, more for valet service. *Marva*, Perón 2000 y Ayacucho; *Lava Ya*, at Libertad 1290 and 832, Paraguay 888, Moreno 417, H Yrigoyen 1294 and Esmeralda 577.

● **Libraries**

Harrods, Florida, 800 block 2nd floor (being remodelled); *Fundación Banco Patricios*, Callao 312, 5th floor, Spanish, English, French and some Italian books, Monday-Friday 1000-1900, membership US$15 per month. See also Biblioteca Nacional, under **Museums**, and **Cultural and Trade Associations**.

● **Places of worship**

(Non-Catholic) The *Holy Cross*, Estados Unidos 3150, established by the Passionists; *St John's Cathedral* (Anglican), 25 de Mayo 282 (services, Sunday 0900 in English, 1030 in Spanish), was built half at the expense of the British Government and dedicated in 1831; *St Paul's, St Peter's, St Michael and All Angels* and *St Saviour's* are Anglican places of worship in the suburbs; *St Andrew's*, Belgrano 579, is one of the 8 Scottish Presbyterian churches. The *American Church*, Corrientes 718, is Methodist, built in 1863, service at 1100; *First Methodist* (American) Church, Santa Fe 839, Acassuso; *Danish Church*, Carlos Calvo 257.

German Evangelical Church, Esmeralda 162; *Swedish Church*, Azopardo 1422; the *Armenian Cathedral* of St Gregory the Illuminator at the Armenian Centre, and the *Russian Orthodox Cathedral* of The Holy Trinity (Parque Lezama) are interesting.

Synagogue: the most important in Buenos Aires are the Congregación Israelita en la República Argentina, Libertad 705 (also has a small museum), and, the oldest, the Templo Israelita at Paso 423 (called the Paso Temple), traditional and conservative. An important orthodox temple is the Comunidad Israelita Ortodoxa, the seat of the rabbis of Argentina, Ecuador 530, T 862-2701. The Comunidad Betel, Elcano 3424, and the B'nai Tikvah, Vidal 2049, are for reformed worshippers. Congregación Emanu-El (reformed sect), Tronador 1455, take bus 140 from Avenida Córdoba to Alvarez Thomas block 1600, then turn right into Tronador.

● **Post & telecommunications**

General Post Office: Correo Central – now privatized, Correos Argentinos, Sarmiento y Alem, Monday-Friday, 0800-2000. *Poste Restante* on 1st floor (US$2.25 per letter), very limited service on Saturday (closes 1300). Fax service US$5 per minute. Philatelic section open Monday-Friday 1000-1800. Centro Postal Internacional, for all parcels over 1 kilo for mailing abroad, at Antártida Argentina, near Retiro station, open 1100 to 1700. Check both Correo Central and Centro Postal Internacional for *poste restante*.

Telecommunications: the city is split into two telephone zones, owned by Telecom and Telefónica Argentina. Local and international calls can be made from *locutorios* which are found throughout the city centre. Local calls can also be made from public telephone boxes, most of which accept *fichas* or *cospeles* (tokens), though some accept coins. *Fichas* cost US$0.50, US$1 for 3, are sold at small tables outside many *locutorios* as well as newspaper stalls, cigarette *kioskos* and Telecom or Telefónica Argentina offices. Many phones now use phone cards costing 5 and 10 pesos: these are sold with in a protective plastic wrapper and you should not accept unsealed cards. The cards of the two companies are interchangeable. International telephone calls from hotels may incur a 40%-50% commission in addition to government tax of about the same amount. For more details see **Postage and Telephone Rates** in **Information for travellers**. During 1998/1989 phone numbers and prefixes will change, see under **Introduction and hints**.

Cybercafe, Maure 1886, Belgrano, reached by bus No 29. Address info@cyber.com.ar.

● **Shopping**

Most shops close lunchtime on Saturday. The main, fashionable shopping streets are Florida and Santa Fe (especially between 1,000 and 2,000 blocks). Visit the branches of *H Stern*, for fine jewellery at the *Sheraton* and *Plaza* hotels, and at the International Airport; *Kelly's*, Paraguay 431, has a very large selection of reasonably priced Argentine handicrafts in wool, leather, wood, etc; *Plata Nativa*, Galería del Sol, Florida 860, local 41, for Latin American folk handicrafts; *Campanera Dalla Fontana*, Reconquista 735, leather factory, fast, efficient and reasonably priced for made-to-measure clothes, ISIC and GO 25 discount. Good quality leather clothes factory at Boyacá 2030, T 582 6909 to arrange time with English speaking owner; *Aída*, Florida 670, can make a leather jacket to measure in 48 hours; *El Guasquero*, Avenida Santa Fe 3117, traditionally made leather goods; *Galería del Caminante*, Florida

844, has a variety of good shops with leather goods, arts and crafts, souvenirs, etc; *XL*, in Paseo Alcorta, Alto Palermo and Alto Avellaneda shopping malls, for leather goods, ISIC and GO 25 discounts; *Marcelo Loeb*, galería at Maipú 466, for antique postcards from all over the world, not cheap, same galería has several philatelic and numismatic shops. C Defensa in San Telmo is good for antique shops; *Pasaje de Defensa*, Defensa 791, is a beautifully restored colonial house containing small shops; *Casa Piscitelli*, San Martín 450, has a large selection of tapes and CDs. *Galerías Broadway*, Florida 575, for cheap electronic goods, CDs, tapes. For cheap fashion clothes try the area round El Once station; *Mega Sports*, Cabildo 1950, for sports clothing, ISIC and GO 25 discounts.

Shopping malls: Patio Bullrich,Libertador 750, entrance also on Posadas, has boutiques selling high quality leather goods but very expensive. **Alto Palermo**, Coronel Díaz y Santa Fe, very smart and expensive. **La Plaza Shopping Centre**, at Corrientes 1600, also has a few restaurants. **Paseo Alcorta**, Figueroa Alcorta y Salguero, 4 levels, cinemas, supermarket, stores, many cheap restaurants (take colectivo 130 from Correo Central). **Galerías Pacífico**, on Florida, between Córdoba and Viamonte, is a beautiful mall with fine murals and architecture, many exclusive shops and fast food restaurants in basement. Also good set-price restaurant on 2nd floor and free lunchtime concerts on lower-ground floor (details in the press).

Camping equipment: good camping equipment and fuel from *Fugate* (no sign), Gascón 238 (off Rivadavia 4100 block), T 982-0203, also repairs equipment. *Outside Mountain Equipment*, Donado 4660, T 541-2084; *Panamericana y Paraná*, Martínez (Shopping Unicenter, 3rd level); *Imperio Deportes*, Ecuador 696, T/F 961-9024, also repairs, very helpful. Good camping stores also at Guatemala

5908 and 5451. Camping gas available at Mitre 1111, *Todo Gas*, Paraná 550, and El Pescador, Paraguay y Libertad. Every kind of battery (including for Petzl climbing lamps) at Callao 373. *Cacique Camping* manufacture camping equipment and clothing, their two shops: Arenales 1435, Barrio Norte, and San Lorenzo 4220, Munro, Provincia Buenos Aires, T 762 0261, F 756 1392, also sell the *South American Handbook*.

Bookshops: many along Avenida Corrientes, west of Avenida 9 de Julio, though most have no foreign language sections. Prices are very high for foreign books. Try *Yenny*, No 571, for new English classics (also 9 other branches) and *Distal*, No 913; also *Fausto*, No 1316 and 1243. *ABC*, Córdoba 685 and Rawson 2105 in Martínez suburb, good selection of English and German books, also sells *South American Handbook*; *Joyce Proust y Cía*, Tucumán 1545, 1st floor, T 40-3977, paperbacks in English, Portuguese, French, Italian; classics, language texts, etc, good prices; *Librería Rodríguez*, Sarmiento 835, good selection of English books and magazines upstairs, has another branch on Florida, 300 block; French bookshop at Rivadavia 743; *Librería Goethe*, Lavalle 528, good selection of English and German books. Italian books at *Librería Leonardo*, Córdoba 335, also newspapers and magazines; *Liber Arte*, Corrientes 1555, also café, alternative press, good video selection, no English books, 10% ISIC discount; *Promoteo*, Corrientes 1916, rare books, ISIC discount; *La Viscontea*, Libertad 1067. *Asatej Bookshop*, Florida 835, 3rd floor, Oficina 320, T 315-1457, and Santa Fe 2450, Loc 93, sells this *Handbook* 'at the best price' with ISIC discount; *El Ateneo*, Florida 340, basement has good selection of English books, other branches including Callao 1380; *Kel Ediciones*, MT de Alvear 1369 and Conde 1990 (Belgrano), good stock of English books and sells *South American Handbook*. *Acme Agency*, Suipacha 245, 1st floor, for imported

English books, also Arenales 885. Prices at *Harrods* on Florida are lower than most. *LOLA*, Viamonte 976, 2nd floor, T 322-3920, Monday-Friday 1200-1900, the only specialist in Latin American Natural History, birdwatching, most books in English; *Librería del Turista*, Florida 937, wide range of travel books including *South American Handbook*, ISIC and GO 25 discounts. **For used and rare books**: *The Antique Bookshop*, Libertad 1236, recommended; *Fernández Blanco*, Tucumán 712; *Casa Figueroa*, Esmeralda 970; and *L'Amateur*, Esmeralda 882. Second-hand English language books from *British and American Benevolent Society*, Catamarca 45 (take train to Acassuso). *Aquilanti*, Rincón 79, esp good on Patagonia; *Juan Carlos Pubill*, Talcahuano 353 (ring bell), and from *Entrelibros*, Cabildo 2280 and Santa Fe 2450, local 7.

For foreign newspapers try the news stands on Florida, and kiosk at Corrientes y Maipú.

Every April the Feria del Libro is held at the Centro De Exposiciones, Figueroa Alcorta y Pueyrredón, Recoleta; exhibitions, shows and books for sale in all languages.

Camera repairs and film developing: film developing to international standards. There are many Kodak labs around Talcahuano. *Fotospeed*, Santa Fe 4838 (20% discount to SAHB owners!) for quality 2-hour service. *Foto Gráfica*, Perón 1253, for black and white developing; *Photo Station*, Díaz Vélez 5504, T 981-1447, 25% ISIC and GO 25 discount. For developing slides Esmeralda 444, fast service, and *Kinefot*, Talcahuano 244. **Camera repairs**: several good shops on Talcahuano 100-400 blocks. Try also *Casa Schwarz*, Perú 989, international brands; *Golden Lab*, Lavalle 630, good prices for film; *Horacio Calvo*, Riobamba 183, all brands and variety of rare accessories, recommended; fast service at Tacuarí 75; for Olympus cameras, *Rodolfo Jablanca*, Corrientes 2589. German spoken at *Gerardo Föhse*, Florida 890, fast, friendly. Note that some types of camera batteries are unavailable, includes Panasonic CR-32.

Markets: for souvenirs, antiques, etc, **Plaza Dorrego**, San Telmo, with food, dancers, buskers, Saturday and Sunday 0900-1700, entertaining, not cheap, an interesting array of 'antiques'. **Feria Hippie**, in Recoleta, near cemetery, big craft and jewellery market, Saturday and Sunday, good street atmosphere, expensive. **Feria Mataderos**, Lisandro de la Torre y Avenida de los Corrodes, Sunday 1100, there is a big gaucho fair with craft stalls and *asado* **Feria de Las Artes** (Friday, 1000-1700) on Defensa y Alsina. Saturday craft, jewellery, etc market, at **Plaza Belgrano**, near Belgrano Barrancas station on Juramento, between Cuba y Obligado, 1000-2000. Handicraft markets at weekends at Parque Lezama, San Telmo. A secondhand book market is at **Plaza Lavalle** in front of Tribunales, a few English titles (ask around), weekdays only. **Plazoleta Santa Fe**, Santa Fe y Uriarte (Palermo) old books and magazines, Saturday 1200-2000, Sunday 1000-2000; plastic arts in the **Caminito**, Vuelta de Rocha (Boca), 1000-2000 summer, 0900-1900 winter. At **Parque Rivadavia**, Rivadavia 4900, around the *ombú* tree, records, books, magazines, stamps and coins, Sunday 0900-1300, **Plazoleta Primera Junta**, Rivadavia y Centenera, books and magazines, Saturday 1200-2000, Sunday 1000-2000. **Parque Patricios**, Caseros entre Monteagudo y Pepiri, 1000-2000, antiques, books, art and stamps. Saturday market in **Plaza Centenario**, Díaz Vélez y L Marechal, 1000-2100 local crafts, good, cheap hand-made clothes.

● **Sports**

Aerobics: try the *Le Parc*, San Martín 645, T 311-9191, expensive, though has cheaper branch at Rivadavia 4615, monthly membership required; *Gimnasio Olímpico Cancillería*, Esmeralda 1042, membership required.

Football in Buenos Aires

Football being the leading sport in Argentina, it is hardly surprising that Buenos Aires has one of the largest numbers of stadia of any city in the world. Although some are old and poorly maintained, those of the bigger clubs, holding 45,000-75,000 spectators, are fine 'theatres' for some of the finest soccer in the world. Over half the first division clubs are based in Buenos Aires. The rivalry between two, Boca Juniors and River Plate, is particularly fierce, and the other big clubs include San Lorenzo, Huracán and Vélez Sarsfield, as well as two more, Independiente and Racing Club, which are from the industrial town of Avellaneda, separated from Buenos Aires by the narrow Río Riachuelo.

Eric Weil

Horseracing: a cheap evening out

Though the Jockey Club in Buenos Aires was targetted by Peronist revolutionaries as one of the bastions of the elite, horseracing is one of the cheapest forms of entertainment in Buenos Aires. There are three main racecourses (*Hipódromos*), two in the city itself and one at La Plata. There is racing on one or other of these courses on virtually every day of the year, usually beginning in the late afternoon and continuing with a race every half-hour until 2300.

All racing takes place on the flat with no jumping and the racetracks are typical North American style ovals. Hipódromo Argentino is the smartest, with grass as opposed to a dirt track, and has the best quality racing. All three racetracks are, however, comparable with the best European courses, much of the racing being held under excellent floodlighting. The quality of horses and riding is also well up to international standard and the stands are large enough to cope easily with the largest crowds. Entry to the course ranges from US$1 at San Isidro to US$5 at Argentino; for a few dollars more you can enter the best stands. Refreshments are also relatively cheap.

There are no on-course bookmakers, betting being by Totalisor only; the large computerised display-board is easy to understand and use, constantly showing the runners and odds. The crowds are enthusiastic and knowledgable. This is a cheap fun night-out in a friendly and unthreatening atmosphere for anyone with the remotest interest in racing or horses.

Philip Horton

Association and rugby football: are both played to a very high standard. Soccer fans should see Boca Juniors, matches Sunday 1500-1800 (depending on time of year), Wednesday evenings, entry US$10 (stadium open weekdays for visits; bus 27), or their arch-rivals, River Plate. Soccer season September-May/June, with a break at Christmas. Rugby season April-October/November.

Chess: *Club Argentino de Ajedrez*, Paraguay 1858, open daily, arrive after 2000, special tournament every Saturday, 1800, high standards. Repairs for pocket chess computers, T 952-4913.

Cricket: is played at four clubs in Greater Buenos Aires between November and March.

Gambling: weekly lotteries. Football pools, known as *Prode*. *Bingo Lavalle*, Lavalle 842, open to 0300.

Golf: the leading golf clubs are the *Hurlingham*, *Ranelagh*, *Ituzaingó*, *Lomas*, *San Andrés*, *San Isidro*, *Sáenz Peña*, *Olivos*, *Jockey*, *Campos Argentinos* and *Hindú Country Club*. Visitors wishing to play should bring handicap certificate and make telephone booking. Weekend play possible only with a member. Good hotels may be able to make special arrangements. Municipal golf course in Palermo, open to anyone at any time.

Horse racing: at Hipodromo Argentino at Palermo and **Hipodoromo San Isidro** in San Isidro. Riding schools at both racecourses.

Ice-hockey: is becoming popular.

Motor racing: Formula 1 championship racing has been restored: the Gran Premier de la República Argentina is held at the Oscar Alfredo Gálvez autodrome on the outskirts of the city in March/April. There are lots of rallies, stock racing and Formula 3 competitions, mostly from March to mid-December.

Polo: the high handicap season is October to December, but it is played all year round (low season April-June). Argentina has the top polo teams. A visit to the national finals at Palermo in November or December is recommended.

Tennis, squash and paddle tennis: are popular – there are five squash clubs. The Argentine Tennis Open is in November, ATP tour. There are many private clubs.

● **Tour companies & travel agents**

Tours: a good way of seeing Buenos Aires and its surroundings is by 3-hour tour. Longer tours including dinner and a tango show, or a gaucho *fiesta* at a ranch (excellent food and dancing, although the gaucho part can be somewhat showy). Bookable through most travel agents, US$50-65. *BAT, Buenos Aires Tur*, Lavalle 1444, T 371-2304, almost hourly departures; *Buenos Aires Vision*, Esmeralda

356, T 394-4682; *Eurotur* (T 312-6170), in English, or *Autobuses Sudamericanos* (TISA), information and booking office at Bernardo de Irigoyen 1370, 1st floor, Offices 25 and 26, T 307-1956/639-4710, F 307-8899. Prices range from US$12 to US$60 (20 night time and *estancia* options), also excursions to Bariloche, Iguazú and Mar del Plata. For reservations in advance for sightseeing tours, with a 20% court esy discount to *South American Handbook* readers, write to Casilla de Correo No 40, Sucursal 1 (B), 1401 Buenos Aires. In USA T (New York) 212-524-0763, First Class Travel Service Ltd. TISA has other branches in Buenos Aires and publishes *Guía Latinoamericana de Omnibus*, organizes Amerbuspass (T 311-7373 for tickets, or USA 602-795-6556, F 795-8180) for bus travel throughout Latin America. At same address *Transporte Aereo Costa Atlántica* (TACA), passenger charter services to Pinamar, Villa Gesell, Bariloche, T 26-7933. Also *Indiana Cars*, T 307-1956/300-5591, for remise, car hire and taxi service with women drivers.

For river tours of Buenos Aires, Charles Cesaire, Dársena Norte, T 553-4380/314-1780, Saturday, Sunday, holidays 1500, 1700, 1900, with bar, US$10.

Travel agents: among those recommended are *Les Amis*, Santa Fe 810, helpful, efficient; *Exprinter*, Suipacha 1107, T 312-2519, and San Martín 170, T 331-3050, Galería Güemes

Argentina...
South America...
The World!

Flyer is an experienced travel agency that gives service to businessmen and backpackers alike.
Flyer can arrange tickets and accommodation at competitive prices

Viajes y Turismo

Reconquista 617 - 8° Piso, Buenos Aires, Argentina
Tel. +54 (1) 313-8224 - Fax+54 (1) 312-1330
E-mail:flyer@impsat1.com.ar

(especially their 5-day, 3-night tour to Iguazú and San Ignacio Miní); *Furlong*, Esmeralda y M T de Alvear, T 318-3200, T 312-3043, Thomas Cook representatives; *ATI*, Esmeralda 561, mainly group travel, very efficient, many branches; *Turismo Feeling*, Alem 762, T 311-9422, excellent and reliable horseback trips and adventure tourism; *Giorgio*, Florida y Tucumán, T 327-4200, F 325-4210, also at Santa Fe 1653; *Inti Viajes*, Tucumán 836, T/F 322-8845, cheap flights, very helpful; *Flyer Viajes y Turismo*, Reconquista 617, 8th floor, T 313-8224, F 312-1330, also at Avenida Fondo de la legua 425, San Isidro, T/F 0512-3101, specialists on *estancias*, fishing, polo, motorhome rental, English, Dutch, German spoken, repeatedly recommended; *Eves Turismo*, Tucumán 702, T 393-6151, helpful and efficient, recommended for flights; *City Service*, Florida 890 y Paraguay, 4th floor, T 312-8416/9; *Travel Up*, Maipú 474, 4th floor, T 326-4648; *Proterra Turismo*, Lavalle 750, 20th floor D, T/F 326-2639; *Folgar*, Esmeralda 961, 3rd floor E, T 311-6937; (see **Tourist offices** in **Information for travellers**). English is widely spoken.

● **Tourist offices**
National office at Santa Fe 883 with maps and literature covering the whole country. Open 0900-1700, Monday-Friday, T 312-2232, 312-5611. There are kiosks at Aeroparque (Aerolíneas Argentinas section), T 773-9891/05, Monday-Friday, 0830-2000 and Saturday 0900-1900, and at Ezeiza Airport, T 480-0224/0011, Monday-Friday 0830-2200.

Municipal office in the **Municipalidad de Buenos Aires**, Sarmiento 1551, 5th floor, T 374-1251, open Monday-Friday 0930-1730, has an excellent free booklet about the city centre and maps. There are municipally-run tourist kiosks on Florida, junction with Diagonal Roque Sáenz Peña, Monday-Friday 0900-1700 and in Galerías Pacífico, Florida y Córdoba, 1st floor, Monday-Friday 1000-1900, Saturday 1100-1900.

For free tourist information anywhere in the country T 0800-5-0016 (0900-2000).

Provincial offices There are also *Casas de Turismo* for most provinces (open Monday-Friday usually, 1000-1800, depending on office). Several are on Avenida Callao: **Buenos Aires**, No 237, T 371-7045/7; others on Callao are **Córdoba**, No 332, T 371-1668, F 476-2615, **Chaco**, No 322, T 476-0961, F 375-1640, **Mendoza**, No 445, T/F 371-7301. Others: **Río Negro**, Tucumán 1916, T 371-7066, F 476-2128; **Chubut**, Sarmiento 1172, T/F 382-0822; **Entre Ríos**, Suipacha 844, T/F 328-9327; **Formosa**, H Irigoyen 1429, T 381-7048, F 381-6290; **Mar del Plata**, Santa Fe 1175, T/F 811-4466; **Jujuy**, Santa Fe 967, 6th floor,

T/F 393-6096; **Misiones**, Santa Fe 989, T 322-0677, F 325-6197; **Neuquén**, Perón 687, T/F 326-6812; **Salta**, Diagonal Sáenz Peña 933, T 326-1314, F 326-0110; **Santa Cruz**, 25 de Mayo 277, 1st floor, T 343-3653, F 342-1667; **Catamarca**, Córdoba 2080, T/F 374-6891; **Corrientes**, San Martín 333, 4th floor, T 394-7432; **La Pampa**, Suipacha 346, T/F 326-0511; **La Rioja** Viamonte 749, 5th floor, T/F 326-1140; **San Juan**, Sarmiento 1251, T 382-5291, F 382-4729; **San Luis**, Azcuénaga 1083, T/F 822-0426; **Santa Fe**, Montevideo 373, 2nd floor, T/F 375-4570; **Santiago del Estero**, Florida 274, T 326-9418, F 326-5915; **Tucumán**, Suipacha 110, T 325-0564; **Tierra del Fuego**, Santa Fe 919, T/F 322-8855.

Other offices: Villa Gesell, B Mitre 1702, T/F 374-5098; Bariloche hotel, flat and bungalow service in Galería at Florida 520/Lavalle 617, room 116 (cheapest places not listed). Calafate bookings for *Refugio and Autocamping Lago Viedma*, excursions with Transporte Ruta 3 and lake excursions with Empresa Paraíso de Navegación booked from Turismo Argos, Maipú 812, 13th floor C, T 392-5460. (For bookings for *Hotel La Loma*, Calafate and further information on the area contact Paula Escabo, Callao 433, 8th floor P, T 371-9123.) **Estancias Turisticas de Santa Cruz**, Suipacha 1120, T/F 325-3098/3102, for information and reservations at *estancias* in Santa Cruz. For tourist information on Patagonia and bookings for cheap accommodation and youth hostels, contact Asatej, see **Useful addresses** below.

● **Tourist information**
On Friday, the youth section of *Clarín* (*Sí*) lists free entertainments; *Página 12* has a youth supplement on Thursday called *NO*, the paper lists current events in *Pasen y Vean* section on Friday; also the weekly, free *Aquí Buenos Aires*, the weekly *La Maga* and Sunday tourism section of *La Nación* (very informative). *Where in Buenos Aires*, a tourist guide in English, published monthly, is available free in hotels,

travel agencies, tourist kiosks on Florida, and in some news stands. The *Buenos Aires Times* is a bilingual monthly newspaper covering tourist topics, available in some hotels. A good guide to bus and subway routes is *Guía Peuser*; there is one for the city and one covering Greater Buenos Aires. Similar guides, *Lumi* and *Guía T*, US$5, are available at news stands, US$10. Also handy is Auto Mapa's pocket-size *Plano guía* of the Federal Capital, available at news stands, US$8, or from sales office at Santa Fe 3117; *Auto Mapa* also publishes an increasing number of regional maps, Michelin-style, high quality. Country-wide maps at Instituto Geográfico Militar, Cabildo 301 (see **Maps** in **Information for travellers**).

● **Useful addresses**
Administración de Parques Nacionales, Santa Fe 680, opposite Plaza San Martín, T 311-0303, Monday-Friday 1000-1700, have leaflets on some national parks. Also library (Biblioteca Perito Moreno), open to public Tuesday-Friday 1000-1700.

Asatej: Argentine Youth and Student Travel Organization, runs a Student Flight Centre, Florida 835, 3rd floor, oficina 320, T 315-1457, F 311-6840; offering booking for flights (student discounts) including one-way flights at bargains prices, hotels and travel (all payments over US$100 must be in US$ cash); information for all South America, noticeboard for travellers, the *Sleep Cheap Guide* lists economical accommodation in Argentina, Bolivia, Chile, Brazil, Uruguay and Peru, ISIC cards sold, English and French spoken; also runs the following: *Red Argentino de Alojamiento Para Jovenes*, same address oficina 309, T 315-1457, F 312-6840, an Argentine hostal association, has a network of hostels around the country; *Asatej Travel Store*, oficina 320 and at Santa Fe 2450, 3rd floor, local 93, selling wide range of travel goods including *South American Handbook* 'at best price'.

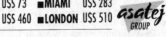

Jorge Newbery

In the years before 1914, before the advent of cinema and sports stars, Jorge Newbery, the son of an American father and an Argentine mother, was one of the first great popular idols of Buenos Aires. In 1900, after studying electrical engineering in the United States, Newbery became Director of Lighting for the city. Dashing, handsome and athletic, it was, however, as a sportsman that he was best known, excelling at rowing, boxing, fencing and wrestling. Owner of one of the city's early motor cars, he was a pioneer of motor racing. His lasting fame, though, was gained as a balloonist and aviator; he was a founding member and the first president of the Argentine Aero Club. In 1909 his balloon, *El Huracán*, broke the South American distance record for ballooning; such was the enthusiasm aroused that the name was adopted by a football club founded shortly afterwards. After achieving the South American altitude record for ballooning, he switched to flying the early monoplanes; in 1914 he set a new world altitude record in a monoplane. He was killed shortly afterwards when his plane crashed following take off from Mendoza in an attempt to cross the Andes. His funeral attracted vast crowds and for years afterwards the date of his death, 1 March, drew mourners to his grave in La Chacarita.

Asociación Ornitológica del Plata, 25 de Mayo 749, T 312-8958, for information on birdwatching and specialist tours, good library.

Central Police Station: Moreno 1550, T 381-8041 (emergency, T 101 from any phone, free).

Comisión Nacional de Museos y Monumentos y Lugares Históricos: Avenida de Mayo 556, professional archaeology institute.

Instituto Antártico Argentino: Cerrito 1248, Buenos Aires, T 816-6313/1689, 0900-1500.

Migraciones: (Immigration), Antártida Argentina 1365 (visas extended mornings only), T 312-3288/7985/8661, from 1230-1700.

Municipalidad: Avenida de Mayo 525, facing Plaza de Mayo.

Oviajes, Uruguay 385, 8th floor, T 371-6137, e-mail oviajes@redynet.com.ar, also offers travel facilities, ticket sales, information, and issues IYHA, ISIC, ITIC, G025 and FIYTO cards, aimed at students, teachers and independent travellers.

Salvation Army: Rivadavia 3255.

Youth Hostel Association: information for all South America, *Asociación Argentino de Albergues de la Juventud*, Talcahuano 214, 3rd floor, T 372-1001 (post code: 1013 Buenos Aires). **NB** A YHA card in Argentina costs US$20, ISIC cards also sold. Secretariat open Monday-Friday 1300-2000. (There are very few hostels near Route 3, the main road south from Buenos Aires.)

YMCA: (Central), Reconquista 439. **YWCA**: Tucumán 844.

● **Transport**
For city transport by bus, metro and taxi see above under **Introduction to the City**.

Local Car hire: expensive, with an additional 20% tax. It is difficult to hire cars during holiday periods, best to book from abroad. Use of Avis Car Credit card with central billing in your home country is possible. See also **Information for travellers**. Driving in Buenos Aires is no problem, provided you have eyes in the back of your head and good nerves. Note that traffic fines are high and police increasingly on the lookout for drivers without the correct papers. **Avis**, Cerrito 1527, T 326-5542, F 326-6992; **A1 International**, San Luis 3138, T 312-9475; **Budget**, Santa Fe 869, T 311-9870, ISIC and GO 25 discount; **Hertz**, Ricardo Rojas 451, T 312-1317. There are several national rental agencies, eg **AVL**, Alvear 1883, T 805-4403; **Ricciard Libertador**, Avenida del Libertador 2337/45, T 799-8514; **Localiza**, Paraguay 1122, T 314-3999; **Unidas**, Paraguay 864, T 315-0777, 20% ISIC and GO 25 discount. **Motoring Associations**: see page 480 for details of service.

INTERNAL TRANSPORT FROM BUENOS AIRES

● **Air**
Domestic flights operate from Aeroparque (Jorge Newbery Airport). See above under **Introduction to the City** for details. Aerolíneas Argentinas, Austral and Lapa offer daily flights to the main cities, for details see text under intended destination, see also page 480 for the Visit Argentina fare. If travelling in the south,

ook ahead if possible with LADE, whose flights e cheaper than buses in most cases.

Buses

ll long-distance buses leave from Retiro termi-al at Ramos Mejía y Antártida Argentina (Subte), T for information 314-2323. Further infor-ation under **Introduction to the City** above. ome bus companies charge extra for luggage legally). Fares may vary according to time of ear and advance booking is advisable Decem-er-March. Some companies may give dis-ounts, such as 20% to YHA or student-card olders and foreign, as well as Argentine teach-s and university lecturers. Travellers have re-orted getting discounts without showing vidence of status, so it's always worth asking. or further details of bus services and fares, look nder proposed destinations.

● Trains

here are 4 main terminals:

Retiro: really three separate stations (Belgrano 311-5287; Mitre T 312-6596; San Martín 311-8704). Services: to Tucumán (run by Tu-umán provincial government) Monday and riday, 1600, returning Thursday and Sunday, 3 hours, US$50 pullman, US$36 1st, US$31 ourist). Suburban services to Tigre, Capilla del eñor, Bartolomé Mitre Zárate and Junin (tickets hecked on train and collected at the end of the ourney).

Constitución: T 304-0021. Frequent services o La Plata (US$1), Ezeiza (US$0.80), Ranelagh US$0.50) and Quilmes (US$0.90). Also subur-an services.(Keep your ticket as you have to how this at your destination.) Services to the ollowing destination are run by Ferrobaires, an gency of the Buenos Aires provincial govern-ment (T 306-7919): to Mar del Plata, daily 0655, 0825, 1530, 1830 (1925 on Friday), 2330, plus dditional Superpullman service Friday 1830, Superpullman US$40, Pullman US$30, First US$19, Tourist US$14 (reduced services out of season); to Bahía Blanca via General Lamadrid, daily except Thursday, 2110, 10 hours, Sleeper US$39, Pullman US$25, First US$20, Tourist US$17. Additional service via Azul, Sierra de la Ventana, Monday, Wednesday, Saturday, 2110; o Necochea, Monday, Wednesday, Friday 2030 (daily in summer), returns Tuesday, Thursday, Sunday, Pullman US$20.50, First US$16, Sec-ond US$14. The Automóvil Club Argentino provides car transporters for its members (see **ACA** in **Information for travellers**).

Once: T 87-0041/2/3, Suburban services and services in Buenos Aires province, including trains to Lujan and Mercedes, run by Trenes de Buenos Aires. Also service to Santa Rosa, run by Ferrobaires, Monday, Wednesday, Friday 2000,

11 hours, Pullman U$$25, First US$20, Tourist US$17.

Federico Lacroze: T 553-5213, suburban serv-ices.

● Hitchhiking

For Pinamar, Mar del Plata and nearby resorts, take bus for La Plata to Alpargatas *rotonda* roundabout. For points further south, take bus 96 to Route 3 – the Patagonia road. Best to hitch from a service station where trucks stop. The police control point at Km 43 (south) is reported to be friendly and will help to find a lift for you. For Mendoza try truck drivers at the wine ware-houses near Palermo Subte station (leaving sta-tion walk northwest, cross the railway line and turn left into Avenida Juan B Justo for the warehouses).

● Passenger boats

The *Buenos Aires Herald* (English-language daily) notes all shipping movements. Flota Flu-vial del Estado (Corrientes 489, T 311-0728) organizes cruises from Buenos Aires, Dársena Sur (dock T 361-4161/0346) up the Paraná river. South Coast, down to Punta Arenas and inter-mediate Patagonian ports, served by the Imp & Exp de la Patagonia. Very irregular sailings. For connections with Uruguay, see below.

TRAVEL INTO NEIGHBOURING COUNTRIES

● By Air

To Brazil: daily services to São Paulo, Rio de Janeiro and other Brazilian cities.

To Chile: foreign and national lines fly daily between Buenos Aires and Santiago, 1½-2 hours.

To Bolivia: services to La Paz and Santa Cruz de la Sierra by Aerolíneas Argentinas and LAB.

To Paraguay: there are daily air services to Asunción by Aerolíneas Argentinas and Lapsa.

To Uruguay: to Colonia del Sacramento: from Aeroparque (Jorge Newbery Airport) to Colonia 12 minutes, several airlines, US$30. Buy tickets directly at the Lapa or Ausa counters preferably in advance especially at weekends when flights are fully booked. Continue by bus to Mon-tevideo, or special transport connecting with Lapa flight, US$3-4 to Montevideo. To Mon-tevideo: from Aeroparque, shuttle service known as *Puente Aéreo* by Aerolíneas Ar-gentinas and Pluna, daily 0730 and 0910, 40 minutes. Book at Aeroparque or T 393-5122/773-0440. To Punta del Este, several flights daily 15 December-1 March with Aerolíneas Argentinas, Pluna and Lapa (Thurs-day-Sunday), 40 minutes, US$90. Out of sea-son, Pluna, Friday only).

● By Road

Four branches of the Pan-American Highway run from Buenos Aires to the borders of Chile, Bolivia, Paraguay and Brazil. The roads are paved except when otherwise stated.

To Chile: via Villa Mercedes, San Luis, and Mendoza, Total: 1,310 km. There are also road connections between Catamarca and Copiapó, Bariloche and Osorno and Puerto Montt, and between Salta and Antofagasta.

Buses Direct services to Santiago, 23 hours, US$70-75, eg Ahumada, El Rápido Internacional and others, 1,459 km; US$70-75 to Valparaíso or Viña del Mar, TAC, Fénix Pullman Norte, cheaper to book to Mendoza and then rebook.

To Bolivia: via Rosario, Villa María, Córdoba, Santiago del Estero, Tucumán, and Jujuy. Total: 1,994 km. The main crossing point is at La Quiaca, but there are also crossings at Aguas Blancas and Pocitos.

Buses There is no direct bus service from Buenos Aires to La Paz but through connections can be booked. Autobuses Sudamericanos, Bernardo de Irigoyen 1370, 1st floor, T 307-1956 and from Retiro terminal, T 315-0204, via La Quiaca, US$135, 52 hours; Atahualpa, T 315-0601, via La Quiaca, US$95, or Pocitos, US$91, daily, but in all cases a single ticket to La Paz or Santa Cruz must be bought once over the frontier. Cheapest route to Pocitos is by bus to Tucumán, US$40 and then re-book for Pocitos, US$25.

To Paraguay: 3 main routes: 1) via Rosario, Santa Fe, Resistencia, Clorinda to Asunción,(via toll bridge). Total: 1,370 km; 2) cross the Zárate-Brazo Largo bridges to Route 12, then head west across Entre Ríos to Paraná and take the tunnel to Santa Fe, or head west across Corrientes province to the bridge between Corrientes and Resistencia and north via Clorinda as above; 3) follow Routes 12 and 14 up the Río Uruguay via Colón and Concordia to Misiones province for Posadas and then take Route 12 to Ciudad del Este via San Ignacio Mini and Puerto Iguazú.

Buses Take 20-22 hours, with 11 companies (all close to each other at the Retiro bus terminal). You have choice between executive (luxury service, 15 hours, US$80), *diferencial* (with food, drinks, 18 hours, US$64) and *común* (without food, but with air conditioning, toilet, 21 hours, US$48). Also 5 companies to Ciudad del Este, US$45; Caaguazú goes to Villarrica, and Expreso Río Paraná and La Encarnaceña go to Encarnación, US$46. Tickets can be bought up to 30 days in advance.

To Brazil: 3 routes: 1) via Puerto Iguazú (above under **To Paraguay**); 2) via Paso de l Libres, reached by following the Puerto Igua route and crossing the bridge between Paso los Libres and Uruguaiana. 3) across the Río la Plata and through Uruguay. This route is a b cheaper, not as long and offers a variety transport and journey breaks.

Buses Direct services to Brazil via Paso de l Libres by Pluma to: São Paulo, 40 hour US$145; Rio de Janeiro, 45 hours, US$16 Porto Alegre, US$71; Curitiba, 38 hour US$128; Florianópolis, 32 hours, US$115. Rio, changing buses at Posadas and Foz c Iguaçu is almost half price, 50 hours. Ticke from Buen Viaje, Córdoba 415, 31-2953, Pluma, Córdoba 461, T 311-4871 or 311-598

To Uruguay: direct road connections by mear of two bridges over the Río Uruguay betwee Puerto Unzué and Fray Bentos and further nor between Colón and Paysandú.

Buses (much slower than the air or sea route given below). '*Bus de la carrera*' (office 65-6 Retiro, T 313-3695) links Montevideo and Bue nos Aires, 8½ hours, US$20. Departure fror each city at 1000, 1015, 2200 and 2230, wit a *dormibus* at 2230 (US$27), via Zárate Gualeguaychú-Puerto Unzué-Fray Bentos-Me cedes.

To Peru: via Mendoza, crossing to Chil through the Redentor tunnel and then nort through Chile via Coquimbo, Arica, Tacna Nasca, Ica, Lima.

Buses Ormeño (T 313-2259) and El Rápid Internacional (T 393-5057) have a direct servic to Lima, from Retiro bus station, 3½ days US$160 including all meals, one night spent i Coquimbo, Chile (if you need a visa for Chile get one before travelling).

● By Boat

To Paraguay: occasional river boats to Asun ción from May to October, 11 days, bed an private bath, food and nightly entertainment US$400, reported good. Details from Tamul Lavalle 388, T 393-2306/1533.

To Uruguay: boats and buses heavily booke December-March, especially at weekends. **NE** No money changing facilities in Tigre, and poor elsewhere. Beware of overcharging by taxis from the harbour to the centre of Buenos Aires. US$3 port tax is charged on all services to Colonia/Carmelo, US$10 port tax in Buenos Aires. Do not buy Uruguayan bus tickets unti you get to Colonia.

Direct to Montevideo, Buquebus, Córdoba 867, T 313-4444, F 313-7636. 'Avión de Buquebus' 4 times a day, 0800, 1130, 150C (1600 Saturday), 1930 (Saturday 1900), Sunday

0800, 1600, 1900, 2350, 3 hours or 2½ hours by K55 (summer schedule), US$47 tourist class, US$59 1st class one way including transport from office to port, vehicles US$93.50-103.50, bus connection to Punta del Este, US$10.

To Colonia del Sacramento, services by 2 companies: Buquebus (US$17-20 depending on vessel) with bus connection to Montevideo (US$5 extra), 6 a day. Ferrylíneas Sea Cat, Córdoba 699, T 394-6800 (port: Dársena Sur, Ribera Este, T 361-4161), Monday-Friday 0800, 1130, 1430, 1830, Saturday 0730, 1030, 1430, 1800, Sunday 0900, 1600, 2000, US$18, 1 hour. Free bus 1 hour before departure from Florida y Córdoba. Connecting bus service from Colonia to Montevideo, US$25 through fare, total journey 4 hours. Ferrylíneas also run a ferry service to Colonia, 3 hours, US$8, with connecting bus to Montevideo, US$15 through fare. Monday-Thursday 0730, 2330, Friday 0730, Saturday-Sunday 0800. Cars are carried on both services. Sailings may be cancelled in bad weather.

From Tigre to Carmelo, boats are operated by Cacciola at 0800, 1730 and 2245, 3 hours, US$11 to Carmelo, and US$18.50 to Montevideo. Cacciola office: Lavalle y Florida 520, oficina 113, T 322-9374/0026 and Estación Fluvial, local 13, Tigre, credit cards accepted. It is advisable to book in advance; connecting bus from offices to port and from Carmelo to Montevideo.

From Tigre to Nueva Palmira, Líneas Delta Argentina, from Tigre 0730, 3 hours, US$14.

THE NORTHERN SUBURBS OF BUENOS AIRES

Northwest of the city along the Plata estuary lie several attractive suburbs, easily reached by train or bus.

Olivos (population about 160,000), the site of the presidential residence is a popular residential district.

From Olivos station, walk up Calle Corrientes with its neocolonial architecture and old, shady trees until you reach the river and the Puerto de Olivos, mainly used for construction materials, but there are a marina (private yacht club) and several parrilladas (popular). On Saturday and Sunday a catamaran sails to Tigre, 2 hours, recommended trip past riverside mansions, sailing boats and windsurfers.

Martínez, nearby, is an attractive residential area, with an interesting shopping area. Sailing and windsurfing are well represented and river launches and other craft may be hired.

San Isidro

(Population 80,000), just beyond Olivos, is one of the most attractive suburbs on the coast and a fashionable nightlife spot, especially along the river bank. There are a number of fine colonial buildings including several quintas (country-mansions). One of these, the **Quinta Pueyrredón**, houses the **Museo Pueyrredón**, which contains artefacts from the life of General Juan Martín Pueyrredón. The church, built in 1895, is in French neogothic style. Also French-inspired is the **Villa Ocampo**, built in 1890 and inhabited by the famous writer Victoria Ocampo. San Isidro is a resort for golf, yachting, swimming, and athletics but is most famous for the **Hipodromo San Isidro**, its magnificent turf racecourse.

TIGRE

(Population 40,000) on the Río Luján about 29 km northwest, is a popular recreational centre. North of the town is the delta of the Río Paraná, the favourite weekend spot for porteños; there are innumerable canals and rivulets, with holiday homes and restaurants on their banks. Regattas are held in November and March. The area is also a profitable fruit growing centre and there is an excellent fruit and handicrafts market at Canal San Fernando on Sunday. The fishing is excellent and the peace is only disturbed by motor-boats at weekends. Regular launch services (lanchas) run to all parts of the Delta, including taxi launches – watch prices for these! – from the wharf. Tourist catamarans, run by Interislena (Lavalle 499, T 731-0261, weekends Lavalle 419, T 731-0264) leave from next to the Cacciola dock, Monday-Friday 1330, 1600, 1½ hours, US$10, different schedule at weekends. Tren de la Costa (see below) also runs luxury catamaran trips. Longer trips (4½ hours) to the open Río de la Plata estuary are available.

Polo

Though the 20th century has seen great swings of fortune for many Argentines, one thing has remained constant: they rule the world at polo, a sport introduced by British railway and meatpacking entrepreneurs. These origins are evident in the Hurlingham Club, the centre of polo in Buenos Aires, which is so English it could have been transplanted from London.

Polo was ideally suited to the flat plains of the pampas and perhaps also to the people: naturally lightweight and brought up in a country founded on horses and cattle, Argentines took to polo like birds to the air. The availability of horses and the skill of the people meant that the sport had a much broader social base than elsewhere where it has remained a game for the rich.

Since 1924 when Argentina first sent a polo team to the Olympic Games and won the gold medal, they have dominated the polo world. Today most good polo teams (there are four in a team) in the world include an Argentine or two. Playing as professionals alongside the other players who are usually amateurs, they are known colloquially in the polo world as "hired assassins". Though polo is a very social sport in England, Argentine professionals have tended not to learn English or to mix socially. Many of those who play in England are country boys who visit for the summer season, taking a string of perhaps a dozen polo ponies with them. Though paid for playing by the team's patron, they sell their ponies at the end of the season to increase their income, before returning home to train more ponies for the following English season. Argentine polo ponies, small thoroughbreds, specially bred for polo, are regarded as among the best in the world.

In a world where money plays an increasing role in sport, polo has been no exception and some Argentine professionals are now breaking into big money: in the 1997 the Heguy brothers, members of Argentina's best polo family, signed up to play for Prince Jefri of Brunei for a reported fee of US$5 million.

Philip Horton

Museums The **Museo Naval**, Paseo Victoria 602, is worth a visit (open Monday-Friday 0800-1230, Saturday and Sunday 1400-1800 US$2, 50% ISIC discount). Covers origins and development of Argentine navy. There are also relics of the 1982 South Atlantic war on display outside.

The **Museo de la Reconquista**, Castañeda y Liniers, T 749-0090, Wednesday-Friday 1000-1200, Saturday/Sunday 14-18, free to ISIC card holders, near the location of Liniers' landing in 1806, celebrates the reconquest of Buenos Aires from the British in 1806-07.

● **Accommodation** There are no good hotels in Tigre itself. On the islands of the Delta: **A3** pp *El Tropezón*, includes meals, an old inn formerly a haunt of Hemingway, now frequented by affluent *porteños*, highly recommended despite the mosquitoes; **A1** *l'Marangatú*, on Río San Antonio, includes breakfast, pool, sports facilities. Delta **Youth Hostel** at Río Luján y Abra Vieja, **F** pp *Canal de San Fernando*, clean, hot showers, table tennis, canoes, ask at Talcahuano 214, Buenos Aires; take all food in advance, there are basic cooking facilities.

● **Places to eat** *Chino*, Cazon 1373, *tenedor libre*, good value. Restaurants on the waterfront in Tigre across the Río Tigre from railway line; cheaper places on Italia and Cazón on the near side.

● **Transport Trains** By train from Buenos Aires to new Estación Tigre, US$0.65 one way, every 10 minutes during peak hours, otherwise every 15 or 20 minutes. Alternatively take train from platform 1 or 2 at Retiro station (FC Mitre) to Bartolomé Mitre and change to the Maipú station (the stations are linked) for the new Tren de la Costa, US$1.50 return, US$2 at weekends, every 12 minutes, 30 minutes journey. Several stations on this line have shopping centres (eg San Isidro) and the terminus, Estación

Delta, will also have a *centro comercial* in 1998, T 732-6200. **Buses** Take No 60 from Constitución: the 60 'bajo' takes a little longer than the 60 'alto' but is more interesting for sightseeing. **Ferries** To Carmelo, Uruguay leave from Cacciola dock (see page 127). Overnight trips to Carmelo (US$72-110 including accommodation) and 3 day trips to Montevideo (US$118 including accommodation) are also available from Cacciola.

ISLA MARTIN GARCIA

(*Population* 200) Situated in the Río de la Plata just off the Uruguayan town of Carmelo and some 45 km north of Buenos Aires, Martín García is now a Provincial Nature Reserve and one of the best excursions from Buenos Aires.

The site of Juan Díaz de Solís' landfall in 1516, the strategic position of the island has given it a chequered history. Defended by gun batteries during the War of the Triple Alliance, it became a military base, was used for quarantining immigrants from Europe and served as a prison: four 20th century Argentine presidents have been detained here including Juan Perón. In 1914 British sailors were interned here, as were survivors from the *Graf Spee* in the Second World War. Evidence of this past can be seen: there are stone-quarries used for building the older churches of Buenos Aires, four gun batteries and a lighthouse (*faro*) dating from 1890. The **Museo Histórico** in the former *pulpería*, houses a display of artefacts, documents and photos.

Wildlife is varied, particularly around the edges of the island and includes laurels, *ceibo* and several species of orchids. Over 200 species of birds visit the island. Take insect repellent.

● **Accommodation** *Hostería Martín García*, owned by Cacciola. For bungalow rental T (0315) 24546. **Camping** *Camping Martín García*, with hostel accommodation.

● **Transport** Boat trips daily except Tuesday and Thursday from Tigre at 0800, returning 1700, 3 hours journey, US$45 including lunch and guide (US$22 transport only), 2-day trip US$120. Reservations can be made through Cacciola, Florida 520, 1st floor, Oficina 113, T 394-5520, who also handle bookings for the inn and restaurant on the island.

ESTANCIAS NEAR BUENOS AIRES

Many *estancias* can be visited relatively easily from Buenos Aires, either to spend a day (*día de campo*) or longer. The following are arranged in order from north to south, with their distance from the capital. A number of others, especially in San Antonio de Areco, are listed under **The Pampas**. Advanced booking for all *estancias* is recommended, either directly or through a specialist travel agency such as *Turismo Flyer*. All offer horseriding.

● **Accommodation L3** pp *Carmen de Sierra*, near Arrecifes, 185 km northwest, T (01)-311-0396. A colonial-style *estancia* dating from 1870; no modern comforts (no lights after 2200) but with lots of style and beautiful surroundings. Carriages and fishing. English spoken. *Día de campo* US$55; **A2** pp *Cabaña los dos Hermanos*, near Zarate, 85 km northwest, T (01)-765-4320. Not really an *estancia* but has a very good *día de campo* with swimming, US$50; **L3** pp *El Cencerro*, T (01)-743-2319. 3 km from Capilla del Señor, 80 km northwest. Carriages, fishing, walking. *Día de campo* US$80. **L2** pp *El Metejon*, near Cañuelas, 51 km southwest, T 0266-21728, F 01-3252197. Modern *estancia*, specializing in polo, English spoken, *día de campo* US$80, also polo classes.

Isla Martín García

1. Comedor
2. Hostería
3. Lighthouse

FROM BUENOS AIRES TO LA PLATA

The 9 de Julio Motorway runs southeast of Buenos Aires, through Avellaneda towards La Plata.

Quilmes

27 km south of Buenos Aires, is named after the Quilmes Indians who were forcibly moved to this site in 1665 from the famous pre-Inca site in Tucumán Province (see page 245). Now an important industrial town, it is the home of one of the world's largest breweries. The **Museo Municipal del Transporte**, Sarmiento 625, houses a collection of carriages and other artefacts from the era of horse-drawn transport; open Monday-Friday 0900-1200, Thursday, Saturday, Sunday 1400-1700.

Florencio Varela

Km 32, is famous as the birthplace of the naturalist and writer W H Hudson. The house is now a museum and forms part of the **Parque Ecológico Guillermo E Hudson**, a small nature reserve covering 42 hectares, notable mainly as a bird sanctuary (over 100 species visit in Spring). Closed in January.

Further south the road passes through the **Parque Pereyra Iraola**, 10,000 hectares of woodland, a former *estancia* expropriated by the Perón government. The park is in three sectors; the central sector includes the **Estación de Cría de Animales Salvajes**, an animal research centre with exotic species, as well as experimental plant nurseries.

LA PLATA

(*Population* 545,000; *Phone code* 021), on the Río de la Plata 56 km southeast of Buenos Aires, is the capital of Buenos Aires province. It is a modern planned city with a university, a port and an oil refinery. A motorway is being built to link the city with Buenos Aires.

History

La Plata was founded in 1882 by Dardo Rocha, Governor of Buenos Aires province as the new provincial capital after the city of Buenos Aires had become federal capital. The site chosen was an estancia; the Paseo del Bosque is the site of park of the estancia. Rocha was inspired by the new urban ideas of Parisian architects and the central grid, 5 km by 5 km, was laid down by Pierre Benoit. His design is notable for its wide avenues and total of 23 squares. An international competition was held to design the public buildings: designs were required to consist of two floors and to use only Argentine materials. Most of the winning designs were by Argentines, but the European influence is strong.

W H Hudson, 1841-1922

The son of immigrants from New England, Hudson was brought up in what was then an isolated spot on the pampas. In *Far Way and Long Ago* (1918), written in old age after serious illness, he described the adventures of a childhood spent wandering the pampas on his pony. His early education at the hands of a series of private tutors was sporadic but he would spend hours alone watching birds and snakes. His life was altered when he caught typhus fever at the age of 15 after a short holiday in Buenos Aires and his health was permanently affected.

In 1869 Hudson sailed for England, never to return because, he later claimed, he believed that large-scale immigration, especially by Italians, had destroyed the birdlife of the pampas. In London he lived in poverty, marrying Emily Wingrave, who was 15 years his elder and who kept boarding houses in Leinster Square and Bayswater. His novels, in the style of utopian romances, achieved little success, but he was soon recognized as a great naturalist, becoming famous for *The Naturalist In La Plata* (1892) and his later works on the English countryside, among them *A Shepherd's Life* (1910). In 1925 a statue was erected in his memory in Hyde Park, London.

Places of interest

The major public buildings are centred around two avenues, Nos. 51 and 53 which run northeast from the Plaza Moreno to the Plaza San Martín and from there to the Paseo del Bosque. On the southeast side of **Plaza Moreno** is the magnificent Gothic **Cathedral**, designed by Benoit, built between 1885 and 1936, and inspired by Cologne and Amiens (visits daily 0900-1300, 1500-1800). The building materials were Argentine but the stained glass windows were made in Germany and France. Its vast interior with its 5 naves holds 12,000 people and covers 7,000m. Opposite is the **Muncipalidad**, in German renaissance style.

Two blocks northeast the **Teatro Argentino** is still under construction after the destruction of the original in a fire in 1977. **Plaza San Martín** is bounded by the **Legislature**, designed by the German architects Heine and Hageman and, opposite, the **Casa de Gobierno** in a mixture French and Flemish renaissance styles. On the northwest side of the plaza is the **Pasaje Dardo Rocha**, designed in Italian renaissance style by the Italian Francisco Pinaroli as the main railway station; it now houses the **Museo Municipal de Bellas Artes** and two theatres. Nearby on Calles 6 and 7 are the imposing **Universidad Nacional** and the **Banco Provincial**.

Among the attractions of the **Paseo del Bosque** are woodlands and an artificial lake as well as the zoological gardens (entry US$2), astronomical observatory and a racecourse but the park is most famous for the **Museo de Ciencias Naturales** (see below).

Museums

Museo de Ciencias Naturales, in the Paseo del Bosque, is one of the most famous museums in Latin America. Founded by Francisco Perito Moreno, it houses an outstanding collection: there are sections on minerology, palaeontology, zoology, anthropology, ethnography, botany and achaeology. The latter includes displays of artefacts from precolumbian peoples throughout the Americas, including a large collection of pre-Inca ceramics from Peru, as well as displays on precolombian civilizations of the northwestern provinces of Argentina. Highly recommended.

Open daily, 1000-1800, US$3, closed 1 January, 1 May, 25 December. Free guided tours, weekdays 1400, 1600, Saturday/Sunday hourly 1030-1630, in Spanish and in English (phone first, T 257744, F 257527).

Museo Provincial de Bellas Artes, Calle 51 No 525. **Museo Dardo Rocha**, Calle 50 No 933. **Museo Casa Almafuerte**, Calle 66 No 530, dedicated to the poet Pedro B Palacios, who was known as Almafuerte.

Excursions

To the **República de los Niños**, 8 km west, an interesting children's village with scaled-down public buildings, built under the first Perón administration; take a green microbus 273 or a red and black 518 to República de los Niños from Plaza San Martín.

To the **Islas del Río Santiago**, north east of the city. To **Punta Lara**, a holiday resort 12 km northeast, where there is a nature reserve protecting the southernmost remaining stretch of riverine forest in South America. In its 31 hectares, over 750 plants species, 150 of them medicinal, 270 bird species, 40 species of mammals and 25 species of reptiles have been identified. Entry is strictly controlled: guided tours on Sunday only 1000-1300 and 1400-1800, T 021-660396 first.

To the **Parque Costero Sur**, a nature reserve 110 km south. Covering 23,500 hectares of marshes along 70 km of coastline, it protects a wide range of birds. It includes several *estancias*, including the **Estancia Juan Géronimo**, T/F (01) 327-0105, which offers accommodation (**L3** pp full board), guided tours, swimming, birdwatching, recommended.

Local festivals

Foundation of the City, 19 November.

Local information
● Accommodation
A3 *Acuarius*, Calle 3 No 731, T/F 214229, with breakfast, small beds; *Corregidor*, Calle 26 No 1026, T 256800, 4-star, modern, air conditioning, snack bar, central, expensive; *San Marcos*, Calle 54 No 523, T 42249, good.

C *Rex*, Avenida 44, No 323, T 212703, modern, air conditioning; *Roga*, Calle 54 No 334, T 219553, three blocks from Paseo del Bosque; *Plaza*, Calle 44 entre Calle 3 y Calle 4, with bath.

● Places to eat
Restaurants rarely open in the evening before 2100. *El Fogón*, Avenida 1 y Calle 49; *Don Quijote*, Plaza Paso, good value, best in town, can get very crowded; Chinese 'tenedor libre' at *Guinga*, Plaza Paso; *La Linterna*, Calle 60 y Avenida 1, upmarket, good value; *El Chaparral*, good *parrillada*, Calle 60 y Calle 117 (Paseo del Bosque). Recommended bar, with steak sandwiches, *El Modelo*, Calle 54 y Calle 5. Best *empanadas* at *La Madrileña*, a hole-in-the-wall on Calle 60 between Avenidas 5 and 6. Best bakery is *El Globo*, Calle 43 y Calle 5.

● Entertainment
Tango and tropical music at *El Viejo Almacén*, on Diagonal 74, Calle 2. There are free concerts during the summer in the *Teatro Martín Fierro* in the Paseo del Bosque.

● Tour companies & travel agents
Turismo San Martín, Calle 51 between Avenidas 7 and 8, recommended.

● Tourist offices
Municipal office Calle 47 No 740 between Calle 9 and Diagonal 74, T 258334; Provincial office, Torre Municipal, Calles 12 y 53, 13th floor, T 295553, F 29554, little information.

● Transport
Trains To/from Buenos Aires (Constitución) run by TMR, frequent, US$1.50. (At Constitución ticket office hidden behind shops opposite platform 6).

Buses To Buenos Aires, 1½ hours, US$3.20, about every 30 minutes. From Buenos Aires from Retiro day and night and from Plaza Constitución, daytime.

THE URUGUAYAN COAST

Along the Uruguayan coast of the Río de la Plata are several attractive little towns, which are growing in popularity as tourist centres. Details of transport from Buenos Aires are given above.

COLONIA DEL SACRAMENTO

(*Population* 22,000; *Phone code* 0522; from Buenos Aires 0222), a Portuguese colonial gem on the east bank of the Río de la Plata, is very popular destination for excursions from Buenos Aires. Jutting into the Río de la Plata, the small historic centre is particularly interesting because there is so little colonial architecture in this part of the continent. The modern town, which extends around a bay, is charming and lively: its are streets lined with plane trees and it has a grand Intendencia Municipal on Méndez y Avenida General Flores, the main street. The best beach is Playa Ferrando, 2 km to the east (buses from General Flores every 2 hours). There are regular sea and air connections with Buenos Aires and a free port.

History
Founded by a Portuguese expedition from Brazil in 1680, Colonia was at the centre of an intense political and military struggle between Spain and Portugal for the next 100 years. Its strategic position opposite Buenos Aires challenged Spanish control of the Río de la Plata and its use as a base for British smugglers undermined Spanish colonial trading restrictions. Within months of its founding it was attacked by troops from Buenos Aires and the settlers were forced to surrender. Refounded in 1683, it was seized by Spain in 1705. It reverted to Portuguese rule under the Treaty of Utrecht (1713) but was temporarily occupied again by Spanish troops in 1735 and 1762, and destroyed in 1777, after which the Treaty of San Ildefonso between the two countries specified the east bank of the Plata estuary as Spanish. It 1807 it was briefly occupied by British troops during the attempted seizure of Buenos Aires.

The Barrio Histórico
With its narrow streets colonial buildings and reconstructed city walls, the Barrio Histórico has been declared Patrimonio Cultural de la Humanidad by Unesco.

The **Plaza Mayor** (Plaza 25 de Mayo) is especially picturesque. At its eastern end is the **Puerta del Campo**, the restored

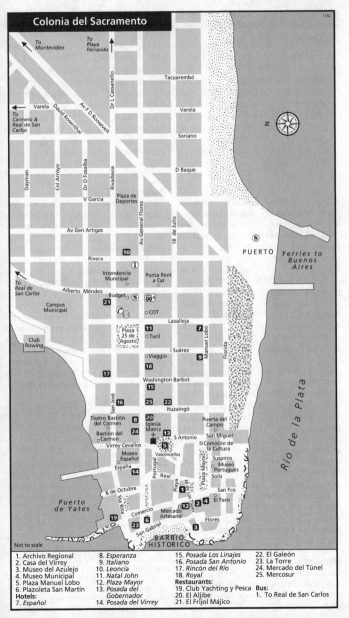

Colonia del Sacramento

Not to scale

1. Archivo Regional
2. Casa del Virrey
3. Museo del Azulejo
4. Museo Municipal
5. Plaza Manuel Lobo
6. Plazoleta San Martín

Hotels:
7. *Español*
8. *Esperanza*
9. *Italiano*
10. *Leoncia*
11. *Natal John*
12. *Plaza Mayor*
13. *Posada del Gobernador*
14. *Posada del Virrey*
15. *Posada Los Linajes*
16. *Posada San Antonio*
17. *Rincón del Río*
18. *Royal*

Restaurants:
19. *Club Yachting y Pesca*
20. *El Aljibe*
21. *El Frijol Májico*
22. *El Galeón*
23. *La Torre*
24. *Mercado del Túnel*
25. *Mercosur*

Bus:
1. To Real de San Carlos

Mihanovic's Folly: Real de San Carlos

Real de San Carlos was the brainchild of Nicolás Mihanovic, an immigrant from Dalmatia who settled in Buenos Aires. Between 1903 and 1912, seeing the potential to attract tourists from Buenos Aires across the Plata estuary to Colonia, Mihanovic built this grand tourist complex, complete with bullring, casino and *frontón* (court) for Basque pelota. Port facilities were built for Mihanovic's vessels and a railway line transported visitors to the resort.

Mihanovic's entrepreneurial zeal did not take into account the political obstacles. In 1912, 2 years after the bullring was completed, the Uruguayan government outlawed bullfighting. The casino, the nearest to Buenos Aires (where gambling was prohibited) prospered briefly until the Argentine authorities imposed a special tax on Mihanovic's vessels.

city gate and drawbridge. On the south side is the **Museo Portugués**; see also the narrow **Calle de los Suspiros**, nearby. At the western end of the Plaza are the **Museo Municipal** in the former house of Almirante Brown (with indigenous archaeology, historical items, paleontology, natural history), the **Casa Nacarello** next door, the **Casa del Virrey**, and the ruins of the Convento de San Francisco (1695), to which is attached the **Faro** or lighthouse) built in 1857 (entry free – tip or donation appreciated).

Just north of the Plaza Mayor is the **Archivo Regional**. From here a narrow street, the Calle Misiones de los Tapes, leads east to the river; at its further end is the tiny **Museo del Azulejo**, housed in the Casa Portuguesa. Two blocks north of here is the Calle Playa which runs east to the Plaza Manuel Lobo/Plaza de Armas, on the northern side of which is the **Iglesia Matriz**, on Vasconcellos, the oldest church in Uruguay, though destroyed and rebuilt several times; the altar dates from the 16th century. Two blocks north of the church on the northern edge of the old city are the fortifications of the **Bastión del Carmen**; just east of it is the Teatro Bastión del Carmen. One block south of the Bastión, at San José y España, is the **Museo Español**, formerly the house of General Mitre.

Museums

All museums open 1130-1830, entry by combined ticket bought from Museo Municipal; not all may be open on the same day.

Real de San Carlos

5 km north around the bay (take blue bus from Flores y Méndez, 30 minutes, US$0.40), is an unusual, once grand but now sad tourist complex. Only the racecourse (Hipódromo) is still operational (US$1 for men, women free) and you can see the horses exercising and swimming in the sea. The elegant **Plaza de Toros** (bullring) is falling apart (it is closed to visitors but a local guide will take you through a gap in the fence); the casino and its hotel are in decay and, though the huge Frontón court can still be used, the building is rotting. There is also a **Museo Municipal**; by the beach are two restaurants. At Parada 20, about 7 stops before Real de San Carlos, is the **Capilla de San Benito**.

Local festivals

In the third week of January, festivities are held marking the founding of Colonia.

Local information
● **Accommodation**

L3 *El Mirador*, Avenida Roosevelt, Km 176½, T 2004, air conditioning, casino, sports facilities.

In Barrio Histórico: **L3-A2** *Plaza Mayor*, Del Comercio 111, T/F 3193, lovely, English spoken; **L3-A2** *Posada del Virrey*, España 217, T/F 2223, suites and rooms; **A1** *Posada del Gobernador*, 18 de Julio 205, T 3018, with breakfast, charming, recommended.

In the centre: **A2** *Esperanza*, Flores 237, T/F 2922, charming; **A2** *Posada Los Linajes*, Washington Barbot 191, T 24181, central, air conditioning, TV, cafeteria, warmly recommended; **A2** *Royal*, Flores 340, T 2169, with breakfast, comfortable, good restaurant, pool, noisy air conditioning but recommended;

A3 *Italiano*, Lobo 341, T 2103, **B** without bath, good restaurant, hot water but no heating, recommended; **A3** *Leoncia*, Rivera 214, T 2369, F 2049, air conditioning, modern, good; **A3** *Natal John*, Flores 382 on plaza, T 2081; **A3** *Posada San Antonio*, Ituzaingó 240, T 5344, with breakfast, **B** during week.

B *Posada de la Ciudadela*, Washington Barbot 164, T 2683, pleasant, air conditioning, simple; **B** *Posada del Río*, Washington Barbot 258, T 3002, shower, with breakfast; **B** *Los Angeles*, Roosevelt 213, T 2335, small rooms, no restaurant, English spoken; **B** *Beltrán*, Flores 311, T 2955, shared bath, comfortable.

Budget accommodation: C-D *Hospedaje Colonial*, Flores 436, T 2906, recommended but noisy, restaurant below. **D** *Hospedaje Las Tejas* Rosenthal y Fray Bentos, T 4096, with breakfast, shower; **D** pp *Español*, Lobo 377, without bath, large dark rooms, lots of character; **D** *Señora Raquel Suárez*, T 2916, has spacious rooms to rent, good value. The municipal sports complex has 2 dormitories with 80 beds, which are sometimes available – ask at the tourist office.

Camping Municipal site at Real de San Carlos, T 4444, US$3.50 per person, **C** in mini-cabañas, electric hook-ups, 100m from beach, hot showers, open all year, safe, excellent, recommended.

● **Places to eat**
La Torre, Flores y Santa Rita, in old town, bar and restaurant, loud disco music, but fine panoramic views especially at sunset; *Pulpería Los Faroles*, just off Plaza Mayor, recommended, friendly. *Yacht Club* (at Puerto de Yates) and *Esperanza* (at hotel) are good; *Mercado del Túnel*, Flores 227, good meat dishes, but encourages eating of fresh vegetables; *Mercosur*, Flores e Ituzaingó, recommended; *El Aljibe*, Flores 248 e Ituzaingó, good fish dishes. Good unnamed *parrillada* and pasta at Ituzaingó 168, nice atmosphere, value for money; *El Galeón*, Ituzaingó y 18 de Julio. *Club Colonial*, Flores 382, good value. *El Frijol Mágico*, Galería Americana at Rivadavia y Méndez, good vegetarian food, 1130-1400.

● **Airline offices**
Lapa, Rivadavia 383, T 2006/2461.

● **Banks & money changers**
Banks open in afternoon only; **Banco Comercial**, on plaza, gives cash against Visa. **Cambio Viaggio**, Flores 350 y Suárez, T 2070, Monday-Saturday 0900-1200, 1300-1800, Sunday 1000-1800 (also outside the ferry dock, with car hire). **Cambio Colonia** and **Banco de la República Oriental del Uruguay** at the ferry port (dollars and South American currencies).

● **Consulates**
Argentina, Flores 215, T 2091, open weekdays 1200-1700.

● **Post & telecommunications**
Post Office: on main plaza.

Telephones: Antel, Rivadavia 420, open till 2300, does not accept foreign money.

● **Shopping**
El Patio, Flores 184, wool, leather, ceramics, Uruguayan stones. *Mercado Artesanal*, del Comercio y de la Plaza, old city; also *Rincón del Turista*, Santa Rita, old city.

● **Tourist office**
Flores y Rivera, T 2182, open Monday-Friday 0800-1830, Saturday and Sunday 0900-2200, good maps of the Barrio Histórico; also at passenger terminal at the dock.

● **Transport**.
Local Car hire: Budget, Flores 472; Punta, Paseo de la Estación L3, on Méndez near Flores; also car hire at airport. Motorcycle and bicycle hire at Flores y Rivera and outside ferry dock, US$5 per hour, US$15 per day, recommended as a good way of seeing the town, traffic is slow.

NB Book in advance for all sailings and flights in summer, especially at weekends.

Air Airport 17 km east along Route 1; for taxi to Colonia, buy ticket in building next to arrivals, US$2. Lapa flies to Aeroparque, Buenos Aires, most days, US$30 including connecting bus services to/from Montevideo. This is generally quicker than hydrofoil.

Buses Bus company offices: COT, Flores 432; Tauril, Flores y Suárez; Tauriño, Flores 436. To **Montevideo**, 2½ hours, COT and Tauril, half-hourly service between the two, US$7.50; Chadre at 0555, 1350; to **Carmelo**, 1½ hours, Tauriño, 4 a day (not Sunday), US$2.50; Chadre/Agencia Central to **Carmelo, Salto**, 8 hours, US$18.75.

Ferries to Buenos Aires are operated by Buquebus (T 0522-2975/3364) and Ferryturismo (T 2919/3145). See under Buenos Aires for details.

NORTHEAST OF COLONIA DEL SACRAMENTO

Route 21 runs northeast through a string of small towns near the Río de la Plata.

Carmelo (*population* 18,000) Km 70, on the banks of the Arroyo Las Vacas, is a pleasant town, connected to Tigre by ferry. It has the church, museum and archive of El Carmen on Plaza Artigas. In the Casa de Cultura, 19 de Abril 246, is a tourist office and museum. On the far side of the river from the centre are the Rowing Club, the Reserva de Fauna (with birds and mammals), the casino, the Yacht Club and Playa Seré, Carmelo's beach at the mouth of the river. In summer, several hundred yachts visit Carmelo.

• **Accommodation A3** *Casino Carmelo*, Rodó sin número, T 2314; **B** *Bertoletti*, Uruguay 171, T 2030, modern; **C** *Rambla*, Uruguay y 12 de Febrero, T 2390; **D** *Palace*, Sarandí 308, T 2622; **D** *San Fernando*, 19 de Abril 161, T 2503, full of character, temperamental showers, recommended. **D** *Oriental*, 19 de Abril 284. **Camping** At Playa Seré, hot showers.

• **Consulates Argentina**, FD Roosevelt 318, T 266.

• **Buses** To **Montevideo**, 1210, 2240, US$8.40, Intertur; to **Fray Bentos** and **Salto**, from main plaza 0710, 1540; to **Colonia**, Tauriño, 4 a day, 1½ hours, US$2.50. **To Argentina**: ferry to Tigre, Cacciola, Constituyente 263, T 8062, 3 a day.

Route 21 continues through **Nueva Palmira** (*population* 7,000) Km 92, a popular yachting resort with a free zone, **La Agraciada**, some 20 km further north, the historic beach famous for the landing of the 33 patriots on 19 April 1825, which led to Uruguayan independence, **Dolores** (*population* 13,000), Km 134, and **Mercedes** (*population* 37,000; *phone code* 0532) Km 177, a yachting and fishing centre during the season. Founded in 1788, its charm (it is known as "the city of flowers") derives from its Spanish-colonial appearance, though it is not as old as the older parts of Colonia.

The Pampas

THIS REGION covers the wide plains of the Pampas, east and south of Buenos Aires, and the Atlantic coast with its many resorts, including Necochea, Bahía Blanca and, the most famous, Mar del Plata. To the south are two ranges of hills, the Sierra de Tandil and the Sierra de la Ventana.

GEOGRAPHY

The pampas, the economic heart of the country, cover some 40 million hectares and extend fanwise from Buenos Aires for a distance of between 550 and 650 km. Apart from two groups of *sierras* or low hills near Tandil and Bahía Blanca, the surface seems an endless flat monotony. In the areas of lowest rainfall, to the south and west, sand dunes, still mobile, can rise to 30m high. Much of this area, known as the *pampa seca* (dry pampa) is desert or semi-desert. There are few native species of trees.

There are few rivers in this area apart from the Río Salado. Many streams peter out in the desert, often disappearing down a series of fault-lines: around Guaminí these fault-lines have produced a series of lakes. Drinking water is pumped to the surface from a depth of from 30 to 150m by the windpumps which are such a prominent feature of the landscape.

FAUNA OF THE PAMPAS

The lagoons and lakes of the pampas offer an overwhelming variety of bird-life, including Chilean flamingos, herons, Roseate spoonbills, Maguari storks, white-faced Ibis, black-necked swans and Coscoroba swans, three species of coots, many species of ducks, the Southern Screamer and the snail kite. Some of the most beautiful birds, such as the Many-coloured Rush-tyrant and the Spectacled tyrant, can be found near aquatic vegetation.

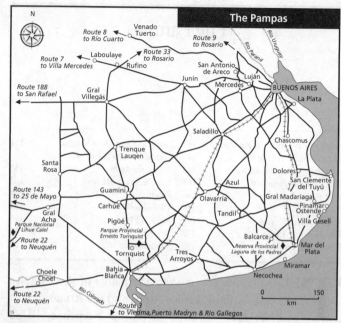

The Pampas

In areas of grassland the Greater Rhea can still be spotted, though more easy to find are the Spotted Tinamou, Southern Lapwing and the Guira Cuckoo. Birds of prey include the Long-winged Harrier, the Chimango Caracara, an opportunistic scavenger and predator. Other species include the Burrowing Owl, the Monk Parakeet, which builds huge communal nests, the Rufous Hornero, which builds an oven nest, the acrobatic Fork-tailed Flycatcher, the colourful Vermilion Flycatcher, the aggressive Great Kiskadee, sandeaters such as the Great Pampa Finch and the Grassland Yellow Finch as well as flocks of cowbirds.

In summer migratory bird species from the northern hemisphere congregate north

Southern Screamer

Rufous Hornero with oven-shaped nest

The Ombu

(*Phytolacca dioica*) Native to Argentine Mesopotamia, this was the first tree introduced to the pampas, a status owed to the shade it offered. A vigorous semi-evergreen, it can grow to 20m high with branches extending over 30m. Deriving its name from the Guaraní word for shade, it is also known as the Red Ink plant or Virginian Poke. It has large poplar shaped leaves with racemes of green flowers and dark purple berries. It is a member of the pokeweed family which are all known for the medicinal properties of their leaves, flowers, and bark.

Jane Norwich

of Punta Rasa in the lowlands around Bahía Samborombon; these include the Red Knot, the Ruddy Turnstone, the White-rumped Sandpiper, the Hudsonian Godwit.

The coypus, a large rodent known locally as the *nutria*, is one of the easiest mammals to find; others include the Pampas Cavy, the hog-nosed skunk, the white-eared opossum and the grey fox. The pampas deer, an endangered species, is specially proteced in the Reserva Campos del Tuyú.

CLIMATE

Over the whole of the pampa the summers are hot, the winters mild, but there is a large climatic difference between various regions, the Atlantic coast being wetter with more moderate temperatures than the interior. South of Buenos Aires around Mar del Plata rain falls all year round and especially in summer. Further south in Bahía Blanca rainfall occurs mainly between October and April. Average daily

temperatures along the coast range from 25° to 14° in Mar del Plata and 30° to 14° in Bahía Blanca in summer to 13° to 5° in Mar del Plata and 13° to 3° in Bahía Blanca in winter. The interior is drier; parts of the western pampas receive as little as 200 mm of rain a year in contrast to over 1,000 mm in Mar del Plata. In Santa Rosa rainfall is heaviest in summer with little in winter. Temperatures in the interior are more variable; summer maxima can reach 40° and minima can be as low as -8°.

ECONOMY

Agriculture is still central to the economy of the pampas. Buenos Aires province accounts for over half of Argentine cereal production: wheat, maize, sorghum, sunflower seed and soyabeans dominate, though barley for the country's breweries is grown in the Sierra de la Ventana. Over 36% of Argentine livestock are also produced in the province, though there is an important regional division of labour; animals are mainly bred in eastern Buenos Aires and western La Pampa and are fattened in the richer pastures of western Buenos Aires and eastern La Pampa. While the coastal areas, especially around Mar del Plata, rely heavily on tourism, Necochea and Mar del Plata have large fishing fleets; the latter is home to three-quarters of Argentina's trawler fleet and to fish processing industries. Mining is centred in the hills around Olavarria, Azul and Tandil while the petrochemical industry is important to Bahía Blanca, which is an important grain exporting port.

Azul	Bahía Blanca	Buenos Aires	Mar del Plata	Necochea	Neuquén	Santa Rosa	Tandil
397							
264	688						
273	464	408					
246	336	513	128				
935	538	1215	1001	874			
803	329	610	871	743	557		
94	335	350	179	163	893	516	

The Pampas: distance chart (km)

Beef, beef and yet more beef

👣 Though Argentina is famous for beef, cattle were not indigenous to the pampas. After Martín de Garay's expedition brought cattle from Paraguay, the animals roamed wild on the plains, reproducing so quickly that by 1780 their numbers were put at 40 million. By then the pampas Indians were driving herds through the Andean passes to trade with the Mapuche of southern Chile, while *gauchos* with dogs and *boleadoras* were slaughtering cattle by the thousand for their hides. These were staked out in the sun to dry, while the meat was left to rot.

Shorthorn

Such wasteful methods came to an end after 1810 with the opening of *saladeros*, or salting-plants. Hides were exported to Europe as was tallow (animal fat) which was used for candles; the meat was turned into *charqui*, strips of beef, dried and salted, which were sold to feed the slaves in Brazil and Cuba. Sources of salt were vital to this process and the routes to the salt flats (*Salinas Grandes*) of southern Buenos Aires province became a key consideration in relations with the Indians.

Hereford

Although technical developments created the opportunity for Argentina to feed the growing demand for beef in Europe, it was also essential that cattle-farmers improve their herds by introducing new breeds to replace the scrawny pampas cattle and alfalfa was sown as it was better fodder than the native grasses.

Aberdeen Angus

The main breeds of cattle which can be seen today were all introduced from Europe. The first Shorthorn bull was imported by the English landowner, John Miller, in 1836. The Hereford, introduced from England in 1862, proved a fine beef animal, hardy and used to the varied climate of the south: it can be distinguished by its red body and white face and legs. The Aberdeen Angus, also a fine beef animal, was favoured by farmers and railway companies as it has no horns and could be transported easier by rail. First introduced in 1879, it is very common throughout Buenos Aires province and is distinguished by its black coat. The Holando Argentino, a mixture of breeds from the Netherlands and Switzerland, is the main milk-producer.

HISTORY

When the Spaniards arrived in Argentina the pampas was covered by tall coarse grasses. The cattle and horses they brought with them were soon to roam wild and in time transformed the Indian's way of life. The only part of the pampas occupied by the settlers was the so-called Rim, between the Río Salado, south of the capital, and the Paraná-Plata rivers. Here, on large *estancias*, cattle, horses and mules in great herds roamed the open range. There was a line of forts along the Río Salado: a not very effective protection against marauding Indians. The Spaniards had also brought European grasses with them; these soon supplanted the coarse native grasses, and formed a green carpet which stopped abruptly at the Río Salado.

In the second half of the 19th century the growing urban population of Europe created a demand for cheap food which spurred the occupation and exploitation of the pampas (as well as parts of the United States, Canada and Australia). Agricultural machinery and barbed wire, well-drilling machines and windpumps, roads, railways, and ocean-going steamships, canning and refrigeration all enabled Argentina to become a major exporter of beef, lamb, wheat and wool. By the 1920s the country was the 'breadbasket of the world', with over 23 million hectares of land under the plough, some 50 million cattle and 30 million sheep.

The transformation of the pampas had important social consequences. Though some politicians argued for colonization schemes which would give immigrants access to smaller landholdings, such schemes were always relegated to poor land, zones near Indian territory or areas some distance from railway lines. From the 1820s onwards governments distributed land, often at very low prices but in such large holdings that only the wealthy could afford to buy. This practice was continued after the 'Conquest of the Wilderness', a war against the Indians in 1878-83 which virtually exterminated them and opened up vast new tracts of the pampas to commercial agriculture. Large *estancias* were often rented out to tenant-farmers who performed the hard work of breaking up the soil by ploughing, destroying pampas grass and

WH Hudson on the Pampas

Some of the best descriptions of the pampas before their transformation by railways and wire, are to be found in the works of WH Hudson.

"We see all round us a flat land, its horizon a perfect ring of misty blue colour where the crystal-blue dome of the sky rests on the level green world. Green in late autumn, winter and spring, or say from April to November, but not all like a green lawn or field; there were smooth areas where sheep had pastured, but the surface varied greatly and was mostly more or less rough. In places the land as far as one could see was covered with a dense growth of cardoon thistles, or wild artichoke, of a bluish or grey-green colour, while in other places the giant thistle flourished, a plant with big variegated green and white leaves, and standing when in flower 6 to 10 feet high."

"On all this visible earth there were no fences, and no trees excepting those which had been planted at the old estancia houses, and these being far apart, the groves and plantations looked like small islands of trees, or mounds, blue in the distance, on the great plain or pampa. They were mostly shade trees, the commonest being the Lombardy poplar, which of all trees is the easiest one to grow in that land. And these trees at the estancias or cattle-ranches were, at the time I am writing about, almost invariably aged and in many instances in an advanced state of decay."

WH Hudson, *Far Away and Long Ago*, Dent, 1985

replacing it with new strains of grass before their tenancies ended. As a result the pampas did not acquire a population of immigrant smallholders or homesteaders as the United States did.

Since the peak of agricultural exports in the 1920s the economy of the pampas has suffered successive crises, brought on by the Great Depression and changes in the world economy. British entry to the European Union deprived Argentina of what had been her most important market just after an epidemic of foot and mouth disease in Britain, traced to a tin of Argentine corned beef, had led to a ban on beef exports to Britain and a stigma

The conquest of the wilderness

Until the 1870s the Indians of the pampas controlled large parts of present-day Argentina, forcing the government in Buenos Aires to defend two frontiers: one in the north which ran west from Santa Fe through Córdoba province and then north towards Santiago del Estero, the other in the south which ran from Azul and Junín west to San Luis and Mendoza. After independence only one campaign was launched against the Indians, in the early 1830s by Rosas in southern Buenos Aires province.

In the 1870s pressure began to grow within the Argentine government for a campaign to defeat the Indians and force their submission to rule from Buenos Aires. The withdrawal of Argentine troops from the frontier to fight in the War of the Triple Alliance led to a series of increasingly audacious Indian raids: in one of these in 1868, the Indian chief Calfucurá led 2,000 warriors in an attack in Córdoba province which made off with 20,000 head of cattle and 200 prisoners. Altogether this province was attacked nine times in 1868.

With the ending of the War of the Triple Alliance, the Argentine government moved to resist the Indians. Adolfo Alsina, Minister of War, drew up a plan for a chain of forts connected by a moat and ramparts, now known as the *Zanja de Alsina*. After Alsina's death in 1877, he was replaced by Julio Roca, who had criticized Alsina's plans as too defensive and had called for a war of extermination.

Roca's campaign of 1879 was launched with 8,000 troops in five divisions, one of them led by Roca himself. In a swift offensive five important Indian chiefs were captured along with 1,300 warriors; 2,300 more were killed or wounded. Roca, who expressed the view that "it is a law of nature that the Indian succumb to the impact of civilised man", destroyed villages and forced the inhabitants to choose between exile in Chile or entering reservations. After the campaign the mountain passes to Chile were closed and remaining Indians were forced onto reservations.

Although victory in the "Campaign of the Wilderness" was portrayed as a personal triumph for Roca, it was due more to technological advances. The spread of the telegraph meant that commanders had intelligence reports to offset the Indians' knowledge of the terrain and helped commanders keep in touch with each other. Railways meant that the troops could be supplied quickly. Remington repeating rifles enabled one soldier to take on five Indians and kill them all.

Roca's campaign had important consequences for the whites of Argentina too. Hailed as a hero, Roca was elected President in 1880 and dominated Argentine politics until his death in 1904. More important in the long run was the distribution of conquered land. Roca's campaign had been financed by mortgaging this land in advance: 4,000 bonds were issued, each redeemable by one square league of land but since no one could buy fewer than four bonds (costing 4 pesos each) every bond-buyer became potential owner of 25,000 acres at least. Over 20 million hectares of land fell into the hands of about 500 people, many of them friends of Roca.

hat Argentina still struggles to cast off: only in 1995 was she able to declare herself free of the disease.

MAJOR ROUTES ACROSS THE PAMPAS

From Buenos Aires several major highways fan out across the Pampas.

SOUTH TO MAR DEL PLATA

Route 2 runs south, past the coastal city of La Plata, through Chascomús and Dolores to Mar del Plata, the most famous Argentine seaside resort.

CHASCOMUS

(*Population* 22,200) 126 km from Buenos Aires, lies on a wide plain on the northern shore of Lago Chascomús, one of a group of lakes known as the Lagunas Encadenadas. Around Plaza Independencia are the colonial-style **Municipalidad** and, next door, the **Teatro Nacional Brazzola**. Southeast of the plaza is the **Capilla de los Negros** (1862) which functioned as a religious centre for the local black community (visits daily 1000-1200, 1700-1900). West of the plaza is the **Parque Libres del Sud**; in the park is the **Museo Pampeano** which focuses on the Battle of Chascomús and has sections on natural history and early colonization. Beyond the park to the south and east along the shores of the lake runs the pleasant costanera. On the far side of the lake is **La Alameda 1789**, a tourist complex based in a former *estancia*, with sports facilities.

Covering 3,000 hectares, Laguna Chascomús swells greatly in size during the rains. Its slightly brackish water is an important breeding place for *pejerrey* fish, though these have declined due to the introduction of carp. Amateur fishing competitions are held in the winter season. There is a boat club and a regatta during Holy Week. Windsurfing is practiced in summer. Further south are two further lakes, La Salada (Km 144) and Lacombe (Km 153), which also offer *pejerrey* fishing, camping and boats for hire.

● **Accommodation** B *Laguna*, Libres del Sur

y Maipú, T 22808; *Los Vascos*, Avenida Costanera, T 22856; *Nuevo Colón*, Libres del Sur 400, T 22567; **C** *El Lago*, Sarmiento y Dolores, T 30879, **D** pp *La Toja*, Libres del Sur 102, T 22268. **Estancia L3** pp *La Mamaia*, 18 km from Chascomús, T/F 0241-24023, full board, covering 1,000 hectares and offering horseriding, swimming pool, cycling and watersports on nearby Lago Chascomús, *día de campo* US$60 per person. **Camping** Seven sites, five on far side of the lake including *La Alameda*, see above.

● **Transport Train** To Buenos Aires (Constitución), 4 daily, US$6 first class. **Buses** To Buenos Aires, US$7, companies: El Cóndor, El Rápido, Río de la Plata, La Estrella and Antón.

DOLORES

(*Population* 30,000; *Phone code* 0245) 204 km from Buenos Aires, was founded in 1818, destroyed by Indians 3 years later, and rebuilt. It is a grain and cattle farming centre.

Museums Museo Libres del Sur, in the Parque Libres del Sur, commemorating the revolt of the district against Rosas in the early 19th century, is interesting and well displayed, Tuesday-Sunday 100-1700. **Museo de Bellas Artes**, Belgrano 134, Wednesday-Sunday 1000-1700.

● **Accommodation** B *Hotel Plaza*, very pleasant; **B-C** *Avenida* Olavarría 362, T 7619, four blocks from Plaza, ugly but OK. *Parrilladas*, *heladerías* and nightlife on Calle Buenos Aires. **Estancias L3** *Haras La Viviana*, 21 km north near Castelli, full board, watersports, birdwatching, fishing, horseriding. Contact Haras La Viviana, Castelli, Gaspar Campos 671, Vicente López CP138, Prov BsAs, T 541-791-2406; **L3** *Dos Talas*, T 3020, F 40887, full board, main house built in 1858, with lovely chapel (copy of Notre Dame de Passy), park designed by Charles Thays, offers horseriding, walking, fishing, cycling, English spoken; día de campo US$65.

● **Transport Local Taxi**: taxi stand at Belgrano y Rico, one block from plaza, T 3507. **Train** Station 15 minutes from centre; to Buenos Aires, 4 daily US$8. **Buses** To Buenos Aires, 3 hours, Río de la Plata, Buenos Aires 285, Cóndor/La Estrella, Buenos Aires 300 block.

SOUTHEAST TO BAHIA BLANCA

Route 3 runs southeast via Azul and Tres Arroyos and then east to Bahía Blanca.

Azul: centre

Not to scale

Av Mitre

Belgrano

H Yrigoyen

Municipalidad

Plaza San Martín

San Martín

Museo Etnográfico

Bolívar

Cathedral

9 de Julio

Roca

To Bus Terminal & Route 3

To Railway station

Rivadavia · Alvear · Colón · Burgos · Uriburu · Moreno · Av 25 de Mayo

Maipú

Av Humberto 1°

To Parque Municipal Sarmiento & Balneario Municipal

Hotels:
1. Argentino
2. Gran Azul

AZUL

(*Population* 62,000; *Phone code* 0281) 264 km southwest of Buenos Aires, is an agricultural centre which holds an annual honey festival in June. Around the attractive Plaza San Martín are the French Gothic-style **Cathedral** (1906) and the neo-classical French-style **Municipalidad**. Southwest of the centre, along the river are the **Parque Municipal Sarmiento**, with over 200 tree species, and the **Balneario Municipal**.

Museums Museo Etnográfico, Alvear y San Martín, two blocks northwest of Plaza San Martín, containing a collection of Mapuche silverware and textiles.

● **Accommodation B** *Gran Azul*, Colón 626, T 22011, excellent cafetería; **C** *Res Blue*, Mitre 983, T 22742, near bus terminal; *Argentino*, Yrigoyen 378, T 25953; *Torino*, San Martín 1000, T 22749. **Camping** Municipal site, in the Balneario Municipal, hot showers, pleasant, US$2 per person.

● **Tourist offices** Avenida 25 de Mayo 619, T 31751.

SOUTHWEST TO NEUQUEN

Route 5 runs southwest via Luján, Mercedes, Chivilcoy, Pehuajó and Trenque Lauquen to Santa Rosa de la Pampa.

LUJAN

(*Population* 56,500; *Altitude* 30m; *Phone code* 0323) 66 km west of the capital, is a place of pilgrimage and a very popular spot for weekend trips from Buenos Aires.

The basilica (1887-1932) rising to 107m, with its twin towers rising to 107m and stained glass windows, stands on Plaza Belgrano. Its bells were made in Italy from guns used in the First World War. Inside the Virgin stands on the High Altar. Each arch of the church is dedicated to an Argentine province, and the transepts to Uruguay, Paraguay and Ireland.

Just off the plaza is the 18th century Cabildo and next to it, the Casa del Virrey, which are now occupied by museums. Behind the Cabildo is the river, with restaurants and pleasant river walks and cruises.

Museums Museo Histórico Colonial, one of the most interesting museums in the country, traces the historical and political development of Argentina and includes sections on Argentine presidents, indigenous peoples and gauchos. Wednesday-Saturday 1200-1730, US$1. **Museo del Transporte**, containing the best collection of carriages in Argentina as well as *La Porteña*, the first railway engine to operate in the country, Wednesday-Sunday 1200-1800. **Salón del**

The Virgin of Luján

In 1620 a terracotta image of the Virgin was being carried by ox cart from church to church in the area. The cart got stuck and the strenuous efforts of men and oxen to move it all failed. This was taken as a sign that the Virgin willed she should stay there. A chapel was built for the image, and around it grew Luján. The Virgin of Luján, adopted as the virgin of Argentina, Paraguay and Uruguay, has made the city into a major pilgrimage spot. The chapel has long since been superseded by an impressive neo-Gothic basilica.

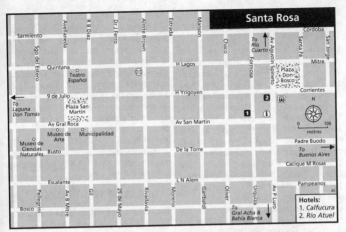

Santa Rosa

Hotels:
1. Calfucura
2. Río Atuel

Automóvil, with a large collection of veteran cars in good condition, daily 1200-1800, US$2. **Museo de Bellas Artes**, poor.

- **Accommodation B** *Centro*, Francia 1062, T 20667, without breakfast; **B** *Eros*, San Martín 129, T 20797, F 21265, without breakfast, good beds; *La Paz*, 9 de Julio 1054, T 24034; **D** pp *Carena*, Lavalle 114, T 23828, poor beds, overpriced. Several others around the terminal including **C** *Venezia*, Alte Brown 100, basic; *City* and *Biarritz*, better.

- **Places to eat** There are numerous restaurants along the river bank and just off the plaza. An excellent one is *L'Eau Vive* on the road to Buenos Aires at Constitución 2112, it is run by nuns, pleasant surroundings.

- **Transport Train** Regular service run by Trenes de Buenos Aires from Once station, Buenos Aires, US$1.50, 2 hours. **Buses** From Buenos Aires (Plaza Once), bus 52, frequent, 2 hours, US$3.70 or direct service, 1 hour, US$5.50. To San Antonio de Areco, 3 a day, US$4, Empresa Argentina, 1 hour.

Mercedes

(*Population* 47,850) 33 km west of Luján, is a pleasant city with many fine buildings. (Not to be confused with Villa Mercedes in San Luis Province – see below.) Tourist office on plaza, very friendly.

- **Accommodation C** *Loren* (no sign), Salta 228, friendly, clean, parking. **Estancia A1** pp *Posada del Campo*, T 0323-28380, F 0324-25987, full board, 100 hectares, swimming pool, horseriding, cycling, birdwatching, good food; *día de campo* US$35.

SANTA ROSA DE LA PAMPA

(*Population* 70,000; *Phone code* 0954) 663 km from Buenos Aires, is the capital of La Pampa province. Founded in 1892, it is a modern city; the **Teatro Español**, Lagos 44, dates from 1908. 10 blocks west of the Plaza San Martín is Laguna Don Tomás and a park with sports facilities.

Museums Museo de Ciencias Naturales, Pellegrini 180, displays on archaeology, flora and fauna, Monday-Friday

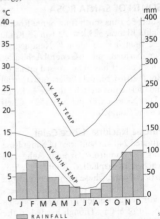

Climate: Santa Rosa

0800-1700. **Museo de Artes**, 9 de Julio 305, Monday-Friday 0800-1200, Saturday 1800-2100.

Excursions To the **Parque Luro**, 32 km south of Santa Rosa. Covering over 6,500 hectares, this provincial park occupies the former estate of Pedro Luro, who created his own hunting grounds and introduced European species such as the Carpathian red deer and the wild boar. Luro's mansion, a central European style *chateau*, can be visited. Opposite is a Centro de Interpretación Ecológico, with displays on the flora and fauna of the Pampas. Nearby is the Museo de Carruajes, with a collection of carriages. Open daily 0900-2000. Campsite.

● **Accommodation** **A2** *Calfucura*, San Martín 695, T 23608, 4-star; **C** *Hostería Río Atuel*, Luro 256, opposite terminal, T 22597, very good; **D** *San Martín*, Alsina 101, clean, restaurant, parking; **D** *Motel Calden*, Eva Perón y Ferinatti, T 24311, large rooms, good restaurant. **Camping** Municipal site near the Laguna Don Tomás.

● **Tourist offices** San Martín y Luro, opposite terminal.

● **Transport Train** To Buenos Aires (Once) Sunday, Tuesday, Thursday 1900, 11 hours, Pullman US$25, First US$20, Tourist US$17. **Buses** Terminal at San Martín y Luro, seven blocks east of Plaza San Martín.

SOUTH OF SANTA ROSA

Route 35 runs south from Santa Rosa to Bahía Blanca, 323 km. At Km 73 Route 152 branches off towards Neuquén: at Km 25 a road leads to **General Acha** after which desert has to be crossed either on Route 20 to Cruz del Desierto and Catriel (no fuel on this stretch), thence on Route 151 to Neuquén, or on Route 152 to Chelforó on Route 22.

Parque Nacional Lihue Calel

Situated 240 km southeast of Santa Rosa and 120 km from General Acha and reached by asphalted Route 152, this national park, whose name derives from the Mapuche for 'place of life', covers 9,901 hectares of low hills which reach a height of 590m. Though located in the middle of desert and receiving only 400 mm of rain annually, the park is home to a wide variety of plant species, including a number of unique species of cactus. Fauna include pumas, the patagonian hare, vizcachas, guanacos and rheas as well as a wide variety of birds. There are geometric cave paintings of Tehuelche origin over 2,000 years old in the Valle de los Pinturas and the Valle de Namencurá. There are also the ruins of the Estancia Santa María. You are required to keep to the authorized footpaths. The park is best visited in Spring.

● **Accommodation** *ACA Hostería* with restaurant, 2 km south of park entrance. **Camping** Site near entrance.

WEST TO SAN LUIS

Route 7 runs west from Buenos Aires via Luján and Junín to San Luis.

Junín

(*Population* 63,700; *Phone code* 0362) Km 256, was founded as a fort in 1827. Its main claim to fame is that Eva Perón lived here between the ages of 11 and 15 before moving to Buenos Aires. Near Junín are several lakes including Laguna de Gómez, 12 km west and Laguna el Carpincho, 4 km west, where there is good fishing.

● **Accommodation** **A2** *Copahue*, Saavedra 80, T 23390, F 29041, faded, ACA discount; *Embajador*, Sáenz Peña y Pellegrini, T 21433.

● **Places to eat** *Paraje del Sauce*, Km 258 on Route 7, picturesque, good food but 'don't stop there if you are in a rush'; *El Quincho de Martín*, B de Miguel y Ruta 7, good.

● **Train** To Buenos Aires (Retiro), Friday, Sunday 1813, 5 hours, First US$9, Tourist US$8.

At **Rufino** (*Population* 15,300), Km 452, is the recommended **L3** *Hotel Astur*, Córdoba 81, **C** with ACA discount. At **Laboulaye**, Km 517, there are several good and cheap hotels, eg *Victoria*, and **B** *Motel Ranquel Mapu*, Km 489, very good, bottled water supplied.

NORTHWEST TO CORDOBA

There are two main routes: Route 9 (713 km) via Rosario (see page 294) and Villa María and the longer Route 8 (835 km) via San Antonio de Areco, Pergamino, **Venado Tuerto** (*Population* 58,000) Km 370 (several hotels) and Río Cuarto. For

The authentic Gaucho town?

Though authentic is an overused word, it best describes San Antonio; a country town set in one of the most fertile areas of the pampas, it has no frills and few hotels; a lick of paint wouldn't go amiss and if you object to flying things or the occasional cockroach in the night, then this isn't for you.

One of the oldest towns in this part of Argentina, San Antonio dates back to the early 17th century and the local school is still run by Irish nuns. In one of the side streets it is still possible to find a *pulpería*: in the dark interior, next to the fruit and vegetables, is a small bar around which there are usually a cluster of present day gauchos, wearing the traditional *bombachas* (baggy trousers) and red neckerchiefs. In the main street there is a silversmith, still making, by hand, the ornamental belt buckles and *facones* (knives) worn by the gauchos. Nearby are several leather shops and a wonderful old saddlery with the ceilings and walls covered with bridles and boots.

Philip Horton

descriptions of Villa María and Río Cuarto see the Central Sierras section.

SAN ANTONIO DE ARECO

(*Population* 15,000; *Altitude* 34m; *Phone code* 0326) 113 km northwest of Buenos Aires) is an attractive town of single-storey buildings, tree-lined streets and a popular costanera. It is a popular centre for visiting *estancias*. Many handicrafts are sold, mainly *gaucho* objects, ceramics, silver, leather, colonial-style furniture.

The **Museo Gauchesco Ricardo Güiraldes**, on Camino Güiraldes y Aureliano, is a modern replica of a typical *estancia* of the late 19th century, containing artefacts associated with gaucho life. Open daily except Tuesday, 1000-1800. Güiraldes himself was born in Paris in 1886. He spent much of his early life on the *Estancia La Porteña*, 8 km from San Antonio. After periods in Paris, where he studied architecture and law, he settled on the estancia. A sophisticated member of Parisian literary circles, Güiraldes was an Argentine nationalist who romanticized *gaucho* life. His best-known book, *Don Segundo Sombra* (1926), was set in San Antonio: the *Estancia La Porteña* and sites in the town such as the old bridge and the *Pulpería La Blanqueada* (at the entrance to the museum), became famous through its pages. Güiraldes died in 1927.

Local festivals *Día de la Tradición*, 10 November, is a *gaucho* festival with traditional parades, games, events on horseback, music and dance. There are celebrations throughout the week beforehand (accommodation is hard to find).

- **Accommodation B** *San Carlos*, Zapiola y Zerbione, T 22401, ask in advance for meals; **D** *Res Areco*, Segundo Sombra y Rivadavia, T 22166, good, comfortable, 15% ISIC and GO 25 discounts; *Res El Hornero*, Moreno y San Martín, T 2733. **Estancias L3** pp *Los Patricios*, 4 km from town, T/F 3833, 200 hectares, horseriding, tennis, swimming pool, English, French, Italian spoken, *día de campo* US$65. Day visits can be made to other *estancias* such as *Cina-Cina*, tour includes typical lunch and riding display, recommended; *La Bomba*, T 0326-4053, and *El Ombú*. **Camping** Municipal site at Zapiola y Zerboni, near river; *Club River* on Costanera; *Auto-camping La Porteña*, T 3402, 8 km from town on the Güiraldes *estancia*, good access roads.

- **Places to eat** Many *parrillas* on the bank of the Río Areco.

- **Tourist office** On the costanera, T 3165, Monday-Friday 0800-1400, Saturday/Sunday 1000-1700.

- **Buses** From Buenos Aires: from Plaza Once, 2 hours, US$4, every hour; also Chevallier from Retiro bus terminal, US$6, 2 hours.

THE SOUTHERN SIERRAS

THE SIERRA DE TANDIL

This range of hills runs southeast from near Azul towards the coast near Mar del Plata, a distance of 340 km.

TANDIL

(*Population* 125,000; *Altitude* 178m; *Phone code* 0293) Situated 350 km south of Buenos Aires and 171 km northwest of Mar del Plata, was founded in 1823 as a fortress. On the south side of the main Plaza Independencia are the neoclassical **Municipalidad** (1923) and **Banco Hipotecario Nacional** (1924) and the **Iglesia del Santisimo Sacramento**, inspired by the Sacre Coeur in Paris. West of the plaza on the outskirts of town is **Cerro Calvario** with the stages of the cross leading to the **Capilla Santa Gemma**, on top. Six blocks south of the plaza, on a hill and offering fine views, is the **Parque Independencia**, with a granite entrance in Moorish style, built by the local Italian community to celebrate the town's centenary. Inside the park is a Moorish style castle, built by the Spanish community to mark the same event. South of the park is the **Lago del Fuerte**, where watersports are practised. Another hill **Cerro Centinela**,

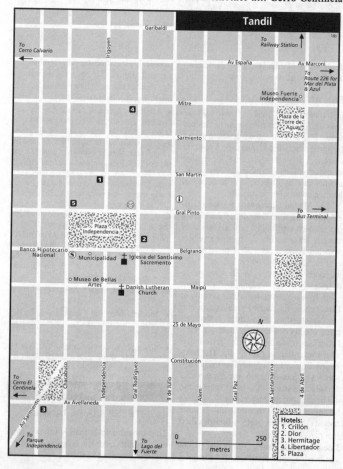

Tandil

Hotels:
1. Crillón
2. Dior
3. Hermitage
4. Libertador
5. Plaza

The legend of El Centinela

In the early days of European settlement at Tandil, some soldiers heard the story of a strange and beautiful girl called Amaika who was able to disappear whenever she realized she was being watched. Amaika, who had been brought up by her white father after her Indian mother had died, was regarded as a kind of goddess by the Indians. An Indian boy, the son of a chief, strong and very tall, sat and watched Amaika every day and, as the two fell in love, she began to leave her hiding place more often to sit with him.

Two white soldiers decided to capture the girl. Her frequent appearances to be with the Indian boy gave them the chance to discover her hiding place and seize her. They carried her off to the fort, but on arrival she escaped into the night. There was a splash in the deep moat surrounding the fort and Amaika was assumed to have drowned, unable to swim because her arms were tied up.

Though Amaika was never seen again, high up on the hill the Indian boy continued to stand in the vain hope that she might appear. As he waited, standing there in all weathers, he began to look more and more like a rock until one day, miraculously, he was transformed into the enormous rock known as 'El Centinela'.

famous for the giant boulder on top, lies southeast of the Parque Independencia (see box, below).

Museums **Museo Municipal de Bellas Artes**, Chacabuco 367, containing works by Argentine artists and a few early 20th century European works. **Museo Fuerte Independencia**, 4 de Abril 485, displaying a collection of local artefacts including carriages and a reconstruction of a *pulpería*.

Excursions To the **Reserva Natural Sierra del Tigre**, 6 km south, 140 hectares, which protects the Cerro Venado, from which there are good views over Tandil. Foxes and guanacos can be seen and there is a small zoo.

Local Festivals Holy Week celebrations are outstanding and attract large numbers of visitors: book accommodation in advance.

● **Accommodation** 3-star hotels including *Dior*, Rodriguez 471, T 31901; **B** *Libertador*, Mitre 545, T 22127, central, good value; **B** *Plaza*, General Pinto 438, T 27160, comfortable and quiet. 2-star: *Austral*, 9 de Julio 725, T 25606; *Crillón*, San Martín 455, T 24159; *Hermitage*, Avellaneda y Rondeau, T 23377. 1-star: **C** *Kaiku*, Mitre 902, T 23114, basic; *Centro*, Sarmiento 591, T 24123; *Cristal*, Rodriguez 871, T 25951. **B** *Cabañas Manantial de las Amores*, T 45701, F 28653, with breakfast, also horseriding, cycle hire, tours. **Estancia** *Acelain*, 54 km north of Tandil, T Buenos Aires 322-2784, Andalusian-style mansion dating from 1922, with gardens inspired by the Generalife in Granada and 800 hectares of park, offering luxury accommodation, horseriding, polo, watersports. **Camping** *Pinar de la Sierra*, south of the Parque Independencia.

● **Places to eat** *El Estribo*, San Martín 759, good atmosphere, recommended. North of Tandil is *Estancia Acelain*, luxury accommodation.

● **Transport** **Air** Lapa flights 3 times a week to Buenos Aires in summer. **Train** To Buenos Aires and Bahía Blanca, daily. **Buses** To Buenos Aires, 6 hours, US$15.

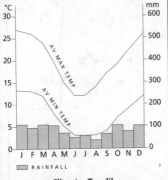

Climate: Tandil

SIERRA DE LA VENTANA

Situated some 100 km north of Bahía Blanca and running northwest to south-east for some 175 km, this is the highest range of hills in the pampas. It is a popular area for excursions from Bahía Blanca.

Tornquist

(*Population* 5,672; *Altitude* 285m) 70 km north of Bahía Blanca by Route 33, with an attractive church on the central plaza and an artificial lake, is a good starting point. Nearby is the Tornquist family mansion, built in a mixture of French styles. Of Swedish origin, Ernesto Tornquist (1842-1908) was the son of a Buenos Aires merchant. Under his leadership the family established the industrial investment bank which still bears his name. Tornquist helped to establish the country's first sugar refinery, meat packing plant and several chemical firms.

● **Accommodation** **B** *Gran Central,* Avenida 9 de Julio, T 091-94005, seedy but friendly; campsite, US$4 per person.

● **Train** To Buenos Aires and Bahía Blanca daily.

Parque Provincial Ernesto Tornquist

25 km east of Tornquist and covering 6,718 hectares, originated with a donation of 3,228 hectares by the Tornquist family to the provincial government in 1937: the entrance is marked by the massive ornate iron gates from the Tornquist family home. Nearby is the Centro de Interpretación Ecológica, which offers displays, videos and talks. From here it is a 3-hour climb to the summit of Cerro Ventana, 1,136m, which offers fantastic views from the 'window' in the summit ridge. Other peaks include Cerro Bahía Blanca, Cerro Chato and Cerro Volante.

Wildlife includes grey foxes, guanacos, pumas and eagles as well as wild horses and red deer. One section of the park is a restricted area in which there are two caves: the **Cueva del Toro** and the **Cueva de las Pinturas Rupestres** which contains petroglyphs. Excursions

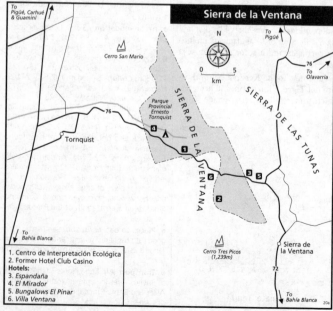

Sierra de la Ventana

To Pigüé, Carhué & Guaminí

Cerro San Mario

To Pigüé

To Olavarría

SIERRA DE LAS TUNAS

Parque Provincial Ernesto Tornquist

SIERRA DE LA VENTANA

Tornquist

To Bahía Blanca

Cerro Tres Picos (1,239m)

Sierra de la Ventana

To Bahía Blanca

1. Centro de Interpretación Ecológica
2. Former Hotel Club Casino
Hotels:
3. *Espandaña*
4. *El Mirador*
5. *Bungalows El Pinar*
6. *Villa Ventana*

Red flags and white flags

Originally a rural trading post, the *pulpería* also served as a bar and social club, selling alcoholic drinks, tobacco and *hierba maté*: a white flag was hung outside to indicate to people at a distance that these were available. A red flag indicated that meat was for sale. The only social institution in many small communities, the *pulpería* also served as a bank, the *pulpero* (or barman) becoming the local money-lender. As the pampas were settled, *pulperías* were often located near railway stations. The name derives from the *pulque*, the Mapuche word for liquor. *Pulperías* were frequently violent places: there were always iron bars to protect the *pulpero* from thieves and discontented customers.

are offered from the Centro de Interpretación on Friday and Sunday 0900 US$2, 5 hours.

Villa Ventana, 10 km east of the Centro de Interpretación on the edge of the park, is a small settlement and the base for climbing Cerro Tres Picos (1,239m), to the south of the park, which is the highest peak in Buenos Aires province. The ruins of the *Hotel Club Casino*, which, when built in 1911 was the most luxurious hotel in Argentina, can be seen; it burned down in 1983. There is an excellent teashop, *Casa de Heidi*, and wholefood is sold at the *Jardín de Aylem*.

● **Accommodation** *El Mirador*, at park entrance, T 941338, 4-star. East of the park on Route 76 are: *La Espadaña*, *Bungalows El Pinar*. **Camping** Campamento Base, near entrance, also has dormitory accommodation, T 091-940288, hospitable; Municipal site in Villa Ventana, all facilities.

Sierra de la Ventana

(*Population* 900; *Altitude* 248m) The town of Sierra de la Ventana, 15 km east of the park at the confluence of the Ríos Sauce Grande, Negro and San Bernardo, is another good centre for exploring the hills. Tres Picos, rising bare and barren from the rich farmlands, is only 6¼ km away. There is a 9-hole golf course, and good trout fishing in the Río Sauce Grande. Excellent tourist information.

● **Accommodation A3** *Provincial*, Drago y Malvinas, T 915025; **D** *La Perlita*, San Martín y Roca, T 915020; **E** pp *Yapay*, Avenida San Martín near bus terminal, quiet, recommended. **Youth hostels** *Albergue Sierra de la Ventana* (sleeping bag necessary). **Camping** Three sites.

● **Buses** To Buenos Aires, La Estrella, 1 a day; to Bahía Blanca, 2 a day (1 on Saturday).

Pigüé

Situated at the northern end of the Sierra, 59 km north of Tornquist, is an alternative base for exploring this area with a car. It has a **Museo Regional**, with photographs of the 'Conquest of the Wilderness'.

● **Accommodation** *Gran Hotel Pigüé*, España 229, T 2460, 3-star; *Central*, San Martín y Belgrano, T 3140.

NORTH OF SIERRA DE LA VENTANA

Route 33 runs north from Pigüé through a group of lakes known as the Lagunas del Oeste, before meeting Route 5, the Buenos Aires-Santa Rosa highway at Trenque Lauquen. The Lagunas del Oeste are popular for fishing: the two main towns for visiting this area are Carhué and Guaminí.

Guaminí

(*Population* 3,500) 202 km north of Bahía Blanca, is a pleasant summer hill resort on the shore of Laguna del Monte.

● **Accommodation** *Res Turis Guaminí*, San Martín y Alem, T 2281. **Camping** Municipal site at the lakeside.

CARHUE

(*Population* 18,000; *Phone code* 0936) Carhué is a resort situated 38 km west of Guaminí. North of the town is Lago Epecuén, which covers over 10,000 hectares and is over 20 times saltier than the sea: its waters, too salty for fish, are recommended for the treatment of chronic rheumatism and skin diseases. The ghost town of Villa Epecuén, a former health resort 8 km north of Carhué, drowned by the lake in 1985, can be visited (unpaved road).

Museums Museo Regional Adolfo Alsina, east of the main plaza, behind the town hall, containing artefacts from the wars against the Indians.

● **Accommodation & services B** *Shalom*, Belgrano 880, T 2503, near terminal,'eccentric but clean', breakfast extra; *Avenida*, Alsina 1185, T 2707; *Termas Carhué*, Dorrego 520, T/F 2887; *Buenos Aires*, Urquiza 313, T 2312; *Res Edith*, Mitre 741, T 2471, heating, cafeteria; *Res Isabel García de Sanz*, Dorrego 659, T 2438; *Res Maruja*, Alvear 730, T 2066; *Res Epecuén*, Martín y Alsina, T 2991, restaurant. Restaurant at bus terminal is reasonable. **Camping** Municipal site nine blocks northwest of main plaza, with *Del Quincho los Almaceneros*, opposite, showers, store. Also at *Balneario La Isla*, on the shores of the lake, full services. *La Chacra*, 5 km east, in 50 hectares of park, full services.

● **Tourist offices** In the town hall on main plaza, T 2233, F 2632.

● **Buses** Terminal one block north of main plaza. To **Buenos Aires**, Empresa Liniers, 9 hours; to **La Plata**, Empresa Liniers, 10 hours; to **Mar del Plata**, Pampa, 10 hours; to **Bahía Blanca**, Ñandú del Sur, 3-4 hours.

COASTAL RESORTS SOUTH OF BUENOS AIRES

Route 36 from Buenos Aires passes La Plata and becomes Route 11 (the *Interbalnearia*) which sweeps around Bahía Samborombón to a string of Atlantic coastal resorts.

SAN CLEMENTE DEL TUYU

(*Population* 8,000; *Phone code* 0252) This is the nearest Atlantic coastal resort to Buenos Aires. A family resort with little nightlife, it is cheaper than the more fashionable resorts further south. To the south of the centre is the **Vivero Cosme Argerich**, a 37 hectare park, with woodlands, plant nursery and sports centre. Open daily 1000-1630. North of the town is **Puerto San Clemente**, a small fishing port with fish restaurants; boats can be hired for fishing trips. North of the port is **Mundo Marino**, the largest oceanarium in South America (T 21071); attractions include two killer whales, dolphins, elephant seals, sea lions and penguins; open

daily from 1000, closes 1530 May-September, 1630 March-April, October-December, 1800 January-February (bus 500 from San Clemente).

Excursions

To **Punta Rasa**, 6 km north, where there are an old lighthouse offering superb views over the coast and a nature reserve owned by the Fundación Vida Silvestre, which, in summer, is home to thousands of migratory birds from the northern hemisphere. Entry US$4.

To the is the **Reserva Campos del Tuyú**, west of San Clemente, near General Lavalle, owned by the Fundación Vida Silvestre, covering 7,500 hectares of riverine habitat. Among the wildlife are pampas foxes and the rare pampas deer as well as 150 species of bird including rheas, American swans and flamingoes.

Coastal resorts south of Buenos Aires

Not to scale

Buenos Aires

320

San Clemente del Tuyú

89

Pinamar

22

Villa Gesell

100

Mar del Plata

53

Miramar

110

Necochea

141

Tres Arroyos

195

Distance in km   Bahía Blanca

Wild Coast

✏️ This coast was known by sailors as the *costa bravía* (wild coast); maritime maps advise sailors to keep their distance to avoid the strong tides, sandbanks and the wreckage of over 50 vessels. Some of these wrecks are still visible: the wreck of the Canadian ship *Her Royal Highness*, sunk in 1883, can be seen at low tide at Las Toninas, as can the remains of the German vessel *Margarethe* at Mar de Ajó. South of Mar de Ajó, near the Punta Médanos lighthouse, the wreck of the French vessel *Karnak*, which went down in 1870 can be seen in the dunes.

The *Margarethe*, wrecked in 1880 when carrying a French theatre company, yielded unusual wreckage. Though crew and passengers were saved, 30 barrels of French wine were lost in the sandbanks. Over 50 years later, when a group of campers drilled a hole for drinking water, their well yielded wine, excellently preserved and extremely drinkable.

Local Information

● **Accommodation**

Best is *Fontainebleau*, Calle 3, No 2290, 4-star. Several on Avenida Costanera including *Stella Marina*, T 21453; *Costanera*, No 2438, T 21110. Several on Calle 1 including **C** *Splendid*, No 2430, T 21316; **B** *Acuario*, San Martín 444, T 21357, including breakfast; **C** *Res Bahía*, Calle 4, between Calle 1 and Calle 15, breakfast included, good. Most close out of season. Several campsites.

● **Places to eat**

Restaurante Yo y Vos, Calle 4 y Calle 17, large and cheap portions, friendly, good.

● **Banks & money changers**

US dollars can be changed at the **Banco de la Provincia de Buenos Aires**, Calle 1 y Calle 4, but travellers' cheques are not accepted anywhere in town.

● **Tourist offices**

Calle 2 y 65, T 21478.

● **Transport**

Buses To **Mar del Plata**, frequent, Empresa Costamar, US$11, 5 hours. To **Buenos Aires**, several companies, US$15-20.

SOUTH OF SAN CLEMENTE

South of San Clemente is a 65 km stretch of coast lined with resorts and known as the *Atlantida Argentina*. The major resorts are **Santa Teresita** (*Population* 9,000; *Phone code* 0246) 17 km south, **Mar del Tuyú** (*Population* 38,000; *Phone code* 0246) 20 km south, **La Lucila del Mar** (*Phone code* 0257) 33 km south, **San Bernardo** (*Phone code* 0257) 35 km south and **Mar de Ajó** (*Population* 13,000; Phone code 0257) 40 km south, which has the largest fishing port on this part of the coast and from where excursions to wrecked vessels are offered.

● **Accommodation** Lots of hotels in Santa Teresita, San Bernardo and Mar de Ajó. In **Santa Teresita**: best is *Golf Internacional*, Calle 27 y Kennedy, T 20469, 4-star. Hotels in centre including *Helénico*, Calle 36 No 238, T 20251; *Playa*, Calle 36 No 270, T 20579; *Sorrento*, Calle 37 No 35, T 20298. Many *hospedajes* including *Alperi*, Calle 2 No 360, T 20411; *El Reloj*, Calle 39 No 250, T 30536; *Stella Maris*, Calle 39 No 216. In **San Bernardo**: best are *Seaboard*, San Bernardo y Chiozza, T 61712, 4-star, and *Neptuno Playa*, La Rioja y Hernández, T 61789; *Res Ileana*, Chiozza 1621, T 60209; few cheap options. In **Mar de Ajó**: 3-star hotels along Avenida Costanera including *Flamingo*, No 343, T 20168; *Mar de Ajó*, No 205, T 20023; *Latinoamericano*, No 55, T 20254; cheaper options including *Catalina*, Avenida Costanera 1270, T 20249; *Dorin's*, Libertador 166, T 20105; *Tupe*, Lebensohn 248, T 20189; *Res Asturias*, Montevideo 338; *Saint James*, Montevideo 370. Elsewhere accommodation is more scarce, in **Mar del Tuyu**: *Santa Rosa*, Costanera y Calle 68, T 20475; *Res Romero*, Calle 58 y 2. In **La Lucila del Mar**: *La Maison*, San Juan 5140, T 62722; *La Morada del Sol*, San Juan 4878, T 62303. **Camping** Lots of sites. North of Santa Teresita is *Autocamping El Carmen*, T 20220. In Mar de Tuyú *Camping Mar del Tuyú*, Calle 94 y Calle 13. In San Bernardo *Weekend*, Gutiérrez y Salta, T 60478. In Mar de Ajó there is a ACA site next to the plaza and a municipal site seven blocks south of the plaza.

PINAMAR

(*Population* 10,000; *Phone code* 0254) 89 km south of San Clemente, is one of the most attractive resorts with 22 km of beaches. It has a golf course and is good for water-skiing. Fish, including conger eel (*congrio*) may be bought on the beach from local fishermen. Nearby is the Reserva Dunícola, with sand dunes up to 30m high. The *Estancias* La Victoria and Dos Montes can be visited.

Ostende (*Population* 2,300) 6 km south, was founded by Belgian entrepreneurs in 1908 but abandoned when the settlers returned to Belgium on the outbreak of the First World War. The only building surviving from that period is the **Viejo Hotel Ostende**, formerly the Hotel Termas, which was a favourite of Antoine de Saint-Exupéry. Another hotel, **Atlantic City**, unfinished in 1914, now functions as a Youth Hostel.

Excursions

To **General Madariaga** (*Population* 17,000), 28 km inland where the *Fiesta Nacional del Gaucho* is celebrated on the first weekend in December with processions, singing and dancing. The **Museo del Tuyú**, in the former railway station, has displays of rural artefacts, paintings and local handicrafts. Nearby is the **Estancia Charles Viejo** where a collection of carriages can be seen. From General Madariaga the **Laguna Salada Grande**, the largest lake in the province and be visited; here there is a 40 hectare nature reserve protecting the southernmost examples of the tala.

Local information
● **Accommodation**
A1 *Playas*, Bunge y de la Sirena, T 82236, F 82226, with breakfast, English spoken. Many, from *Arenas*, Bunge 700, T 82444, 4-star, to *Berlín*, Rivadavia 326, T 82320; *Sardegna*, Jasón 840, T 82760; *Boulogna*, Jasón 523, T 82242, all 1-star. All hotels fully booked throughout January-March. Houses and apartments can be rented from December-March: 2-room flats about US$1,000 per month, up to US$5,000 for a mansion. In March rates are halved. **In Ostende**: best is *Savoia*, Biarritz y Progreso, T 86453, 4-star; *Viejo Ostende*,

Biarritz y El Cairo, T 86081, 3-star; *Rambla*, Biarritz 16, T 86028. **Youth hostels** Nuestras Malvinas y Sarmiento, T 82908. **Camping** Three sites all in Ostende (take green *Montemar* bus from terminal): *Saint Tropez*, US$18 per site; *Quintana* and *Nuestras Malvinas*.

● **Tourist offices**
Bunge 700.

● **Transport**
Train To Buenos Aires (Constitución), US$23 first, US$18 *turista*.

Buses Terminal four blocks north of main plaza. To **Buenos Aires**, Antón, US$20, Río de la Plata US$23, Plusmar *coche cama* US$26.

VILLA GESELL

(*Population* 16,000; *Phone code* 0255) 22 km south of Pinamar, is a modern resort named after the man who planned it in the 1940s, the furniture manufacturer, Carlos Gesell. It is particularly popular with younger people; it has a chocolate factory, fine beaches, watersports facilities and over 100 hotels. In season it is very busy: in January 1994 it attracted 700,000 visitors. Villa Querandi, south, is more simple and peaceful. The **Reserva Forestal y Parque Gesell**, at the northern end of Avenida 3, includes the Casa Histórica, Carlos Gesell's mansion, which functions as a museum. West of the reserve is an open-air amphitheatre where performances are given.

Local information
● **Accommodation**
Most hotels are between Avenida 3 and the beach. *Terrazas Club*, 4-star, suite accommodation, Avenida 2 entre Calle 104 y 105, T 63214; *Colón*, 1-star, Avenida 4, Calle 104, T 62310, restaurant; **B** *Hostería Gran Chalet*, Paseo 105 No 447 y Avenida 4-5, T 62913, recommended; **C** *Bero*, Avenida 4 y Calle 141, T 66077, opposite bus terminal; **E** pp *Hosp San Hector*, Avenida 8, No 641, T 62052. Many others of all classes. Many apartments for rent (rates as Pinamar).

Youth hostels *Albergue Camping El Coyote*, Alameda 212 y 306, Barrio Norte, T 68418.

Camping Many sites, including three off Avenida Buenos Aires, north of the centre.

● **Sports**
Horseriding: *Tante Puppi*, Boulevard y Paseo 102.

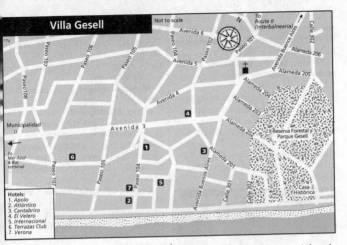

Villa Gesell

Not to scale

Hotels:
1. Apolo
2. Atlántico
3. Cantábrico
4. El Velero
5. Internacional
6. Terrazas Club
7. Verona

● **Tourist offices**
In the Municipalidad on Avenida 3.

● **Transport**
Air From Buenos Aires, Austral, US$85, LAER, US$60.

Buses Terminal at Avenida 3 y Paseo 140, south of town. Direct to Buenos Aires, US$21, Empresa Antón and Río de la Plata, book in advance at weekends.

MAR DEL PLATA

(*Population* 502,000; *Phone code* 023) The most famous Argentine resort, dating from the turn of the century, is 100 km further south and 400 km from the capital. With its 8 km of beaches, it attracts about

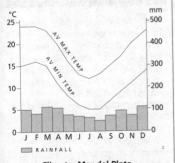

Climate: Mar del Plata

2 million visitors every summer (when the night-life continues all night). For the rest of the year the town is fairly quiet and good value.

Places of interest
The most famous area of the city is around **Playa Bristol** where a broad promenade, the **Rambla**, runs past the fine **Casino** (upper floor open to the public) and the **Gran Hotel Provincial**, both of which were designed by Bustillo and date from the late 1930s. Six blocks north along Avenida San Martín is the **Plaza San Martín**, flanked by the attractive cathedral The Rambla runs southeast along Playa Bristol towards Punta Piedras, where, on the headland, stands the **Torreón del Monje**, a Norman style mansion built in 1904. Three blocks inland from Punta Piedras on top of the hill are other examples of the *pintoresque* architecture of the early years of this century, among them the Norman style **Villa Ortiz Basualdo** (1909) and the mock Tudor **Villa Blaquier** (1905).

South of Punta Piedras are the rocky promontory of **Cabo Corrientes** and the fashionable **Playa Grande**, with its private clubs and the summer mansions of wealthy *porteños*. Further south is the port, reached by bus, 15 minutes from terminal. There is a large fishing fleet and a huge sealion colony can be seen from the *Escollera Sur* (southern breakwater). Beyond the port are the **Punta Mogotes** lighthouse, built in 1891 (open Thursday 1330-1700) and the **Bosque Peralta Ramos**, a 400 hectares forest of eucalyptus and conifers.

North of Playa Bristol at **Punta Iglesias** there is a large rock carving of Florentino Ameghino, the palaeontologist. Further north is **Playa La Perla**, with moderately priced hotels. The wooded municipally-owned **Parque Camet**, 8 km north of the centre, has polo grounds and playing fields.

Mar del Plata Orientation

Route 2 to Buenos Aires

Parque Camet

Route II to Santa Clara del Mar, Mar Chiquita & Villa Gesell

Route 226 to Laguna de los Padres & Balcarce

Atlantic Ocean

See detail

Playa La Perla

Route 88 to Necochea

Punta Iglesias

Playa Bristol

Punta Piedras

N

Playa Varese
Cabo Corrientes

Playa Chica

Playa Grande

Port

Escollera Sur

El Bosque Peralta Ramos

Punta Mogotes

0   2
km

Route II to Miramar

Museums

Museo de Hombre del Puerto – Cleto Ciocchini, Padre Dutto 383, Thursday/Friday/Saturday 1500-1900, US$2, shows the history of the port and its first Sicilian fishermen.

Museo Municipal de Ciencias Naturales, Libertad 2999, small but interesting.

Museo Municipal de Arte, Colón 1189, is housed in the Villa Ortíz Basualdo, which dates from 1909; upper floors of the mansion can be visited, art exhibitions on the ground floor, open weekdays except Wednesday 1200-1700, Saturday/Sunday 1400-1900, US$2, free Tuesday.

Centro Cultural Victoria Ocampo, Matheu 1851, is housed in the Villa Victoria, a beautiful early 20th century wooden house prefabricated in England, where the famous author spent her summers until her death in 1979; inside are artefacts from her life and temporary exhibition, daily 1400-2000, US$2, ISIC cards US$1.

Villa Mitre, Lamadrid 3870, in the former mansion of a son of Bartolomé Mitre; inside are an eclectic collection of artefacts including photos of the city at different points in its history.

Excursions

To **Santa Clara del Mar**, a quiet resort 18 km north, where the **Museo Paleontológico Pachamama**, Niza 1065, can be visited. Beyond, 34 km north, is the **Mar Chiquita**, a lagoon joined to the sea by a narrow channel, offering good beaches,

Florentino Ameghino

Born in Luján of Italian parents in 1854, Ameghino started collecting bones and fossils as a boy. Though he lacked any formal scientific training, his reputation spread after he presented his theories to an international congress of archaeologists in Paris in 1878. Before his death in 1911, he published nearly 200 books and articles and became Director of the *Museo de Ciencias Naturales* in La Plata. He aroused great controversy with his theory that humanity originated and spread from the Argentine pampas.

fishing and boating. Also to the Laguna de los Padres and to Balcarce (see below).

Local festivals

10 February (Foundation of City); 10 November (Day of Tradition); 22 November (Sta Cecilia).

Local information
● **Accommodation**

Hotel prices

L1	over US$200	L2	US$151-200
L3	US$101-150	A1	US$81-100
A2	US$61-80	A3	US$46-60
B	US$31-45	C	US$21-30
D	US$12-20	E	US$7-11
F	US$4-6	G	up to US$3

Unless otherwise stated, all hotels in range **D** and above have private bath. Assume friendliness and cleanliness in all cases.

There are over 700 hotels and all other categories of accommodation. During summer months it is essential to book in advance. Many hotels open in season only. Out of season, bargain everywhere. *Provincial*, Boulevard Marítimo 2500, T 916376, 4-star grand hotel overlooking Playa Bristol; **A1** many 4-star including *Argentino*, Belgrano 2225, T 32223, also apartments, highly recommended; *Dos Reyes*, Colón 2129, T 912714; *Hermitage*, Boulevard Marítimo 2657, T 519081, 150 rooms; *Gran Dora*, Buenos Aires 1841, T 912594; *Astor*, Entre Ríos 1649, T 921616, small, no credit cards, 3 minutes from beach.

Among the 3-star hotels (**A2**) are: *Benedetti*, Colón 2198, T 30031/2, recommended; *Gran Continental*, Córdoba 1929, T 48432; *Presidente*, Corrientes 1516, T 28819; **A3** *O Sole Mío*, Avenida Independencia 1277, T 26685, half board, Italian run, highly recommended.

B *Cosmos*, Buenos Aires 2481, T 933544, with breakfast; **B** *Boedo*, Almirante Brown 1771,

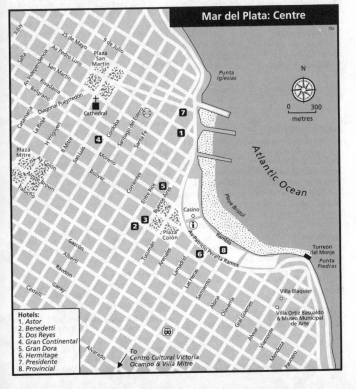

Mar del Plata: Centre

Hotels:
1. Astor
2. Benedetti
3. Dos Reyes
4. Gran Continental
5. Gran Dora
6. Hermitage
7. Presidente
8. Provincial

Bathing in the 19th century

The fashion for bathing spread from Europe to Argentina in the late 19th century; just as in Europe it raised moral concerns as the *Reglamento de Baño* (Bathing Regulations) of 1888 indicated:

● "Unaccompanied men may not approach bathing women but must maintain a distance of at least 30m."
● "Nude bathing is forbidden. The bathing costume **must** cover the body from the neck to the knees."
● "The use of theatre or opera glasses or similar is forbidden during bathing hours."
● "It is prohibited to use words or actions which are dishonest or contrary to decorum."

Breaches of the Regulations could lead to a fine of 2 to 5 pesos or imprisonment for 24-48 hours for a first offence (and 5 to 10 pesos or 48-96 hours imprisonment for a second offence). A third offence could lead to the offender being banned from the beaches for a month.

T 24695, hot water, good value, near beaches (open January-February only); **B** *Canciller*, Gascon 1639, T 512513, with breakfast; **B** *Sousas*, Alsina y Rawson, T/F 511549, without breakfast; **B** *Piemonte*, Buenos Aires 2447, T 954113, with breakfast, good beds; **C** *Monterrey*, Lamadrid 2627, T 23266, good; **C** *Niza*, Santiago del Estero 1843 (**E** out of season), safe, recommended.

Budget accommodation: the area around the bus terminal is full of cheaper places: try especially Alberti, Sarmiento and La Madrid. **B** *Alpino*, Balcarce y La Rioja, T 931034, with breakfast, family run, clean, central, open all year; **B** *Europa*, Arenales 2735, T 40436, quiet, hot water; **C** *Hosp Paraná*, Lamadrid 2749, T 42825; **C** *Paley*, Alberti 1752, T 955036, comfortable, open all year, recommended, good value restaurant; **D** pp *Lima*, Sarmiento 2452, T 518895, without breakfast, poor beds; **D** pp *Wilton Palace*, Las Heras, T 514456, without breakfast, adequate; **D** pp *Ushuaia*, Gascón 1561, T 510911, with breakfast, pleasant.

Apartment rental: There are many houses and apartments for rent. Monthly rates for summer exclude electricity, gas etc. Flats US$4,200-600, chalets US$550-1,000, houses US$800-1,800. The tourist office has a list of companies.

Youth hostels   D pp *Pergamino*, Tucumán 2728, T 957927, near terminal, friendly, clean, small IYHA discount.

Camping *Pinar de la Serena*, Ruta Provincial 11 y Calle 3. Near Punta Mogotes are *El Griego*, 3 km, T 823471, also cabins, cycle hire; *El Faro*, 1.5 km, T 660268, also cabins. Other sites, reasonable prices. Several on the road south.

● **Places to eat**
There are many seafood restaurants in the modern Centro Comercial Puerto, three blocks from the fishing port. *El Caballito Blanco*, Rivadavia 2534, excellent, German decor; *Gruta de Capri*, Belgrano 2161, not cheap but excellent value; *La Paella*, Entre Ríos 2025, good. Seafood restaurants in the Centro Comercial Puerto including *La Caracola*, good but not cheap; *La Piazetta*, Plaza San Martín, good pasta and salads, vegetarian options; *Teresa*, San Luis 2081, fresh pasta dishes, good value; *Lo de Terri*, Gascón y San Luis, good *parrilla*; *Raviolandia*, Colón y Las Heras, good, cheap, try the seafood with rice. Many *tenedor libre* restaurants of all kinds along San Martín. *Los Inmortales*, Corrientes 1662, good, moderately priced. Good value meals at *La Nueva Glorieta*, Alberti 1821, and *El Nuevo Hispano*, Alberti 1933. Many cheap restaurants along Rivadavia.
Vegetarian: *El Jardín*, San Martín 2463, *tenedor libre*, and *La Huerta*, San Martín 2300.

● **Bars**
Marienplatz, Belgrano y Entre Rios, most stylish *confitería* in town, highly recommended but expensive; smart bars around Calle Alem, popular in summer and weekends.

● **Airline offices**
Aerolineas Argentinas, Rambla Hotel Provincial, Local 1, T 28725; **Austral**, Rambla Hotel Provincial, Local 65.

● **Banks & money changers**
Lloyds Bank, Avenida Luro 3101. Open 1000-1600, cash advances on Visa. *Casas de Cambio* **Jonestur**, San Martín 2574, best rates for travellers' cheques; **Amex**, Colón 2605, does not cash travellers' cheques; **La Moneta**, Rivadavia

Victoria Ocampo

Born into a wealthy Buenos Aires family in 1890, Victoria Ocampo was an essayist and critic who used her wealth to support the arts. In 1931 she launched *Sur*, a cultural journal and later opened a publishing house of the same name. She argued that the aim of Argentine writing should be to blend and mix the modern literatures from all over the world. Her magazine sought to offer these bridges between cultures through translation (see her own translations of Virginia Woolf, one of her literary models). Ocampo also wrote a highly evocative autobiography and 26 volumes of essays which stressed quotation, translation and interpretation of the universal literary canon in an accessible, almost conversational style.

Her work earned her recognition as the first woman to be elected to the Argentine Academy of Literature. Important writers, including Albert Camus, Graham Greene, Aldous Huxley and Rabindranath Tagore, were made welcome at her house and had their works published by her.

An outspoken opponent of both Fascism and Communism, she came into conflict with Juan Domingo and Evita Perón: her imprisonment in 1953 led to a storm of protest abroad. Though she supported women's suffrage and feminism, she was attacked by the left for what they regarded as her elitist views and for her hostility to the Castro regime in Cuba. Argentine nationalists were equally hostile, criticizing her as *extrangerizante* (a lover of everything foreign).

2623; **Mar del Plata Cambio**, Buenos Aires 1910; Visa ATM, Santa Fe y Rivadavia.

● **Cultural centres**
La Cultura (formerly Sociedad de Cultura Inglesa), San Luis 2498, friendly, extensive library.

● **Entertainment**
Reduced price tickets are often available for theatre performances etc from *Cartelera Baires*, Santa Fe 1844, local 33 or from *Galería de los Teatros*, Santa Fe 1751.

Casino Central: open December to end-April, 1600-0330; 1600-0400 on Saturday. Winter opening, May-December, Monday-Friday 1500-0230; weekends 1500-0300. Entrance US$5. Three other casinos operate in summer.

Cinemas: *Cine Arte* at Centro Cultural Pueyrredón, 25 de Mayo y La Rioja, every Monday, US$1.50, followed by discussion; Wednesday 50% discount at all cinemas.

Discos: most are on Avenida Constitución.

● **Laundry**
Laverap, Buenos Aires 2680, Colón 1716, Entre Ríos y Rivadavia and Moreno y Corrientes.

● **Post & telecommunications**
Post Office: Luro 2460, poste restante, also international parcels office (open till 1200).

Telecommunications: Luro y Santiago del Estero; many *locutorios* around the town.

● **Sports**
Fishing: fishing is good all along the coast and *pejerrey, corvina* and *pescadilla* abound; you can charter a private launch for shark fishing.

● **Tourist offices**
Boulevard Marítimo 2267, T 41325, open 0800-2000 (later in summer), English spoken, good information, including bus routes to all sites of interest; kiosk in Plaza San Martín.

● **Tours & boat trips**
City tours leave from Plaza San Martín and Plaza Colón. Tours also to Miramar and the sierras. Boat trips visiting Isla de los Lobos, Playa Grande, Cabo Corrientes and Playa Bristol leave from the harbour, US$7, 40 minutes, summer and weekends in winter. Longer cruises on the *Anamora*, 1130, 1400, 1600, 1800, US$10, T 840103.

● **Useful addresses**
Immigration Office: Chile y Alberti, open am.

● **Transport**
Local Car hire: **Primer Mundo**, Jujuy 967, T 739817; **Rent A Car Internacional**, Hotel Dora, Buenos Aires 1841, T 910033; **Weekend**, H Yrigoyen 1967, T 922627; **Dollar**, Córdoba 2270, T 933461; **Avis**, at airport, T 702100; **Budget**, Bolívar 2628, T 956579. Rates for small Fiat including insurance and tax start at US$65 per day. Also **cycle hire**.

Air Camet airport, 10 km north of town. Many flights daily to **Buenos Aires**, Austral, Lapa (T 922112) and AR. Southern Winds to **Córdoba**, **Tucumán** and **Salta**. *Remise* taxi from airport to town, mini bus US$3.50.

Juan Manuel Fangio: gentleman of the track

👣 Considered by many the greatest racing driver of all time, Juan Manuel Fangio was born in Balcarce of Italian immigrants in 1911. His racing debut came in 1936 in a modified taxi but the suspension of the sport in the Second World War interrupted his career and he was aged 37 before he raced in Europe. Despite this he won the world championship in 1951 and dominated the sport until he suddenly retired in 1958, arguing that champions, actors and dictators should always quit at the top.

Fangio's record is still unrivalled: he won the world championship a record five times, four of them in succession (1954-1957). He won 24 of the 51 Grand Prix races he entered and 102 of the 186 international races he drove in. His greatest triumph came in the German Grand Prix in 1957: after a pit-stop left him nearly a minute behind the leaders, he broke the lap record nine times to win, despite having to wedge himself into the car with his knees after the seat broke. At Monaco in 1950, noticing that the crowd were not watching him as he approached a bend, he braked and was able to avoid a pile up of cars around the corner.

Long before his international triumphs Fangio was a legend in Argentina. In the early 1940s a tango described him as "king of the wheel" though some people later criticized him for cooperating too much with Perón. In 1958 Fidel Castro's guerrillas kidnapped him in Cuba, but he was released 2 days later and reported that they served his breakfast in bed.

In an epoch when drivers competed for the sake of the sport and gave way to faster rivals with a smile and a wave of the hand, Fangio was renowned for his humility and sense of fairness. A modest family man, he was never accused of driving dangerously. However, foul play can take many forms. Before one important European Grand Prix, Fangio's rivals sent a beauty queen to his room to ensure he would have a short night's sleep. No one knows what ensued, but next day Fangio drove as though he had slept like a log all night, and maybe he really had.

After his retirement from racing, he returned to Balcarce to live in the house where he had been born. He died in 1995.

With thanks to Federico Kirbus.

Train To **Buenos Aires** (Constitución) from Estación Norte, Luro 4599, about 13 blocks from the centre. Buses to/from centre 511, 512, 512B, 541. Services at 0750, 1020, 1715, 1820, Superpullman US$40, Pullman US$25, First US$19, Tourist US$14. Booking offices in bus terminal, Monday-Saturday 0800-2000 and at Córdoba y Rivadavia. To Miramar, from Estación Sur, J B Justo y Olazábal, daily except Sunday, 0500, 1830, 1½ hours.

Buses Terminal in former railway station at Alberti y Las Heras, central. To **Buenos Aires**, 6 hours, US$26, Micromar, Costera Criolla, also has coche cama, Empresa Argentina, Chevallier; to **Miramar**, hourly, 45 minutes, US$4; El Cóndor and Rápido Argentino to **La Plata**, US$20; La Estrella to **San Martín de los Andes**, US$56; to **Bariloche**, US$60 (none direct, change at Bahía Blanca or Tres Arroyos); to **Bahía Blanca**, only Pampa, 6 daily, US$25, 5½ hours; to **San Clemente del Tuyú**, Empresa Costamar,

frequent, US$11, 5 hours. To **Puerto Madryn** and **Trelew**, Wednesday and Saturday night. For hitchhiking south, take a colectivo to the monument to El Gaucho.

INLAND FROM MAR DEL PLATA

Route 226 runs northwest to Balcarce and Tandil. The **Reserva Provincial Laguna de los Padres** (entry 19 km from Mar del Plata), contains a reconstruction of the **Reducción de Nuestro Señora del Pilar**, a Jesuit mission founded in 1746 and abandoned due to Indian attacks in 1751. Nearby in the park is the **Estancia Laguna de los Padres**, which houses the **Museo Tradicionalista José Hernández**; the writer lived here as a youth and his experiences are said to have inspired Martín Fierro. One section of the park is a natural reserve protecting the *curro*, a rare spikey bush. At Sierra de los Padres, Km 33, there is a mini-zoo and golf club. The **Laguna Brava**, Km 38, at the foot of the Balcarce hills, offers *pejerrey* fishing.

Balcarce

(*Population* 32,000; *Altitude* 108m) 68 km west of Mar del Plata, is a centre for visits to the Cerros Cinco Dedos, five strangely shaped hills. Balcarce is the birthplace of Juan Fangio: just off the Plaza Libertad is the **Museo Juan Manuel Fangio**, which houses all his trophies including a silver cup the same height as Fangio himself. Also on display are many of the racing cars he drove as well as photos and other artefacts associated with the sport. Open daily 1100-1800, US$5, recommended.

- **Accommodation** B *Balcarce*, Calle 17, T 22055, good.

- **Transport** Frequent buses from Mar del Plata.

MIRAMAR

(*Population* 17,500; *Phone code* 0563) Lies 53 km southwest of Mar del Plata along the coast road. Known as the 'city of bicycles', it is cheaper than Mar del Plata; the cliffs backing the beach are higher and the surrounding hills more picturesque. Founded in 1888, the town was badly damaged by storms in 1911 and 1921. There is a fine golf course at *Hotel Golf Roca* and a casino. Immediately south of the city limits is the **Vivero Dunícola Florentino Ameghino**, an 502 hectare forest park on the beach whose vegetation stays green and blooming throughout the year, despite winter night-time temperatures below freezing. Inside the park is the **Museo Municipal**, with displays of animal fossils and of Querandí Indian artefacts.

Mar del Sur, 14 km south, among dunes and black rocks (*Hotel Boulevard Atlántico*) is a peaceful resort with good fishing in a lagoon and bathing on the beach.

- **Accommodation** Dozens of hotels and apartments. B *Santa Eulalia I*, Calle 26 No 851, T 20808, friendly but run down; B *Villa Cruz*, Calle 19, No 864, friendly, clean, near the beach; *Gran*, Calle 29, No 586 esquina 12, T 20358, 2-star; *Palace*, Calle 23, No 774, T 20258, 3-star. **Camping** F pp *El Durazno*,

3 km from town, good facilities, shops, restaurant, take bus 501 marked 'Playas'. Many sites, reasonably priced.

- **Tourist offices** On central plaza, has maps.

- **Transport Trains** Ferrobus daily except Sunday to Mar del Plata, 0630, 2000. **Buses** To Buenos Aires, Chevallier, Micromar and Costera Criolla, 8 a day, US$31; to Mar del Plata, US$4, Rápido del Sud, Pampa; to Necochea, Pampa.

NECOCHEA

(*Population* 60,000; *Phone code* 0262) Situated about 110 km further southwest along the coast, is another famous resort, known as the 'Pearl of the South': its 24 km long beach is one of the best in the country. There is a large Danish community, Danish club and consulate. The town which lies on the west bank of the Río Quequén, is in two parts, with the centre 2 km inland from the seafront area. On the opposite bank of the river lies **Quequén** (*Population* 14,000), one of the most important grain exporting ports in the country. The two towns are linked by three bridges, one of them a 270 km hanging bridge built in Cherbourg in 1929.

Places of interest

In the seafront area of Necochea, four blocks southwest of the Plaza San Martín, is the **Parque Miguel Lillo** (named after the Argentine botanist), comprising

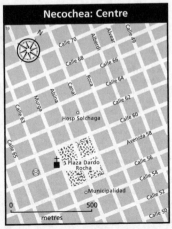

Necochea: Centre

0   500
metres

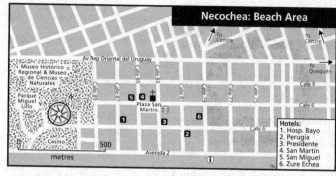

Necochea: Beach Area

Hotels:
1. Hosp. Bayo
2. Perugia
3. Presidente
4. San Martín
5. San Miguel
6. Zure Echea

nearly 600 hectares of conifers, nature park, swan lake with paddle boats, an amphitheatre, go-cart track and two museums: the **Museo Histórico Regional** and the **Museo de Ciencias Naturales**. Nearby there is a municipal recreation complex, with a large casino deteriorating in the salt air (open summer daily and winter weekends 2200-0400), various sports facilities, including skating rink, swimming pool, bowling, a cinema, discoteque and children's play area. East of Quequén harbour there is a lighthouse built in 1921 (open daily 1600-2000) and fine beaches, particularly the Balneario La Villazón.

Excursions

Southeast of Necochea are miles of sanddunes, little visited by tourists. Visits can also be made up the Río Quequén to the Cascadas de Quequén, small waterfalls 13 km north; nearby is the forested Parque Cura-Meucó.

Local information
● Accommodation
The Hotel Association is at Avenida 79 y Calle 4. Most hotels are in the seafront area from Calle 2 (parallel with beach) north between Avenida 71-91. There are at least 100 within 700m of the beach. Most close off-season when it is worth bargaining. Best is *Presidente*, Calle 4 No 4040, T 23800, F 25974, 4-star; **A3** *Hostería del Bosque*, Calle 89 No 350, T/F 20002, five blocks from beach, quiet, upper rooms better, nice bar and garden, parking next door. On Plaza San Martin: *San Miguel*, Calle 85 No 301, T/F 25155, open all year and *San Martín*, Calle 6 No 4198, T/F 37000, restaurant, open all year; **A3** *Perugia*, Calle 81, No 288, T 22020,

air conditioning, open all year; **B** *Asturias*, San Martín 842, T 24524; **B** *Doramar*, Calle 83, No 329, T 25815, family run, helpful; **D** *Zure Echea*, Calle 79 No 355, T 22167, open all year; **E** *Hosp Bayo*, Calle 87, No 338, T 23334.

In the Centre: C *Hosp Solchaga*, Calle 62, No 2822, T 25584, excellent, open all year; **C** *Center*, Calle 59, No 2966, T 22013; **D** *Gala*, Calle 57, No 2815, T 22447. Several in Quequén including *Costa Azul*, *Continental*, *Quequén*. The tourist office has a list of companies which rent apartments.

Camping *Río Quequén*, Calle 22 y Ribera Río Quequén, T 22145, sports facilities, bar, cycle hire; *Las Grutas*, Avenida 2 y Las Grutas; *Puelches*, Calle 111 y Avenida 32, 500m from sea, pool. Campsites on beach reported expensive in season. Also in Quequén are: *Doble Jota*, Calle 502 y 529, T 26058; *Monte Pasuvio*, Calle 502 sin número, T 26064; *El Gringo*, Calle 519 y 520, T 25449.

● Places to eat
Centro Basko, Calle 65, T 24939, typically Basque, good; *Rex*, Calle 62, 'a trip to 1952 Paris', not cheap.

● Post & telecommunications
Post Office: in centre, Avenida 58, No 3086, near beach, Calle 6, No 4099.

Telecommunications: *Telefónica*, Calle 61, No 2432.

● Language schools
Instituto Argentino de Idiomas, Galería Monviso, local 8, Calle 62 y 63, recommended.

● Sport
Fishing: for fishing by boats three companies: *La Trucha*, Calle 10 y Calle 59, T 28601; *El Gordo*, Calle 10, No 3060, T 27812; *El Cornalito*, Calle 59, No 441, T 29570.

Horseriding: *Caballo's*, Villa Marítima Zabala y Avenida 10, T 23138.

● **Tourist offices**
On beach front at Avenida 79 y Avenida 2, T 38333, English spoken. **ACA**, Avenida 59, No 2073, T 22106.

● **Transport**
Air Airport 12 km northwest of town. To **Buenos Aires**, Aerolineas Argentinas and LAER, US$60-80.

Train Station in Quequén. To **Buenos Aires** (Constitución) daily, 7 hours, Pullman US$17, First US$12, Tourist US$10; additional service Monday, Wednesday, Friday.

Buses Terminal at Avenida 47 y Calle 582, 4 km from the centre; bus 513, 517 from outside the terminal to the beach. Taxi to beach area US$3. To **Buenos Aires**, US$44, La Estrella, Plus-Mar and Costera Criolla; to **Mar del Plata**, Pampa, US$10; to **Bahía Blanca**, Pampa, US$22; to **Tres Arroyos** US$10.

TRES ARROYOS

(*Population* 44,500; *Altitude* 107m; *Phone code* 0983) 141 km west of Necochea, lies in an important cattle and wheat growing area. The town was a centre of Dutch immigration (Dutch consulate and school). There is also an important Danish colony, with school, club and consulate. Around the Plaza San Martín are the **Municipalidad**, in French Bourbon style, and the **Iglesia Nuestra Señora de Carmen**, which is vaguely French gothic. The **Museo de Bellas Artes**, a block southwest, contains a collection of paintings by Argentine artists.

South of Tres Arroyos are three pleasant resorts. **Claromecó**, reached by a 68 km paved road, is a fishing port with a beautiful beach of dark sand backed by high dunes. **Orense**, further east, is a centre for watersports, including surfing, wind-surfing and water-skiing. **Reta**, west of Claromecó, is set among eucalyptus and pine plantations.

● **Accommodation & places to eat At Tres Arroyos**: **A3** *Parque*, Pellegrini 23, T 31350, restaurant, recommended; **B** *Alfil*, Rivadavia 140, T 27002, restaurant; *Andrea*, Istilart 228, T 26214, good. *Restaurant Di Troppo*, Moreno 133, good; *Tres Amigos*, Chacabuco 102, popular *parrilla*. **At Claromecó**: several hotels and restaurants. **Camping at Claromecó**: good campsite, *Dunamar*, ACA, US$6 per person, hot showers, fire pits and laundry facilities.

● **Buses** Modern terminal on the outskirts of Tres Arroyos. To Claromecó twice daily off season, extra buses from mid-December in season; to Mar del Plata, Pampa, 4½ hours. From Buenos Aires to Claromecó, La Estrella, US$40.

BAHIA BLANCA

(*Population* 260,000; *Phone code* 091) The most important centre south of Mar del Plata and an important route centre, stands at the head of a large bay at the mouth of the Río Naposta. The major grain exporting port in the country, the city is also Argentina's most important petrochemical centre. South of the city are several ports, the most important of which are Puerto Ingeniero White, which handles oil and chemicals, and Puerto Galván (grain). Puerto Belgrano, 29 km southeast, is Argentina's most important naval base.

History

Bahía Blanca was founded in 1828 as a fort, the **Fortaleza Protectora Argentina**, both to control Indian cattle rustling and to protect the coast from Brazil whose navy had landed in the area in 1827. Though the native population of the area was defeated in the campaigns of Rosas, the fortress was attacked several times, notably by 3,000 Calfucurá warriors in 1859. An important centre of European immigration, it became a major port with the building of railways connecting it with grain-producing areas of the pampas.

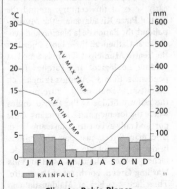

Climate: Bahía Blanca

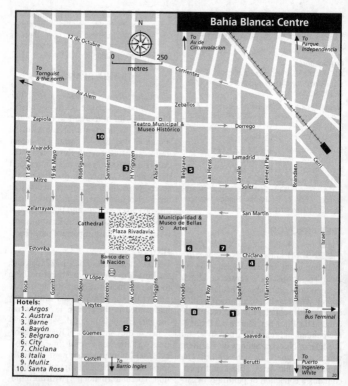

Bahía Blanca: Centre

Hotels:
1. Argos
2. Austral
3. Barne
4. Bayón
5. Belgrano
6. City
7. Chiclana
8. Italia
9. Muñiz
10. Santa Rosa

Places of interest

The major public buildings date from the early years of this century: around the central **Plaza Rivadavia** are the **Municipalidad**, the **Banco de la Nación** and neoclassical **Cathedral**; three blocks north is the **Teatro Municipal**. There is a modest **Jardín Zoológico** in Parque Independencia, Ruta 3 y Avenida Pringles, on the outskirts. South of the centre, just over the railway bridge is the **Barrio Inglés** where the foremen and technicians of the port and railway construction teams lived; Brickman Street, just past the railway bridge, is a row of late Victorian semi-detached houses. Managers lived at **Villa Harding Green**, northeast of the centre. There are beaches at Maldonado and Colón, both 3 km south of the city.

Museums

Museo del Puerto, Torres y Carrega, at Ingeniero White, in former customs building, excellent displays of domestic artefacts from the early 20th century. Serves as a *confitería* on Sunday. Bus 500, 504. Highly recommended. Monday-Friday 0900-1200, Saturday/Sunday 1530-1930.

Museo Histórico, in the Teatro Municipal, Alsina 425, including sections on the pre-conquest period, the conquest and interesting photos of early Bahía Blanca. Daily 1600-2000. Outside is a statue of Garibaldi, erected by the Italian community in 1928.

Museo de Bellas Artes, in basement of Municipalidad, Alsina 65, small, free. Tuesday-Saturday 0930-1300, Thursday-Sunday 1600-2000.

Museo de Arte Contemporánea, Sarmiento 450, Tuesday-Friday 1000-1300, 1600-2000.

Excursions

To **Puerto Belgrano**, Argentina's most important naval base, 29 km southeast, which can be visited daily.

To **Pehuén-Có**, a quiet resort 84 km southeast, reached by a turning off Route 3; accommodation is available in the *Hotel Cumelcan* and there are several campsites.

To **Monte Hermoso** (*Population* 2,900), another fine resort 106 km east. Near Monte Hermoso are Sauce Grande, another resort 4 km east along the coast road and Laguna Sauce Grande, a large lake 10 km northeast, where there is *pejerrey* fishing and boats can be hired.

● **Accommodation** Several hotels including *La Goleta*, Costanera y Calle 10, T 81142, 3-star; *América*, Valle Encantado 91, T 81005; *Santa Isabel*, Bahía Blanca 55, T 81030. Hotels open only January-March. **Camping** Several sites including *El Americano*, good facilities, and *las Dunas*, 30 minutes' walk west along the beach, US$3 per person, a friendly spot run by an elderly German couple.

Local holidays

11 April (Foundation of the City); 24 September (Our Lady of Mercy); 10 November (Day of Tradition).

Local information
● **Accommodation**

Most hotels charge extra for parking. **A1** *Austral*, Colón 159, T 20241, F 553737, 4-star, restaurant; **A3** *Ameghino*, Valle Encantado 60, T 81098, near beach; **A3** *Argos*, España 149, T/F 40001, 3-star; **A3** *ACA Motel Villa Borden*, Avenida Sesquicentenario, entre Rutas 3 y 35, T 40151, T 21098; **A3** *Santa Rosa*, Sarmiento 373, T/F 20012.

B *Belgrano*, Belgrano 44, T/F 20240/30498, without breakfast, restaurant; **B** *City*, Chiclana 226, T 30178, without breakfast, overpriced; *Italia*, Brown 181, T 20121, simple, restaurant; *Muñiz*, O'Higgins 23, T 20021, central; **B** *Barne*, H Yrigoyen 270, T 30864, F 550513, with breakfast, helpful, family run, recommended; **B** *Bayón*, Chiclana 487, T 22504, safe; **B** *Victoria*, Gral Paz 82, T 20522, basic, hot water, recommended.

C *Chiclana*, Chiclana 370, T 30436, **D** without bath, basic, poor beds; **C** *Del Sur*, 19 de Mayo 75, T 22452, with restaurant, noisy with traffic; **C** *Res Roma*, Cerri 759, T 38500, cheaper without bath; **C** *Hosp Andrea*, Lavalle 88, air conditioning; **D** *Los Angeles*, Chiclana 367, basic. Other *residenciales* near railway station, eg **D** *Los Vascos*, Cerri 747, T 29290.

Camping *Balneario Maldonado*, 4 km south, T 29511, US$5 per tent, US$1 per person, next to petrochemical plant, salt water swimming pool, bus 514 along Avenida Colón every hour but only when beach is open, ie when sunny and not in evening. *Cala Gogo*, Sarmiento 4000.

● **Places to eat**

La Cigala, Cerri 757, very good; *Il Vesuvio*, San Martín 337, good lunch, cheap; *Sergio*, Gorriti 61, good food, large portions, good value; *Café La Bahía*, Chiclana 548, good value, recommended. A few good fish restaurants at the harbour, eg *Cantina Royal*. Very good seafood and fish at Ingeniero White. *Northwestern Café*, Alsina 236, American bar, pizzas, happy hour 1600-1800.

● **Airline offices**

Aerolineas Argentinas, San Martín 198, T 26934; LADE, Darregueira 21, T 37697; TAN, San Martín 216, Galería Visión 2,000, Local 80, T 33610.

● **Banks & money changers**

Lloyds Bank (BLSA), Chiclana 102; Citibank, Colón 58; Amex, Fortur, Soler 38, T 26290, poste restante, English spoken. Casas de Cambio: Pullman, San Martín 171, changes US$, travellers' cheques to US$ notes, 3% commission on travellers' cheques, good rates (closes 1600); Viajes Bahía Blanca, Drago 63, good rates. All casas de cambio closed at weekends.

● **Consulates**

Chile, Güemes 102, T 550110, F 258803; Italy, Colón 446, T 551633; Spain, Drago 70, T 22549.

● **Laundry**

Laverap, Villarrino 87 and at Perú 122; Daimar, Mitre 184.

● **Post & telecommunications**

Post Office: Moreno 34.

Telephones: Telefónica, O'Higgins 249.

● **Shopping**

Municipal market, Donado 151.

● **Tourist offices**

In town hall on main plaza, Alsina 43, T 550110, F 558803, Monday-Friday 0800-1200. Also in airport in January/February, helpful.

● **Transport**

Local Bus: US$0.65, but you need to buy carnets (cards) from kiosks for 1, 2 or 4 journeys.

Air Comandante Espora, 11 km northeast of centre. Austral and Lapa (T 46566) to **Buenos Aires**. To **Comodoro Rivadavia**, **Río Gallegos** and **Río Grande**, Austral and Kaiken. Lapa and TAN to **Neuquén**.

Train Station at Avenida Gral Cerri 750, T 21168. To **Buenos Aires** (Constitución), via Sierra de la Ventana and Azul, 2000 daily, 12 hours, Sleeper US$39, Pullman US$26, First US$20, Tourist US$17.

Buses Terminal in old railway station 2½ km from centre at Estados Unidos y Brown, T 29616. Buses 505, 514, 517 to centre, no hotels nearby. To **Buenos Aires** frequent, several companies, 10 hours, US$30-34, shop around; to **Mar del Plata**, Río Paraná, US$25, 5½ hours; to **Córdoba**, US$44, 12 hours; to **Neuquén**, 6 a day, 8 hours, US$20; to **Nechea**, Pampa, 5 hours, US$22; to **Zapala**, 3 daily, 11 hours, US$25, El Valle; to **Río Colorado** US$8, **Viedma**, 3 a day, 4 hours; to **Trelew**, 3 a week, US$32, 12 hours; to **Río Gallegos**, Don Otto, US$80.

To **Tornquist**, US$4, 0600, 1300, 1720, 1 hour, last return 2020; to **Sierra de la Ventana** (town) 0600, 2040 (not Saturday).

Hitchhiking South or west from Bahía Blanca is possible but not too easy. Most southbound traffic takes Route 22 via Río Colorado. North to Buenos Aires on Route 3 is 'virtually impossible'.

FROM BAHIA BLANCA TO NEUQUEN

Route 22 runs direct from Bahía Blanca, cutting across the southern tip of La Pampa to **Río Colorado** (campsite with all facilities), on the river of the same name (Bus to Buenos Aires 0100, 11 hours, US$30.) It then runs through northern Río Negro to **Choele Choel** on the Río Negro itself, 308 km from Bahía Blanca. Large fruit growing areas at Choele Choel and Villa Regina are irrigated from the Río Negro dam. An unbroken series of groves of tall trees shelter the vineyards and orchards.

● **Accommodation Choele Choel**: B *ACA Motel* on edge of town, T/F 0946-2394, Ruta Nacional 22, Km 1,006; fine modern *Hotel Choele Choel*; several other hotels. **Camping** Free municipal site beside Río Negro, shady, excellent, no showers. Good restaurant at bus terminal.

The Central Sierras:
Córdoba and San Luis

THE PROVINCES of Córdoba and San Luis are notable for several ranges of hills: while the Sierras de Córdoba are a popular tourist area, the Sierras de San Luis are much less visited. The city of Córdoba, Argentina's second city, has some colonial architecture and is an important route centre, especially for bus travel to the northwest.

GEOGRAPHY

While the pampas extend across southern and eastern Córdoba province and the southern part of San Luis provinces, to the north and west five ranges of hills run from north to south. Further detail of these sierras are given in the text. The two provincial capital cities lie on the edge of these hills, Córdoba to the east and San Luis to the west. North of Córdoba and to the east of the sierras is a broad plateau which declines gently from 600m towards Laguna Mar Chiquita in the northwest of the province.

The sierras are drained by five major rivers flowing east. Though usually known as the Ríos Primero, Segundo, Tercero, Cuarto and Quinto, their prehispanic names are sometimes also used. The two most northerly of these, the Ríos Primero (or Suquía) and Segundo (or Xanaes) flow northeast and empty into Laguna Mar Chiquita, a large inland sea. Further south the Ríos Tercero and Cuarto flow into the Río Saladillo, which as the Río Carcarañá empties into the Paraná. The Río Quinto, the main river draining the Sierras de San Luis,

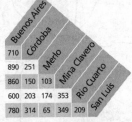

Buenos Aires					
710	Córdoba				
890	251	Merlo			
860	150	103	Mina Clavero		
600	203	174	353	Río Cuarto	
780	314	65	349	209	San Luis

The Central Sierras: distance chart (km)

flows southeast and disappears into the pampas. Two other rivers in San Luis are worth noting, the Río Conlara, which flows north before drying up, and the Río Salado which drains the west of the province and forms the boundary with the province of Mendoza. The main rivers have been dammed forming a number of artificial lakes, which provide irrigation, hydro-electric power and water sports facilities. These are particularly important in Córdoba: the province has 15 dams, nine of which generate electricity.

Of the two provinces, Córdoba has far the higher population, over 75 million; San Luis has under 300,000 inhabitants.

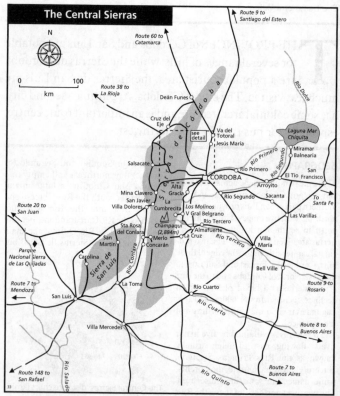

The Jesuits in Córdoba

Though less well known than the missions of Paraguay and the Argentine province of Misiones, Córdoba was one of the most important Jesuit centres in Latin America. The first Jesuits arrived in the city in 1587 and, shortly afterwards Córdoba became the headquarters of the Order's activities in South America. The need to train priests led to the foundation of a Jesuit College in the city, which in 1621 became the University of San Carlos, one of the first universities in the continent. Novices studied Latin, theology and the arts; tuition was free. The University became the focus of local cultural life and by the 18th century *Córdoba Docta* (learned Córdoba) was recognized as the cultural capital of the Viceregency of La Plata.

The cost of maintaining the University with its 40 Jesuit teaching staff was met from the produce of nearby farms and *estancias* which were bequeathed to the University. Several of these can still be seen today: at Alta Gracia, Jesús María, Santa Catalina and La Candelaria.

CLIMATE

This area enjoys a dry continental climate. Average daily temperature in the two provincial capitals range from 4° to 18° in winter and from 17° to 30° in summer, but temperatures are lower in the sierras and higher in the plains to the south and east. Rainfall occurs mainly in summer, being higher in the sierras and lower in the plains where it drops to 200 mm a year. Some areas in the sierras, notably Merlo, enjoy special microclimates. The city of San Luis is noted for a strong southerly wind, the *Viento Chorrillero*, which blows almost daily.

ECONOMY

The city of Córdoba is one of the most important industrial centres in the country, the home of Argentina's car and aviation industries: there are Renault, Iveco and Fiat car plants, as well as a Lockheed aircraft maintenance centre. While the south and east of Córdoba province and the south of San Luis province are areas of cereal production and cattle ranching, agriculture in the sierras is more varied with olives, vines, cotton and honey being produced. The sierras are also of growing importance for mining, marble being extensively mined in Córdoba, wolfram, quartz, feldspar, mica, graphite, onyx and gold in San Luis.

CORDOBA

(*Population* 1.2 million; *Altitude* 440m; *Phone code* 051) Córdoba, Situated on the Río Primero, is capital of Córdoba Province and Argentina's second largest city. It is a major route centre and industrial city. Though it has several important colonial buildings, it is a busy modern city with two universities and a flourishing shopping centre. Despite the size of the modern city, the old centre around Plaza San Martín is relatively peaceful.

History

Founded in 1573 by an expedition from Santiago del Estero led by Jerónimo Luis

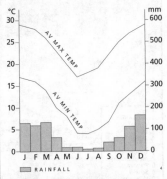

Climate: Córdoba

de Cabrera, Córdoba was an important city in colonial times, situated at the junction of the routes from Chile and Alto Peru to Buenos Aires. In 1810 when Buenos Aires backed independence, the leading figures of Córdoba voted to remain loyal to Spain. After independence the city was a stronghold of opposition to Buenos Aires. Since the 1940s Córdoba has grown from a cultural, administrative and communications centre into a large industrial city.

Places of interest

A walking tour of the old city Most of the older buildings lie within a few blocks of the **Plaza San Martín**, which has a fine statue of the Liberator. On the west side is the former **Cabildo**, dating from 1610 and built around two interior patios. It has served as a prison, courthouse, local legislature and police headquarters. Part is now occupied by tourist offices; the interior patios form the Casa de la Cultura. Next to it stands the **Cathedral**, the oldest in Argentina, built 1697-1782, with a neo-baroque interior, attractive stained-glass

windows and a richly-decorated ceiling: see the remarkable cupola. Just south of the Cathedral at Independencia 122 is the 17th century **Carmelite convent** and chapel of **Santa Teresa**. The convent, dating from 1628, has a fine portal built in 1770.

From Plaza San Martín walk west one block to the pleasant **Plaza del Fundador**, where there is a statue to the city founder Jerónimo Luís de Cabrera. On the west side of the Plaza is the convent and church of **Santa Catalina de Siena**, founded in 1613 but rebuilt in the late 19th century. From here walk two blocks south along Obispo Trejo to the former Jesuit church of **La Compañía**. Though its façade was rebuilt in the 20th century, the church dates from about 1650: the barrel vaulted ceiling and cupola of its Capilla Doméstica, built entirely of Paraguayan cedar, are unique. Next to La Compañía are two other former Jesuit institutions, the main building of the **Universidad Nacional de Córdoba** and the **Colegio Nacional de Montserrat**. One block west of the latter at Vélez Sarsfield 351 is the neo-classical **Teatro Libertador**

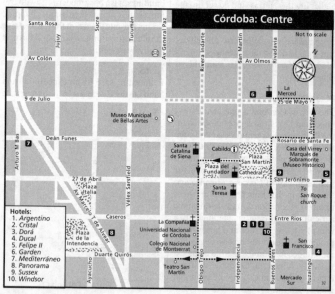

Córdoba: Centre

Not to scale

Hotels:
1. *Argentino*
2. *Cristal*
3. *Dorá*
4. *Ducal*
5. *Felipe II*
6. *Garden*
7. *Mediterráneo*
8. *Panorama*
9. *Sussex*
10. *Windsor*

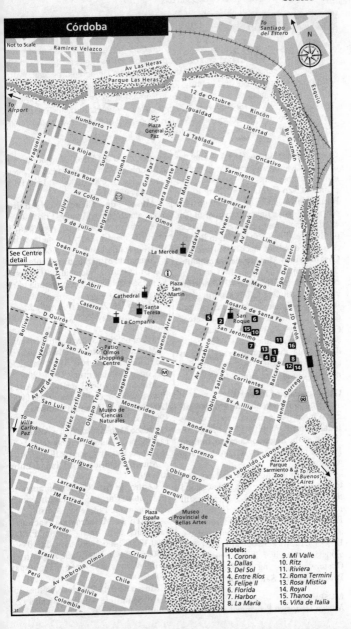

Córdoba

Not to Scale

N

To Santiago del Estero

To Airport

To Villa Carlos Paz

To Buenos Aires

Ramírez Velazco
Av Las Heras
Parque Las Heras
12 de Octubre
Igualdad
Rincón
Humberto 1°
Plaza General Paz
La Tablada
Libertad
La Rioja
Sucre
Tucumán
Oncativo
Santa Rosa
Av Gral Paz
San Martín
Sarmiento
Jujuy
Av Colón
Belgrano
Catamarca
9 de Julio
Av Olmos
Rivera Indarte
Av Maipú
Lima
Deán Funes
Rivadavia
Alvear
Salta
La Merced
25 de Mayo
Sgo Del Estero
27 de Abril
Plaza San Martín
Esquiú
Bv Guzmán
Cathedral
Caseros
Santa Teresa
Rosario de Santa Fe
San Roque
La Compañía
San Jerónimo
D Quirós
Bv San Juan
Patio Olmos Shopping Centre
Entre Ríos
Bolívar
Ayacucho
Buenos Aires
Av Chacabuco
Obispo Salguero
Corrientes
Balcarce
Allende Dorrego
Av MT de Alvear
Av Vélez Sarsfield
Independencia
Bv A Illia
San Luis
Obispo Trejo
Montevideo
Museo de Ciencias Naturales
Av H Yrigoyen
Laprida
Ituzaingó
Rondeau
Parană
Rodríguez
San Lorenzo
Larrañaga
Obispo Oro
Av Leopoldo Lugones
Parque Sarmiento & Zoo
JM Estrada
Derqui
Peredo
Plaza España
Museo Provincial de Bellas Artes
Brasil
Crisol
Perú
Av Ambrosio Olmos
Chile
Bolivia
Colombia

MT Alvear
Fragueiro
Achaval

See Centre detail

Hotels:
1. Corona
2. Dallas
3. Del Sol
4. Entre Ríos
5. Felipe II
6. Florida
7. Harbor
8. La María
9. Mi Valle
10. Ritz
11. Riviera
12. Roma Termini
13. Rosa Mística
14. Royal
15. Thanoa
16. Viña de Italia

Radical Córdoba

Always at odds with Buenos Aires, Córdoba has acquired a reputation for opposition to the central government and support for the Radical party. Its most famous hour came in 1969 when disturbances in the city ignited opposition to military rule throughout the country. The *Cordobazo* of May 1969 began with student protests in support of their fellows in Corrientes, but gained support among the car workers who took over the city and were only defeated by the use of the army. More recently, Córdoba has been the stronghold of Radical party opposition to the Peronist government of Carlos Menem.

General San Martín (1891). From the Colegio Nacional walk two blocks east to Calle Buenos Aires; the convent and church of **San Francisco** at Entre Ríos y Buenos Aires, dating from the late 18th century, contains fine examples of Indian woodcarving. From here walk two blocks north across Plaza San Martín to Rosario de Santa Fe and one block east to reach the **Casa del Virrey Marqués de Sobramonte**, the sole remaining colonial house in the city which houses the Museo Histórico Provincial. Continue one block north along Ituzaingó and then one block west along 9 de Julio to reach the basilica of **La Merced** at 25 de Mayo 83; built in the early 19th century, it has a fine gilt wooden pulpit dating from the colonial period. On its exterior, overlooking Rivadavia, are fine murals by local artist Armando Sica.

Other places of interest

The church of **San Roque**, Obispo Salguero y San Jerónimo, is notable for its Indian-carved pulpit. The neo-gothic church of the **Sagrado Corazón**, built in 1933, at Buenos Aires y Yrigoyen, is also worth a visit.

The magnificent **Mitre railway station**, near the bus terminal, is now closed though its beautiful tiled *confitería* is still in use. South of the centre in the large **Parque Sarmiento** is a good zoo, with animals in clean spacious environments, US$3. On the western outskirts of the city alongside the river is the **Parque del Oeste**, with sporting facilities, and the **Parque General San Martín**.

Museums

Museo Histórico Provincial, in the 18th century Casa del Virrey Marqués de Sobremonte, Rosario de Santa Fe 218, Tuesday-Friday 0900-1300, 1500-1900, Saturday 0900-1300.

Museo de Ciencias Naturales, Yrigoyen 115, open Monday-Friday 0800-1900, Saturday 0900-1200, good guided tours (in Spanish, entry free, 'interesting skeletons of prehistoric glyptodonts').

Museo de Mineralogía y Geología of the Universidad Nacional de Córdoba, Vélez Sarsfield 299, open Monday-Friday, 1400-1600.

Museo de Zoología, same address, open Monday-Friday 0900-1200, Wednesday-Friday 1600-1800, many birds but poorly displayed with no labels.

Museo del Teatro y de la Música, in the Teatro San Martín, Vélez Sarsfield 365, open Monday-Friday 0900-1200.

Museo Provincial de Bellas Artes, Plaza España, open Tuesday-Friday 0900-1300, 1500-2000, Saturday/Sunday 1500-1900, good.

Museo Municipal de Bellas Artes, Gral Paz 33, open Tuesday-Friday 0930-1330, 1630-2030, Saturday/Sunday 1000-2000.

Museo Histórico de la Ciudad, Entre Ríos 40.

Centro de Arte Contemporáneo, in the Chateau Carreras, a late 19th century mansion in the Parque San Martín.

Museo de Meteorología Nacional, San Luis 801, open Tuesday-Friday 0900-1300, 1400-1800, Saturday 0830-1230; nearby in Laprida is Argentina's main observatory, open Wednesday 2000-2200.

Museo de Arte Religioso, in the convent of Santa Teresa, Independencia 122, Saturday 1030-1230.

Local holidays

6 July (Foundation of the City); 30 September (St Jerome), 7-10 October.

Local information

Note that Boulevard Perón is often referred to as Boulevard Reconquista.

● **Accommodation**

Hotel prices

L1	over US$200	**L2**	US$151-200
L3	US$101-150	**A1**	US$81-100
A2	US$61-80	**A3**	US$46-60
B	US$31-45	**C**	US$21-30
D	US$12-20	**E**	US$7-11
F	US$4-6	**G**	up to US$3

Unless otherwise stated, all hotels in range **D** and above have private bath. Assume friendliness and cleanliness in all cases.

More expensive hotels, mainly in the centre: *Córdoba Park*, H Yrigoyen y Boulevard Illia, 4-star, modern; **L3** *Panorama*, Alvear 251, 4-star, good, pool, central, new; **A3** *Cañada*, Alvear 580, T 37589, good, including conference facilities with full technical back-up, air conditioning, restaurant, laundry; **A3** *Windsor*, Buenos Aires 214, T 224012, comfortable, very good. On San Jerónimo: **A2** *Felipe II*, No 279, T 214752, bar, good; **A3** *Ritz*, No 495, T 45031, with breakfast, 'clean but dilapidated'; **A3** *Sussex*, No 125, T 229071, comfortable, roomy, discounts for ACA members; **A3** *Dallas*, No 339, T/F 216091, with breakfast, parking, air conditioning, recommended; **A3** *Viña de Italia*, No 611, T/F 226589, with breakfast, parking, restaurant, good value; **A3** *Del Sol*, Balcarce 144, T 33961, fan, air conditioning extra, recommended; **A2** *ACA Hotel Dr Cesar C Carman*, Avenida Sabattini (Ruta 9) y Bajada del Pucará, T 243565, **A1** for non-members, very good.

Cheaper hotels On Corrientes: **C** *Bristol*, No 64, T 236222, air conditioning; **C** *Res Mi Valle*, No 586, fan, small, nice, family-run, recommended. On San Jerónimo: **B** *Felipe II*, No 279, T 44752, adequate; **B** *Corona*, No 574, T 228789, without breakfast; **D** *La María*, No 628, parking, good value; **D** pp *Rosa Mistica*, No 532, also monthly rates; **E** pp *Res Thanoa*, No 479, T 222807, with bath, old fashioned, good value. On Balcarce: **B** *Mallorca*, No 73, T 39234, quite clean and near bus terminal, noisy; **B** *Riviera*, No 74, T 223969, with breakfast, parking; **D** *El Progreso*, No 140, basic. On Entre Ríos: **B** *Regins*, No 627, T 232825, without breakfast; **B/C** *Roma Termini*, No 687, without breakfast, air conditioning, spotless, welcoming, recommended; **B/C** *Entre Ríos*, No

567, T 230311, with breakfast, parking, family run, good value. **Elsewhere**: **C** *Florida*, Rosario de Santa Fe 459, T 26373, recommended, some rooms with air conditioning; **B** *Royal*, Bv Perón 180, T 215000, F 553492, with breakfast and parking; **B** *Garden*, 25 de Mayo 35, T 44739, central, secure, highly recommended; **C** *Harbor*, Paraná 126, T/F 217300, without breakfast, good value; **E** pp *Gral Paz*, 25 de Mayo 240, with bath, run down, clean.

The following offer 10% discount to ISIC card holders: *del Sol*, Balcarce 144 (see above) and on Arturo Illia, *del Boulevard*, No 182, *Heydi*, No 615.

Camping: Municipal site, Gral San Martín, at the back of the Complejo Ferial (bus 31).

● **Places to eat**

There are numerous places, including grills, suitable for meals out-of-doors when the weather is good in the Cerro de las Rosas district, on the northern outskirts. Many cheap restaurants along San Jerónimo including *San Carlos*, No 431, good food and service; *Casino Español*, Rivadavia 63, good; *La Mamma*, La Cañada y Santa Rosa, excellent Italian, pricey; *Il Gatto*, Gral Paz y 9 de Julio, great pasta and pizzas, reasonably priced; *Romagnolo*, Perón y San Jerónimo, opposite the Mitre railway station, recommended; *Betos*, San Juan 494, best *lomitos* in town, *parrilla*, recommended, pricey; *Fancy Café*, Andarte 317, good, cheap; *Firenze*, 25 de Mayo 220, busy, pleasant, traditional café; *Meeting*, 27 de Abril 248, good café; *Sorocabana*, corner of Plaza San Martín, 24-hour café. Excellent fruit juices (*licuados*) at *Kiosco Americano*, Tucumán 185 and at Gral Paz 242. Good *empanadas* at *La Vieja Esquina*, Belgrano y Caseros; *Empanadería La Alameda*, Obispo Trejo near University, reasonable food, good student atmosphere, set 2200-2400. Ice-cream at branches of *Dolce Neve* throughout town; *Soppelsa's* ice cream is also highly recommended, with several outlets.

● **Airline offices**

Aerolíneas Argentinas, Colón 520, T 216041; Austral, Buenos Aires 59, T 228529; Lapa, Caseros 355, T 220033; LAB and Alitalia, 25 de Mayo 6625, 3rd floor; KLM, General Paz 159.

● **Banks & money changers**

Lloyds Bank (BLSA), Buenos Aires 23; Citibank, Rivadavia 104, poor rates; Banco Sudameris buys Amex travellers' cheques at 1% commission; Banco Feigin for Mastercard; Banco de Galicia on Sucre for Amex cards. Amex, Simonelli Viajes, Alcorta 50, T 26186. Many *cambios* on Rivadavia just off Plaza San Martín; shop around for best rate. See also **Currency** in **Information for travellers** for *bonos*.

● **Cultural centres**

Asociación Argentina de Cultura Británica, San Juan 137, good library, poor reading room, open Monday-Friday 0900-1200, Monday, Wednesday, Friday 1600-1945, Tuesday, Thursday 1500-1945; **Goethe Institut**, Illia 356, open Tuesday-Friday 1700-2100.

● **Consulates**

Austria, J Cortés 636, T 720450; Belgium, F Posse 2533, T 813298; Bolivia, Castro Barros 783, T 732827; Chile, Crisol 280, T 609622; Finland, Chacabuco 716, T 605049; Germany, Eliseo Conton 1870, T 890809 (Honorary Consul: Carlos Oechsle); Italy, Ayacucho 131, T 221020; Paraguay, 9 de Julio 573, T 226388; Peru, Poeta Lugones 212, T 603730. Spain, Chacabuco 875, T 605013; Sweden, Alvear 10, T 240094; Switzerland, Entre Ríos 185, local 10, T 226848.

● **Entertainment**

Cinema: modern multi-screen ones in new shopping centres. *Cine Teatro Córdoba*, 27 de Abril 275, foreign language films, slightly cheaper, nice atmosphere. Programmes in local newspaper, *La Voz del Interior*.

Discotheques: several on Avenida H Yrigoyen, expensive; late night rock music at *Música Pura*, Montevideo 100, Thursday-Saturday. Several in Cerro de las Rosas including *Estación Victorino*, Nuñez y Victorino Rodriguez, fashionable.

Folk music: at *Pulpería El Viejo Rincón*, Dumesnil y Mendoza, excellent music till 0500. **Tango** in *Confitería Mitre*, Mitre railway station, Sunday 2130.

● **Hospitals & medical services**

English-speaking doctor, *Ernesto J MacLoughlin*, Centro Asistencial Privado de Enfermedades Renales, 9 de Julio 714, home Pérez del Viso 4316, T 814745. Dentist, *Dra Olga Olmedo de Herrera*, Fco J Muñiz 274, T 804378, daughter speaks English.

● **Language schools**

Comisión de Intercambio Educativo, San José de Calasanz 151, T 243606, offers classes mainly pre-arranged in Germany. (Contact Kommission für Bildungsaustausch, Wrangelstr 122, DW-2000 Hamburg 20.) *Interswop*, Sucre 2828, Alta Cordoba, T 710081, F 220655, organizes stays abroad and language classes (about US$180 per week, 25 hours of classes) and accommodation at about US$10 per day, also exchange programmes for any nationality. Applications and details: Interswop, Bornstrasse 16, 20146 Hamburg, Germany, T/F 40-410-8029.

● **Laundry**

Chacabuco 320; *Laverap*, Chacabuco 301, Rivera Indarte 285, and Paraná y Rondeau; *La Lavandería*, Avellaneda 182, local 4; also in bus terminal.

● **Post & telecommunications**

Post Office: Colón 201, parcel service on the ground floor beside the customs office.

Telecommunications: General Paz 36 and 27 de Abril 27.

● **Shopping**

In the centre the main shopping area, with lots of *galerías*, is off Plaza San Martín. Three modern shopping malls: *Patio Olmos*, Vélez Sarsfield y San Juan, varied shops, smart; *Córdoba Shopping Centre*, Barrio Villa Cabrera, with good views of the city, 12-screen cinema; *Nuevocentro Shopping*, 4-screen cinema, Avenida Duarte Quirós, Barrio Santa Ana. Handicraft market in Rodríguez y Canada, Saturday/Sunday 1500-2130, ceramics, leather, woodcrafts and metalware. *Librería Blackpool*, Dean Funes 395, for imported English books. Health food shops in *galería* on 27 de Abril opposite Plaza Fundador.

● **Tour companies & travel agents**

Carolina, San Jerónimo 270, local 13/14, good value excursions, minimum of 6 people; *El Delfín*, Gral Paz 250, local 140, 1st floor; *Argentina Turística*, Vélez Sarsfield 30, T/F 234520, recommended; *Alexandria*, Belgrano 194, planta alta, T 237421/247503, for budget travel.

● **Tourist offices**

Dirección Provincial de Turismo, Tucumán 25. Provincial and municipal tourist offices in the old *Cabildo*, on Plaza San Martín. Exhibition of gauchismo on floor above. Offices also at bus station, has free maps, extensive information on accommodation and camping in the province, helpful, open Monday-Friday 0700-2100, Saturday/Sunday 0800-2100, and at airport. For free tourist information (in Spanish) on the province T 0800-4-0107. A useful information booklet is the free monthly, *Plataforma 40*, published by Nueva Estación Terminal de Omnibus de Córdoba (Netoc).

Club Andino: Deán Funes 2100, open Wednesday after 2100, closed January.

● **Transport**

Local Bus: municipal buses and electric buses (trolleys) do not accept cash; you have to buy tokens (*cospeles*) or cards from kiosks, normal US$0.65, *diferencial* US$1.30. **Car hire**: Avis, Corrientes 452, T 227384, F 222483 and airport, T 816473; **A1**, Entre Ríos 70, T 224867; **Budget**, Figeroa Alcorta 50, T 244822; **Dollar,**

Chacabuco 185, T 210426; **Localiza**, Castro Barros 1155, T 747747. At the airport are **Avis**, **A1**, **Hertz**, **Localiza** and **American Remis**.

Air Pajas Blancas airport, 13 km north of city, has shops, post office, a good restaurant and a *casa de cambio* (open Monday-Friday 1000-1500). Taxi to airport, US$15. Minibus (*combi*) service between airport and hotels, US$3, run by Turismo Pampa de Achala, Alvear 481, T/F 254773. Alternatively take local bus No 55 from Santa Rosa y Avellaneda (Plaza Colón), allow 1 hour. Several flights to **Buenos Aires** daily, about 1 hour; Andesmar fly to **Tucumán**, **La Rioja**, **Salta** and **Mendoza**; to **Puerto Iguazú**, Southern Winds, US$147. Southern Winds also fly to **Mendoza**, **Tucumán**, **Salta**, **Neuquén**, **Bariloche**, **Mar del Plata** and **Rosario**. AR, TAN and Kaiken fly to most major Argentine cities. International flights with TransBrasil and Varig to Brazil, with Americana to Peru, and to Uruguay direct, others via Buenos Aires.

Trains A tourist train, the Tren de la Sierra, runs intermittently in high season only (Holy Week, July, summer), from Rodríguez del Busto station (15 km out of town) to Capilla del Monte. Departs 0830, returns 1530, Tuesday, Thursday, Friday, Saturday, Sunday depending on demand, US$10 one way, including taxi transfer from bus terminal to Rodríguez del Busto.

Buses Large terminal conveniently situated at Boulevard Perón 300. In the basement are a bank (does not change travellers' cheques), post office and phones; the ground floor has booking offices, tourist information and a *casa de cambio*; there are shops and cafés on the first floor and a restaurant, supermarket, laundry and left luggage lockers on the top floor. Very busy at peak travel periods.

To **Buenos Aires**, Ablo, Costera Criolla, Chevallier or Cacorba, 10 hours, US$30 *común*, US$50 *diferencial*: to **Salta** (US$41) and **Jujuy** (US$45), Panamericano, 4 daily, La Veloz del Norte twice, about 12 and 15 hours. To **Mendoza**, 10 hours, 6 a day with TAC, slow, 1 daily with Uspallata US$40, avoid La Cumbre; to **Tucumán**, US$30, 8 hours, about 8 a day, Panamericano has more than other companies; to **Posadas**, Expreso Singer, Crucero del Norte (very good buses), Encon, US$43, 18 hours; to **Santa Fe**, frequent, 5½ hours, US$18; to **Trelew** (US$60, 17 hours), **Comodoro Rivadavia** (US$75, 24 hours) and **Río Gallegos** (US$100, 36 hours) Taqsa; to **Mar del Plata** US$45-55; to **La Rioja**, 4 a day, 6½ hours, US$15; some go on to Catamarca, US$16; to La Rioja-Aimogasta-**Tinogasta**- **Fiambalá**, El Cóndor, daily 1500, 2320 (Fiambalá Monday, Thursday only); to **La Rioja**, Chevallier, 6½ hours, US$15, also *coche cama*; to **Catamarca**, Chevallier, 4 a day, US$16, 6

hours; to **Belén** (Catamarca), La Calera, Monday, Wednesday, Friday, 2100. To **Villa Carlos Paz**, Cacorba, fast, efficient,1 hour, every 15 minutes, continues to **Cosquín**, US$3.60, and **La Falda**, US$5, in the Sierras de Córdoba. To **Villa Carlos Paz**, also Car-Cor minibus service, from town centre (Humberto 1° 57) every 40 minutes, US$3.

International services To **Asunción** (Paraguay) direct, Brújula, 4 times a week, and Cacorba 19 hours, US$55. To **Montevideo** (Uruguay), US$57, departs 1700, Monday, Wednesday, Friday and Sunday, Encon, 15 hours, and Cora, 4 days a week. To **Santiago** (Chile), US$32, 16 hours. To **Lima** (Peru), El Rápido, via Mendoza and Chile, 60 hours, US$100. To **Pocitos** (Bolivian border) with Panamericano. In general, it is best to travel from Córdoba if you are going north, as it may be hard to get a seat if boarding en route.

THE SIERRAS DE CORDOBA

Three ranges of undulating hills rise from the pampas, their lower slopes often wooded, particularly in the south. The central range, Sierra Grande, is the longest and highest, extending for some 600 km and including the peaks of Champaquí (2,790m), Los Gigantes (2,370m), La Bolsa (2,260m) and Las Ovejas (2,206m). To the east is the Sierra Chica with its highest peak, Uritorco (1,949m) and to the west is the Sierra de Guasapampa and its continuation, the Sierra de Pocho. In some places the peaks are separated by high plains, known as *pampas*. West of Córdoba the three ranges are 150 km wide.

At the foot of the Sierra Chica the rivers have been dammed to form large lakes: Lago San Roque on the Río Primero, the Embalse Los Molinos on the Río Segundo, and a sequence of four lakes on the Río Tercero. There are two other large dams in the hills, at Cruz del Eje and La Viña. They provide power and irrigation, and the lakes themselves are attractive. Sailing and fishing are popular.

A network of good roads gives pleasant contrasts of scenery. The climate is dry, sunny and exhilarating, especially in winter. There are innumerable good hotels and *pensiones*; names are therefore not always given. Many services are closed out of season.

SOUTHEAST OF CORDOBA

From Córdoba two routes run southeast across the Pampas towards Buenos Aires. Route 9 (713 km) passes through **Villa María** (*population* 65,000), Km 130, a prosperous agricultural town and important route centre at the junction of Route 9 with the highway linking central Chile with Paraguay, Uruguay and Brazil.

- **Accommodation B** *City*, Buenos Aires 1184, T 20948; **C** *Alcázar*, Alvear y Ocampo, T 25948, near bus station, good value.

The other route, Route 38 runs across flatlands and rolling hills to Río Cuarto, where it joins Route 8. About half-way the road runs across the retaining wall of the great Río Tercero dam. The town of **Río Tercero** (*population* 42,657; several hotels) is a modern industrial centre with an armaments factory and petrochemical works.

RIO CUARTO

(*Population* 138,000; *Altitude* 439m) Km 203, is situated on the river of the same name. Founded in 1786, it has a fine Municipalidad (1932) and Cathedral (1890). The **Museo Histórico Regional**, Fotheringham 178, contains displays on early white settlement and the wars against the Indians. In April/May one of the country's biggest motor races is held here.

- **Accommodation** *Opera*, 25 de Mayo 55, T 634390, 4-star; **B** *Gran*, Sobremonte 725, T 33401, 3-star; **C** *Alihué*, Sarsfield 58, good value, very friendly, big rooms. Near bus terminal on Sobremonte 100-200 block are three cheap *Residenciales*, *El Ciervo*, *Hosp El Bambi*, *Res Monge*, all **C**. **Camping** Municipal site, *El Verano*.

- **Banks & money changers** Lucero Viajes, Constitución 564, T 33656, only place changing travellers' cheques, 3% commission.

- **Buses** To Buenos Aires, US$34, frequent service; to Mendoza, US$24; to Córdoba, US$10; to Santiago, Chile, frequent.

NORTH AND EAST OF CORDOBA

NORTH TO ASCOCHINGA

Provincial route 57 runs north from Córdoba through pleasant little townships such as Villa Allende, Río Ceballos, Salsipuedes and La Granja. At El Manzano, Km 44, an unpaved road branches west to La Cumbre. At **Candonga** (*Altitude* 1,000m), 15 km along this road, there is a chapel built in 1730 as an oratory of the Jesuit Estancia of Santa Gertrudis (open Tuesday-Sunday 0900-1300, 1500-1800).

Ascochinga, 61 km north of Córdoba and 20 km west of Jesús María, is an unremarkable village but 14 km further north is **Santa Catalina**, which was the most important Jesuit *estancia* in the Sierras de Córdoba. Founded in 1622, the site includes the church with its twin towers and elegant façade, the cemetery with a baroque gateway and the residence. Only the church can be visited: the key is kept at the house to its right. Buses from Jesús Maria, twice a day.

- **Accommodation** In Río Ceballos: **D** *La Gloria*, Avenida San Martín 5495, affiliated to IYHA, warmly recommended. Three campsites. Several campsites also at **Salsipuedes**. In Candonga: *Hostería Candonga*, good meals. In Ascochinga: **B** *Hostería El Cortijo*, full board only, good value, small swimming pool and river outside, horses for rent, US$1 per hour; campsite at Tres Cascadas falls, 5 km west, open all year.

North and East of Córdoba

Not to scale

Villa de María

Parque Cerro Colorado ○— 12 —│ 22

104

Santa Catalina
│ 14
Ascochinga ○— 20 —○ Jesús María
│ 6
La Granja ○
│ 11
Candonga ○— 15 —○ El Manzano
To La Cumbre (30 km) ← │ 10
│ ○ Río Ceballos
Villa Allende ○ │ 51
│ 17
└— 17 —
Distance in km   Córdoba

NORTH ALONG ROUTE 9

Route 9 is the main road north to Santiago del Estero.

Jesús María

(*Population* 21,000; *Altitude* 533m; *Phone code* 0525) 51 km north of Córdoba, is the site of another former Jesuit *estancia*: though dating from the 16th century, most of the buildings are 18th century. Apart from the fine church and the former residence, there is, in the cloisters, an excellent **Museo Jesuítico**, one of the best on the continent; it also has an important archaeological collection (Monday-Friday 0800-1200 and 1400-1900, Saturday and Sunday 1600-2000). The remains of the famous winery can also be visited: wine from Jesús María was reputed to have been the first American wine served to the Spanish royal family. South of the town centre is the **Casa de Caroya**, another former Jesuit property now housing the excellent **Museo de Inmigración**, which focuses on the settlement of the large Italian community in **Colonia Caroya**, 3 km south Jesús María. At **Sinsacate**, 4 km north of Jesús María, is a fine colonial posting inn, with long, deep verandah and chapel attached, which is now occupied by the **Museo Rural de la Posta** (summer Tuesday-Sunday 1500-1900; winter Tuesday-Sunday 1400-1800). Each January Jesús María celebrates a popular gaucho and folklore festival, lasting 10 nights from 2nd week. Good fishing in winter.

- **Accommodation** *Rizzi*, Tucumán 664, T 20323, 2-star; *Napoleón I*, España 675, T 21273; *Hosp Del Plata*, Tucumán y Colón. **Camping** *Los Nogales*, on western outskirts near river.

- **Buses** Direct to Córdoba, US$2, 1½ hours; to Buenos Aires, TAC, US$30.

Parque Arqueológico y Natural Cerro Colorado

This provincial park covering 3,000 hectares, contains about 30,000 rock paintings scattered among some 200 sites, some of them underground. Painted by the Comechingones Indians between the 10th century and the arrival of the Spanish, the paintings, in red, black and white, portray animals, hunting scenes and battles against the Spanish. There is also a small archaeological museum (US$1, includes guide). Wildlife in the park includes eagles, white woodpeckers and foxes.

In the centre of the park there is a village: among the houses is the former home of the Argentine folklore singer and composer Atahualpa Yupanqui, now a museum, which can be visited, US$2, ask in the village for the curator.

The park can only be visited with a guide: guides available from the administration building, tour 1-1½ hours. There is a hostería and campsite.

- **Access** By an unpaved road, 12 km, which branches off Route 9 at Rayo Cortado, 104 km north of Jesús María. Daily bus from Jesús María at 1610.

Villa de María

(*Population* 2,400; *Altitude* 440m) 136 km north of Jesús María, is the birthplace of Leopoldo Lugones, a poet of country life. His house is a museum.

LAGUNA MAR CHIQUITA

211 km northeast of Córdoba, on the southern margin of the Chaco and about 320 km southeast of Santiago del Estero, this large salt-lake is fed by three rivers: from the north by the Río Dulce which flows through a large area of marshland known as the **Bañados del Río Dulce** and from the south by the Ríos Primero and Segundo from the Sierras de Córdoba. At times the water is so salty you can float in it. As the lake is shallow (maximum depth 12m) and has no outlet, its size varies – 65 to 80 km by 30 to 40 km – according to rainfall patterns.

The lake and its coastline form the **Reserva Natural Bañados del Río Dulce y Laguna Mar Chiquita**, an important nature reserve providing a feeding area in summer for migratory birds from the northern hemisphere. The vegetation is similar to the wetlands of the Chaco. There is fishing for *pejerrey* all year round and during the summer it is very popular with visitors; its salt waters are used in the treatment of rheumatic ailments and skin diseases. Park administration is situated in **Miramar** (*population* 2,000; *altitude* 75m) on the southern shore.

NB This Mar Chiquita and Miramar should not be confused with the other Mar Chiquita and Miramar on the Atlantic coast.

• **Accommodation** *Savoy*, San Martín y Sarmiento, cheap, very friendly. **Camping** *Autocamping Lilly*, Bahía de los Sanavirones.

THE PUNILLA VALLEY

Situated between the Sierra Chica to the east and the Sierra Grande to the west, the Punilla valley is the most popular tourist area of the Sierras de Córdoba. Its rivers are drained by two reservoirs, Lago San Roque, 27 km west of Córdoba, in the south, and Embalse Cruz del Eje, in the north. From Villa Carlos Paz Route 38 runs north along the valley through a string of resorts where there are many hotels and campsites.

VILLA CARLOS PAZ

(*Population* 46,000; *Altitude* 642m; *Phone code* 0541) Villa Carlos Paz, situated on Lago San Roque 35 km west of Córdoba, is a large and rather uninteresting resort with many hotels and often crowded. Tours available on catamarans to the two dams on the lake (daily 1500, US$10, 1½ hours); launch trips also available. A chair-lift runs (0900-1900) to the summit of the Cerro de la Cruz, which offers splendid views. There is also a museum of meteorites, entry US$2.

Excursions

To **Los Gigantes** (*Altitude* 2,374m) 33 km west, a paradise for climbers, reached by an unpaved road which runs through **Tanti** (*population* 3,200; *altitude* 900m; accommodation) over the Pampa de San Luis to Salsacate. Two-day treks possible. Local buses from Tanti. Club Andino has a *refugio*; details in Villa Carlos Paz. Further west at Km 65 a road branches off to **La Candelaria**, 25 km north, where there is a former Jesuit *estancia* and a church dating from 1693. From here a road runs west to La Higuera.

To the **Observatorio Bosque Alegre**, 31 km south (see under Alta Gracia for details).

• **Accommodation** Plenty of hotels in all price categories. **C** *El Monte*, Caseros 45, T 22001, F 22993, very good, recommended; **C** *Mar del Plata*, Esquiú 47, T 22068, recommended; **C** *Villa Carlos Paz Parque*, Santa Fe 50, T 25128, full board available, recommended. **Camping** ACA site, San Martín y Nahuel Huapi, T 22132; *Club de Pesca*, España y Avenida Atlántica, and *Los Pinos*, Curros Enríque y Lincoln, open all year. Many others.

• **Banks & money changers** Banco de Córdoba, San Martín, accepts US$ cash only.

• **Laundry** San Martín y Libertad.

• **Post & telecommunications** Post Office and telephone: San Martín 190.

• **Shopping** Best buys: leather mats, bags, pottery.

• **Tour companies & travel agents** *Recep Tur Carlos Paz*, in bus terminal, T 21725, offer tours to Capilla del Monte US$13, to La Cumbrecita US$24.

• **Tourist offices** San Martín 400, near terminal, T 21624.

• **Buses** Terminal at San Martín y Belgrano, near centre. To Córdoba every 15 minutes in summer, US$2; taxi to/from Córdoba airport, US$10.50. To/from Buenos Aires, Ablo, US$26; also Cacorba, Chevallier, General Urquiza.

COSQUIN

(*Population* 16,400; *Altitude* 720m) 26 km north of Villa Carlos Paz, 63 km from Córdoba, on the banks of the Río Cosquín, Cosquín is known as the National Folklore Capital. It is the site of Argentina's most important folklore festival, beginning in the last week in January. There is also a national *artesanía* festival in the same month. There are good views over the Punilla valley from Cerro Pan de Azúcar (1,260m), situated 7 km east of town in the Sierra Chica. Chairlift to top (all year round).

Museums **Museo de Artesanías**, Tucumán 1031. **Museo Camin Cosquín** on Route 38, 3 km north of centre, minerals and archaeology, recommended.

• **Accommodation** Several places near the bus terminal including: **C** *La Serrana*, P Ortiz 740, T 51306, good; **C** *Italia*, Ternengo y Vértiz, T 52255, recommended; **D** *Ideal*. Several campsites.

• **Tourist offices** Plaza Próspero Molino; 0700-2100 daily in high season, 0800-2000 daily off season.

Buses To Córdoba, US$3.60, Empresa La Calera direct or La Capillense 1½ hours via Carlos Paz.

LA FALDA

Population 14,000; *Altitude* 933m; *Phone code* 0548) 82 km north of Córdoba, is a good centre for walks in the surrounding hills. The **Hotel Edén**, built 1897 as a grand hotel, visited by illustrious figures early this century, but closed since the 1960s, can be visited (guided tours only; daily 0930-1200, 1600-1900 in season, 1000-1200, 1500-1800 off season, US$3).

Museums Model Railway Museum at **Las Murallas Zoo** Las Murallas 200, daily 0930-2000 in season, Saturday/Sunday only 1000-1200, 1500-1900 off season; **Museo Arqueológico Ambato**, Cuesta del Lago 1467, privately run, well displayed, open Thursday-Sunday and public holidays 0900-2000, US$0.50.

Excursions To **Valle Hermoso** (*Altitude* 850m), 5 km south. The old restored chapel of San Antonio is a little gem. There is a small museum; displays include palaeontology and archaeology. Horseriding. To **Huerta Grande** (971m), 3½ km north, a bathing resort with good fishing and medicinal waters. To the *Estancia El Silencio*, 11 km east, T 24809, which offers trekking and horseriding.

A good circular route is to the **Cascadas de Olaén** via a road west from La Falda; at Km 16 turn left and follow for 2 km to the crossing marked 'Cascadas de Olaén', from where it is 4½ km further to the falls via the Capilla Santa Bárbara, a Jesuit chapel dating from 1747. Return to the crossing and turn right; follow dirt road for about 12½ km until you reach Route 38 from where it is a further 12 km north to La Falda.

● **Accommodation** About 80 hotels in all categories, all full in December-February holiday season; La Falda is visited mostly by the elderly, many hotels belong to pension funds. 4-star: **A1** *Nor Tomarza*, Edén 1603, T 22004 and **A1** *Tomaso di Savoia*, Edén 732, T 23013. **C** *Res Atenas*, Rosario 329, T 22424, comfortable, recommended; **D** *Hostería Los Abrojos*, Goya sin número, Valle Hermoso, T/F 70430, hot water, also full board, sports, excursions; **E** pp *Malvinas*, 2 blocks from terminal, meals available. Houses for rent 1 March to 30 November on a monthly basis. **Camping** *Balneario 7 Cascadas*, T 23869, west of centre, hot water, cafeteria.

● **Places to eat** *El Bochín*, España 117, good, cheap; *Pachamama*, 9 de Julio 160, vegetarian.

● **Banks & money changers** Banco de la Nación and Banco de Suquía for exchange.

● **Post & telecommunications Post Office**: Avenida Argentina y 9 de Julio. **Telecommunications**: Telecom, San Martín 6.

● **Tour companies & travel agents** *Aventura Club*, 9 de Julio 541, T/F 23809, trekking, jeep tours, camping, birdwatching etc. *Wella Viajes*, Avenida Edén 412, loc 12, T 0548-21380, offers 15% discount to ISIC and youth card holders for trekking, climbing, etc to Cerro Champaquí.

● **Tourist offices** Avenida España y de la Torre and at bus terminal.

● **Buses** To Córdoba, US$4, 2 hours; to Buenos Aires, Cacorba, Cita, US$40.

LA CUMBRE

(*Population* 6,500; *Altitude* 1,141m) 12 km north of La Falda, offers fine views from the statue of Christ the Redeemer on the hill. Trout streams with good fishing from November to April. Swimming, golf, tennis; hang gliding and parapenting nearby at Cuchi Corral. The **Estancia El Rosario**, 6 km southeast of La Cumbre, offers horseriding, parapenting, excursions and sports, daily 0830-1830. **Cruz Chica**, 2 km north of La Cumbre (*Altitude* 1,067m), is a wealthy residential area with English-style houses and gardens in pine woods. The **Museo Manuel Mujica Laínez**, occupies the former house of the Argentine writer, US$3, in season daily, off season at weekends only 1400-1800. **Los Cocos**, 8 km north of La Cumbre, is a popular mountain resort with good hotels and many holiday houses. Climb up El Mastil and beyond for the views and birds.

● **Accommodation & places to eat La Cumbre**: **A1** *Lima*, Moreno y Dean Funes, with breakfast, T 51722, excellent facilities, pool, quiet; **C** pp *Victoria*, Posadas sin número, T 51412, charming, small; *Res San Antonio*, Caraffa 449, T 51338; **C** *Res Peti*, Paz y Rivadavia, good. *Pizza Luis*, Rivadavia 267, recommended. **At Los Cocos**: *Blair House*, Grierson, T 92147, English-style, recommended; *Host Walcheren*, T/F 92049; *Host del Mediterraneo*, Los Tulipanes sin número,

T 92023; *Los Pinos*, Grierson sin número, T 92002, F 92188; *Los Molles*, Grierson sin número. T 92001. **Camping** *El Cristo*, Cabrera sin número, T 51839.

• **Tourist offices** Caraffa 300, near bus terminal.

• **Buses** To Córdoba, US$4.50.

CAPILLA DEL MONTE

(*Population* 7,620; *Altitude* 979m; *Phone code* 0548) 109 km north of Córdoba, is the best centre for exploring this part of the Sierras. The location of many sightings of unidentified flying objects, the area is popular for 'mystical tourism' and there are tours to meditation and 'energy' centres. There are good opportunities for walking, windsurfing on the El Cajón reservoir, parapenting from Cerro Las Gemelas and rock-climbing. Horse riding costs US$20 per half day.

Excursions To **Cerro Uritorco** (*Altitude* 1,979m), 6 km northeast, 4-hour climb, via La Toma, 4 km, where there are medicinal waters and from here there are further walking opportunities. To **Los Alazanes** dam (*altitude* 1,400m). At **San Marcos Sierra** (*altitude* 680m), 22 km west, known as *capital de la miel* for the quality of its honey, there is an 18th century church (several hotels and campsite). From here it is another 12 km northwest to the Cruz del Eje dam; there are parakeets and small farmhouses and good views along the way. The **Quebrada de la Luna**, 14 km north, is the highest point in the Sierra Chica.

• **Accommodation A3** *Cerro Uritorco*, Alem 671, T 82069, pool, trekking, horseriding and camping; **B** *Hosp Italia*, Rivadavia 54, clean, showers, opposite bus terminal; **D** pp *la Loma*, Frías 123, T 81138, pool; *Roma*, Corrientes 387, T 81083, pool, air conditioning; **D** pp *Los Gemelos*, Alem 967, T 81186, F 81239, half board; **C/D** *Hosp Centro*, Irigoyen y Funes, T 82116. Many others in all categories. **Camping** Municipal site *Calabalumba*, 600m north of the centre, **E** per tent, hot water, recommended, also *cabañas*; *Witcoin* on road to La Toma, T 81801; *Cabañas La Toma*, US$10 per tent.

• **Tourist offices** In old railway station, T 81341, open daily 0830-2030, some English spoken.

• **Buses** To Córdoba, 3 hours, US$10; to Buenos Aires, many companies, US$38.

Cruz del Eje

(*Population* 25,500; *Phone code* 0549) 39 km further northwest near the dam, is an uninteresting town, famous for its olives Boats for hire on the reservoir where there is good fishing.

• **Accommodation A3** *Posta de las Carretas*, Ruta 38 y Rua Moyano, T 2517, good, service station and restaurants; **C** *España*, Caseros y Alsina, T 2702, friendly, family-run. **Camping** Possible at foot of dam.

THE TRASLASIERRA VALLEY

Situated west of the Sierra Grande and east of the Sierra de Guasapampa, this valley is much less developed than the Punilla Valley and offers better opportunities for the independent traveller. Its name, meaning 'Across the Sierra', implies an isolation from Córdoba on the other side of the Sierra Grande. Sandy soils limit agriculture in the valley but potatoes, olives and grapes are grown. Three rivers, the Ríos Los Sauces, Mina Clavero and Panaholma, provide irrigation. From Cruz del Eje a road runs south through the valley to Villa Dolores and into San Luis province.

THE ROUTE FROM CORDOBA

Known as the **Camino de las Altas Cumbres**, this is the most spectacular route in the Sierras. The road, running southwest from Villa Carlos Paz passes **Ycho Cruz**, by the Río San Antonio (**D** *Hostería Avenida*, with bath; several campsites) before climbing into the Sierra Grande and crossing the Pampa de Achala, a huge desert plateau of grey granite and descending into the Traslasierra valley near Mina Clavero.

The **Parque Nacional Quebrada de los Condoritos**, along a 7 km track south from the former Hotel El Cóndor (Km 64), covering 40,000 hectares, was created in 1995 to protect the spectacular Quebrada de los Condoritos, an 800m deep gorge. This is the easternmost habitat of the condor which nests in the walls of the gorge: they are best seen from a rocky

The Museo Rocsen

The Museo Rocsen is perhaps one of the most unusual museums in Argentina. The life's work of Juan Santiago Bouchon, a native of Brittany, France, it contains over 12,000 items arranged under 56 themes. Though there are sections on archaeology, geology, anthropology and oceanography, it also contains European furniture, musical instruments, vehicles, machinery and much more.

At the age of 8 Bouchon discovered a clay figure of a Roman soldier 2,000 years old while digging in a Roman amphitheatre: the discovery changed his life. After studying anthropology and fine arts and teaching himself natural sciences, he moved to Argentina in 1950 with 8,000 kg of luggage. Working for the French tourist office in Buenos Aires, he travelled the country, before settling in Nono in 1959. The first museum building, covering 100 sq m, was opened in 1969; it now occupies 1,325 sq m. The great façade of the building is marked by 49 human statues, designed by Sr Bouchon to trace human history; not one is of a military figure; the last is of Martin Luther King. The museum is staffed by members of Sr Bouchon's family.

Though his museum may appear to be a collection of everything and anything, Sr Bouchon is clear about his aim, believing that single-theme museums bore most visitors, and he plans to extend the museum by a further 2,700 sq m.

outcrop known as *El Balcón*. Information from *guardaparques* or from Club Andino in Córdoba.

● **Accommodation B** pp *La Posta*, Km 101, T/F 0544-70887, with breakfast; **A1** pp full pension, beautifully situated, great views, also has an *Albergue*, **C** pp, with breakfast, without bath, reservations advisable.

● **Buses** From **Córdoba** to Ycho Cruz, US$2, Cotap; to El Cóndor US$5.

SOUTH OF CRUZ DEL EJE

The road from Cruz del Eje passes through several uninteresting towns and across the flat Pampa de Pocho before reaching Mina Clavero (Km 139). South of Salsacate a road branches off east across the Sierra Grande to Villa Carlos Paz via Los Gigantes (see above) and another branches west towards Chepes via the **Quebrada de la Mermela**, Km 87, a gorge which is entered by passing through five tunnels. Beyond the gorge, at Km 107 a turning leads off to the **Parque Natural Chancani**, 4,920 hectares, which protects one of the last remnants of *Chaqueño* forests in this area.

MINA CLAVERO

(*Population* 5,100; *Altitude* 915m; *Phone code* 0544) 140 km west of Córdoba at the confluence of the Ríos Panaholma and Mina Clavero and at the foot of the

Camino de Las Altas Cumbres, is a good centre for exploring the high *sierra*. Black ceramics are a traditional product of this area. There is a fascinating museum, **Museo Rocsen**, 13 km south and about 5 km from the village of Nono, open daily 0900 till sunset, US$3. The road south of Nono, near the Embalse La Viña, a reservoir surrounded by forests, is lined with hotels and campsites.

● **Accommodation & places to eat** There are over 70 hotels, though many close off season. **B** *La Posada*, Sarmiento 1394, T 70179, with breakfast; **C** *Ferrari*, Oviedo 1334, T 70172, with breakfast; **C** *Marengo*, San Martín 518, T 70224, with breakfast; **D** pp *La Morenita*, Urquiza 1142, T 70347, with breakfast, parking; **D** pp *Las Leñas*, Muiño 1208, T 70714; **E** pp *El Parral*, Vila 1430, T 70005; **E** pp *Res Jonathan II*, Mitre 1208, opposite terminal, with breakfast. **Camping** Several sites including *La Siesta*, at north end of town and three sites west of centre. On the road south of Nono: **C** *Las Mil y Una*, Km 13, T 98167, excellent, restaurant, helpful; **D** pp *Castillo Villa La Fontana*, Km 20, between Los Hornillos and Los Rabanes, **E** pp without bath, in beautiful 1920s Italianate palace, attractive gardens, English spoken, cooking and laundry facilities, highly recommended.

● **Places to eat** *Rincón Suizo*, **C** Champaquí 1200, serves good pastries.

● **Sports Climbing**: *Traslasierra Turismo*, Mitre y Merlo, T/F 70929, organize day trips to

Champaquí, minimum 4 persons, US$40 per person including equipment. **Horseriding**: *Mis Montañas*, at Los Hornillos, Km 22 south, T 0544-49015, F 0544-94435, German and English spoken.

● **Buses** Terminal in centre at Avenida Mitre 1191. To **Córdoba**, US$10, 6 a day, 3 hours; to **Buenos Aires**, TAC, US$40, 12 hours; to **Mendoza**, 8½ hours, US$26.

VILLA DOLORES

(*Population* 21,000; *Altitude* 529m) An uninteresting town 45 km south of Mina Clavero and 187 km southeast of Córdoba, is the most important town in the valley. The **Museo de la Ciudad**, Sarmiento y San Martín, contains displays on natural history and archaeology and a model of the Sierras de Córdoba, Monday-Friday 0800-1200, 1500-1900. South of here the road continues to Merlo and Villa Mercedes.

● **Accommodation B** *Sierras Grandes*, San Martín 9, T/F 20088, without breakfast, gloomy, overpriced; **D** pp *Vila Plaza*, on Plaza, T 21691, without breakfast, parking, poor beds; **D** *Hosp Cáceres*, Brizuela 390; **D** *Res Champaquí*, F Germán 166, T 22358; **D** pp *Hosp Sonia*, Brizuela 415, T 22938, opposite terminal, without breakfast. At Las Tapias, 10 km east is **B** pp *La Posta de Mistal*, T 20893, half board, pool, tennis, restaurant. **Camping** Nearest site at Piedra Pintada, 6 km northeast, pleasant village well situated for walks into mountains.

● **Tourist office** 25 de Mayo 1, Monday-Friday 0800-1400.

● **Buses** Terminal at Brizuela y Tomás Edison. To **Buenos Aires**, Chevallier *cama*, US$40, 12 hours; to **San Luis** 5¼ hours; to **Córdoba**, several companies, US$8-10, 5 hours; to **Mendoza**, TAC, US$26, 8 hours; to **Mina Clavero**, frequent, US$3, 1½ hours.

CHAMPAQUI

The highest peak in the Sierras (2,884m), Champaquí is topped by a bronze bust of San Martín. It can be climbed from Las Rosas, 15 km east of Villa Dolores, or from San Javier, 12 km southeast. The route from San Javier goes by La Constancia, a ruined *estancia* set in a river valley with pine and nut trees. To the summit takes 8-10 hours, the descent to La Constancia 4 hours. Neither route should be attempted in misty weather. The easiest way to climb Champaquí is from Villa General

Belgrano in the Calamuchita valley.

2 km south of San Javier, at the foot of Champaquí, in a region of woods and waterfalls is **Yacanto**, which has curative waters.

● **Accommodation** Available in both San Javier and Las Rosas. A good base is *Vai Kunta* (Postal address 5885 Las Rosas), 2-hour walk from Los Molles, run by Rolf Graf (Swiss), good food, guides. Taxis to Los Molles from *pizzería* near bus station in Las Rosas.

THE CALAMUCHITA VALLEY

Situated south of Córdoba west of the Sierra Chica and east of the Sierra Grande, this valley is a prosperous agricultural zone, producing cereals, alfalfa and fruit. It provides fine walking opportunities in wooded countryside. Route 5 runs from Córdoba south past Alta Gracia before climbing through the hills around the Embalse Los Molinos and continuing to the artificial lakes of the Río Tercero, 117 km south of Córdoba.

ALTA GRACIA

(*Population* 39,000; *Altitude* 580m; *Phone code* 0547) 39 km southwest of Córdoba, occupies the site of a 17th century Jesuit *estancia*. With the arrival of the railway and the building of the Hotel Sierras (1908), the town became a popular resort for sufferers from respiratory diseases, among them the young Che Guevara.

The major buildings of the *estancia* are situated around the plaza. The church, completed in 1762, with a baroque façade but no tower, is open for services only (summer Monday-Saturday 2000, Sunday 1000 and 1800; winter Monday-Saturday 1800, Sunday 1000 and 1800). To the north of the church is the former Residence, built round a cloister and housing the **Museo del Virrey Liniers**, open Tuesday-Friday 0900-1300, 1500-1830, Saturday, Sunday 0930-1230, 1530-1830, US$1 (all day in summer). To the south of the church are the former workshops, now occupied by a school. North of the residence is the **Tajamar**, an artificial lake built by the Jesuits. The clock tower, on its corner, dates from 1938: its figures include those of a gaucho, an Indian, a Jesuit and a conquistador.

Northwest of the centre in parkland is the abandoned Sierras Hotel, and, beyond it, the **Museo Manuel de Falla** on Pellegrini, closed Monday, entry US$0.30, in the house where the Spanish composer spent his final years. There are beautiful views from the Gruta de la Virgen de Lourdes, 3 km west of town.

Excursions To the **Observatorio Bosque Alegre**, 17 km northwest, which at the time of construction contained the largest telescope in South America. Open Thursday 1600-1800, Sunday 1000-1200 and 1600-1800. The surrounding area affords good views over Córdoba, Alta Gracia and the Sierra Grande.

● **Accommodation** *Covadonga*, Quintana 265, T 21456; *Hostería Reina*, Urquiza 229, T 21724, good. **Camping** *Los Sauces* in the Parque Federico García Lorca.

● **Tourist offices** Tourist office inside clock tower by Lago Tajamar.

● **Buses** To Córdoba, US$1.50, every 15 minutes, 1 hour.

VILLA GENERAL BELGRANO

(*Population* 4,500; *Altitude* 840m; *Phone code* 0546) This is a very German looking town 85 km south of Córdoba. Founded in the 1930s, its German character was boosted by the arrival of interned seamen

The Graf Spee

The *Graf Spee*, a German 'pocket' battleship launched in 1934, was small enough to avoid the restrictions put on the German navy in 1919 but was more heavily gunned than any cruiser afloat and faster than any vessel which could outgun her. In 1939, the *Graf Spee* sank nine merchant ships in the Atlantic before being cornered on 13 December by three British cruisers. After a 14 hour battle in which one British ship was badly damaged, the *Graf Spee's* commander, Captain Hans Langsdorff, retreated into the neutral port of Montevideo, where the 36 German crewmen killed were buried. Langsdorff asked to stay in Montevideo for 2 weeks to repair his ship; the Uruguayan government, under British pressure, gave him 2 days. On 17 December the *Graf Spee* sailed out to sea. Crowds, lining the shore in fading light to watch the expected battle, saw the vessel sink within minutes. All the remaining crew and 50 captured British seamen on board were rescued. Hitler had given the order to scuttle the vessel rather than allow it to be captured. Two days later, in Buenos Aires, Langsdorff wrapped himself in the flag of the Imperial German Navy and committed suicide.

Most of the crew were interned in Argentina where they were warmly welcomed by the German community of Buenos Aires. British pressure forced the Argentine government to disperse them: groups were sent to Mendoza, Córdoba, San Juan, Santa Fe and Rosario and over 200 were kept on Isla Martín García. Their reception in the towns of the interior varied: in Córdoba they were welcomed by the governor, while in Mendoza they were stoned by locals and beaten up by the police. Many of the officers escaped and returned to serve with the German navy, much to the annoyance of the British who suspected Argentine government connivance. The German embassy, meanwhile, tried to enforce military discipline and to prevent the men from getting friendly with local women.

In 1945 the US and British governments demanded the repatriation of all the men to Germany. Nearly 200 sought to avoid this by marrying Argentine women and a further 75 escaped, but in 1946 the British navy deported over 800 men to Germany. Many, after 6 years in Argentina, had no wish to return to a country shattered by defeat and within 2 years all those who wished to return to Argentina were allowed to do so.

from the *Graf Spee*, some of whom later settled here. There is a monument to the crew in the Plazoleta Graf Spee. A pleasant and popular resort in attractive countryside, it is a good centre for excursions in the surrounding mountains. Genuine German smoked sausages and cakes are sold.

Museums Museo Arqueológico Ambrosetti, collection of artefacts from Comechingon Indians, the original inhabitants of the valley; **Museo del Carruaje**, old carriages and cars; **Museo Ovni**, on southern outskirts, dedicated to unidentified flying objects.

Excursions To **La Cumbrecita** (*Altitude* 1,450m) a German village 40 km west, where there is good walking and riding. At Km 6 there is an 18th century chapel, the oldest in the valley. South of La Cumbrecita is **Villa Alpina**, a small resort 55 km west along a poor gravel road and the base for climbing Champaqui.

Local festivals *Oktoberfest* beer festival in October; *Fiesta de la Masa Vienesa*, Easter week; *Festival del Chocolate Alpino* in July.

● **Accommodation A3** *Bremen*, Route 5 y Cerro Negro, T 61133, restaurant, sports facilities; **A2** *Edelweiss*, Ojo de Agua 295, T 61317, F 61387, pool, excellent food; *Berna*, V Sársfield 86, T/F 61097; **B** *Hostería Alfred*, Uruguay y Roca, T 61119, with breakfast, very good, French spoken, horseriding; **C** *Res Alpino*, Roca y 25 de Mayo, T 61355, F 62177, without breakfast, kitchen facilities. **At Villa Berna**, 25 km west: *Cougar Hill*, T 0546-87018, English, French, German spoken, very helpful. **At La Cumbrecita**: **A3** *Cascadas*, T 81015, with pool, tennis etc; **A3** *Panorama*, higher up hill (T 98406); *La Cumbrecita*, T 98405, F 81052; *Las Verbenas*, T 81008. **At Villa Alpina**: chalets; youth hostel, T 0571-21947. **Youth hostels C** *El Rincón*, in beautiful surroundings near town, cooking and laundry facilities, highly recommended (reservations: Patricia Mampsey, Casilla 64, T 61323); *Estancia Alta Vista*, T 62238, 14 km from town on route to La Cumbrecita, both offer discounts to ISIC and YHA card holders (20% and 25% respectively). **Camping** *San José*, 2 km north of town, T 62496; *Camping Arroyo* and municipal site, both near Arroyo El Sauce.

● **Buses** To **Córdoba**, 2 hours, US$4, frequent (sit on the left); to **Mendoza**, US$28; to **Buenos Aires**, San Juan Mar del Plata, daily 2000, 11 hours, US$48, several other companies. To **La**

Cumbrecita by taxi (US$33, 1-1½ hours) or by bus, Sunday only.

SAN LUIS PROVINCE

South of the city of San Luis is flat and of little interest but in the northern part of the province three ranges of hills run from north to south: the Sierra de las Quijadas in the west, the Sierra de San Luis in the Centre and the Sierra de Comechingones to the east.

SAN LUIS

(*Population* 110,000; *Altitude* 765m; *Phone code* 0652) 770 km west of Buenos Aires, is the provincial capital. Founded by Martín de Loyola, the governor of Chile, in 1596, it is a modern city and good centre for exploring the Sierra de San Luis.

Places of interest

On the south side of Plaza Independencia is the **Convento de Santo Domingo**, the oldest building in the city, dating from the 18th century; the adjacent church is modern. Visit the **Centro Artesanal San Martín de Porras**, next to the monastery, where rugs are woven. Open Monday-Friday 0700-1300.

Excursions

Just outside the city are two artificial lakes,

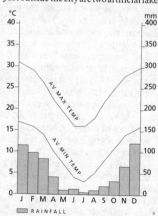

Climate: San Luis

San Luis centre

not to scale

To Bus Terminal

Bolívar

Lavalle

Av Presidente Illia

Pedernera
Municipalidad

Junín

Plaza Pringles

Pringles

Belgrano

Rivadavia

Chacabuco

San Martín

Mitre

Caseros

Constitución

Falucho

Lafinur

Ayacucho

Palacio de Gobierno

9 de Julio

Plaza Independencia

25 de Mayo Convento Santo Domingo

Centro Artesanal

Balcarce

Hotels:
1. Aiello
2. Gran Hotel España
3. Grand Palace
4. Gran San Luis
5. Quintana

Embalse Potrero de los Funes, 15 km northeast, surrounded by woods and picnic areas, and Embalse Cruz de Piedra, 10 km east, which offers good fishing. Just north of the latter is El Volcán, a *balneario* with camping and picnic.

Local information
● Accommodation

On Pres Illia: **A2** *Quintana*, No 546, T/F 38400, 4-star, best, without breakfast, large rooms, restaurant; **A3** *Aiello*, No 431, T 25609, F 25694, with breakfast, air conditioning, spacious, garage, recommended; **A3** *Gran San Luis*, No 470, T 25049, F 30148, with breakfast, restaurant, pool; **A3** *Gran Hotel España*, No 300, T 37700, F 37707, also cheaper rooms **B**, gloomy but clean.

Elsewhere: **A3** *Grand Palace*, Rivadavia 657, T 22059, with breakfast, parking, central, spacious, gloomy, good lunches; *Intihuasi*, La Pampa 815 (behind Casa de Cultura), spotless, TV, lounge, highly recommended; **C** *Iguazu*, Ejercito de los Andes 1582, T 22129, basic; **C** *Rivadavia*, Rivadavia 1470, T 22437, without breakfast, good beds, gloomy, opposite bus terminal; next door is **D** *17 de Octubre*, which should be avoided, gloomy, basic, run down; **D** *San Antonio*, Ejército de los Andes 1602, T 22717, without breakfast, restaurant; *Res Buenos Aires*, Buenos Aires 834, T 24062; *Res Los Andes*, Ejercito de los Andes 1180, T 22033.

Outside the city: **L3** *Hotel Potrero de los Funes*, T 30125/20889, F 23898 (Buenos Aires, 25 de Mayo 516, 11th floor, T 313-4886, F 312-3876), luxury resort and casino on lake of the same name, sports and watersports, lovely views; *Villa Andrea*, at El Volcán, F 94009, pool, restaurant. Several hotels along Route 20 to El Volcán.

Camping Three sites in El Volcán: *El Volcán*, T 27447, F 21337; *El Rincón*, and *Salto Colorado*.

● Places to eat
Most close at weekends; hotel restaurants are closed Sunday, *San Luis'* closes Saturday too. *El Cantón de Neuchatel*, San Martín 745, opposite Cathedral on main plaza, is open Sunday, modest; *Michel*, Lafinur 1361, good food and service; *Campo La Sierra*, 18 km west on Route 20, Swiss run, also offers horseriding and trekking.

● Banks & money changers
Very difficult to change travellers' cheques, try **Banco de Galicia**, Rivadavia y Belgrano, 1.5% commission.

● Tourist offices
Junín y San Martín, excellent.

● Transport
Bus terminal at Vía España between San Martín y Rivadavia. To **Buenos Aires**, US$30 (US$37 *coche cama*); to **Santiago** (Chile), 9-10 hours, Turbus US$30, Tas Choapa US$25; to **Mendoza**, US$16, 3 hours; to **Córdoba**, US$20, 7½ hours.

ROUTES The most direct route to Córdoba, is by Route 146 which runs north from San Luis to the west of the Sierras de Córdoba through San Francisco del Monte de Oro, Luján and Villa Dolores. An alternative is Route 20 which runs east through La Toma to meet Route 148 (see above) which follows north to Villa Dolores along the western edge of the Sierras. Route 7 leads across the pampas to Buenos Aires via Villa Mercedes, 99 km southeast.

PARQUE NACIONAL SIERRA DE LAS QUIJADAS

Situated in the northwestern corner of the province, 97 km northwest of San Luis, the park covers 150,000 hectares including the **Potrero de Aguada**, a huge natural amphitheatre of nearly 4,000 hectares surrounded by steep red sandstone walls, eroded into strange shapes. Archaeological remains include evidence of dinosaurs and pterosaurs. Flora and fauna are those of a transitional zone between wooded sierra and open, Chaco-type terrain: the vegetation is largely scrub though species such as the *quebracho*. Fauna include guanaco, collared peccaries, cougars, tortoises, crowned eagles and peregrine falcons and condors. There are no facilities and no wardens: take everything with you including water. Access is by an unpaved road which turns off from Route 147 (San Luis to San Juan) at Hualtarán. Excursions can be organized from San Luis.

THE SIERRA DE SAN LUIS

Situated northeast of the city of San Luís, this range of hills is little known to travellers but is becoming more accessible with the building of paved roads. The sierra is a centre for mining green onyx.

SAN LUIS TO CAROLINA

The western edge of the sierras can be visited by taking Route 9 north from San Luís.

El Trapiche

Km 42, is an attractive village set on the Río Trapiche in wooded hills; there are summer homes, hotels and picnic sites. Nearby is the La Florida reservoir which offers good fishing. Bus from San Luis, US$4 return.

● **Accommodation A2** *Hostería Los Sauces*, T 93027; *El Parque*, T 93058; *Hostal Los Pinos*, T 93009. **Camping** Municipal, south near the Embalse La Florida; *Schmidt*, further north by the river.

Carolina

Km 84, is a former gold-mining town at the foot of Tomolasta (2,018m) which offers great views; accessible by 4WD vehicle. Though the goldmine is closed, it can be visited. A statue of a gold miner overlooks the main plaza. Gruta de Intihuasi, 21 km southeast, is a cave formed by a natural arch. The paved road ends at Carolina: an unpaved track leads north over the Cuesta Larga to San Francisco del Monte de Oro, from where it is possible to follow Route 146 to Villa Dolores.

● **Accommodation** *Hostería Las Verbenas*, T 24425.

SAN LUIS TO SAN MARTIN

The central part of the Sierras is best reached by Route 20 to La Toma, from where a paved road runs north to San Martín.

La Toma

84 km east of San Luís, is the cheapest place to buy green onyx. From here you can make an excursion to Cerros Rosario, interesting hills and rock scenery, 10 km northwest. **Accommodation C** *Italia*, Belgrano 644, T 21295, hot showers.

Libertador General San Martín

(Known as San Martín) 75 km north of La Toma, is a good centre for exploring the rolling hills of the northern sierra. The Dique La Huerta, 7 km west, offers good fishing for *pejerrey*. From San Martín an unpaved road runs north to reach Route 146.

The Sierra de San Luis

Distance in km

- **Accommodation** **E** pp *Hostería Eva Perón*, with bath and breakfast, meals served, good value, recommended.
- **Buses** From San Luis 1 daily; from Villa Mercedes 2 a day in summer.

EASTERN SAN LUIS

VILLA MERCEDES

(*Population* 77,000; *Altitude* 515m; *Phone code* 0657) Founded in 1856 as a fortress, is an important route centre with little of interest. The old municipal market (Chacabuco y Mitre) is now an arts and community centre.

- **Accommodation & places to eat** ACA hotel **B** *San Martín*, Lavalle 435, T 22358, restaurant, parking. Cheaper places on Mitre, eg **C** *Res Cappola*, No 1134, recommended.
- **Transport** **Air** Airport at Villa Reynolds, southeast. **Buses** Terminal on Plaza San Martín opposite Municipalidad. To Buenos Aires US$28; to **Villa Dolores** 1 hour.

THE CONLARA VALLEY

Lying east of the Sierra de San Luis and west of the Sierra de Comechingones, this broad valley runs into the Traslasierra Valley to the north. From Villa Mercedes Route 148 runs north through **San José del Morro**, Km 49, where there is an 18th century chapel. Nearby is the Sierra del Morro, the remnants of a collapsed giant volcano; inside its crater are small volcanic cones (there is a model in the Museo de Ciencias in Buenos Aires). Lots of rose-quartz can be found here. From here Route 148 follows the Río Conlara north towards Villa Dolores (see page 182). More scenic is Provincial Route 1 which runs parallel to the east along the base of the Sierra de Comechingones through a string of pretty villages like Villa Larca, Cortaderas, Carpintería and Merlo.

MERLO

(*Population* 6,000; *Altitude* 895m; *Phone code* 0656) Situated almost at the San Luis-Córdoba border, some 150 km north of Villa Mercedes, is a small town on the steep western slopes of the Sierra de Comechingones. A popular holiday centre, Merlo claims a special microclimate: its altitude makes it cooler than the pampas and it is sheltered from the humidity of the damp easterly winds. Locals claim that it also benefits from specially high levels of ionization, atmospheric ozone and nitric oxide, which are purported to be beneficial for the nervous system. These high concentrations are explained by the presence of uranium in the local rocks. The area is being promoted for its rich wildlife, particularly birds. On the plaza is the church dating from 1720, though the town itself was only founded in 1797. There are many good walks especially in the Sierra (eg the climb to Cerro Linderos Alto via the hill with a cross; the Circuito de Damiana Vega, 3-4 hours) and excursions to *balnearios*, waterfalls and other attractions. 8 km north of Merlo is **Piedra Blanca**, a small settlement in attractive surroundings. Nearby is a giant *algarrobo* tree, known as the *agarrobo abuelo*.

- **Accommodation** In Merlo and nearby are many hotels, *hosterías* and *residenciales* though many open in summer only. Most in Merlo are along Avenida del Sol. **A2** *Rincón del Este*, T 75306, 3-star, 5 km from centre, recommended; **A1** *Parque*, Avenida del Sol 821, T 75110, with breakfast, tennis, golf, pool. At Villa Elena, 26 km south, is **B** pp *Posada del Sol*, T 20017 (Buenos Aires 522-1406), half-pension, pool, tennis, restaurant, English spoken.
- **Tour companies & travel agents** *Valle del Sol*, T 76109, tours to Sierra de las Quijadas US$45 per person, minimum 6 persons. For tours to the Sierra del Morro contact Carlos Lasalle, Hostería Naschel, T 91277.
- **Tourist office** On southern outskirts.
- **Buses** Terminal 3 blocks from the plaza. Frequent services to **San Luis**; to **Buenos Aires**, TAC, Sierras Cordobesas and Chevallier, US$35, 12 hours; to **Córdoba**, TAC, 7 hours.

The West:
Mendoza, San Juan
and La Rioja

THREE PROVINCES which span the Pampas and the heights of the Andes: Mendoza, on the main Andean crossing between Argentina and Chile, is a centre of wine making, fruit growing, winter sports and climbing; San Juan and La Rioja, further north, are less popular with travellers but offer diverse and spectacular landscapes.

GEOGRAPHY

The western parts of these three provinces are dominated by the two ranges of the Andes: the *Cordillera Principal* or western range and the *Cordillera Frontal* or eastern range. Between them are high upland valleys. The western range, which is the highest and forms the frontier with Chile, declines in altitude south of Mendoza. The mountain passes are over 3,000m in Mendoza but over 4,000m further north. Highest peaks are Aconcagua (6,959m), Tupungato (6,800m), Ramada (6,410m), de la Pollera (6,235m), del Plomo (6,120m), San Juan (6,111m), Marmolejo (6,070m), San José (6,099m) and Juncal (6,060m) in northern Mendoza, Mercedario (6,770m) in southern San Juan and Pissis (6,882m), Bonete (6,759m), Veladero (6,436m), Reclus (6,335m), Olivares (6,220m), El Toro (6,160m), Los Gemelos (6,130m), De Las Tórtolas (6,105m), Famatina (6,097m) and Calinga (6,028m) in La Rioja.

East of the Andes lie discontinuous ranges of mountains, rising as high as 4,000m and known as *precordillera*: between these and the Andes, running north-south, are high valleys such as Uspallata, Uco, Calingasta, Iglesia and Vinchina. The eastern half of these provinces is arid steppe, part of a great geological depression into which flow the

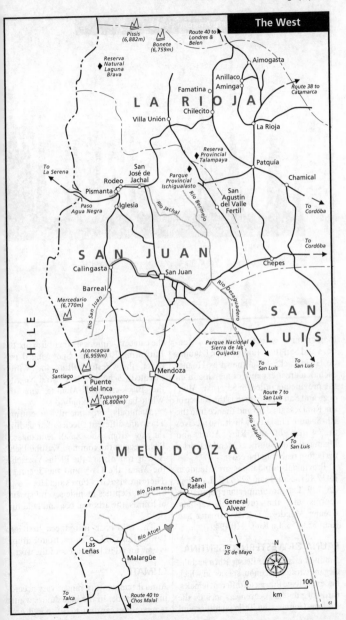

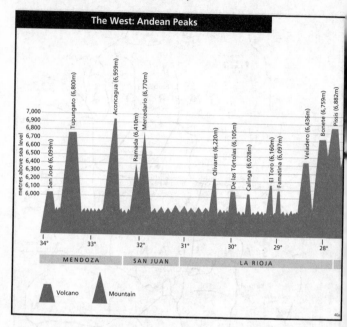

The West: Andean Peaks

MENDOZA   SAN JUAN   LA RIOJA

Volcano   Mountain

major rivers. Two of these, the Ríos Mendoza and San Juan, flow into the Lagunas de Guanacache (also known as Huanacacha), a great expanse of marshland on the provincial borders of San Juan, Mendoza and San Luis, which is the source of the Río Desaguadero and thence into the Río Salado. The latter, which also receives the waters of the Ríos Atuel and Diamante from southern Mendoza, dries up before reaching the coast.

Provincial populations are Mendoza 1,412,481, San Juan 528,715, La Rioja 220,729. The most important population centres are the provincial capitals: Greater Mendoza 773,559; Greater San Juan 353,456; La Rioja 110,494.

FAUNA OF WESTERN ARGENTINA

Among birds are the Lesser Rhea and the elegant Crested-tinamou, species in which males incubate the eggs of different females. Birds of prey and scavengers include the Andean Condor, the Turkey-vulture and the caracara. Amongst other birds are the Burrowing Parrot, the Spot-winged Falconet, the Crested-gallito, the White-throated Cacholote, the Austral Negrito, the Black-crowned Monjita and the White-banded Mockingbird.

Mammals are mainly nocturnal. There are different species of armadillo, ranging from the small endangered Pichiciego to the common Wailing Pichi. Among rodents are the Plains Vizcacha, the Mara, the Cavy and the Tucotuco. There are also Grey Foxes and Hog-nosed Skunks. Reptiles include several species of lizards, the arboreal boa and land turtles.

The wild boar, introduced first into Parque Luro in La Pampa, from Europe, is now found in large areas of the west.

CLIMATE

Annual temperature ranges vary according to altitude. In the high Andes winter temperatures can drop to -30° though even

Andean condor

Burrowing Parrots

in winter daytime temperatures can rise rapidly. On the plains maximum summer temperatures range from 36° to 43° in La Rioja: winters in the plains are cool, but rarely below -3°. The high valleys west of the *cordillera frontal* often enjoy the most pleasant climate with winter minima of -14° in July and summer maxima of around 30° in February.

Sheltered from the Pacific Ocean by the Andes, these three provinces generally receive little rain; rainfall is lowest in La Rioja, especially in the eastern steppe and highest in southern Mendoza. Although snow falls in the mountains of Mendoza in winter, snow is less common in San Juan or La Rioja. Rainfall is concentrated in the summer months and often falls as heavy storms.

ECONOMY

In this area of slight rainfall, little can be grown except under irrigation. In Mendoza only 4% of the 15 million hectares of land are cultivated, most of it in the two important oases formed by the Ríos Mendoza and Tunuyán in the north and around the Ríos Diamante and Atuel, 160 km to the south around San Rafael. Wine dominates the provincial economy: of the cultivated area 40% is given over to vines, 25% is under alfalfa grown for cattle, and the rest is devoted to olive groves, fruit trees and vegetables. Petroleum is produced in the south of the province, and there are important uranium deposits. The main manufacturing industries are petrochemicals, chemicals and machinery.

The Zonda

Though the *zonda*, a warm, dry, westerly wind, can occur throughout western Argentina and at any time of year, it most commonly affects Mendoza and San Juan between August and October. Beginning over the Pacific as a wet wind, the *zonda* deposits its humidity on the Chilean side of the Andes; as it drops on the eastern side of the *cordillera*, its temperature increases 1° for every 100m. By the time it reaches the plains it is very dry and very warm, in winter causing an unseasonal increase in temperatures and provoking snowfalls in the mountains. Though it blows away the dust in the atmosphere, allowing you to see clearly over long distances, Argentines often stress its negative effects: apart from the physical damage to houses and crops, it is said to cause headaches and sickness. The *Pirelli* guide to Argentina warns that it provokes "emotional instability, an increase in delinquency and even alterations in sexual behaviour!"

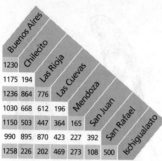

	Buenos Aires	Chilecito	Las Rioja	Las Cuevas	Mendoza	San Juan	San Rafael
Chilecito	1230						
Las Rioja	1175	194					
Las Cuevas	1236	864	776				
Mendoza	1030	668	612	196			
San Juan	1150	503	447	364	165		
San Rafael	990	895	870	423	227	392	
Ischigualasto	1258	226	202	469	273	108	500

The West: distance chart (km)

San Juan and La Rioja are less fortunate. San Juan relies heavily on agriculture and is Argentina's second largest wine producer; La Rioja is more varied: agriculture is important, but there is also considerable mining activity for gold, silver, copper, lead, zinc and other minerals and industry includes food processing, textiles, chemicals and electronics.

MENDOZA

(*Population*: of city 121,000, of Gran Mendoza 773,559; *Altitude* 756m; *Phone code* 061) Mendoza is situated 1,060 km from Buenos Aires at the foot of the Andes. Around it is the broad plain of the Río Mendoza; intensive cultivation and irrigation has made this the heartland of Argentine wine production. An important route centre, especially for travel to Chile, it lies at the centre of the largest conurbation in western Argentina: the other towns in *Gran Mendoza* are Guaymallén (200,000), Godoy Cruz (179,000) Las Heras (146,000), Maipú (72,000) and Lujan del Cuyo (54,000).

History

Founded from Chile in 1561, the city was named after García Hurtado de Mendoza, then governor of Chile. In the colonial period it was of little significance, being governed from Chile and having little contact with modern-day Argentina. The city was completely destroyed on Easter Saturday 1861 by an earthquake which killed some 4,000 of its 12,000 inhabitants. After 1861 a new centre was planned, several blocks to the west; this modern city with its broad avenues and attractive plazas was planted with trees watered by a network of irrigation channels 500 km long.

Places of interest

The centre of the city is the **Plaza Independencia**, a large square in the middle of which are the Museo de Arte Moderno and a theatre. On the western side and dating from the 1920s is the *Plaza Hotel*, which accommodated Argentine presidents, including Juan Perón and Evita, on their visits to the city; though run down, it is worth a visit. Next door is the Teatro Independencia, which can also be visited. Off the corners of Plaza Independencia are four smaller squares: of these the most attractive is the **Plaza España**, pleasantly tiled and with a mural displaying historical episodes and scenes from *Don Quijote* and *Martín Fierro*.

East of Plaza Independencia and linked to it by pedestrianized Paseo Sarmiento is **Avenida San Martín**, the city's main boulevard and a popular meeting place: it is closed to public transport which passes instead along 9 de Julio and San Juan. Most of the

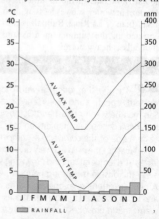

Climate: Mendoza

Mendoza and San Juan

🐚 "To be between San Juan and Mendoza" is an Argentine expression for alcoholic excess. Yet of the two provinces, it is Mendoza which dominates wine production: in an average year 71% of all Argentine wine is made within its boundaries (23% comes from San Juan) and almost all the leading wineries are based in Mendoza. Lying at about the same southern latitude as the northern latitudes of France, Italy and California, the province is favoured by its temperate climate, clearly defined seasons and lack of extremes of temperature.

The 130,000 hectares of vineyards in the province are located in two main regions: in the north centred around the provincial capital and in the south around San Rafael. A third area, semi-separated from Mendoza, can be found tucked at the foot of the Andes, due west of the capital around the small town of Tupungato. While a few vineyards are found below 500m, the best, in the departments of Maipú and Lujan del Cuyo, are situated at between 700m and 1,000m. Tupungato vineyards are at 900m to 1,300m. The local soils are sandy and/or calcareous, often with pebbles and limestone, and occasionally clay. The vineyards, in common with all Argentine vineyards except for a few exceptions in Salta, are planted on flat, slightly sloping land, so as to allow for efficient irrigation.

Grape picking is still almost entirely by hand, mechanical harvesting being rare. The season starts in the second half of February and ends in the first 10 days of April, though the dates vary slightly from area to area. As a result Argentine wines are ready about 6 months before European wines in any given year. A picturesque wine festival is held in Mendoza during the first week of March, with a crowning of the Festival Queen as a spectacular closing act to a monster show held in an open air amphitheatre in the Parque San Martín.

Dereck Foster

city's public buildings lie five blocks south of Plaza Independencia in the *Barrio Cívico*. The original city centre, destroyed in 1861, now known as the **Area Fundacional**, is about 10 blocks north of the centre: here there are a museum and the ruins of the Jesuit church of **San Francisco**. The best shopping centre is **Avenida Las Heras**, where there are good souvenir, leather and handicraft shops. At **Plaza Pellegrini**, Avenida Alem y Avenida San Juan, an attractive little square, wedding photos are taken on Friday and Saturday nights.

10 blocks west of Plaza Independencia are the wrought iron entrance gates to the great **Parque San Martín**, covering some 420 hectares and containing over 50,000 trees of 750 species, as well as watercourses, a 1 km-long artificial lake, where regattas are held, a sports stadium, an amphitheatre and the **Jardín Zoológico** (US$1). There are views of the Andes (when the amount of floating dust will

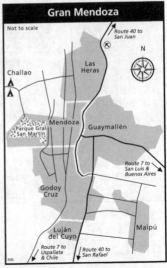

Gran Mendoza

allow) rising in a blue-black perpendicular wall, topped off in winter with dazzling snow, into a china-blue sky. On a hill above the park is the **Cerro de la Gloria**, crowned by the **monument to San Martín**: a great rectangular stone block with bas-reliefs depicting various episodes in the equipping of the Army of the Andes and the actual crossing. In front of the block, San Martín bestrides his charger.

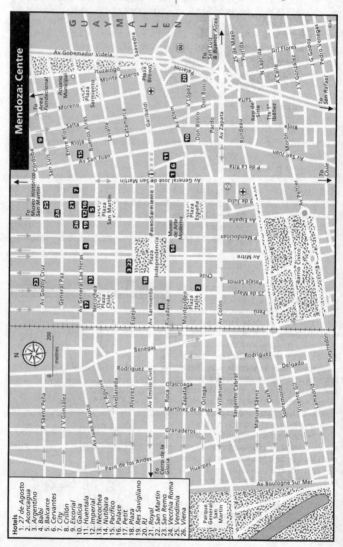

Mendoza: Centre

Hotels
1. 27 de Agosto
2. Aconcagua
3. Argentino
4. Balbi
5. Balcarce
6. Cervantes
7. City
8. Crillón
9. Escorial
10. Gran
11. Huentala
12. Imperial
13. Necochea
14. Nutibara
15. Pacífico
16. Palace
17. Petit
18. Plaza
19. Res Savigliano
20. RJ
21. Royal
22. San Martín
23. San Remo
24. Vecchia Roma
25. Vendimia
26. Viena

To reach the park entrance take bus 110 from Sarmiento west of Plaza Independencia or the *trolley* from Sarmiento y 9 de Julio. An hourly bus ('Oro Negro') runs to the top of the Cerro de la Gloria from the east end of the park, on Avenida Libertad – it's a long walk (45 minutes).

Tours

Official tours of the city are generally poor value. A large sign in Plaza Independencia shows a walking tour which takes about 2 hours. The Municipal Tourist Office runs a bus service (*Bus Turístico*) around the city, with commentary by the driver, daily 1000-2000, US$10, children under 12 US$5. There are 14 stops (clearly marked) and the bus waits for 15 minutes at Cerro de la Gloria: tourists can leave or join the bus at any point; tickets are valid for 24 hours. Map of route available from municipal tourist office.

Museums

Museo del Area Fundacional, Alberdi y Videla Castillo, history of Mendoza, Tuesday-Saturday 0800-1400, 1630-2230, Sunday afternoon only, contains the mummified body of a child found on Aconcagua, US$2, best organized museum in Mendoza, recommended.

Museo Histórico San Martín, Avenida San Martín 1843, containing artefacts from San Martín's campaigns and other items, poorly organized, open Monday-Friday 0900-1200, US$1.

Museo del Pasado Cuyano, Montevideo 544, large collection including sections on San Martín and history of Mendoza, open Tuesday-Saturday 0930-1230, US$0.50.

Museo de Ciencias Naturales and **Museo Arqueológico** (in the Ciudad Universitaria), Playas Serranes, Parque San Martín, Tuesday-Friday 0900-1200, 1400-1800, Saturday-Sunday 1500-1900.

Museo Municipal de Arte Moderno, underground (*subsuelo*) in Plaza Independencia, US$1.50, very small unless there is a special exhibition.

Acuario Municipal, underground at Buenos Aires e Ituzaingó, small but worth a visit, US$0.50, open Monday-Friday 1000-1200 and 1530-2000, Saturday and Sunday same times in the morning.

On the road south of the city to Luján de Cuyo (bus 200, 40 minutes) is the excellent Museo Provincial de Bellas Artes Emiliano Guiñazu, **Casa de Fader**, dedicated to Argentine artists, surrounded by sculpture in gardens, admission US$1.50, open Tuesday-Friday 0930-1330, 1500-1900, Saturday, Sunday 1630-2030, T 960224. For the **Museo Nacional del Vino**, see below.

Wine

Many *bodegas* welcome visitors; visiting times available from Tourist Office. Most *bodegas* are outside the city but one which is close is **Bodegas Escorihuela**, Belgrano 1188, Godoy Cruz, T 220157, reached by Bus T from Godoy Cruz y Garibaldi; tours Monday-Friday 0900, 1130, 1230, 1300, 1430, 1530.

La Colina de Oro

The Giol bodega, *La Colina de Oro* occupies a special place in the development of the Mendoza wine industry. Once the largest *bodega* in the world, it was named after the birthplace of Bautista Gargantini, who, with Juan Giol, founded *Bodegas Giol* in 1896. Oak casks for storage were imported from France, one of which, with a capacity of 75,000 litres was the largest in the world. Selling its wines under the labels *La Colina* and *El Toro*, the company expanded rapidly: at its height it employed over 800 workers, 400 of them making barrels, 180 as carters and 220 in the *bodega* itself. Some 1,200 mules were used for transport and the first aerial *vinoducto* (wine aqueduct) in the world, 3 km long, was built between the winemaking plant and one of its *bodegas*. Juan Giol eventually sold out to the Banco Español and in 1954 the company was taken over by the state. It was split up and privatized in 1988; the *bodega* is now owned by a cooperative of local vinegrowers.

San Martin the Liberator

Among the independence heroes of Spanish America José Francisco de San Martín stands equal to Simon Bolívar. Like Belgrano, he advocated a monarchy rather than a republic and like Bolívar he hoped to unite Spanish America after independence. Though he failed to achieve either aim, his military genius played a major role in securing independence. This genius lay mainly in his grasp of detail and his organizational ability even when leading troops scattered by large distances and mountainous terrain. His epic crossing of the Andes in 1817 was a turning point in the Wars of Independence; the campaigns which followed in Chile and Peru ended Spanish rule in South America.

Born in Yapeyú, Corrientes in 1778 and educated in Spain, San Martín served in the Spanish army in North Africa, Spain and France, gaining his first combat experience at the age of 15. In 1811 he resigned from the army and sailed for London where he made contact with Francisco de Miranda and other supporters of South American independence. Arriving in Buenos Aires the following year, he was appointed to train a new cavalry regiment. In December 1813 he replaced Belgrano as commander of the northern armies. Arguing against the view that the way to defeat the Spanish stronghold of Peru was by an offensive through Alto Peru (Bolivia), San Martín resigned in 1814. His request to be appointed governor of Cuyo province, based on Mendoza, was granted and he spent the next 2 years preparing to carry out his plan for the capture of Peru by means of a giant flanking movement through Chile and then up the coast to Lima.

The nucleus of his Army of the Andes was drawn from regular troops sent by Buenos Aires. Financed by reorganizing the taxation system of Cuyo, the army was armed by setting up arms factories around Mendoza. San Martín personally reconnoitred the mountain passes to plan the crossing to Chile. Realizing the importance of deception, he called a meeting of Pehuenche Indian chiefs in September 1816 and asked permission to cross their territory to invade Chile via the passes south of Mendoza; as expected spies carried this news across the Andes, leaving San Martín free to use a more northerly route. Though the main force crossed by the Los Patos and Uspallata passes, smaller columns crossed further

---

Several are southeast of Mendoza in **Maipú** (where you should see the lovely square and eat at the *Club Social*, good simple food): **La Colina de Oro**, Ozamis 1040, T 972090, reached by 151 bus marked 'Maipú', every hour, 0900-1230, 1500-1800 from terminal, US$1, short tour, good tasting, nearby is the **Museo Nacional del Vino**, in the Casa de Giol, Ozamis 914, T 975255; **López**, Ozamis 375, T 973610; **'La Rural' (Bodega Rutini)**, Montecaseros sin número, Coquimbito, T 973590, a small bodega, is worth visiting, bus 170, tours 0900-1100, 1600-1800, tasting, Museo del Vino (fascinating), open Monday-Friday 0800-1100, 1500-1800 (very sales oriented). In **Guaymallén**, east of Mendoza: **Santa**

Ana, Roca y Urquiza, T 211000, visits 0800-1700; **Toso**, JB Alberdi 808, T 380244, is small, old-fashioned, has excellent wines and an interesting, free guided tour, some tasting, highly recommended.

South of the city: **Chandon**, Ruta Provincial 15, Km 29, T 980830, tours Monday-Friday 0930, 1100, 1230, 1400, 1530, Saturday 0930, 1100, 1230. The **Orfila** bodega in San Martín, T (0623) 20637, 40 km east, located in the house of the Libertador, also has a wine museum.

Wine tastings are also available at **La Cava**, Benegas 776, Monday-Saturday 0900-1300, 1630-2100, Sunday 1000-1300. Prices at the *bodegas* have roughly a 100% mark-up from supermarket prices. Many

north and south. Setting out on 18-19 January 1817, 3,778 men with equipment, support services and 10,791 horses and mules crossed the Andes in 21 days, arriving on time at their intended destinations. Within days the army defeated the Spanish at Chacabuco and entered Santiago in triumph, but conclusive victory was delayed until the Battle of the Maipú (5 April 1818). With Chilean independence secure, San Martín led his forces by sea to Peru in 1820. Avoiding battle against the larger Spanish forces, he negotiated a truce and encouraged enemy desertions. Finally entering Lima in triumph, in July 1821, he assumed political and military command of the new republic of Peru.

San Martín's three meetings with Simon Bolívar in Guayaquil, Ecuador, in July 1822 are one of the most famous, and mysterious, episodes of his career. Afterwards San Martín returned to Lima, resigned his post and returned to his small farm in Mendoza. In 1824 he left for Europe, settling first in Brussels and later in Grand Bourg, France. He died in Boulogne-sur-Mer in 1850. In 1880 his remains were returned to Buenos Aires and placed in the Cathedral. Symbolizing to many Argentines the virtues of sacrifice, bravery and lack of personal gain, he is remembered by countless statues in squares across the country and by street names in even the smallest towns.

Bank note showing José de San Martín

tourist agencies include the *bodegas* in their half-day or day-long tours (US$10-13) but these visits are too short, with too few guides and little tasting – only of the cheaper wines, usually in plastic cups.

Excursions
To the thermal springs at **Cacheuta**, 29 km west and at **Villavicencio**, 47 km north (see **From Mendoza to Chile** below).

To **Embalse El Carrizal**, an artificial lake 60 km south, where there are yachting and fishing, campsites and picnic areas.

Local holidays
18 January (Crossing of the Andes); 25 July (Santiago Apóstol); 8 September (Virgin of Carmen de Cuyo). Hotels fill up fast

at the beginning of March for the *Fiesta de la Vendimia* (wine vintage festival). Prices rise at this time, and in July (the ski season) and September (the spring festival).

Local information
● Accommodation

Hotel prices			
L1	over US$200	L2	US$151-200
L3	US$101-150	A1	US$81-100
A2	US$61-80	A3	US$46-60
B	US$31-45	C	US$21-30
D	US$12-20	E	US$7-11
F	US$4-6	G	up to US$3

Unless otherwise stated, all hotels in range **D** and above have private bath. Assume friendliness and cleanliness in all cases.

L3 *Aconcagua*, San Lorenzo 545, T 204455, F 311085, 4-star, good service, good but expensive restaurant, pool, tourist advice and bookings available; *Huentata*, Primitivo de la Reta 1007, T 240766, 4-star, good; *Cervantes*, Amigorena 65, T/F 201782, central, modern.

A range: *Crillón*, Perú 1065, T 245525, F 248079, small, clean but overpriced; **A1** *Plaza*, Chile 1124 on main plaza, T/F 233000, elegant but faded, air conditioning; **A2** *Nutibara*, Mitre 867, T 295428, F 296628, central, air conditioning, parking, with breakfast, pool, recommended; **A3** *Palace*, Las Heras 70, T/F 234200, air conditioning, with breakfast, good beds, central; *San Martín*, Espejo 435, T 380677, recommended; *Vecchia Roma*, España 1615, T 232529 (next door to restaurant of same name), comfortable, safe; **A2** *Balbi*, Las Heras 340, T 233500, F 380626, pool, air conditioning, nice rooms, helpful; **A3** *Argentino*, Espejo 455, Plaza Independencia, T/F 254000, with breakfast, garage; **A3** *1° de Mayo*, Garibaldi 82, T 204296, F 204820, with breakfast, good beds, restaurant, recommended; **A3** *Milena*, Babilonia 17 (off San Juan), T 202738, with breakfast, small rooms, quiet; **A3** *Gran Ritz*, Peru 1008, T 235115, with breakfast; **A3** *Vendimia*, Godoy Cruz 101, T 250675, F 233099, good.

B range: *Acapulco*, Patricias Mendocinas 1785, T 230454, F 320124; *Center*, Alem 547, T/F 237234, with breakfast, parking, poor beds; *Imperial*, Las Heras 84, T 234671, old fashioned, central, with breakfast; *City*, General Paz 95, T 251343, including breakfast, helpful; *27 de Agosto*, Amigorena 36, T 200035, F 200023, with breakfast; *Petit*, Perú 1419, T 232099, without breakfast, recommended; *RJ*, Las Heras 212, T/F 380202, with breakfast, comfortable, helpful, English spoken, recommended; *Pacífico*, San Juan 1407, T/F 235444, modern, comfortable, good value; *Balcarce*, San Martín 1446, T 252579, old fashioned, with breakfast; *Andino*, Patricias Mendocinas 1528, T 202609, F 290059, with breakfast, parking, comedor; *Royal*, 9 de Julio 1550, T 380522/380675, breakfast included, air conditioning; *El Libertador*, España 247, T 290921, good; *Las Viñas*, Martinez de Rosas 1668, T 232501.

C range: *San Remo*, Godoy Cruz 477, T 234068, with breakfast, quiet, small rooms, rooftop terrace, secure parking, highly recommended; *El Piño Azul* apartments, San Martín 2848, T 304240; *Mayo*, 25 de Mayo 1265, T 254424, including breakfast, good value; *Zamora*, Perú 1156, T 257537, reasonable; *Necochea*, Necochea 541, T 253501, pleasant, cheerful, English spoken; *Escorial*, San Luis 263,

T 254777, recommended; *Viena*, Las Heras 240, T 20046, with breakfast. On Juan B Justo *Ideal*, No 270, T 256842, transport to bus terminal; *Embajador*, No 365, T 259129, air conditioning, good value; *Margal*, No 75, T 252013, central, safe, good, with fan.

D *Galicia*, San Juan 881, near Alem, T 202619, gloomy, kitchen facilities, air conditioning; *Hosp Los Andes*, de la Reta 1051, with bath, gloomy, basic; *Res Alberdi*, Alberdi 51, T 234110, run down; **E** pp *Res Savigliano*, Palacios 944, T 237746, near bus terminal, without bath, with breakfast, kitchen facilities, rooftop terrace, highly recommended 'best hostel in South America' (Heiner Muth, Freiburg, Germany); **E** pp *Hosp Eben-Ezer*, Alberdi 580, T 312635, quiet, German spoken; **E** pp *El Descanso*, Gral Paz 463; **E** pp *Dam-Sire*, Viamonte 410, near terminal; **E** pp *Hosp Doñas Carmen*, de la Reza 1047, 1st floor, T 203439, central, good for long stay; **E** pp *Alicia*, Alem 431, T 237799, without breakfast, near terminal.

Youth hostels **E** *Veris Tempus*, Tirasso 2170, T 263300, often has school groups, take bus 26B, 'Paraguayo', 20 minutes, ask driver; **E** pp, *Campo Base*, Lavalle 2028, Guaymallén, T 457661, buses 52, 54, 56 and T, small dormitories, camping, cooking and laundry facilities, climbing wall, information on climbing and permits for Aconcagua, recommended.

Camping In Parque General San Martín, T/F 296656. Two cheaper sites at El Challao, 6 km west of the city centre, reached by colectivo No 110 leaving every hour: *El Challao Camping*; *Camping Suizo*, T 302576, US$10 per site, modern with pool, barbecues, hot showers, friendly, recommended. At Guaymallén, 9 km east: *Saucelandia*. Take insect repellent. White gas (*bencina blanca*) can be bought at *Ferretería Alsina*, Catamarca 37.

● **Places to eat**
La Marchigiani, Patricias Mendocinas 1550, good varied menu, expensive; *Trevi*, Las Heras 70, good food and service, recommended; *Posta Las Marías*, San Martín 914, English spoken, speciality is roast kid, pricey but good; *Sarmiento*, Avenida Sarmiento 658 (*parrilla*), good; *Parrillada Arturito*, Chile 1515, good steak, good value, popular with locals; *Montecatini*, Gral Paz 370, wide variety, good food, good value, recommended; *Mesón Español*, Montevideo 244, good food and atmosphere, pricey, Charlie the blind pianist plays requests; *Centro Catalá*, San Juan 1437, good fixed menu, recommended; *La Reja 14*, San Lorenzo 65, good meat, recommended; *Club Alemán*, Necochea 2261, Godoy Cruz, recommended. Ice cream at *Soppelsa*, Las Heras y España and at Paseo Sarmiento, recommended. *Sr Cheff*,

restaurant/confiteria at *Hotel 1 de Mayo*, Garibaldi 80. *Il Tucco*, Emilio Civit 556, also in centre at Paseo Sarmiento 68, excellent Italian restaurants, reasonable prices; *Boccaduro*, Mitre 1976, *parrilla*, good. Good value, and big 'super pancho' sandwiches in many places, including *Pizzería Sebastián*, Alem 431; *Pizzería Mi Querencia*, Las Heras 523, good pasta dishes and atmosphere; *Aranjuez*, Lavalle y San Martín, nice café, good meeting place; *Mankie Snack Bar*, Las Heras y Mitre, excellent breakfasts; several good snack bars (known as *carrito* bars): *Tío Paco*, Salta y Alem; *Torombola*, San Juan 1348; *Don Claudio*, Benegas 744; *El Gran Lomo*, San Martín y Pedro Molina, open 24 hours, recommended. There are several cheap eating places near the terminal along Alem opposite the hospital.

Vegetarian: *Comedor Línea Verde*, Montecaseros 1177, *tenedor libre*; *Date Cuenta*, Montecaseros 1177; *Las Vías*, Catamarca 76.

● **Airline offices**
Aerolíneas Argentinas and **Austral**, Paseo Sarmiento 82, T 204100; **Andesmar**, Espejo 189, T/F 380654 and bus terminal; **Lapa**, España 1012, T 291061; **Lapsa**, España 1057, 7th floor, Of 10, T/F 296287; **TAN**, España 1012, T 340240; **Dinar**, Paseo Sarmiento 69, T/F 205138; **Ladeco**, Sarmiento 144, T 291868; **Interaustral**, San Martín 92, T 202200.

● **Banks & money changers**
Lloyds Bank (BLSA), General Gutiérrez 72, cash advance on Mastercard, no commission; **Banco de Crédito Argentino**, España 1168, cash advance on Visa card, high commission; **Citibank**, Avenida San Martín 1099, gives US$ cash for travellers' cheques. **Banco Roberts**, Espejo 9 de Julio, low commission and good rates on travellers' cheques (go to counter marked 'inversiones'). Many *casas de cambio* along San Martín, including **Exprinter**, No 1198, 2% commission on travellers' cheques; **Santiago**, No 1199, recommended; **Maguitur**, No 1203, 1.5% commission on travellers' cheques. *Casas de cambio* open till 2000 Monday-Friday, and some open Saturday morning.

● **Cultural centres**
Alianza Francesa, Chile 1754; **Instituto Dante Alighieri** (Italy), Espejo 638; **Instituto Cultural Argentino-Norteamericano**, Chile 985; **Instituto Cuyano de Cultura Hispánica** (Spain), Villanueva 389; **Goethe Institut**, Morón 265, Monday-Friday, 0800-1200, 1600-2230, German newspapers, Spanish classes, very good.

● **Consulates**
Bolivia, Eusebio Blanco y 25 de Mayo, T 292458; **Chile**, Emilio Civit 599, T 255024; **Belgium**, Cuadros 156, Godoy Cruz, T 396338; **Spain**, Agustín Alvarez 455, T 253947; **Italy**, Perú 1396, T 231640, F 380714; **France**, Houssay 790, T 231542; **Germany**, Montevideo 127, 1st floor D6, T 296539; **Finland**, Boulogne Sur Mer 889, 6th floor, T 972388; **Israel**, Olascoaga 838, T 380642.

● **Entertainment**
Casino: 25 de Mayo 1123, daily 2100-0300.

Cinema: *Cine de Arte Eisenchlas*, 9 de Julio 500, Thursday-Sunday 2200.

Discotheques: *Saudades*, Barraquero y San Martín; *Kalatraba*, Perú 1779.

● **Hospitals & medical services**
Central hospital near bus terminal at Alem y Salta, T 248600. There is a private gynaecological clinic at Gral Paz 445; helpful and relatively inexpensive.

● **Language schools**
Sra Inés Perea de Bujaldon, Rioja 620, T 290429, teaches Spanish to German speakers, recommended.

● **Laundry**
Coin-operated laundromat, at corner of San Juan and Rondeau. *Laverap*, Avenida Colón 547, recommended; *La Lavandería*, San Lorenzo 338.

● **Post & telecommunications**
Post Office: Avenida San Martín y Avenida Colón, unreliable *poste restante*.

Telephone: *Telefónica de Argentina*, Chile 1584. There are many *locutorios* around the centre.

● **Shopping**
Mercado Central, Avenida Las Heras y Patricias Mendocinas, clean, well-stocked, closes 1300-1630. *Centro Comercial Plaza Mendoza*, on the eastern outskirts, has supermarkets, shops, fast food and cinemas. Leather goods good and cheap, try *Alain de France*, Olegario V Andrade 147. English language magazines and *Buenos Aires Herald* usually available from kiosks on San Martín.

● **Sports**
Gymnasium: San Juan y Buenos Aires.

Mountain climbing: information from Tourist Office. Club Andinista, F L Beltrán 357, Gillén, T 319870. There is a 3-day (Thursday-Saturday) climbing and trekking expedition via Godoy Cruz and Cacheuta to Cerro Penitentes (4,351m), sleeping in mountain refuge, food included. See also page 203.

River rafting: is popular; ask agencies for details.

Skiing: ski resorts near Mendoza are: Los Penitentes, 165 km west and Vallecito, 79 km west, both on the route to Chile (see below) and Manantiales, 63 km west of Tunuyán (south of Mendoza). The best skiing in the province is at Las Leñas, south of San Rafael (see page 206). Equipment hire *Piré*, Las Heras 615, T 257699 and other agencies.

● **Tour companies & travel agents**
Lots, especially on Paseo Sarmiento. *Cuyo Travel*, Paseo Sarmiento 162, 10% discount for ISIC and youth card holders for trekking and climbing on Aconcagua. *Turismo Cóndor*, 25 de Mayo 1537, T 234019 (also at bus terminal), recommended for tours in and around the city, and to El Cristo Redentor statue, good guides, Spanish only; *Mylatours*, Paseo Sarmiento 133, T 380717, recommended; *Turismo Sepeán*, San Juan 1070, T 204162, friendly and helpful, have branch in Santiago (Chile); *Turismo Cultural*, Rivadavia 211, T 242579, helpful; *Servicios Especiales Mendoza*, Annette Schenker, c/o Hotel Cervantes, Amigorena 65, 5500 Mendoza, F (061) 244721, 240131, or Radio, code 548, 242162/244505, guided tours, many languages spoken, waterskiing on El Carrizal lake, climbing Aconcagua and Andes, trekking and other specialist programmes; *Road Runner*, in bus teminal, trekking, horseriding, rafting; *José Orviz*, Juan B Justo 550/536, T/F 256950, guides, mules, transportation and hire of mountain trekking equipment. Many agencies, including those in the terminal, run tours in high summer to the *Cristo Redentor* statue via Puente del Inca, US$28, 12 hours, only 15 minutes at statue. Other local tours offered include Mendoza city tour, US$20; wine tour US$13; Puente del Inca, US$28. Agencies also offer longer excursions including to the Valle de la Luna, US$80, 22 hours and to San Luis province, US$39, 15 hours.

● **Tourist offices**
Provincial office, San Martín 1143, T 202800. Municipal offices at Paseo Sarmiento/Garibaldi y San Martín, T 201333, central, very helpful, open 0900-2100, and at Las Heras 670. Also at airport, T 306484, helpful (frequently closed). They have a list of reasonable private lodgings and a hotel booking service (**B** range and upwards), and other literature including lists of *bodegas* and an excellent free town and province map.

● **Useful addresses**
ACA, San Martín y Amigorena; *Migraciones*, España 1425, T 380569; *Travelling Student*, San Martín 1366, local 16, T 290029/30.

● **Transport**
Local Buses: all city buses have two numbers, one is large and ends in zero (eg 140); below it is a smaller number (eg 141, 142, 143, etc), which is the one to look for. Local directions will usually give both numbers, eg 140, sub-número 145. **Car hire**: Herbst, in *Hotel Plaza*, Chile 1124, T 289403, reliable vehicles from US$70 per day including mileage and insurance, recommended; *Avis*, La Rioja 1462, T 255601; **Lis Car**, San Lorenzo 110, T 291416; **Localiza**, at airport and Necochea 425, T 491491; **Al Rent a Car**, San Juan 1012, T/F 304040. **Bicycles**: *El Túnel*, at exit from bus terminal, buys and sells cycles, also repairs, friendly. **Motorcycle repairs**: César Armitrano, Rubén Zarate 138, 1600-2100, highly recommended for assistance or a chat; he will let you work in his workshop.

Air   El Plumerillo, 8 km north of centre, T 487128, has *casa de cambio* and a few shops. Reached by *remise* taxis (US$7, including US$1 to enter airport grounds) and bus No 68 from San Juan y Alem which takes you close to the terminal (10 minutes' walk); make sure there is an 'Aeropuerto' sign on the driver's window. To **Buenos Aires**: 1 hour 50 minutes, with AR, Lapa, Austral, Interaustral and Dinar. National and Ladeco to **Santiago**, daily. To **Córdoba**, AR, Austral, Interaustral and Andesmar; Andesmar also to **Tucumán**, US$129, **Salta**, US$149, and **Neuquén**. Kaiken serves many destinations in the south. AR, Dinar and Lapa to **San Juan**. To **Malargüe**, TAN and TAPSA. TAN to **Neuquén**. Southern Winds to **Córdoba**, **Tucumán** and **Salta**.

Buses Terminal on east side of Avenida Videla, 15 minutes' walk from centre, T 313001, with shops, post office, tourist information and supermarket (open late). To **Buenos Aires**, 15 hours, second class US$30-40, first class, US$55, companies including Chevallier, TAC, Jocoli, El Rápido, Expreso Uspallata, La Cumbre, La Estrella; to **Bariloche**, Andesmar daily, TAC, 3 a week, US$70, 22 hours, book well ahead; to **Córdoba**, Colta, TAC and La Cumbre, 9 hours, US$35 (for scenery go via Las Altas Cumbres in daylight); to **San Rafael**, many daily, Empresa Uspallata, 3½ hours, US$10; to **Malargüe**, Empresa Uspallata, 5½ hours, US$19; to **San Luis**, Jocoli, US$14, 3 hours, frequent; to **San Juan**, Colta, ESMA, La Cumbre and TAC, frequent, US$11, 2 hours; to **La Rioja**, US$25, 10 hours, La Estrella and Libertador; similarly to **Catamarca**, 12 hours, daily, US$25; to **Tucumán**, Andesmar, La Estrella, Libertador, TAC, US$29; to **Salta**, Andesmar and Bosio (via Tucumán), 20 hours, US$52; to **Puerto Iguazú** at 1930, Monday, Wednesday, Saturday with Cotal, US$70, 38 hours; alternatively take daily

Villa Marta bus to Santa Fe and change, about 40 hours including waiting time; to **Comodoro Rivadavia**, daily with Andesmar, at 2000, US$100, 32 hours including four meal stops; the Tuesday and Saturday departures continue to Río Gallegos, arriving 1450 Thursday; to **Rosario**, US$30, 12 hours. 20% student discount on some routes (eg Comodoro Rivadavia).

Transport to Santiago, Chile: cars and minibuses run by Chiar – some adverse reports – and Nevada, US$30, fast, friendly, 5½-6 hours. When booking, ensure that the car will pick you up and drop you at your hotel; have this written on your receipt, if not you will be dropped at the bus terminal. Regular bus services, daily, several companies, El Rápido, Tur Bus and TAC have been recommended, mixed reports on other companies. Most buses are comfortable and fast (6½-8 hours) and charge US$20-25, those with air conditioning and hostess service (including breakfast) charge more, worth it when crossing the border as waiting time can be a matter of several hours. Passport required when booking, tourist cards given on bus. Children under 8 pay 60% of adult fare, but no seat; book at least 1 day ahead, shop around. The journey over the Andes is spectacular. If you want to return, buy an undated return ticket Santiago-Mendoza; it is cheaper. Taxi to Santiago costs about US$90 for 4-5 people.

Other international buses: to **Viña del Mar**, TAC, CATA and El Rápido daily, US$20-25; to **Valparaíso**, 2 daily, US$20-25; to **La Serena**, via Agua Negra pass, El Rápido, CATA, summer only; to **Lima**, El Rápido, Monday, Wednesday, Saturday 0900; also Ormeño, 3 a week; to **Montevideo**, Tas Choapa, El Rápido, Gral Artigas, 1 a week each, US$66.

Hitchhiking: between Mendoza and Buenos Aires is quite easy. If hitching to San Juan, take bus No 6 to the airport which is near Route 40. Hitching from Mendoza to Los Andes (Chile) is easy; go to the service station in Godoy Cruz suburb (bus No 6), from where all trucks to Chile, Peru and elsewhere leave.

FROM MENDOZA TO CHILE

From Mendoza Route 7 runs west to Chile via the international tunnel. This route is sometimes blocked by snow in winter (June-October): if travelling by car in these months enquire about road conditions from ACA in Mendoza. Officially, driving without snow chains and a shovel is prohibited between Uspallata and the border. ACA and Chilean Automobile Club sell, but do not rent, chains, but ask at YPF station in Uspallata about chain rental. If driving in mountains remember to advance the spark by adjusting the distributor, or weaken the mixture in the carburettor, to avoid the car seizing up in the rarified air.

There are two alternatives of Route 7 from Mendoza as far as Uspallata; the southern route following the Río Mendoza

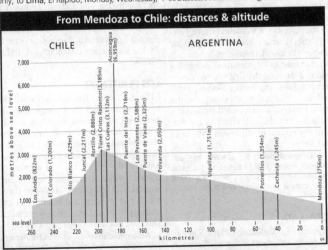

From Mendoza to Chile: distances & altitude

via Cacheuta, being much easier than the northern one via **Villavicencio** (*altitude* 1,700m), Km 47, where there are hot springs, much frequented by tourists, and pleasant walks nearby. The *Gran Hotel* is under restoration, but the park can be visited. Beyond Villavicencio the road is unpaved over the spectacular Cruz del Paramillo (*altitude* 3,050m), offering views of Aconcagua, Tupungato and Mercedario, and round the *Caracoles de Villavicencio*, 365 bends which give the route its name, *La Ruta del Año* (Route of the Year).

Cacheuta

(*Altitude* 1,245m) 42 km west of Mendoza along the southern route to Uspallata, has thermal springs, US$8 entry (indoor thermal baths for a variety of ailments, for residents only).

● **Accommodation**   L *Hotel Termas*, T 316085, full board; *Hostería Mis Montañas*, 400m west. **Camping** Two sites: *Camping Termas de Cacheuta*, T 259000; *Camping Don Elias*, 4 km west.

● **Buses** TAC and Empresa Uspallata from Mendoza.

Potrerillos

(*Altitude* 1,354m) Km 58, is a charming resort situated at the foot of the Cordón del Plata mountains, excellent birdwatching in summer. A 21 km road turns off here for the ski resort of **Vallecito** (season July-September) which has a ski-lodge, four *refugios*, ski school, restaurant. In summer you can hike to Vallecito from Potrerillos taking 2 days: on the first you see desert scenery, blooming cactus flowers, birds and an occasional goat or cow; on the second you walk surrounded by peaks, a steep but not difficult climb to the San Antonio refuge, usually open with beds and meals.

● **Accommodation & places to eat** A1 *Gran Hotel*, T 0624-82010 or via *Hotel Plaza*, Mendoza, with meals, 3-star. **Camping** ACA campsite. *Restaurant Armando*, recommended.

USPALLATA

(*Population* 3,000; *Altitude* 1,751m) Km 100, is the only settlement of any size between Mendoza and the Chilean frontier. A former silver and zinc mining town, it lies in the valley of the Río Uspallata: a road follows the valley north to Barreal (108 km) and Calingasta (see page 212), unpaved for its first part and tricky when the snow melts and floods it in summer. North of the town are Las Bóvedas, several metal foundries built of *adobe* and an Inca *tambería*; there is a small, interesting museum.

● **Accommodation** A2 *Valle Andino*, Ruta 7, T (0624) 20033, good rooms and restaurant, heating, pool, including breakfast, ACA discount; A3 *Uspallata*, T 20003, nice location, but run down, good service; C *Hostería Los Cóndores*, T 20002, good restaurant; *Donde Pato*, Ruta 7, good food and service. **Camping** Municipal site, US$3 per tent, hot water.

● **Buses** From Mendoza, 0700, 1000, US$10.

WEST OF USPALLATA

The road crosses a vast, open, undulating plain, wild and bare. On all sides stand the grey, gaunt mountains. On the far side of this plain the valley narrows till Río Blanco is reached, the road climbs steeply and the mountain torrents rush and froth into the river. The majestic cone of **Tupungato**, one of the giants of the Andes, rising to 6,800m, can be seen by looking left up the Tupungato valley about 2 km after Punta de Vacas. Walking tours in the Tupungato area can be arranged by Quinche Romulo, Alte Brown, Tupungato (a town 73 km southwest of Mendoza), T 0622-88029.

LOS PENITENTES

(*Altitude* 2,580m) Km 165, is a small ski resort named after the majestic mass of pinnacled rocks; from their base (easily reached with a guide from Puente del Inca – see below), the higher rocks look like a church and the smaller, sharper rocks below give the impression of a number of cowled monks climbing upwards. Skiing is good with few people on slopes: there are 28 pistes with a total length of 24 km and eight lifts. Open May-September. Daily ski hire US$35, lift pass US$30.

● **Accommodation**   A3-B *Ayelén*, T 259990, comfortable; C *La Taberna del*

Gringo, Km 151, Villa Los Penitentes, recommended; *Hostería Penitentes*, and others; **B** *Cruz de Caña* ski club, 1 km west, only open in season, with comfortable dormitories, including meals, and a good restaurant. The owner organizes trekking expeditions to Plaza de Mulas on Aconcagua; US$50 a day full board during expedition, and US$20 per mule.

PUENTE DEL INCA

(*Population* 100; *Altitude* 2,718m) Km 172, is a sports resort set among mountains of great grandeur. The natural bridge after which the resort is named is one of the wonders of South America; it crosses the Río Mendoza at a height of 19m, has a span of 21m, and is 27m wide, and seems to have been formed by sulphur-bearing hot springs. Watch your footing on the steps; extremely slippery. There are hot thermal baths just under the bridge, a little dilapidated but a great place to soak your feet. Puente del Inca is the best point for horseriding excursions into the higher Andean valleys. West of the village (you can walk along the old railway), to the right, there is a fine view of Aconcagua sharply silhouetted against the sky. Los Horcones, the Argentine customs post, is 1 km west. To visit the Laguna Horcones in the Parque Provincial Aconcagua see below.

● **Accommodation A3-B** *Hostería Puente del Inca*, T 380480, less off-season, very pleasant atmosphere, friendly service, good food, more expensive if booked in Mendoza; **E** pp *Parador del Inca*, with breakfast, dormitories, sleeping bag essential, cheap meals; **E** pp *La Vieja Estación*, old railway station, dormitory, kitchen facilities, meals served. **Camping** *Los Puquios*, 1 km east; also possible next to the church, if your equipment can withstand the winds. Better site near Laguna de los Horcones in the Parque Provincial Aconcagua.

● **Buses** Expreso Uspallata from Mendoza, US$8, 4 hours, 0700 and 1000, returning from Puente del Inca 1130 and 1615; local buses also go on from Puente del Inca to Las Cuevas, Expreso Uspallata, US$12 return (**NB** Take passport). Most buses from Mendoza to Santiago de Chile refuse to drop passengers here but El Rápido will do so if you book in advance. Some buses for Santiago stop here and may take passengers if they have seats.

ACONCAGUA

(*Altitude* 6,959m) The highest peak in the world outside Asia, gets its name from the Quechua for 'stone sentry'. Five great glaciers hang from its slopes. While its north face is relatively easy to climb (the list of successful ascents includes two Italians on bicycles in 1987 and four blind climbers in 1994) the south face is almost impossible. The north face was first climbed by Zurbriggen of the Fitzgerald Expedition in 1897. In 1985, a complete Inca mummy was discovered at 5,300m. Best time for climbing is from end-December to February.

The **Parque Provincial Aconcagua**, 75,000 hectares, includes 30 other peaks over 4,000m, nine of them over 5,000m. Entry is via the Valle de los Horcones, 2 km west of Puente del Inca; here is a Ranger station, excellent views of Aconcagua, especially in the morning; free camping, open climbing season only. From here the route leads past the Laguna de los Horcones with reflections of Aconcagua in its green waters. At Confluencia (3,200m), 3 hours further walking, there is a campsite (recommended if pacing yourself). Confluencia is the meeting point of two valleys: Horcones Superior and Horcones Inferior, which lead to the Plaza de Mulas and Plaza de Francia base camps respectively. There is no drinking-water after Confluencia: take your own.

At Plaza de Mulas (4,370m), 38 km from Puente del Inca, there is the highest hotel in the world (see below), and a rescue patrol, crowded in summer. Plaza de Francia (4,200m), 25 km from Puente del Inca, is less crowded in summer.

Permits For trekking or climbing a permit is required: these must be obtained in advance from Dirección de Recursos Naturales Renovables, Parque Gral San Martín, Mendoza, T 252090. 7-day trekking January US$40, December/February US$30, rest of year US$10. For climbing a 20-day permit is required (foreigners: January US$120, December/February US$80, rest of year US$30, Argentines half-price).

ACCESS Allow at least 1 week for acclimatization at lower altitudes before attempting the summit. The north face is climbed from the Plaza de Mulas base camp (4 days). The south face, which should only be attempted by very experienced climbers, is reached from Plaza de Francia. Mules can be hired at Puente del Inca for the journey to the base camp (shop around; large differences in muleteers prices; more economical to travel with a group); you have to pay for 3 days there and back (1 day rest) and for the muleteer.

● **Accommodation** Hotel Plaza de Mulas, **L3** pp full-board, **B** pp without meals, good food, information, medical treatment, recommended, also camping area.

● **Equipment** Take a tent able to withstand 100 miles per hour winds, and clothing and sleeping gear for temperatures below -40°C. Equipment hire at hotel.

● **Climbing information** Trekking and climbing programmes can be booked through agencies in Mendoza and Buenos Aires (eg Proterra Turismo, Lavalle 750, p 20 D, T/F 326-2639). Prices from US$990 to US$1,890 for 10 days. Treks and climbs are also organized by Sr Fernando Grajales, the famous climber, in Hostería Puente del Inca, by Roger Cangiani at Campo Base in Mendoza or at Moreno 898, 5500 Mendoza, Telex 55-154. Information also from Eduardo Enrique Esteban, Emilio Civit 320, Maipú, Mendoza, CP 5515, T/F (61) 973393 and Carlos and Amalia Cuesta, Los Gateados, near Cementerio de los Andinistas, 1 km before Puente del inca (December-February, or T Mendoza 391080/290410), recommended for details on mules, trekking and climbing (see also under Mendoza, **Tour companies & travel agents**). Further information from Dirección de Recursos Naturales Renovables.

LAS CUEVAS

(Altitude 3,112m) Km 188, a collection of eight buildings, is advertised as a skiing resort (though there is no ski-lift as yet). Beyond, the road goes through the 3.2 km Cristo Redentor Tunnel to Chile (US$2 for cars and VW buses). Before the opening of the tunnel the route led over La Cumbre pass and the statue of **El Cristo Redentor** (Christ the Redeemer) at 4,200m, erected jointly by Chile and Argentina in 1904 to celebrate the British arbitration in 1902 of boundary disputes between the two countries. The statue, 8m high, is completely dwarfed by the landscape. Though the pass is now closed, the statue may be visited by taking the old road, though this is closed in winter. To walk from Las Cuevas, allow 4½ hours up, 2 hours down: you should be in good condition and the weather should be fine. Agencies in Mendoza also offer 12-hour excursions in summer (see above for details).

● **Accommodation & places to eat A3** Hostería Las Cuevas, half-board, warm rooms, food OK. Food available at kiosk at Expreso Uspallata bus stop.

FRONTIER WITH CHILE

● **Argentine immigration**
The Chilean border is beyond Las Cuevas, but all Argentine entry and exit formalities are dealt with at Punta de Vacas, 30 km east of Las Cuevas.

● **Argentine customs**
A new customs post, Ingeniero Roque Carranza has been built near Los Horcones, 2 km west of Puente del Inca. Customs at the frontier are open 0700-1830 (1800 in summer).

● **Chilean customs**
Thorough search of vehicles entering Chile for fruit, vegetables and dairy products.

● **Crossing by private vehicle**
Car drivers can undertake all formalities in advance at Uspallata while refuelling. Members of ACA need only the Libreta de Pasos por Aduana, otherwise you need the Documento de Exportación to enter Chile.

● **Chilean consulate**
See under Mendoza. **NB** No visas into Chile are available at the border. Tourist cards are given out on international buses.

● **Hitchhiking**
You can hitchhike, or possibly bargain with bus drivers for a seat, from Punta de Vacas to Santiago, but if you are dropped at the entrance to the tunnel in winter, one cannot walk through. Travellers report that customs officers may help by asking motorists to take hitchhikers through to Chile.

SOUTHERN MENDOZA

The main settlements in southern Mendoza lie in the oases of the valleys of the Ríos Atuel and Diamante where irrigation has made large-scale fruit growing possible. West of the main city of San

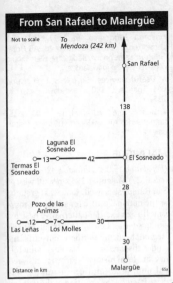

From San Rafael to Malargüe

Not to scale

To Mendoza (242 km)

San Rafael

138

Laguna El Sosneado

Termas El Sosneado — 13 — — 42 — El Sosneado

28

Pozo de las Animas

Las Leñas — 12 — 7 — — 30 — Los Molles

30

Malargüe

Distance in km

65a

Rafael lie the ski resort of Las Leñas and the small town of Malargüe.

SAN RAFAEL

(*Population* 95,000; *Altitude* 688m; *Phone code* 0627) San Rafael, the second city in the province and a service centre for this agricultural area, lies north of the Río Diamante, 273 km southwest of San Luis, 242 km south of Mendoza. The **Parque Mariano Moreno**, 2 km south of the centre on Isla del Río Diamante (reached by Iselin bus along Avenida JA Balloffet) includes botanical gardens, a zoo and the **Museo Municipal de Historia Natural**, with displays on anthropology, archaeology, and palaeontology, Tuesday-Sunday 0800-1200, 1500-1900, free. Visits can be made to two wine *bodegas*: **Bianchi**, at Montecaseros y Civit, recommended, and **Suter** on Route 143 west of the centre.

Excursions

Southwest to the **Cañon de Atuel**, a spectacular gorge with polychrome rocks. In the space of some 50 km the Río Atuel drops some 500m, cutting through the rocks of the Bloque de San Rafael. Most of the gorge lies between two lakes 46 km apart, Valle Grande (508 hectares) and El Nihuil (9,600 hectares) formed by damming the river to generate electricity. A *ripio* road runs through the gorge offering fantastic and changing views. The area is a centre for adventure tourism, rafting, horseriding and fishing. From San Rafael three buses a day go to the Valle Grande at the near end of the gorge, 35 km, US$3 but there is no public transport through the gorge to the El Nihuel dam. Around Valle Grande there is plenty of accommodation and campsites, river rafting and horse riding. Travel agencies in Mendoza run all-day excursions to the canyon, but these involve long hours of travel.

- **Accommodation** *España*, San Martín 292, T 24055, 2-star; **C** *Kalton*, Yrigoyen 120, T 30047, excellent, safe, good value; **D** pp *Hosp Rex*, Yrigoyen 56, T 22177, with breakfast; **D** pp *Hosp Jardin*, Yrigoyen 283, T 34621, with breakfast; *Hosp Cerro Nevado*, Yrigoyen 376, T 28209. **Hostels E** pp *Albergue Municipal*, El Pino sin número, with breakfast. **Camping** *El Parador*, 2 km south on Isla Río Diamante. Several campsites near the Valle Grande dam.

- **Sports** *Complejo Turistico Portal del Atuel* at Valle Grande, T/F 23583, offers varied activities including rafting, trekking, canoeing.

- **Tour companies & travel agents** Many including *Ever Green*, San Martín 265, T 21950; *Rumbo*, Coronel Day 45, T 24871.

- **Tourist offices** At Yrigoyen y Balloffet, very helpful, T 24217. Ask for Aldo or Hector Seguín at España 437 for trekking and climbing information. **ACA**, Yrigoyen y 9 de Julio.

- **Buses** Buses to **Mendoza**, frequent, US$9; to **Neuquén**, US$20.

FROM SAN RAFAEL TO LAS LEÑAS

A paved road leads from San Rafael west across the plain of the Río Atuel, passing saltflats and marshland.

El Sosneado, Km 138, set on the Río Atuel near oilwells, is the only settlement along this road. A *ripio* side road leads off and follows the valley of the Río Atuel northwest to Laguna El Sosneado, 42 km, the Termas el Sosneado, 55 km (the *Hotel Termas El Sosneado* is in ruins) and the Overo volcano (4,619m).

- **Accommodation** **D** pp *Hosteria El Sosneado*, T 0627-71971, with breakfast, good beds.

The Route to Las Leñas

166 km southwest of San Rafael, a *ripio* road follows the Río Salado west into the Andes. It passes **Los Molles**, Km 30, where there are thermal springs and accommodation. Opposite Los Molles a *ripio* road leads to the *refugio* of the Club Andino Pehuenche and on 8 km to the **Laguna de la Niña Encantada**, a beautiful little lake and shrine to the Virgin. At Km 37 are the **Pozo de las Animas**, two natural pits, both filled with water (the larger is 80m deep); when the wind blows across the holes, a ghostly wail results, hence the name (from the Spanish *anima* or soul).

Las Leñas

(*Altitude* 2,250m) Km 49, is an international ski resort, the most expensive in Argentina (season July-October). Set in the middle of five snow-capped peaks, it has 41 pistes with a total length of 65 km and 11 ski-lifts. Beyond Las Leñas the road continues into Valle Hermoso, a beautiful valley accessible December-March only.

● **Accommodation** In **Las Leñas**: **L2** *Piscis*, 5-star; *Aries, Escorpio, Acuario* and *Geminis*, T for all 71100. There are cheaper apart-hotels and *dormy houses*, US$1,200 per week for 5

Alive!

Some 8 km from the *Hotel Termas El Sosneado* a plaque marks the site of the crash of an Uruguayan airforce plane in October 1972. The plane, a Fairchild F-27 en route from Montevideo to Santiago, carried 45 passengers and crew, including the members of a rugby team. The pilot, co-pilot and several passengers died on impact. Despite the efforts of the Chilean and Argentine airforces, the wreckage was not found. Two of the survivors crossed the mountains to Chile and finally brought help to the remaining 14 survivors who had spent 70 days on the Las Lágrimas glacier. The incident inspired the best-selling book 'Alive' by Piers Paul Read and the films 'Survive' (1976) and 'Alive' (1992).

---

people. For cheaper accommodation you have to stay in **Los Molles** where there are: **A3** pp *Hostería Lahuen-co*, T/F 0627-27171, full pension, run down, old fashioned; **A3** *Hotel Hualum*, same phone. Budget travellers should consider staying in Malargüe.

● **Useful services** Ski passes: high season US$40 per day, US$30 per half-day. Daily ski hire US$20.

● **Buses** From San Rafael, daily 1000, US$5; from Buenos Aires, 15 hours, in skiing season only.

MALARGUE

(*Population* 15,000; *Altitude* 1,426m; *Phone code* 0627) Malargüe, 196 km southwest of San Rafael, sees itself, somewhat grandly, as the national centre for adventure tourism. It is an excellent alternative base for skiing at Las Leñas. The small **Museo Regional**, on the northern outskirts, includes displays on archaeology, minerology and local history. Nearby is a restored old mill, used until cereal-growing was devastated by the eruption of the volcano Descabezado in 1932.

Excursions To the **Fortín Malal Hue**, ruins of a fort dating from 1847, 12 km south.

To the **Caverna de las Brujas**, privately owned caves 70 km southwest (last 7 km *ripio*, difficult in wet weather) which take 2-3 hours to visit; own vehi-

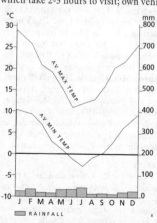

Climate: Malargüe

Malargüe

Not to scale

To San Rafael

Museo Regional

N

Alfonso Capdevilla

Batalion Nueva Creación

Satumino Torres

Plaza General San Martín

Turimalal

Municipalidad

Rodríguez

General Villegas

San Martín

Manuel Ruibal

Eusebio Adad

Adolfo Puebla

Fray Luis Bellrán

Av General Roca

Presidente Safás

Adrián Illega

General Uribura

Emilio Civit

Av Rufino Ortega

Karen Travel

4th Division

To Neuquen à Chile

Hotels:
1. Bambi
2. El Cisnie
3. Portal del Valle
4. Río Grande
5. Rioma
6. Turismo
7. Valle Hermoso

40 north, T 71589, with breakfast, pleasant; **A3** Reyen, San Martín 938, T/F 71429, with breakfast; **B** Hotel del Turismo, San Martín 224, T/F 71042, with breakfast, heating, good restaurant, comfortable, recommended; **B** Portal del Valle, Route 40 north, T 71294, F 71811, sauna, pool, restaurant, also suites; **B** Llancanelo, T 70689, with breakfast; **B** Rioma, Inalicán 68, T 71065, with breakfast, heating; **C** Valle Hermoso, Torres 151, T 71360, F 70470. Several others. **Camping** Polideportivo Marlargüe, T/F 71060; La Costa, Route 40 south, Km 7.

● **Sports** Caving: Epecuén, Fortín Malargüe y Meneses, T 71747. **Climbing**: Kieniv Aventuras, Pueblas 157, T 71297. **Cycling**: Ciclotours, Pueblas 908, T 70336. **Horseriding**: Pincheira Aventuras, Ortega 423, T 71823; Yaima, Ortega 1043, T 71202.

● **Tour companies & travel agents** AGAPE Mendoza, Asociación Grupo Antropo-Paleonto-Espeleológico, contact Dora de and Héctor Rofsgaard, Beltrán 414, T 71536; Expresos Payún, Avenida Roca 430, T 71426; Karen Travel, San Martín 1056, T 70342, horseriding, trekking, rafting, excursions; Turimalal, San Martín 193, T/F 70812, offer rock climbing, US$10 per person per half day, horseriding, cycle hire, skiing and fishing equipment hire; Extremis, San Martín 550 and several other shops on same street also rent out skiing and fishing equipment.

● **Tourist offices** Route 40 on the northern outskirts, T 71659.

● **Transport Air** Airport on southern edge of town, T 71265. Flights with TAN, T 71600, and Tapsa, T 71763, to Mendoza and Neuquén. Also Austral in skiing season. **Buses** TAC and Expreso Uspallata from Mendoza.

South of Malargüe

Route 40 continues to Chos Malal (see under **The Lake District**), 294 km (road ripio from Km 114). At Km 72 a dirt road turns off to the petrified forests of **Llano Blanco**.

FRONTIER WITH CHILE: PASO PEHUENCHE

Paso Pehuenche (2,553m) is reached by a ripio road which branches off Route 40, 66 km south of Malargüe. On the Chilean side the road continues down the valley of the Río Maule to Talca. The border is open December-March 0800-2100, April-November 0800-1900.

cle plus guide essential, hire in Malargüe US$20.

To **Laguna Llancanelo**, 37 km southeast, one of the main Argentine nesting areas of the Chilean flamingo. The lake is best visited in spring when the birds arrive. Details from the tourist office. Fishing licences from the Dirección de los Bosques, next to the tourist office.

● **Accommodation** High season (January/February and July/August) prices given: off-season prices much lower. **A3** El Cisne, Villegas 278, T 71350, good value, recommended; **A3** Bambi, San Martín 410, T/F 71237, with breakfast, overpriced; **A3** Río Grande, Route

SAN JUAN PROVINCE

Some 90% of the population of this province live in the valley of the Río San Juan, which also contains 90% of the cultivated land in the province. The only other population centre in the province is the Río Jáchal valley, some 180 km north. North of the Río Jáchal is uninhabited and inaccessible. Over 65% of cultivated land is used for growing vines and much of the remainder for olives.

SAN JUAN

(*Population* 122,000; *Altitude* 650m; *Phone code* 064) San Juan, the provincial capital, 168 km north of Mendoza, was founded 1562 by Don Juan Jufré de Loaysa y Montese and moved to its present site in 1593 to avoid the flooding of the Río San Juan. An earthquake which struck San Juan on 15 January 1944 was the most powerful in Argentine history, measuring 7.8° on the Richter Scale. Over 10,000 people were killed and the aftershocks continued for months afterwards. At a fund-raising event at Luna Park in Buenos Aires for the victims of the tragedy, Juan Perón met Eva Duarte, the radio actress who became his second wife. The rebuilt city has a well laid-out centre, with tree-lined streets and a modern cathedral.

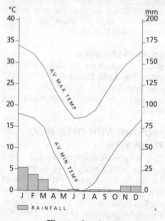

°C / mm

AV MAX TEMP
AV MIN TEMP

J F M A M J J A S O N D

RAINFALL

Climate: San Juan

Places of interest
One of the country's largest wine producers, *Bodegas Bragagnolo*, on the outskirts of town at Route 40 y Avenida Benavídez, Chimbas, can be visited (bus 20 from terminal; guided tours daily 0830-1330, 1530-1930, not Sunday). **Escuela de Fruticultura y Enología**, Sarmiento 196 (bus going west on Avenida San Martín), students show visitors round.

Museums
Museo Casa de Sarmiento, Sarmiento y San Martín, open Tuesday-Saturday 0830-1900; birthplace of Domingo Sarmiento.

Museo de Ciencias Naturales, Avenida San Martín and Catamarca, includes fossils from Ischigualasto Provincial Park (see below), open Monday-Saturday, 0830-1230, 1630-2030, Saturday 0900-1200, US$0.50.

Museo Histórico Sanmartiniano, Laprida 96 Este, including the restored cloisters and two cells of the Convent of Santo Domingo, destroyed in 1944. San Martín slept in one of these cells on his way to lead the crossing of the Andes, closed Sunday, US$0.40.

Excursions
To the **Parque Sarmiento**, 10 km northwest on the banks of the Río San Juan, where there is a small zoo. The **Embalse de Ullum**, 7 km further, offers rowing, sailing and fishing.

To the **Parque de Zonda**, 17 km west, which includes the Quebrada de Zonda, a 4 km long gorge and the **Museo Geografico Municipal Albert Einstein**, situated in a tunnel under the hill.

To the **Museo Arqueológico** of the University of San Juan at La Laja, 26 km north, open Monday-Friday, 0900-1830, Saturday, Sunday, 1000-1300 (1000-1730 summer) US$2, which contains an outstanding collection of prehispanic indigenous artefacts, including several well-preserved mummies. Inexpensive thermal baths nearby. Bus No 20 from San Juan, 2 a day, but you need to take the first (at 0830) to give time to return.

To **Vallecito**, 64 km east, the site of a famous shrine to the **Difunta Correa**, an unofficial saint whose infant (according

Sarmiento

Born, the son of a soldier, in 1811, San Juan's most famous son Domingo Faustino Sarmiento was the colossus of Argentine public life in the 19th century. In a career which extended over some 60 years as writer, educator, journalist, historian, linguist, diplomat and politician, he consistently advocated education as the solution to Argentina's problems. While still a teenager he taught in local schools, but was forced to flee to Chile in 1829 after fighting in the defeated Unitarist forces against the Federalists. An early advocate of women's education, he founded a girls' secondary school in San Juan after his return to the city in 1836. He also started a newspaper, 'El Zonda', in which he put forward his ideas on education and agriculture. In 1840, as a result of his opposition to Rosas, he was again forced into exile in Chile, where he was on friendly terms with prominent politicians and writers. Head of a teacher training college and tirelessly promoting his educational theories, he was an important influence on the development of the Chilean educational system.

Sarmiento's fame as a writer is based primarily on his work, *Facundo: Civilisation and Barbarism*, published in 1845. Focussing on the career of Juan Facundo Quiroga, the Federalist *caudillo* (military leader) of La Rioja, the book was a passionate attack on Rosas. Expressing the views of a sector of the Argentine elite which opposed Rosas attempts to close the country to outside influences, Sarmiento presented the struggle in terms of a war between civilization and barbarism. The latter was equated with the backward interior, provincial *caudillos*, the *gaucho* as an inferior social type and introverted nationalism. Civilization could be found in adopting European patterns in the political, cultural and social spheres. Argentina had to open up its trade to the rest of the world, attract European immigrants and acquire values of sociability and respectability that would lead the country out of fragmentation caused by excessive individualism.

Rosas replied by trying to have Sarmiento extradited, but the Chilean government sent him to study educational methods in Europe and the United States. Though he participated in the overthrow of Rosas, he soon fell out with his successor, Urquiza. In 1855 he became head of education for Buenos Aires province, though his support for universal public education with an emphasis on science and gymnastics for both boys and girls met with fierce opposition. After serving as Senator for San Juan he was sent as a diplomat to Peru and the United States.

As President of Argentina, 1868-1874, he encouraged European immigration, greater trade, improvements in public health and the building of schools, public libraries, roads and railways. His presidency was, however, not without its ironies: despite his lifelong hostility to *caudillos*, he exhibited many of the characteristics of the personalist leader; though a native of the frontier province of San Juan, he strengthened the power of the Federal Government, crushing provincial opponents; an advocate of the rule of law, he ruled by decree when he deemed the law inadequate.

Between leaving office and his death in 1888 he worked tirelessly in a succession of government posts and still found time to found a newspaper and an educational journal. His complete writings filled 53 volumes. Somewhere he found time to marry, leave his wife for another woman and father a son who was killed fighting against Paraguay in the War of the Triple Alliance.

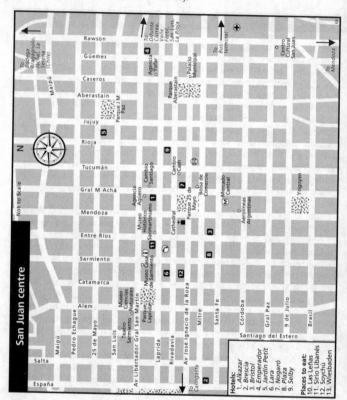

San Juan centre

Hotels:
1. Alkázar
2. Brescia
3. Bristol
4. Emperador
5. Jardín Petit
6. Lara
7. Nogaró
8. Plaza
9. Selby

Places to eat:
10. Las Leñas
11. Sirio Libanés
12. Joychú
13. Wiesbaden

to legend) survived at her breast even after the mother's death from thirst in the desert. Some 700,000 pilgrims visit the shrine every year, up to 100,000 of them in Holy Week, some crawling 100m on their knees. See the remarkable collection of personal items left in tribute, including number plates from all over the world and even one policeman's detective school diploma! For information, consult Fundación Vallecito at Caucete. Accommodation includes *Res Difunta Correa*.

Local information
● Accommodation
A1 *Alkázar*, Laprida 82 Este, T 214965, F 214977, including breakfast, garage, good; **A2** *Nogaró*, de la Roza 132 Este, T 227501/5,

pool, air conditioning, central, TV, parking (ACA and US AAA discounts); **A3** *Capayan*, Mitre 31 Este, T 214222, with breakfast, very good; **A3** *Central*, Mitre 131 Este, T 223174, quiet, good beds, welcoming owner; **A3** *Jardín Petit*, 25 de Mayo 345 Este (ACA discount with cash), T 211825, hot water, pricey, parking next door.

B *Bristol*, Entre Rios 368 Sur, T 222629, air conditioning, hot water; **B** *Plaza*, Sarmiento 344 Sur, T 225179, noisy disco behind; **A3** *Embajador*, Rawson 25 Sur, T 225520, large rooms, pleasant, café, good value. Several residenciales (**B**) along Avenida España, blocks 100-600 Sur.

C *Jessy-Mar*, Sarmiento 8 Norte, T 227195, small rooms, noisy; **C** *Res 12 de Diciembre*, Sarmiento 272 Norte.

Camping Site in the Parque Sarmiento; also *Camping Municipal Rivadavia*, in the Parque Zonda, free, no facilities. Take insect repellent.

● Places to eat

Wiesbaden, Circunvalación y San Martín, German-style, pleasant setting; *Soychú*, de la Roza 223 Oeste, excellent vegetarian food; *Club Sirio Libanés 'El Palito'*, Entre Rios 33 Sur, pleasant decor, good food; *Las Leñas*, San Martín 1670 Oeste, *parrilla*, pricey, recommended; *El Castillo de Oro*, de la Roza 199 Oeste, central, reasonable; *Comedor Central*, de la Roza 171 Este, not luxurious but good *locro* (stew) and *chivito* (goat); *Parrilla Bigotes*, Las Heras e de a Roza, inexpensive 'all you can eat' meat, chicken, salads; *Listo el Pollo*, San Martín y Santiago del Estero, very good. Many *pizzerías*, *confiterías*, and sidewalk cafés. *Lomoteca San José*, San Martín 179, grills, inexpensive, late night music at weekends; *El Clavel de Oro*, Santa Fe y Entre Ríos, snacks, drinks; *Marilyn Bar*, San Martín y Mendoza, late night drinks. Eat under thatched shelters (*quinchos*) at *Las Leñas*, San Martín, 1600 Oeste.

● Banks & money changers

Banks open 0700-1200. Banco de San Juan, Mendoza y Rivadavia, for Mastercard advance, no commission. None of the ATMs accept international credit cards. Good rates at Cambio Santiago, General Acha 52, weekdays until 2100, Saturday until 1300; Cambio Cash, Tucumán 210 Sur; Montemar, Laprida 133 Sur; Multicrédito, Laprida y Mendoza; Bolsa de Comercio, Gral Acha 278 Sur.

● Cultural centres

Centro Cultural San Juan: Gral Paz 737 Este, concerts and other events.

● Laundry

Marva, San Luis y Avenida Rioja.

● Shopping

Mercado Artesanal at Avenida España y San Luis, worth a visit.

● Sports

Bicycle repairs: *Ruedas Armado*, San Martín y La Rioja, helpful.

● Tour companies & travel agents

Yafar Turismo, Caseros y Laprida, T 214476 (no tours); *Mario Agüero Turismo*, General Acha 17 Norte, T 220864, tours to Ischigualasto subject to demand, US$50 per person plus US$3 National Park entry fee; *Fascinatur*, San Martín 2918 (Oeste), Rafael Joliat recommended for 4WD treks to remote areas, F 230058, also via Corvalle bus office at terminal.

● Tourist offices

Sarmiento Sur 24 y San Martín, helpful, good brochures, open Monday-Saturday, 0900-1330, 1430-2100, Sunday 0900-1300; also at bus terminal. Arranges tours in summer only. Large-scale provincial maps available at bookshops.

ACA, 9 de Julio 802 Este, useful information on routes, helpful.

● Transport

Local Car hire: Parque Automotor, España y San Martín, T 226018. Cash discount on request. Localiza, España 274 (Sur), T 229243.

Air Chacritas Airport, 11 km southeast. From Buenos Aires with AR (T 220205), Dinar and Lapa (T 216039). AR and Dinar also from Mendoza.

Buses Terminal at Estados Unidos y Santa Fe, nine blocks east of centre (buses 33 and 35 go through the centre). To La Rioja, 9 hours, US$19, or go via Chepes, 0900 daily US$6, with connecting service from Chepes, Monday, Wednesday, Sunday at 1600, 4 hours, US$10, Catamarca (660 km over secondary roads, US$17, with connection to Salta, US$29), Tucumán (3 a day, 13 hours, Libertador is cheapest), Córdoba, Santa Fe, Mar del Plata, Bahía Blanca and BsAs (Autotransporte San Juan, US$47). To San Agustín at 1800, US$11. 15 departures daily to and from Mendoza with TAC and El Cumbre, 2 hours, US$11, try to sit in the shade (on west side in the morning, east in the afternoon). Also services to provincial tourist destinations. To Chile: only connection with Santiago (Chile) is via Mendoza; catch the TAC bus at 0600, arrives in Mendoza 0830 in time for bus to Santiago.

Hitchhiking To La Rioja, take route 141 to Chepes (ACA *Hostería*), then north to Patquía; more traffic on provincial Route 29, a well paved, but less interesting road than that via San Agustín or Jachal (see below).

THE CALINGASTA VALLEY

Situated some 100 km west of San Juan and separated from the city by the Sierra del Tontal, this valley is drained by the Río de los Patos and the Río Castaño Viejo, which join to form the Río San Juan. Inhabited since at least 10,000 BC, the valley formed part of the route of the Camino del Inca, which ran south to the Uspallata Valley and north to the Iglesia Valley. In the 19th century mining was important: abandoned mine workings can still be seen. From the 1930s it became the centre of the Argentine cider industry, before losing out to the Río Negro valley in the 1970s.

The valley is reached from San Juan by the scenic Provincial Route 12 (open westbound Sunday-Friday 0400-1300,

Saturday 0400-1430, eastbound Sunday-Friday 1500-2000, Saturday 1630-2000) which follows the Río San Juan. Provincial Route 412 runs along the valley, linking it to Uspallata in the south and Iglesia in the north. About half way between Calingasta and Barreal, this passes, to the east, the Cerros Pintados, a range of red, white and grey stratified hills.

CALINGASTA

(*Population* 2,000; *Altitude* 1,430m) Calingasta lies at the confluence of the Ríos de los Patos and Calingasta, 135 km west of San Juan. Set in attractive surroundings, it produces cider and hold an annual cider festival in April. Nearby are sulphate and aluminium mines. The Jesuit chapel of Nuestra Señora del Carmen dates from 1739.

● **Accommodation B** *Calingasta*, T 22014, remodelled, pool, full board available; **C** *La Capilla*, T 21033, including breakfast, basic but very clean, family run, the family also sells the TAC bus tickets, and has the only public telephone in the village. **Camping** Municipal site. Take insect repellent.

North of Calingasta

Route 412, unpaved from Calingasta, climbs the valley of the Río Castaño Viejo. At **Villa Nueva**, 33 km north, the **De Cordelier** cement plant can be visited. Here the road forks: Route 412 continues north to Iglesia and Las Flores, a route described as scenic but lonely, while the other fork continues up the valley to disused gold mines at Mina Castaño Viejo.

BARREAL

(*Population* 1,800; *Altitude* 1,650m; *Phone code* 0648) Barreal lies 40 km south of Calingasta, 108 km north of Uspallata. From here excursions can be made east into the Sierra de Tontal, rising to 4,000m with views over San Juan, Mercedario and Aconcagua, and south following the valley of the Río de los Patos to Las Hornillas (54 km) where there is fishing and a *refugio* and then runs west towards the Chilean frontier and Mercedario (see below).

● **Accommodation A3** *Barreal*, San Martín sin número, T 41000, reservations through *Nogaró* in San Juan, T 227501, poor restaurant,

pool, riding; *Cabañas Alamos-Cordilleranos*, T 41025/41139, on plaza next to *Supermercadito El Angel*; *Cabañas Doña Pipa*, Mariano Moreno sin número, T 41004, sleep 5, with bath, kitchen, sitting room, comfortable; **E** *Hotel Jorge*, clean, very simple; *Posada San Eduardo*, San Martín y Los Enamorados, T 41046, colonial-style and patio with old trees, small, most rooms with bath, pleasant and relaxing. Accommodation with Sr Patricio Sosa or Sr Cortez. **Camping** Municipal site, also *cabañas*, T San Juan 223745.

● **Places to eat** *Isidoro*, Roca sin número, owned by local baker and sandyacht champion, reasonable, good set meals; food also available at *Mama Rosa*.

● **Tour companies & travel agents** For rafting trips contact Sr Eduardo Conterno. Sr Ramón Luis Ossa, physical education teacher at the high school, runs mule treks into the Andes, crossing the foothills in summer, from 10 to 21 days between November and April; contact via *Cabañas Doña Pipa*, address above.

● **Buses** From San Juan daily, El Triunfo, 0700, plus Monday, Wednesday, Friday, Sunday at 2030 (return Monday, Wednesday, Friday, Sunday 1330, 1600, Tuesday, Thursday 1400, Saturday 1600), 5 hours, US$11. *Remise* service San Juan-Calingasta-Barreal, US$17 per person, T San Juan 262121 daytime or 252370 1900-2300; in Barreal, Sr Pachá, *Restaurante Isidoro*; also Silvio, T San Juan 252370, Barreal 41257, US$14, recommended. Omnibus Vitar from Mendoza (Las Heras 494, T 232876) Thursday and Saturday via Uspallata, continuing to Tamberías and Calingasta (return Friday and Sunday); fare Barreal-Calingasta US$7.

Reserva Natural El Leoncito

Covering 76,000 hectares of the eastern slopes of the Sierra de Tontal and rising to over 4,000m, this reserve includes two observatories (visits daily 1000-1100, 1600-1800, US$3; no public transport; tours can be arranged from San Juan, Avenida España 1512 Sur, T 213653, or at *Hotel Barreal*). To the west there are fine views of Mercedario and other peaks in the *cordillera*. The environment is semi-arid; fauna includes guanacos, red and grey foxes, and peregrine falcons.

ACCESS Access is from an unpaved road (17 km) which turns off the Route 412, 22 km south of Barreal. Ranger post at entrance; no facilities, take all supplies.

MERCEDARIO

Known in Chile as El Ligua and rising to 6,770m, Mercedario lies southwest of Calingasta. It was first climbed in 1934 by a Polish expedition which went on to climb the nearby peaks of Pico Polaco (6,050m), La Mesa (6,200m), Alma Negra (6,120m) and Ramada (6,410m). No authorization is required, but it is advisable to inform the Gendarmería Nacional at Barreal.

From Barreal go to Casas Amarillas on the Río Blanco, about 100 km on a gravel road. It may be possible to hire a Unimog 4x4 from the Gendarmería Nacional; guides (*baqueanos*) may also be hired, they can provide mules if necessary. The best time is mid-December to end-February; the types of terrain encountered are gravel, snow and rock. There is no rescue service.

- **Information** From Club Andino Mercedario, 9 de Julio 547 Este, 5400 San Juan, or *Antonio Beorchia Nigris*, director, Ciadam (Research Centre for Andean Archaeology), República del Líbano 2621, 5423 San Juan. **NB** It is illegal to cross the frontier to/from Chile in this region.

Northern San Juan

Not to scale

To Reserva de la Biosfera San Guillermo

Angualasto

To Villa Unión (144 km)

To Paso Agua Negra (94 km)

Rodeo — 42 — San José de Jachal

20

22

Pismanta

5

Las Flores

10

Iglesia

111

100

55

San Juan

Distance in km

NORTHERN SAN JUAN: THE RIO JACHAL VALLEY

The valley of the Río Jachal is an oasis some 180 km north of the provincial capital. Flowing south from the mountains of La Rioja through the valley of Iglesia, the Jachal flows east through a narrow gorge (the **Quebrada del Jachal**) before continuing southeast into the Río Bermejo. The river has been dammed to create an artificial lake, the Embalse Cuesta del Viento, covering 3,000 hectares. The main town is San José de Jachal, east of the gorge.

From San Juan the Jachal valley is reached by Route 40, the principal tourist route on the East Andean slope. At Talacasto, Km 55, Route 436 branches northwest towards Iglesia (Km 166), Las Flores (Km 180) and the Chilean border at Paso Agua Negra (see below).

SAN JOSE DE JACHAL

(*Population* 15,000; *Altitude* 1,157m) San José de Jachal, an oasis town 157 km north of San Juan by Route 40, is a wine and olive-growing centre with many adobe buildings. From here, the undulating Route 40, runs north to Villa Unión (see below), crossing dozens of dry watercourses; it is unpaved north of the La Rioja border.

- **Accommodation & places to eat** C *Plaza*, San Juan 545, T 20256; *San Martín*, Juan de Echegaray 387, T 20431. **Camping** *El Chato Flores*, restaurant, good; another site 3 km west.

- **Buses** Expreso Argentino bus from San Juan at 0730 arrives at 0940.

RODEO

(*Population* 1,600; *Altitude* 1,900m) Rodeo, lies 42 km west of San José along a scenic road which runs through several tunnels as it passes through the Quebrada de Jachal. There are good facilities for fishing and water sports. Ing Meglioli raises guanaco and vicuña, and sells local produce and crafts. From here a *ripio* road runs north along the Jachal valley to **Angualasto**, Km 20, where the **Museo Arqueológico Luis Benedetti**, contains a 400-year-old mummy.

RESERVA DE LA BIOSFERA SAN GUILLERMO

Situated north of Angualasto, this park protects 860,000 hectares of the upper valley of the Río Blanco, rising from 3,300m to peaks of over 5,000m. Vegetation is sparse, consisting mainly of steppe grasses and cacti, but the park is home to over 5,000 vicuña as well as vizcachas, guanacos, pumas, grey foxes, white eagles, falcons and condors. The park is also the site of important archaeological remains: several burial sites of prehispanic peoples have been found. The park is best visited between October and April and is inaccessible when the Río Blanco is high.

ACCESS Access is from Angualasto. Register with the police in Angualasto and report to the rangers in the park. Guides are available in Angualasto and Las Flores.

PISMANTA

(*Altitude* 1,724m) 22 km southwest of Rodeo, 182 km north of San Juan, is an oasis town with thermal springs. There is a Jesuit chapel, dating from 1640, 3 km away. Nearby are other thermal springs, Termas Rosales and Termas Centenario, but these have few facilities.

● **Accommodation** B *Termas de Pismanta*, T 227501, with breakfast, rooms for 120 guests, thermal baths between 38° and 44°C, a large swimming pool, medical attention, bowling, bingo occasionally, covered parking, good value. Reservations in Buenos Aires (Maipú 331) and San Juan (San Martín y Sarmiento); E *La Olla*, family run, clean, restaurant.

● **Buses** From San Juan, TAC, 2 daily, Empresa Iglesia 4 weekly; also from Mendoza.

FRONTIER WITH CHILE: PASO AGUA NEGRA

Paso Agua Negra (4,600m; different maps give different altitudes) is 100 km west of Pismanta, the first 60 km is poor asphalt, the last 35 km *ripio*. The crossing is spectacular, particularly the views of fields of *penitentes* (ice needles) about 5 km east of the pass. This route is only open January to early April; in winter it is closed by snow, in summer it may be closed by rain. On the Chilean side the road continues to Vicuña, 172 km west, and La

Serena, 238 km west. First fuel is at Rivadavia, 154 km west.

● **Immigration** Argentine immigration and customs at Las Flores, open 24 hours for entry, 0800-1700 only for departures. Police checkpoint 40 km west of Las Flores. Chilean immigration and customs are at Las Juntas, 84 km west of Paso Agua Negra, open 0800-1700; US$2 per vehicle 1700-2200.

● **Transport** No public transport on this route. Check road conditions with ACA in Las Flores.

● **Accommodation** First accommodation in Chile at Huanta (Guanta on some maps), 126 km west, **G**, clean, basic, ask for Guillermo Aliaga. No food between the frontier and Huanta.

NORTH AND EAST OF SAN JUAN

Two of the most popular attractions in this region are the Parque Provincial Ischigualasto and the Reserva Provincial Talampaya, situated near each other on the San Juan/La Rioja provincial border (Ischigualasto is in San Juan; Talampaya

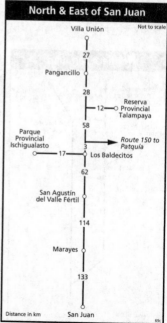

North & East of San Juan

Not to scale

- Villa Unión
  - 27
- Pangancillo
  - 28
  - 12 — Reserva Provincial Talampaya
  - 58
- Parque Provincial Ischigualasto
  - 17 — Los Baldecitos
    - 3 — Route 150 to Patquia
  - 62
- San Agustín del Valle Fértil
  - 114
- Marayes
  - 133
- San Juan

Distance in km

69c

in La Rioja). From San Juan these are reached by taking Route 141, which runs east towards La Rioja province, and then turning north onto Route 510 (paved but poor) just after Marayes, Km 133.

San Agustín del Valle Fértil

(*Population* 3,000; *Altitude* 870m) 102 km north of Marayes along Route 510, is a textile-weaving town which has become a base for visiting the parks. There is fishing in the nearby Embalse San Agustín. Tourist information on the plaza. Local weavers sell ponchos and blankets.

● **Accommodation** **A3** *Hostería Valle Fertil*, Rivadavia sin número, T (0646) 20015-7, new, good, overlooking Dique San Agustín; *Res Andacollo*; *Res Los Olivos*; **D** *Hosp Romero*; **E** pp *Hosp Santa Fe*, with bath, welcoming, recommended; private houses also provide lodging; **E** pp *Hosp Ischigualasto*, Mitre y Aberstain, T 20146, with bath, clean, fan. **Camping** Municipal site next to the Embalse.

● **Buses** From San Juan, US$9; from La Rioja, Monday-Friday 1215, US$10, 4 hours.

PARQUE PROVINCIAL ISCHIGUALASTO

Popularly known as the **Valle de la Luna** (Valley of the Moon), this park covers 62,000 hectares of spectacular desert landforms, the site of important archaeological discoveries. Named after a Huarpe Indian chief, the site occupies a large basin, formerly filled by a lake, lying, at an average altitude of 1,200m, between the red Cerros Los Colorados to the east and the green, black and grey rocks of Los Rastros to the west. Many of the rocks have bizarre shapes and are named accordingly, eg the submarine, the kiosk, the mushroom. Fossils from all the geological periods of the last 250 million years old have been found; among these have been fossils of the oldest dinosaurs known, including *Eoraptor*, 225 million years old and discovered in 1993. Vegetation is scrub and bushes; fauna include guanacos, vizcachas, patagonian hares, red foxes, pumas and rheas.

ACCESS The entrance is at Cerro El Morado, 1,800m, reached by a side road 17 km long, turning off Route 510 at a police checkpoint near Los Baldecitos, 56 km north of San Agustín del Valle Fértil. Entry US$5.

● **Transport** All private vehicles must be accompanied by rangers whose knowledge and interest vary greatly; fee US$2 per person. There are two circular routes on unpaved roads: 30 km (2 hours) and 50 km (3 hours): these visit only a small part of the park, though they cover most of the interesting sites. Local bus from San Juan Monday and Friday to police checkpoint and on Saturday afternoon, if demand is sufficient. Tours from San Juan, US$50 (not including lunch); from San Agustín US$18 for a guide (ask at tourist office). Guide Barros Lito, US$40 for full day tour of both Ischigualasto and Talampaya in private car, pay him afterwards; although he says he speaks English, he doesn't. Taxi US$55 (recommended if there are 4-5 people), more out of season.

RESERVA PROVINCIAL TALAMPAYA

Extending over 215,000 hectares at an altitude of 1,200m, Talampaya occupies a basin between the Cerros Los Colorados to the west and the Sierras de Sañogasta to the east. Though the park's fossils have been less significant to scientists than those of Ischigualasto, the rock formations are just as interesting and in some places petroglyphs can be seen. The most popular part is the gorge of the Río Talampaya, the walls of which rise to 143m. At one point the gorge narrows to 80m wide; here

Cactus,
Parque Provincial Talampaya

Talampaya

"There are 600-year-old petroglyphs with pictures depicting animals. The whole area is said to have been covered with water long ago; now there are two visible strata, the *tarjado* and the *talampaya*. After that one enters a canyon with 'balconies', sheer overhanging walls. Coming out of the canyon there are rocks shaped like a cathedral, a bird, a castle, a chessboard, a monk, and three kings on a camel."

Herbert Levi

there is a 'botanical garden'. Vegetation and fauna are similar to Ischigualasto.

ACCESS Access is by a paved side road, 12 km long, which turns off Provincial Route 26, at Km 144, 61 km north of the police checkpoint at Los Baldecitos and 55 km south of Villa Unión. Entry US$3, open 0800-1630, entrance US$3. Best time to visit in the morning, avoiding strong winds in the afternoon.

● **Accommodation** *Refugio* near the entrance, sleeping bag essential; free campsite next to park administration. In Pagancillo, a village 28 km north on Route 26, accommodation can be arranged by Sr Páez, Park Director (eg with **D** pp *Familia Flores*, including breakfast and dinner).

● **Transport** Chilecito-San Juan buses pass Talampaya. Patquía-Villa Unión buses pass through Pagancillo. Tours through the gorge of the Río Talampaya in 4WD vehicles are operated by park rangers, five tours of different lengths offered, prices per truck, US$30-110, not including entrance. Tours arranged through Dirección Provincial de Turismo in La Rioja, through the tourist office in Chilecito or Sr Páez, Park Director, in Pagancillo.

LA RIOJA PROVINCE

The eastern part of the province consists of a plain which stretches south and east to the Sierras de Córdoba. Extending over some 4 million hectares, and including large areas of saltflats, this area is sometimes known as the *Llanos de los Caudillos*. Water is sparse and vegetation is scrub and poor grassland, used for cattle ranching.

To the west several ranges of mountains run north-south, extending to the Andes in the far west. Between these ranges lie two valleys, the Valley of Famatina and the Valley of Vinchina. Communications between these valleys are difficult. About 50% of the population live in the capital.

LA RIOJA

(*Population* 106,000; *Altitude* 498m; *Phone code* 0822) La Rioja, the provincial capital, is situated on the edge of the plains at the foot of the Sierra de Velasco. Founded in 1592, it is known as 'City of the Orange Trees', but there are also many specimens of the contorted, thorn-studded *palo borracho* tree. Despite a major earthquake in 1894, some colonial buildings survive.

Places of interest

The city centres on Plaza 25 de Mayo; here are the early 20th century Cathedral and the neo-colonial Casa de Gobierno. The **Convent of San Francisco**, one block northwest at 25 de Mayo y Bazán y Bustos, contains the Niño Alcalde, a remarkable image of the infant Jesus as well as the cell (*celda*) in which San Francisco Solano lived and the orange tree, now dead, which he planted in 1592. To visit the tree when the church is closed, ring the bell at 25 de Mayo 218 next door. The **Convent of**

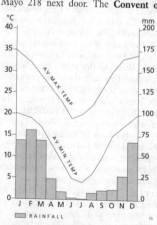

Climate: La Rioja

La Rioja: Centre

Not to scale

Hotels
1. Imperial
2. King's
3. Libertador
4. Plaza
5. Talampaya
6. Turismo

Santo Domingo, Luna y Lamadrid, is the oldest surviving temple in Argentina, dating from 1623. The **Casa González**, at Rivadavia 950, is a brick 'folly' in the form of a castle. On the outskirts of the city, 3 km west, is the **Parque Yacampis**, with a swimming pool and zoo.

Museums
Museo Folklórico, P Luna 811, Tuesday-Friday, 0900-1200, 1600-2000, Saturday, Sunday, 0900-1200, US$1.50.

Museo Arqueológico Inca Huasi, Alberdi 650, owned by the Franciscan Order, contains a huge collection of fine Diaguita Indian ceramics, open Tuesday-Friday, 0800-1200, 1500-1900, US$1.

Museo Histórico de la Provincia, Dávila 87, opening hours variable.

Museo Municipal de Bellas Artes, Copiapó 253, works by local, national, and foreign artists.

Excursions
The most popular excursions are to Los Padercitos and the Embalse Los Sauces, west of the city (see below).

Local information
NB Avoid arriving on Saturday night as most things are shut on Sunday.

● Accommodation
Accommodation can be difficult to find, particularly in the lower price ranges.

A2 *Plaza*, Mitre y 9 de Julio, T 25215, recommended but street noisy; **A3** *King's*, Quiroga 1070, T 25272; *Libertador*, Buenos Aires 253, T 27474, good value; *Talampaya*, Perón 951, T 24010; *Turismo*, Perón y Quiroga, T 25240, parking.

B *Imperial*, Moreno 345, T 22478, helpful; **B** *Res Petit*, Lagos 427, basic, hospitable.

C *Savoy*, Roque A Luna 14, T 26894, excellent value, hot shower; **C** *Pensión 9 de Julio*, Copiapó y Vélez Sarsfield, recommended; **C** *Res Florida*, 8 de Diciembre 524, basic. Tourist

Office keeps a list of private lodgings, such as Sra Vera, Dávila 343.

Camping ACA site in the Parque Yacampis; at Balneario Los Sauces, 15 km west.

● **Places to eat**
Café Corredor, San Martín y Pelagio Luna, good, cheap; *Il Gatto*, Plaza 25 de Mayo, good pastas and salads; *Club Atlético Riojano*, Santa Fe between 9 de Julio and Buenos Aires, no atmosphere but cheap; good open air *churrasquería* next to *Hotel de Turismo*; *La Casona*, Rivadavia 449, very good and reasonably priced, recommended; *Taberna Don Carlos*, Rivadavia 459, good fish and service; *Comedor Sociedad Española*, 9 de Julio 233, excellent pastas, inexpensive; *La Pomme*, Rivadavia y San Martín, open-air terrace, popular meeting place.

● **Banks & money changers**
US$ cash changed at **Banco de Galicia**, Plaza 25 de Mayo (no commission on Visa cash advance), and **Banco de Crédito**, San Nicolás 476. Travellers' cheques difficult to change – try **Banco de la Provincia**, Bazán y Bustos, commission 8%. Better to change plenty before arriving (see note on provincial bonds used as currency, page 468).

● **Laundry**
Laverap, Perón 944.

● **Post & telecommunications**
Post Office: Perón 258.
Telecommunications: Perón 764.

● **Tour companies & travel agents**
Yafar Turismo, Lamadrid 170, tour to Ischigualasto and Talampaya parks. To visit the parks by private car with guide costs US$190 for up to 5 people, plus park entry fees.

● **Tourist offices**
Perón y Urquiza, T 28834.

● **Transport**
Air To/from **Buenos Aires**, Aerolíneas Argentinas (T 27257) and Lapa (T 35197); Lapa also to **Catamarca**, Aerolíneas Argentinas to **Tucumán**, Andesmar to **Córdoba** and **Mendoza**.
Buses Terminal seven blocks south of the Cathedral at Artigas y España. To **Buenos Aires**, General Urquiza, US$47, combine with Ablo, via Córdoba; to **Córdoba**, Chevallier, 6½ hours, US$15, also *coche cama*. To **Mendoza** (US$25) and **San Juan** (US$19), La Estrella, Libertador and Andesmar, 8 hours. To **Tinogasta**, 0620, 2200, daily, US$11. To **Tucumán** (US$15), with Bosio and La Estrella. To **Salta**, Andesmar, 10 hours, US$33. Also provincial services.

NORTHEASTERN LA RIOJA

Two roads head north from La Rioja: Route 38 runs northeast to Catamarca; at Km 33, Provincial Route 9 (later 10) branches off north for Villa Mazán, Km 99. 7 km north of Villa Mazán is **Termas Santa Teresita**.

● **Accommodation A3** *Hostería Termas Santa Teresita*, T 20445, with breakfast, open air thermal pool, thermal baths in all rooms, good set menu, highly recommended.

The other road, Route 1 to Aimogasta is more interesting, passing through Villa Sanagasta, Aminga and Anillaco.

Las Padercitas
Km 8, is the site of the remains of the 16th century adobe building where San Francisco converted the Indians of the Yacampis valley. The ruins are protected by a stone temple. Beyond is the **Quebrada de los Sauces**, the gorge of the Río Los Sauces, and an artificial lake, Km 15, with swimming and fishing. The **Cerro de la Cruz** (1,680m), Km 27, is a centre for hang-gliding, where condors and falcons may be sighted.

Northeastern La Rioja

Not to scale

Aimogasta — Termas Santa Teresita — Villa Mazán — Anillaco — Aminga — Chuquis — Villa Sanagasta — Los Sauces — Las Padercitas — La Rioja

To Catamarca

Distance in km

70a

Menem and Anillaco

At the beginning of this century there was only a crystalline brook at this spot (*yaco* or *llaco* is Quechua for water and *ani* is Quechua for shade). Shortly afterwards a Syrian immigrant family called Menehem settled here and started a vineyard, its fine grapes, pressed at their own *bodega*, producing a tasty white wine. When the eldest son, now calling himself Menem, first became Governor of La Rioja province, he convinced the Argentine Automobile Club to build a handsome *hostería* in his hometown. Today Anillaco is a kind of unofficial second capital of Argentina, where the now-President Carlos Menem celebrates cabinet meetings and press conferences. Menem, who plans to retire here, has built a spacious private residence and a mountain retreat nearby. The building of an airstrip for medium sized commercial jets a few kilometres from town has fuelled criticism and allegations of misuse of public funds.

Marlú Kirbus

Villa Sanagasta

(*Population* 1,600; *Altitude* 1,000m) Km 32, is attractively set among orchards; there is a chapel dating from 1801. From here the road climbs steeply over the Cuesta de Huaco (1,800m) and runs north; at Km 83 a turning (2 km) leads to **Chuquis**, where there there is a small museum.

Aminga

(*Population* 600; *Altitude* 1,360m) Km 88, has several wine *bodegas*; the vines are grown between rows of orange and walnut trees. The **De La Fuente** *bodega* may be visited.

Anillaco

(*Population* 900; *Altitude* 1,300m) 3 km off the road at Km 93, is the hometown of President Carlos Menem. This small town, with two fine hotels is becoming a tourist attraction: it styles itself *Capital de la Fe* on account of its proximity to the *Señor de la Peña* (Our Lord of the Rock), a giant boulder 25 km west said to resemble the figure of Christ; it is a site of Holy Week pilgrimages.

● **Accommodation** *ACA Hostería*, restaurant; *Hostería Los Amigos*. **Camping** Municipal site, US$2 per person.

Aimogasta

(*Population* 7,700; *Altitude* 830m; *Phone code* 0827) Km 117 at the junctions of Routes 1, 9 and 60, is the largest town in this part of the province. Known as the 'National olive capital', it holds the

National Olive Festival on May 24. Nearby at Arauco there is an olive tree dating from the 16th century, which has the distinction of having escaped the royal decree of 1770 to cut down all the olive trees in the Spanish colonies.

● **Accommodation** *Hostería Brigite*, on plaza; *Hostería Arauco*, T 20206. **Camping** *Los Nacimientos*.

THE FAMATINA VALLEY

This valley lies between two ranges of hills: to the east the Sierra de Velasco, rising to 4,257m, separates it from La Rioja; to the west is the Sierra de Famatina. From La Rioja the valley is reached via Patquía, 69 km south of the capital. Previously an important mining area, the valley is famous for its tasty wines, olives and walnuts.

CHILECITO

(*Population* 20,000; *Altitude* 1,074m; *Phone code* 0825) Chilecito, is the second town in the province. Founded in 1715, its name derives from the influx of Chilean miners in the 18th and 19th centuries. There are good views of the Sierra de Famatina, especially from the top of El Portezuelo, an easy climb from the end of Calle El Maestro. It is also a base for climbing Cerro Negro Overo (6,097m) in the Famatina massif. On the southern outskirts of town you can see the first station of the cable car system to the La Mejicana mine; the first station has a small historical museum. At

Chilecito: Centre

Los Sarmientos, 2 km north of town, is a chapel, dating from 1764, with a fine wooden door, the work of Indian craftsmen.

Museums

Samay Huasi, 2 km southeast of town, the house of Joaquín V González, founder of La Plata University, open 0800-1200 and 1500-1800, contains the **Museo de Ciencias Naturales**, and the **Museo de Mineralogía y Arqueología**, pleasant gardens, and good views of Chilecito and the Sierra de Famatina.

Molino San Francisco y Museo de Chilecito, J de Ocampo 63, has archaeological, historical and artistic exhibits, open Monday-Friday 0800-1300, 1400-1900.

Local information
● **Accommodation**

A3 *Chilecito*, Dr L Martínez y 8 de Julio, T 2201/2, good, no credit cards, safe parking, pool, good restaurant; **A3** *Hostería ACA*, Gordillo y Ocampo, **B** for members, friendly, clean.

B *Riviera*, Castro Barros 133, recommended, hot showers.

C *Americano*, Libertad 68, T 8104; **C** *Belsavac*, 9 de Julio y Dávila, T 2877, good but thin walls; **C** *Wamatinag*, Galeria Victoria, west side of Plaza Sarmiento, T 2977, pleasant, best value in town. The Tourist Office has a list of families offering accommodation, but not for singles.

Camping At Santa Florentina, 6 km northwest of Chilecito and Las Talas, 2 km beyond.

● **Places to eat**

El Gallo, Perón e Illia, excellent. On Plaza Sarmiento are: *Chaplin*, best in town; *Robert Snak Bar*, light meals and drinks; *Vanesa*, good home-made ice-cream; *Toscanini*, Fátima y San Martín, good Italian food, inexpensive; *Ferrito*, Avenida Luna 661, very good.

● **Tour companies & travel agents**

For tours in the Reserva Natural Laguna Brava (see below) contact Jorge and Adriana Llanos, T 22171, or Adolfo and Daniel at *Laguna Brava ETV*, T 22348, F 23330. For treks, and trips to see gold washers at Famatina or to Talampaya, ask for Carlos de Caro, or enquire at tourist office.

● **Tourist offices**

Libertad e Independencia, T 2688, very helpful.

● **Transport**

Air J Facundo Quiroga airport at Anguinán, 7 km south. Líneas Aéreas Riojanas to **La Rioja**, 20 minutes.

Buses To San Juan, Tuesday, Thursday, Saturday at 2200; to Tinogasta (Catamarca), Monday-Friday, direct at 0700 via route 11, returning same day at 0600; to **La Rioja**, 3 times daily, Cotil; to Villa Unión daily at 1345, Cotil; to Catamarca and Córdoba via La Rioja only.

North of Chilecito

Route 40 continues north from Chilecito. **Famatina** (*Population* 2,000; *Altitude* 1,470m), Km 31, is a sleepy hamlet amid nut

La Mejicana

The La Mejicana cable car gives some idea of Chilecito's importance as a mining centre in the early 20th century. Built in 1903-5, it linked the La Mejicana mine in the Sierra de Famatina with the foundry at Santa Florentina and the railhead in Chilecito, and replaced mules as the only means of supplying the mine and transporting the ore. Built by the Bleichert company of Leipzig, Germany, it was, at the time, the longest cable railway in the world, 34.6 km long and climbing from 1,075m in Chilecito to 4,063m at the mine. There were 262 towers, 9 stations, a tunnel 160m long and a viaduct; the two ends were linked by one of the first telephone systems in the country. 450 wagons, each with a capacity of 250 kg, carried the gold, silver and copper ore from the 40 mine workings, at a speed of 8 km per hour, powered by a steam engine fed by *quebracho* wood brought from Santiago del Estero.

After the mine closed in 1926, some regular maintenance was carried out by railway company until 1974. In 1990 the municipal government began restoration work: tourist services are operated on special occasions between Chilecito and the Santa Florentina foundry on a branch line 6 km away.

plantations (*hostería*, restaurants). From here Provincial Route 11 (*ripio*) goes north to Tinogasta, while Route 40 heads north to **San Blas** (*Population* 2,800; *Altitude* 1,050m), which has a church dating from 1734. 12 km further north Route 40 meets Route 60, the Aimogasta-Tinogasta road.

WESTERN LA RIOJA

The westernmost inhabited valley in La Rioja is that of the Río Vinchina, which flows along the west side of the Sierra de Famatina. The valley is reached from the provincial capital via Patquía and Route 150, then north along Route 26 via the Talampaya Provincial Park, or from Chilecito by Route 40, which branches off, at Nonogasta, 16 km south and runs westwards through the Cuesta de Miranda, one of the most spectacular routes in the province. Winding its way between the Sierra de Famatina to the north and the Sierra de Sañogasta to the south, it rises to 2,010m and drops again, passing through 320 bends in its 11.5 km.

Villa Unión

(*Population* 3,500; *Altitude* 1,240m) 92 km west of Nonogasta, is the largest settlement in the valley and is a base for visits to the Talampaya Provincial Park, 67 km south.

● **Accommodation** *Dayton*, main street; **E** *Hosp Paola*, main street opposite police station, basic; next door is **E** *Hosp Changuito*, restaurant.

NORTH OF VILLA UNION

Provincial Route 26, unpaved, runs along the Río Vinchina valley. From **Vinchina** (*Population* 1,900; *Altitude* 1,490m; several

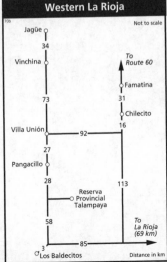

Western La Rioja

Not to scale

High water

✒ "Between Bonete and Veladero there is a crater filled by a lake, 5,319m high, until recently believed to be of volcanic origin but now established as having been caused by a meteorite 4 km in diameter. This region is probably one of the last white patches on the maps of the world. Along the route small stone refuges like snailshells can be seen, built in the mid-19th century for the drivers of oxen along this route to Chile. Vicuñas, guanacos and flamingoes may be seen along the route."

Federico Kirbus

basic *hospedajes*), Km 73, it passes through the Quebrada de la Troya before reaching **Jagüe** (*Population* 200; *Altitude* 2,000m), Km 117.

Reserva Natural Laguna Brava

This park covers some 405,000 hectares of mountain-valleys, rising from 3,800m to 4,360m. Laguna Brava, a salt lake, 4,271m, 16 km long, 3 km wide, lies further northwest, beyond the Portezuelo del Peñón, which offers superb views over the lake, with some of the mightiest volcanoes on earth in the background. From the left these are the perfect cone Veladero (6,436m), Reclus (6,335m), Los Gemelos (6,130m), Pissis (6,882m) the highest volcano in the world, though inactive, and Bonete (6,759m) which is visible from Villa Unión and Talampaya. The park is home to flamingoes and over 3,000 vicuñas. The building of a new international road to Chile, planned to run through the park, along the north side of Laguna Brava and through the Paso de Pircas Negras (4,195m), will make this area much more easily accessible.

ACCESS Access is from Jagüe, 4WD vehicle essential. Entry US$10. For tours in this area see under Chilecito.

The Northwest

THE PROVINCES of Catamarca, Santiago del Estero, Tucumán, Salta and Jujuy provide major contrasts. The west of the region, Catamarca, Salta and Jujuy, offer Andean landscapes, particularly around the major tourist centre of Salta. Further east are the provincial capitals of Santiago del Estero and Tucumán as well as Argentina's three cloudforest parks. One of the few areas in the country with an Amerindian minority, this is also a region of prehispanic ruins, especially at Tafí del Valle, Quilmes and Santa Rosa de Tastil.

GEOGRAPHY

In the northwest the crest of the Andes rises to include some of the highest peaks in the Americas. East of the Andes lies the *puna*, a windswept, stony and treeless plain, geologically a remnant of the Brazilian massif of hard ancient crystalline rocks. Parts of the *puna* are not drained by rivers: rainfall and snowfall collects in lakes and forms large areas of saltflats. Rivers flow east from the *puna* through steeply cut valleys or *quebradas*, which are particularly important as routes to the *puna*. East of the *puna* and running north-northeast to southsouthwest are several ranges of hills. Between these ranges are lowlands known as the *valles*. The easternmost ranges fall steeply towards the plains of the Chaco

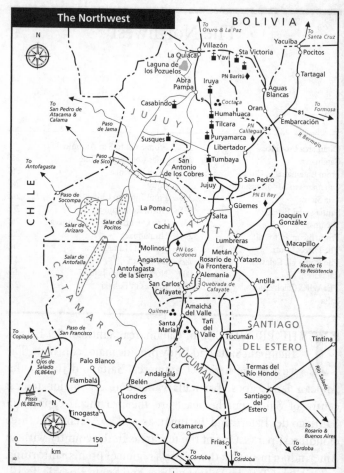

The Northwest

which occupy the southeasternmost parts of this region.

Though many rivers and streams flow east from the *puna*, they feed into three main rivers: the Bermejo, the Juramento and the Dulce. The Bermejo is easily the largest, flowing south from Bolivia and receiving the waters of the Río San Francisco, which flows north from Salta, and of the smaller rivers which flow east in Jujuy. The Dulce flows south into Laguna Mar Chiquita in Córdoba province while the Juramento feeds into the Río Salado and is part of Argentina's longest river system, the Paraná.

The highest peaks in this region are: Ojos del Salado (6,864m), Tres Cruces (6,749m), Walther Penk (6,683m), Incahuasi (6,638m), Nacimientos (6,493m), El Muerto (6,488m), Pico Ata (6,445), El Cóndor (6,373m), De Los Patos (6,239m) and San Francisco (6,016m) in Catamarca; Llullaillaco (6,739), Antofalla (6,440m), Cachi (6,380m), Socompa (6,031m) and

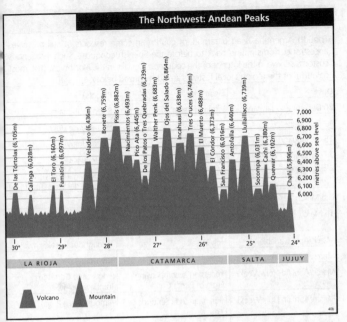

The Northwest: Andean Peaks

De las Tórtolas (6,105m)
Calinga (6,028m)
El Toro (6,160m)
Famatina (6,097m)
Veladero (6,436m)
Bonete (6,759m)
Pissis (6,882m)
Nacimientos (6,493m)
Pico Ata (6,445m)
De los Patos o Tres Quebradas (6,239m)
Walther Penk (6,683m)
Ojos del Salado (6,864m)
Incahuasi (6,638m)
Tres Cruces (6,749m)
El Muerto (6,488m)
El Condor (6,373m)
San Francisco (6,016m)
Antofalla (6,440m)
Llullaillaco (6,739m)
Socompa (6,031m)
Cachi (6,380m)
Quewar (6,102m)
Chañi (5,896m)

metres above sea level
7,000
6,900
6,800
6,700
6,600
6,500
6,400
6,300
6,200
6,100
6,000

30° 29° 28° 27° 26° 25° 24°

LA RIOJA   CATAMARCA   SALTA   JUJUY

▼ Volcano   ▲ Mountain

Quewar (6,102m) in Salta and Chañi (5,896m) in Jujuy.

ECONOMY

The economy of the northwest is as varied as its landscapes. Tucumán and eastern Jujuy are the centres of Argentine sugar production, while tobacco is also an important crop. Cafayate is renowned for its

Cushion-shaped vegetation
of the High Andes

wines and the valleys of western Catamarca also produce grapes and other fruit. Industry tends to be limited to food-processing but minerals are important in some parts of the northwest, particularly in Jujuy: antimony and tin are mined in Rinconada, while Sierra del Aguilar and Nevado del Chañi have the richest deposits of lead, zinc, silver and iron in Argentina and iron ore from the Zapala mine is processed at Palpalá. Oil is extracted from around Libertador General San Martín in eastern Salta. Tourism is also important for the local economy, especially in Salta which has become one of the major tourist centres in Argentina.

CLIMATE

There are distinct climatic zones. In the *puna* wide variations in daytime temperatures occur: from 35°C to -2°C in summer; from 15°C to -26° in winter. Though snow falls on the mountains above 5,500m, rainfall is low, in some area below 50 mm a

Festivals of the Northwest

Though Argentina is an ultramodern country in some respects, it still preserves ancestral customs dating back to before the Spanish conquest. Such indigenous customs survive in the interior of the country, especially in the Northwest. The most colourful of the region's local festivals are summarized below:

Date	Event	Place(s)
20 December-6 January	Virgin of Belén	Belén (Catamarca)
1-15 January	Pre-Carnival festivities	Humahuaca (Jujuy)
15-31 January	January festival	Tilcara (Jujuy)
2 February	Virgen of Candelaria	Humahuaca
6 February	Pachamama (Mother Earth)	Purmamarca (Jujuy); Amaichá del Valle (Tucumán)
Feb/March (variable)	Carnival	Humahuaca
19 March	San José (patron saint of workers)	San José and Cachi (Salta)
March/April (variable)	Holy Week	Throughout the Northwest
March/April (in Holy Week)	Festival of Yavi	Yavi (Jujuy)
March/April (in Holy Week)	Procession accompanying Virgin of Punta Corral	From Punta Corral to Tumbaya (Jujuy)
March/April (in Holy Week)	Pilgrimage to El Señor de la Peña	Aimogasta (La Rioja)
4 May	Santa Cruz	Uquía (Jujuy)
24 June	San Juan, Rinconada, Conchinoca, Santa Catalina	San Juan Bautista (John the Baptist)
24/25 July	Santiago Apóstol (St James)	Humahuaca
26 July	Santa Ana	Tilcara (Jujuy)
15 August	Toreo de la Vincha (only bullfight in Argentina)	Casabindo (Jujuy)
30 August	Santa Rosa de Lima (Patron-saint of America)	Purmamarca (Jujuy)
15 September	Our Lord and the Virgen of the Miracle	City of Salta
First Sunday in October	Adoration of the Cachis	Iruya (Salta)
Third Sunday in October	Fiesta de las Ollas (pots)	La Quiaca (Jujuy)
1, 2 November	All Souls Day; Day of the Dead	Towns in the Quebrada de Humahuaca (Jujuy)
8 December	Virgen del Valle (Virgen of the Valley)	City of Catamarca
December-January	Adoration of the Child Jesus (nativity plays)	Many places in the Northwest.

Federico Kirbus

Fauna of the Northwestern Highlands

Vicuñas

👣 The *puna* is home to a variety of birdlife including the Lesser Rhea, a non-flier which compensates by running fast, the Andean Lapwing, the Puna Plover, the Mountain Caracara and the Andean Condor. The lakes of the *puna*, which attract different species according to the season, are outstanding for bird-watchers. There are huge flocks of Flamingoes (three species of which the Chilean is the most common), Andean Geese, Puna Ibis, Andean Gulls and various species of coots and ducks including the Puna Teal and the Crested Duck.

Camelids are the most impressive mammals, with herds of wild vicuña and guanaco as well as the domesticated Llama. Rodents include the chinchilla.

In the valleys of the *prepuna* you can see Andean Woodpeckers, Grey-hooded Parakeets, Giant Hummingbirds, Ghiguano Thrushes and seedeaters such as the Green Yellow-finch, the Black-hooded Sierra-finch and the Black Siskin. Lesser Rheas, Andean Geese, guanacos and vicuñas can be seen in winter.

Santiago de La Vega

year. In the valleys temperatures are less extreme; rainfall is heavier in the eastern valleys. The eastern hills experience a very different climate, with heavy rainfall, up to 2,000 mm a year, carried by easterly winds from the Atlantic. Temperatures in the east rise rapidly with declining altitude. Rainfall throughout the northwest occurs mainly in summer, when many roads become impassable.

HISTORY

The northwest was one of the most important areas of prehispanic settlement as the extensive archaeological sites of Quilmes, Tafí del Valle and Santa Rosa de Tastil indicate. This was also one of the first areas of Spanish settlement. The first Spanish expedition, led by Diego de Almagro from Cuzco (Peru), entered Argentina in 1536.

Colonial churches of Salta and Jujuy

👣 Some of the most attractive colonial churches in Argentina are to be found in the provinces of Salta and Jujuy. Despite the ravages of time, natural disasters, war and restoration work, many retain their charm, especially away from the two provincial capitals.

The main influence on church architecture in this region was the city of Sucre (today in Bolivia), which was capital of the *audiencia* of Chuquisaca and seat of an archbishop. The architecture of Sucre, in its turn, was influenced particularly by the medieval churches of Seville. The basic structure, with adobe walls and wooden-framed roof, had a single nave with side-chapels, sacristy and a single tower. In the valleys, where the population was entirely Amerindian, an atrium or covered area outside was added in front of the church: this was used for teaching the unconverted and often became the social centre of the village.

Away from the cities, the easiest churches to visit are those in the Valles Calchaquís and the Quebrada de Humahuaca. Among the less accessible are some of the most outstanding, notably Casabindo and Yavi in northern Jujuy.

Cafayate	Catamarca	Jujuy	Humahuaca	La Quiaca	Salta	San Antonio de los Cobres	Santiago del Estero	Tafí del Valle	Tinogasta	Tucumán
441										
299	650									
413	676	126								
577	961	292	166							
190	540	97	223	387						
324	676	233	359	525	136					
387	370	834	1,001	126	486	622				
122	235	566	692	858	312	464	235			
335	278	928	1,054	1,220	836	741	665	517		
229	212	459	585	749	328	464	158	107	508	

A little later a better and lower route was discovered through the Quebrada de Humahuaca. Along this new route the Spanish founded a group of towns: Santiago del Estero, Tucumán, Salta, and Jujuy. Throughout the colonial period these were the centres of white settlement. Attempts to subdue the Amerindian population of the valleys included the imposition of *encomiendas*, the establishment of Jesuit and Franciscan missions and military conquest, but resistence was fierce, especially in the Calchaquí and Humahuaca valleys.

Trade followed the pattern of Spanish advance into the northwest: just as the area had been settled from the north, colonial trade was oriented towards Potosi and other mining areas. Trade was largely in mules and other goods were carried by mules. The larger cities of the northwest grew in importance as they served this route. Mules were bred mainly in the plains between Rosario, Santa Fe, and Córdoba, and driven to Salta for the great fair in February and March. In 1679 Crown officials estimated that 40,000 cattle and 20,000 mules were passing through Salta each year on their way north. Tucumán was strategically important: the routes of the Ríos Salado and

Dulce forced mule traffic to pass through it on the way to Salta. Jujuy was intended to protect the trade route from attacks by the Humahuaca and Calchaquí indians.

Although the economy of the cities continued to rely on the trading route to Bolivia, by the 18th century the Spanish had developed cattle ranching, tobacco, wheat, oranges and rice in the valleys. The break up of the Spanish empire and the loss of trade links with Bolivia and Peru hit the area badly. Jujuy was invaded 11 times by royalist forces and was badly devastated during the wars of independence. The whole area suffered from the political instability which followed.

CATAMARCA PROVINCE

Catamarca can be divided into three areas: the eastern sierras, the *Alta Cordillera* or High Andes, and the *puna*. The eastern part of the province is crossed from north to south by several ranges of hills. There are three main valleys: the Valle de Catamarca, the most populated part of the province, situated between the Sierra de Ancasti and the Sierra de Ambato; the Campo de Belén, a wide basin west of the Sierra de Ambato and south of the Sierra de Belén; and the valley of the Río

Abaucán between the Sierra de Fiambalá and the Sierra de Narváez. West of the Sierra de Fiambalá is another valley, the Valle de Chaschuil, almost uninhabited, west of which tower the High Andes. North of Belén, the northern part of the province is *puna*, a high rolling, largely barren plain. The province is scattered with thermal springs.

Economy
Cattle, fruit, grapes and cotton are the main agricultural products, but it is also renowned for hand-woven ponchos and fruit preserves. There are traces of Amerindian civilizations, including extensive agricultural terraces (now mostly abandoned), throughout the province.

CATAMARCA

(*Population* 111,000; *Altitude* 522m; *Phone code* 0833), known officially as San Fernando del Valle de Catamarca, lies on the Río del Valle, 153 km northeast of La Rioja and 240 km south of Tucumán. Founded in 1683, it is the provincial capital. Many of the public buildings date from the late 19th century and were designed by the Italian architect Luigi Caravati.

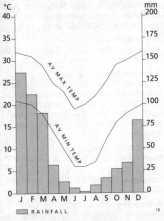

Climate: Catamarca

Places of interest
On the Plaza 25 de Mayo are the **Cathedral** (1878) and the **Casa de Gobierno** (1891), both designed by Caravati. One block north of the plaza is the **Convento de San Francisco** with a church dating from 1891. Fans of Caravati should visit the **Seminario Concillar**, with its double bell-tower and Italianate façade, four blocks east of the plaza. Visitors can also see the place where murdered student, María Soledad Morales, was found in 1990. (The affair led to lengthy criminal proceedings – as yet unresolved – and the site has become a shrine.)

Museums
Instituto Cultural Esquiú, Sarmiento 450, with important archaeological section, Monday-Friday 0700-1300, 1430-2000, Saturday, Sunday, morning only.

    Museo Folklórico, underground (*subsuelo*), Paseo Gral Navarro.

    Museo de Bellas Artes, Mota Botello 239, Monday-Friday 8000-1300.

Excursions
To the **Capillas del Valle**, churches in the Valle de Catamarca, just north of the city. The first of these, at **San Isidro**, 5 km east, was designed by Caravati. At **Villa Dolores**, 1 km further north, there is a church built in colonial style in 1847, **San Antonio**, 3 km further, dates from 1802, but was remodelled in 1830 and 1845. Nearby is a **zoo** with guanacos, vicuñas, alpacas and llamas in a park. **San José**, 4 km further north, is another colonial style early 19th century church while **La Señora del Rosario**, 2 km east, is the the real thing, a simple white building dating from 1715. **Los Milagros**, another 3 km north (1793) has a 19th century tower.

    To **Dique Las Pirquitas**, a lake with good fishing and watersports in the same valley, 25 km north of Catamarca.

● **Bus** No 1A from bus terminal stops at *Hostería de Turismo* (with restaurant) at Villa Pirquitas, about 45 minutes' walk. Five morning buses from 0700, last returns at 2200. Opening hours Monday-Friday 1000-1900, Saturday, Sunday and holidays 0830-1900.

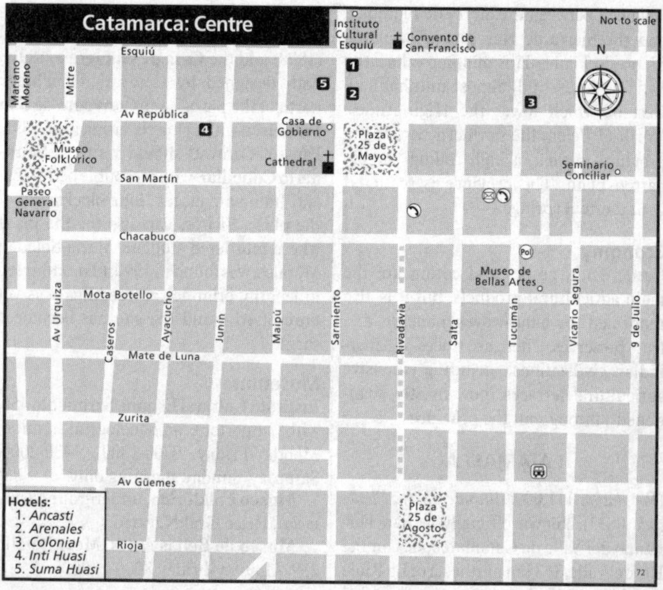

Catamarca: Centre

Hotels:
1. Ancasti
2. Arenales
3. Colonial
4. Inti Huasi
5. Suma Huasi

Local festivals

Pilgrimages to the church of the Virgen del Valle. In July, regional handicrafts are sold at Festival del Poncho, a *feria* with 4 nights of music, mostly folklore of the northwest.

Local information

● **Accommodation**

A3 *Ancasti*, Sarmiento 520, T 25001/4, 3-star, restaurant.

B *Arenales*, Sarmiento 544, T 303307, 3-star; **B** *Inti Huasi*, República 297, T 24664, 3-star.

Budget accommodation: **C** *Colonial*, República 802, T 23502, no food, recommended, welcoming, good value; **C** *Delgado*, San Martín 788, basic; **C** *Suma Huasi*, Sarmiento 547, T 22301, avoid TV lounge and rooms above it; **D** *Las Cumbres*, Plaza 25 de Agosto. Many *Residenciales* on Avenida Güemes. Discounts to ACA members at *Ancasti*, *Inti Huasi*, and *Suma Huasi*. Provincial tourist office has a list of families who rent rooms.

● **Places to eat**

Sociedad Española, Urquiza 703; *La Cabaña*, Tucumán 1115, has folk dancing. *Las Tinajas*, Sarmiento 533, excellent, pricey, live music, warmly recommended; *Pizzería Maryeli*, Esquiú 521, basic (but good *empanadas*);

Sociedad Italiana, M Moreno, pastas, inexpensive; *Comedor Unión Obrera*, Sarmiento 857, good value, speciality *cabrito*; *Parrilla de Adrián*, Güemes block 500, good *asado*; *Montmartre*, Paseo General Navarro, good food, reasonably priced; *Marco Polo Bar*, Rivadavia 916, drinks, snacks. Many cheap restaurants along Avenida Güemes, bars and cafés along Rivadavia (pedestrian street).

● **Airline offices**

Aerolíneas Argentinas, Sarmiento 589, T 24450; *Lapa*, Sarmiento 506, T 34772.

● **Banks & money changers**

Banco de Catamarca, Plaza 25 de Mayo, changes US$ cash but not travellers' cheques; Banco de Galicia changes travellers' cheques, US$10 commission. (See note on provincial bonds used as currency under **Information for travellers**.)

● **Post & telecommunications**

Post Office: San Martín 753, slow, open 0800-1300, 1600-2000.

Telephones: Rivadavia 758, open 0700-2400, daily.

● **Shopping**

Catamarca specialities from: *Cuesta del Portezuelo*, Sarmiento 575; *Maica Regionales*, next to Aerolíneas Argentinas; *Casa*

Valdés, Sarmiento 586; and *Suma Regionales*, Sarmiento y Esquiú. *Mercado Artesanal*, Urquiza 945, wide range of handicrafts, open 0700-1300, 1400-2000, reached by infrequent colectivo 23 from centre.

● **Tour companies & travel agents**
Enrique Lovell, at *Huellas Andinas*, T 31930, offers overland tours in 4WD to the Antofagasta de la Sierra region.

● **Tourist offices**
Provincial tourist office, **Roca y Virgen del Valle**, T/F 22520, Monday-Friday 0700-1300, 1400-2000. Offices in bus terminal and airport. In small towns in the province, go to the municipalidad for information and maps.

● **Transport**
Air Aeropuerto Felipe Varela, 20 km south. Aerolíneas Argentinas and Lapa to Buenos Aires and La Rioja.

Buses Terminal 5 blocks southeast of plaza at Güemes y Tucumán. To **Tucumán**, 4-5 daily, Bosio, 4½ hours, US$10, several other companies; to **Buenos Aires**, US$50, 2nd class at 2200, 1st class at 1900, daily; to **Córdoba**, Chevallier, 4 daily, 6 hours, US$16; to **Belén** via Cerro Negro, Coop Catamarca, 8 hours; to **Santiago del Estero**, 1630, US$12; to **Mendoza**, several daily.

Buses to Santiago del Estero province: no service over the Cuesta del Portezuelo to Lavalle but some buses to Frías, further south use this route (bus No 9), Coop de Transportes de Catamarca, departing 0500 Tuesday, Thursday, Friday and Saturday, 5 hours, returning 1400. From Frías buses run to Lavalle and on to Santiago del Estero. To Frías via Totoral, No 18 Monday, Wednesday, Friday, Saturday 0500, 5½ hours, returning 1330. To Lavalle via Totoral, same No 18, leaves Tuesday, Thursday, and Sunday 1100, 4 hours.

FROM CATAMARCA TO SANTIAGO DEL ESTERO

Provincial Route 42 (paved) runs northeast over the Sierra de Ancasti towards **Lavalle** and Santiago del Estero. At the village of El Portezuelo (*altitude* 600m), Km 18, there is a police checkpoint before the road climbs up the famous **Cuesta del Portezuelo**, 20 km long and rising to 1,680m, through 13 hairpin bends. There are panoramic views over the Valle de Catamarca. From the top the road continues via El Alto (*altitude* 950m; *hosteria*), near which is the Dique Ipizca (good *pejerrey* fishing) to Lavalle. For buses along this route see above.

FROM CATAMARCA TO CHILE

Route 60 (later Route 45) runs northwest along the provincial border with La Rioja passing through Aimogasta (see above under **The West**) before following the Río Colorado to Tinogasta.

TINOGASTA

(*Population* 9,000; *Altitude* 1,203; *Phone code* 0837), 277 km west of the provincial capital, is a former-copper mining town in in the broad valley of the Río Abaucán. An oasis of vineyards, olive groves, and poplars, this was an important area of pre-hispanic settlement. There are 2 small archaeological museums: the **Museo Arqueológico Municipal**, in the Casa de la Cultura, Constitución y Eva Perón, which dsiplays objects from the fortress of Batungasta; and the **Museo Doctor Alaniz**, Copiapó y Tucumán. Excursions may be made to the the Termas de Aguadita, 15 km west and to the Diaguita indian archaeological site of **Batungasta**, 24 km north on the road to Fiambalá, from where it is possible to walk west through an impressive red sandstone gorge.

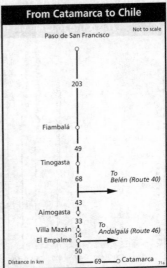

From Catamarca to Chile

Not to scale

Paso de San Francisco

	203
Fiambalá	
	49
Tinogasta	
	68	To Belén (Route 40) →
	43
Aimogasta	33
Villa Mazán	To Andalgalá (Route 46) →
El Empalme	14
	50

Distance in km ——— 69 ——— Catamarca

71a

• **Accommodation A3** *Provincial de Turismo*, Romero y Gordillo, T 23911, clean but run down, restaurant; **C** *Hostería Novel*, near airport, friendly. **Camping** At Balneario Municipal.

• **Places to eat** *Persegani*, Tristán Villafañe 373; *Rancho Huairapuca*, on Moreno.

• **Tour companies & travel agents** *Varela Viajes*, Copiapó 156, T/F 20428 for 4WD excursions to the Alta Cordillera; Omar Monuey, La Espiga de Oro, 25 de Mayo 436 for expeditions and horse riding.

• **Buses** To Tucumán, Empresa Gutiérrez, Tuesday, Friday, Sunday 1700, Monday, Tuesday, Friday, Sunday 0615, Friday 0845, US$22; return Tuesday, Friday, Sunday. To Catamarca 1700 and 0030 daily; to **La Rioja** and **Córdoba** 0930, El Cóndor, US$11. Services twice a week to **Chubut**, **Comodoro Rivadavia**, and **Caleta Olivia**, with Empresa Ortiz, reflect that this is the source region for labour in the Patagonian oilfields.

FIAMBALA

(*Population* 1,800; *Altitude* 1,550) 49 km further north in the Abaucán valley in an area of vineyards, is the last town before the frontier. It was founded in 1702 near the site of a mission. The church of San Pedro on the outskirts 2 km south dates from 1702. Near the plaza is the **Museo**

del Hombre with indian mummies found recently in the Alta Cordillera. There are thermal springs nearby: the **Termas de Fiambalá**, 14 km east, temperatures from 30°C to 54°C, can be visited by taxi,(make sure taxi fare includes wait and return) and the **Termas de Saujil**, 15 km north.

• **Accommodation C** *Hostería Municipal*, good value, also restaurant; small, basic *pensión* (unsigned – ask), near which is a good restaurant. **Camping** At the Termas de Fiambalá.

• **Tour companies & travel agents** For excursions into the Alta Cordillera on foot or in 4WD contact Jonson and Ruth Reynoso, T 0766-90271/90170, F 0837-96154 (check state of vehicles). 4WD vehicles may be hired in Fiambalá: ask at the Intendencia.

• **Buses** Empresa Gutiérrez daily at 1345 to Catamarca via Tinogasta (1500) and Cerro Negro junction (1610), connect with Coop Catamarca bus to Belén (from Catamarca), about 2 hours by bad road. Also 0530 departure from Fiambalá.

Climbing in the Alta Cordillera

Fiambalá and Tinogasta are the starting points for expeditions to several inactive volcanic peaks along this part of the frontier near the San Francisco pass. These include **Pissis** (6,882m), the second highest mountain in South America, first

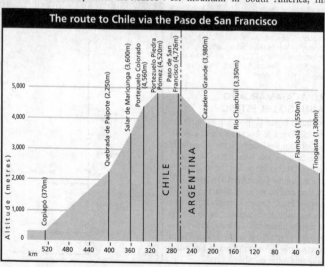

The route to Chile via the Paso de San Francisco

climbed in 1937. You have to register at the police station outside Fiambalá, take passport. Other climbing possibilities include: Bonete (6,759m) Walther Penck (6,658m), El Fraile (6,062m), Incahuasi (6,638m), Nacimientos (6,493m), Tres Cruces (6,749m), El Muerto (6,488m) and San Francisco (6,016m). Ojos del Salado (6,864m) is best attacked from the Chilean side. The most favourable periods for climbing are short: November-December and March-April. In winter temperatures in this area can drop to to -35°C.

FRONTIER WITH CHILE: THE PASO DE SAN FRANCISCO

Fiambalá is the starting-point for the crossing to Chile via the Paso de San Francisco (4,726m), 203 km northwest along a road described as "quite some washboard" (Hannes Scheiner) though not requiring 4WD vehicle Officially open all year, this route is is liable to be closed by snow between June and October; take enough fuel for at least 400 km as there are no service stations from Fiambalá to just before Copiapó.

● **Argentine immigration & customs**
At La Gruta, 21 km east of the pass.

● **Into Chile**
On the Chilean side roads run to El Salvador and Copiapó. Chilean customs are near the Salar de Maricunga, 100 km west of the pass.

CATAMARCA TO ANTOFAGASTA DE LA SIERRA

Two roads, Route 46 to Andalagá and Route 40 to Belén and Antofagasta de la Sierra run north to give access to the valleys of western Catamarca. Route 46 (paved) branches off Route 60 at El Empalme and runs northwards between the Sierra de Ambato to the east and the saltflats of the Salar de Pipanaco to the east.

ANDALGALA

(*Population* 7,800; *Altitude* 962m; *Phone code* 0835), the main town along this road, lies 134 km north of El Empalme, in an area of olives, walnut trees and fruit growing which is renowned for its strong alcoholic drinks. Originally a fortress, the town is situated at the foot of Mount Candado (5,450m) in a zone rich in archeological

remains. There are two archeological museums: the **Museo Arqueológico Provincial**, Belgrano y Mercado (Monday-Friday 0900-1300), and the **Museo Privado Malli**, Núñez del Prado 510. At Minas Capillitas, 66 km north of the town, rhodochrosite, Argentina's unofficial national stone is quarried; it can be bought at shops around the plaza.

● **Accommodation** Hotel de Turismo, T 2210, often full; Res Galileo, T 2247. **Camping** Autocamping La Aguada, with pool, US$5 per tent.

● **Transport** 3 bus lines to Catamarca.

BELEN

(*Population* 8,800; *Altitude* 1,240m; *Phone code* 0835) lies 85 km west of Andalgalá along Route 46 at the junction with Route 40 which runs north from Route 60 at Cerro Negro, 79 km west of El Empalme. Founded in 1681 at the entrance to the gorge of the Río Belén, the town lies north

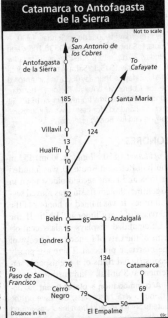

Catamarca to Antofagasta de la Sierra

Not to scale

To San Antonio de los Cobres

Antofagasta de la Sierra

To Cafayate

185

Santa María

Villavil 124

13

Hualfín

10

52

Belén — 85 — Andalgalá

15

Londres

76   134

Catamarca

To Paso de San Francisco

Cerro Negro — 79

69

50

El Empalme

Distance in km

69c

at the northern edge of a wide basin, the Campo de Belén and is noted for its olives, walnuts and peppers. This region is also famous for its weavings, ponchos, saddlebags and rugs: Belén is known as national capital of the poncho. There are good views from the new statue of the Virgin of Belén, 450m above the town, at the summit of the path beginning at Calle General Roca. The **Museo Condor Huasi**, contains one of the largest collection of Diaguita artefacts in the country. North of Belén there are thermal springs at La Ciénaga, 22 km along Route 40.

Local festivals Fiesta de Nuestra Señora de Belén, 20 December-6 January; Festival Nacional del Poncho, July/August.

● **Accommodation & places to eat** **A3** *Samay*, Urquiza 349, T 61320, recommended; *C Turismo*, cheap and good, recommended; *Provincial*, dilapidated. **Camping** At Balneario Municipal. Good breakfast at bus terminal; *Restaurant Dalesio*, near YPF gas station, excellent and cheap; *El Amigazo*, behind church, good.

● **Buses** To **Catamarca** via Andalgalá; Coop Catamarca via Saujil, Poman, Chumbicha, Tuesday, Thursday 1000, Friday, Sunday 1300, 8 hours; to **Santa María** Tuesday 1330, Friday and Sunday 2020; return Tuesday and Thursday 0930, Sunday 1945; to **Salta** via Hualfín, Santa María, Cafayate Thursday 0600; to San Antonio de los Cobres via Villavil, Tuesday, Thursday, Sunday 0800 (returns from Villavil at 1830). Sit on right-hand side for best views of impressive canyon and Río Bolsón reservoir.

LONDRES

(*Population* 1,850; *Altitude* 1,300m) 15 km south of Belén on Route 40, was founded in 1558 and is the second-oldest town in Argentina, though its site was moved several times. It was named in honour of the marriage of Mary Tudor and Philip II: the municipalidad displays a glass coat-of-arms of the City of London and a copy of the marriage proposal. There are poorly reconstructed ruins of a prehispanic settlement at Shinkal, 4 km northwest.

● **Accommodation & places to eat** No hotels, but several hospedajes. Campsite on the route to Shinkal. Snacks from the shops around the plaza.

NORTH OF BELEN

There are two routes north to Salta. The most direct is via Route 40 which runs northeast another 176 km, largely unpaved, to Santa María at Tucumán provincial border (see page 244), and on to Cafayate (page 245) and Salta.

The alternative is via Route 43, which branches west off Route 40 at a point 52 km north of Belén and runs across the high *puna* to Antofagasta de la Sierra and San Antonio de los Cobres (see page 265)). This route is almost impassable for passenger cars after heavy rains: the stretch just after the junction with Route 40 is very difficult with 37 km of fords. At Km 87 is Cerro Compo (3,125m), from which the descent is magnificent; at Km 99 the road turns right to Laguna Blanca, where there is a small vicuña farm (don't go straight at the junction). There are thermal springs along this road: at Hualfín 10 km north of the junction, and at **Villavil**, 13 km further north (open January-April). For buses along this route see under Belén.

NB This route requires enough fuel for 600 km at high altitudes on unmaintained roads: fuel consumption of carburettor engines at these altitudes is almost double that in the lowlands (fill up at Hualfín and San Antonio de los Cobres).

ANTOGAGASTA DE LA SIERRA

(*Population* 900; *Altitude* 3,365m), is the main township in sparsely populated northwest Catamarca. Situated on the Río Punilla 260 km north of Belén and 557 km northwest of the provincial capital, it is surrounded by lunar landscapes and volcanoes. To the west are the salt flats of the Salar de Antofalla. There are many peaks over 5,000m, including Cerro Galán (5,912m) a volcano with a giant caldera 40 km x 25 km. Deposits of marble, onyx, sulphur, mica, salts, borates, and gold can be found in the area. Wildlife includes vicuña, guanaco, vizcacha, flamingos, foxes and ostriches. No petrol station, but fuel obtainable from *intendencia*. North of Antofagasta the road continues via the Salar de Hombre Muerto to San Antonio de los Cobres.

- **Accommodation & Places to eat E** pp *Pensión Darío*, blue door just off main square; *Res Florida*, Catamarca 6; *Almacén Rodríguez*, Belgrano y Catamarca, serves meals, including breakfast.

- **Buses** From Belén Tuesday, Thursday, Sunday 0800, or hire a pickup or hitch.

SANTIAGO DEL ESTERO

(*Population* 201,000; *Altitude* 200m; *Phone code* 085), situated on the Río Dulce on the western edge of the Chaco, lies 435 km north of Córdoba. On the opposite bank of the river is the town of **La Banda** (*population* 71,000). Capital of its namesake province, it is a commercial centre for the Chaco.

Founded in 1553 by Francisco de Aguirre, Santiago was at one time an important city: it was the base for expeditions to found six other cities in the northwest. In 1570 it became a bishopric and in 1577 was made capital of the Spanish province of Tucumán. Sited near large Indian communities it was a centre of Jesuit missionary activity. Though Santiago proudly sees itself as the oldest city in Argentina, virtually none of this past has survived.

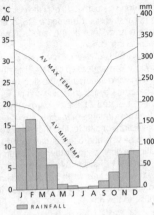

Climate: Santiago del Estero

Santiago del Estero: Centre

Hotels:
1. *Libertador*
2. *Gran*

Andres Chazarreta

Celebrated as the man who put Argentine folk music and dance "on the map", Andres Chazarreta was born in Santiago del Estero in 1876. From early childhood he learned to play the guitar and other instruments by ear. His first formal musical studies, at the age of 26, oriented him towards European opera and the light classics, then all the rage in Argentina which looked to France and Italy for musical inspiration.

In 1905, however, Chazarreta became fascinated by gaucho literature. Inspired by José Hernández's epic poem "Martín Fierro" and the novels of Eduardo Gutierrez which were adapted for the stage and performed by travelling groups of players, Chazarreta began arranging and performing traditional folk tunes, beginning with the celebrated Zamba de Vargas. In 1911 in Santiago del Estero he produced a stage performance of traditional music and dance by a group of rural artists. Despite predictions of disaster, the show was a great success, but Chazarreta and his troupe of musicians and dancers had to wait another decade until they achieved their ultimate goal, a similar triumph in Buenos Aires.

In 1941 Chazarreta founded the Academy of Native Dance in Buenos Aires and by the time of his death he had made over 250 records. His versions of traditional songs and dances, mainly based on Santiago, continue to dominate Argentine folk music to this day.

Nigel Gallop

Places of interest

On the **Plaza Libertad** stand the **Municipalidad** and, next to it, the **Jefatura de Policia**, built in 1868 in the style of a colonial cabildo. On the west side is the **Cathedral**, the fifth on the site, dating from 1877. The fine modern **Casa de Gobierno** is on Plaza San Martín, four blocks northwest. Two blocks southeast of the plaza, at Urquiza y 25 de Mayo, is the convent of **Santo Domingo**, containing one of two copies of the 'Turin Shroud', given by Philip II to his 'beloved colonies of America'. On Plaza Lugones, three blocks east of Plaza Libertad, is the church of **San Francisco** (1895), at the back of which is the cell of San Francisco Solano, patron saint of Tucumán, who stayed in Santiago in 1593. East of the centre on the banks of the Río Dulce, is the pleasant **Parque Francisco de Aguirre**.

Museums

Museo Arqueológico, Avellaneda 353, containing a large collection of Indian pottery and artefacts, the lifework of Emilio and Duncan Wagner, the sons of a French diplomat. Born in Scotland and educated in Switzerland, the brothers arrived in the city in 1885 and dedicated themselves to collecting artefacts from pre-conquest Indian civilizations in the Chaco. Their collection of over 90,000 pieces, formed the basis of the museum. Monday-Friday, 0800-1300, 1400-1900, Saturday, 0900-1200, free.

Museo Histórico, Urquiza 354, containing artefacts from wealthy local families, Monday-Friday, 0830-1230, 1530-1830, Saturday 0900-1200.

Museo de Bellas Artes, Independencia between 9 de Julio and Urquiza, Monday-Friday, 0900-1300.

Museo Andrés Chazarreta, Mitre 127, in the musician's former house and displaying artefacts from his life, daily 1000-1200.

Local festivals

Carnival when virtually everything throwable gets thrown by everyone at everyone else.

Local information

● **Accommodation**

A3 Gran, Avellaneda e Independencia, T 224563, 4-star; **Libertador**, Catamarca 47,

T 218730, 3-star; **A3** *Rodas*, Gallo 432, T 218804, safe.

Budget accommodation: **C** *Res Emausi*, Avenida Moreno 600 block, good value; *Santa Rita*, Santa Fe 273, near bus terminal, basic.

Camping *Las Casuarinas*, Parque Aguirre, T 211390. Insect repellent essential.

● **Places to eat**
Restaurant Sociedad Española, Independencia 236, popular, good value; *Centro de Viajes*, Buenos Aires 37, good value lunches; *Mía Mamma*, 24 de Septiembre 16, on Plaza, good restaurant/salad bar, pricey.

● **Airline offices**
Aerolíneas Argentinas, Buenos Aires 60, T 224088; Austral, Libertad 766, T 214612.

● **Banks & money changers**
Banco Francés, 9 de Julio y 24 de Septiembre; Noroeste Cambio, 24 de Septiembre 220, good rates. Amex, El Quijote Paladea Turismo, Independencia 342, T 213207.

● **Tourist offices**
On Plaza Libertad, T 214243.

● **Transport**
Air Mal Paso airport on northwestern outskirts. Austral to Buenos Aires and Jujuy.

Buses Terminal at Gallo 480, four blocks from centre. To **Buenos Aires**, several daily, 12 hours, US$37, Cacorba, La Unión and Atahualpa; to **Resistencia**, 3 a day, El Rayo, via Quimili and Roque Sáenz Peña, 8 hours, US$25; to **Córdoba**, 12 a day, 7 hours, US$16; to **Tucumán** via Río Hondo US$8; 4 a day to **Salta**, US$23, Panamericano, 5½ hours, and to **Jujuy**, 7 hours.

TERMAS DE RIO HONDO

(*Population* 25,000; *Altitude* 265m; *Phone code* 0858), situated 65 km north of Santiago del Estero on the Río Dulce, is the most popular spa town in Argentina. The thermal waters, over 30°C are recommended for blood pressure and rheumatism and good to drink. There are 2 pools: La Olla near the river and the Pileta Municipal in the Parque Güemes, both southeast of the centre. The huge Río Hondo dam, 4 km west on the Río Dulce, forms a lake of 33,000 hectares, used for sailing and fishing.

● **Accommodation** There are over 170 hotels, but at national holiday periods, and especially in August, accommodation is hard to find, so book well in advance. *Grand Hotel Río Hondo*, Yrigoyen 552, T 21195; *Los Pinos*, Maipú 201, T 21043, pleasant; **B** *Ambassador*,

Libertad 184, T 21196; *Aranjuez*, Alberdi 280, T 21108. **Camping** 2 sites, both on Yrigoyen y Ruta 9: *Del Río*, US$5 rent a tent, US$4 own tent, very well run; *La Olla*, opposite. Also ACA site 4 km from town; *El Mirador*, Ruta 9 y Urquiza.

● **Tourist office** Caseros 132, T 21721.

● **Buses** Terminal Las Heras y España, north of centre near Route 9. To **Santiago del Estero**, 1 hour, US$2 and to **Tucumán**, 2 hours, US$4; several to **Buenos Aires** US$38.

TUCUMAN

(*Population* 400,000; *Altitude* 450m; *Phone code* 081), full name San Miguel de Tucumán, lies 159 km northwest of Santiago del Estero on a broad plain on the west bank of the Río Sali: to the west towers the Sierra de Aconquija. Capital of the smallest province in Argentina, it is the largest and most important city in the north. Summer weather can be very hot and sticky.

History
Founded in 1565 and transferred to its present site in 1685, Tucumán became an important centre for mule trains on the routes from Bolivia to Buenos Aires and Mendoza. With a colonial economy based on sugar, citrus fruit and tobacco, it developed a landed aristocracy distinct from those of Buenos Aires and Córdoba. The Congress of Tucumán, which met from

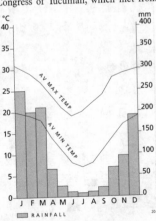

Climate: Tucumán

1816 to 1820, was attended by 29 representatives from 14 provinces, including three which are now part of Bolivia.

Although unable to agree on a constitution, its famous independence declaration on 9 July 1816 was an important statement

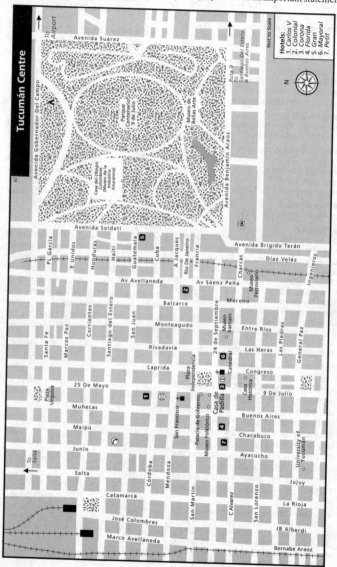

Tucumán Centre

Not to Scale

Hotels:
1. Carlos V
2. Colonial
3. Corona
4. Florida
5. Gran
6. Mayoral
7. Petit

of the aims of the leaders of the movement against Spanish rule. The city was the site of an important battle during the Wars of Independence: Belgrano's victory here over a royalist army ended the Spanish threat to restore colonial rule over the River Plate area. In the 19th century the province received relatively few immigrants, retaining its colonial flavour and traditional social structure into the 20th century when it began to industrialise with the growth of sugarmills, chemical plants, distilleries and textile mills.

Places of interest

The oldest building on the main **Plaza Independencia** is the neoclassical **Cathedral** (1852) with its distinctive cupola. Inside, near the baptismal font, is an old rustic cross, used when founding the city. On the west side is the ornate **Palacio de Gobierno** (1910): next to it is the church of **San Francisco** (1891), with a picturesque façade and tiled cupola.

South of the plaza, on Calle Congreso, is the **Casa Histórica**: only the original room where the Declaration of Independence was drafted remains, the rest being a modern reconstruction housing a museum (see below): a bas-relief on the museum walls shows the delegates proclaiming independence. There is a *son et lumière* programme nightly (not Tuesday, except in July) at 2030 in the garden (adults US$2, children US$1, tickets from tourist office on Plaza Independencia, no seats).

Several of the former mansions of wealthy families are now occupied by museums, including the **Casa Padilla**, Plaza Independencia, and the **Casa Sortheix**, San Lorenzo y Lillo. East of the centre is the **Parque Nueve de Julio**, 190 hectares, formerly the property of Bishop Colombres: his house is a museum and the park includes a lake and sports facilities. There are fine views over the city from Cerro Jabriel, reached by bus 118.

Museums

Casa Histórica (see above), Calle Congreso, Tuesday-Friday 0830-1330, 1500-1930, Saturday 0830-1300, US$0.40.

Museo de la Industria Azucarera, in Bishop Colombres's house in the Parque 9 de Julio. Outside is his first mill, while inside there is a display on sugar-making, open Tuesday-Friday 0900-1200, 1730-2030.

Museo de Antropología y Etnografía, 25 de Mayo 265 in University building, fine collection, Monday-Friday, 0800-1200, 1600-2000.

Museo Folklórico Provincial, 24 de Septiembre 565, Monday 1730-2030, Tuesday-Friday, 0900-1230, 1730-2030, Saturday, Sunday, 1800-2100, free.

Instituto Miguel Lillo, San Lorenzo y Lillo, associated with the natural sciences department of the University, has a small but well-presented museum containing sections on geology and biology with some stuffed animals and a dinosaur skeleton, Monday-Friday, 0900-1200, 1500-1800.

Museo de la Ciudad, in the Casa Padilla, Plaza Independencia, houses a collection of international art and antiques.

Museo Histórico de la Provincia (Casa de Avellaneda) Calle Congreso 56, Monday-Friday, 0900-1230, 1700-2000, Saturday-Sunday, 1700-2000.

Museo Iramaín, Entre Rios 27, memorial to the sculptor Juan Carlos Iramain, Monday-Friday, 0900-1900.

Museo de Bellas Artes, 9 de Julio 48, entre 24 de Septiembre y Alvarez, Tuesday-Friday, 0900-1300, 1630-2100, Saturday-Sunday, 0900-1200, 1730-2030.

Museo Ferroviario, Charcas y Saenz Peña, small railway museum in former Belgrano station.

Excursions

To **El Cadillal** dam, in the gorge of the Río Sali, 26 km north, which supplies electricity and water for the city and permanent irrigation for 80,000 hectares. There are places to eat, a good ACA campsite, good swimming, and a small archaeological museum at the dam. **Bus** Sierras y Lagos, every 1½ hours approximately, US$1.50, 45 minutes, last buses back 1715 and 1945).

To **Simoca**, 45 km south on Route 157, which is known as the *capital del sulky* because of the widespread use of sulkies (carriages). It has a Saturday morning handicrafts and produce market. **Bus** Posta bus, several, 1½ hours, US$2.50; essential to get there early.

To **Horco Molle**, 14 km west on the edge of the Sierras de Aconquija, where there is the **Reserva Biológica San Javier**, covering 14,172 hectatares, with subtropical plants. **Bus** at 1130 (the only one) returns immediately. Further west in the Sierras are **San Javier**, *altitude* 1,220), Km 34 and, to the south, **Villa Nougués**, Km 36, the summer residence of the well-to-do Tucumanos). Both are reached by San Javier bus 1300.

During the sugar cane harvest (*zafra*) some *ingenios* (mills) offer tours: ask the tourist office for details. The easiest to visit is **Ingenio Concepción**, on the outskirts of Tucumán, guided tours (in Spanish) Monday-Saturday, 0930 and 1030, no booking required. Take Aconquija bus for Santo Cristo US$0.60, 15 minutes.

Local holidays

24 September, Battle of Tucumán; 29 September, San Miguel; 10 November, Día de la Tradición.

Local information
● **Accommodation**
L3 *Grand de Tucumán*, Avenida Soldati 380, T 245000, 5-star, opposite Parque 9 de Julio, rooms with even numbers quieter, outstanding food and service, pool (open to non-residents), tennis courts, disco.

A1 *Carlos V*, 25 de Mayo 330, T/F 221972, central, good service, air conditioning, bar, restaurant, recommended; **A2** *Metropol*, 24 de Septiembre 524, T 311180, F 310379, run down, helpful; **A3** *Gran Hotel Corona*, 24 de Septiembre 498 on corner of Plaza Independencia, T 310985, good location and facilities; **A3** *ACA Motel Tucumán*, Avenida San Martín 2080, T 266037; **A3** *Premier*, Alvarez 510, T 310381, air conditioning, good; **A3** *Colonial*, San Martín 35, T 311523, modern, fan, laundry service, good breakfast, recommended; **A3** *Mediterraneo*, 24 de Septiembre 364, T 310025, F 310080, 20% discount to *South American Handbook* readers.

Budget accommodation: **B** *Viena*, Santiago del Estero 1050, T 310004; **C** *La Vasca*, Mendoza 281, T 211288, safe, recommended; **C** *Casa de Huéspedes María Ruiz*, Rondeau

1824, safe, recommended; **C** *Florida*, 24 de Septiembre 610, T 221785, good value, poorly-lit rooms, helpful; **C** *Independencia*, Balcarce, entre San Martín y 24 de Septiembre, with fan quiet, poor water supply on 1st floor; **C** *Palace*, 24 de Septiembre 233, recommended; **C** *Petit*, Alvarez 765, T 214902, spacious, old fashioned, without bath.

Near terminal: **D** *Alcázar*, Saenz Peña 33, not very clean; **E** *Estrella*, Araoz 38, very hospitable.

Outside the city: at San Javier **A3** *Hostería San Javier* T 929004, F 229241, beautiful location, clean, pool, restaurants; at Villa Nougués **A3** *Hostería Villa Nougués*, T 310048, small, excellent, great views.

Camping Avoid the sites in the Parque 9 de Julio. Two roadside camp sites 3 km east and northeast of city centre.

● **Places to eat**
There are several popular restaurants and cafés in Parque 9 de Julio and on Plaza Independencia. *El Fondo*, San Martín 848, T 222161, good service, 'best steak house ever'; *Ali Baba*, Junín 380, Arab specialities (Syrian owners), intimate, inexpensive, recommended, closed lunchtime; *El Fogón*, Marcos Pez 600, good; *El Alto de la Lechuza*, 24 de Septiembre y Avellaneda; *La Leñita*, 25 de Mayo 377, expensive, smart, good meat; *La Parrilla de La Plaza*, San Martín 391, excellent, reasonable prices; *Las Brasas*, Maipú 740, good but not cheap; *Augustus*, 24 Septiembre y Buenos Aires, good café; *Pastísima Rotisería*, Mendoza y Laprida and at San Martín 964, good cheap snacks, take out service. Set lunches near bus terminal good value. *Panadería Villecco*, Corrientes 751, good bread, also 'integral'. In this part of Argentina 'black beer' (eg Salta Negra) is available.

● **Banks & money changers**
American Express, Chacabuco 38, T 217269, does not change cash or travellers' cheques, but very helpful; **Noroeste Cambios**, San Martín 775, accepts travellers' cheques; **Dinar**, San Martín 645 and 742, cash only, and **Maguitur**, San Martín 763, good rates for cash, accepts travellers' cheques. (See note on provincial bonds used as currency, page 468.)

● **Cultural centres**
Alliance Française, Mendoza 255, free events in French; **Instituto Italiano di Cultura**, Salta 60; **Aticana** (North American Centre) including J F Kennedy Library, Salta 581, open Monday-Friday, 0800-1200, 1700-2100; *Peña Cultural El Cardón*, Las Heras 50, library, exhibition centre, snacks served.

● **Entertainment**
Casino: Sarmiento y Maipú, open Friday, Saturday, Sunday, 2100-0230.

● **Laundry**
Lava Norte, Mendoza 375, also at Buenos Aires y San Lorenzo, open 0800-2200, wash and dry US$5; *Mi Lavadero*, Ayacucho 115.

● **Post & telecommunications**
Post Office: Córdoba y 25 de Mayo, open 0700-1300, 1600-2000 Monday-Friday, 0800-1300 Saturday.

Telecommunications: Telecom, Maipú 360, open 24 hours, best after 1900.

● **Shopping**
Artesanía El Cardón, Alvarez 427, excellent handicrafts; *Mercado Artesanal*, at the tourist office in Plaza Independencia, small, but nice selection of lace and leather work. All shops close 1200-1630. There is a lively fruit and vegetable market, *Mercado de Abasto*, at San Lorenzo y Lillo, worth a visit.

● **Tour companies & travel agents**
Tours may be difficult to arrange out of peak season (eg September) owing to shortage of passengers. *Patsa Turismo*, Chacabuco 38, T 217269, F 310490.

● **Tourist offices**
In Plaza Independencia at 24 de Septiembre 484, 0800-1800, 1700-2200, with electronic displays on provincial tourist attractions. For free tourist information, T 0800-5-8828.

● **Transport**
Local Car hire: Avis, Congreso 76, T 875674, F 31184 and airport; **Liprandi**, 24 de Septiembre 524, T 311210/212665; Movil Renta, San Lorenzo 370, T 218635/310550, F 310080 and at airport; **Localiza**, San Juan 959, T 311352. **Car repairs**: Rubén Boss, Avenida Aconquija 947, recommended esp for Volkswagen. **Motorists**: should not park on the street overnight; pay US$5 for garage parking.

Air Aeropuerto Benjamín Matienzo, 10 km east of town. Bus connection for each flight, US$1.50, starts from *Hotel Mediterraneo*, 24 de Septiembre 364. Taxi US$10. To Buenos Aires, AR, Lapa (T 305530) and Dinar. To Córdoba and Salta Andesmar, Lapa and Dinar. Southern Winds to **Córdoba**, **Salta**, **Mendoza**, **Rosario**, **Neuquén**, **Bariloche** and **Mar del Plata**.

Buses Modern terminal on Avenida Benjamín Araoz with a huge shopping complex; to **Cafayate**, 6½ hours, US$20, Aconquija, 4 daily via Tafí (2½ hours, US$9) and Santa María, sit on left-hand side; direct to **Salta** (not via Cafayate), 4½ hours, several daily, eg La Estrella, Veloz del Norte, US$21, 4½ hours. See below on routes to Salta. Plenty of buses to **Jujuy**, eg Veloz del Norte, 0900, 6 hours.
To **Buenos Aires**, Chevallier, La Estrella, Veloz del Norte, 16 hours, air conditioning, bar, video, 3 stops; book in advance; fares

US$40-70; to **Posadas**, La Estrella, US$55, 19 hours, 1600 daily; to **Mendoza**, La Estrella, US$29, 3 a day (14 hours), via Catamarca, La Rioja, and San Juan; to **La Rioja**, 7 hours, US$15; to **Catamarca**, 5 a day with Bosio, plus other lines; to **Santiago del Estero**, US$8; to **Córdoba**, US$30, 7 hours, many companies including Sol, El Tucumano and Panamericano; to **Pocitos**, frontier with Bolivia, US$25.

Trains Service to Buenos Aires run by Tucumán provincial government, Thursday and Sunday, 23 hours, US$50 pullman, US$36 first, US$31 tourist, returning, Monday and Friday, 1600.

FROM TUCUMAN TO SALTA

There are two routes from Tucumán to Salta: the road via Rosario de la Frontera and Güemes is quicker, but far less scenic or interesting than the route via Cafayate, which offers the chance to visit the archaeological sites of Tafí del Valle and Quilmes and the beautiful Quebrada de Cafayate.

Tucumán to Salta: the direct route

Not to scale

Distance in km

THE DIRECT ROUTE

Route 9 runs north from Tucumán, east of the Sierra de Aconquija via Rosario de la Frontera and Metán to Güemes, where it forks: Route 34 continues towards Jujuy and the Bolivian frontier; Route 9 branches off west, through the mountains to Salta.

ROSARIO DE LA FRONTERA

(*Population* 18,000; *Altitude* 769m; *Phone code* 0876; Km 134, is famous mainly for the thermal springs which lie 8 km east of town. These are the site of the oldest spa hotel in Argentina, built in 1884, with thermal swimming pool and golf course; nearby is an artificial lake owned by Club Caza y Pesca. Excursions may be made to **El Naranjo**, 19 km northwest, a former Jesuit mission; the church contains images and carvings made by Indians.

● **Accommodation A3** pp *Termas*, Route 34, T 81004, full board, rambling place, good food but many rooms without private bath (taxi from bus terminal US$7). Baths US$1.50. About 1 km from *Hotel Termas* is **ACA hostería**, T 81143. **C Real**, Güemes 185, T 81067, basic, clean, not all doors close.

● **Buses** To Tucumán, Güemes, Salta and Jujuy, frequent.

At Km 153 a road runs east 2 km to the **Posta de Yatasto**, a historic staging post, where there is a museum; campsite. At Km 173, 2 km north of **Metán** (*population* 23,000; *altitude* 858m), Route 16, known as the *Transchaco*, heads east across the Chaco to Resistencia (see **The Northeast**). At Lumbreras, Km 206 Route 5 runs northeast and then north, meeting Route 34 south of Embarcación and Orán.

PARQUE NACIONAL EL REY

Situated 160 km north of Rosario de la Frontera and 196 km east of Salta, this park covers 44,162 hectares of the eastern foothills of the Andes rising to 1,600m.

Parque Nacional El Rey

Not to scale

N

Serrania del Creston del Gallo

Cerro Puntudo ▲

Cerro Piquete ▲

Serrania el Chañar

Cerro Bayo ▲

Serrania del Piquete

Cerro El Chañar ▲

Río Popayán

Río del Valle

Cerro Maldonado ▲

To Route 5 to Salta & Tucumán

▲ peak
⌂ park ranger post

43c

The park is bounded by two ranges of hills: the Cresta del Gallo to the northwest and the Serrania del Piquete to the southeast: between these ranges clear streams with fishing feed the Río Popayán. There are several small lakes.

Vegetation varies with altitude, humidity and rainfall. The lower parts of the park are covered with Chaco-type scrub, including algarrobos and talas; higher up is cloudforest (see under **Horizons** for more detail). Fauna include the red-legged seriema, the Chaco chachalca, the coati as well as foxes, tapirs, brockets and peccaries. The rivers are inhabited by river-otters and *mayuato* (crab-eating racoons) and there are 152 species of birds. Mosquitoes, ticks and chiggers thrive; take lotion. Horse-riding is available. The best time to visit is May to October.

● **Climate** Mean temperatures range from 12°C in winter to 27°C in summer. Mean annual rainfall is 600-700mm in the valleys, and up to 1,800 mm in the upper areas of the park. Most rainfall is in summer, when the park can be inaccessible.

● **Access** is via a poor road which branches off Route 5, 44 km east of Lumbreras and runs north 46 km, fording the river nine times; passable for ordinary cars except in the wet season.

● **Accommodation** None while *Hostería El Rey*, 12 km north of the entrance, is closed (it is due to be transferred to private hands). Camping is free, there are several sites, but few facilities.

● **Information** Park office, España 366, 3rd floor, Salta (helpful). There are *guardaparques* at the park entrance.

● **Transport** No public transport; ask the park office in Salta about alternatives, or take a tour from an agency, US$50pp for at least 6.

THE ROUTE VIA CAFAYATE

Route 38 runs southwest from Tucumán towards Catamarca; at Km 42 Route 307 branches off northwest towards Cafayate, climbing through sugar and citrus fruit plantations before passing through the **Quebrada del Río los Sosa**. At Km 69 there is a statue to El Indio, with picnic area.

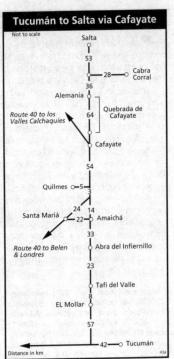

Tucumán to Salta via Cafayate

Not to scale

Salta
53
28 — Cabra Corral
36
Alemanía
Route 40 a los Valles Calchaquíes 64 Quebrada de Cafayate
Cafayate
54
Quilmes o—5
3
24 14
Santa Mariá 22 — Amaichá
33
Route 40 to Belen & Londres Abra del Infiernillo
23
Tafí del Valle
8
El Mollar
57
42 — Tucumán

Distance in km 43a

TAFI DEL VALLE

(*Population* 2,600; *Altitude* 2,100m; *Phone code* 0867), Km 107, lies about half-way along the valley of the Río Tafí, known to archaeologists as a holy valley of the precolumbian Indian peoples. Southwest of the town is the **Capilla Jesuítica y Museo La Banda** in the 16th century chapel of San Lorenzo (open Monday-Saturday 1000-1600, Sunday 900-1200). The southern part of the valley is filled by an artificial lake, Embalse La Angostura; south of this are **El Mollar** (*population* 1,300; *altitude* 2,000m) and the **Parque de los Menhires**, a park with 129 standing stones marked with engraved designs of unknown significance. There are good views but in winter the valley is often shrouded in fog caused by clouds from the humid lowlands (best to visit in the morning).

The Sacred Valley

As in other parts of the ancient world, the dependence of the early inhabitants on crops and wildlife and the ever-present risk of drought, floods or some other type of natural disaster meant that appeasing the gods assumed great importance. They built sacred sites and erected statues as images of the gods.

Situated in a hollow covering 100 square km at an altitude of 2,000m and surrounded by hills, Tafí del Valle was densely populated: the sides of the valley were covered in agricultural terraces and traces of the large numbers of underground dwellings can still be seen. Curiously they have a floral pattern, each of the circular rooms leading off a circular central patio. The many ritual circles can be identified by the circles of stones with a larger rock in the centre. What stands out above all are the *menhires*. These were gods which protected the fields and the dwellings. Due to the number of these Tafí is thought to have been the most sacred place of the indigenous population of northwestern Argentina.

A complete circuit of the valley can be made by road, a distance of 38 km, beginning in Tafí and passing through La Banda, San Isidro, El Rincón, El Mollar and La Angostura. At the last of these, on a hill, there are 129 *menhires*, brought together from all over the valley in the early years of this century. Smooth, hand-worked or sculptured, each dolmen is a small work of art, each worthy of being studied in the context of the large population that which once lived in Tafí.

Federico Kirbus

- **Accommodation   A1** *Lunahuana*, T 210330, half pension, expensive restaurant; **A1** *El Mirador*, 3-star, excellent views; **A3** *Hostería ACA*, T 21027, run down, restaurant, garden; **C** *Colonial*, T 21067, near bus station, closed out of season, no singles; **C** *Atep*, Los Menhires, in winter, recommended; *Pensión*, opposite *Colonial*, in billiard hall, ask in advance for hot water; **E** pp *hostal* run by Celia Correa, near church, recommended. Hotels and bungalows (**B**) at El Pinar del Ciervo. At La Banda, 1 km southwest of town is **A1** *La Hacienda Le Pepe*, including breakfast, English and French spoken, horses for rent. **Camping** *Autocamping Los Sauzales*, T 21084, US$4, run down.

- **Places to eat** *El Rancho de Félix*, recommended; *El Portal de Tafí*, good, has video room (movies in summer only); *La Rueda*, at southern entrance to village, inexpensive, recommended; *Los Faroles*, pleasant cafe. Try local cheese.

- **Estancia B** *Estancia Los Cuartos*, T 081-22-6793/0867-21444, offers accommodation, lunches and activities including horseriding.

- **Tour companies & travel agents** Tours to El Mollar and Tafí are available from several agencies in Tucumán, US$15 each for 4 people minimum. For tours throughout the northwest from Tafí, contact Margarita and Bruno Widmer, T/F (0867) 21076, highly recommended. Off season contact the tourist office to arrange excursions by taxi, US$15 per person.

- **Buses** To Tucumán, Aconquija, sit on right side, 4 a day, 3½ hours, US$9. To Cafayate 4 a day, 4 hours, US$10. Tafí-El Mollar daily 1215, returns 1330, US$1. Tucumán-Cafayate buses stop at El Mollar on request.

NORTHWEST OF TAFI DEL VALLE

From Tafí Route 307 continues northwest. At Km 130 it crosses the Abra del Infiernillo (3,042m) and then runs down through the attractive arid landscape of the valley of the Río del Amaichá to join Route 40 which follows the Río Santa María north to Cafayate.

Amaichá del Valle

(*Population* 400; *Altitude* 2,200; *Phone code* 0892), Km 163, claims to have 360 sunny days a year. It has an important Pachamama festival at end of Carnival. The road forks here: Route 357 continues north 14 km to the junction with Route 40 while Route 337 branches off south to join Route 40 at Santa María.

- **Accommodation   Hostal** *Colonial*, T 21046; *Casa del Piedra*, new, semi-luxurious.

- **Buses** To Tucumán, US$7.

The fall and rise of Quilmes

Of all the indigenous peoples of northwestern Argentina, perhaps the most tragic fate was that which awaited the inhabitants of Quilmes. At the heart of the resistance to Spanish rule, in the 17th century Quilmes had a population of some 3,000, though it is estimated that 7,000 people in the surrounding area were also under its rule. Defeated by being cut off from water and food supplies, the 270 surviving families were marched out of the northwest and were settled in a reservation 27 km south of Buenos Aires. Forced to work in a quarry, most lost their lives in a smallpox epidemic in 1718. By 1730 only 141 remained and when the reservation was closed in 1812 there were no survivors.

Today the Quilmes are chiefly remembered by the name of the largest brewery in Argentina, which gets its name from the town built on the site of the reservation.

Santa María

(*Population* 7,500; *Altitude* 1,800m), 22 km south of Amaichá, lies on the Río Santa María on the site of a Franciscan mission. The **Museo Arqueológico Eric Boman**, on the plaza is small but interesting. From Santa María Route 40 leads north along the valley to Cafayate (55 km) and south to Belén (176 km, see page 233). Along this road are several archaeological sites which can be visited including Ampajango, 27 km south, Fuerte Quemado 15 km north and Quilmes (see below).

• **Accommodation A3** *Plaza*, San Martín 350, T 20309, on plaza, small rooms; **B** *Provincial de Turismo*, San Martín y 1 de Mayo, T 20240, recommended, dining room; **C** *Res Inti-Huaico*, Belgrano 146, with bath, clean, friendly, lovely gardens, recommended. **Campsite** Municipal campsite at end of Sarmiento.

• **Buses** To Tucumán 6 hours, 0220, 0800, US$8.50; to Cafayate, 4 hours, El Indio daily 0700 at excluding Thursday at 1030, US$10. Empresa Bosio to Catamarca, Saturday; via Tucumán Sunday 1230, 9 hours; Cayetano to Belén 4 hours, Monday, Wednesday, Friday 0500.

Quilmes

32 km north of Santa María, 5 km along a dirt road off Route 40, Quilmes is one of the most important archaeological sites in Argentina. Situated on the slopes of the Sierra de Quilmes at an altitude of 1,850m, were a central fortification flanked to north and south by two other fortresses which controlled the valley. Its strategic situation and the width of its walls, up to 3m, made it impregnable. Southeast of the main ruins are others which stretch as far as a dam several kilometres distant. Best seen 1600-1700, there are splendid views and interesting cacti (guide 0700-1730, entry US$2). Near the entrance there is an archaeological museum.

• **Accommodation & services A2** *Parador Ruinas de Quilmes*, T (0892) 21075, at the site, comfortable, underfloor heating in winter, air conditioning in summer, owners are tapestry and ceramics experts; shop selling good indigenous crafts, particularly textiles; good restaurant, bar and camping facilities.

• **Transport** For a day's visit take 0630 Aconquija bus from Cafayate to Santa María, alight at site, or take 0700 bus from Santa María; in each case take 1100 bus back to Cafayate. Taxi from Cafayate US$60 return.

CAFAYATE

(*Population* 8,432; *Altitude* 1,660m; *Phone code* 0868) 231 km northwest of Tucumán, lies 78 km down the valley from Santa María. Founded in 1863 on the site of Jesuit and Franciscan missions, it is a popular holiday centre for Argentines in January. Surrounded by vineyards, it is an important centre of wine production and home of several renowned *bodegas*. North of the town is Ceramica Cristófani, where you can watch the whole process of making pots.

Vineyards

Several *bodegas* can be visited. North of town are **La Banda** (next to ACA *hosteria*), interesting because it is the oldest in the valley, English spoken, and **La Rosa**, reached by turning right 500m past the

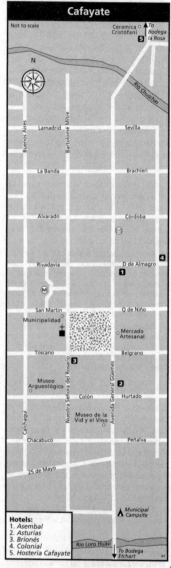

Cafayate

Not to scale

Ceramica Cristófani — To Bodega la Rosa

Rio Chuschas

Lamadrid — Sevilla

Bartolomé Mitre

Buenos Aires

La Banda — Brachieri

Alvarado — Córdoba

Rivadavia — D de Almagro

Nuestra Señora del Rosario

San Martin
Municipalidad

Q de Niño

Toscano — Mercado Artesanal

Belgrano

Museo Arqueológico

Colón — Hurtado

Museo de la Vid y el Vino

Avenida General Güemes

Chacabuco — Peñalva

25 de Mayo

Municipal Campsite

Hotels:
1. Asembal
2. Asturias
3. Briones
4. Colonial
5. Hosteria Cafayate

Rio Loro Huasi — To Bodega Etchart

ACA *hostería*, visits Monday-Friday, 0800-1230, 1500-1830, weekend mornings only, no need to book, 30-minute tours and

tasting; nearby is an old water mill which is still in use. **Etchart**, 2 km south on Ruta 40, T 21310/2, offers tours Monday-Friday 0800-1830.

Museums

Museo de la Vid y El Vino on Avenida Güemes, two blocks south of the plaza, in an old *bodega*, includes a collection of old equipment and a display on the history of wine, well laid out, US$1.

Museo Arqueológico Rodolfo I Bravo, Calchaquí y Colón, local collection of the late Sr Bravo, includes pre-Inca funeral urns and 19th century domestic artefacts, US$1.

Excursions

To **Cerro San Isidro**, 5 km west where there are cave paintings and fine views across the Aconquija chain in the south and Nevado de Cachi in the north

Local festivals

Serenata Cafayateña, just after Carnival, the most important music festival in the area.

Local information
● Accommodation

Accommodation is hard to find at holiday periods (especially in single rooms). Prices are much lower off season.

A3 *Asturias*, Güemes 158, T 21328, with breakfast, pool, recommended; **A3** *Briones*, Toscano 80, main plaza, T 21270, comfortable, accepts Amex; **A3** *Hostería Cafayate* (ACA), T 21296, on northern outskirts, modern, quiet (but cold), colonial-style, covered parking, good food, but restaurant may be closed.

B *Asembal*, Güemes y Almagro, T 21065, nice rooms, good restaurant; **B** *Gran Real*, Güemes 128, T 21016, without breakfast, pool, pleasant, recommended; **B** *Tinkunaku*, Diego de Almagro 12, one block from plaza, recommended.

Budget accommodation: **C** *Colonial*, Almagro 134, T 21233, charming patio; **C** *Confort*, Güemes 232, T 21091, clean, comfortable, member of Red Argentina de Alojamiento para Jóvenes; **C** *La Posta del Rey*, Güemes 415, T 21120; **C** *Pensión Arroyo* (no sign), Niño 160, recommended. **D** *Familia Herrero*, Vicario Toscano 237, T 21269, recommended. **E** pp *Youth Hostel*, Avenida Güemes 441, T 21440, small, hot water, stores luggage, tours arranged, English and Italian spoken; another,

Pachamama

Pachamama, the goddess of mother earth is a deity venerated for the fertility of the earth, animals and crops. Pachamama is important throughout the Andes, but there are great regional variations in beliefs and practices. While the term Pachamama is Quechua, it is widely used by Spanish speakers. Ironically Quechua speakers in rural Bolivia refer to her by the Spanish term *Virgen*. Although after the conquest llamas replaced humans as sacrificial victims, today Pachamama usually has to make do with offerings of cigarettes, alcohol and coca leaves. As she is also the deity of travellers, it is particularly important to make offerings to her before setting out on a journey. It is also customary, on reaching a mountain pass, to add a rock to the *apacheta* (pile of stones) built up over the centuries.

Of the few surviving pachamama festivals in the northwestern Argentina that in Amaichá is reckoned to be the most important. Celebrated over several days, the final day is particularly colourful. A woman chosen from the most elderly of the village takes on the role of Pachamama: dressed up, she is mounted on a horse or on a cart drawn by oxen. She is accompanied by other deities, El Yastay, the god of animals and hunting, La Nusta, a young maiden celebrating fertility, and El Pujillay, the fawn-like spirit of carnival. At the height of the festivities Pachamama offers everyone wine from the new harvest and is in turn toasted by the people.

E pp, at Buenos Aires 930, T 239910; **E** pp Rosario 165, T 21098, dormitory style, basic, kitchen. Accommodation in private houses is available.

Campsite Municipal site *Lorohuasi* on southern outskirts, hot water, pool, well maintained, bungalows for rent, **D** for 4 people; private site opposite ACA *hostería*.

● **Places to eat**
Several good ones on the main plaza: *Cafayate*; *Confitería La Barra*; *El Gordo*; *La Carreta de Don Olegario*, Güemes y Quintana, recommended; *El Criollo*, Güemes 254, clean, good, recommended; *La López Pereyra*, Güemes 375, good food, friendly. Several *comedores* along Rivadavia (two blocks north of Plaza), where the locals eat. Only the more expensive restaurants are open late.

● **Banks & money changers**
Banco de la Nación, main plaza, for cash; travellers' cheques and credit cards not accepted.

● **Shopping**
Handicrafts are made in the town: tapestries are interesting but very expensive, visit the Calchaquí tapestry exhibition of Miguel Nanni on the main plaza. For silver work try Jorge Barraco, Colón 147. Oil paintings, woodcarving, metalwork and ceramics by Calixto Mamani can be seen in his gallery, Rivadavia 452, or contact him at home (Rivadavia 254). Handicrafts in wood and silver by Oscar Hipaucha near the Bodega Encantada. Pancho Silva has a workshop on 25 de Mayo selling and their own and locals' handicrafts. Local pottery is sold in the *Mercado Municipal de Artesanía* on the plaza. Souvenir prices are generally high

● **Tourist offices**
Kiosk on the main plaza.

● **Transport**
Local Bicycles: hire from Rentavel, Güemes 175 US$2 per hour, US$15 per day. **Horses**: can be hired from La Florida, Bodega Etchart Privado, 2 km south of Cafayate, or from Tito Stinga (ask around).

Buses To Tucumán, Aconquija, daily 0600, 8 hours, US$20, also Saturday 1500. Alternatively go to Santa María on 1100 El Indio bus, or 0630 Aconquija bus, 2 hours, US$10, and then take bus to Tucumán; to **Salta** via the Quebrada de Cafayate, El Indio, 0545, 0900, 1830, 4 hours, US$11 (worth travelling in daylight); to **Angastaco**, El Indio, 1100 daily except Sunday, US$4, sit on the right, leaves Angastaco for the return journey at 0630. **Tours** Cafayate can also be visited by organized excursion from Salta, US$40, including lunch and visit to a *bodega*.

NORTH OF CAFAYATE

North of Cafayate the Río Santa María joins the Río Calchaquí to form the Río de las Conchas which flows north into the Embalse Cabra Corral. Route 40 climbs the Calchaquí valley northwest from Cafayate to San Antonio de los Cobres. (For a description of this route see the **Valles Calchaquíes** below). Route 68 branches off north of Cafayate and follows the Río de las Cochas northeast to Salta, passing through the spectacular Quebrada de Cafayate.

The Quebrada De Cafayate

The gorge of the Río de las Conchas, known as the Quebrada de Cafayate, starts about 20 km north of Cafayate and extends for about 65 km. For most of its length it is a desert landscape, with rocks of contrasting colours: the winding road offers constantly changing views and many wild birds, including *ñandúes* (rheas) can be seen. The gorge is particularly famous for the unusual rock formations found in the southern section, all signposted. These include *Los Castillos* (The Castles) Km 20, *El Obelisco* (The Obelisk), Km 23, *El Fraile* (The Friar) Km 29, *El Sapo* (The Toad) Km 35, *El Anfiteatro* (The Amphitheatre) Km 48, and *La Garganta del Diablo* (The Devil's Throat) Km 49.

One way of seeing the Quebrada is by taking the El Indio bus towards Salta and then walk back (catching a returning bus from Salta) from Los Loros, Km 32, or the Garganta del Diablo; alternatively hire a bike in Cafayate and take it on the 0545 El Indio bus and then cycle back. **NB** The sun is very hot, take lots of water.

Embalse Cabra Corral

North of the Quebrada the road runs along the west side of the Embalse Cabra Corral through Col Moldes and El Carril to Salta. Cabra Corral, 81 km south of Salta, is one of the largest artificial lakes in Argentina; water skiing, fishing, camping site, restaurant and sailing club; the **B** *Hostería Cabra Corral*, T 231965, is 4 km from the lake, half board, swimming pool, 'delightful', recommended.

THE VALLES CALCHAQUIES

Rising at above 5,000m on the slopes of the Nevado de Acay, the Río Calchaquí flows south between the Sierra de Pastos Grandes to the west and Cumbres del Obispo to the east. In its 210 km course before its

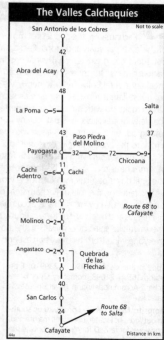

The Valles Calchaquíes

Not to scale

San Antonio de los Cobres

42

Abra del Acay

48

La Poma ○—5—○ Salta

43

Paso Piedra del Molino

37

Payogasta ○—32—○—72—○—9
Chicoana

11

Cachi Adentro ○—6—○ Cachi

Route 68 to Cafayate

45

Seclantás ○

17

Molinos ○—2—○

41

Angastaco ○—2—○ Quebrada de las Flechas

11

40

San Carlos ○

24 Route 68 to Salta

Cafayate

Distance in km

confluence with the Río Santa María just north of Cafayate, the river drops some 3,400m and gathers the waters of 34 streams and rivers. Originally it continued south along the Río Santa María and into the Quebrada de Belén.

History

The valleys of the Río Calchaquí and its tributaries were densely populated in prehispanic times. After the defeat of the indigenous population in the Calchaquí Wars, the Spanish established missions and *haciendas* in the valley. Some of these *haciendas* survived until the 20th century, before being seized by the Perón government in the 1940s. During the colonial period the valley prospered, providing pasturage for mules-trains and herds of cattle en route over the mountain passes into Chile and Alto Perú (Bolivia). After independence lower parts of the valley became the chief wheat

The Calchaquí Wars

The Calchaquí valleys were the scene of the strongest resistance to Spanish rule in the Argentine northwest. In 1630, following the failure of Jesuit missionaries to christianize the local indigenous peoples, the Spanish Governor of Tucumán tried to bring them under control of Spanish landowners. The uprising which ensued quickly spread beyond the valley and was only ended with the arrival of reinforcements from Chile. Chamelin, the Indian leader of the uprising, was hanged and quartered, his head being exhibited in La Rioja and his right arm in Londres.

A second uprising in 1657 was sparked by the arrival of a Spanish adventurer, Pedro de Bohórquez, who claimed to be a descendent of the last Inca. The response of the Governor of Tucumán was to clear the valleys of their inhabitants: 5,000 people were taken prisoner and 11,000 more were dispersed throughout the northwest as gifts to Spanish settlers.

growing and wine producing area for the provincial capital but the local economy declined in the late 19th century when the building of railway lines linking Salta with the south brought cheap wheat from the pampas and when local wines were hit by the expansion of wine production in Mendoza.

Route 40

From Cafayate Route 40 climbs up the valley to the Abra del Acay and then continues to San Antonio de los Cobres. The road is mainly gravel and can be very difficult after rain, but the views of the Andean-foothills with their strange rock formations and unexpected colours, are fascinating. Most of the villages along the road grew up around colonial *haciendas*. Fuel is available in Cachi, Molinos and Angastaco.

SAN CARLOS

(*Population* 1,500; *Altitude* 1,710m), Km 24, was the most important village in the valley until the growth of Cafayate. The first settlement on the site in 1551 was destroyed by Indians and three further attempts met a similar fate. Its church, completed in 1854, is the largest in the valley; its zinc roof replaced the original made of cactus which was destroyed by an earthquake in 1930. There is a small archaeological museum on the plaza and nearby are artisans' shops and workshops and a craft market.

● **Accommodation** C *Hostería*, T 218937; E pp *El Bagualero*. Several *hospedajes*. Municipal campsite.

● **Buses** El Indio, on the Salta-Cafayate-Angastaco run, arrive in San Carlos by noon and on the return journey at 0745.

The Quebrada de las Flechas.

This gorge, just south of Angastaco, is bypassed by a new section of Route 40. Formed by the Río Calchaquí and remarkable for its formations and colours, the quebrada is named after the arrow-shaped rocks found particularly about 10 km south of Angastaco.

Wine label

ANGASTAGO

(*Population* 600; *Altitude* 1,900m) 2 km off Route 40 at Km 77, is a modern village, with a small archaeological museum in the civic building. The church is modern but a much older one, the **Iglesia del Carmen de Angastaco** (1800) lies about 8 km further north on the Finca El Carmen. This area is famous for *vino patero*, a sweet wine, red or white, which is supposed to be made by treading the grapes in the traditional manner: sample it in a house close to the bridge in Angastaco. The Fiesta Patronal Virgen del Valle is held on the second weekend of December, with processions, folk music, dancing, many gauchos and rodeos.

- **Accommodation** C *Hostería*, T 222826, negotiable in low season, good meals on request, pool, knowledgeable, highly recommended; **F** pp *Res El Cardón*, good, clean, comfortable.

- **Buses** To Cachi and Salta (US$5.50), Friday, 1100 only; daily bus to San Carlos and Cafayate 0545 (Saturday and holidays 0630). Taxi to Molinos US$40, ask at police station for address of Orlando López; no transport for hitching.

Molinos

(*Population* 500; *Altitude* 2,000m) 2 km off Route 40 at Km 118, was founded in 1659. The church, with its fine twin-domed bell-towers, built about 1720, contains the mummified body of the last Royalist governor of Salta, Don Nicolás Isasmendi Echalar (to protect it from visitors plucking its hair, this relic can no longer be viewed by the public). The priest is very knowledgeable about local history. A pleasant walk is down from the church, crossing a creek and then climbing a gentle hill, from which there are good views of Molinos and surrounding country. Fiesta del Poncho in February.

- **Accommodation** A3 *Hostería Molinos*, T 214871, recommended, with breakfast, good meals, in Casa de Isasmendi, which also contains a small museum. *Sra de Guaymas* (known as 'Sra Silvia') runs a restaurant and rents rooms, **E**, basic, clean. There are other rooms to rent around the main plaza.

- **Buses** To Salta via Cachi, Thursday, Friday, Saturday, Monday at 0645, also Monday, Thursday, Saturday at 1315, Marcos Rueda; 2 hours to Cachi, US$4.50, 7 hours to Salta. To Angastaco, Thursday morning.

Seclantás

(*Population* 183; *Altitude* 2,200m) Km 135 is a small village with a church dating from 1835. Many of the houses are in colonial style with verandas in front. No accommodation. 8 km south along the old road are a disused mill and the archaeological site of Churcal.

CACHI

(*Population* 1,400; *Altitude* 2,280m; *Phone code* 0868), Km 180, is a beautiful little town at the foot of the Nevado del Cachi (6,380m). Founded in 1694, it is renowned for its weaving, other crafts and invigorating climate. The roof of the 18th century church is made from the wood of the *cardón* cactus. The **Museo Arqueológico** (Monday-Saturday, 0800-1800, Sunday, holidays 0900-1200) presents a small but interesting survey of pre-colonial Calchaquí culture, US$1. There are fine views from the Cemetery, 10 minutes walk from the village.

Excursions

To **Cachi Adentro**, 6 km west, for more fine views where horses can be hired, US$5 per hour and fishing is also possible. Three buses a day from Cachi.

To the Indian ruins at **Las Pailas**, 18 km northwest; in themselves not especially impressive but the view is breathtaking, with huge cacti set against snow-topped Andean peaks. The ruins can be reached on foot (4 hours one way), or by bus from Cachi. Ask for directions or a guide in Las Pailas village. There is another archaeological site at **La Paya**, reached by a 4 km road which turns off Route 40 10 km south of Cachi.

- **Accommodation** A3 *ACA Hostería Cachi*, T 210001, on hill above the town, good, pleasant; **D** pp *El Cortijo*, clean, friendly, good breakfast; **E** pp *Res Pajarito*, with bath, basic; **E** *Albergue Municipal*, also has good municipal campsite with swimming pool and barbecue pits, on hill at south end of town. **At Cachi Adentro**, **B** *Hostal Samay Huasi*, a restored *hacienda*, pleasant and helpful owners, heating and hot water at all times; **A1** *El Viejo Molino de Cachi Adentro*, a restored working mill,

Cardoons

Cardoons

(*Trychocereus pasacana*) This slow-growing cactus is found only at altitudes between 2,000 and 3,500m and is very susceptible to changes in climate. Full grown cardoons reach a height of 6m and are thought to be 100-200 years old. Its wood, which is marked by long thin holes, is so hard that it has been used for centuries for making furniture and building houses: many older churches in the Andes have ceilings of cardoon. Overexploitation of such a slow growing plant has led to restrictions on its use.

There are many stories about the cardoon: according to one from the War of Independence, General Belgrano's troops used to clothe cardoons in ponchos and hats to hide their numerical inferiority from the opposing Spanish armies.

beautiful views, horse riding, recommended, minimum stay 3 days, book in advance, Buenos Aires T 8039339, F 4762065, Salta T 213968, F 233122.

● **Buses** To Salta, 1530 daily except Wednesday, also at 0900 Thursday, Friday, Saturday, Monday, 5 hours, US$14; to Molinos 1200 daily; El Indio from Cafayate Thursday morning only, returning Thursday afternoon.

La Poma

(*Population* 300; *Altitude* 3,015m) 5 km off Route 40 at Km 234, is the last village in the valley. Situated near two extinguished volcanoes and with views over the Nevado de Palermo (6,172m), it was destroyed by an earthquake in 1930: the ruins lie 2 km north of the modern village. **Accommodation** F *hosteria*.

From La Poma to San Antonio de los Cobres

North of La Poma Route 40 continues over the Paso Abra del Acay (4,900m), Km 282, the highest pass in South America negotiable by car. Road conditions vary depending on the weather and whether the bulldozer has passed recently; high clearance vehicle advisable. The critical part is south of the pass at Mal Paso, Km 257, where summer rains can wash the road away. There are no buses on this road. North of the pass the road runs across the *puna* to San Antonio de los Cobres (see below), Km 324.

FROM CACHI TO SALTA

At Payogasta (new *Hostería*), 11 km north of Cachi, Route 33 (gravel) turns off Route 40 and runs east along a dead-straight stretch of 10 km known as **La Recta del Tin-Tin** and over the Piedra del Molino pass (3,347m), Km 43, before dropping through the Cuesta del Obispo. This part of the road runs through the **Parque Nacional Los Cardones**, a new national park covering 70,620 hectares at altitudes between 2,700 and 5,000m and intended to protect the huge candelabra cacti. If you want to spend some time in the park, take the 0700 Marcos Rueda bus from Salta towards Cachi, get off at La Recta del Tin-Tin and catch returning bus around 1600.

From the end of the Cuesta del Obispo the road runs through the **Quebrada de Escoipe**, a narrow gorge 34 km long, which can be flooded in wet weather. The road is paved from Chicoana, Km 115, 5 km east of the gorge (*hostería*); it joins Route 68 at El Carril, 119 km from Cachi and 37 km south of Salta.

SALTA

(*Population* 375,000; *Altitude* 1,280m; *Phone code* 087), situated on the Río Arias in the wide Lerma valley, lies in a mountainous and strikingly beautiful district.

1,600 km north of Buenos Aires, Salta was founded in 1582 and still possesses a number of fine colonial buildings. Capital of its province, it is a great handicraft centre and the major starting place for tours of the northwest.

Places of interest

An interesting pedestrian tour of the centre is marked by ceramic pavement plaques. The central **Plaza 9 de Julio** is one of the most outstanding squares in the country and the only one with verandas all round. The **Cathedral** (open mornings and evenings), on the north side was built 1858-1878; it contains the images of the Cristo del Milagro and of the Virgin Mary and has a rich interior mainly in red and gold, as well as a huge late baroque altar. Opposite the cathedral is the **Cabildo**, built in 1783 (the upper floor was added in 1807; the arches are slightly out of line).

One block west of the Cabildo are three colonial mansions: the **Casa Leguizamón**, Caseros y Florida, the **Casa Arias Rengel**, next door (now housing the **Museo de Bellas Artes**) and the **Casa Hernández**, Florida y Alvarado; a fourth, the **Casa Uriburu** (see below under Museums) lies one block east of the Plaza at Caseros 421. Just beyond is the **San Francisco** church, at Caseros y Córdoba (1796), one of the city's landmarks with its magnificent façade and red, yellow and grey coloured tower (1882) rising above the city centre skyline (open 0700-1200, 1730-2100, in theory). Two blocks further east is the Convent of **San Bernardo**, Caseros y Santa Fe, built in colonial style in 1846; it has a famous wooden portal of 1762. Nuns still live here so the inside of the convent is not open to visitors.

East of the city centre is the **Cerro San Bernardo** (1,458m), at the foot of which is an impressive **statue** by Víctor Cariño, 1931, **to General Güemes**, whose *gaucho* troops repelled seven powerful Spanish invasions from Bolivia between 1814 and 1821. The top of the hill can be climbed by a steep path (1,136 steps) with Stations of the Cross from behind the nearby Museo Antropológico or by cable car (*teleférico*), daily except Thursday, 1400-2000, US$6 return, children US$3, from Parque San Martín. At the top there is an old wooden cross, together with restaurant and artificial waterfalls. At the bottom near the *teleférico* station is a lake where rowing boats can be hired (US$3 for 20 minutes).

Museums

In summer check opening times at tourist office as many close.

Museo Histórico del Norte, in the Cabildo Histórico, Caseros 549, colonial, historical and archaeological museum,

The miracle of Salta

According to legend the famous images of Christ and the Virgin Mary in Salta cathedral were found in a box floating in the sea off Callao, Peru, in June 1592 and later given to the city. Their fame comes from their intervention during a series of terrifying earthquakes which hit the city in September 1692. In a dream José Carrión, a priest, received the revelation that only when the images were paraded through the streets would the earthquakes cease. The apparent success of this strategy is celebrated every year between 6 and 14 September, culminating on 15 September when the images repeat their historic journey through the city.

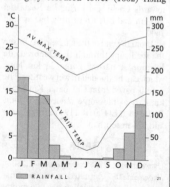

Climate: Salta

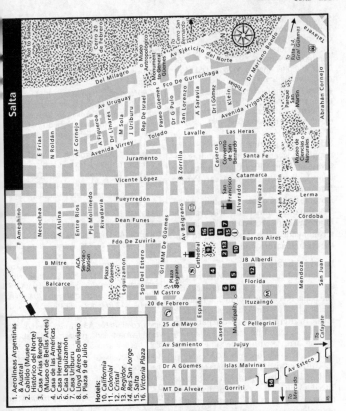

1. Aerolíneas Argentinas & Austral
2. Cabildo (Museo Histórico del Norte)
3. Casa Arias Rengel (Museo de Bellas Artes)
4. Casa de las Américas
5. Casa Hernández
6. Casa Leguizamón
7. Casa Uriburu
8. Lloyd Aéreo Boliviano
9. Plaza 9 de Julio

Hotels:
10. California
11. Colonial
12. Cristal
13. Regidor
14. Res San Jorge
15. Salta
16. Victoria Plaza

guided tour in Spanish, recommended, Monday-Friday 0930-1330, 1530-2030, Saturday/Sunday 0930-1330, 1630-2030, US$1.

Museo Antropológico, Paseo Güemes, behind the statue, large and important collection including many objects from Tastil (see page 259), Tuesday-Friday 0830-1230, 1430-1830, Saturday 1500-1830, Sunday 1600-1830, US$1.

Museo de Bellas Artes, Florida 20, Monday-Saturday 0900-1300, 1700-2100, Sunday 0900-1200, US$0.60 (closed January).

Casa Uriburu, Caseros 421, Tuesday-Saturday, 1000-1400, 1530-1930, US$0.60, has relics of one of the most distinguished *salteño* families.

Museo Folklórico Pajarito Velarde, Pueyrredón 106.

Museo de Ciencias Naturales, in Parque San Martín, has a full display of over 150 regional stuffed birds and an interesting display of armadillos, recommended, Tuesday-Sunday 1400-2000, US$0.25.

Museo de la Ciudad 'Casa de Hernández', La Florida 97, Tuesday-Saturday, 0900-1230, 1600-2030.

Excursions

To **San Lorenzo**, a wealthy neighbourhood 11 km northwest of Salta.

● **Accommodation** *El Castillo*, T 921052, also good restaurant in high tower, closed Monday, free taxi service for 4-6 people; **A2** *Hostal*

Selva Montana, Alfonsina Storní 2315, T 921184, luxurious, highly recommended; camping and picnicking beside rocky stream and natural woodland. Sibylle Oeschger and Hansruedi Hintermann, T 921080, rent 1 room (**E** pp) and offer horseriding tours, US$24 per person per half-day.

● **Buses** Hourly bus service from Salta terminal, Empresa Chávez, platform 15, 30 minutes, US$1. Bus stops in front of *Quebrada* restaurant (good food, quite expensive). Last bus back about 2330.

Salta is the starting point for several popular longer excursions, including **Cafayate** and the **Valles Calchaquíes** (see above), allow 2 to 3 days by car; **Parque Nacional El Rey** (see above) and **San Antonio de los Cobres** (see below). Agencies also offer tours to the **Quebrada de Humahuaca** (see below) but these are not recommended: it is much better to visit the quebrada from Jujuy.

Local festivals

15 September, Cristo del Milagro (see above); 24 September, Battles of Tucumán and Salta. 16-17 June, Commemoration of the death of Martín Güemes, with folk music in afternoon and *gaucho* parade in mornings around his statue. Salta celebrates Carnival with processions on the four weekends before Ash Wednesday at 2200 in Avenida Belgrano (seats optional at US$2-4); also Mardi Gras (Shrove Tuesday) with a procession of decorated floats and dancers with intricate masks of feathers and mirrors. It is the custom to squirt water at passers-by and *bombas de agua* (small balloons to be filled with water) are on sale for dropping from balconies.

Local information
● **Accommodation**

Hotel prices

L1	over US$200	**L2**	US$151-200
L3	US$101-150	**A1**	US$81-100
A2	US$61-80	**A3**	US$46-60
B	US$31-45	**C**	US$21-30
D	US$12-20	**E**	US$7-11
F	US$4-6	**G**	up to US$3

Unless otherwise stated, all hotels in range **D** and above have private bath. Assume friendliness and cleanliness in all cases.

Salta is a favourite convention town. Some hotels close for a vacation during the Christmas season until January 10, so check. Accommodation is scarce in the last 2 weeks in July because of holidays and around 10-16 September because of the celebrations of Cristo de Milagro.

A1 *Portezuelo*, Del Turista 1, T 310133 F 310133, breakfast extra, some rooms air conditioned, English, German, French, Italian spoken, pool, helpful, good restaurant recommended; **A2** *Salta*, Buenos Aires 1, in main plaza, T 21101/413, 1st class, pool, good restaurant; **A2** *California*, Alvarado 646 T 216266, one block from main plaza, recommended; **A2** *Victoria Plaza*, Zuviría 16, T 310334, expensive but good restaurant, the foyer overlooking the plaza is one of the centres of *salteño* life; **A3** *Colonial*, Zuviría 6, T 310760, air conditioning, recommended, but 1st floor rooms good, 2nd floor rooms cheaper but poor; **A3** *Cristal*, Urquiza 616, T 222256, helpful; **A3** *Las Lajitas*, Pasaje Calixto Guana 336, T 233796, modern, good value, ACA reduction, recommended; **A3** *Petit*, H Yrigoyen 225, T 213012, pleasant, small, expensive breakfasts, rooms around courtyard with small swimming pool, air conditioning extra, French spoken; **A3** *Regidor*, Buenos Aires 10, T 222070, English-speaking owner, good value lunch, comfortable; **A3** *Cristian*, Islas Malvinas, with breakfast, parking, clean, English spoken, highly recommended.

B *Astur*, Rivadavia 752, T 311305, recommended; **B** *España*, España 319, T 217898, central but quiet, simple, recommended; **B** *Florida*, Florida y Urquiza 718, T 212133, stores luggage, recommended; **B** *Italia*, Alberdi 231, T 214050, next to jazz club/casino, recommended; **B** *Res Elena*, Buenos Aires 256, T 211529, quiet, 'charming', safe, try to get there early; **B** *Res Balcarce*, Balcarce 460, T 218023, friendly, clean; *Res Provincial*, Santiago del Estero 555, T 219438, hot water.

Budget accommodation: D pp *Res Crisol*, Ituzaingó 166, T 214462, good meeting place; **D** pp *Sanyor* San Martín 994, T 214440, laundry facilities; **D** pp *Res San Jorge*, Esteco 244 y Ruiz de los Llanos 1164 (no sign), T/F 210443, with bath (**E** pp without), parking, safe deposit, laundry and limited kitchen facilities, central heating, parking, homely, guide for climbing, horse-trekking advice by proprietor, also organizes local excursions by car, good value, highly recommended (take buses 3 and 10 from bus terminal to San Martín y Malvinas); **D** *Casa de familia de María del Toffoli*, Mendoza 915 (about 10 blocks from bus station), T 320813, nice atmosphere, comfortable, roof terrace, cooking facilities, also rooms at Nos 917 and 919, **D-C**, belonging to Sra Toffoli's sisters (reservations at No 917), all highly recommended; *Sra Dora de Batista*, Mendoza 947, T 310570, recommended, laundry facilities; **E** pp *María Galleguillos*, Mendoza 509, T 318985, with breakfast, recommended; *Mercedes Anchezar*, 20 de Febrero 197, 5th floor, T 320701, F 313595, without breakfast; **E** *Hosp Doll*, Pasaje Ruiz de los Llanos 1360 (seven blocks from centre), with bath, safe, recommended. Many other cheap hotels near railway station (eg **E** *Internacional*, Ameghino 651, hot water, basic, with good cheap restaurant), but few near bus terminal.

Youth hostel **E** pp *Backpackers*, Buenos Aires 930, T 314305, bus 12 from bus terminal or 30 minutes walk, **E** pp in dormitories, laundry and kitchen facilities, stores luggage, budget travel information, bar,English, Greek and Hebrew spoken, frequently recommended, noisy, crowded and popular; **E** pp *No Me Olvides*, Avenida de los Pioneros, Km 0.800, shared rooms, cooking facilities, recommended. **NB** Do not be tempted by touts at the bus terminal offering convenient accommodation.

Outside Salta: B pp *Hostería de Chicoana*, in Chicoana, 47 km south, T/F 807003, pool, gardens, English and German spoken, horses for hire, recommended.

Estancias (in Salta *estancias* are known as *fincas*): *Finca San Antonio*, El Carril, T/F 908034, accommodation, pool, horseriding, other activities; **B** *Finca Los Lapachos*, at Perico, north of Salta on Route 66, a sugar estate, comfortable; **L3** pp *Finca El Bordo de las Lanzas*, at El Bordo, 45 km east of Salta, 12 km from General Güemes, T 310525, full board, excursions, recommended; **A3** pp *Finca Arnaga*, T 921478, F 921513, cycling, walking, French and English spoken, recommended; **L3** pp *Finca Los-Los*, 4 km from Chicoana, 47 km south, T 317258, F 310253, full board, horseriding, trout fishing; **L3** pp *Finca El Manantial*, 30 km from Salta, T/F 395506, beautiful views, swimming, sports, recommended.

Camping Casino Provincial municipal grounds, by river, 300m artificial lake (popular December-February). Bus 13 to grounds. There is no signposting: leave the city heading south on Calle Jujuy, after 3 km you will see the Coca Cola plant on your left; turn left before the plant and then take the first road right. Charges US$3 per tent plus US$2 per person. Free hot showers available if there is gas (not often), safe, bathrooms run-down, disappointing. At ACA's *Motel Huaico*, Bolivia y P Costas, T 310571. *Municipal Campsite* at Campo Quijano, 30 km west of Salta, at the entrance to Quebrada del Toro gorge, hot showers, bungalows, plenty of room for pitching tents, recommended, bus from Salta bus terminal.

● **Places to eat**
El Monumento, Gurruchaga 20 (opposite Güemes monument), good food, slow service, good atmosphere, reasonably priced; *La Posta*, España 476, food and atmosphere both excellent, reasonable prices, highly recommended; *El Viejo Jack*, Virrey Toledo 145, good meat dishes, huge portions; *Palacio de la Pizza*, Caseros 459, "best pizza of all anywhere" (Federico Kirbus); *Cantina*, Caseros y 20 de Febrero, pizzas, steaks; *9 de Julio*, Urquiza 1020, excellent lunch; *El Mesón de Pepe*, Rivadavia 774, fish specialities, good but pricey. Several good places on Plaza 9 de Julio. Pleasant outdoor restaurants in Parque San Martín, at foot of Cerro San Bernardo; *Sociedad Española*, Balcarce 653, excellent cuisine; *de Pablo*, Mitre 399, excellent set lunch; *JT*, San Martín y Yrigoyen, good food; *Santana*, Mendoza y Catamarca, good; *Alvarez*, Buenos Aires y San Martín, cafetería style, cheap and good; *La Casona del Molino*, Caseros 2600, colonial house, good food and drink, good value, entertainment provided by guests; *Pub Yo Juan*, Balcarce 481, popular, live music at weekends; *Dali* and *Café Van Gogh*, both on Plaza 9 de Julio, good breakfasts; *Cafemania*, Caseros 860, good breakfasts; *Café del Paseo* at *Hotel Colonial*, Zuviría 6, open 24 hours, superb breakfast, good value (ask for Té Paseo); *Cafe Río*, Mitre 40, good breakfasts. Cheap restaurants near the bus terminal, which is also the cheapest places for breakfast. Many restaurants are lunch only, especially on San Martín near the Municipal Market. Cheapest food is from the numerous *superpanchito* stalls.

● **Airline offices**
Austral, Caseros 475, T 310258; Lapa, Caseros 492, T 317080; Dinar, Buenos Aires 46, T/F 310606; Lloyd Aéreo Boliviano, Buenos Aires 120, T 217753 (will hold luggage and schedule a *colectivo* taxi).

● **Banks & money changers**
Banks, open 0730-1300, do not advance cash against credit cards as all have ATMs. **Banco de la Nación**, Balcarce y España; **Banco Provincial de Salta**, España 526 on main plaza, low commission on travellers' cheques; **Banco de Credito Argentino**, Alvarado 777, for Mastercard and Visa; **Banco Nacional de Lavoro**, Florida y Urquiza, cash on Mastercard; **Banco de Galicia**, Balcarce y Belgrano; **Banco Roberts**, Mitre 143, good rates, no commission on Amex travellers' cheques, changes Thomas Cook travellers' cheques (go

to *Comercio Exterior* desk); **Chicoana Turismo**, Belgrano y Zuviria 255, Amex agent, cashes small travellers' cheques. Many *cambios* on España including **Maguitur**, No 666, only cash. **Golden Life**, Mitre 95 (Plaza 9 de Julio), local 1, 1st floor, best rates for cash. Difficult to buy US$ on cards or travellers' cheques. See also **Currency**, in **Information for travellers** for note on provincial bonds.

● **Cultural centres**
Alliance Française, Santa Fe 20, T 210827.

● **Consulates**
Bolivia, Dr Mariano Boedo 32, T 223377, open Monday-Friday, 0900-1300 (unhelpful, better to go to Jujuy); **Chile**, Santiago del Estero, T 215757; **Paraguay**, Boedo 38, friendly; **Peru**, 25 de Mayo 407, T 310201; **Spain**, Las Heras 1329, T 221420; **Italy**, Alvarado 1632, T 213881; **France**, Santa Fe 20, T 213336; **Germany**, Córdoba 202, T 216525, F 311772, consul Juan C Kühl, who also runs travel agency (see below), helpful.

● **Entertainment**
Music: folk music show and evening meal at *Boliche Balderrama*, San Martín 1126; *Gauchos de Güemes*, Uruguay 750; *Casa Güemes*, España 730. For something less touristy try *Manolo*, San Martín 1296 or *La Casa del Molino*, Luis Burela y Caseros, T 316079, folk music and *empanadas*. Some bars charge around US$7 per person for music, but don't display charges.

● **Laundry**
Sol de Mayo, 25 de Mayo 755, service wash. *Laverap*, Santiago del Estero 363 (open Sunday morning) good, fast service, US$6 for one load; *Marva*, Juramento 315; *La Baseta*, Alvarado 1170.

● **Post & telecommunications**
Post Office: Deán Funes 160, between España and Belgrano *poste restante* charges US$1.15 per letter.

Telephone: Belgrano y 20 de Febrero, 24 hours; international calls at Vicente López 146, 0800-1930.

● **Shopping**
Mercado Municipal, San Martín y Florida, for meat, fish, vegetables, *empanadas*, *humitas* and other produce and handicrafts, closed 1200-1700 and Sunday. Good supermarket, *Disco*, Alberdi y Leguizamon. **Mercado Artesanal** on the outskirts of the city in the Casa El Alto Molino, a late 18th century mansion, at San Martín 2555, T 219195, Monday-Friday 0800-2000, Saturday 0900-2000 (sometimes closes in summer) take bus 2, 3, or 7 from Avenida San Martín in centre and get off as bus crosses the railway line. Excellent range of goods but expensive. Woodcarvings of birds etc from *Tres Cerritos*, Santiago del Estero 202. For objets d'art and costume jewellery made of onyx, visit *Onix Salta*, Chile 1663. **Feria del Libro**, Buenos Aires 83; *Librería Rayuela*, Buenos Aires 96, foreign-language books and magazines; *Plural Libros*, Buenos Aires 220, helpful. Arts and handicrafts are often cheaper in surrounding villages. Camping shops: *HR Maluf*, San Martín y Buenos Aires, and one at La Rioja 995.

Hairdressing: cheap hairdressing by students at the *Academía de Peluquería Miguel Angel*, Alvarado 911.

● **Tour companies & travel agents**
All agencies charge similar prices for tours (though some charge extra for credit card payments): Salta city US$15; Quebrada del Toro US$18; Cachi US$45; Humahuaca US$50 (too long in the bus: go from Jujuy); San Antonio de las Cobres US$75; Cafayate (1 day) US$40; 2-day tour to Cafayate, Angastaco, Molinos, Cachi, US$80. Out of season, tours often run only if there is sufficient demand; check carefully that tour will run on the day you want. *Movitren*, Caseros 431, T 316174, F 311264, for Tren a las Nubes and full programme of tours; *Saltur*, Caseros 525, T 212012, F 311622, very efficient and recommended for local tours (no English-speaking guides). *Puna Expediciones*, Braquiquitos 399, T 341875 (well qualified and experienced guide Luis H Aguilar can also be contacted through the *Res San Jorge*), organizes treks in remote areas, US$25 a day including transport to trekking region, food, porters, highly recommended. *Ricardo Clark Expeditions*, Caseros 121, T 215390, specialist tours for bird watchers, English spoken, books on flora and fauna in several languages sold, highly recommended; *Hernán Uriburu*, organizes trekking and horseriding expeditions, Rivadavia 409, T 310605, expensive but highly professional. *Juan Kühl*, Córdoba 202, T 216525, F 311772 tours by light aeroplane, horseback, caravan, boat, German and English spoken, highly recommended, also runs photographic company; *Martín Oliver*, T 321013, F 91052, adventure tourism guide. *Movitrack*, Hostal Selva Montana, Alfonsina Storni 2315, San Lorenzo, Salta, T 921184, F 921433, offer one day safaris in a 4x4 truck, to San Antonio de los Cobres, then north along Route 40 via Salinas Grandes and the Quebrada de Purmamarca to the Quebrada de Humahuaca and thence back to Salta, German, English spoken, depart 0600, 14½ hours, US$95 plus US$15 for refreshments, 2 or 3 times a week, May-September, book in advance direct from company, not through travel agencies which have their own tours and may tell you trip is full.

● **Tourist offices**
Provincial Tourist Office (Emsatur), Buenos Aires 93 (one block from main plaza). Open every day, except Sunday, till 2100. Very helpful, gives free maps. Municipal Tourist office, Buenos Aires 61, closed Sunday, helpful, free maps. Both offices arrange accommodation in private houses in high season (July) and can arrange horse-riding, US$50 full day, US$30 half-day including guide and meals, recommended. Office at bus terminal, friendly, no maps.

● **Useful addresses**
Immigration Office: Maipú 35, 0730-1230.

● **Transport**
Local Car hire: very expensive. **Avis**, Alvarado 537, T 317575, F 311184, US$100 per day, recommended; **Rent A Car**, Caseros 489 and 221; local companies reported to be cheaper: **ALE**, Caseros 753, T 223469; **López Fleming**, Buenos Aires 33, T 211381, new cars, cheapest, friendly; **Ruiz Moreno**, Caseros 225, in Hotel *Salta*, good cars, helpful; **Renta Autos**, Caseros 400, also good. It may be cheaper and more convenient to hire a taxi for a fixed fee. **Bicycles**: *Pogoni*, España 676, helpful; *Parra*, Caseros 2154, T 225326, helpful; *Manresa*, Pellegrini 824, imported equipment. Helpful mechanic, *S Fernández*, Urquiza 1051.

Air Airport 12 km south, reached by bus 22 from San Martín; don't be fooled by taxi touts who tell you there is no bus. Taxi from airport to bus terminal US$9. LAB to **Santa Cruz** (Bolivia) twice a week, once via Tarija, continuing to Cochabamba. Austral, Dinar and Lapa fly to **Buenos Aires**, 2 hours, minimum. Dinar, Lapa, Andesmar to Tucumán. Andesmar also to **Córdoba** and **Mendoza**. Southern Winds to **Córdoba**, **Tucumán**, **Rosario**, **Mendoza**, Neuquén, Bariloche and Mar del Plata.

Buses Terminal is eight blocks east of the main plaza (T 214716 for information). Behind terminal is a 24 Shell station serving cheap snacks. To **Buenos Aires**, several daily, US$80, 19 hours

The railway line to the clouds

The line from Salta to the Chilean frontier at Socompa, a distance of 570 km, is one of the great feats of South American railway construction. Begun in 1921 on the basis of French plans drawn up in 1911, it was the most outstanding achievement of Richard Maury, an engineer from Pennsylvania who arrived in Argentina in 1906 and who is commemorated by the station at Km 66 which bears his name. Though in 1922 President Yrigoyen ordered its completion within 500 days, it would be 1948 before this occurred, by which time developments in road and air transport had reduced its importance. Delays were not only the result of construction difficulties: on several occasions work was halted through lack of funding.

Some idea of the problems faced by Maury can be gained from the statistics. The line includes 21 tunnels, with a total length of 3.2 km; 19 of them are on the 178 km stretch between Campo Quijano and the La Polvorilla viaduct; there are also 31 bridges, 13 viaducts and 1,279 bends.

From the station in Salta (1,487m) the line runs to Campo Quijano (Km 40, 1,520m) and then climbs steeply up the Quebrada del Toro. At El Alisal (Km 50) and Chorrillos (Km 66) there are switchbacks as the line climbs the side of the gorge. At Km 122 and Km 129 the line goes into 360° loops before reaching Diego de Almagro (3,304m). At Abra Munaño (3,952m) the road to San Antonio can be seen below to the left, zig-zagging its way up the Quebrada del Toro. From here the line drops slightly on its way across the *puna* to San Antonio, Km 196.

The viaduct at La Polvorilla, 22 km further west, is one of the most spectacular engineering feats on the line: 224m long, 63m high and curved, it weighs 1,724 tons and is held up by six towers. Built in Italy, it was erected in 1929-1930. The highest point on the line, Abra Chorrillos (4,475m), is reached 13 km further west, from where the line runs across the *puna*, 3,500-4,000m above sea level, for another 335 km before reaching Socompa (3,865m). On the Chilean side the line continues to Calama and Antofagasta, 901 km west of Salta. For further details of the building of this line see Federico Kirbus's book: *El Fascinante Tren A Las Nubes* (Ateneo, 1996).

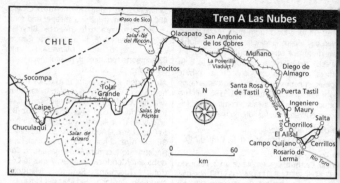

Tren A Las Nubes

(Atahualpa, La Estrella, including snacks, dinner and breakfast in restaurant, comfortable, recommende, 4 daily) US$86 with La Veloz del Norte (20% ISIC discount); to **Córdoba**, 4 a day, 12 hours, US$41, Expreso Panamericano (T 212460), twice daily, Veloz del Norte; to **Santiago del Estero**, 6 hours, US$23; to **Tucumán**, 4 hours, several firms (La Veloz del Norte recommended, La Estrella), US$18; to **Puerto Iguazú**, via Tucumán, US$70; to **Mendoza** via Tucumán, several companies, daily, US$52, 20 hours; to **Embarcación** daily with Atahualpa at 0700, US$14.50; to **Tartagal**, Veloz del Norte, Atahualpa (poor buses), US$22; to **Jujuy**, Balut Hnos, or Atahualpa hourly between 0700 and 2300, 'directo', US$7, 2 hours; to **La Rioja**, US$33; to **Belén**, Wednesday, US$26.

To **Cafayate**, US$11, 4 hours, El Indio, 4 a day; to **Santa María**, El Indio, 6½ hours, 0700; to **Cachi**, 5 hours, US$14, **Angastaco** (depart Thursday 1300) and **Molinos** (7 hours) Marcos Rueda daily (except Tuesday, Thursday) at 1300, unreliable on Sunday (sit on left); to **Rosario de la Frontera**, US$5, 2½ hours. To **San Antonio de Los Cobres**, 5½ hours, El Quebradeño, Monday-Saturday 1600, Sunday 1930, US$14. Extra service on Thursday 1030 continues to the Tincalayu mining camp (arrives 2140), returning to Salta on Friday 1200, passing San Antonio at 1800. This bus is the only public transport going further into the *puna* than San Antonio.

To Paraguay: Salta provides the most reliable cheap land connection between Bolivia and Paraguay. Direct service to Asunción, Empresa Sol, US$42, overnight, 14 hours. Alternatively travel to **Resistencia**, buses daily 1700, US$40 with La Veloz del Norte (20% reduction for students), Sáenz Peña or Panamericano, 12 hours, then change. For description of road, see page 317. Salta-**Formosa** with Atahualpa, which provides the quickest route to Asunción (change at Orán), operates only twice weekly because of the state of the road – Wednesday and Sunday at 0630, 12 hours, US$40.

To Chile: services to Calama, San Pedro de Atacama (both US$55), Antofagasta (US$60) Iquique (US$72) and Arica (US$75), Tramaca Tuesday and Friday in winter, plus Sunday in summer, at 0700, 12 hours, via Jujuy (0900) with three meals. Book well in advance, may be difficult to get a reservation, so try just before departure for a cancellation. Be prepared for delays at the frontier and take warm clothes (at night ice sometimes forms on the insides of bus windows), plenty of water, food, a sheet to protect luggage against dust (**NB** Chilean customs will not allow fruit in). This route is usually closed for at least part of the winter and is liable to closure at other periods of the year.

To Bolivia To **La Quiaca**, on Bolivian frontier, about 10 buses daily, Atahualpa, US$27, 11 hours (via Jujuy, prolonged stop), can be very cold, dusty, not recommended, best change to Panamericano in Jujuy. Also Balut, 3 a day, US$23, 7 hours. To **Orán** (see page 257), 6 hours, and Aguas Blancas for Bermejo, Bolivia; thence road connection to Tarija. To Yacuiba, via **Pocitos** (Bolivian frontier, see page 142), for Santa Cruz, US$17 with Atahualpa to Pocitos, 7-10 hours, very full, road paved.

Trains Station at 20 de Febrero y Ameghino, nine blocks north of Plaza de Armas, taxi US$2. Trains only on the line to Socompa on the Chilean frontier (see below for a description of the line). On all journeys on this line beware of *soroche* (altitude sickness): do not eat or drink to excess.

The Tren a las Nubes (Train to the Clouds) between Salta and La Polvorilla viaduct operates every other Saturday from April to October, weather permitting, and on additional days in the high season (July/August) depart 0700, return to Salta 2215, US$95, without meals, credit cards not accepted, US$250 from Buenos Aires (planned to run every Saturday throughout the year). The train is well-equipped with oxygen facilities and medical staff, restaurant car and snack bar. Explanations are available in English, Spanish, French and Italian. Book in advance (especially in high season) through *Movitren*, address above, **Veloz del Norte**, Esmeralda 320, 4th floor, T 326-9623, Buenos Aires, or through any good travel agency (seats are limited and booking in Salta can be difficult as the train is often booked up from Buenos Aires). There is also a new service to the Quebrada del Inca, with folklore show, on Wednesdays, shorter and cheaper than the Tren a las Nubes, details and booking through Movitren.

Regular services Freight trains run between Campo Quijano and the borax mine at the Salar de Pocitos, but they are not supposed to carry passengers. There is also a weekly freight train with one or two passenger carriages which leaves Salta Fridays about 0900 for San Antonio, 12 hours, and Socompa, 26 hours, returns Sunday: tickets from office to right of station entrance from 0800 on day of departure or in advance from yellow building to left of entrance. Officially this train is restricted to locals only; if refused passage in Salta boarding is usually possible in Campo Quijano and Rosario de Lerma (reached by bus from Salta 1800): ask in the brake van and offer the guard yerba mate, sugar and cigarettes. Restaurant car, no heating, extremely cold; long delays are common and you may do much of the journey in the dark. Take food, water, sleeping bag and warm clothing. Fare US$30. From Socompa irregular freight trains run to Augusta

Victoria, Baquedano or Antofagasta in Chile: officially the Chilean railway authorities do not permit passengers to travel on this line. Options are to return to Salta or wait, perhaps for several days, for a lift by train or truck. There is no food or accommodation in Socompa; if stuck try the Chilean customs building.

FROM SALTA TO SAN ANTONIO DE LOS COBRES AND CHILE

San Antonio and the Chilean frontier can be reached by road and by rail (though see above for problems of rail travel). Note that the roads are all *ripio* or dirt, apart from the section of Route 51 between Salta and Campo Quijano.

Route 51, which is being upgraded, runs west from Salta. From **Campo Quijano**, Km 30, it climbs along the floor of the Quebrada del Toro, fording the river repeatedly before reaching **Ingeniero Maury** (*altitude* 2,350m), Km 65, where there is a police control point. From Km 96 Route 51 climbs the Quebrada de Tastil, leaving the railway which continues through the Quebrada del Toro.

Santa Rosa de Tastil (*altitude* 3,200) Km 103, is the site of a pre-hispanic village and a small museum (US$0.50), recommended.

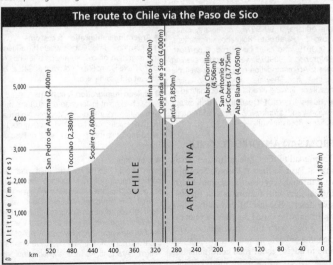

The route to Chile via the Paso de Sico

- **Accommodation & places to eat In Santa Rosa**: basic accommodation next door to the museum, no electricity or heating, take food, water and candles. Try the *quesillo de cabra* (goat's cheese) from Estancia Las Cuevas. **At El Alfarcito**, 5 km south of Santa Rosa there is a good restaurant with one double room.

- **Transport** El Quebradeño bus (see below). Alternatively take a tour from Salta, or share a taxi.

Beyond Tastil the road climbs over the Abra Blanca pass (4,050m), though the old route, over the Abra Muñano in a long series of steep zig-zags, is still passable. At the top of the pass, the road drops and runs across the *puna*, offering views of Chañi (5,896m) to the left, Acay (5,716m) to the right, and Quewar (6,102m) in the far distance. At Km 123 Route 51 meets Route 40, the road from La Poma over the Abra del Acay.

SAN ANTONIO DE LOS COBRES

(*Population* 2,200; *Altitude* 3,750m; *Phone Code* 087), 136 km northwest of Salta, is a squat, ugly mining town situated in a hollow in the *puna* surrounded by hills.

- **Accommodation C** pp *Hostería de las Nubes*, on the eastern outskirts, T 909058 (or Esmeralda 320 Buenos Aires, T 326-0126), modern, including breakfast, restaurant, comfortable, recommended; *Res Inti Huasi*, opposite Aduana, T 909997/8, restaurant, clean; *Hosp El Palenque*, Belgrano sin número, T 909019, also café, family run. **E** pp *Hosp Belgrano*, T 909025, very friendly, evening meals. Accommodation may also be available in the school. Beware *soroche*: avoid eating heavily or drinking alcohol until acclimatised.

- **Buses** To Salta, El Quebradeño, daily except Thursday and Saturday, 5½ hours, US$14; stops at Santa Rosa de Tastil.

FROM SAN ANTONIO TO CHILE

There road to the Chilean frontier crossings at Paso de Sico at Paso de Socompa runs through very beautiful scenery, crossing saltflats with flamingos and impressive desert. Because of snowfalls, these routes may be closed 2-3 times a year, for 2 or 3 days each time. Immigration and customs officials in San Antonio may be able to advise about road conditions but truck drivers using it are more reliable.

Obtain sufficient drinking water before setting out from San Antonio. Most traffic uses the Paso de Sico crossing: there is virtually no traffic on the other road. A third crossing, via the Paso de Huaytiquina, shown on many maps, is closed. **NB** Hitchhiking along these roads is not recommended.

Route 51 continues across the *puna*; at Km 149 there is a turning which runs below the La Polvorilla railway viaduct. At Km 163 the highest point on the road, the Abra de Chorrillos (4,650m) is reached. At Cauchari (3,993m), Km 204 on the southern edge of the Salar de Cauchari, the road forks. One branch, Route 27 follows the railway line south and west across the giant Salar de Arizaro to the Chilean frontier at Paso de Socompa. At Pocitos, 40 km south of Cauchari, Route 17 branches off Route 27 and runs south to Antofagasta de la Sierra. Route 51 continues west from Cauchari before forking again at Km 210, where Route 70 leads off north towards the Chilean frontier crossing at Paso de Jama while Route 51 runs to the frontier at Paso de Sico (4, 079m).

FRONTIER WITH CHILE: PASO DE SICO AND PASO DE SOCOMPA

- **Argentine immigration & customs**
In San Antonio de los Cobres where the aduana and migration offices are at opposite ends of town. There is a police checkpoint at Catúa, 26 km east of Paso de Sico.

- **Chilean immigration & customs**
Police checkpoint in Toconao but customs and immigration in San Pedro de Atacama. Note that fruit, vegetables and dairy products may not be taken into Chile (search 20 km west of Paso de Sico).

- **Into Chile**
From Paso de Sico the road the road continues on the Chilean side via Mina Laco and Socaire to Toconao (road very bad between these two points), San Pedro de Atacama and Calama. From Paso de socompa a poor road runs to Pan de Azúcar from where there are roads west to the Pan American Highway south of Antofagasta and north via the Salar de Atacama to San Pedro de Atacama. No fuel is available until San Pedro or Calama.

JUJUY PROVINCE

FROM SALTA TO JUJUY

There are two routes: the direct road, Route 9 (92 km) via La Caldera and El Carmen, is more interesting. North of La Caldera it winds through the Sierra de Chañi, passing through areas of cloudforest before reaching the Abra de Santa Laura (1,600m) and dropping to El Carmen. The other route via Güemes is better for hitchhiking.

JUJUY

(*Population* 182,000; *Altitude* 1,260m; *Phone code* 0882) is located on the edge of a broad valley at the southern end of the Quebrada de Humahuaca. Though the original city was sited between two rivers, the Ríos Grande and Xibi Xibi (or Chico), it has sprawled south beyond the latter. Founded first in 1561 and then in 1575, when it was destroyed by the Indians, the city was finally established in 1593. Wars and earthquakes have ensured that the city has few colonial remains. Capital of one of the smallest, and poorest, provinces in the country, Jujuy is a pleasant stop en route to or from Bolivia and a convenient stepping off point for excursions into the *puna* and to the national parks further northeast.

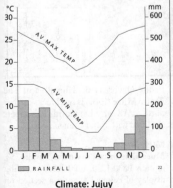

Climate: Jujuy

History

The province of Jujuy bore the brunt of fighting during the Wars of Independence: between 1810 and 1822 the Spanish launched 11 invasions down the Quebrada de Humahuaca from Bolivia. In August 1812 General Belgrano, commanding the republican troops, ordered the city to be evacuated and destroyed before the advancing Spanish army. This event is marked on 23-24 August by festivities known as *El Exodo Jujeño* with gaucho processions and military parades. As a tribute to the city for obeying his orders, Belgrano donated a flag which is displayed in the Casa de Gobierno: a painting of this ceremony can be seen inside the Cathedral.

Places of interest

In the eastern part of the city is the **Plaza Belgrano**, a fine square lined with orange trees. On the south side of the plaza stands the **Casa de Gobierno**, an elaborate 17th century French-style palace, built in 1920. Inside, in the Salón de la Bandera, is the flag donated to the city by Belgrano (open Monday-Friday, 0800-1200, 1600-2000, but not always). Around the building are 4 statues representing Justice, Liberty, Peace and Progress by the Argentine sculptor, Lola Mora. On the west side is the **Cathedral**, dating from 1765 (the tower was built in 1906) which has been heavily restored. Inside are several fine 18th century paintings as well as a superb gold plated wooden pulpit, carved by Indians in the Jesuit missions, a colonial

---

What's in a name?

The city's formal title is San Salvador de Jujuy and it is usually referred to by locals as San Salvador. Jujuy is said to be corruption of Xibi Xibi, one of the rivers on which the city is sited. The two previous cities founded by the Spanish on this site went by the names of La Ciudad de Nieva (after the then-Viceroy of Peru), 1561, and San Francisco de la Nueva Provincia de Alava, 1575. Travellers usually refer to the city as Jujuy (pronounced 'Hoo-Hooey').

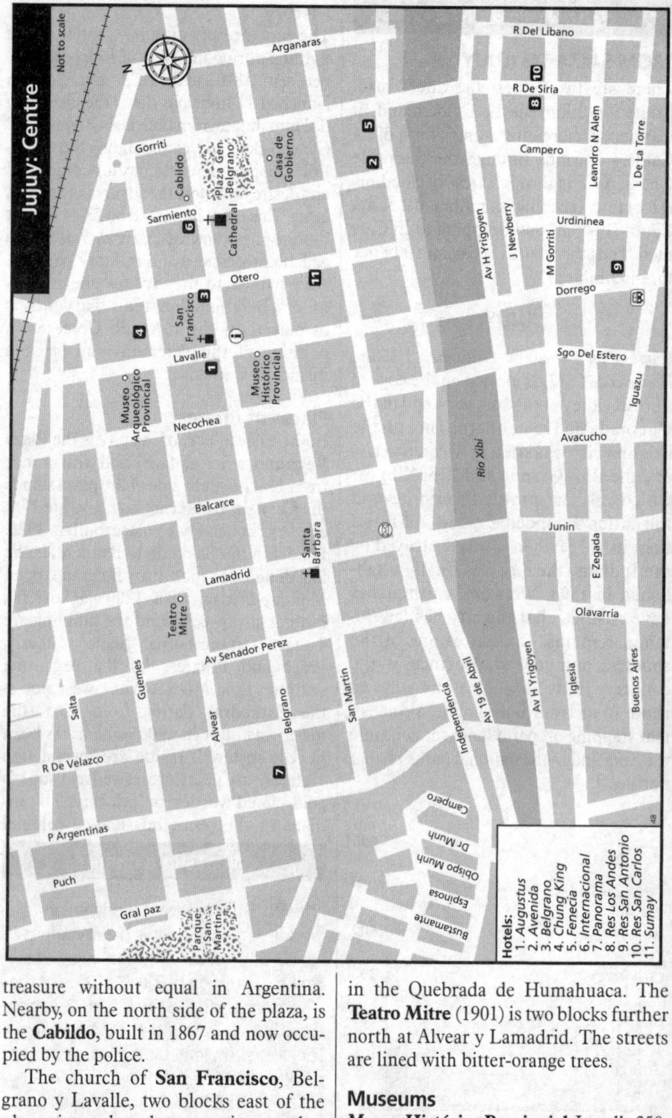

Jujuy: Centre

Not to scale

Hotels:
1. Augustus
2. Avenida
3. Belgrano
4. Chung King
5. Fenecia
6. Internacional
7. Panorama
8. Res San Andrés
9. Res San Antonio
10. Res San Carlos
11. Sumay

treasure without equal in Argentina. Nearby, on the north side of the plaza, is the **Cabildo**, built in 1867 and now occupied by the police.

The church of **San Francisco**, Belgrano y Lavalle, two blocks east of the plaza, is modern but contains another fine colonial pulpit. The church of **San Bárbara**, San Martín y Lamadrid (1777) is similar in style to the colonial churches in the Quebrada de Humahuaca. The **Teatro Mitre** (1901) is two blocks further north at Alvear y Lamadrid. The streets are lined with bitter-orange trees.

Museums

Museo Histórico Provincial, Lavalle 250, in daily 0830-1230, 1500-2000, including display of colonial art and a section on General Juan Lavalle, an opponent of Rosas,

Belgrano

Though among Argentine independence heroes, General Manuel Belgrano stands second only to San Martín, his plans to establish a constitutional monarchy after independence were a failure and his military career was marked more by defeat than victory. He is, however, honoured as the creator of the Argentine flag although when he first unfurled the now familiar blue and white banner on the banks of the Río Paraná in 1812, he was reprimanded by senior officers who opposed what they saw as a declaration of independence from Spain.

Born into a wealthy merchant family in Buenos Aires in 1770, Belgrano was educated in Spain, returning to become a leading figure in a circle of intellectuals influenced by the European enlightenment. As secretary of the Buenos Aires merchant guild, he promoted ideas of free trade through his writings. He was therefore an enthusiastic supporter of moves to break away from Spanish colonial rule with its trading restrictions. In 1811 he commanded a military expedition to Paraguay; convinced that the Paraguayans would support his cause, his force of 700 men was overwhelmed by 5,000 Paraguayans and defeated. Placed in command of the northern armies, he defeated royalist forces at Tucumán (September 1812) and Salta (February 1813). His attempt to end Spanish control over Upper Peru (Bolivia) by siezing Potosi failed: defeated, he was forced back to Tucumán, where he was replaced by San Martín.

In 1815 Belgrano was sent to Europe to pursuade Spain to accept Argentine independence under a king from the Spanish royal family. After the failure of this mission he participated in the Congress of Tucumán; though he successfully argued for a declaration of independence, his schemes for a monarchy under a descendent of the Incas were again rejected. After a further period with the northern army he died in Buenos Aires in 1820.

Bank note showing Manuel Belgrano

who was killed here in 1841. According to the story, he was hit by a bullet which passed through the door as he approached it from the other side. The door in the museum is a copy; the original is in the Museo de Historia Nacional in Buenos Aires. Entry US$1.

Museo de Paleontología y Mineralogía, part of the University of Jujuy, Avenida Bolivia 2335, Monday-Friday 0800-1300. Also here is the **Estación Biológica de Fauna Silvestre**, open Sunday (for private tours on other days, contact Dr Arturo A Canedi, T 25617-25845), very interesting.

Museo de Bellas Artes, Güemes 956, Monday-Friday, 0800-1200, 1700-1900.

Museo Histórico Policial, in the Cabildo, Monday-Friday 1000-1300,

1500-2100, Saturday 1030-1230, 1830-2100, Sunday 1830-2100.

Museo de la Iglesia San Francisco, Belgrano y Lavalle, including 17th century paintings from Cusco and Chuquisaca.

Museo Arqueológico Provincial, Lavalle 434, Monday-Friday 0800-1300, 1500-2000, Saturday/Sunday 0900-1300.

Excursions

To **Termas de Reyes**, 19 km northwest, a thermal resort with the *Hotel Termas de Reyes*, a grand neo-classical hotel set among magnificent mountains. Non-residents can use the Hotel's thermal pool, US$3 (weekends US$5), and there are also municipal baths, US$1, open daily 0800-1200 and 1400-1700 (Thursday 1400-1700 only).

● **Accommodation A3** *Termas de Reyes*, T 0882-35500, with breakfast or half-board, **A2** full board, run down, restaurant. Camping US$5 per person with use of thermal pool, take insect repellent.

● **Buses** 6 a day from Jujuy bus terminal between 0630 and 1945, returning 0700-2040, US$1 1 hour.

Local festivals

Festival on 6 November. El Exodo Jujeño, 23/24 August (hotels fully booked).

Local information
● **Accommodation**

Panorama, Belgrano 1295, T 30183, 4-star, highly-regarded; **A2** *Augustus*, Belgrano 715, T 22668, 3-star, VIP section very good, standard section overpriced, modern, comfortable but noisy; **A2** *Internacional*, Belgrano 501 (Plaza Belgrano), T 22004; **A3** *Fenicia*, 19 de Abril 427, T 28102, quiet; **A3** *Avenida*, 19 de Abril 469, T 22678, on riverside, with good restaurant (**C** off season, cafeteria only); **A3** *Hostería Posta de Lozano*, Route 9, Km 18, good restaurant, pools with fresh mountain water, covered parking; **A3** *Sumay*, Otero 232, T 22554, central, friendly, recommended; **A3** *Alto La Viña*, Route 56, Km 5, on northeastern outskirts, T 26588, attractive, swimming pool; **B** *Res Los Andes*, Siria 456, T 24315, hot water, a bit prison-like. Opposite is **B** *Res San Carlos*, Siria 459, T 22286, modern, some rooms air conditioned, parking.

Budget accommodation: **C** *Belgrano*, Belgrano 627, T 26459, old fashioned, hospitable, noisy. On Alvear: **C** *Chung King*, No 627,

T 28142, dark, very noisy, many mosquitoes, good restaurant; **D** *Res Norte*, No 444, T 222721, basic; **D** *El Aguila*, Alvear 400, basic. Near the bus terminal only **C** *San Antonio*, Lisandro de la Torre (opposite), modern, recommended. **D** *Res Río de Janeiro*, Avenida José de la Iglesia 1536, very basic, run down.

Camping *Camping Municipal*, Avenida República de Bolivia west of town near the Río Grande, US$4 per tent, ask for a cheaper rate for one person; *Autocamping*, 3 km north outside city at Huaico Chico. Buses 4 or 9 frequent, hot showers (if you remind the staff), laundry facilities, very friendly.

● **Places to eat**

El Cortijo, Lavalle y San Martín, interesting salads, good vegetarian food, reasonably priced; *Sociedad Española*, Belgrano y Pérez, elegant setting, good set price meals; *Bar La Royal*, Belgrano 770, good but expensive; *La Victoria*, Avenida El Exodo 642, away from centre, good; *Confitería Carena*, Belgrano 899, old-fashioned, good for breakfast; *La Ventana*, Belgrano 751, good cheap menu, good service, a-la-carte menu is expensive; *La Rueda*, Lavalle 320, good food and service, very popular, expensive; *Madre Tierra*, Belgrano y Otero, vegetarian, fixed price lunch, recommended; *Krysys*, Balcarce 272, excellent atmosphere, good food, pricey; *Cybercafé*, Belgrano y Balcarce; *Ruta 9*, Costa Rica 968, Barrio Mariano Moreno (take taxi), good local food, Bolivian owners. Cheaper places on Santiago del Estero and Alem behind bus terminal. Very good ice cream at *Helados Xanthi*, Belgrano 515, made by Greek owner. *Opus-Café*, Belgrano 856, good coffee, music and atmosphere. Good bread and cake shop at Belgrano 619. Good sandwiches at *Rada Tilly*, 2 locations on Belgrano.

● **Banks & money changers**

At banks: **Banco de la Provincia de Jujuy**, Lamadrid, changes US$ cash only; Amex travellers' cheques can only be changed at **Banco Quilmes**, Belgrano 904, 1% commission while **Banco de Galicia**,Alvear, charges US$10 commission; nowhere to change Thomas Cook travellers' cheques; **Horus**, Belgrano 722, good rates for cash; **Dinar**, Belgrano 731. Travel agencies on Belgrano also change cash. If desperate, ask the dueña of the *confitería* at bus station, rates not too unreasonable. (See note on provincial bonds used as currency, page 468.)

● **Consulates**

Bolivia, Patricinio Argentino 641, T 23156, visa US$5, pay no more; **Spain**, Rua de Velasco 362, T 28193; **Italy**, Avenida Fascio 660, T 23199; **Paraguay**, Tacuarí 430, T 28178.

● **Entertainment**
Chung King, Alvear 627, live music and dancing at weekends.

● **Laundry**
Laverap, Belgrano y Rua de Velazco.

● **Post & telecommunications**
Post Office: at Independencia y Lamadrid, in Galería Impulso, Belgrano 775.
Telecom: Senador Pérez 141, open 0700-0100.

● **Shopping**
Handicrafts are available at reasonable prices from vendors on Plaza Belgrano near the cathedral; *Regionales Lavalle*, Lavalle 268; *Centro de Arte y Artesanías*, Balcarce 427; *Librería Rayuela*, Belgrano 636, good maps and travel guides; *Librería Belgrano*, Belgrano 602, English magazines and some books; *Farmacia Avenida*, Lavalle y 19 de Abril, 0800-2400.

● **Tour companies & travel agents**
Many along Belgrano: *Alicia Viajes*, No 592, T 22541; *Giménez*, No 775, T 2924; *Turismo Lavalle*, No 340; *Pasajes Turismo* No 722; *Grafitti*, No 731; *Be Dor Turismo*, No 860 local 8, 10% for ISIC and youth card holders on local excursions. All offer tours along the Quebrada de Humahuaca, 12 hours, US$25.

For information on bird watching, contact Mario Daniel Cheronaza, Peatonal 38, No 848-830, Viviendas 'El Arenal', Jujuy.

● **Tourist offices**
Belgrano 690, T 28153, very helpful, open till 2000.

● **Useful addresses**
Migración: Antardida 1365.

● **Transport**
Local Car hire: Avis, *Hotel Jujuy Palace*, T 911501, F 311184 and airport.

Air Aeropuerto El Cadillal, 32 km southeast, T 91505; Tea Turismo vans leave *Hotel Avenida* to meet arrivals, 1 hour, US$4.50. Austral flies to **Buenos Aires**, 1 a day direct, **Salta** and **Santiago del Estero**. LAB to Tarija twice a week. Austral offers bus connection with its Buenos Aires flight to Tartagal (in the northeast of the province) via San Pedro and Embarcación.

Buses Terminal at Iguazú y Dorrego, six blocks south of centre. To **Buenos Aires**, US$89, several daily with Balut, La Estrella, La Internacional; to **Córdoba**, Panamericano and La Veloz del Norte, daily; to **Tucumán** 5 hours, US$25, and Córdoba, 14 hours US$45, Ledesma; to **Puerto Iguazú**, 2 a week, US$80, 30 hours; to **Salta** hourly from 0700, 2¾ hours, US$6; to **La Quiaca**, 6½ hours, several companies, US$16, reasonably comfortable, but very cold at night, best is Veloz del Norte, fastest is El Quiaceño; to **Humahuaca**, US$7, 3 hours, sit on left side; to

Tilcara 1½ hours, US$5; to **Orán** daily at 1700; to **Embarcación**, US$7 Balut, via San Pedro; to**Purmamarca** and **Susques**, Thursday and Sunday, returning from Purmamarca at 1330 on Wednesday and Saturday.

To Chile To Antofagasta via the Paso de Jama, San Pedro de Atacama and **Calama** (15 hours), Tramaca, Tuesday and Friday, US$50 including cold meal, breakfast; to **Iquique**, Wednesday and Saturday, Panamericano, US$50. Check weather conditions in advance.

FROM JUJUY TO CHILE

This route via the Paso de Jama, an alternative to the route via the Paso de Sico (see above), is now the road most used by traffic, including trucks, crossing to northern Chile. **NB** No fuel is available between Jujuy and San Pedro de Atacama except at Susques and then only if they have electricity.

Near Purmamarca (see below), 61 km north of Jujuy on Route 9, Route 52 (*ripio*) leads west through the quebrada de Purmamarca and over the Abra Potrerillos (4,170m) to reach the *puna*. From here the road runs northwest, crossing, at Km 127, Route 40, which runs between San Antonio de los Cobres and Abra Pampa. At Km 131-136 the road crosses Salinas Grandes (3,500m), one of the largest areas of salt-flats in the country (fantastic views especially at sunset). In the winter months, on

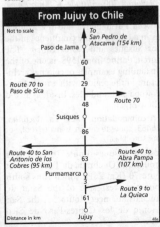

From Jujuy to Chile

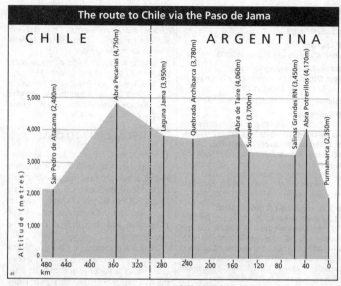

The route to Chile via the Paso de Jama

CHILE | ARGENTINA

San Pedro de Atacama (2,400m) · Abra Pecanas (4,750m) · Laguna Jama (3,950m) · Quebrada Archibarca (3,780m) · Abra de Taire (4,060m) · Susques (3,700m) · Salinas Grandes RN (3,450m) · Abra Poterillos (4,170m) · Purmamarca (2,350m)

Altitude (metres): 5,000 / 4,000 / 3,000 / 2,000 / 1,000 / 0

km: 480 440 400 360 320 280 240 200 160 120 80 40 0

49

both sides of the road, three different ancient types of salt mining by hand can be seen. At Km 180-200 the road winds through the Quebrada de Mal Paso crossing the Tropic of Capricorn several times.

Susques

(*Population* 700; *Altitude* 3,700m; *Phone code* 0882), Km 213, the only settlement between Purmamarca and the frontier, lies in a hollow at the confluence of the Ríos Susques and Pastos Chicos. The church, dating from 1598, is one of the outstanding examples of colonial architecture in the region, with a roof of cactus-wood and mud tiles. Inside is an old bellow-organ.

● **Accommodation** *Res La Vicuñita*, T 26463, opposite church, thatched roof, hot water, breakfast.

West of Susques Route 16 continues through the Quebrada de Taire to meet Route 70 (Km 261), which runs south along the west side of the Salar de Cauchari to meet Route 51, the San Antonio de los Cobres-Paso de Sico road.

FRONTIER WITH CHILE: PASO DE JAMA

The pass (4,750m) 360 km west of Jujuy, is reached by a 60 km road which branches off Route 70. Argentine customs and immigration are at Susques. On the Chilean side the road continues (unpaved) to San Pedro de Atacama (Km 514), where fuel and accommodation are available, and Calama. Chilean customs and immigration are at San Pedro de Atacama.

NORTH FROM JUJUY

Route 9 runs north from Jujuy, through the Quebrada de Humahuaca and then across the *puna* to the Bolivian frontier at La Quiaca. **NB** Drivers heading off main roads in this area should note that service stations are far apart: there are ACA stations at Jujuy, Humahuaca and La Quiaca and YPF stations at Tilcara and Abra Pampa. Spare fuel and water must be carried. In the rainy season (January-March) ask the highway police about flooding on the roads.

● **Buses** There are frequent bus services along the Quebrada which stop at the main towns; most services from Jujuy to Humahuaca, fewer north of Humahuaca. Companies: Panamericano, Veloz del Norte, Cotta Norte, Balut, Atahualpa.

THE QUEBRADA DE HUMAHUACA

The road through this gorge offers some of the most attractive landscapes in the Northwest; the rocks are a spectacular variety of colours and giant cacti grow in the higher, drier parts.

The Quebrada de Humahuaca has some of the most interesting festivals in the region. The pre-Lent carnival celebrations are picturesque and colourful. At Easter in Tilcara and Humahuaca pictures of the Passion are made of flowers, leaves, grasses and seeds and a traditional procession on Holy Thursday at night is joined by thousands, especially in Yavi.

Tumbaya (*Population* 150; *Altitude* 2,094m), Km 51, has a church originally built in 1796 and rebuilt in 1873.

From Jujuy to La Quiaca

50a   Not to scale   Distance in km

PURMAMARCA

(*Population* 200; *Altitude* 2,100m), 3 west of Route 9 at Km 61, lies on Route 52 to Paso de Jama (see above). Overlooking the village to the west is a hill: seven contrasting colours can be distinguished in the rock strata (best seen in the early morning or at least before noon. Inside the church of Santa Rosa (1648, rebuilt 1778) are frescos of scenes from the life of the saint. Next to the church is an *algrarrobo* tree thought to be 500-years-old.

● **Accommodation** E pp *Ranchito del Rincón*, Sarmiento, new, owners Yolanda and Zulma are helpful, highly recommended; also 2 rooms in shop, **F** pp, ask at the police station for the address; *comedor* on main square has good, cheap, local food and helps find accommodation.

Maimará

(*Population* 1,600; *Altitude* 2,150m), Km 75, offers more views of colourful rock strata, known as *La Paleta del Pintor*. 3 km south is **La Posta de Hornillos**, one of the chain of colonial posting house which used to extend from Buenos Aires to Lima. Restored, the building now houses a transport museum (open, in theory, Wednesday-Monday 0900-1800, free).

● **Accommodation** C *Pensión La Posta*, the owners' son is a tourist guide and has helpful information, 5 km from Maimará.

TILCARA

(*Population* 2,900; *Altitude* 2,460m; *Phone code* 088), Km 84, lies near the confluence of the Ríos Grande and Huasamayo. 2 km south of the village overlooking the Río Grande is a *pucará*, or Indian fortress, uncovered in 1903 and reconstructed in the 1950s. Beautiful mountain views, recommended. At the entrance there are botanical gardens containing only high altitude and *puna* plants.

Museums Museo Arqueológico, attached to the University of Buenos Aires, contains a fine collection of precolumbian ceramics from the Andean regions of present day Argentina, Bolivia and Peru, Tuesday-Sunday 0900-1200, 1500-1800, highly recommended, US$2, free entry Tuesday. Admission includes entry to the *pucará* and vice-versa.

Local festivals *Fiestas* on weekends in January.

• **Accommodation B** *Turismo*, Belgrano 590, swimming pool (usually dry); **D** *El Antigal*, Rivadavia, pleasant, good restaurant, colonial style, stores luggage, recommended; **E** *Hostería La Esperanza*, spacious room, arranges walking tours; **E** *Res Frami*, Lavalle y Bolívar, T 955045; **E** *El Pucará*, three blocks from plaza, cosy, friendly, recommended; **E** *Edén*. **Youth hostel E** *Malka*, San Martín sin número, five blocks from plaza, good views, tours offered, kitchen facilities, IYHA affiliated, horse and bike rental, meals provided; also at Radio Pirca, **E** pp, three blocks from plaza, use solar energy. **Camping** Municipal campsite, dirty; *Camping El Jardín*, US$5, clean, hot showers.

• **Places to eat** *Pucará*, good value; *Café del Museo*, good coffee.

• **Shopping** There are excellent craft stalls and shops around the main plaza, selling ponchos, sweaters and wooden items.

Huacalera

(*Population* 100; *Altitude* 2,700), Km 90, is 2 km north of the Tropic of Capricorn: a sundial 20m west of the road marks the exact location. The church, several times restored, has a cactus-wood roof.

Uquía

Km 105, has one of the oldest churches is the region: built in 1691, the walls of the naves are hung with 17th century paintings of winged angels in military dress: the so-called *ángeles arcabuceros*. Note also the barroque altarpiece.

• **Accommodation A3** *Hostal de Uquía*, T 0887-90508, half board, clean, English spoken.

HUMAHUACA

(*Population* 6,000; *Altitude* 2,940m; *Phone code* 0877), Km 126, is the largest and most important town between Jujuy and the Bolivian frontier. Founded in 1591 on the site of a prehispanic settlement, it has the air of the archetypal Andean colonial town with narrow streets and one-storey *adobe* buildings: in fact it was mostly rebuilt in the late-19th century. Coach trips from

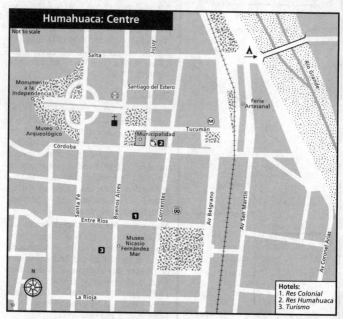

Humahuaca: Centre

Not to scale

Salta
Jujuy
Monumento a la Independencia
Santiago del Estero
Feria Artesanal
Río Grande
Museo Arqueológico
Córdoba
Tucumán
Municipalidad
Santa Fé
Buenos Aires
Corrientes
Av Belgrano
Av San Martín
Av Coronel Arias
Entre Ríos
Museo Nicasio Fernández Mar
La Rioja
N

Hotels:
1. *Res Colonial*
2. *Res Humahuaca*
3. *Turismo*

Salta and Jujuy congregate here at midday but few tourists stay for more than a couple of hours. It is an attractive and peaceful centre from which to explore the Quebrada de Humahuaca.

Places of interest

The church, **La Candelaria**, completely rebuilt in 1873-80, has a bell from 1641. The modern **Cabildo**, in Californian neocolonial style is incongruous: from it a mechanical figure of San Francisco Solano blesses the town at 1200. Overlooking the town is the massive **Monumento a la Independencia Argentina**, made of bronze and weighing 60 tons, built in 1936-50 and sited here because the valley was the scene of the heaviest fighting during the Wars of Independence. There is a good **Feria Artesanal** on Avenida San Martín (on the far side of the railway line), but avoid the middle of the day when the coach parties arrive.

Museums

Museo Folklórico Regional, Buenos Aires 435, run by Sixto Vásquez, traditional customs, US$5 including guide, recommended.

Museo La Casa, Buenos Aires 296, daily 1000-2000, US$3, guided tours in Spanish only, insights into 19th century social customs, recommended.

Museo Ramoneda, Salta y Santa Fe, private collection of contemporary art.

Museo Arqueológico Municipal, at one side of Independence monument, Monday-Friday 0800-1200, 1400-1700.

Museo Nicasio Fernández Mar, Buenos Aires, opposite *Hotel de Turismo*, memorial to the sculptor, open daily, free.

Excursions

To **Coctaca**, 10 km northeast, where there is an impressive and extensive (40 hectares) series of pre-colonial agricultural terraces, the largest archaeological site in Jujuy (puzzling because the terrain is not very hilly).

Local festivals

2 February, La Candelaria. Carnival celebration is one of the most outstanding in the northwest.

Local information

● **Accommodation**

C *Provincial de Turismo*, Buenos Aires 650, T 12, run down, poor service, modern building sadly out of keeping with surroundings; **C** *Res Humahuaca*, Córdoba y Corrientes, one block north of bus terminal, **D** without bath, some air conditioning, traditional, recommended; **C** *Res Colonial*, Entre Ríos 110, near bus terminal, T 21007, some windowless rooms, **D** without bath, laundry facilities; **E** pp *Posada del Sol*, over bridge from terminal, cooking facilities, recommended.

Youth hostel E pp *Albergue Humahuaca*, Buenos Aires 447, T 21064, clean, laundry and very limited cooking facilities, cafeteria, cold, special price for ISIC and youth card holders. Offers tours, all with accredited local guides to popular and lesser-known sites, horse riding, trekking, local festivals, also to the Pacific via Lagunas Colorada and Verde (Bolivia) and the Ruta de Che Guevara (Bolivia).

Camping Across bridge by railway station, small charge including use of facilities.

● **Places to eat**

Most restaurants open only during the day, difficult to find breakfast and the mediocre restaurant at the bus terminal is often the only place open in the evenings. Beware of *soroche*: eat light meals and avoid alcohol until acclimatised. *La Cacharpaya*, Jujuy 295, excellent, pricey, Andean music; *Humahuaca Colonial*, Tucumán 22, good regional cooking, good value, but invaded by coach parties at midday; *El Rancho*, Belgrano sin número, just around the corner from market, lunches only, where the locals eat.

● **Banks & money changers**

Bank. Try the handicraft shops on the main plaza, or the *farmacia* at Córdoba 99. Better rates at Youth Hostel, but best to change elsewhere. Credit cards are not accepted anywhere.

● **Tourist offices**

Kiosk in main plaza in high season.

● **Buses**

To **Jujuy**, US$7; to **La Quiaca**, US11.

NORTH OF HUMAHUACA

Route 9 climbs out of the Quebrada de Humahuaca and runs across the bleak and barren *puna* to La Quiaca on the Bolivian border. The road is unpaved from Km 146 where a road turns off northeast to **Iturbe** (**F** *Pensión El Panamericano*, basic) and then over the 4,000m Abra del Cóndor before dropping steeply into the Quebrada de Iruya to Iruya.

IRUYA

(*Population* 300; *Altitude* 2,713m), 77 km from Humahuaca, is a beautiful walled village wedged on a hillside. Probably founded in 1741, it was a colonial stopover point for mule trains to Bolivia. It is a pleasant and friendly centre for horseback or walking trips in the area (take sleeping bag). At Titiconte 7 km away, there are unrestored pre-Inca ruins (take guide). There is a colourful Rosario festival on the first Sunday in October.

● **Accommodation & places to eat** F pp *Albergue Belén*, very basic; F pp *Hosp Tacacho*, clean, friendly, *comedor*, on the plaza. Food at *Comedor Iruya*.

● **Tour companies and travel agents** *Puna Expediciones* (see Salta page 256) runs a 7-day trek, Salta-Iruya-Nazareno-La Quiaca, walking between Iruya and Nazareno along remote paths, sleeping in local schoolhouses; rest of route is by truck.

● **Buses** Daily bus service from Jujuy and Humahuaca to Iturbe by Panamericano, 1400 and 1900, 45 minutes; in Iturbe you may be able to get a seat on a truck. Empresa Mendoza bus from Humahuaca, 0730, Monday, Wednesday and Saturday, 3½ hours, US$7 one way, waits 2-3 hours in Iruya before returning; service varies according to time of year and is suspended in rainy season (esp February and March) details from *Almacén Mendoza*, Salta y Belgrano, Humahuaca.

Tres Cruces

(*Altitude* 3,693m), Km 190, is where customs searches are made on vehicles from Bolivia. From here a private paved road runs south to the Mina Aguilar where lead zinc and silver are mined.

● **Accommodation** E pp *El Aguilar* (no sign) without bath, clean, basic.

ABRA PAMPA

(*Population* 4,000; *Altitude* 3,484m), Km 217, is an important mining centre originally known as Siberia Argentina. Route 9 continues north from here to La Quiaca and three roads branch off: southwest to Casabindo, west to Cochinaca and northwest to the Laguna de los Pozuelos and Rinconada. At Miraflores 15 km south west of Abra Pampa on the Casabindo road is a vicuña farm, the largest in Argentina. Information offered, photography permitted; buses Monday-Saturday mornings from Abra Pampa.

● **Accommodation** F pp *Res El Norte*, Sarmiento 530, shared room, clean, hot water, good food; *Res Cesarito*, clean, restaurant.

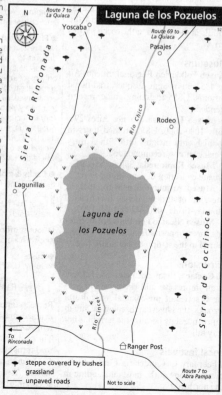

Laguna de los Pozuelos

Route 7 to La Quiaca
Yoscaba
Route 69 to La Quiaca
Pasajes
N
Sierra de Rinconada
Río Chico
Rodeo
Lagunillas
Laguna de los Pozuelos
Sierra de Cochinoca
Río Cincel
To Rinconada
Ranger Post
Route 7 to Abra Pampa

🌲 steppe covered by bushes
ᴠ grassland
— unpaved roads
Not to scale

El Toreo de la Vincha

Each year on 15 August Casabindo celebrates the Assumption of the Virgin by holding El Toreo de la Vincha, the only *corrida de toros* (bullfight) held in Argentina. Bullfighting was outlawed in Argentina shortly after independence, but this is no ordinary bullfight. To start with, the bull is not killed; instead, in front of the church, he challenges onlookers to take a ribbon and silvercoins which he carries on its horns. The coins are offered to the Virgin. The event is said to symbolize the struggle between the Virgin (whose defenders are the men) and the Devil (the bull). There is, however, another aspect to the celebrations: just before the *toreo*, in another part of the village, coca leaves and alcohol are buried as a tribute to *Pachamama*.

Casabindo

(*Altitude* 3,500m) 62 km southwest of Abra Pampa, was founded in 1602. Its magnificent church with twin towers dates from 1772 and is sometimes called 'the cathedral of the Puna': (Federico Kirbus): inside are frescos of archangels in military uniforms (*angeles arcabuceros*).

● **Buses** La Quiaqueña bus daily on Route 40 from Jujuy to La Quiaca passes through Casabindo.

LAGUNA DE LOS POZUELOS

(*Altitude* 3,650m) 50 km northwest of from Abra Pampa, is a flamingo reserve extending over 16,245 hectares. Some 36 bird species have been identified. Temperatures can drop to -25°C in winter; if camping warm clothing, drinking water and food are essential. There is a ranger station at the southern end of the Laguna with a campsite nearby. At Lagunillas, further west, there is smaller lagoon, which also has flamingos.

● **Access** Southern entrance is from the Abra Pampa-Casabindo road. There is also an entrance north of Guayatayoc, northwest of the Laguna and 5 km east of Route 7.

● **Buses** Monday-Friday 0930, 2 hours, US$3.

LA QUIACA

(*Population* 11,500; *Altitude* 3,442m; *Phone code* 0885), 292 km north of Jujuy, lies on the Río La Quiaca (usually dry), which forms the Bolivian border: it is linked with Villazón on the Bolivian side by a bridge. A modern town, it dates from the opening of the railway line in 1907. Most commercial activity has moved to Villazón where everything is cheaper.

Excursions

To **Yavi** (*population* 300; *altitude* 3,300m), 16 km east along a good paved road. Founded in 1667, this provided the crossing point to Bolivia until rail and road connections were built through La Quiaca. The church of **San Francisco** (1690) is a colonial gem: although the roof has been replaced. it has magnificent gold decoration and windows of onyx. (Find the caretaker at her house and she will show you round the church, open Tuesday-Sunday 0900-1200 and Tuesday-Friday 1500-1800). Opposite is the **Casa del Marqués Campero y Tojo**, the austere former mansion of the family who were granted large parts of the *puna* by Philip V of Spain.

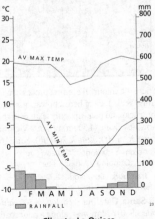

Climate: La Quiaca

La Quiaca & Villazón

Not to scale

- **Buses** From Jujuy to Santa Catalina via La Quiaca, 19 hours, Monday and Friday.

Local festivals

The Mancafiesta, or the festival of the pots, on the Third Sunday in October.

Local information

● **Accommodation**

B *Turismo*, Siria y San Martín, T 2243, recommended, modern, comfortable, hot water 1800-2400, heating from 2030-2400 in winter, restaurant.

C *Cristal*, Sarmiento 543, T 2255, **D** without bath, run down, hospitable; **C** *Victoria*, opposite railway station, good hot showers; *Alojamiento Pequeño*, Avenida Bolívar 236, cheap, basic; **C** *Res La Frontera*, Belgrano y Siria, also restaurant, good.

Camping is possible near the control post on the outskirts of town; also at the ACA service station about 300m from the frontier.

● **Places to eat**

Sirio-Libanesa, near *Hotel Frontera*, good, cheap set meal.

● **Banks & money changers**

No facilities for changing travellers' cheques. Rates are better in Villazón. If arriving in Argentina note that the Province of Jujuy issues it own paper currency (valid only in the province), so be sure to ask for *pesos nacionales*. (See under **Information for travellers**).

● **Hospitals & medical services**

There is a good hospital south of the centre. *Farmacia Nueva*, half a block from Church, has remedies for *soroche* (mountain sickness).

● **Buses**

Terminal at España y Belgrano, luggage storage. To **Salta**, 6-8 a day (10 hours, US$27; cheapest company Balut, US$23) via Humahuaca (5 hours, US$11) and Jujuy (5 hours) with change in Jujuy; to **Jujuy**, US$21.50, 6½ hours, Panamericano, 5 a day, some meal breaks, but take own food, as sometimes long delays; to **Buenos Aires**, via Jujuy, US$89 including meals, 28 hours.

FRONTIER WITH BOLIVIA

The frontier bridge is 10 blocks from La Quiaca bus terminal, 15 minutes' walk (taxi US$2). This crossing is the scene of a lot of illegal (but tolerated) smuggling: searches of locals are thorough. Contrary to popular belief, there is no fee to cross the border either way, and any attempts to levy a surcharge or tax are illegal. This does not prevent some officials (especially

There is a colourful evening procession in Holy Week. East of here a precarious road for trucks and pick-ups only leads over the Abra de Lizoite (4,500m) to Santa Victoria (*population* 700; *altitude* 2,200m), Km 116.

● **Accommodation** Available in private houses. **Camping** Municipal site.

● **Transport Taxi**: from La Quiaca, US$25 return, including 1 hour wait.

To **Santa Catalina** (*population* 200; *altitude* 3,900) 67 km west, along a poor road, where there is a 19th century church.

on the Bolivian side) attempting to extort money from unknowing visitors. You should be on your guard at all times at this border crossing; stories of illegal practices are rife.

● **Argentine immigration & customs**
Offices open 0700-2000 (signature needed from customs officer, who may be out for lunch); on Saturday, Sunday and holidays there is a special fee of US$3 which may or may not be charged. Buses arriving outside these hours have to wait, so check before travelling.

Formalities for those entering Argentina are usually very brief but thorough customs searches are made 100 km south at Tres Cruces. Avoid carrying items such as packets of coca leaves or similar derivatives of the plant.

● **Bolivian immigration in Villazón**
The Bolivian office is on Avenida República de Argentina immediately after the frontier bridge; open 0700 to 1900, Monday-Saturday.

● **Time difference**
Bolivia is 1 hour behind Argentina from October to April. From May to September Argentina loses an hour and keeps Bolivian time.

● **Argentine consulate in Villazón**
Three blocks south of the main plaza at the intersection of Avenida República de Argentina and Calle Río. Open weekdays 1000-1200 and 1400-1700, closed weekends and holidays.

● **Bolivian consulate in La Quiaca**
República Arabe Siria y San Juan; open 0830-1100 and 1400-1700 weekdays, Saturday 0900-1200 (in theory). Travellers who need a visa to enter Bolivia are advised to get it before arriving in La Quiaca.

INTO BOLIVIA: VILLAZON

(*Population* 13,000; *Altitude* 3,443m), an uninspiring town lies on the north bank of the river 898 km south of La Paz.

● **Accommodation**
Villazón has a surprising number of lodgings, all very cheap and offering little beyond the basic amenities. Dollars, bolivianos and Argentine pesos are accepted, but not credit cards.

D *Residencial El Cortijo*, 20 de Mayo 338, T 696209, the best of the lot, intermittent hot water, restaurant; **F** pp *Grand Palace*, behind bus terminal, safe; **F** *Res Martínez*, opposite *Grand Palace*, T 696562, hot water, recommended; next door is **F** *Residencial 10 de Febrero*, very basic; **F** *Res Panamericano*, Avenida República de Argentina, laundry facilities, recommended; **F** *Hotel Bolivia*, one block

from border, small rooms, run down, good value breakfast, hot showers extra.

● **Places to eat**
The town's culinary offerings are limited. The only bona fide restaurant is *Charke Kan*, next door to the *Hotel Grand Palace*. Off the plaza is *Snack El Pechegón*. There are also a handful of dubious-looking food stalls near the bus terminal, all of which are equally unappetizing. Most travellers suggest crossing the border to eat in La Quiaca.

● **Banks & money changers**
There is no bank in town: change money at one of the four *casas de cambio* on Avenida República de Argentina approaching the border: *Cambio Porvenir* is rumoured to be the best, but rates vary. Hotels and shops probably change small amounts only. Difficult to change travellers' cheques and terrible rates offered. Credit cards are not accepted anywhere.

● **Post & telecommunications**
Post Office and **Entel** are in the same building, on Avenida República de Argentina opposite bus terminal. Both are open weekdays 0700-1800 (Entel sometimes until 2100) and Saturday 0800-1200.

● **Transport**
Buses Terminal is near the plaza, five blocks north of the border. To **Potosí**, several between 0830 and 1830, 10-15 hours, US$7-8 (up to 24 hours in wet weather); to **Tupiza**, 0700 and 1500, US$2.50; to **Tarija**, a beautiful journey but most buses go overnight only, daily at 1900/2000, US$6.50, 6 hours; to **La Paz**, several companies, 25 hours, US$17.25, even though the buses are called 'direct', you may have to change in Potosí, perhaps to another company. A taxi to the border is US$0.35, or hire a porter, US$1, and walk across.

Trains Station about 1 km north of the frontier on the main road; taxi US$2.50. To **Oruro** (very dusty and cold), via Tupiza, Atocha and Uyuni, Monday and Thursday at 1630, US$5.60; Tuesday and Friday at 1600, US$7.50. Latest reports suggest that trains go no further than Uyuni. The ticket office opens at 0800; expect long queues.

NORTHEAST FROM JUJUY

Route 34 runs northeast, following the valley of the Río San Francisco which flows along the base of the eastern foothills and into the Río Bermejo. The road provides alternative routes to Bolivia and access to two of Argentina's three cloudforest parks.

SAN PEDRO DE JUJUY

(*Population* 50,000; *Phone code* 0844) is a sugar town, 63 km east of Jujuy. The Ingenio La Esperanza, 4 km east, is a sugar-mill with hospital, housing and a recreation centre, formerly owned by the English Leach brothers.

● **Accommodation B** *Hotel Alex 2*, Rua Leach 467, T 20269, fan; *Alex 1*, Tello 436, T 20299; **E** *Vélez Sarsfield*, V Sarsfield 154, T 20446.

● **Places to eat** Excellent restaurant at *Sociedad Sirio-Libanesa* on the plaza.

● **Buses** To Jujuy, US$2.50, 1½ hours; to Embarcación, Atahualpa, US$6.50, 2½ hours.

LIBERTADOR GENERAL SAN MARTIN

(*Phone code* 0866) Km 113, is another sugar town with a big sugar mill, the Ingenio Ledesma, on the southern outskirts. Of little interest, it is the stepping off point for the Parque Nacional Calilegua.

● **Accommodation E** *Res Gloria*, Urquiza 270, hot water; **E** *Ledesma*, Jujuy 473 just off plaza, large rooms but no keys, local radio station opposite so can be noisy.

● **Places to eat** *Sociedad Boliviana*, Victoria 711, where the locals eat.

● **Banks & money changers** On Plaza San Martín, Banco Roberts changes dollars at a good rate.

● **Tourist offices** At bus terminal.

PARQUE NACIONAL CALILEGUA

125 km northeast of Jujuy, this park, covering 76,360 hectares protects an area of peaks, sub-tropical valleys and cloudforest on the eastern slopes of the Serranía de Calilegua. The highest peaks are Cerro Amarillo (3,720m) and Cerro Hermoso (3,200m). Several rivers flow southeast

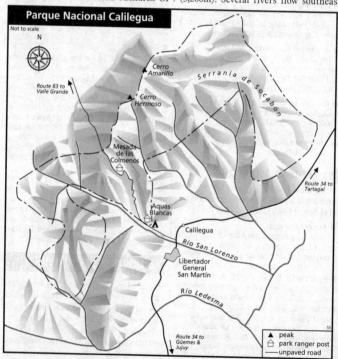

Parque Nacional Calilegua

Not to scale

N

Cerro Amarillo

Serranía de Socabón

Route 83 to Valle Grande

Cerro Hermoso

Mesada de las Colmenos

Route 34 to Tartagal

Aquas Blancas

Calilegua

Río San Lorenzo

Libertador General San Martín

Río Ledesma

Route 34 to Güemes & Jujuy

▲ peak
⌂ park ranger post
— unpaved road

across the park into the Río Ledesma. Vegetation varies dramatically according to altitude. There are over 300 species of bird including the red-faced guan and the condor. Among the 60 species of mammal are tapirs, pumas, otters and *taruca* (Andean deer).

Route 83 (unpaved) climbs northwest across the park, providing access to the southeast sections and splendid views. The best trek is to the summit of Cerro Amarillo, 3 days round trip from the entrance. At Alto Calilegua near the base of Cerro Amarillo, there is an interesting shepherds' settlement. It is possible to walk west from the park to Humahuaca and Tilcara (allow at least 3 days; these walks are described in *Backpacking in Chile and Argentina* by Bradt Publications).

● **Climate** Subtropical with a dry season. Mean temperatures range from 17,198C in winter to 28°C in summer. Mean annual rainfall is 2,000 mm, falling mainly in summer.

● **Access** Park entrance is at Aguas Negras, 12 km northwest of Libertador General San Martín, reached by Route 83 which runs off Route 34 just north of town. Hitching possible. Best time for visiting is outside the rainy season (November-March).

● **Park services** Park headquarters are on San Lorenzo sin número, in Calilegua, 4 km northeast of Libertador, T (0886) 22046. There are two ranger stations, at Aguas Negras and at Mesada de las Colmenas, 13 km further northwest along Route 83.

● **Camping** site at Aguas Negras (drinking water from river nearby, and some cooking facilities and tables). To camp at Mesada de las Colmenas ask permission at Aguas Blancas.

● **Transport** Trucks run by Empresa Valle Grande, Libertad 780, leave Libertador, Tuesday, and Saturday, 0730, 6 hours if road conditions are good, very crowded, returning Sunday and Thursday 1000. Check with Sr Arcona (the driver, everyone knows him) in Libertador whether the truck is going. Weather is unpredictable. Or contact Gustavo Lozano at Los Claveles 358, Barrio Jardín, T 21647, who will contact Angel Caradonna to pick you up.

ROUTES TO BOLIVIA

VIA POCITOS

From Libertador General San Martín, Route 34 runs northeast 244 km, to the Bolivian frontier at Pocitos.

Embarcación

(*Population* 13,000; *Phone code* 0878) 217 km northeast of Jujuy, was built as the western terminus of the Trans-Chaco railway line to Formosa which no longer operates. 2 km out of town is the Loma Protestant mission for Matuco and Toba Indians, who sell unpainted pottery.

● **Accommodation & places to eat** C *Punta Norte*, España 277, clean, air conditioning, friendly. Restaurant of *Sociedad Sirio-Libanesa*, H Yrigoyen and 9 de Julio, cheap and good.

● **Buses** To **Orán**, 1 hour, US$1.70; to **Pocitos** change at Tartagal, making sure your ticket is stamped with the next bus time or you won't be allowed on it; to **Buenos Aires** US$91; to **Salta** US$14.50, 3 a day; to **Formosa** daily at 1300, 17 hours, US$40, Atahualpa, but frequently cancelled; alternative is to take bus to Pichanal, US$1.25, several companies, change for J V Gonzales, US$10, 1600, and change again for Resistencia, 2215, then take a bus to Formosa.

Tartagal

(*Population* 35,000; *Altitude* 350m; *Phone code* 0875), Km 306, is an agricultural centre with a small museum featuring displays on animals of the Chaco and regional folk art. The director, Ramón Ramos, is very informative about the region. Animal masks and pottery are made by Indians at Campo Durán, 32 km north.

● **Accommodation** B *Tropico*, Rivadavia 571, T 21341, expensive but clean; B *Argentino*, San Martín 54, T 21327, 3-star; B *Espinillo*, San Martín 122, T 21007; *Res City*, Alberdi 79, T 21558. **Camping** At the Complejo Deportivo, southeast of centre.

FRONTIER WITH BOLIVIA: POCITOS

Pocitos lies on the frontier 56 km north of Tartagal and 362 km northeast of Jujuy. Crossing can take time here, depending on the availability of officials. Argentine customs and immigration at the frontier. Beware that theft at customs has been reported.

● **Accommodation** E *Hotel Buen Gusto*, just tolerable.

● **Buses** Daily service to **Buenos Aires**, via Salta, La Internacional; frequent services to **Tartagal** and **Embarcación**.

Fauna of the cloudforest

Birdlife in cloudforests varies according to altitude, latitude and season, but the Blue-crowned Trogon, Plush-crested Jay, Olive-golden Woodpecker and Yellow-striped Bullfinch are worth looking out for. As in most Neotropical forests, the most common mammals are bats and rodents; one unusual rodent is the *Coendú* or Tree-Porcupine, which has a prehensile tail for climbing in the trees. Other mammal species include Capuchin Monkeys, tapirs, Crab-eating foxes, Coatís, armadillos, brockets, peccaries and species of cats such as the Margay. Among endangered species are the jaguar and, at the highest altitudes, the *taruca* or North Andean deer.

For a description of cloudforest vegetation, see **Horizons**.

Santiago de la Vega   Coati

● **Into Bolivia**
The road continues via Yacuiba, 4 km north of the frontier, to Tarija, 280 km north. From Yacuiba there are regular bus services to Tarija and Santa Cruz de la Sierra, departing mainly 1700-1900.

VIA AGUAS BLANCAS

At Pichanal, 88 km northeast of Flamingos, 16 km before Embarcación, Route 50 crosses Route 34 and runs along the valley of the Río Bermejo to the Bolivian frontier at Aguas Blancas 69 km north.

Orán

(*Population* 35,000; *Altitude* 350m; *Phone code* 0878), Km 20, formally San Ramón de la Nueva Orán is the only town along this road but is of little interest.

● **Accommodation** B *Gran Hotel Orán*, Pellegrini 617, T 21214; and several *residenciales*, including **C** *Res Crisol*, López y Planes, hot water, friendly, recommended.

● **Buses** To **Aguas Blancas** every 45 minutes, US$2; to **Güemes**, 8 a day, US$10; to **Salta**, Veloz del Norte and Atahualpa, 3 daily each, US$17.50; to **Tucumán**, direct, at 2130, connecting for Mendoza bus which leaves at 1300; to **Jujuy** at 1200 daily; to **Formosa** (connection for Paraguay), US$28, 14 hours, leaving Tuesday, Thursday, Saturday at 0930; to **Embarcación**, US$3; to **Tartagal** daily at 0630 and 1800. Note that buses are subject to searches for drugs and contraband and long delays are possible.

FRONTIER WITH BOLIVIA: AGUAS BLANCAS

Aguas Blancas lies 49 km north of Orán on the west bank of the Río Bermejo, opposite the Bolivian town of Bermejo to which it is linked by a bridge. There is no accommodation, nowhere to change money and Bolivianos are not accepted in Argentina south of here. There are shops and several restaurants including *El Rinconcito de los Amigos*.

● **Argentine customs & immigration**
Open from 0700 to 1200 and 1500 to 1900; insist on getting an exit stamp. There is no exit tax.

● **Buses**
To Orán every 45 minutes, US$2, luggage checks on bus.

● **Into Bolivia**
Bermejo (*population* 13,000; *altitude* 415m) has several hotels and 2 *casas de cambio*, both on the main street. From Bermejo the road continues (unpaved except for 50 km) following the east bank of the Río Bermejo towards Tarija, 210 km north. The views are spectacular (sit on the left). This route is not recommended during or just after the rainy season. There are buses to Tarija, twice daily, 5 hours.

PARQUE NACIONAL BARITU

Situated northwest of Aguas Blancas on the west bank of the Río Bermejo, this is one of the most inaccessible parks in the country. Covering 72,439 hectares of the

Parque Nacional Barítú

Not to scale

N

To Los Toldos

Río Lipeo

Río Bermejo

BOLIVIA

Río Bermejo

To Aguas Blancas

To Aguas Blancas

Serranía de las Pavas

Sierras del Porongal

Sendero Angosto

Río Pescado

— unpaved road
····· footpath
⌂ park ranger post

eastern slopes of the Andean foothills and rising to around 2,000m, the park is crossed by several streams which feed north into the Río Lipeo (and thence into the Bermejo) and south into the Río Pescado. Most of the park is covered by cloud-forest, vegetation varying with increasing altitude. Fauna is also abundant and varied. There are no facilities apart from ranger posts and campsites at the entrances.

● **Climate** Mean temperatures vary from 21°C in winter to 30°C in summer. Mean annual rainfall is 2,000 mm, with the heaviest rainfall in summer.

● **Access** There are three entrances, all of them difficult to reach: at Sendero Angosto, reached by a dirt road which runs west, 30 km, from near the customs post in Aguas Blancas; at Los Pozos, north of the park, which can be reached by crossing into Bolivia from Aguas Blancas, following the road north along the Río Bermejo and then recrossing the frontier at La Mamora; from Los Toldos to the west of the park, reached by following the same route through Bolivia and recrossing the river further north. Access is difficult during and immediately after wet weather.

The Northeast

NORTHEASTERN ARGENTINA consists of the basins of the Paraná and Uruguay rivers which meet north of Buenos Aires to form the Río de la Plata. Three routes are followed: the Río Uruguay, with excursions into Uruguay; the Ríos Paraná/Paraguay to Asunción (Paraguay), and the Río Alto Paraná with the Jesuit missions near Posadas (in particular San Ignacio Miní). There are also sections on the Chaco and on the magnificent Iguazú falls on the border with Brazil.

GEOGRAPHY

The northeast is dominated by the river systems of the Paraná/Paraguay and the Uruguay. Between the rivers, a distance which varies from about 210 km near Santa Fe to 390 km in northern Corrientes, lies Argentine Mesopotamia: the provinces of

Entre Ríos, Corrientes, and Misiones. The landscape of these three provinces differs markedly. Most of Entre Ríos is covered by plains of rich pasture land not unlike those of Uruguay. The province of Corrientes is marshy and deeply-wooded, with low grass-covered hills rising from the marshes. The normal rainfall is about

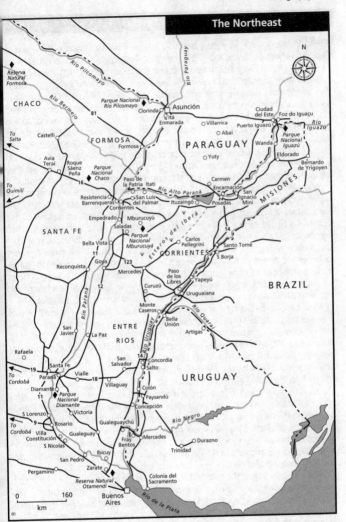

The Northeast

2,000 mm, but the rains are not spread uniformly and drain off quickly through the sandy soil. Misiones is a narrow strip of land between the Uruguay and the Alto Paraná rivers, 80-100 km wide and about 400 km long. Situated on the edge on the Paraná Plateau the province's hilly landscape, with its red soil, much of it covered with forests of pine and cedar and broad-leaved trees, is reminiscent of parts of Brazil.

On the west bank of the Paraná the pampas extend north across most of Santa Fe province, the soil becoming gradually poorer further north. North of Santa Fe is the Argentine Chaco, a great

The Real Mission

Between 1609, when they built their first *reducción* or mission in the region of Guaíra in present day Brazil, and 1767 when they were expelled from Spanish America, the Jesuits founded about 50 missions around the upper reaches of the Ríos Paraná, Paraguay and Uruguay. Though some of these were in areas inhabited by the native Americans of the Chaco, the most famous were the 32 among the Guaraní in present-day Paraguay, Northeast Argentina and Southern Brazil. In 1627 the northern missions around Guaíra were attacked by the slave-hunting *Bandeirantes* from São Paulo, forcing them to flee southwards: 10,000 converts, led by the priests, floated on 700 rafts down the Río Parapanema into the Paraná, only to find their route blocked by the Guaíra Falls. Pushing on for 8 days through dense virgin forest on both sides of the river, they built new boats below the falls and continued their journey. Some 725 km from their old homes, they reestablished their missions and trained militias which protected them from further attacks.

Copying the layout of Franciscan missions, the Jesuits built their *reducciones* around a central square, with the church in the middle of one side: alongside the church were the cloisters, workshops, priests' quarters and the cemetery. The living quarters of the Guraraní occupied the remaining three sides. Each mission was run by two priests, other Europeans being strictly excluded. Often occupying rich lands and efficiently organized, the missions prospered: the Guaraní grew traditional crops such as manioc, sweet potatoes and maize, plants imported from Europe like wheat and oranges as well as looking after herds of cattle, horses and sheep. The missions became major producers of *yerba maté*, favoured by the Jesuits as an alternative to alcohol. Apart from the common lands, used for crops and animals, the Guaraní farmed individual plots.

The decision by Carlos III to expel the Jesuits from South America in 1767 was made under conditions of the highest secrecy: sealed orders were sent to the colonies with strict instructions that they should not be opened in advance. On the appointed date over 2,000 members of the order were put on ships for Italy after which Jesuit property was auctioned. The Jesuit schools and colleges were taken over by the Franciscans and Dominicans; the missions fell into disuse and many were destroyed in 1817 on the orders of the Paraguayan dictator Rodríguez de Francia.

Controversial since the founding of their first missions, the Jesuits had attracted many enemies: the wealth and economic power of the missions angered land-owners and traders; their control over Guaraní annoyed landowners short of labour; rumours circulated that the missions contained mines and hoards of precious metals. A treaty between Spain and Portugal in 1750 settling their border disputes in the area placed seven missions under Portuguese control: the Jesuits resisted with arms, justifying Spanish and Portugese suspicion of the power of the order.

Disagreement over the role of the Order has continued to the present day: some, such as R B Cunninghame Graham, saw them as a 'vanished arcadia' and a kind of primitive socialism; others have accused the Jesuits of enslaving the Guaraní and forcing them to adopt Christianity. The Order's supporters stress its role in defending the Guaraní from enslavement and exploitation by the Spanish and Portugese and refer to missions as 'lost cities'.

Visiting the Missions Only four of the missions show signs of their former splendor: San Ignacio Mini in Argentina, Jesús and Trinidad in Paraguay and São Miguel in Brazil. The first three can be visited with ease from Posadas or Encarnación, as can several others, including Santa Ana, Loreto and San Cosmé y Damián, all of which are described in the text.

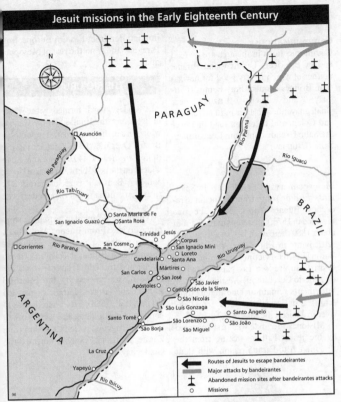

Jesuit missions in the Early Eighteenth Century

Routes of Jesuits to escape bandeirantes
Major attacks by bandeirantes
† Abandoned mission sites after bandeirantes attacks
○ Missions

plain which stretches west from the Paraná to the foothills of the Andes.

CLIMATE

Winters are mild; summers are hot with rain falling in short, sharp storms. Both Entre Ríos and Corrientes often suffer from summer drought. In Misiones the rainfall is heavy: twice as heavy as in Entre Ríos. The days are hot, and the nights cool.

ECONOMY

Santa Fe is an important agricultural province, producing some 35% of the country's wheat and over 50% of its sunflower seeds; other crops include flax, lentils, soya and potatoes. Much of Entre Ríos and Corrientes is still pastoral, a land of large *estancias* raising cattle and sheep. Maize is largely grown in southern Entre Ríos, which is also the most important producer of linseed and poultry in Argentina. The northeastern part of the province, around Concordia, is the main citrus fruit area in the country; rice is also grown in this area and commercial forestry is important. In Corrientes, along the banks of the Paraná between the cities of Corrientes and Posadas, rice and oranges are grown. Misiones is the largest producer of *yerba mate*: 180,000 hectares are dedicated to its cultivation. Citrus, tobacco, timber and tung oil are also produced. The Chaco is mainly devoted to cattle ranching, though tannin and cotton are also cultivated.

Communications

Communications in the area are by road and by the rivers Uruguay and Paraná, neither of which is very good for navigation. Bridges connect Fray Bentos (Uruguay) and Puerto Unzué, near Gualeguaychú, and Paysandú (Uruguay) and Colón, and there is a road link over the Salto Grande dam from Concordia to Salto (Uruguay).

HISTORY

Mesopotamia was first colonized by Spaniards pushing south from Asunción to reoccupy Buenos Aires; Santa Fe was founded in 1573, Corrientes in 1588. From about 1880 there were Jewish agricultural settlements in Entre Ríos, promoted by Baron Hirsch for victims of pogroms in the Czarist Empire (see 'Los gauchos judíos' by Alberto Gerchunoff). Vestiges of these settlements remain at Domínguez (museum) and Basavilbaso, and across the river in Moisesville (Santa Fe).

Misiones Province was first occupied by the Jesuit Fathers fleeing from the Brazilian Alto-Paraná region with their devoted Indian followers. During th[is] century Misiones has attracted large scal[e] immigration from Eastern Europe, from Paraguay and from the rest of Mesopotamia.

THE RIO URUGUAY

The Río Uruguay is formed by the water[s] of two rivers, the Pelotas and the Canoas which rise in the Serra do Mar in souther[n] Brazil. Over 1,600 km long in total, i[t] drains an area of 440,000 sq km. At it[s] widest, on the bend between Puerto Unzu[é] and Fray Bentos, it is 25 km across. Th[e] river is Argentina's eastern boundary with Uruguay and Brazil.

There are no regular passenger shipping services. From Buenos Aires Route 9 runs northwest to Zárate, where the Paraná de las Palmas and Paraná Guazú rivers, and the Isla Talavera which lies between, are crossed by the beautiful Zárate and Brazo Largo suspension bridges (toll US$6). From here Route 14 continues north along the west bank of the Río Uruguay. At Ceibas, 76 km from Zárate, Route 12 branches northwest to Gualeguay.

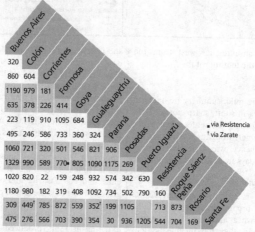

Buenos Aires												
320	Colón											
860	604	Corrientes										
1190	979	181	Formosa									
635	378	226	414	Goya								
223	119	910	1095	684	Gualeguaychú							
495	246	586	733	360	324	Paraná						
1060	721	320	501	546	821	906	Posadas					
1329	990	589	770■	805	1090	1175	269	Puerto Iguazú				
1020	820	22	159	248	932	574	342	630	Resistencia			
1180	980	182	319	408	1092	734	502	790	160	Roque Sáenz Peña		
309	449†	785	872	559	352†	199	1105		713	873	Rosario	
475	276	566	703	390	354	30	936	1205	544	704	169	Santa Fe

■ via Resistencia
† via Zarate

The North East: distance chart (km)

GUALEGUAYU

(*Population* 30,000; *Phone code* 0444), 134 km from Zárate, on the west bank of the Río Gualeguay, is situated in the centre of one of the richest cattle and sheep ranching regions in Entre Ríos. Inside the **Iglesia San Antonio**, on the central Plaza Constitución, there are frescos which include reproductions of works by Rafael, Rembrandt and Rubens.

Museum

Museo Histórico Regional, San Antonio Norte 230.

● **Accommodation A3** *Gran Gualeguay*, Monte Caseros 217, T 23085, poor value; **E** *Italia*, Palacios 1, T 24575, with bath, friendly. There is a municipal **campsite**.

● **Places to eat** In the centre there are practically no restaurants, but the *Jockey Club* and the *Club Social*, both on the main square close to the *Gran Hotel Gualeguay*, cater also for non-members. The *Club Social* has a very nice atmosphere, good food, and you might be invited to see films on certain nights.

● **Fishing** There is good fishing at the confluence of the Ríos Gualeguay and Pavón, 43 km south. Excursions are offered in launches, minimum 2 days, details from tourist office.

● **Tourist office** on eastern outskirts of town, eight blocks east of centre.

GUALEGUAYCHU

(*Population* 64,500, with a large German contingent; *Phone code* 0446) 220 km north of Buenos Aires, lies 13 km east of Route 14 on the west bank of the Río Gualeguaychú, 19 km above its confluence with the Río Uruguay. A pleasant town, with an attractive *costanera*, it has become a popular weekend resort for *porteños* since the opening of the Zárate-Brazo Largo Bridges. On the opposite bank of the river is the Parque Unzué, 110 hectares, with sports facilities and sailing clubs.

Museums

Museo de la Ciudad, San Luis y Jujuy, in a former mansion built in 1835, US$1.

Museo Arqueológico, in the Casa de la Cultura, 25 de Mayo 734, with artefacts from indigenous cultures of the Uruguay basin.

Solar de los Haedo, San José y Rivadavia (on Plaza), in the oldest house in the city, which served as Garibaldi's headquarters when he sacked the city in 1845. Filled with artefacts of the Haedo family, guided tour (Spanish) US$1, Wednesday-Saturday 0900-1145, Friday/Saturday also at 1600-1945.

Museo Ferroviario, Piccini y Rocamora, open air railway museum in the former station.

Local festivals

Lively pre-Lenten Carnival.

Local information

● **Accommodation**

Accommodation is scarce at weekends (when few single rooms are to be found) and during carnival. The tourist office has a list of family accommodation.

A3 *Embajador*, San Martín y 3 de Febrero, T 24414, casino; **A3** *Alemán*, Bolívar 535,

The Río Uruguay

Not to scale

Distance in km

```
Yapeyú
  │
  58
  │
Paso de los Libres ○─4─○ Uruguaiana
                         (Brazil)
  │
  96
  │
Monte Caseros ○
  │
  240
  │              Termas del
  │              Arapey
  ○──────────○   (Uruguay)
  │
  96
  │
Concordia ○─39─○ Salto (Uruguay)
  │
  53           10
  │            ○ Termas del
  │              Daymán
Parque Nacional ○  (Uruguay)
El Palmar
  │
  51
  │
Colón ○─13─○ Paysandú
  │           (Uruguay)
  45
  │
Concepción ○
del Uruguay
  │
  74
  │
Gualeguaychú ○─44─○ Fray Bentos
  │                  (Uruguay)
  70
  │
Gualeguay ○─64─┤
  │
  76
  │
  ○ Zárate
  │
  90
  │
  ○ Buenos Aires
```

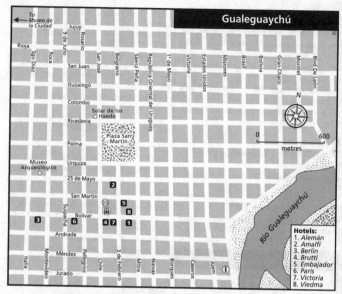

Gualeguaychú

Hotels:
1. Alemán
2. Amalfi
3. Berlin
4. Brutti
5. Embajador
6. Paris
7. Victoria
8. Viedma

T 26153, German-spoken, without breakfast, recommended; **A3** *Paris*, Bolívar y Pellegrini, T 23850, F 26260, with breakfast, fan, restaurant, comfortable; **A2** *Berlin*, Bolívar 733, T/F 25111, German spoken, with breakfast, comfortable; **A3** *Viedma*, Bolívar 530, T 24262, garage extra. **B** *Victoria*, Bolívar 565, T 26469, opposite terminal, small rooms, modern, with breakfast.

Budget accommodation: C *Brutti*, Bolívar 591, T 26048, shabby, good value, without breakfast, fan; **C** *Amalfi*, 25 de Mayo 571, T 25677, with breakfast, good beds; **D** *Mayo*, 3 de Febrero y Bolívar, T 27661, uncomfortable beds, with bath.

Camping *La Delfina* in the Parque Unzué, T 22293; *Costa Azul*, T 23984; *Puerta del Sol*, T 23700, and *Playa Chica*, T 25709, all near river; *Ñandubaysal*, 15 km east, T 26009, best.

● **Banks & money changers**
Banco Internacional Cooperativa, 25 de Mayo y Perón, changes cash; *Casa de Cambio*: Daniel, 3 de Febrero 128.

● **Tourist offices**
Costanera y 25 de Mayo, open 0800-2000.

● **Transport**
Air Airport west of town.

Buses Terminal in centre of town at Bolívar y Chile. To **Fray Bentos**, 1 hour, US$3, 2 a day,

ETA; to **Mercedes**, 1½ hours, US$4, 2 a day, ETA; to **Concepción del Uruguay, Colón** and **Concordia**; to **Buenos Aires** US$15, 4 hours, Flechabus and El Rápido, 6 a day each.

FRONTIER WITH URUGUAY: LIBERTADOR GENERAL SAN MARTIN BRIDGE

Situated 33 km south of Gualeguaychú, this bridge (5.4 km long) provides the most southerly route across the Río Uruguay, to Fray Bentos. Vehicle toll US$4; pedestrians and cyclists can only cross on motor vehicles, though officials may arrange lifts.

● **Customs & immigration**
At opposite ends of the bridge. This is a very uncomplicated crossing: formalities take about 10 minutes.

● **Argentine consulate**
Sarandí 3195, Fray Bentos.

● **Transport**
For buses see above under Gualeguaychú. Passport details are noted when booking tickets and passed to officials at border. Passports inspected on the bus.

INTO URUGUAY: FRAY BENTOS

(*Population* 22,000), 44 km south east of Gualeguaychú and 7 km west of the international bridge, is the southernmost port on the east bank of Río Uruguay. A friendly little town with an attractive *costanera*, Fray Bentos is famous for its meat-packing factory (*frigorífico*) known as **El Anglo**, which has been restored as the **Museo de La Revolución Industrial**, open daily except Monday, entry by guided tour only, US$1.50, 1000, 1430 (more frequently in summer), tour 1½ hours in Spanish, may provide leaflet in English.

There are beaches to the northeast and southwest and also at Las Cañas, 8 km south (where there is a tourist complex including motels, T 2597, **C**, campsite, sports facilities and services).

Local information

● Accommodation

A2 *Gran Hotel Fray Bentos*, Paraguay y Zorilla, T 2358, overlooking river, casino; **B** *Plaza*, 18 de Julio y 25, T 2363, comfortable; **D** *Colonial*, 25 de Mayo 3293, T 2260, attractive old building with patio; **E** pp *25 de Mayo*, 25 de Mayo y Lavalleja, T 2586, basic.

Camping At the *Club Remeros*, near the river and at Colegio Laureles, 1 km from centre, T 2236.

● Places to eat

Enramada, España y 25 de Agosto, the best; several cafés and pizzerías on 18 de Julio near Plaza Constitución.

● Banks & money changers

Cambio Fagalde, Plaza Constitución, open Monday-Friday 0800-1900, Saturday 0800-1230.

● Tourist offices

In Museo Solari, Plaza Constitución, T 2233, very friendly.

Fray Bentos: corned beef and oxo

To generations of British people brought up in the early and mid-20th century, Fray Bentos means corned beef: the name was the most famous trademark of what for many was a staple part of the diet. Dating from 1859 and situated on the edge of one of the best natural harbours on the Río Uruguay, the *frigorífico* (meat-packing plant) became the first factory in Uruguay to produce a meat extract by a method invented by the German chemist Julius Leibig. This extract was sold in Britain under the name *Oxo*. Operating with British capital the Leibig Extract of Meat Company expanded the *frigorífico* until by the 1930s it was employing some 5,000 workers of the town's population of 12,000. By then 2,500 cattle were being killed by every 8 hour shift of 200 workers and over 6,000 tons of meat were being processed daily and loaded straight onto vessels in the plant's own port. Peak production periods were during the two World Wars as the *frigoríficos* tried to meet the demand for corned beef and other products to feed the armed forces. Nothing was wasted: animal remains were turned into fertilizers and it was said that the only part of an animal not used was the 'moo'.

The *frigorífico* was sold off to the Uruguayan government in 1961, though the Fray Bentos name had long been turned into a trade mark for products which had no connection with the town. The factory was closed, at very short notice, in 1980. 10 years later work began to turn it into a museum and business park.

There were many other *frigoríficos* in this part of South America, some of which, now modernised, still operate. What makes Fray Bentos unusual, if not unique, is the preservation of buildings and machinery from its heyday. Covering some 55 hectares, the buildings include the offices, beautifully restored and lacking only personnel. Much of the machinery, though old, is still in working order. Outside, in the Barrio El Anglo, the workers' and managers' housing can be seen. Among the 30 enterprises to move into the business park have been a restaurant, *Wolves*, and a discotheque called *Fuel Oil*.

Urquiza

The most important figure in the history of Entre Ríos, Justo José de Urquiza, a contradictory figure. While his fame rests on his role in the overthrow of the dictator Rosas, Urquiza was a provincial *caudillo* whose decision to resist Rosas was based more on political calculation and personal interest than on principle. An autocrat who, after the defeat of Rosas was known in Buenos Aires as 'the other Rosas', Urquiza was a lifelong advocate of educational improvement and in later life an enthusiastic promoter of railway-building.

Born in 1801, Urquiza's early life was perhaps typical of the landowner of the period: mixing business with provincial politics and playing a leading role in the warfare between provincial *caudillos* of the 1830s and 1840s, he became provincial governor in 1841. Business interests as well as political rivalry brought him into conflict with Rosas: though the biggest landowner in the province and owner of meat-salting plants, his landholdings were of little value as long as Rosas blockaded the Río Paraná to enforce the dominance of Buenos Aires.

After his victory over Rosas at Caseros (1852), Urquiza led his troops into Buenos Aires where they massacred Rosas's supporters. Named director of the Argentine Confederation, he later became its first president. Following the defeat of the Confederation armies by Buenos Aires in 1861, he retired to the Palacio San José, where he dedicated himself to his business and philanthropic interests. By 1869 his personal fortune was said to include 600,000 cattle, 500,000 sheep, 20,000 horses and nearly a million hectares of land. Like so many *caudillos* he met a violent death, assassinated in 1870 in his own house by agents paid by his former ally, López Jordán, the *caudillo* of Santa Fe.

● **Transport**

Terminal at 18 de Julio y Blanes, but do not get off here as buses also call at company offices around Plaza Constitución. To **Montevideo**, ETA, 4½ hours, 6 a day, US$9, also Chadre; to **Mercedes**, ETA, US$1, frequent, 30 minutes; to **Paysandú**, US$4.75; to **Buenos Aires**, *bus de la carrera*, 3½ hours, US$18; to **Gualeguay-chú**, 1 hour, US$3, 2 a day.

CONCEPCION DEL URUGUAY

(*Population* 65,000; *Phone code* 0442), known locally as Concepción, is situated 74 km north of Gualeguaychú opposite several islands on the Río Uruguay. It is a major port and service centre for a prosperous agricultural region. Founded in 1783, it was capital of Entre Ríos province between 1813-21 and 1860-1883.

Places of interest

The old town is centred on **Plaza Ramírez**; on its west side is the Italian neoclassical-style **Basílica de la Concepción Inmaculada**, which contains the remains of General Urquiza. Next to it is the **Colegio Superior del Uruguay**, considered the first secular school in the country, though sadly its 19th century buildings were largely replaced in 1935. **Banco Pelay**, 5 km northeast, is a 3 km stretch of beach, considered the longest riverine beach in South America.

Museums

Museo Casa del Delio Panizza, Galarza y Supremo Entrerriano, in a mansion dating from 1793, containing 19th century furnishings and artefacts.

Museo Don Andrés García, personal collection, open daily 0900-1200, 1500-1800.

Excursions

To the **Palacio San José**, the former mansion of General Urquiza, 35 km west of the town. Now a museum with artefacts from Urquiza's life and a collection of period furniture, the palace stands in a beautiful park with an artificial lake. Open Monday-Friday 0900-1300, 1400-1800, Saturday/Sunday 0900-1245, 1400-1745,

US$1.50, written explanations in Spanish, French and English, highly recommended. Reached by Itape buses to 3 km from the Palacio, US$3, 45 minutes.

Local festivals

Fiesta Nacional de la Playa, second half of January, with water and beach sports; carnival.

Local information

● **Accommodation**

B *Res Fiuri*, Sarmiento 779, T 27016, attractive; **B** *Carlos I*, Eva Perón 117, T 26776, 2-star.

C *Gran*, Eva Perón 114, T 22851; **C** *Virrey*, González 2075, T 25017, F 25007; **C** *Ramírez*, Martínez 50, T 25106, above bus terminal.

E *Hosp Los Tres Nenes*, Galarza 1233, near terminal, good.

Camping *Banco Pelay*, 5 km northeast, T 24003.

● **Places to eat**

El Canguro, opposite terminal, good food, reasonably priced; *Rocamora*, Rocamora y Millán. Bus terminal bar for *tenedor libre* meals.

● **Tourist offices**

9 de Julio 844, T 25820.

● **Buses**

Terminal at Rocamora y Los Constituyentes, 11 blocks west of Plaza Ramírez (bus 1 to centre or remise, US$1). To **Buenos Aires**, frequent, 4½ hours, US$15; to **Paraná**, 5 hours; to **Colón** 45 minutes; to **Paysandú** (Uruguay) 1 hour, US$4.

COLON

(*Population* 15,000; *Phone code* 0447) 45 km north of Concepción del Uruguay, was founded in 1863 as a port for the Swiss colony of San José, 10 km north. The river is more picturesque here with an attractive *costanera*, 7 km of sandy beaches, and cliffs visible from a considerable distance. Nearby is a bridge linking Colón with Paysandú, Uruguay. The town is known for *artesanía* shops along 12 de Abril, and there is a large handicrafts fair at Carnival time.

● **Accommodation L3** *Quirinale*, Quirós sin número, T 21978, 5-star (with casino); **A3** *Plaza*, 12 de Abril y Belgrano, T 21043, with breakfast, air conditioning, modern; **A3** *Holimasú*, Belgrano 28, T 21305, F 21303, with breakfast; **B** *Palmar*, Ferrari 285, T 21952, good; **B** *Vieja Calera*, Bolívar 344, T 21139,

with breakfast, air conditioning; **C** *Ver-Wei*, 25 de Mayo 10, T 21972, without breakfast, new ownership. **Families** rent rooms – the Boujon family, Maipú 430, **C**, good breakfast and other meals extra, recommended. **Apartments** for rent from Sr Ramón Gallo, Paysandú, T 472 3280, with kitchen, bathroom, hot showers, close to bus terminal. **Camping** Two sites on river bank: **Camping Municipal Norte**, T 21484, excellent facilities, cheapest; **Piedras Coloradas**, T 21408.

● **Places to eat** *Comedor El Rayo*, Paysandú 372; *Pizzería Luisa*, San Martín 346; *La Rueda*, San Martín y 3 de Febrero; *Marito*, Gral Urquiza y Andrade.

● **Tourist office** Avenida Costanera y Gouchón.

● **Buses** Terminal at Paysandú y Sourigues. To **Buenos Aires**, 4 a day, US$18, 5 hours; to **Concepción del Uruguay**, Copay and Paccot, 4 a day, 2 on Sunday, US$2; to **Concordia**, US$6 (2½ hours) and **Paraná** daily; to **Córdoba** 4 a week; to **Paysandú**, Uruguay, US$3, 45 minutes.

FRONTIER WITH URUGUAY: GENERAL JOSE ARTIGAS BRIDGE

7 km south of Colón, the bridge gives access to the Uruguayan city of Paysandú. Toll US$4.

● **Customs & immigration**

Argentine and Uruguayan formalities are both dealt with at Argentine end of the bridge. Easy crossing.

● **Transport**

Regular bus services between Colón and Paysandú, for details see above. Passports are collected on the bus.

INTO URUGUAY: PAYSANDU

(*Population* 100,000; *Phone code* 0722), situated on the east bank of the Río Uruguay 6 km from the international bridge, was an important meat-packing town in the early 20th century. There is a golf club, and a rowing club which holds regattas.

There are several fine late 19th and early 20th century buildings: note particularly the **Teatro Florencio Sánchez** (1876), the **Jefatura de** Policia and the **Basílica de Nuestra Señora del Rosario** dating from 1860. Also worth a look is the **Monumento a la Perpetuidad**, the old cemetery.

Museums include **Museo de la Tradición**, north of town at the Balneario

Municipal, Tuesday-Friday 1230-1700, Saturday 0900-1200, Sunday 1330-1700, reached by bus to Zona Industrial, gaucho articles, worth a visit. **Museo Salesiano**, Florida 1278, attached to Cathedral, interesting, open Monday-Friday 0830-1130.

Excursions To the **Río Quequay waterfalls**, 25 km north. To the **Termas del Guaviyú** thermal springs 50 km north with four pools, restaurant, motel accommodation and excellent cheap camping facilities, entrance to springs US$0.50. **Buses** (1½ hours, US$2.50, 4 a day).

Local festivals During Holy Week (book hotels in advance).

● **Accommodation** There is a range of hotels: **L3** *Gran Hotel Paysandú*, 18 de Julio y 19 de Abril, T 3400, air conditioning, with breakfast, comfortable; **A3** *Lobato*, Gómez 1415, T 2241, with breakfast, air conditioning, modern, good; **B-C** *Rafaela*, 18 de Julio 1181, T 5053, with breakfast, large rooms, modern; **C** *Concordia*, 18 de Julio 984, T 2417, **D** without bath, old-fashioned, pleasant patio; **D** *Sarandí*, Sarandí 931, T 3465, good, comfortable; **E** pp *Victoria*, 18 de Julio 979, T 4320, highly recommended, cheaper without bath, very helpful. **Youth hostel** Liga Deportiva de Fútbol, Baltasar Brum 872, T 4247, US$1 per person, neither clean nor well-maintained. Cabins for 5 or more people. **Camping** Balneario Municipal, 2 km north of centre, by the river, no facilities. Also at the Parque Municipal, south of centre, some facilities.

● **Places to eat** *Artemio*, 18 de Julio 1248, "best food in town"; *Asturias*, Pereda 917, very popular, good food, recommended. *Los Tres Pinos*, Avenida España 1474, *parrillada*, very good.

● **Banks & money changers** Several *casas de cambio* on 18 de Julio, including **Cambio Fagalde**, No 1004; **Cambio Bacacay**, No 1008; both change travellers' cheques, open Saturday 0830-1230. Also **Banco de la República**, 18 de Julio y 19 de Abril.

● **Embassies & consulates** Argentina, Gómez 1084, T 2253, Monday-Friday 0800-1300; **Brazil**, Herrera 932, T 2723.

● **Post & telecommunications** Post Office: 18 de Julio y Montevideo. **Antel**: Montevideo 875.

● **Tourist offices** Plaza de la Constitución, 18 de Julio 1226, Monday-Friday 0800-1900, Saturday-Sunday 0800-1800.

● **Transport Air** Aviasur flights to Montevideo (US$80 return); Pluna, Florida 1249, T 3071). **Buses** Terminal at San Martín y Artigas. To **Montevideo**, US$14.70 (Núñez), 15.50 (Copay), 5-6 hours, also Chadre/Agencia Central, many buses; to **Salto** US$5, 6 a day; to **Rivera**, US$15. To **Fray Bentos**, 4 a day, 1½ hours direct, 4 hours via Young, US$5; to **Colonia del Sacramento** Chadre, 1700, 6 hours, US$7.50. It can be difficult to get a seat on long-distance buses going north.

PARQUE NACIONAL EL PALMAR

51 km north of Colón and 53 km south of Concordia, on west bank of the Río Uruguay, the Park occupies a former *estancia* and covers 8,500 hectares of gently undulating grassland and mature palm forest, which includes Yatay palms up to 12m

Yatay Palm

(*Syagrus yatay*). This tall and graceful palm is now mainly confined to the El Palmar National Park to which it gave its name. This palm was once found across the entire Pampas region, but particularly close to the Río Uruguay and its tributaries. The introduction of widespread cattle ranching was to prove devastating: the young seedlings were just as tasty as the grass and now only full grown 150-200 year old palms are to be found except in protected areas where seedlings and young specimens of less than 30 years old may be found. The palms grow in groves or *palmares* and the trunks may reach 12m in height with the fronds or leaves some 2m in length.

Jane Norwich

Yatay Palms

Parque Nacional El Palmar

(map labels)
To Concordia
N
Arroyo Ubalay
Arroyo Los Loros
Entrance
Visitors' Centre
URUGUAY
Arroyo El Palmar
Río Uruguay
Arroyo El Espina
Route 14
To Colón & Buenos Aires
83

high, some of which are hundreds of years old. Along the Río Uruguay and the streams (*arroyos*) which flow into it, there are gallery forests of subtropical trees and shrubs. There are also Indian tombs; on the edge of the Río Uruguay there are beaches and the remains of an 18th century quarry and port. Fauna includes capybaras, foxes, otters and vizcachas as well as rheas, monk parakeets and several species of woodpecker. It is best to stay overnight as wildlife is more easily seen in the early morning or at sunset. Very popular at weekends in summer.

● **Access** Buses from Colón, 40 minutes, US$2.50, will drop you at the entrance and it is easy to hitch the last 6 km to the park administration. Entry US$5.

● **Services** The administration centre is in the east of the park, near the Río Uruguay. Nearby there are camping facilities (US$6 per person, electricity, hot water) with restaurant opposite, and a small shop. There is a small hotel 8 km north of the Park

CONCORDIA

(*Population* 93,800; *Phone code* 045) 104 km north of Colón, lies a little downriver from Salto, Uruguay. Founded in 1832, Concordia soon became the most prosperous Argentine city on the Río Uruguay. At Salto Grande, 18 km north, there is a large Argentine-Uruguayan hydro-electric dam, which creates an artificial lake, 80,000 hectares, with excellent fishing. The dam provides a crossing to the city of Salto, Uruguay. Above Salto Grande the river is generally known as the Alto Uruguay.

Places of interest

South west of the main **Plaza 25 de Mayo** is the Cathedral (1899). In the streets around the plaza there are some fine buildings, notably the French-style **Palacio Arruabarrena**, seven blocks north west on Plaza Urquiza. 5 km northeast is **Parque Rivadavia**, 70 hectares of gentle hills and woodlands, in the centre of which are the ruins of the **Palacio San Carlos**. In 1888, 2 years after his arrival in Concordia, the Conde Eduardo de Machy, son of a French banker, bought the lands of the Parque Rivadavia from the descendents of the Urquiza family. After ordering the

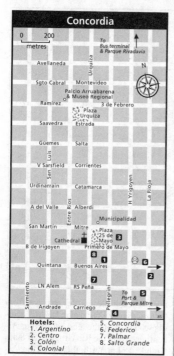

Concordia

0   200
metres

To Bus terminal & Parque Rivadavia

Avellaneda

Urquiza

Sgto Cabral   Montevideo

Palcio Arruabarena & Museo Regional

Ramírez   3 de Febrero

Plaza Urquiza

Saavedra   Estrada

Güemes   Salta

San Luis

V Sarsfield   Corrientes

Urdinarrain   Catamarca

H Yrigoyen

La Rioja

A del Valle   Alberdi

Entre Ríos

San Martín   Mitre   Municipalidad

Plaza 25 de Mayo

Cathedral   3

B de Irigoyen   Primero de Mayo

8

Quintana   Buenos Aires   6

LN Alem   RS Peña   7

2

Sarmiento

Pellegrini

Andrade   Carriego

To Port & Parque Mitre   5

4

Hotels:
1. Argentino
2. Centro
3. Colón
4. Colonial
5. Concordia
6. Federico
7. Palmar
8. Salto Grande

building of a mansion, he set up factories producing jams and ice, bringing in the best machinery from Europe and employing over 700 building workers. 3 years later, in 1891, the Count left for Europe, never to return. The factories and the *palacio* were sold several times, before being burned down in 1938. The park offers good views of the river and there is also a motor-racing track. Take bus No 2, one block from Plaza 25 de Mayo, to corner of Avenida Justo and Avenida Salto Uruguay, from where entrance is one block north.

Museums

Museo Regional, Plaza Urquiza, in the Palacio Arruabarrena, local and natural history collections, open 0800-2100 daily, entry free.

Local Festivals

Fiesta Nacional de la Pesca de la Boga, a fishing festival, 3rd week in January. Fiesta Nacional de Citricultura (citrus fruit festival), December, includes crowning of the national citrus fruit queen.

Local information
● Accommodation

A1 *Salto Grande*, Urquiza 581, T/F 210034, with breakfast, comfortable; **A2** *Palmar*, Urquiza 521, T 216050, F 215020, bright, comfortable, also **B** in older part, with breakfast; **A3** *San Carlos*, Parque Rivadavia, T 216725; **A3** *Federico 1°*, 1° de Mayo 248, T 213323, with fan; **A3** *Centro*, La Rioja y Buenos Aires, T 217776, F 217746, air conditioning, comfortable, *comedor*.

Budget accommodation B *Colón*, Pellegrini 611, T 215510, fan, attractive but run down, poor beds; **B** *Embajador*, San Lorenzo 75, T 213018, near bus terminal, neat; **C** *Argentino*, Pellegrini 560, T 215767, with bath, old fashioned, nice patio; **C** *Central*, 1° de Mayo 148, T 212842, reasonable, but shared bathrooms not too clean; **C** *Colonial*, Pellegrini 443, T 221448, without breakfast, fan, pleasant; **C** *Concordia*, La Rioja 518, T 216869, with fan, good; **C** *Victoria*, Urquiza y San Lorenzo, two blocks from terminal, recommended.

Camping *La Posada de Suárez – Club Viajantes* on Avenida Costanera south of Parque Mitre, warmly recommended, with good *parrillada* alongside, but beware the cats; also site in Parque Rivadavia. North of the city near Salto Grande are: *La Tortuga Alegre*, Km 14, T 211340, with restaurant, store; *Las Palmeras*, Km 18, T 218359; *Punta Viracho*, Km 18.

● Places to eat

La Estancia, Plaza 25 de Mayo, good value; *Comedor Las Dos Naciones*, Plaza 25 de Mayo y Avenida 1° de Mayo, good, moderate prices, large portions; *Mafalda*, corner of Plaza Urquiza and Entre Ríos, very good home made ice cream and cakes.

● Banks & money changers

Banco Río de la Plata, on plaza, no commission on Visa advances; Casa Julio, 1 de Mayo, half a block from plaza; Casa Chaca, on plaza; Tourfé on Mitre.

● Post & telecommunications

Post Office: La Rioja y Buenos Aires.

Telephone: San Luis 700 block, open 24 hours.

Internet: Dampermic, Sarmiento 55, US$8 per hour.

● Tourist offices

Plaza 25 de Mayo, open 0700-2400 daily.

● **Transport**

Buses Terminal at Justo y Yrigoyen, 13 blocks north west of Plaza 25 de Mayo, which is reached by No 2 bus. To **Buenos Aires**, 6 daily, US$17, 6½ hours; to **Córdoba**, US$25, Expreso Singer, at 2200 and 0300, 9 hours; to **Paraná** 5 a day, to **Posadas** at 1800 and 2300, Expreso Singer (8½ hours, US$32), to **Iguazú** at 1810, 13½ hours, to **Corrientes** US$11; to **La Paz** (Entre Ríos) – see page 303, 1100, US$10.50, 8 hours; to **Paso de los Libres** direct, El Recreo 1500 Monday, Saturday and several at 0300, US$11, 3½ hours.

Ferry to Uruguay: passenger service to Salto operated directly by Sancristobal and Río Lago, US$3-4, 5 departures Monday-Friday, 4 departures Saturday, 2 departures (0800 1800) Sunday, 20 minutes, tickets obtainable at a small kiosk, which shuts 15 minutes before departure, outside building marked 'Resguardo'. To reach port take No 4 bus from terminal marked 'Puerto'.

FRONTIER WITH URUGUAY: SALTO GRANDE

Bus service via Salto Grande dam, Flecha Bus and Chadre 2 a day each, US$3, all formalities on Argentine side, passports checked on bus. **Bicycles**: note that cycles are not allowed to cross the international bridge but officials will help cyclists find a lift.

INTO URUGUAY: SALTO

(*Population* 80,000) Situated on the east bank of the Río Uruguay, 13 km south of Salto Grande and 39 km by road from Concordia, Salto is a centre for cultivating and processing citrus fruit. The town's commercial area is on Calle Uruguay, between Plazas Artigas and Treinta y Tres. The port is on Calle Brasil. See the beautiful but run down **Parque Solari** (on Ruta Gral Artigas, northeast of the centre) and the **Parque Harriague** (south of the centre) with an open air theatre and a zoo (free, closed Monday, seven blocks from centre, feeding time 1400-1500).

Museums Museo de Bellas Artes, in the French style mansion of a rich *estanciero*, Uruguay 1067, opens at 1400, well worth a visit. **Museo de Historia Natural**, Zorrilla de San Martín y Brasil. Nearby is the **Museo de Tecnología** in the old Mercado Central.

Excursions To the **Salto Grande** dam and hydroelectric plant; a tour can be arranged with the tourist office, US$5, minimum 5 people, every 30 minutes, 0700-1400.

To the **Salto Chico**, south of Salto Grande, where there is a beach, fishing, camping. Reached by launch. Nearby is the resort of Salto Chico.(**A1** *Hotel Horacio Quiroga*, T 34411, sports facilities, staffed by nearby catering school).

Local festivals Shrove Tuesday carnival.

● **Accommodation** Hotels include: **A3** *Gran Salto*, 25 de Agosto 5, T 34333, with breakfast, best, air conditioning, recommended, good restaurant, reasonably priced; **A3** *Los Cedros*, Uruguay 657, T 33984, with breakfast, air conditioning, comfortable; **B** *Argentina*, Uruguay 892, T 29931, with breakfast, air conditioning, cafetería, comfortable; **B** *Biasetti*, San Martín 94, T 32141, old-fashioned, large rooms; **C** *Artigas Plaza*, Artigas 1146, T 34824, run down, log fire in winter, some rooms without windows; **C** *Plaza*, Plaza Treinta y Tres, T 33744, simple, old-fashioned; **D** *Pensión 33*, Treinta y Tres 269, basic, central. **Youth hostels** *Club Remeros de Salto*, Rambla Gutiérrez y Belén (by the river) T 33418, open all year, friendly, no cooking facilities, pool (US$5 per day), US$5, US$6.50 without IYHA card; *Club de Leones*, Uruguay 1626, need a student to sign you in.

● **Places to eat** *Pizzería Las Mil y Una*, Uruguay 906, popular, good atmosphere; *Don Diego*, Chiazzaro 20, pasta; *Club de Uruguay*, Uruguay 754, good breakfast and good value meals.

● **Banks & money changers** Banco Pan de Azúcar does cash advances on Visa and Mastercard; Banco de Crédito, Mastercard only; both on Calle Uruguay. Several Casas de Cambio on same street.

● **Embassies & consulates** Argentina, Artigas 1162, T 32931, open Monday-Friday 1300-1700.

● **Post & telecommunications Post Office**: Treinta y Tres y Artigas.

● **Tourist offices** Uruguay 1052, T 4096, open 0800-2000, Sunday 0800-1200, free map.

● **Transport Air** To Montevideo, Aviasur, US$80 return. Bus to airport, US$2. **Buses** Terminal 6 blocks south of centre at Latorre y Larrañaga. To **Montevideo**, 7½ hours, 4 a day, US$20, TTN good service, also El Norteño, Núñez and Chadre; to **Termas del Arapey**, 2 hours, daily, US$5.25. **Paysandú** US$5, 2 hours, 6 a day; to **Bella Unión**, 2 hours, US$6,

6 a day; to **Colonia**, Chadre, 0555, 1555, 8 hours, US$18.75; to **Fray Bentos**, same times, US$10.

Not far from Salto are three sets of **hot springs**: at **Fuente Salto**, 6 km north of the city, there are medicinal springs. **Termas del Daymán**, 10 km south, beautifully laid out with eight swimming pools (**entrance**: US$0.35, towel US$0.50, locker US$0.10; it is cheaper to buy combined bus/entrance ticket in Salto). **Bus** No 4 every 30 minutes from Artigas, US$0.15. **Termas del Arapey**, 96 km northeast of Salto, lie on the Río Arapey south of Isla Cabellos (Baltazar Brum). The waters at these famous thermal baths (five pools) contain bicarbonated salts, calcium and magnesium. Both Daymán and Arapey have hotels (full details from the tourist office, or in the *South American Handbook*).

NORTH OF CONCORDIA

Route 14 continues north, inland from the giant Salto Grande lake, and then runs northwest following the west bank of the Río Alto Uruguay. Above Monte Caseros and Bella Unión, the river forms the boundary between Argentina and Brazil.

MONTE CASEROS

(*Population* 19,600) 240 km north of Concordia, is a small port near the confluence of Ríos Quarem and Alto Uruguay. On the opposite bank of the Alto Uruguay is the Uruguayan town of Bella Unión, on the Brazilian border.

- **Accommodation** *Paterlini*, Colón y Salta, T 219; *Conte*, Salta 463; *Cortez*, 2 de Febrero 1663.
- **Ferry** Regular lauches cross to Bella Unión.

INTO URUGUAY: BELLA UNION

(*Population* 12,000) Situated just south of the frontier between Uruguay and Brazil, Bella Unión lies 144 km north of Salto. The Brazilian frontier is crossed by the Barra del Cuaraim bridge.

- **Accommodation** 3 hotels and a campsite in the Parque Fructuoso Rivera (T 0642-2261), insect repellent needed.
- **Consulate** Brazil, Lirio Moraes 62, T 54.

- **Buses** to **Salto**, US$6, 2 hours; to **Montevideo**, US$26.15, El Norteño, Chadre. Buses to Barra del Cuareim (the 'town') leave every 30 minutes, US$0.60, from Plaza 25 de Agosto.

PASO DE LOS LIBRES

(*Population* 34,000) lies 96 km north of Monte Caseros; on the opposite bank is the larger Brazilian town of Uruguaiana: a bridge joins the two. Paso de los Libres was founded in 1843 by General Madariaga; it was here that he crossed the river from Brazil with his 100 men and annexed Corrientes province for Argentina.

Local festivals Colourful carnival celebrations.

- **Accommodation A3** *Alejandro I*, Coronel López 502, T 24100, pool, cable TV, best; **C** *Uruguay*, Uruguay 1252, T 25672, not clean but friendly, good *comedor*; opposite is **C** *26 de Febrero*. Near terminal are **C** *Capri*, T 24126, with bath, and several others. **Camping** Camping Municipal, near the international bridge in a park with views over the river and Uruguaiana; also nearby at Laguna Mansa.
- **Tourist offices** Near Argentine customs office at end of the bridge.
- **Transport Air** Líneas Aéreas Entre Ríos (LAER) to **Buenos Aires**, **Paraná**, **Gualeguaychú**, and **Concordia**, very low fares. **Buses** Terminal 1 km south of town centre, on road to the frontier. To **Buenos Aires**, US$25.

FRONTIER WITH BRAZIL: PASO DE LOS LIBRES

The international bridge, 1.5 km long, lies 2 km south of the centre of Paso de los Libres.

- **Customs & immigration**
Argentine and Brazilian formalities are carried out at opposite ends of the bridge. Exchange and information are available in the same building as Brazilian immigration (exchange rates are better in Uruguaiana than at the border).

- **Transport**
Minibuses run between Paso de los Libres and the bridge, US$0.60. Buses run between the town centres and bus terminals, every 30 minutes, but do not wait at immigration posts and bus tickets are not transferable. No bus service on Sunday – taxi charges US$20.

INTO BRAZIL: URUGUAIANA

(*Population* 117,460), just over the international bridge on the east bank of the Río

Uruguay, is an agro-industrial city serving western Río Grande do Sul.

- **Accommodation A1** *Hotel Glória*, Rua Domingos de Almeida 1951, T 412-4422, good; **D** *Palace*, Praça Rio Branco, without breakfast. *Fares Turis Hotel*, Pres Vargas 2939, T/F 412-3358, may let you leave your bags while you look around town.

- **Buses To Uruguay**, Planalto buses run from Uruguaiana via Barra do Quaraí/Bella Unión (US$4.50) to Salto and Paysandú.

YAPEYU

(*Population* 1,200) 58 km north west of Paso de los Libres, is the site of a Jesuit mission (1626) little of which remains. It is famous as the birthplace of the liberator, José de San Martín. Part of the house where he was born is preserved as a museum. There is also an interesting Jesuit Museum.

- **Accommodation B** *San Martín*, next to the *Municipalidad*, T 93120; camping by the river; **B** *Bungalows*, near river, *cabañas*, good; the Carillo family on the main plaza rent rooms, **E**, good.

BUENOS AIRES TO PARAGUAY: THE RIOS PARANA AND PARAGUAY

The Río Paraná is formed by the rivers Paranahyba and Grande which rise in Brazil. From their confluence the Paraná flows 2,570 km before entering the Río de la Plata: its total length is 3,470 km and it drains an area of 1,510,000 square km. Its major tributary, the Río Paraguay, which flows south from central Brazil across the Pantanal, drains an area of 1,095,000 sq km. Slow-moving due to its low gradient, the river is braided south for the 440 km south from Diamante to the outskirts of Buenos Aires. The only long-distance passenger services up the Río Paraná from Buenos Aires are to Asunción, Paraguay.

BUENOS AIRES TO ROSARIO

Route 9 heads north west out of the capital and runs north west along the west bank of the Paraná to Rosario.

RESERVA NATURAL OTAMENDI

Situated off Route 9 at Km 68, this reserve covers 2,600 hectares on the banks of the

Río Paraná. Vegetation varies from medium-sized trees such as willows, *ceibos* and alders to areas of tall grasses. Parts of the reserve are regularly flooded; here there are rushes, tussock grass and white grass. Fauna include the thick-tailed opossum, the capybara and the marsh-deer. Over 240 species of birds have been identified, including two banded warblers, rufous-capped antshrikes, rushbirds, rush-tyrants, coots, ducks and swans. A trail leads from the Administration Centre to an observation sight which offers extensive views over the floodplains.

ZARATE

(*Population* 77,000; *Phone code* 0328), Km 90, an industrial centre with large *frigoríficos* and paper works on the west bank.

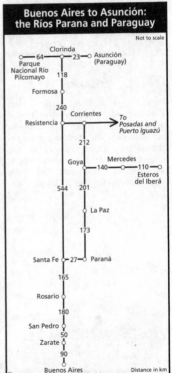

Buenos Aires to Asunción: the Ríos Parana and Paraguay

Not to scale

Clorinda — 64 — ○ — 23 — ○ Asunción (Paraguay)

Parque Nacional Río Pilcomayo — 118

Formosa

240

Resistencia — ○ Corrientes → *To Posadas and Puerto Iguazú*

212

Goya — ○ Mercedes — 140 — ○ — 110 — ○ Esteros del Iberá

544 — 201

La Paz

173

Santa Fe — ○ 27 — ○ Paraná

165

Rosario ○

180

San Pedro ○

50

Zarate ○

90

Buenos Aires ○

Distance in km

Route 14 branches off here and runs north across the Zarate and Brazo Largo bridges.

● **Accommodation B** *San Martín*, Ameghino 773, T 22713. **Camping** Several sites over the Zarate bridge on Isla Talavera including *Camping Club La Isla*.

● **Places to eat** *Restaurant La Posta de Correa*, cheap, good service. Along the waterfront are many *parrillas* and restaurants.

● **Buses** From Buenos Aires (Plaza Once) US$3, every 30 minutes.

SAN PEDRO

(*Population* 35,500) 50 km further north west on the edge of the Laguna San Pedro, this is the most attractive town on this part of the Paraná. The town is centred on Plaza Constitución, in the centre of which is the **Iglesia de Nuestra Señora del Socorro** (1872). On the corner of the plaza, in the Municipalidad, is the **Museo Histórico Regional**.

● **Accommodation** *Turismo*, Boulevard Paraná 450, T 25459, 3-star; *Obligado*, Mitre 425, T 24225, 3-star. **Camping** Many sites along the edge of the laguna.

ROSARIO

(*Population* 1 million; *Altitude* 24m; *Phone code* 041), 320 km north of Buenos Aires, is the third largest city in Argentina and one of the most important industrial and export centres in the country. Rarely visited by travellers, it has a lively cultural scene and is the home of many popular rock musicians

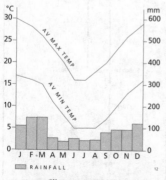

Climate: Rosario

and modern artists. It has a racecourse, two boat clubs and a golf club.

Routes from Buenos Aires

There are two routes: the best is by Route 8 (marked Córdoba) to Pergamino, and then, following signs, by Route 188, and then 178 to Rosario. This is better than lorry-packed Route 9.

Climate

From October to early March it is warm, and from December to the end of February uncomfortably hot. Changes of temperature are sudden.

History

Unlike most Spanish American cities, Rosario was never officially founded. Though a fort was established in 1689 by Luis Romero de Pineda, it remained little more than a port for the export of mules and tobacco throughout the 18th century. The opening of a railway line connecting the port with Córdoba in 1870 and the growth of shipping along the Paraná led to its sudden growth in the late 19th century: its port became a major exporter of grain and beef, while new industries were established, including metal-working, breweries, grain mills, textiles, leather industries and chemical works. By the 1920s it was being compared with Chicago as a major grain-exporting centre with a large immigrant population from Italy.

Places of interest

The old city centres on the Plaza 25 de Mayo. Around it are the **Cathedral**, in somewhat eclectic style and containing the Virgen of Rosario, and the **Palacio Municipal**. One block east is the **Monumento de la Bandera**, an imposing and austere memorial built between 1930 and 1955 on the site in which General Belgrano who raised the Argentine flag for the first time. The tower, 75m high, reached by lift (US$0.50), offers the best available views over the city, the river and its islands. Below is the Sala de las Banderas, containing the flags of all the American states (except Canada).

The demolition of the old railway and warehouse facilities along the river has

The golden age of Rosario

🏖️ At the height of its prosperity (1880-1950), Rosario became a city noted for its French and Italian-inspired architecture. Sadly, serious damage was done in the 1970s as some of the finest buildings were demolished and replaced by ugly 10 and 12 storey tower blocks, destroying the harmony and uniformity of the streets and replacing it with a untidy and irregular appearance.

Interesting examples of its former glory remain however. Some of the mansions of the rich can be seen along Boulevard Oroño, one of the finest avenues in the city. The stretch of Calle Córdoba which runs from Boulevard Oroño to Avenida San Martín has been titled the **Paseo del Siglo**; plaques (in Spanish) identify some of the most important surviving buildings. Note particularly the Victoria shopping mall, Córdoba y San Martín, and the Falabella store, Córdoba y Sarmiento, which occupies the former La Favorita building, once the great department store of Rosario. Further west, at Córdoba y Corrientes, is the Bolsa de Comercio (stock exchange); opposite is La Fénix, the former mansion of one of the cities grain exporting barons. See the Paseo del Siglo at night, when it is a very popular spot especially at weekends.

opened up this area. South of the Monumento de La Bandera is is the **Parque Urquiza**, with sports facilities. Further north, at the foot of the monument, is the **Parque de la Bandera**, beyond which is the **Parque de España**, a modern development which incorporates the old railway arches as an exhibition centre (Tuesday-Sunday 1500-2000, US$1) and offers fine views over the Río Paraná. Further north is the bar *Aux de Magaux*, a good spot for resting and watching passing boats. Beyond, another park is under construction.

Boulevard Oroño runs southwest to the **Parque Independencia**, 126 hectares, with lakes and monumental gardens and several museums (see below).

Museums
Museo Histórico Provincial, Parque Independencia, Monday-Friday 0900-1230, 1400-1730, Saturday/Sunday 1500-1800.

Museo de Bellas Artes J B Castagnino, Pellegrini 2202, just outside the Parque Indepdendencia. Houses a large collection of European paintings, particularly French impressionist, Italian barroque and Flemish works as well as individual works by El Greco and Goya and one of best collections of Argentine paintings. Tuesday-Saturday 1200-2000, Sunday 1000-2000.

Museo de la Ciudad, Parque Independencia, Tuesday-Friday 1000-1300, Saturday/Sunday 1600-1900.

Centro Cultural Bernardino Rivadavia, San Martín 1080, 0800-2000 daily, free, contemporary art, also cinema, theatre.

Museo de Arte Decorativo Firma y Odilio Estévez, Santa Fe 748, former private collection including 16th century Flemish tapestries, silverware from 18th century Potosi and pre-Columbian ceramics from Peru as well as a replica of Titian's famous portrait of Philip II. Few explantions, all in Spanish. Thursday-Sunday 1500-2000.

Museo Provincial de Ciencias Naturales, Moreno 750, Tuesday-Friday 0900-1200, Saturday-Sunday 1500-1800

Museo del Paraná y Sus Islas, Belgrano y La Rioja. Monday, Tuesday, Thursday 0900-1100, Sunday 1600-1900.

Excursions
To **Balneario La Florida**, about 8 km north, where there is a beach, swimming.

To the **islands in the Río Paraná**. Launches run regularly every 15 minutes in summer, less frequently off season, summer US$2 return winter US$1 return. The islands can also be visited at weekends on board the *Ciudad de Rosario*, which leaves the Estación Fluvial near

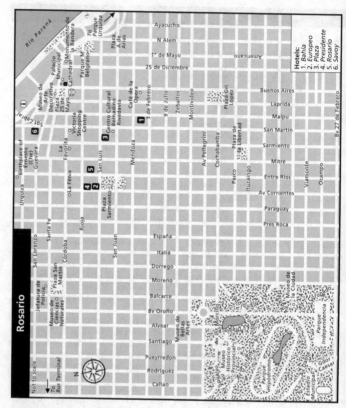

Rosario

the Monumento de la Bandera, Saturday/Sunday 1400, 1630, also Sunday 1000.

To the **Estancia La Margarita**, near Victoria, on the opposite bank of the Río Paraná, T 0436-22159, F 0435-21623, accommodation (**L3** pp), homemade food, horseriding, fishing, watersports, beautiful surroundings, recommended.

To **San Lorenzo** (*population* 38,000), 28 km north, the site of one of the largest chemical works in Argentina. In the centre near the river is the restored former Franciscan monastery **of San Carlos de Borromeo**. Nearby is the **Campo de la Gloria**, site of the battle of San Lorenzo (3 February 1813), at which, Spanish troops disembarking from their boats, were attacked and routed by San Martín's forces, who had been concealed behind the monastery. The monastery, built in 1780 and used as a hospital during the battle, is now a museum: visitors can see the room used by San Martín as well as a pine tree grown from a cutting of the tree under which the Liberator rested after the battle. The chapel contains paintings and sulptures from the 17th and 18th centuries.

Local holidays

Fiesta de las Colectividades, first 2 weeks of November, with music, dance and food in front of the Monumento de la Bandera. In the second week of September the Sociedad Rural hosts a large fair.

Ernesto 'Che' Guevara

Rosario is strangely coy about its links with Guevara, one of the most famous Latin Americans of the 20th century, perhaps because his parents soon moved with their asthmatic child to the healthier climate of the Sierras de Córdoba. The future revolutionary was born in 1928 in a house at Entre Ríos y Urquiza into a middle class family.

After attending medical school in Buenos Aires, he travelled through Latin America in 1952-1953: the diaries of part of this trip were published recently in English. In Mexico he joined Fidel Castro's small band of men who landed in Cuba in 1956 and overthrew the dictator, Batista. Though, as head of the Cuban Central Bank, he played an important role in implementing the economic policies of the new government, Guevara became more famous for his support for revolution elsewhere in Latin America. In his book, 'Guerrilla Warfare' (1960) he offered a practical guide for hopeful revolutionaries, advocating the use of guerrilla warfare to overthrow governments. His attempt to lead a guerrilla campaign in Bolivia, intended to spark off a revolution throughout the continent, led to his death in 1967. Lacking support from local people, his small force wandered the steep valleys of eastern Bolivia for several months before being ambushed by Bolivian troops. Guevara was executed and buried in an unmarked grave; his body was exhumed and returned to Cuba in 1997.

His early death confirmed his status as the revolutionary poster and T-shirt image of the 1960s and continued to inspire would-be revolutionaries in Latin America in the 1970s. In the very different circumstances of the 1990s his life and views have attracted renewed interest in his native country.

Local information
● Accommodation

Hotel prices

L1	over US$200	L2	US$151-200
L3	US$101-150	A1	US$81-100
A2	US$61-80	A3	US$46-60
B	US$31-45	C	US$21-30
D	US$12-20	E	US$7-11
F	US$4-6	G	up to US$3

Unless otherwise stated, all hotels in range **D** and above have private bath. Assume friendliness and cleanliness in all cases.

A1 *La Paz*, Barón de Mauá 36, T 210905, quiet, recommended; **A1** *Presidente*, Corrientes 919, T 242854, good; **A1** *Plaza*, Barón de Mauá 26, T 47097; **A1** *Riviera*, San Lorenzo 1460, T 252058, air conditioning; **A2** *Europeo*, San Luís 1364, T 240382, with breakfast, modern; **A3** *Benidorm*, San Juan 1049, T 219368, with breakfast, central, overpriced; **B** *Colonial*, Maipú y Zeballos, T 219041, with breakfast; **B** *Rosario*, Corrientes 900, T 242170, with breakfast, parking, large rooms, good beds.

Budget accommodation: **C** *Río*, Rivadavia 2665, T 396421, pleasant; **C** *Normandie*, Mitre 1030, T 212694, helpful, central; **D** pp *Bahía*, Maipú 1262, T 217271, without breakfast, poor beds; **D** *Savoy*, San Lorenzo y San Martín, T 480071, built 1900 and retaining old-fashioned bathrooms, cheap restaurant, good value.

Around terminal: on Avenida Santa Fe: **B** *Micro*, No 3650, T 397192, uninspiring; **B** *América*, No 3746, T 386584, without breakfast, best value on this street; **B** *Casas*, No 3600, T 304717, without breakfast, air conditioning, pleasant, recommended; **B** *Confort*, No 3500, T 380486, poor beds; **B** *Embajador*, No 3554, T 384188, with breakfast, air conditioning extra, good; **B** *Nahuel*, No 3518,

Canallas and leprosos

Rosario is the home of two of Argentina's oldest and most famous football clubs: Rosario Central and Newell's Old Boys. Central, founded in 1889 by workers on the Central Argentine Railway, draw their support mainly from the north of the city. Newells, who were founded by ex-pupils of the Anglo-Argentine school led by the Englishman Isaac Newell, are supported mainly by the southern part of the city.

Rivalry between the two clubs is understandably intense and, if partly based on social class, is heavily influenced by tradition. At their peak Central won the championship 4 times, once fewer than Newell's. On Sundays the city divides in more ways than one: fans of Central head north to Lisandro de la Torre to watch their team, while Newell's fans go to their stadium in the Parque Independencia. Fans are easily distinguishable: Central wear blue and white, while Newell's wear red and black. Travellers should perhaps exercise care in using the nicknames commonly used: Central are known as the *canallas* (politely translated as 'rabble') while Newell's are less than affectionately known as *leprosos* or lepers.

T/F 397292, with breakfast, gloomy, modern; **B** *Le Nid*, Iriondo 660, T 388762, without breakfast, air conditioning, modern, pleasant, recommended.

Camping At Balneario La Florida, 8 km north.

● **Places to eat**
Don Rodrigo, Sante Fe 968, and *Fénix*, Santa Fe next to Citibank, are both very good; *La China*, Santa Fe 1882, US$5 *tenedor libre*; *Gaucho*, Roca 725, churrasquería; *Capote*, Corrientes y Urquiza; *Mamacita*, 9 de Julio 2246, Mexican; *Vegetariano*, Mitre 710; *Casa Uruguaya*, Alvear 1125 (T 69320), away from centre, good; *Marialronn*, Santa Fe y Pres Roca, recommended for dancing. Excellent quality and value meals at the supermarket at Tucumán y Corrientes. Along the river are good cheap restaurants and fishing club barbecues, good atmosphere. Several parrillas and ice-cream parlours along Pellegrini.

● **Airline offices**
Aerolíneas Argentinas, Santa Fe 1410.

● **Banks & money changers**
Lloyds Bank (BLSA), La Rioja 1205; Citibank, Santa Fe 1101; **First National Bank of Boston**, Córdoba y Mitre. Open 1000-1600. Most banks charge 2% commission on cheques and cash. Amex, Grupo 3 de Turismo, Córdoba 1147, T 244415. Casas de Cambio: Transatlántica, Córdoba 992; Exprinter, Córdoba 960; Carey, Corrientes 802; Carbatur, Corrientes 840.

● **Entertainment**
Bars: *Café de la Opera*, Mendoza y Laprida, next to *Teatro El Círculo*, cabaret, live music, highly recommended, friendly; *La Puerta*, Entre Ríos 639, *La Nuestra*, San Luis y Rosas; *Berlín*, Pasaje Zabala (Sarmiento 300); *Pasaporte*, Maipú 509, very good.

Several good bars along the *Paseo del Siglo* (Córdoba 1600 to 1800) and nearby including *Miscelánea*, Roca 755; *Play Off*, Santa Fe y Roca, as well as on Tucumán 800 to 1,000 blocks in the El Bajo district.

Discoteques: *L'Infierno*, Córdoba 2300; *María*, Santa Fe y Roca.

● **Laundry**
Santa Fe 1578.

● **Post & telecommunications**
Post Office: Córdoba y Buenos Aires.

Telecommunications: San Luis, between San Martín and Maipú.

● **Shopping**
Main shopping street is the pedestrianised Avenida Córdoba. There is a handicrafts fair in front of the tourist office, Saturday and Sunday from 1500.

Bookshop: *Stratford*, Mitre 726, for imported English books.

● **Tourist offices**
ETUR, Belgrano y Buenos Aires, T 802230/1, 0800-2000 daily, helpful, maps, English spoken.

● **Useful addresses**
Scrivanti, Corrientes 653, 6th floor, T 253738, for budget travel information.

● **Transport**
Air Fisherton airport, 8 km west of centre. Minibus operated by Transportes Ayolas, Dean Funes 1525, T 839863, connects with flights, US$4, to and from hotels and AR office. Taxi or *remise* US$10. Several flights daily to **Buenos Aires** with Aerolíneas Argentinas and Austral; Andesmar to **Córdoba** and **Mendoza**; Southern Winds to **Córdoba**, **Tucumán**, **Salta**, **Neuquén**, **Bariloche** and **Mar del Plata**.

Buses Terminal at Santa Fe y Caferatta, about 25 blocks west of the *Monumento de la Bandera*. Bus to centre 115, 119, US$0.50, taxi US$4. Terminal has post office, shops and restaurants. To **Buenos Aires**, Chevallier hourly, US$20-22, 3-4 hours, also Ablo, General Urquiza, La Unión; to **Córdoba**, 6½ hours, US$18, several companies; to **Santa Fe**, US$10; to **Mendoza**, US$30, 10 hours; to **mar del Plata**, TIRSA, US$47, 12 hours; to **Bariloche**, TIRSA, US$97, 24 hours; to **Puerto Iguazú**, US$50.

Trains The Buenos Aires-Tucumán service stops in Rosario; to Tucuman, US$15, 13 hours, Monday and Friday.

Ferry To Victoria, on the east bank of the Río Paraná, which has a municipal campsite.

SANTA FE

(*Population* 350,000; *Altitude* 26m; *Phone code* 042), 165 km north of Rosario, lies near the confluence of the Ríos Santa Fe and Salado in a low-lying area with lagoons and islands just west of the Río Paraná. The city is capital of its province and the centre of a very fertile region. Founded by settlers from Asunción in 1573 and transferred to its present site in 1660, it was, in the colonial period, one of the main centres of Jesuit and Franciscan influence in the country and an important port on the voyage between Buenos Aires and Asunción. After independence it suffered badly from the struggles between provincial *caudillos*.

Places of interest

The southern part of the city, around the **Plaza 25 de Mayo** is the historic centre.

Santa Fe: cradle of the constitution

Santa Fe calls itself the "Cradle of the Constitution" and the "city of conventions". It was here that the constitution of 1853 was drafted; though replaced by Perón in 1949, and abused, suspended and broken at will by military governments, it is still in force. Conventions to consider reforms to the constitution have also met in the city, in 1860, 1866, 1957 and 1994.

On the Plaza itself is the **Cathedral**, dating from 1751 but remodelled in 1834, with its twin towers capped by blue cupolas. On the east side is **Iglesia de Nuestra Señora de los Milagros**, dating from 1694, richly decorated with an ornate dome. Next door is the **Colegio de la Inmaculada Concepción**, established by the Jesuits. On the northern side is the majestic **Casa de Gobierno**, built in 1908 in French-style on the site of the historic Cabildo in which the 1853 constitution was drafted.

One block south of the plaza is the **Iglesia y Convento de San Francisco** built in 1680. The church has walls nearly 2m thick and fine wooden ceilings, built from timber floated down the river from Paraguay, carved by indigenous craftsmen and fitted without the use of nails. Inside are the remains of Estanislao López (see below). The pulpit and altar are 17th century baroque. A block west of the Plaza at 3 de Febrero y 9 de Julio is the **Iglesia de Nuestra Señora del Rosario**, part of the 19th **Convento de Santo Domingo**, which has a fine patio and museum; north of the centre at Javier de la Rosa 623, is the modern neo-gothic style **Iglesia de Nuestra Señora de Guadalupe**, with attractive stained glass windows (open daily 0730-2000, bus 4 from the centre, 20 minutes).

Museums

Museo de San Francisco, in the Convent (see above) includes a reconstruction with wax figures of the Consitutent Congress of 1852-1853, daily 1000-1200, 1500-1800.

Museo Histórico Provincial, 3 de Febrero y San Martín, in a building dating from 1680 (one of the oldest surviving civil buildings in the country), includes pieces from the former Jesuit mission of San Javier, as well as artefacts associated with the dictator Rosas and with Urquiza, who overthrew him. There are portraits of both men and of Estanislao López, Rosas's ally who ruled Santa Fe, Tuesday-Friday 0830-1230, 1430-1900, Saturday/Sunday 1500-1800.

Museo Etnográfico y Colonial, 3 de Febrero y 25 de Mayo, includes large collection of artefacts from Santa Fe La

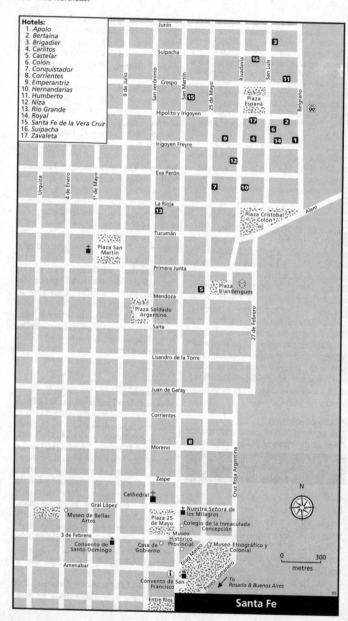

Hotels:
1. *Apolo*
2. *Bertaina*
3. *Brigadier*
4. *Carlitos*
5. *Castelar*
6. *Colón*
7. *Conquistador*
8. *Corrientes*
9. *Emperantriz*
10. *Hernandarias*
11. *Humberto*
12. *Niza*
13. *Río Grande*
14. *Royal*
15. *Santa Fe de la Vera Cruz*
16. *Suipacha*
17. *Zavaleta*

Santa Fe

Vieja (the original site of the city) and items from indigenous cultures in the Santa Fe area, Monday-Friday 0900-1200, 1530-1900, Saturday 1530-1830, Sunday 1000-1200, 1530-1830.

Museo de Bellas Artes, General López, Tuesday-Sunday 1730-2030, exhibitions of local artists' work.

Local holidays

30 September (San Jerónimo); 15 November (Foundation of City).

Local information
● **Accommodation**

A1 *Conquistador*, 25 de Mayo 2676, T/F 551195, sauna, pool, gym; **A2** *Río Grande*, San Gerónimo 2586, T 551025, modern, recommended; **A2** *Corrientes*, Corrientes 2520, T 592126, with breakfast, garage, restaurant, comfortable; **A2** *Hostal de Santa Fe de la Vera Cruz*, San Martín 2954, T 551740, best, genial, well-kept and run; **A3** *Castellar*, 25 de Mayo y Falucho, T 520141, air conditioning, parking; **A3** *Hernandarias*, Rivadavia 2680, T 529752, fan, gloomy; **A3** *Suipacha*, Suipacha 2375, T 521135, safe, recommended air conditioning, garage, pleasant; **B** *Niza*, Rivadavia 2755, T 522047, very nice, without breakfast, air conditioning; **B** *Emperatriz*, Irigoyen Freyre 2440, T 530061, pleasant, good value.

Near the terminal: **A3** *Bertaina*, H Yrigoyen 2255, T/F 553068 parking, air conditioning, good beds, well maintained; **A3** *Zavaleta*, H Yrigoyen 2349, T/F 551840, cafeteria, with breakfast; **B** *Colón*, San Luis 2862, T 545167, **D** without bath, pleasant, large rooms; **B-C** *Royal*, Irigoyen Freyre 2256, T 527359, OK, fan, gloomy; **C** *Apolo*, Belgrano 2821, T 527984, old fashioned, gloomy, poor beds, basic; **B** *Brigadier*, San Luis 3148, T 537387, two blocks from bus station, good, air conditioning, some English spoken, parking; **B-C** *Carlitos*, Irigoyen Freyre 2336, T 531541; **C** *Humberto*, Crespo 2222, T 550409, without breakfast, poor beds, basic.

Camping Several sites on the lakes and rivers outside town including: *Náutico Sur*, on the Río Santa Fe; *Luz y Fuerza*, 7 km north near Laguna Guadelupe; *Cámara del Hogar*, 4 km east on Route 168; *Túnel Subfluvial*, 300m before the Hernandarias tunnel to Paraná, 17 km east.

● **Places to eat**

Many good ones, offering excellent meals with good wine. *El Quincho de Chiquito*, Obispo Príncipe y Almirante Brown, excellent and good value, classic fish restaurant, huge helpings. Excellent grills including *surubí* (local fish) at

Gran Parrillada Rivadavia, Rivadavia 3299. *Surubí* also at *España*, San Martín 2644. *Baviera San Martín*, San Martín 2941, good salads; *Café de la Paix*, San Martín y Santiago del Estero.

● **Banks & money changers**

Lloyds Bank (BLSA), 25 de Mayo 2501, open 0715-1315; **Citibank**, San Martín 2609. **Amex** representative, *Vacaciones Felices*, San Martín 2347. **Casas de Cambio: Camsa**, 25 de Mayo 2466; **Carbatur**, San Martín 2520; **Tourfé**, San Martín 2901,Saturday 0830-1230, changes travellers' cheques.

● **Laundry**

Servi Rap, Rivadavia 2834 (open Saturday 0800-1300); *Laverap*, San Martín 1687.

● **Sports**

Swimming: on river at Guadalupe beach; local bus.

● **Tourist offices**

San Martín 2836 and at the bus terminal: maps, friendly.

● **Transport**

Air Airport at Sauce Viejo, 17 km south. Daily Aerolíneas Argentinas flights to Buenos Aires, T 599461.

Buses Terminal near the centre at Belgrano 2910. To **Córdoba**, US$18, 5 hours; to **Buenos Aires**,many companies, US$19-28; to **Paraná**, Etacer and Fluviales del Litoral, frequent US$2, 1 hour; to **Rosario** very frequent, 2½ hours by *autopista*, US$10; to **Mendoza** daily; to **Posadas**, 12 hours, US$30, several companies; to **Santiago del Estero/Tucumán** (2010); to **Concordia** 4½ hours, US$16.50; to **Asunción** (Paraguay), daily overnight, La Internacional US$31, común, US$57 diferencial.

The Route between Santa Fe and Paraná

The two cities do not face one another, but are 27 km apart and are separated by several islands, linked by bridges and the Hernandarias tunnel, 2.9 km long. From Santa Fe the route runs northeast crossing Laguna Guadeloupe onto Isla Crucesitas and then across the Río Colastine (Km 8) onto Isla Santa Candida. The tunnel is at Km 19, toll US$2 per car. Trucks with dangerous loads cross the river by a launch which also carries pedestrians and operates Monday-Saturday, 0600-2100, 20-minutes journey, frequency depending on demand from trucks.

PARANA

(*Population* 210,000; *Altitude* 63m; *Phone code* 043), capital of Entre Ríos province, is situated on the east bank of the Río Paraná, 495 km north of Buenos Aires. Although the area was populated long before, the city was founded in 1730 by settlers from Santa Fe. From 1853 to 1862 the city was capital of the Argentine Confederation.

Places of interest

The centre is situated on a hill offering fine views over the river and beyond to Santa Fe. Though nothing remains from the colonial period, there are many fine 19th and 20th century public buildings. In the centre is the **Plaza Primero de Mayo**, where there are fountains and a statue of San Martín. On the east side is the **Cathedral**, notable for its fine stained glass windows, its portico and its interior. Just around the corner from the cathedral is the **Colegio del Huerto**, seat of the Senate of the Argentine Confederation between 1853 and 1861. Also on the plaza are the **Municipalidad** (1890) and the **Club Social** (1906), for years the elite social centre of the city. Several blocks north of the plaza are the **Teatro 3 de Febrero** (1908), the **Casa de Gobierno** (1900), on the Plaza Carbo, which has a grand façade and the **Iglesia San Miguel** (1895) on Plaza Alvear.

The city's glory is **Parque Urquiza**, northwest of the centre. Extending over

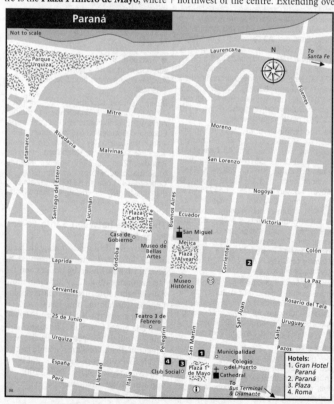

44 hectares and planted with lapachos, palos borrachos and pines, it has an enormous statue to General Urquiza, and a bas-relief showing the battle of Caseros, at which he finally defeated Rosas; also an open-air theatre. There are pleasant walks along the river bank and around the fishing port of **Puerto Sánchez**.

Museums
Museo de Bellas Artes, Buenos Aires 355. **Museo Histórico**, Buenos Aires y Laprida, including a fine collection of silverware, open Tuesday-Friday, 0700-1300, 1500-2000, Saturday, 0900-1200, 1600-1900 (winter), 1700-2000 (summer), Sunday, 0900-1200.

Excursions
To the **Parque Nacional Diamante**, 44 km south. Covering 2,458 hectares of marshland and riverine forest 6 km south of the town of Diamante, this new park is a good spot for birdwatching: over 140 species have been identified. Before visiting you must contact the *quardaparque* at H Yrigoyen 396, Diamante.

Local information
● **Accommodation**
There is a shortage of hotel space, especially at peak periods (Semana Santa and July), when the tourist office arranges accommodation with families. There is a greater selection of hotels – at lower prices – in Santa Fe.

A1 *Mayorazgo*, Etchevehere y Córdoba, on Costanera Alta, T 230333, 5-star, with fine view of park and river, has casino and swimming pool; **A2** *Paraná*, 9 de Julio 60, T 231700, with breakfast, pleasant; **A2** *Gran Hotel Paraná*, Urquiza 976, T 223900; **B** *Super Luxe*, Villaguay 162, T 232835.

Budget accommodation: **C** *Bristol*, Alsina 221, T 313961, close to the bus terminal, basic; **C** *Plaza*, San Martín 915, T 210720; **C** *Roma*, Urquiza 1069, with bath, basic, central.

Camping *Balneario Thompson*, just west of the tunnel; *Balneario Los Arenales*, east of the tunnel.

● **Laundry**
Laverap, Belgrano 650 and San Juan 273.

● **Tourist offices**
25 de Mayo 44.

● **Transport**
Air General Urquiza airport, 12 km south east of town.

Buses New terminal 1 km southeast of centre on Avenida Ramírez. East across Entre Ríos to **Concordia** on Río Uruguay, 5 a day, 5 hours. To **Buenos Aires**, US$22.

NORTH OF SANTA FE AND PARANA

Two roads lead north, one on either side of the Río Paraná. East of the river Route 12 runs from Paraná to Corrientes passing through small towns such as La Paz, Goya and Bella Vista while Route 11 runs to the west of the river through Reconquista to Resistencia.

La Paz
(*Population* 16,700; *Phone code* 0437), 173 km north of Paraná, is a small port in an area popular for fishing. It has a regional museum, riverside park and golf club.

● **Accommodation** Milton, Italia 1029, T 22232, 2-star; Res Plaza, San Martín 862, T 21208; others. **Camping** El Eucaliptal, information from España 1157, T 21496, F 21918, also cabins, sleep 4-6.

Goya
(*Population* 56,700; *Phone code* 0777), Km 374, is the second town of the Province of Corrientes, situated at the centre of a tobacco-growing region. There is a vehicle ferry across the river to **Reconquista** (*population* 34,800; several hotels). Further north still, at **Bella Vista** (*population*

Camilla

Though no traces remain of the house in which they lived, Goya provided refuge for two famous fugitives, whose story formed the basis of the film *Camilla* by Maria Luisa Bemberg. Camilla O'Gorman, the daughter of one of the most aristocratic families in Buenos Aires, eloped with a priest. Escaping the moral disapproval of Buenos Aires, they lived here incognito for several months, but were recognized, arrested and shot on the orders of Rosas. Their fate shocked many people who disapproved of their morals and contributed to the overthrow of the dictator.

21,000; campsite, no accommodation) river crossing is possible at the port 5 km away.

● **Accommodation In** Goya: *Cervantes*, Gómez 723, T/F 22864, 3-star; *Turismo*, Mitre 860, T/F 22926, 3-star; *Colón*, Colón 1077, T 22682, 1-star; several others. **Camping** Many sites including *Club Social y Deportivo*, on road to port, T 22735.

Mercedes

(*Population* 20,750), 140 km east of Goya, is a good base for visiting the Esteros del Iberá. About 27 km south of Mercedes are the strange Ita Pucú rock formations, remnants of a mountain massif long disappeared.

● **Accommodation** *Turismo*, Caaguazú y Sarmiento, T 317; *Plaza*, San Martín 699, T 13, cheapest.

RESERVA PROVINCIAL DEL IBERA

This reserve protects nearly 800,000 hectares of marshland known as the **Esteros del Iberá**. Similar to the Pantanal in Brazil, the Esteros are the old course of the Río Paraná. From their outlet into the Río Corrientes, which flows south west into the Río Paraná, the marshes extend some 250 km northeast to Ituzaingó on the Alto Paraná and are some 150 km wide at their greatest extent. Though the waters are under 5m deep, there are several deep lagoons along the southeastern edge. Fauna are very similar to the Wet Chaco (see below): species include the endangered *aguará-guazú* (maned wolf), the marsh deer and the broad nosed caiman as well as capybaras, brocket deer, curiyús (yellow anaconda) and tegú lizards. About 300 species of bird have been identified, among them the Yabirú (or Juan Grande) stork – the largest stork in the western hemispere, southern screamers and several species of ducks.

● **Access** is 2 km from **Colonia Carlos Pellegrini**, 110 km northeast by dirt road from Mercedes. Here there is a visitors centre, camping and shop. The tap water here is not drinkable, but bottled water can be bought.

● **Accommodation A3** *Posada de la Laguna*, T/F 076-929532, also meals, English spoken; also rooms in the house of Pera Roque, **E** pp, basic.

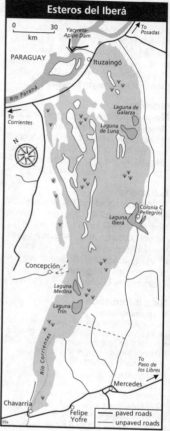

Esteros del Iberá

0 — 30 km

To Posadas
Yacyreta-Apipe Dam
PARAGUAY
Ituzaingó
Río Paraná
To Corrientes
Laguna de Galarza
Laguna de Luna
Colonia C Pellegrini
Laguna Iberá
Concepción
Laguna Medina
Laguna Trin
Río Corrientes
To Paso de los Libres
Mercedes
Chavarría
Felipe Yofre

— paved roads
— unpaved roads

● **Buses** Daily bus and minibus from Mercedes.

● **Tours** can be arranged through agencies in Mercedes and Corrientes: in Corrientes try Marcus Moncada, of *Turismo Aventura 4WD*, Junín 1062, Loc 4. Workers at the visitors centre take boat trips in small punts, US$10 per hour, a recommended way of discovering the wildlife quietly.

● **Estancias** for *estancias* on the northern edge of Iberá see under Ituzaingó.

PARQUE NACIONAL MBURUCUYA

Situated north of the Esteros del Iberá and and south east of the city of Corrientes,

Mburucuyá

Almost unpronounceable in Spanish or English, Mburucuyá is the Guaraní name for the passion flower (*Passiflora caerula*), found in hot climates across the world. Its Spanish name *pasionaria* was given by missionaries who saw similarities with the Passion of Christ: its three stigmas representing the three nails, the five anthers the five wounds, the corona the crown of thorns, the ten tepals the faithful apostles (no Judas or Peter), and the lobed leaves and tendrils by which it climbs the hands and scourges of the persecutors.

Passion flower

Well adapted to its environment, it secretes a sweet substance which attracts ants, which defend the plant from caterpillars and insects. It flowers over a long period during the summer and its orange/red berries are poisonous.

Jane Norwich

this park covers 15,060 hectares, stretching north from the marshlands of the Río Santa Lucía, which forms its southern limit. Formerly two *estancias*, the park includes varying natural environments, ranging from Wet Chaco to *Espinal* types. Flora includes yatay and caranday palms and quebrachos as well as areas of savanna. Fauna includes the rare *aguará guazu* (maned wolf), monkeys, mountain foxes and about 300 bird species. No infrastructure.

● **Access** is by Provincial Route 86, 12 km east of the town of Mburucuyá, 107 km northwest of Bella Vista. The *guardaparque* lives in Mburucuyá.

CORRIENTES

(*Population* 268,000; *Altitude* 55m; *Phone code* 0783), capital of Corrientes province, lies 586 km north of Paraná, about 40 km south of the confluence of the Ríos Paraguay and Alto Paraná. Founded on a relatively high promontory in 1588 by an expedition from Asunción, it became important as a port on the route between Buenos Aires and Asunción. Several Franciscan missions were built nearby to settle the Indians.

The city is mainly a service centre for its agricultural hinterland which produces beef, cotton, tobacco, rice and *yerba maté*. It is also an important route centre, linked with Resistencia, 25 km west, by

the General Belgrano bridge, 1.7 km long, across the Río Paraná (toll US$1 per car) and with Posadas and the Iguazú falls by Route 12. The river can make the air heavy, moist and oppressive, but in winter the climate is pleasant.

Places of interest

The main **Plaza 25 de Mayo** is one of the best preserved in Argentina. On the north side is the **Jefatura de Policia**, built in 19th century French style. On the east side are the Italianate **Casa de Gobierno** (1881-6) and the **Ministerio de Gobierno** (1882). On the south side is the church of **La Merced**, while the **Casa Lagraña**, built in 1860 for the governor, lies one block south. Two blocks east at Quintanta y Mendoza is the **Convento de San Francisco**, rebuilt in 1861 on the site of the original which dated from 1608. The **Cathedral**, built in 1874 is on Plaza Cabral where there is a statue to the sergeant who saved San Martín's life at the battle of San Lorenzo. The church of **La Cruz de los Milagros** (1897) houses *La Madera*, a miraculous cross placed there by the founder of the city, Alonzo de Vera – Indians who tried to burn it were killed by lightning from a cloudless sky.

Calle Junín is pedestrianized, with restaurants and shops, crowded at night. The attractive Avenida Costanera, lined with *lapachos* and *palos borrachos*, leads

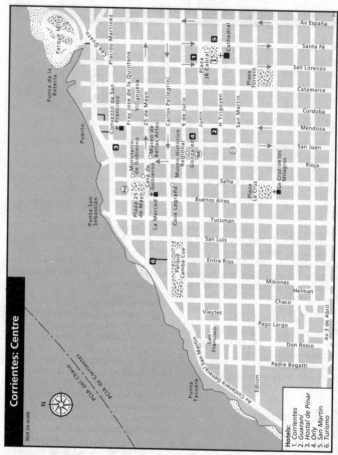

Corrientes: Centre

Not to scale

Av España
Santa Fé
San Lorenzo
Catamarca
Cordoba
Mendoza
San Juan
Rioja
Salta
Buenos Aires
Tucuman
San Luís
Entre Rios
Misiones
Helman
Chaco
Vieytes
Pago Largo
Don Rosco
Padre Bogatti

Av 3 de Abril

Cathedral
Plaza JB Cabral
Plaza Torrent
Plaza La Cruz
La Cruz de los Milagros

Convento de San Francisco
Villanueva
Fray Jose de la Quintana
Placido Martinez
25 de Mayo
Carlos Pellegrini
9 de Julio
Junin
H Yrigoyen
San Martin
Gonzalez
Museo Histórico Regional
Museo de Bellas Artes
Casa de Gobierno
Ministerio de Gobierno
Plaza 25 de Mayo
La Merced
Casa Lagraña

Puerto
Punta San Sebastián
Punta de la Batería
Parque Mitre
Punta Tacuara

Parque Camba Cua

Av Costanera General / San Martin
San Francisco
San Martin
Edison

PCIA del Chaco
PCIA de Corrientes

N

Hotels:
1. Corrientes
2. Guarani
3. Hostal de Pinar
4. Orly
5. San Martin
6. Turismo

along the Río Paraná to **Parque Mitre**, from where there are good views of sunsets over the river. Up river from the bridge to Resistencia, is a **zoo** with animals of the region.

Museums

Museo Histórico Regional, 9 de Julio 1044, Tuesday-Friday 0800-1200, 1600-1800, Saturday 0900-1200, US$1.

Museo de Bellas Artes, San Juan 643, Tuesday-Friday, 0800-1200, 1600-2100, Saturday, Sunday, 0900-1200, 1800-2000.

Museo de Ciencias Naturales, San Martín 850, daily except Tuesday, 0800-1200, 1600-2000.

Museo de Artesanía, Buenos Aires y Quintana, Monday-Friday, 0730-1200, 1500-2000, Saturday 0900-1200, 1600-1900.

Excursions

There are several interesting towns northeast along Route 12.

Santa Ana de los Guacarás, Km 17, is the site of a 17th-century Fransiscan mission. The chapel, restored in 1889, dates

Graham Greene in Corrientes

Corrientes is the setting of one of Greene's most famous novels, *The Honorary Consul* (1973), the story of the kidnapping of the British Honorary Consul by opponents of the Paraguayan dictator, General Stroessner (never named in the novel). In his memoirs, *Ways of Escape* (1980), Greene explains how he first visited Corrientes in 1966 en route to Asunción to research his novel *Travels With My Aunt*; the boat stopped for half an hour:

"A few lights along the quay, a solitary sentinel outside a warehouse, a small public garden with something resembling a classical temple and the slow tide of the great river". (*Ways of Escape*, Penguin 1981.)

Returning for 2 weeks 5 years later, Greene found the inspiration for *The Honorary Consul* from a newspaper story. The Paraguayan consul in a town near Corrientes was kidnapped by mistake for the Paraguayan Ambassador; General Stroessner, on a fishing holiday in Argentina, refused to respond. However, although several characters in the novel were also based on people Greene met, there are few descriptions of the city:

"The city was beginning to wake up for the evening hours after the long siesta of the afternoon. A chain of cars drove by along the riverside. The white naked statue in the belvedere shone under the lamplight, and the Coca Cola sign glowed in scarlet letters like the shrine of a saint. Through the darkness the ferry boat was screaming a warning to the Chaco shore". (*The Honorary Consul*, Penguin 1974).

---

from 1771. The old railway station has been preserved as a museum to the Ferrocarril Provincial El Económico, a narrow-gauge railway line which operated from 1890 to 1960.

Paso de la Patria (*population* 2,200) Km 38, lies on the Alto Paraná opposite its confluence with the Río Paraguay. A paradise for *dorado* fishing, it is very popular during the *Fiesta del Pesca Dorada* in August. **Accommodation A3** *Hostería Don Julián*, T 94021, full board. Lots more including cabins.

Itatí (*population* 5,700; *phone code* 0783), Km 73, is a tiny port on the Alto Paraná and the site of a festival (June 16) which celebrates the crowning of the Virgin of Itatí. According to one version of the story, the Virgin appeared before local Indians who were attacking the settlers in Itatí and persuaded them to cease fighting. The Basílica, built in 1942, has a dome 83m high, 26m diameter and it seats 9,000 people. **Accommodation** *Antártida*, 25 de Mayo sin número, T 93060; *El Promesero*, 25 de Mayo sin número, T 93129; *El Colonial*, Desiderio Sosa 672, T 93050. **Camping** 2 sites.

Local festivals
Carnival is very colourful. Corrientes is the national capital of Carnival.

Local information
● **Accommodation**

More expensive than Resistencia, **A2** *Gran Hotel Guaraní*, Mendoza 970, T 23663, F 24620, with breakfast, very good, air conditioning, restaurant; **A3** *Corrientes*, Junín 1549, T 65019, F 65025, with breakfast, air conditioning, parking, good value for Corrientes, good restaurant; **A3** *Turismo*, Entre Ríos 650, T 23841, pool US$3 a day to non-residents; **A3** *Hostal de Pinar*, Martínez y Italia, T 69060, modern, parking, sauna; **A3** *Orly*, San Juan 867, T 27248, with breakfast, air conditioning, parking; **A3** *San Martín*, Santa Fe 955, T 65004, F 32326, with breakfast, good beds, restaurant, parking.

Budget accommodation: is difficult to find. In the centre **C** *Robert*, La Rioja 437, basic, clean, without bath. Several near the terminal including **C** *Caribe*, Avenida Maipú Km 3, T 69045.

Camping Near bus terminal is *Camping-club Teléfono*, Avenida Maipú, hot showers or bath, friendly. Four sites along Route 12 heading east.

● **Places to eat**
El Nuevo Balcón, Pellegrini 962, good food, clean, reasonable prices; *Las Brasas*, Avenida Costanera y San Martín (near beach). Many

others, and various *pizzerías*. Several tea rooms on San Juan, and on Junín. Try *chipas* (maize delicacies).

● **Banks & money changers**
Banco de la Provincia, 9 de Julio y San Juan, cash advance on Mastercard; **Banco de Iberá** for cash advance on Visa and Mastercard; **Casa de Cambio El Dorado**, 9 de Julio 1343.

● **Entertainment**
Nightclubs: *Metal*, Junín y Buenos Aires; *Savage*, Junín y San Lorenzo.

● **Posts & telecommunications**
Post Office: San Juan y San Martín.
Telecommunications: Pellegrini y Mendoza.

● **Tour companies & travel agents**
Turismo Aventura 4WD, Galería Paseo del Sul, Junín 1062, T 27698, F 33269, Amex. *Quo Vadís*, Carlos Pellegrini 1140, T 23096.

● **Tourist offices**
Plaza Cabral.

● **Transport**
Local Car hire: Avis at *Gran Hotel Guaraní* and airport; only credit cards accepted from foreigners.

Air Camba Punta Airport, 10 km east of city reached by Route 12. Bus No 8 from Avenida Costanera y La Rioja. Austral (T 27442) and Lapa (T 31625) to Buenos Aires and Formosa.

Buses To **Resistencia** US$1.30, Cota, every 15 minutes, 40 minutes journey, labelled 'Chaco', leaving from Avenida Costanera y La Rioja. Terminal 5 km south of centre, bus No 6 or 11 from Avenida Costanera y La Rioja, US$0.50. To **Posadas** US$18, 5½ hours, road paved; to **Buenos Aires**, US$30, but there are more services from Resistencia to Buenos Aires, Rosario and Santa Fe; to **Paso de los Libres**, 5 hours, US$10; to **Concordia** US$11, Empresa Gualeguaychú, 2 a day; to **Asunción** (Paraguay) US$18.

RESISTENCIA

(*Population* 228,000; *Altitude* 52m; *Phone code* 0722) the hot and energetic capital of the Province of Chaco, is situated 544 km north of Santa Fe on the Río Barranqueras, 6 km from its confluence with the Río Paraná. Founded in 1750 near the site of a Jesuit mission, it was abandoned after the expulsion of the Jesuits and refounded by immigrants from Fruili, Italy, in 1878. With the port of Barranqueras, just south on the Río Paraná, Resistencia is the commercial centre for the Chaco region. It is also an important route centre for travellers between Asunción, Salta and Iguazu. A city of little architectural interest, it is known as the 'city of the statues', there being many of these in the streets.

Places of interest
The **Fogón de los Arrieros**, Brown 350 entre López y French, is a famous club very interesting. Open to non-members Monday-Saturday, 0800-1200, Tuesday, Wednesday, Thursday only, 2130-0100, US$2, highly recommended.

Museums
Museo Histórico Regional, Donovan 425, Monday-Friday, 0800-1200, 1600-1800, in the Escuela Normal Sarmiento, traces the development of the city.

Museo de Ciencias Naturales, Pellegrini 802 (former railway station), Monday-Friday, 0830-1230, 1600-2000, Saturday 0900-1200.

Museo de Bellas Artes, Mitre 150, Tuesday-Saturday, 0730-1200, 1500-1900, collection of 19th and 20th century local works

Museo Regional de Antropología, Las Heras 727 in the Universidad Nacional del Nordeste, Monday-Friday 0800-1200, 1600-2100.

Museo Del Hombre Chaqueño, Illia 655, sections on indigenous peoples,

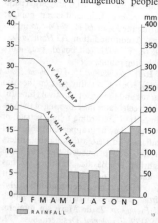

Climate: Resistencia

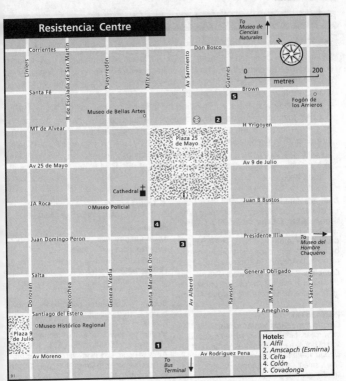

Resistencia: Centre

Hotels:
1. Alfil
2. Amscapch (Esmirna)
3. Celta
4. Colón
5. Covadonga

European immigration and the fauna of the Chaco.

Museo Policial, Roca 233, Monday-Friday 0800-1200, 1500-2000, Saturday 0800-1200, sections on marijuana and other drugs.

Excursions

To the **Parque Nacional Chaco**, see page 318.

To the **Reserva Natural Colonia Benitez**, 13 km north, which protects 10 hectares of wet Chaco marshlands with savanna and Caranday palms.

To the **Isla del Cerrito**, an island 63 km northeast of Corrientes at the confluence of the Ríos Paraná and Paraguay, which forms a provincial nature reserve of 12,000 hectares, covered mainly with grassland and palm trees. At the eastern end of the island, on the Río Paraná, is Cerrito, a tourist complex with white sand beaches, accommodation and restaurants, which is very busy during the *Fiesta de la Pesca Dorada* in Paso de la Patria.

- **Access** Follow Route 16 east and turn north just before the bridge to Corrientes: from here a road, the last 20 km of which are dirt, leads to a bridge, from where it is 17 km further to Cerrito. A ferry service connects Cerrito with Paso de la Patria.

Local information

● Accommodation

A3 *Colón*, Sta María de Oro 143, T 22862, old fashioned, comfortable; **A3** *Covadonga*, Güemes 182, T 44444, F 43444, small rooms, air conditioning, *Tabaré* snack bar; **B** *Hotel AMCSAPCH* (known as Esmirna), H Yrigoyen 83 on corner of Plaza, T 22898, owned by local police, with bath, good value, air conditioning.

The Fogón de los Arrieros

Unique in Argentina and with few parallels in South America, the Fogón de los Arrieros was founded in the late 1930s by a group of friends led by the poet and sculptor Juan de Dios Mena. The club building, with bar, library and workshop, is decorated with local art and 'objets'. A meeting-place for artists and other local characters, it welcomes visits from travellers.

The Fogón was also the inspiration for the city's statues and murals. In 1961, deciding to promote an 'open air art gallery', the club began to promote the placing of statues and sculptures in the streets and plazas: there are now nearly 200, including 26 in Avenida Sarmiento alone, some by local artists, some by outsiders. This, along with the murals in the city's public buildings, can be seen as an expression of the club's view that art is an important part of the development of the city and of the Chaco.

Budget accommodation: **C** *Alfil*, Santa Maria de Oro 495, T 20882, air conditioning extra, English spoken; **C** *Celta*, Alberdi 210, T 22986, with bath, basic; **C** *Res San José*, Rawson 304, basic; **C** *Res Alberdi*, Alberdi 317, **E** without bath, basic but clean, restaurant, recommended; **D** *Aragón*, Santiago del Estero 154.

Camping 2 sites north of town: *Parque Dos de Febrero*, Avenida Avalos, very pretty, near artificial lake, US$3 per tent; *Parque Avalos*, free.

Places to eat

Círculo Residentes Santafecinos, Vadia 150, tasty meals, family style. Try *chupin de surubí*, a sort of bouillabaisse, delightful. *Restaurant Sociedad Italiana*, Yrigoyen 204, excellent cuisine, smart, pricey; *Charly*, Güemes 215, snacks, good breakfast.

● **Banks & money changers**

Banco del Chaco, Plaza 25 de Mayo, cash only; **Banco de Crédito**, Justo 200 block, cash advance on Mastercard. **Banco de Iberá** changes travellers' cheques (3% commission); **Banco Corrientes**, Alberdi 300 block, cash on Visa card; **Cambio El Dorado**, 9 de Julio 201, changes travellers' cheques at reasonable rate.

● **Laundry**

Tokio, Güemes y Brown.

● **Post & telecommunications**

Post Office: Plaza 25 de Mayo, Monday-Saturday, 0700-1200, 1500-2000.

Telecommunications: Justo y Paz.

● **Shopping**

Regionales Pompeya, Güemes 154, sells local handicrafts and has an Indian handicraft display. Excellent leather goods at *Chac*, Güemes 160.

● **Tour companies & travel agents**

Puerto Aventura, Saavedra 557, T/F 32932, very helpful.

● **Tourist offices**

Justo 135; kiosk in Plaza 25 de Mayo.

● **Transport**

Local Car hire: Avis, French 701 and at airport. Localiza, Roca 460, T 39255.

Air Airport 8 km west of town (no bus). AR (T 22859/25360), Austral (T 44550) and Lapa (T 30201) to/from Buenos Aires; Lapa to Formosa.

Buses To **Corrientes** over the Río Paraná bridge, every 15 minutes from Avenida Alberdi near Plaza 25 de Mayo, 40 minutes, US$1.30. Modern terminal 5 km east of centre (bus 3 or 10 to centre, US$0.60; remise US$4). To **Buenos Aires** 14 hours, US$35 several companies, most services overnight; to **Santa Fe**, 8 hours, US$26; to **Córdoba**, 12 hours, US$43; to **Formosa** 2½ hours, US$10; to **Puerto Iguazú** US$30; to **Posadas**, 5½ hours, US$18; to **Tucumán** El Rayo, 1930 and 2200, 12 hours, US$21; to **Salta**, Veloz del Norte and Central Sáenz Peña, daily 1700, 14 hours, US$40.

To Paraguay To **Clorinda** and border US$17, 4 hours; to **Asunción** daily, via Formosa, La Internacional, 6 hours, US$21.

To Bolivia To frontier at Aguas Blancas/Bermejo, take bus for Salta, change at Güemes, for direct connection to Orán (Atahualpa buses every 2 hours approximately), from where it is 45 minutes to border.

NORTH OF RESISTENCIA

Route 11 runs north to Formosa and the Paraguayan frontier near Clorinda. Crossing low lying pastures with streams and Caranday palms, this route offers views of the diverse birdlife of the Wet Chaco and is particularly beautiful in the evening.

FORMOSA

(*Population* 155,000; *Phone code* 0717), 240 km north of Corrientes, is the capital of Formosa Province and the only Argentine port of any note on the Río Paraguay. Boats cross the river to **Alberdi**, a Paraguayan duty-free spot, which can be visited only if you have a multiple entry visa.

Museums

Museo Histórico Regional, 25 de Mayo y

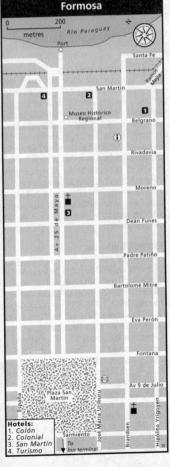

Formosa

Belgrano, Monday-Friday 0730-1200, 1500-1930, entry free, large collection of artefacts with no particular logic.

Local information

● Accommodation

A2 *Turismo*, San Martín 759, T 26004, best, parking, air conditioning; **A1** *Colón*, Belgrano 1068, T 26547, noisy, air conditioning, colour TV, spacious, **B** without air conditioning, good, with breakfast; **B** *San Martín*, 25 de Mayo 380, T 26769, air conditioning, with breakfast, run down; **B** *Plaza*, Uriburu 920, T 26767, 2-star.

Budget accommodation: **C** *Rivas*, Belgrano 1395, T 20499, **E** without bath, cold water, basic, run down; **C** *Colonial*, San Martín 879, T 26345, basic, air conditioning, parking; **C** *Casa de Familia*, Belgrano 1056, good. Opposite bus terminal is **D** *Hosp El Extranjero*, Gutnisky 2660, T 28676, modern, air conditioning, with bath, also short stay.

Camping *Club Caza y Pesca* southwest of town, on the Río Paraguay southwest of town. To the south of Formosa, reached by Route 11: *Camping Banco Provincial*, Km 4, good facilities including pool, tennis courts, T 29877; *Las Arianas*, 10 km south (turn off Route 11 at El Pucu, Km 6), T 27640.

● Places to eat

Ser San, 25 de Mayo y Moreno, good; *Pizzería Italia*, 25 de Mayo y Rivadavia. Also on 25 de Mayo: *El Tono María*, No 55, good Italian food, nice atmosphere, expensive; *Parrillada La Cascada*, No 335.

● Banks & money changers

Banks close at noon and there are no *casas de cambio*; buy pesos in Asunción or Clorinda.

● Tour companies & travel agents

Turismo de Castro, Brandzen 75, T 34777; *Turinfort*, Moreno 58, T 27011.

● Tourist offices

Brandzen 117, T 26502, also at bus terminal very helpful.

● Transport

Air El Pucu airport, 7 km north; Austral and Lapa (T 35979) to Buenos Aires.

Buses Modern bus terminal on western outskirts (bus 4 or 11 to/from centre). To **Asunción**, 0400, 0800 and 1730, 3 hours, US$10.50; easier to go to Clorinda on the border (US$6.50) and then take a bus to Asunción. To **Resistencia**, 6 a day, US$10; to Buenos Aires US$41, La Internacional. Bus services to **Embarcación** are frequently cancelled (scheduled daily 1200; do not rely on this as a route to Bolivia, better to go from Resistencia to Salta and then north).

Trains There are no longer passenger services on the line across the Chaco to Embarcación.

CLORINDA

(*Population* 40,000; *Phone code* 0718) 118 km north of Formosa, lies on the Río Pilcomayo, 13 km upstream from its confluence with the Río Paraná. It has a banana festival in early October.

● **Accommodation** **B** *Embajador*, San Martín 166, T 21148; **C** *Helen*, San Martín 320, T 21118; **C** *Res 9 de Julio*, San Martín y Roque Sáenz Peña, T 21221, with air conditioning; *Res San Martín*, 12 de Octubre 1150, T 21211.

● **Buses** From Argentine end of Puente Loyola: to **Formosa**, 10 a day; **Resistencia**, US$14, 4 a day, and **Santa Fe/Rosario/Buenos Aires** 3 daily.

PARQUE NACIONAL RIO PILCOMAYO

Situated 65 km northwest of Clorinda, this park covers 48,000 hectares of Wet Chaco environment on the western bank of the Río Pilcomayo. The western part, near the entrance, is mainly marshland; further east is savanna studded with groves of trees including quebrachos, caranday palms and palos borachos. Along the Río Pilcomayo are areas of riverine forest. Among the protected species are aguará-guazú, giant anteaters and tapirs. Caimans, tagú lizards, black howler monkeys, rheas and a variety of birds can also be seen. You need at least a day to visit the western parts of the park and must be accompanied by *guardaparques*. Vehicles should have 4WD.

● **Access** Buses run to Laguna Blanca, 4 km from the Park Entrance; 3 km further is the *guardaparque* office, near which camping is permitted.

FRONTIER WITH PARAGUAY: CLORINDA

There are two routes into Paraguay.

● **By Road**

The easiest crossing is via the Puente Loyola, 3 km north of Clorinda. From Puerto Falcón, at the Paraguayan end of the bridge, the road runs 20 km east and crosses the Río Paraguay to reach Asunción.

● **Immigration**

Formalities for entering Argentina are dealt with at the Argentine end, those for leaving Argentina at the Paraguayan end. Easy crossing, open 24 hours.

● **Transport**

Buses Local services to Asunción, Empresa Falcón US$1, every hour, last bus to the centre of Asunción 1830.

By Ferry From Puerto Pilcomayo, close to Clorinda (bus US$0.40) there is is a vehicle ferry service to Itá Enramada (Paraguay), US$0.65, 20 minutes journey every 30 minutes. Then take bus 9 to Asunción.

● **Immigration**

Argentine immigration at Puerto Pilcomayo, closed at weekends for tourists. Paraguayan immigration at Itá Enramada.

INTO PARAGUAY: ASUNCION

(*Population* over 1.2 million; *Phone code* 021) The capital and largest city in Paraguay, Asunción has expanded south and east far beyond its original site on the shore of a bay on the eastern bank of the Río Paraguay. Most of the public buildings are near the river, but none is older than the last half of the 19th century. The central plazas of the city are drenched in colour during July-August with the prolific pink bloom of the *lapacho* trees, which grow everywhere. Dwelling houses are in a variety of styles; new villas in every kind of taste have replaced the traditional one-storey Spanish-style house, except in the poorer quarters.

Places of interest

Most of the public buildings can be seen by following El Paraguayo Independiente southeast from the **Aduana** (Customs House). The first is the **Palacio de Gobierno**, built 1860-1892 in the style of Versailles (open Sunday). In Plaza **Independencia** or **Constitución** stands the **Congreso Nacional** (debates can be attended during the session from April to December, on Thursday and sometimes Friday). On the northwest side of the Plaza is the **Antiguo Colegio Militar**, built 1588 as a Jesuit College and now housing the Casa de la Cultura and the military history museum (see below). On the southeast side of the Plaza is the **Catedral**. Two blocks southwest, along Calle Chile, is **Plaza de los Héroes**, with the

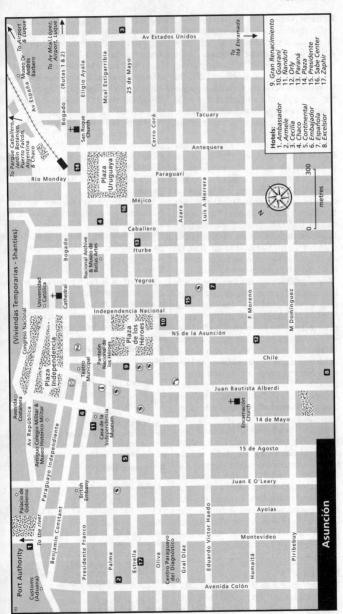

To Airport
& Luque

To Mcal López,
Airport, Luque

To Av España
(Rutas 1 & 2)

Museo Dr Andrés
Barbero

Av Estados Unidos

To Itá Enramada

Hotels:
1. Ambassador
2. Armele
3. Cecilia
4. Chaco
5. Continental
6. Embajador
7. Española
8. Excelsior
9. Gran Renacimiento
10. Guaraní
11. Nanduti
12. Orly
13. Paraná
14. Plaza
15. Presidente
16. Sabe Center
17. Zaphir

Eligio Ayala

Mcal Estigarribia

25 de Mayo

Tacuary

Cerro Corá

Antequera

Paraguarí

Luis A Herrera

Azará

Méjico

Caballero

Iturbe

Yegros

Independencia Nacional

NS de la Asunción

Chile

F Moreno

M Dominguez

Juan Bautista Alberdi

14 de Mayo

15 de Agosto

Juan E O'Leary

Ayolas

Montevideo

Piribebuy

Humaitá

Eduardo Victor Haedo

Gral Díaz

Centro Paraguayo
del Diagnóstico

Oliva

Estrella

Palma

Presidente Franco

British Embassy

Benjamin Constant

Paraguayo Independiente

Antiguo Colegio Militar &
Museo Histórico Militar

Av Republica

Avenida Costanera

Congreso Nacional

Universidad
Católica

Cathedral

Nacional Archive
& Museo de
Bellas Artes

Bogado

Plaza
Uruguaya

Río Monday

San Roque
Church

Bogado

To Parque Caballero,
Jardín Botánico,
Puerto Falcón,
Argentina & Chaco

To the river

Customs
(Aduana)

Port Authority

Palacio
de Gobierno

Plaza
Independencia

Teatro
Municipal

Casa de la
Independencia Museum

Plaza
de los
Héroes

Panteón
Nacional de
los Héroes

Encarnación
Church

Avenida Colón

(Viviendas Temporarias - Shanties)

Asunción

metres
300
0

N

Panteón Nacional de los Héroes based on Les Invalides in Paris, begun during the War of the Triple Alliance and finished in 1937. Near the **Plaza Uruguaya** is the railway station, built 1856, and a steam engine, the *Sapucai*, dating from 1861. The **Cementerio Recoleta**, the national cemetery resembling a miniature city with tombs in various architectural styles, is on Avenida Mariscal López, 3 km southeast of the centre.

The best of several parks is **Parque Carlos Antonio López**, set high to the west along Colón and, if you can find a gap in the trees, with a grand view. The **Jardín Botánico** covering 250 hectares is 6 km east, on Avenida Artigas y Primer Presidente, reached by bus (Nos 2, 6, 23, and 40, US$0.15, about 35 minutes from Luis A Herrera, or Nos 24, 35 or 44B from Oliva or Cerro Corá). The gardens lie along the Río Paraguay and contain only trees (no labels, but nice and shady), an 18-hole golf course, and a little zoo, which has inspired some unfavourable comments and protests. Entrance fee US$0.50. In the gardens are the former residences of two Presidents: that of Carlos Antonio López, a one-storey typical Paraguayan country house with verandahs, which now houses a **Museo de Historia Natural** and a library, and that of Francisco Solano López, a two-storey European-inspired mansion which is now the **Museo Indigenista** (both museums open Monday-Saturday 0730-1130, 1300-1730, Sunday 0900-1300, both free, neither is in good condition). The beautiful church of **Santísima Trinidad** (on Santísimo Sacramento, parallel to Avenida Artigas), dating from 1854 with frescoes on the inside walls, is well worth a visit. It is a 10-minute walk from the zoo entrance. The **Maca Indian reservation** is north of the Gardens (take bus 42 or 44, entrance US$0.15, guide US$0.80); the Indians, who live in very poor conditions, expect you to photograph them (US$0.25).

Museums

Museo Nacional de Bellas Artes, Iturbe y Mariscal Estigarribia, a good collection of Spanish paintings including works by Tintoretto and Murrillo; also an interesting selection of 20th century Paraguayan art, open Tuesday-Friday, 0700-1900, Saturday-Sunday 0800-1200.

In the **Casa de la Independencia** (14 de Mayo y Presidente Franco) is an interesting historical collection; open Tuesday-Friday 0700-1200 and 1430-1830, Saturday and Sunday 0800-1200, entry free.

Museo Histórico Militar in the Antiguo Colegio Militar, on Plaza de la Independencia, open Monday-Friday 0730-1200, 1330-1800, Saturday-Sunday 0800-1200, containing collections focussing on the War of the Triple Alliance and the Chaco War.

Museo Dr Andrés Barbero, España y Mompox, open Monday-Friday 0700-1100, and Monday, Wednesday, Friday 1500-1700, anthropological, free, with a good collection of tools and weapons, etc, of the various Guaraní cultures, recommended.

Centro de Artes Visuales, at Isla de Francia, access via Avenida Gral Genes, bus 30 or 44A from the centre, open daily, except Sunday and holidays, 1600-2030; contains **Museo Paraguayo de Arte Contemporáneo**, with some striking murals, **Museo de Arte Indígeno** and **Museo de Barro**, containing ceramics, highly recommended.

Museo del Ferrocarril, Mariscal López y Antequera, Monday-Friday 0700-1300.

Local information

For fuller details on Asunción including restaurants, embassies, travel agents and excursions see the *South American Handbook*.

● **Accommodation**

Hotel prices

L1	over US$200	**L2**	US$151-200
L3	US$101-150	**A1**	US$81-100
A2	US$61-80	**A3**	US$46-60
B	US$31-45	**C**	US$21-30
D	US$12-20	**E**	US$7-11
F	US$4-6	**G**	up to US$3

Unless otherwise stated, all hotels in range **D** and above have private bath. Assume friendliness and cleanliness in all cases.

The hotel bill does not usually include a service charge. Check out time is usually 1000.

In Asunción: **L3** *Chaco*, Caballero 285 y Estigarriba, T 492066, F 444223, with breakfast, parking nearby, rooftop swimming pool, good restaurant (US$15-20); **L3** *Guaraní*, Oliva e Independencia Nacional, T 491131/139, F 443647, efficient, courteous, central, good value, reasonable restaurant with good buffet; **L3** *Sabe Center*, 25 de Mayo y México, T 450093, F 450101, has luxury suites, central, on busy corner; **L3-A2** *Excelsior*, Chile 980, PO Box 2863, T 495632, best, conference facilities, etc; **A1** *Cecilia*, Estados Unidos 341, T 210365, F 497111, very smart, comfortable, recommended, good restaurant; **A2** *Continental*, 15 de Agosto 420 y Estrella, T 493760, 1st class, all rooms air conditioning, TV, swimming pool, restaurant, recommended cafetería, bars, laundry service; **A3** *Gran Armele*, Palma y Colón, T 444455, F 445903, with breakfast, good restaurant, air conditioning, used by tour groups, recommended; **A3** *Gran Renacimiento*, Chile 388 y Estrella, T 445165, central, air conditioning, good service; **A3** *Paraná*, Caballero y 25 de Mayo, T 444236, F 494793, with breakfast, central, secure, helpful, discounts negotiable, restaurant recommended, also short-stay.

B *Orly*, Humaitá 209, T 491497, F 442307, good value (**D** for stays over 2 months), *City* cafetería in lobby is good; **B** *Presidente*, Azara y Independencia Nacional, T 494931, F 496500, with breakfast and air conditioning; **B-C** *Embajador*, Pdte Franco 514, T/F 493393, with breakfast, air conditioning, **C** with fan, central, parking.

Specially for German-speaking travellers: **L3-A3** *Westfalenhaus*, M Benítez 777 y Stma Trinidad, T 292374/293323, F 291241, e-mail westfalenhaus@pla.net.py, TV, comfortable, German run, swimming pool, air conditioning; **B** *Zaphir*, Estrella 955, T 490025, small, comfortable, good value.

C *Española*, Herrera y Yegros, T 447312, parking, highly recommended; **C** *Ñandutí*, Pdte Franco 551, T 446780, with breakfast, comfortable, luggage stored, recommended; **C** *Plaza*, Eligio Ayala y Paraguarí, T/F 444772, **D** without bath, spacious rooms, air conditioning, luggage stored, highly recommended.

E *Ambassador*, Montevideo 111, T 445901, on riverbank, with bath, dirty showers, fan, kitchen and laundry facilities, run down, basic, noisy. There are many hotels and *residenciales* in our **D** and **E** ranges on Calle Cerro Corá, eg **D** *Amigo*, Cerro Ceró u Caballero, without bath, with breakfast, cooking and laundry, facilities, cheap, recommended but noisy.

Near Bus Terminal on Avenida F de la Mora: **C** *Adelia*, on corner with Lapacho, T 553083, with breakfast, modern; **C-D** *Yasy*, No 2390, T 551623, with fan. Many more behind these in Dolores eg **C-D** *Anahi*, T 554943, with breakfast and fan; **E** *El Paraíso*, Lapacho 236, T 555948, shower, quiet, safe, no breakfast.

Camping The pleasant site at the Jardín Botánico charges US$1.50 per person plus tent, cars also permitted, cold showers and 220v electricity, busy at weekends. If camping, take plenty of insect repellent. You can camp at rear of *Restaurant Westfalia*, T 331772, owner speaks English, French, German, very knowledgeable, US$1 per night for car, hot showers, clothes washing facilities, noisy, animals. Take Avenida Moreno, towards Ciudad del Este, turn right after going under two bridges into General Santos. *Rest Westfalia* is 3 km further, 5 km from Asunción (bus 19, 23 or 40).

● **Embassies**

Argentina, España y Perú, T 212320, visas issued at Edificio Banco Nacional de Argentina, Palma 319, 1st floor, open 0800-1300, 2 hour service, photo needed.

● **Tourist offices**

Dirección General de Turismo, Palma esquina Alberdi, open Monday-Friday 0800-2000, T 441530, F 491230. Free map, information on all parts of Paraguay, but you may need to be persistent. Another map is sold in bookshops.

● **Useful addresses**

Immigration: O'Leary 625, 8th floor. Ministerio de Relaciones Exteriores, O'Leary y Presidente Franco.

● **Transport**

Local City buses: the system is extensive, running from 0600-2400; Buses stop before every street corner; in the city there are bus-stop signs. Journeys within city, US$0.30. For buses to the new bus terminal, see below. Buses only recommended outside rush hours, with light luggage. Keep your ticket for inspection until you leave bus. **Taxis**: minimum fare in the city is US$0.70 plus US$0.05 for every 100m. About 30% more at night. The average journey costs about US$2, there is an extra charge for luggage. Hire by the hour; minimum US$10, up US$20 outside the city. Radiotaxi recommended, T 550116, or 311080.

Air Silvio Pettirossi Airport, 15 km northeast of centre. Several agencies have desks where you can book a taxi to your hotel, US$15. Bus 30A goes every 15 minutes between the red bus stop outside the airport and Plaza de los Héroes, US$0.30, difficult with luggage, allow 30-45 minutes. Minibus service from your hotel to airport run by Tropical, T 84486, book in advance, US$8.

Buses Terminal, south of the centre at República Argentina y Fernando de la Mora, reached by taking local bus No 8 (the only direct one), on Oliva, Haedo, or Cerro Corá in the centre and get off outside the terminal, US$0.20. In the centre get off at Chile y Díaz. Allow 30-40 minutes (other buses Nos 10, 25, 31, 38 and 80, follow very circuitous routes). Taxi to/from centre, recommended if you have luggage, US$4, journey time depends on traffic, minimum 20 minutes. The terminal has a bus information desk, free city/country map, restaurant (quite good), café, casa de cambio (poor rates) and shops. Bus company offices on the top floor are in three sections: short-distance, medium and long. There are services to all parts of Paraguay as well as to Argentina (see below), Chile, Brazil and Bolivia. Hotels nearby: turn left from front of terminal, 2 minutes walk.

THE ARGENTINE CHACO

The Chaco is a vast low-lying plain some 900 km across and covering about half of Paraguay, areas of Bolivia and Brazil and parts of northern Argentina. The Argentine Chaco stretches between the Andean foothills in the west and the Ríos Paraná and Paraguay in the east, comprising the entire provinces of Formosa and Chaco, parts of Salta, Santiago del Estero and Santa Fe, and a tiny corner of the province of Córdoba. Its southern limit is the Río Dulce valley, which forms a segment of the

The Quebracho

Though large areas of quebracho forest have been destroyed, the tree continues to symbolize the Chaco. There are in fact two species of quebracho: white (Aspidosperma quebracho blanco) and red (Schinopsis Balansae). White quebracho is found throughout northern Argentina. Growing as high as 23m, it has a grey trunk up to 1m in diameter and pointed leaves. The Indians used its bark for medicinal purposes. The red quebracho, found only in the Chaco, has very hard wood and is the purest known source of tannin (up to 30%) which has made it of great value for curing leather.

Jane Norwich

border between Santiago del Estero and Córdoba provinces. Though this sprawling alluvial lowland rises gradually from east to west, its rise is so gentle (200m in 900 km) that the rivers which cross it are slow and meander.

There are two distinct zones: the Wet Chaco along the Ríos Paraná and Paraguay and the Dry Chaco further west. Each has its own fauna and flora. The Wet Chaco is covered mainly by marshlands with savanna and groves of Caranday palms. Further west, as rainfall diminishes, scrubland of algarrobo, white quebracho, palo borracho and various types of cacti are found. Little visited by travellers, its wildlife makes it a worthwhile destination for nature lovers. Though poor roads and lack of public transport make much of the Chaco inaccessible, there are several parks: two are described below while a third, the Parque Nacional Pilcomayo, near Clorinda, is described above.

The Chaco is one of the main centres of indigenous population in Argentina: it is home to two of the largest minorities, the *Tobas* and the *Wichi* or *Mataco* as well as the less numerous Mocovi.

Climate.
Rain falls mostly in summer; in the east annual rainfall is about 1,200 mm, dropping to 400-700 mm in the centre. Higher rainfall (1,700 mm a year) occurs in the far west near the Andean foothills, but most is lost through evaporation. South America's highest temperatures, exceeding 45°C, have been recorded here, but winters are mild, with an occasional touch of frost in the south.

Economy
The Chaco is mostly cattle country, with large *estancias* and low stocking rates: some estimate that the minimum size for an *estancia* to return a profit is 7,500 hectares. Tannin and cotton are the traditional industries, although acreage planted to sunflowers has increased dramatically, along with maize and sorghum. Tannin is struggling against competition from synthetic tannin and

Fauna of the Wet Chaco and Iberá marshlands

The open landscapes of the Wet Chaco and the Iberá marshlands offer incredible opportunities for observing wildlife. Reptiles include the Yellow Anaconda, Black Caiman and Broad-snouted Caiman, the Tegu-lizard and the water turtle. Bird-life is outstanding; among species which may be seen are the Greater Rhea, Jabiru and Wood storks, Roseate spoonbills and White-necked Herons, Red-legged Seriema, the Chaco Chachalaca, the Anhinga, the Plumbeous Rail, the Wattled Jacana, Black-headed Parakeets and Turquoise parrots, Scarlet-headed Blackbirds, Yellow-winged Blackbirds and Screaming Cowbirds. Species of ducks include the Muscovy and Tree-ducks. Amongst the birds of prey are the Black-collared Hawk and the Savannah Hawk.

Capybaras

The Chaco and Iberá are also probably the best environments in Argentina for viewing land mammals. Worth watching out for are the Capybara, the largest rodent in the world, the Black Howler Monkey and the Crab Eating Fox. There

Maned Wolf

are also armadillos and two species of brockets. Peccaries, tapirs and Collared Anteaters are more difficult to find. Endangered species are the long-legged Maned Wolf, the Giant Anteater and the Marsh Deer, which is restricted mainly to the marshlands of Iberá.

Most of these mammals can also be found further west in the dry Chaco, though here you may also find the Peccari Quimilero as well as endangered species such as the Giant Armadillo and the Jaguar. The dry Chaco is also home to reptiles such as the Red Ground Lizzard, an arboreal boa and other species of birds, notably the Black-legged Seriema.

Santiago de la Vega.

the huge mimosa plantations in South Africa. The more accessible eastern forests have nearly disappeared; deforestation of all species is proceeding rapidly in the north and west of the province, which produces charcoal for a military steel foundry in Jujuy. Small roadside factories also produce custom furniture.

Cities in the Chaco

The most important cities are on the edge of the Chaco: Resistencia and Formosa are on the west bank of the Ríos Paraná and Paraguay and are described above. For Santiago del Estero, on the western edge

of the Chaco, see the North West section. The other towns are located along the two main routes which cross the Chaco, Route 16 and Route 81. Most roads in the Chaco are poor.

ROUTE 16

Running northwest from Resistencia through Roque Sáenz Peña to Salta province where it connects with Route 9, the main northern highway, at a point north of Metán, this is the best route between Paraguay and Northwest Argentina. It is mostly paved, several tolls.

Penetrating the inpenetrable

El Impenetrable is the name sometimes given to a large northwestern expanse of the Argentine Chaco. Covering some 4 million hectares and largely unihabited, it has resisted attempts at settlement and commercial exploitation during the past century.

In the years before the First World War two railway lines were begun across the Chaco, from Barrancas to Métan, and from Formosa to Embarcación. These were intended to open the Chaco up for settlement and for transporting the products of the region out to the ports of the Río Paraná. Towns were built along these lines and the new settlers, attracted by the rise in world cotton prices during the First World War, turned the area into a major producer of cotton. In the 1950s competition from natural fibres, soil exhaustion and changes of government policies led to a collapse in cotton production and the abandonment of towns and villages.

The railways struggled on, though lack of investment, declining revenues and competition from road transport, made their timetables ever more fictional. By the early 1990s the trip from Formosa to Embarcación, 20 hours in a *cochemotor* with wooden seats and no refreshments, was decidedly for the adventurous, though those who made it reported that the birdlife was wonderful. The 1994 decision of the Argentine government to transfer responsibility for passenger rail services to the provinces dealt the final blow to passenger trains on these two lines.

PARQUE NACIONAL CHACO

Situated 115 km west of Resistencia and extending over 15,000 hectares, this protects one of the last remaining untouched areas of the Wet Chaco. Along the banks of the Río Negro, which crosses the park, are areas of riverine forest. There are 10 km of tracks, which lead through different types of environment including lagunas and streams, savanna with Caranday palm groves and forests of quebracho and palo borracho. It is a good place to see the region's abundant birdlife. The *guardaparques* offer a 1-2-hour walk, explaining the region's plants and animals, recommended. The park is best visited in autumn and spring. "The mosquitos are more voracious than we've ever encountered in Asia or South America, but the birds were good" (Tim Woodward and Phaik Hua Tan, Hong Kong).

● **Access** The park is reached by Provincial Route 9, which branches off Route 16, 56 km west of Resistencia. Route 9 is paved for 15 km, but the remaining 23 km to the park entrance are unpaved and difficult in wet weather. Entry US$5.

● **Accommodation** Camping facilities, good, free, cold showers, but the nearest supplies are in Capitán Solari, 6 km from the park entrance.

● **Buses** From Resistencia 4 daily, 2½ hours, US$6, as far as Capitán Solari from where local transport is available, ask around.

PRESIDENCIA ROQUE SAENZ PENA

(*Population* 65,000; *Altitude* 93m; *Phone code* 0714), 160 km northwest of Resistencia, is the major centre on Route 16. Founded in 1912, in the 1920s it attracted large number of immigrants from Central Europe. Since the early 1980s it has acquired the status of a spa town: its thermal waters, 35-42°C are 30% more salty than the sea and are claimed to be the best in the country. Its principal attraction is the **Parque Zoológico**, 3 km south of the centre and covering 28 hectares, one of the best in the country, containing a wide variety of animals native to the Chaco, as well as a botanical reserve of local species. The **Museo Histórico de la Ciudad**, San Martín y Sarmiento, displays on the founding and early growth of the city, Tuesday-Friday 0730-2000, Saturday/Sunday 1430-2100. The **Casa de la Cultura**, Calles 12 y 9, has exhibitions of indigenous handicrafts, archaeology, anthropology.

Excursions To **Quitilipi**, 23 km east along Route 16, where there is a Toba community and a free municipal camp-site. To **Castelli** (*population* 13,000) 114 km north, where there is a large Toba Indian community and an *artesanía* shop. **Accommodation E** *Hotel Guc*, basic. **Buses** Central Sáenz Peña services at 1100, 1530 and 2000.

● **Accommodation A2** *Gualok*, San Martín 1198, T 20521, including use of thermal baths (also available to non-residents for a small charge); **A3** *Augustus*, Belgrano 483, T 22809, air conditioning; **B** *Orel*, San Martín 130, T 20101; *Res Asturias*, Belgrano 402, T 20210, fair; *Res Sáenz Peña*, Sub Palmira 464, T 20320, near bus station, cheap. **Camping El Descanso**, municipal site, 1 km east of centre.

● **Entertainment Thermal baths**: Brown 541, with sauna, massage and other services.

● **Buses** To Buenos Aires, daily 2000, US$40 (from Buenos Aires also daily 2000), La Estrella and La Internacional alternate days; to Santiago del Estero and Tucumán, Empresa El Rayo daily; to Resistencia (connection for Salta 1700 daily), 2 hours, US$4.

NORTHWEST OF ROQUE SAENZ PENA

At **Avia Terai**, 31 km northwest of Roque Sáenz Peña, the road forks. Provincial Route 94 goes southwest to General Pinedo, then continues paved as National Route 89 to Quimilí and Santiago del Estero. Along this road, near Gancedo, 141 km south of Avia Terai on the border of Chaco and Santiago del Estero provinces is the **Campo del Cielo**, a meteorite impact field about 15 km by 4 km where about 5,000 years ago a planetoid broke before landing into 30 main pieces. Some of the meteorites are on display in Buenos Aires (the Rivadavia Museum and the Planetarium), but the largest, 'El Chaco' (33.4 tonnes), is on display at the Campo. Access is by a 15 km dirt road south from Gancedo.

From Avia Terai, Route 16, runs straight northwest through **Pampa del Infierno**, Km 232, to the Santiago del Estero border. In Santiago province the road is good as far as Los Tigres, Km 387, then less good to the Salta border. From this border to **Macapillo**, Km 539, it is straight and well-paved. From Macapillo

the road runs north following the Río Juramento to **Joaquín V González**, Km 575, around which it is appalling and difficult after rain. From here it continues through Ceibalito and El Tunal to meet Route 9 just north of Metán. At Km 585 and Km 593, roads run north to connect with provincial Route 5 (passing Parque Nacional El Rey, see page 242) and Route 9 at Lumbreras. The Joaquín V González stretch can be avoided by a dust-road which branches off just past Macapillo and runs to El Tunal, via Corral Quemado.

Route 16: The Trans Chaco Highway

Route 9 to Tucumán — Route 9 to Salta and Jujuy

90
8 — To Route 5
10 — Joaquín V González
28 — El Quebrachal
8 — Malcapillo
76 — Taco Pozo
49 — Monte Quemado
27 — Los Tigres
84 — Pampa de los Guanacos
71 — Pampa del Infierno
To Santiago del Estero
48 — Avia Terai
31 — Roque Saenz Peña — 114 — Castelli
16 — Quitilipi
81 — 38 — Parque Nacional Chaco
56 — Resistencia

Not to scale
Distance in km

- **Services** There are service stations at Roque Sáenz Peña, Pampa del Infierno (ACA *Hostería*), Pampa de los Guanacos (good hot, clean and free showers at the YPF station, and good value set dinner at the *comedor* next door), **Taco Pozo** (basic *Hospedaje* half a block from ACA station), **El Quebrachal** (gaucho festival in late November) and J V González (last fuel before Güemes en route to Salta). Fuel cannot be pumped during frequent power cuts.

ROUTE 81

Running northwest across the Chaco from Formosa to Embarcación, this is the other route across the Chaco. It is paved as far as Las Lomitas, Km 299, from where it is dirt and often in very poor condition, especially after rain.

RESERVA NACIONAL FORMOSA

Situated 210 km northwest of Las Lomitas and some 500 km north west of Formosa, this park stretches between the Río Teuquito to the north and the Río Bermejo to the south. Covering 10,000 hectares and located at the heart of the Dry Chaco, the park covers 10,000 hectares of woodlands broken by the floodplains of the Río Teuquito. The park is one of the few habitats in Argentina of the endangered *tatú carreta* (priodontes maximus), the largest surviving species of armadillo. Other fauna include carayá monkeys, mountain foxes, pumas, peccaries and a wide variety of bird species.

The best times to visit are spring and autumn.

- **Access** Park entrance is reached by Provincial Route 39 which runs 62 km south from Ingeniero Juárez, situated 459 km northwest of Formosa. 4WD vehicle advisable. No accommodation, take supplies from Ingeniero Juárez.

ALONG THE ALTO PARANA

At the confluence of the two rivers above Corrientes the Río Paraguay comes in from the north, the Alto Paraná from the east. The Alto Paraná is difficult to navigate, being shallow in parts, braided in others, its various channels embracing mid-stream islands. Much rice is grown on its banks. Yerba mate, tea and tobacco are grown in the area around Posadas.

ITUZAINGO

(*Population* 10,000; *Altitude* 72m) lies 227 km east of Corrientes on the northern edge o the Esteros del Iberá. There are good view of the birdlife of Iberá from the road. It is modern town serving the nearby Yacyreta Apipé hydroelectric project, which can b visited: free buses run to Centro de Relacio nes Públicas, where a video is shown an other information given.

- **Accommodation** Several hotels, eq **A3** *Ituzaingó*, Entre Rios y Iberá, T 20601 **E** *Hosp Dos Hermanos*, Pellegriní y Posadas clean, friendly.

- **Estancias** *San Gará*, Route 12, Km 1237 about 15 km west, full board **A2** pp, or ir dormitory with hammock-style accommoda tion, **C** pp, including pool and all excursions intc the Iberá marshes, by boat, jeep or on horseback a lovely place with extraordinary hospitality recommended. Book in advance: T 0786 20550, in Posadas 0752-27217, in Buenos Ai res, 01-811-1132, F 476-2648 (office a

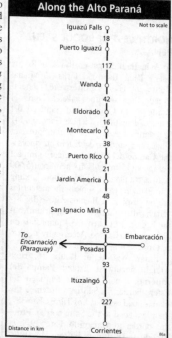

Along the Alto Paraná

Not to scale

Iguazú Falls
  18
Puerto Iguazú
  117
Wanda
  42
Eldorado
  16
Montecarlo
  38
Puerto Rico
  21
Jardín America
  48
San Ignacio Mini
  63   Embarcación
To Encarnación (Paraguay) ← Posadas
  93
Ituzaingó
  227
Distance in km Corrientes

86a

Avenida Alvear 1668, 5th floor); ask for owner Sr Pablo Prats. Take any bus between Posadas and Ituzaingó and walk 1.5 km from turning to the *estancia*; **A2** pp *San Juan Poriahú*, on the northern edge of the Iberá marshes, near Loreto, 83 km southwest of Posadas, 16,500 hectares, devoted to cattle ranching and cereals. Full board accommodation. Tours are offered in boats to see a superb array of animals and birds. Also horseriding, fishing. Open March-November to groups of 4-12. Transport from Corrientes US$45. T/F Buenos Aires 791-9511, from US$75 per person per day, advance booking essential.

POSADAS

(*Population* 211,000; *Altitude* 82m; *Phone code* 0752) the main Argentine port on the south bank of the Alto Paraná, is 320 km east of Corrientes. Founded in 1879, the city flourished as a river port and is now capital of Misiones.

Places of interest

The centre of the city is the Plaza 9 de Julio on which stand the **Cathedral** and the **Gobernación**, in French neogothic style. There are fine views over the river from the **Parque Río del Paraguay**, 11 blocks north, where there is also a good **Mercado Artesanal** (Monday-Friday, 0800-1200). A good way of seeing the city is to take the No 7 bus ('Circunvalación') from Calle Junín. On the opposite bank of the river lies the Paraguayan town of Encarnación, which can be reached by the San Roque bridge.

Museums

Museo Regional, Alberdi 606 in the Parque Río del Paraguay, open 0800-1200, 1400-2000, rather neglected.

Museo del Hombre, General Paz 1865, open Monday-Friday, 0700-1300, 1400-1900, housing archaeological pieces from the areas to be flooded by the Yacyretá hydroelectric project and a section on the Jesuit missionary era.

Museo de Ciencias Naturales, San Luis 384, open Monday-Friday, 0800-1200, 1500-1900, Saturday/Sunday (summer) 0900-1200, US$1, including sections on the Guaraní, Jesuit missions especially San Ignacio Miní, European colonization and endangered species.

Museo de Bellas Artes, Sarmiento 1815, open 0700-1230, 1400-1830, entry US$2.

Excursions

To **San Miguel Apóstoles** (*phone code* 0758), 65 km south, a prosperous town founded by Ukrainian and Polish immigrants, where a maté festival is held in November. **Accommodation D** *Hotel Misiones*.

To **Estancia Santa Inés**, 20 km south (Route 105), T 0752-36194, F 0752-39998, 2,000 hectares, much of which grows *yerba maté*. Activities include walking, horseriding and, between February and October, helping in *maté* cultivation. Accommodation **A3** full board; half-day activities US$20, taxi from Posadas, US$15.

Local information

NB After alterations to street numbering, all buildings have old and new numbers.

● **Accommodation**
Cheaper accommodation is available in Embarcación. Best is **A2** *Libertador*, San Lorenzo 2208, T 37601, F 39448, with breakfast, also cheaper rooms for travellers; **A2** *Continental*, Bolívar 314, T 38966, F 35302, comfortable but noisy, restaurant, parking, breakfast; **A2** *Posadas*, Bolívar 1949, T 40888, F 30294, garage, air conditioning, TV, comfortable, good service, snack bar, laundry, highly recommended; **B** *Turismo*, Bolívar 171, T 37401,

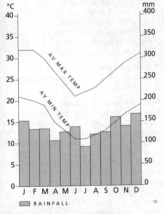

°C / mm

Climate: Posadas

RAINFALL

Posadas

Hotels:
1. City
2. Continental
3. Gran Misiones
4. Horianski
5. Libertador
6. Posadas
7. Turismo

modern, air conditioning; **B** *City*, Colón 280, T 33901, air conditioning, central, good value, good restaurant.

Near bus terminal: **B** *Carioca*, Mitre 2437, T 24113, next to expreso Singer; **B** *Colonial*, Barrufaldi 2419, T 36149; **B** *Horianski*, Líbano 2655, T 22675, garage, fan, poor value; **C** *Res Misiones*, Azara 382, basic, helpful; **C** *Gran Hotel Misiones*, Líbano y Barrufaldi, T 22777, run down, with breakfast; **B** *Res Marlis*, Corrientes 234, T 25764, German spoken, highly recommended; **B** *Le Petit*, Santiago del Estero 1630, T 36031, parking. **C** *Res Andresito*, Salta 1743, T 23850, youth hostel style, noisy.

Camping Municipal site, Avenida Gendarmeria Nacional, on the river, off Route 12, electric showers, dirty, shop, reached by buses 4 or 21 from centre;.

● **Places to eat**
El Tropezón, San Martín 185, good, inexpensive; *El Encuentro*, San Martín 361, good value; *La Ventana*, Bolívar 1725, excellent; *Sociedad Española*, La Rioja 1848, good food, popular lunches; *El Estribo*, Tucumán y Ayacucho, good cooking in attractive atmosphere, recommended;

La Querencia, Bolívar 322, on Plaza 9 de Julio, good value, recommended; *Pizzería Los Pinos*, Sarmiento y Rivadavia, excellent and cheap; *Pizzería La Grata Alegría*, Bolívar y Junín, good; *Sukimo*, Azara near San Martín, good for breakfast. The restaurant at San Martín 1788 serves excellent meals, good value. Several cheap places on Mitre near the bus terminal, near the market and on the road to the port.

● **Airline offices**
Lapa, Junín 2054, T 40300; **Austral**, Ayacucho 264, T 32889.

● **Banks & money changers**
Banco de Iberá, Bolívar 1821 (main plaza), changes Amex travellers' cheques (4-5% commission); **Banco de La Nación**, Bolívar 1799, opens 0700-1215; **Banco Francés**, San Martín y San Lorenzo, Visa cash advance (morning only); **Banco Nacional del Lavoro**, Plaza 9 de Julio, ATM accepts Mastercard and Visa. **Cambio Mazza**, Bolívar 1932 and Buenos Aires 1442, open Saturday 0800-1200, travellers' cheques accepted. Amex agent, *Express Travel*, Félix de Azara 2097, T 237687 Street money changers on southwest corner of Plaza

9 de Julio. If stuck when banks and *cambios* are closed, cross the river to Encarnación and use the street changers.

● **Consulates**

Brazil, Mitre 631, T 24830, 0800-1200, visas issued free, photo required, 90 days given; **Paraguay**, San Lorenzo 179.

● **Entertainment**

Discos: *Los Años 60*, San Lorenzo y Entre Ríos; *Power*, Bolívar between 3 de Febrero y 25 de Mayo. Another at San Martín y Jujuy, open 0100-0500 Thursday-Sunday.

● **Laundry**

Lavemaster, Santiago del Estero y San Lorenzo, efficient.

● **Post & telecommunications**

Post Office: Bolívar y Ayacucho.

● **Tour companies & travel agents**

Viajes Turismo, Colón 1901, ask for Kenneth Nairn, speaks English, most helpful, good tours to Iguazú and local sights.

● **Tourist offices**

Colón 1985 y La Rioja, T 24360, helpful, maps and brochures in English of Posadas, Formosa and Iguazú Falls. Municipal kiosk on Plaza 9 de Julio, open 0800-1200, 1400-2000 daily. Hotel listings for Misiones province.

● **Transport**

Air General San Martín Airport, 12 km west, reached by Bus No 8 or 28 from near bus terminal (ask at kiosk opposite terminal) in 20 minutes, taxi US$13. To **Buenos Aires**, Lapa and Austral, both once a week via Corrientes; Lapa also to **Iguazú**, Austral to **Formosa**.

Buses Terminal at Uruguay y Mitre. Expreso Singer and Tigre terminal is at Mitre 2447 (T 24771/2) 5 minutes walk from the main terminal To **Buenos Aires**, 15 hours, shop around off season for best deal; Singer and Tigre each have several buses a day: *común* US$47.50, *diferencial* US$58, *ejecutivo* (with hot meal) US$70; some go via Resistencia, some via Concordia. From the Argentine side of the international bridge bus tickets to Buenos Aires are sold which includes taxi to bus terminal and breakfast. Frequent services to San Ignacio Miní, 1 hour, US$3.50, and Puerto Iguazú, *servicio común* US$16, 7 hours, *expreso*, US$23, 5 hours; to **Córdoba**, Singer and Litoral on alternate days at 1200, 19 hours; to **Corrientes** US$15; to **Formosa**, US$8; to **Tucumán**, La Estrella, daily 1600, 19 hours, US$55; to **Resistencia**, 6-7 hours, US$18; to **Concordia**, Singer, US$32, 2100 daily, 10 hours; to **Concepción del Uruguay**, Singer, US$29, 11 hours.

International For buses to *Encarnación* see below under Frontier Crossing. To **Asunción**, Singer, daily 1400, 7 hours, and Empresa Godoy, US$14; to **Montevideo**, a roundabout journey because the main Asunción-Montevideo route passes through Corrientes; alternative is Singer to the junction for Colón, at Villa San José (ACA hostel, C), local bus to Colón, bus over the bridge to Paysandú, then on to Montevideo. To Brazil via Uruguaiana, Singer, US$10-14, 6 hours, 3 daily to **Paso de los Libres**, then cross the international bridge. Singer to **Porto Alegre**, via Oberá, Panambí, Santo Angelo and Carazinho, Tuesday, Thursday, Sunday at 1400, arriving 0345 next day.

FRONTIER WITH PARAGUAY: PUENTE SAN ROQUE

This is the only route between the two cities: the ferry service across the river is for locals only (no immigration facilities). Pedestrians and cyclists are not allowed to cross the bridge; cyclists must ask officials for assistance. Pesos are accepted in Encarnación, so no need to change them back into dollars. **NB** Paraguay is 1 hour behind Argentina, except during Paraguayan summer time.

● **Immigration & customs**

Formalities are conducted at respective ends of the bridge. Argentine side has different offices for locals and foreigners; Paraguay has one for both. Delays are common entering Argentina.

● **Buses**

Buses leave from opposite terminal every 15 minutes, *servicio común* US$1.50, *servicio diferencial* (faster service at frontier) US$3; buses do not wait for formalities; alight, keep your ticket and luggage, and catch a later bus. Taxi US$5.

INTO PARAGUAY: ENCARNACION

(*Population* 60,000) situated some 371 km southeast of Asunción, Encarnación is the third largest city in Paraguay. Founded in 1614, it exports the products of a rich agricultural area: timber, soya, *maté*, tobacco, cotton, and hides. The old centre is due to be drowned when the Yacyretá-Apipé dam is completed: though badly neglected, it forms the main commercial area, selling a wide range of cheap goods to visitors from Argentina and Brazil. A modern, but less intersting, centre has been built on higher ground. The cost of living is higher than in most other parts of Paraguay, but at present tourist goods, electrical equipment and accommodation are much cheaper than in Posadas.

Excursions to Jesuit Missions

To **Trinidad**, the hilltop site of a Jesuit *reducción*, 28 km east of Encarnación by Route 6. Founded in 1706 and designed by the architect Juan Bautista Prímoli, it is now a Unesco World Cultural Heritage site. The Jesuit church, once completely ruined, has been partially restored. Note the restored carved stone pulpit, the font and other masonry and relief sculpture. Also partially rebuilt is the bell-tower which is near the original church (excellent views from the top). You can also see another church, a college, workshops and the Indians' living quarters. For information, or tours, contact Sr Augusto Servián Goana, the curator who lives close by. **Accommodation** You can stay at the Centro Social, food and shower available, take sleeping gear; camping permitted at the souvenir stall. Hotel under construction. **Buses** From Encarnación take any bus to Ciudad del Este, US$1 (beware overcharging). A taxi tour from Encarnación costs about US$30.

To **Jesús**, a small town with the ruins of another mission, 10 km northwest of Trinidad, along a rough road (which turns off 300m north from Trinidad entrance). In the five years between settling here in 1763 and being expelled, the Jesuits commenced a massive construction programme including church, sacristy, *residencia* and a baptistry, on one side of which is a square tower. There is a fine front façade with three great arched portals in a Moorish style. Beautiful views in all directions. Opening hours as for Trinidad, entry US$1. Camping permitted at entrance to ruins. **Buses** Unreliable service from Trinidad, 30 minutes, US$1, last return bus 1700, also collective taxis, US$4.25. Enquire locally as taxis try to overcharge.

To **San Cosmé y Damián**, another Jesuit site about 90 km west. Although founded as a Jesuit mission in 1632, it was moved to the present site in 1760. When the Jesuits were expelled seven years later, the great church and ancillary buildings were unfinished. A huge completion project has recently been carried out following the original plans. Open 0700-1100, 1300-1700, entry US$0.25. **Accommodation E** *hospedaje* opposite Antel building, dirty. Camping is possible in the school grounds but ask first. **Buses** from Encarnación, La Cosmeña, US$4.25, 2 hours, 0830, also services by Perla del Sur.

Local information
● **Accommodation**

Generally better value than Posadas.

A2 *Novohotel Encarnación*, first class, on outskirts Route 1, Km 2, T 4131, comfortable, very well run, highly recommended; **B** *Paraná*, Estigarribia 1414, T 4440, good breakfast, helpful, recommended.

Budget accommodation: C *Acuario*, Mallorquín 1550, T 2676, with breakfast, central, pleasant, parking; **D** *Central*, Mariscal López 542, T 3454, with breakfast, nice patio, German spoken; **D** *Germano*, Cabañas y Carlos A López, opposite bus terminal, T 3346, **E** without bath, German and Japanese spoken, small, very accommodating, highly recommended; **D** *Hotel Liz*, Independencia 1746, T 2609, comfortable, restaurant, parking, recommended; **D** *Viena*, PJ Caballero 568, T 3486, beside Antelco, with breakfast, German spoken, food, garage; **E** *La Rueda*, Carlos A López y Memmel near bus terminal, a bit run down but OK.

● **Places to eat**

Rubi, Estigarribia 519, good Chinese; *Parrillada las Delicias*, Estigarribia 1694, good steaks, comfortable, Chilean wines; *Rancho Grande*, Estigarribia y Cerro Corá, large parrillada, live music; *Cuarajhy*, Estigarribia y Pereira, terrace seating, good food, open 24 hours; *Ñasaindy*, Estigarribia 900, for snacks; *Tokio*, Estigarribia 472, good Japanese, real coffee.

● **Banks & money changers**

Most banks are in the upper town, eg *Banco Continental*, Estigarribia 1418, Visa accepted; Lloyds Bank, Villarrica y Estigarribia, open Monday-Friday 0845-1215; *Banco Unión*, Estigarribia 1404, changes travellers' cheques (with purchase receipt), cash advance on Visa. Money changers at the Paraguayan side of the bridge but it is best to change money in town. Several *Casas de cambio* for cash on Estagarribia (eg *Cambios Guaraní* at No 307, *Cambio Iguazú* at No 211).

● **Consulates**
Argentina, Mallorquín y Cabañas; Brazil, Memmel 452; Germany, Memmel 627; Japan, Carlos A López 1290.

● **Laundry**
Laverap, 25 de Mayo 552.

● **Post & telecommunications**
International Phone: Antelco, Capitán PJ Caballero y Mariscal López, 0700-2200, very unfriendly.

● **Tourist offices**
Wiessen 345, three blocks from bus terminal, helpful, open 0800-1200; street map of city. In the afternoon a map of city can be obtained from the Municipalidad, Estigarribia y Kreusser, oficina de planificación.

● **Transport**
Buses Terminal is at Estigarribia y Memmel; good cheap snacks. To Asunción, Alborada, Flecha de Oro, Rysa, Nuestra Señora de la Asunción, all except last named at least 4 a day, 6 hours, US$15. Stopping (común) buses US$9, but much slower (6-7 hours). To Ciudad del Este, US$9, several daily, 4 hours.

SAN IGNACIO MINI

(*Population* 4,300m; *Altitude* 240m; *Phone code* 0752), 63 km east of Posadas is a small town which is the site of the most impressive remains of a Jesuit mission in the Misiones region. It is a good base for visiting other Jesuit ruins nearby and for walking. There is also a small **Museo Provincial**, which contains a collection of artefacts from Jesuit reducciones, open 0700-1900 daily.

History

San Ignacio Mini ('small' in comparison with San Ignacio Guazu – 'large' – on the Paraguayan side of the Río Paraná) was founded on its present site in 1696. At the height of its prosperity in 1731, the mission housed 4,356 people but after the expulsion of the Jesuits in 1767 its decline was rapid: by 1784 there were only 176 Guaraní and by 1810 none remained. In 1817, by order of the Paraguayan dictator, Rodriguez de Francia, San Ignacio was set on fire. The ruins, like those of nearby Santa Ana and Loreto, were lost in the jungle until discovered again in 1897. In 1943 control over the site was handed to an agency of the Argentine government.

Some of the craft work produced at San Ignacio can be seen in two museums in Buenos Aires: the Museo colonial Isaac Fernández Blanco and the municipal Museo de Arte Colonial.

Visiting the San Ignacio ruins

Like other Jesuit missions San Ignacio Mini was constructed around a central plaza: to the north, east and west were about 30 parallel one-storey buildings, each with a wide veranda in front and each divided into ten small, one-room dwellings. The roofs have gone, but the massive metre-thick walls are still standing except where they have been torn down by the *ibapoi* trees. The public buildings, some still 10m high, are on the south side of the plaza: in the centre are the ruins of the church, 71m x 28m, finished about 1724. To the right is the cemetery, to the left the cloisters, the priests' quarters and the workshops. The masonry, a red sandstone, was held together by a sandy mud. There is much bas-relief sculpture, mostly of floral designs.

The **Centro de Interpretación Jesuítico-Guaraní**, generally known as the 'Museo Vivo', 200m inside the entrance to the ruins, is an exhibition which includes representations of the lives of the Guaraní before the arrival of the Spanish, the work of the Jesuits and the consequences of their expulsion, as well as a fine model of the mission in its heyday; well laid out.

● **Entry** The site is maintained by UNESCO as a National Monument (open 0700-1900, entry US$2.50, US$10 with guide, tip appreciated if the guards look after your luggage). Allow about 1½ hours for a leisurely visit. Go early to avoid crowds. There are heavy rains in February. Mosquitoes can be a problem.

● **Son et-lumière** show at the ruins, 2000 (not Monday or Tuesday) US$2.50, weekends only out of season, cancelled in wet weather, Spanish only, tickets from museum.

Excursions

To the ruins of the mission of **Loreto**, reached by a 3 km dirt road (signposted) which turns off the main road 6 km west of San Ignacio. Moved to its present site in 1686, it was the site of the first printing

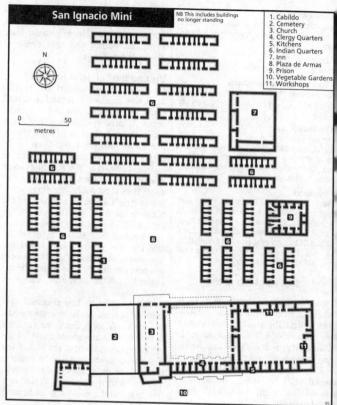

San Ignacio Mini

NB This includes buildings no longer standing

1. Cabildo
2. Cemetery
3. Church
4. Clergy Quarters
5. Kitchens
6. Indian Quarters
7. Inn
8. Plaza de Armas
9. Prison
10. Vegetable Gardens
11. Workshops

N

0   50
metres

press in the area. Little remains of this once large establishment other than a few walls, though excavations are in progress. Note the number of old trees with stones encased between their buttresses and main trunk. **Accommodation** *Colonial*, at entrance, secluded, recently opened.

To **Santa Ana**, the ruins of another Jesuit mission, 16 km west. Moved to its present site in 1660, Santa Ana was the site of the Jesuit iron foundry. Much less well preserved than San Ignacio, the ruins are 1½ km along a path from the main road (signposted), entry US$1.

To the **Casa de Horacio Quiroga**, the former house of an Argentine writer born in Uruguay, situated 2 km southwest of

town in beautiful gardens, entry US$2, recommended. From here the path leads to Puerto Nuevo on the Río Paraná, from where, during summer, boats cross to Paraguay.

To the **Parque Provincial Tetú-Cuare**, 11 km south, a 75 hectare reserve which includes the Peñon Tetú-Cuare, a 150m high hill also known as the Peñon Reina Victoria because of its supposed resemblance to the facial profile of the British queen; there are panoramic views over the Río Paraná. From here the path continues 1 km to a riverside picnic spot.

Local festivals

30-31 July.

Local information

● **Accommodation**

B *Hostería San Ignacio*, T 70064, with breakfast, nice rooms, pleasant grounds. **C** *San Ignacio*, San Martín 823, T 70047, good, *cabañas*; **C** *Hosp El Descanso*, Pellegrini 270, T 70207, modern, quiet, owner speaks German, recommended, excellent camping. **D** pp *El Sol*, Chatsa 73, with breakfast, nice garden. **E** *Hosp Italia*, San Martín 1291, artists' house, dormitory style, laundry facilities, recommended. **F** pp *Hosp Alemán Los Salpeterer*, Sarmiento y Centenario, 100m from bus terminal, without bath, kitchen, nice garden, run down but pleasant, 'pool', recommended, English and German spoken.

Camping At Hosp Alemán Los Salpeterer and house opposte. Two pleasant sites by small lake about 5 km south of San Ignacio, on Route 12, cold showers only.

● **Places to eat**

Restaurant Don Valentín, good and cheap lunches. Opposite the entrance to the ruins are several *comedores* and a shop selling huge homemade ice creams.

● **Tour companies & travel agents**

Tours and excursions on foot, on horseback and by canoe are offered by Dante and Eva Perroue, details from tourist information. Also Jorge and Diana, in house opposite Hosp Alemán Los Salpeterer, offer horses, canoeing, tours.

● **Buses**

Though some buses leave from the terminal at Sarmiento y Quiroga, many through services stop only at the entrance to San Ignacio. Buses to/from **Posadas** every 30 minutes-1 hour, US$3.50, last return bus at 2100; to **Puerto Iguazú**, US$14; to **Buenos Aires**, US$35 including meals, 24 hours, 1800, 1900.

SAN IGNACIO TO PUERTO IGUAZU

Route 12 continues northeast, parallel to the Río Alto Paraná, towards Puerto Iguazú. It passes through **Jardín América**, Km 48 (*Salto Tabei* campsite 2 km off Route 12, excellent, swimming, fishing, restaurant, cabins, recommended), **Capioví** (restaurant, *Salto*, and campsite, with a room with beds for budget travellers, pleasant, near Capioví Falls; owner speaks German and English) and **Puerto Rico** (*population* 12,000; *altitude* 205m) Km 69 (hotel, restaurants, poor campsite).

Montecarlo (*population* 12,500; *altitude* 130m; *Phone code* 0751) Km 107, has is a

zoo and a *yerba mate* packing plant which can be visited.

● **Accommodation** *ACA hostería*, T 97023, highly recommended; **C** *Ideal*; **C** *Kayken*. **Camping** Good site with pool.

ELDORADO

(*Population* 38,000; *Altitude* 218m; *Phone code* 0751), Km 123, is a prosperous small town surrounded by flourishing *mate*, tung, citrus, eucalyptus and tobacco plantations. The ACA office is very helpful and has a large illuminated map of Eldorado and its surroundings. For information on the **Misiones Rainforest Reserve**, contact Daphne Colcombet, T (0751) 21351.

● **Accommodation** **A3** *Hostería ACA*, T 21370, pool, good facilities; **B** *Alfa*, Córdoba y Rioja, T 21097; **C** *Atlántida*, San Martín 3087, T 21441, air conditioning, pool, parking, good restaurants, recommended; **C** *Esmeralda*, San Martín, Km 8, basic; **C** *Ilex*, San Martín, Km 9, safe; *Gran Riojano*, San Martín 314, T 22217, 5 minutes walk from main road crossing, with restaurant. **Camping** Municipal site in Parque Schweim, San Martín, Km 1, T 2154, free, good.

● **Banks & money changers** *Cambio Fonseca.*

● **Estancia** **A1** pp *Las Mercedes*, 7 km from town, T 31511, F 31448, 620 hectares of maté and pine plantations, plus cattle, offers birdwatching, horseriding, swimming pool, fishing, canoeing, English, German, Russian spoken, recommended.

WANDA

(*Population* 7,500; *Altitude* 120m) Km 165, is famous as the site of two open-cast amethyst and quartz mines which sell gems. There are free guided tours to one of them, Tierra Colorada, daily.

● **Accommodation** **C** pp *Hotel Las Brisas*, at Puerto Esperanza, Swiss owned, English and German spoken, discount for Swiss nationals.

● **Buses** Between Posadas and Puerto Iguazú stop near the mines and the hotel.

THE INTERIOR OF MISIONES

An alternative route through Misiones is along Provincial Route 14 which runs from San José, 42 km south of Posadas, northeast through the heart of Misiones to Bernardo de Yrigoyen, on the Brazilian

Subtropical rainforest of Misiones

frontier. Along this route several roads connect with Route 12.

At **Leandro N Alem** (*population* 15,600; *altitude* 290m), 52 km east of San José, Provincial Route 4 runs south to **San Javier** (*population* 6,500) 43 km south on the Río Uruguay, in an area famous for sugar cultivation and fishing. Cerro Monje, a hill 6 km north, is the site of a chapel, which attracts pilgrims in Holy Week. There is a **Museo Histórico** and just west of town are the ruins of the Jesuit mission of San Francisco Javier. Some 26 km west along Provincial Route 2 (unpaved) are the ruins of another Jesuit Mission, Santa María La Mayor. **Accommodation** *ACA Hotel*, Plaza del Cerrito. **Transport** Frequent ferry service across the river to Porto Xavier in Brazil from the port, 4 km from town. Buses to Posadas.

OBERA

(*Population* 42,000; *Altitude* 310m; *Phone code* 0755) 79 km northeast of San José (95 km from Posadas) is located in an area of tea and *yerba-maté* plantations: the factories for drying the leaves can be visited. One of the biggest centres of 20th century European immigration in the province, it is the second largest town in Misiones. Its immigrant origins can be seen in its different churches. East of the centre is the **Parque de Naciones**, with houses to commemorate the 17 nationalities who settled here. Nearby, at Haiti y Diaz de Solís, is the

Criadero de Pájaros Wendlinger, housing a collection of local birds. There are waterfalls, Salto Berrondo, set in a park 6 km west on Route 103. In the first week of October there is a *Fiesta Nacional del Inmigrantes*.

There are two museums: the **Museo de Ciencias Naturales**; Gobernador Barreyra y José Ingenieros, Tuesday-Friday 0600-1200, 1600-1800, Saturday 0600-1200 and the **Museo Municipal**, in the Municipalidad, Gobernador Barreyra y José Ingenieros, with displays on the foundation of the town, Monday-Friday 0600-1200, 1700-2000.

● **Accommodation** *Premier*, 9 de Julio 1164, T 21214, 3-star; *Cuatro Pinos*, Sarmiento 853, T 21306, good value; *C Real*, opposite bus terminal, T 22761, basic, hot showers; *Res Anahí* Santiago del Estero 36, T 21127, many others cheap accommodation at Centro Deportivo. **Camping** Santa Rita, Route 14m 3 km from town; Salto Berrondo, at the falls, swimming pool.

● **Places to eat** *Enqüete* restaurant, Cabeza de Vaca 340, good; excellent *empanadas* at *Bar Terminal* next to bus terminal.

● **Tourist office** Plazoleta Güemes, Libertad 90, open 0700-1900, Saturday 0700-1300, very helpful, lots of maps.

● **Buses** To **Posadas**, 2 hours, US$5.50, Singer; once a day to/from **Puerto Iguazú**, 5 hours.

FROM OBERA TO BERNARDO DE YRIGOYEN

Route 14 continues northeast from Oberá, passing through a string of small towns including **Aristobolo del Valle** (*population* 6,000; *altitude* 400m; *phone code* 0755), Km 135, and **Dos de Mayo** (*C Hotel Alex*, clean), Km 159.

At **Paraíso** Km 243, Provincial Route 21 (a dirt track) runs south 82 km to the Río Uruguay and the **Saltos del Moconá**, an alternative route is via El Soberbio, reached by paved Provincial Route 212 which turns off Route 14 at San Vicente (Km 178), but whichever route you take if you want to see the falls you will get wet: at least to your knees in the dry season while in wet weather it is impossible. The area has been declared a provincial park and there is fine fishing but no infrastructure.

Fauna of the subtropical rainforest

Coati

Although birds and mammals are not easily seen by visitors, the fauna of subtropical rainforests is the most diverse in Argentina. Some 500 species of birds have been identified in the forests of Misiones. Among mammals are the tapir, the largest mammal in South America, as well as brockets, peccaries, Brown Capuchin Monkeys, Crab-eating Racoons and several species of cats, including the puma, the Ocelot, the Margay and the Yaguarundi. Most species of bats, rodents and opossums can be found: the easiest to spot are the Coatí, the Grey Squirrel and the Paca. Among endangered species are the Jaguar (the largest cat in the Americas), the Giant Otter, the Bush-dog, the Giant anteater, the Harpy Eagle (the most powerful eagle in the world), the Brazilian Merganser (a duck with a serrated bill) and the Broad-snouted Caiman (now recovering from near extinction).

Santiago de la Vega

Beyond the Paraíso Route 14 continues to **San Pedro** (*population* 6,500; *altitude* 510) Km 255, 9 km north of which Route 20 (paved) runs north and joins up with Route 17 which runs west through lovely vegetation to Eldorado; Route 14 becomes a dirt track leading through **Tobuna**, where there are the Alegría falls to Bernardo de Yrigoyen.

● **Accommodation At San Pedro: C** *American Hotel*, Güemes 670, T 3364, meals served; at **Palmera Boca**, 3 km from San Pedro **C** *Posada Itaroga*, T 0751-70165, a family farm with log houses beside a lake, swimming and rowing boats, includes breakfast, cooking facilities, peaceful, relaxed and friendly, recommended, also camping.

Bernardo de Yrigoyen

(*Population* 3,700; *Altitude* 805m; *Phone code* 0741), on the Brazilian frontier is situated in the highest part of the hills of Misiones. From here the direct (dirt) road north to Puerto Iguazu, 142 km, crosses the National Park of Iguazú, via the quiet attractive villages of Andrecito, Cabuneí and San Antonio, offering fine views of rainforest. The **Reserva Natural San Antonio**, 600 hectares of forest on the banks of the Río San Antonio, protects one of the few remaining areas of Paraná pine, which

only 40 years ago covered large areas of the province.

● **Accommodation At Bernardo de Yrigoyen: C** ACA *Motel*, Ruta Nacional 14, Km 1435, T 0751-92026, clean, friendly; *Yrigoyen*, Libertad sin número. **At Andrecito**: **C** *Res Los Robles*, clean, quiet, nice.

● **Buses** There are services to B Yrigoyen from Eldorado and Oberá; local buses also run in dry weather from Yrigoyen to Puerto Iguazú through the national park.

IGUAZU

The Iguazú Falls, the most overwhelming and spectacular waterfalls in South America, are one of the most popular attractions in Argentina. Situated on the Río Iguazú (in Guaraní *guazú* is big and *I* is for water), which is the border between Argentina and Brazil, they lie 19 km upstream from the confluence of the Río Iguazú with the Río Alto Paraná. Bridges connect the Argentine town of Puerto Iguazú with the Brazilian city of Foz do Iguaçu and that city in turn with the Paraguayan city of Ciudad del Este. Both Argentine and Brazilian sides of the falls are described below: this is followed by descriptions of Puerto Iguazú, Foz do Iguaçu and Ciudad del Este.

THE IGUAZU FALLS

The Iguazú river basin extends over some 62,000 sq km. The river rises in the Brazilian hills near Curitiba at an altitude of around 1,200m, from where it flows for some 1,300 km across the Paraná Plateau, a thick layer of very hard basalt lava formed as a result of a massive Triassic volcanic erruption over 100 million years ago. On its way it receives the waters of about 30 rivers before reaching the falls which lie at an altitude of 160m at the edge of the plateau. Above the main falls the river, sown with wooded islets, opens out to a width of 4 km. There are rapids for 3½ km above the falls: a 60m precipice, over which the water plunges in 275 falls over a frontage of 2.7 km at an average rate of 1,750 cubic metres a second (in 1992 after heavy rains the rate rose to 29,000 cubic metres a second). The most spectacular part is the Garganta del Diablo, visited from the Argentine side (see below). Downstream is a 28 km long gorge stretching to the Río Alto Paraná and formed as the river has eroded its way back up the river. The falls are 20m higher than Niagara and about half as wide again.

Above the impact of the water upon basalt rock hovers a perpetual 30m high cloud of mist in which the sun creates blazing rainbows. Viewed from below, the tumbling water in its setting of begonias, orchids, fern and palms with toucans, flocks of parrots and cacique birds, swifts (*vencejos*) dodging in and out of the very falls, and myriad butterflies (at least 500 different species), is majestically beautiful, especially outside the cool season (when the water is much diminished, as are the birds and insects).

History

The first European visitor to the falls was the Spaniard Alvar Núñez Cabeza de Vaca in 1541, on his search for a connection between the Brazilian coast and the Río de la Plata: he named them the Saltos de Santa María. Though the falls were well known to the Jesuit missionaries, they were forgotten, except by local inhabitants, until the area was explored by a Brazilian expedition sent out by the Paraguayan president, Solano López in 1863. In the 20th century, the falls have become recognised globally as a major attraction though this did not impress Malcolm Slesser in the 1960s: "Except for a night or the tiles in Rio de janeiro, Brazil's greatest tourist attraction is the Iguaçu falls_This huge cataract eclipses Niagara. These falls are a splendid frolic of three hundred falls 270 feet high, almost three miles wide, filling the place with spray_Here is a large government hotel, luxurious with absolutely nothing to do except eat, drink and lounge - and look at the falls. We did not go, on the principle that a waterfall was a waterfall" (*Brazil: Land Without Limit*, George Allen and Unwin, London, 1969, pages 151-2).

How to visit

Most of the falls lie in Argentina, leading to the Argentine saying "Argentina puts on the show and Brazil charges for the view". There are National Parks on both sides of the falls; in both of them the subtropical rainforest benefits from the added humidity in the proximity of the falls, creating an environment rich in vegetation and fauna. Given the massive popularity of the falls, the remaining areas of the national parks are surprisingly little visited.

The Brazilian park offers a superb panoramic view of the whole falls and is best visited in the morning when the light is better for photography. The Argentine park (which requires a day to explore properly) offers closer views of the individual falls and is much more interesting from the point of view of seeing the forest with its wildlife and butterflies, though to appreciate these properly you need to go early and get well away from the visitors areas. Transport between the parks is via the Ponte Tancredo Neves as there is no crossing at the falls themselves. Both parks can, if necessary, be visited in a day, starting at about 0700, but the brisk pace needed for a rapid tour is exhausting for the non-athletic in the heat. Sunset from the Brazilian side is a worthwhile experience.

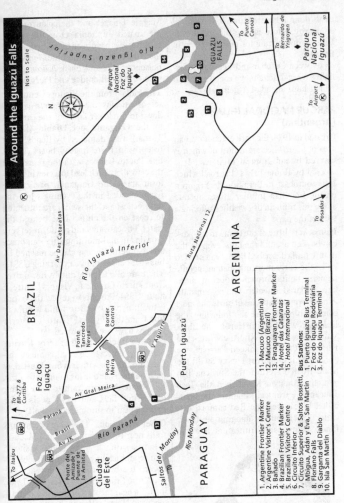

Around the Iguazú Falls

Not to Scale

1. Argentine Frontier Marker
2. Argentine Visitor's Centre
3. Bañado
4. Brazilian Frontier Marker
5. Brazilian Visitor's Centre
6. Circuito Inferior
7. Miguito Superior & Saltos Bossetti, Miguito, Adán y Eva, San Martin
8. Floriano Falls
9. Garganta del Diablo
10. Isla San Martin
11. Macuco (Argentina)
12. Macuco (Brazil)
13. Paraguayan Frontier Marker
14. *Hotel das Cataratas*
15. *Hotel Internacional*

Bus Stations:
1. Puerto Iguazú Bus Terminal
2. Foz do Iguaçu Rodoviária
3. Foz do Iguaçu Terminal

Busiest times are holiday periods and on Sunday, when helicopter tours over the falls from the Brazilian side are particularly popular (and noisy). Both parks have visitors' centres, though the information provided by the Argentine Centre is far superior to that in the Brazilian Centre. Despite the massive popularity of the falls, the remaining parts of the parks are surprisingly little visited.

There are many advantages in staying in Foz and commuting to the Argentine side (better and cheaper hotels and restaurants, for example). If you decide to stay in Brazil, do not rely on spending *reais* in Argentina; they are accepted, but at very poor rates. It is better to change dollars into pesos for the day, which is easily done at Puerto Iguazú bus terminal or nearby before taking the bus to the Falls. A poorer rate for pesos is given in Brazil.

Between October and February (daylight saving dates change each year) Brazil is 1 hour ahead of Argentina.

PARQUE NACIONAL IGUAZU (Argentina)

Created in 1934, the park extends over an area of 67,620 hectares, most of which is covered by sub-tropical rainforest. It is crossed by Route 101, a dirt road which runs southeast to Bernardo de Yrigoyen on the Brazilian frontier. Buses operate along this route in dry weather, offering a view of the park.

Fauna Very little of the fauna in the park can be seen around the falls: even on the nature trails described below you need to go in the early morning. Fauna include jaguars, tapirs, brown capuchin monkeys, collared anteaters and coatimundi. Among over 400 species of birds, the most commonly visible are the following: the Black-Crowned Night Heron, the Black Vulture, the Plumed Kite; the White-eyed Parakeet; the Blue-winged Parrolet, the greater Ani, the Great Dusky Swift, the Scale Troated Hermit, the Surucua Trogon, the Amazon Kingfisher, the Toco Toucan, the tropical kingbird, the Boat-billed Flycatcher, the Red-rumped Cacique which builds hanging nests on Pindo palms, and fruiteaters like the

Toco Toucan

Magpie Tanager and the colourful Purple-troated Euphonia. Over 100 species of butterflies have been identified, among them the colourful shiny blue *Morpho*, the poisonous red and black *heliconius* and species of Papilionidae and Pieridae.

The Falls From the Visitors Centre two sets of catwalks (the *Circuito Inferior*) lead down to the lower falls but the catwalks to the **Garganta del Diablo** (Devil's Throat) were damaged by floods, most recently in 1986. Instead boats (US$4) link Puerto Canoas with the remains of the catwalks which lead to a viewing platform above the Garganta, particularly recommended in the evening when the light is best and the swifts are returning to roost on the cliffs, some behind the water. The catwalks and platform get very crowded in mid-morning after tour buses arrive. Puerto Canoas can be reached by bus – see below – or by car, parking US$1). There are also trips by dinghy down river from Puerto Canoas to Visitors Centre, 1 hour, US$4. Projects to renew the entire catwalk network and to build a railway line from the Visitors' Centre to Puerto Canoas have been approved.

Below the falls a free ferry leaving regularly subject to demand, connects the Circuito Inferior with **Isla San Martín**. A path on the island leads to the top of the hill, where there are trails to some of the less visited falls and rocky pools (take bathing gear in summer to cool off).

Other attractions There are two nature trails near the falls: the Sendero Macuco 4 km, starting from near the Visitors' Centre and leading to a natural pool (El Pozón) fed by a waterfall and good for swimming; the Sendero Yacaratia, leading from near the start of the Macuco trail to Puerto Macuco (this has been criticised as not being a 'serious' nature trail).

● Activities

Iguazú Jungle Explorer offer a range of activities are offered, which can be booked through agencies in Puerto Iguazú or in the park. These include: *Aventura Náutica*, a journey by launch along the lower Río Iguazú to the foot of the falls, US$15; *Safari Náutico*, a 4 km journey by boat from Puerto Canoas to Puerto Marías along the Río Iguazú above the falls, US$10; *La Gran*

Papilionidae Butterfly

Aventura, a 7 km trip by jeep along the Yacaratia Trail, then up the lower Río Iguazú by boat to the canyon of the Garganta del Diablo, followed by a visit to Isla San Martín US$30; *Full Day*, which includes the *safari náutico*, *aventura náutica* and a visit to the Garganta del Diablo, US$25 or US$40 with lunch at the *Hotel Internacional*.

There are also night-time walking tours between the *Hotel Internacional* and the falls when the moon is full; on clear nights the moon casts a blue halo over the falls. Mountain bikes and boats can also be hired, US$3 an hour. For serious birdwatching and nature walks with English speaking guide contact Daniel Samay (*Explorador* agency) or Miguel Castelino through the Visitors' Centre, highly recommended.

Clothing In the rainy season, when water levels are high, waterproof coats or swimming costumes are advisable for some of the lower catwalks and for boat trips. Cameras should be carried in a plastic bag. Wear shoes with good soles, as the rocks can be very slippery in places.

Services Entry US$5, payable in pesos or dollars only (guests at *Hotel Internacional* should pay and get tickets stamped at the hotel to avoid paying again). Visitors' Centre includes a museum of local fauna and an auditorium for periodic slide shows (on request, minimum 8 people), no commentary, only music; it also sells a good guide book on Argentine birds.

Food and drinks are available in the Park but are expensive so best to take your own. **Camping** Camping Puerto Canoas 600m from Puerto Canoas, tables, but no other facilities, nearest drinking water at park entrance. Camping sometimes permitted at the school just inside the Park entrance.

● **Transport**
Transportes Cataratas buses run every 30-45 minutes from Puerto Iguazú bus terminal, stopping at the National Park entrance for the purchase of entry tickets and continuing to Puerto

Canoas. Fares US$2 to Visitors' Centre, US$2 to Puerto Canoas, payable in pesos, dollars or reais. First bus 0640, last 1700, last return 1900, journey time 30 minutes. These buses are sometimes erratic, especially when it is wet, even though the times are clearly indicated. There are fixed rates for taxis, US$30, up to 5 people. A tour from the bus terminal, taking in both sides of the Falls, costs US$40. Hitchhiking to the Falls is difficult, but you can hitch up to the Posadas intersection at Km 11, then it is only 7 km walk. For transport between the Argentine and Brazilian sides see below under Puerto Iguazú. Motorists can park overnight in the National Park, free.

PARQUE NACIONAL FOZ DO IGUAÇU (Brazil)

The Brazilian National Park was founded in 1939 and the area was designated a World Heritage Site by Unesco in 1986. The park covers 170,086 hectares, extending along the north bank of the Rio Iguaçu, then sweeping northwards to Santa Tereza do Oeste on the BR-277.

Fauna Most frequently encountered are little and red brocket deer, South American coati, white-eared opossum, and a sub-species of the brown capuchin monkey. The following are also present, but much harder to see: jaguar, ocelot, jaguarundi, puma, margay, white-lipped peccary, bush dog and southern river otter. The endangered tegu lizard is common. Over 100 species of butterflies have been identified, among them the electric blue *Morpho*, the poisonous red and black *heliconius* and species of Papilionidae and Pieridae.

The birdlife is especially rewarding for the birdwatcher. Five members of the toucan family can be seen: toco and red-breasted toucans, chestnut-eared araçari, saffron and spot-billed toucanets. In the bamboo stands you may see: spotted bamboowren, grey-bellied spinetail, several antshrikes, short-tailed antthrush. In the forest: rufous-thighed kite, black-and-white hawk-eagle, black-fronted piping-guan, blue ground dove, dark-billed cuckoo, black-capped screech-owl, surucua trogon, rufous-winged antwren, black-crowned tityra, red-ruffed fruit-crow, white-winged swallow, plush-crested jay, cream-bellied gnatcatcher,

The Macuco Safari

'After about 20 minutes ride on the trailer you get off and begin hiking your way down the side of the Iguaçu gorge to the Macuco Falls which cascade into a deep dark plunge pool. Steps cut into the rock allow you to descend to the foot of the falls but beware: they are slippery and steep. Stout walking shoes are a must. The tour is taken at a relaxed pace and there is no pressure to rush back up those steps. After the falls you descend to the banks of the river, where you take to water in inflatable rafts capable of carrying 20 people. The ride is bumpy, but make sure you look up at the steep sides of the gorge. As the boat comes up to the edge of the falls there is a deafening roar from above as the boat begins to turn and the spray is so powerful you have to shut your eyes. You will get very wet. Plastic raincoats are sold at the launch site and plastic bags are provided for cameras if you ask. The view of the falls is unbeatable. Once back on dry land you are whisked up to the top of the canyon by jeep to rejoin the trailer to the entrance. From here a free shuttle bus transfers you through the park to the top of the falls.'

Naomi Peirce

black-goggled and magpie tanagers, green-chinned euphonia, black-throated and utlramarine grosbeaks, yellow-billed cardinal,red-crested finch. (Bird and mammal information supplied by Douglas Trent, *Focus Tours*; see **Specialist Tour Operators**, see page 493.

From opposite the *Hotel das Cataratas* a 1½ km paved walk runs part of the way down the cliff near the rim of the Falls, giving a stupendous view of the whole Argentine side of the falls. It ends almost under the powerful Floriano Falls: from here an elevator carries visitors to the top of the Floriano Falls (from 0800; US$0.50) and to a path leading to Porto Canoa (if there is a queue it is easy and quick to walk up). Waterproof clothing can be hired although it is not absolutely necessary.

The **Macuco Safari Tour**, US$32 (Amex accepted), leaves from near the falls, with trailers taking the visitors down the trail (see box below); guides speak Portuguese, English and Spanish; take insect repellent, highly recommended. *Macuco Safari de Barco*, Caixa Postal 509, 85851-001, Foz do Iguaçu, Paraná, T (045) 574-4244. Expeditions can also be organized, by prior arrangement, for photographers, botanists and others, and boat hire can be arranged for up to 80 people, by the hour, or by the day.

Helicopter tours over the falls leave from *Hotel das Cataratas* at US$50 per person, 7 minutes. Apart from disturbing visitors, the helicopters are also reported to present a threat to some bird species which are laying thinner-shelled eggs: the altitude has been increased, making the flight less attractive.

There is a small museum 10 km from the Falls (1 km from park entrance is a side road to the museum, look for sign 'Centro de Visitantes' near the Policia Militar post) and opposite it are some steps that lead down the steep slope to the river bank. This is a beautiful walk. Park entry US$6, payable in *reais* only at the entrance. If possible, visit on a weekday when the walks are less crowded.

● **Places to eat** Non-residents can eat at the *Hotel das Cataratas*, US$27.50 midday and evening buffets.

● **Transport** Buses leave Foz do Iguaçu, from the *Terminal Urbana* on Avenida Juscelino Kubitschek, opposite Infantry Barracks. There are 2 services: Dois Irmãos (marked 'Cataratas') to the falls every hour, 0800-1800 at weekends, holidays and in high season, Monday-Friday, past airport and *Hotel das Cataratas*, 40 minutes US$1.20 one way, payable in *reais* only (the driver waits at the Park entrance while passengers purchase entry tickets); Transbalan (marked 'Parque Nacional'), every 30 minutes, to the park entrance only (from where you will need to take a 'Cataratas' bus for the rest of the way which works out more expensive). Both buses can also be picked up at any of the stops on Avenida Juscelino Kubitschek. Return buses 0700-1800,. Taxi US$6, plus US$2.50 per hour for waiting.

Many hotels organise tours to the Falls: these have been recommended in preference to taxi rides. If visiting Brazilian side from Puerto Iguazú by bus, ask driver to let you off shortly after the border at the roundabout for road to the falls (BR 469), where you can get another bus.

PUERTO IGUAZU

(*Population* 19,000; *Altitude* 210m; *Phone code* 0757) is situated 18 km northwest of the falls high above the river on the Argentine side near the confluence of the Ríos Iguazú and Alto Paraná. A modern town which serves mainly as a centre for visitors to the falls, its prosperity has varied in relation to the difference in prices between Argentina and Brazil. The port lies to the north of the town centre at the foot of a hill: from the port you can follow the Río Iguazú downstream towards Hito Argentino, a *mirador* with views over the point where the Ríos Iguazú and Alto Paraná meet and over neighbouring Brazil and Paraguay.

Museum

Museo Mbororé, San Martín 231, Monday-Saturday 1700-2100, US$1, exhibition on Guaraní culture, also sells Guaraní made handicrafts, cheaper than shops.

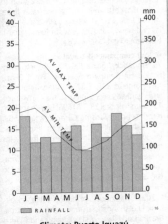

Climate: Puerto Iguazú

Local information
● Accommodation

Crowded during summer (January-February), Easter and July holiday periods. Accommodation is expensive but there is plenty of choice; outside the high season be prepared to shop around and to bargain.

L2-L3 *Internacional Iguazú*, T 20748, F 20311, 5-star, pool, casino, good restaurants, business facilities, overlooking the falls, rooms with garden views cost less, excellent, check-out can take ages. Reservations at Avenida Eduardo Madero 1020 (T 311-4259, or 313-6292), Buenos Aires (in UK through Utell Internacional); *Cataratas*, Route 12, Km 4, T 21000, F 21090, 5-star, pool, gymnasium.

A1 *Esturión*, Tres Fronteras 650, T 20020, clean, comfortable, swimming pool, good restaurant, reservations at Belgrano 265, 10th floor, Buenos Aires; **A3** *Alexander*, Córdoba 685, T 20249, T 20566, opposite bus station, air conditioning, includes breakfast, pool, recommended; **A3** *La Cabaña*, Tres Fronteras 434, T 20564, with breakfast, air conditioning, good, with an older part and a new annexe, swimming pool, recommended; **A3** *Las Orquídeas*, Ruta 12, Km 5, T 20472, very comfortable; **A3** *Saint George*, Córdoba 148, T 20633, F 20651, with breakfast, comfortable, pool and garden, good, expensive restaurant, **B** in older part, highly recommended.

B *Hostería Casa Blanca*, Guaraní 121, T 21320, two blocks from bus station, with breakfast, fan, large rooms with phone, recommended. Behind *Saint George* is **B** *Hostería Los Helechos*, Amarante 76 (off Córdoba), T 20338, with breakfast, owner speaks German, pleasant, fan, motel-style accommodation, 10% discount for ISIC and YHA card holders, pool; **B** *Gloria*, Uruguay 344, pool, quiet; **B** *Libertador*, Bompland 110, T 20416, modern, central, helpful, large bedrooms and public rooms, rooms at back have balconies overlooking garden and swimming pool; **B** *Tierra Colorada*, Córdoba y El Urú 265, T 20649, very good, with fan, trips arranged.

C *Res Lilian*, Beltrán 183, T 20968, two blocks from bus terminal, helpful, safe, recommended; **C** *Res Río Selva*, San Lorenzo 147, T 21555, laundry facilities, large garden, pool, communal barbecue, highly recommended; **C** *King*, Victoria Aguirre 209, T 20917, pool, hot showers, good value; **C** *Misiones*, Victoria Aquirre 304, T 20991, with breakfast, fan; **C** *Res Paquita*, Córdoba 158, T 20434, opposite terminal, nice setting, some rooms with terrace, recommended; **C** *Res San Fernando*, Córdoba y Guaraní, T 21429, near terminal, popular, **D** in low season.

Puerto Iguazú

Not to Scale

N

Hotels:
1. Alexander
2. Gloria
3. Libertador
4. Los Helechos
5. Misiones
6. Res Paguita
7. Saint George
8. Tierra Colorada

Places to eat:
9. La Rueda

To Turismo Dick, Telephone Office, Brazilian Consul, Hotel King & Iguazú Falls

Youth hostel: *Hosp Uno*, Beltrán 116, T 20529, **E** pp with bath, also dormitory accommodation, IYHA reduction, friendly, clean, recommended, tour to Itaipú, Foz de Iguazú and Brazilian side of falls. The Tourist Office has a list of family accommodation (**E** pp), though it may be reluctant to find private accommodation unless the hotels are full.

Camping For site in the National Park see above. Municipal site, 1 de Mayo y Entre Ríos, reported 'grim'. **Camping El Pindo**, Avenida Aguirre, Km 3 at the southern edge of town, US$1.60 per person, plus charge for tent and for use of pool, friendly, but very run down. There are also facilities at Complejo Turístico Americano, Route 12, Km 5, T 2782 including pool (open to non-guests, US$2.50) in pleasant, wooded gardens, but no food; US$3 per person, US$3 per car, US$3 per tent.

● **Places to eat**
La Rueda, Córdoba 28, good food at reasonable prices; *Pizzería Ser*, Aguirre 453, good pizzas; *Charro*, Córdoba 106, good food, popular with locals, no credit cards; *Don Nicola*, Bompland 555, good; *El Criollito*, Tres Fronteras 62, recommended; *Casa de Comercio*, Aguirre 327; *Tomás*, Córdoba y Misiones, at bus terminal, open 24 hours, *tenedor libre*; *Chapa*, behind bus station, cheap, highly recommended; *Fechoria*, Ing Eppens 294, good *empanadas*; *Panificadora Real*, Córdoba y Guaraní, good bread.

● **Airline offices**
Aerolíneas Argentinas, Brasil y Aguirre, T 20194; **Lapa**, Bompland 110, loc 7, T 20214.

● **Banks & money changers**
Three *casas de cambio* opposite the tourist office and several on Aguirre towards the outskirts of town towards the falls including **Dick**, changes travellers' cheques, at high commission (up to 10%). Kiosk at the bus terminal poor rates. Rates vary so shop around. Alternatively change US$ in Foz do Iguaçu and buy pesos in Puerto Iguazú. Nowhere to get cash on Visa.

● **Tour companies & travel agents**
Turismo Dick, Aguirre 226, T 20556, also in Foz do Iguaçu; *Reinhard Foerster*, Privat Servis, Tres Fronteras 335, T 2774, offers naturalists' and birdwatchers' programmes; *Macuco Tur*, Terminal, local 23, T 21696, English spoken, recommended; *Turismo Caracol*, Aguirre 563, T 20064, does all-day tour of both sides of falls, includes good meal in Brazil, but mainly for 'non-English speaking clients with an interest in shopping'. *Turismo Cuenca del Plata*, Amarante 76, T 20338, offers 10% discount to ISIC and youth card holders on local excursions. Recommended taxi-guide, Juan Villalba, T 20973 (radiotaxi 044), good value, speaks basic English. Agencies arrange day tours to the Brazilian side (lunch in Foz), Itaipú and Ciudad del Este (US$25) though more time is spent

shopping than at the falls, and to a Wanda gem mine, San Ignacio Miní and a local zoo (10 hours driving time, US$30, not including entry fees, may be cheaper for more than 2 in a taxi or hired car); *Kurtz*, at terminal, T/F 21599, helpful, recommended; *Africana Tours*, Esmeralda 358, Buenos Aires T/F 394-1720, recommended for their complete package, by plane or bus, including all tours, hotels and half-board (US$167-598 depending on hotel). Many agencies eg *Flyer Turismo*, run tours from Buenos Aires, starting at US$75 for 1-day.

● **Tourist office**
Aguirre 396, T 20800, open Monday-Friday 0800-1200, 1500-2000, Saturday/Sunday 0800-1200, 1630-2000.

● **Transport**
Local Car hire: Avis at airport. Localiza, at airport and Aguirre 279, T 20975. Cars may be taken to the Brazilian side for an extra US$5.

Air Airport south of Puerto Iguazú near the Falls. Expreso del Valle buses (T 20348) between airport and bus terminal connect with plane arrivals and departures, US$3; check times at Aerolíneas Argentinas office. Taxis charge US$10 to *Hotel Internacional*, at least US$18 to Puerto Iguazú, US$14 to Foz do Iguaçu and US$25 to the Brazilian airport.

Aerolíneas Argentinas and Lapa fly direct to/from Buenos Aires, 2 hours, flights are very crowded. For best view on landing, sit on right side of aircraft.

Buses To/from Buenos Aires, 21 hours, Expreso Singer, Expreso Tigre, Expreso Iguazú and other companies daily, US$39-45 *común*, US$65 *cama* (some offer student discounts). It is cheaper to take a local bus to Posadas and then rebook. To Santiago del Estero, Wednesday and Saturday 0130, 20 hours, Cotal, gives student discount; to Córdoba, via Posadas, 23 hours, US$45, Singer or El Litoral or Cruzero del Norte *semi-cama*; to Rosario daily except Thursday, US$50; to Posadas, stopping at San Ignacio Miní, frequent, 5 hours, US$23, *expreso*, 7 hours, US$16 *servicio común*; to San Ignacio Miní, US$14 *servicio común*, US$17 *rápido*; to Resistencia daily 1430 and 2200, 11 hours, US$30 (change there for Bolivian border at Aguas Blancas/Bermejo, via Güemes and Orán); to El Dorado, 2 hours, Cotal US$5; to Salta, via Tucumán, Tuesday, Thursday, Sunday 1100, Itatí, 12 hours, US$80.

FRONTIER WITH BRAZIL

This crossing via the Puente Tancredo Neves is straightforward. If crossing on a day visit no immigration formalities are required. Argentine immigration is at the Brazilian end of the bridge. If entering Argentina buses stop at immigration.

● **Brazilian Consulate**
In Puerto Iguazú, Guaraní y Esquiu, 0800-1200.

● **Transport**
Buses leave Puerto Iguazú terminal for Foz do Iguaçu every 20 minutes, US$2 but do not wait at the frontier so if you need exit and entry stamps keep your ticket and catch the next bus (bus companies do not recognize each other's tickets). Taxis: between the border and Puerto Iguazú US$15; between the border and *Hotel Internacional Iguazú* US$35.

FRONTIER WITH PARAGUAY

Ferry service from the port in Puerto Iguazú to Tres Fronteras is for locals only (no immigration facilities). Crossing to Paraguay is via Puente Tancredo Neves to Brazil and then via the Puente de la Amistad to Ciudad del Este. Brazilian entry and exit stamps are not required unless you are stopping in Brazil. There is a US$3 tax to enter Paraguay.

● **Paraguayan Consulate**
Bompland 355.

● **Transport**
Direct buses (non-stop in Brazil), leave Puerto Iguazú terminal every 30 minutes, US$2, 45 minutes, liable to delays especially in crossing the bridge to Ciudad del Este. Taxi from Puerto Iguazú to Ciudad del Este, US$70 one way.

FOZ DO IGUAÇU (Brazil)

(*Population* 188,190) A rapidly developing and improving town, with a wide range of accommodation and good communications by air and road with the main cities of southern Brazil, and with Asunción, Paraguay.

Excursions

To the **Itaipu dam**, on the Río Paraná 12 km north, the largest single power station in the world built jointly by Brazil and Paraguay. The Paraguayan side may be visited from Ciudad del Este.

Tours

Bus marked Canteira da Obra from Terminal Urbana (stand 50 Batalhão) goes every 40 minutes to the Public Relations office at the main entrance (US$0.35), Conjunto C-via Norte or via Sul bus goes more frequently to within 250m. Visits are free, but in groups only. In the Visitors' Centre (T 520-5252) a short video presentation, apparently available in English but

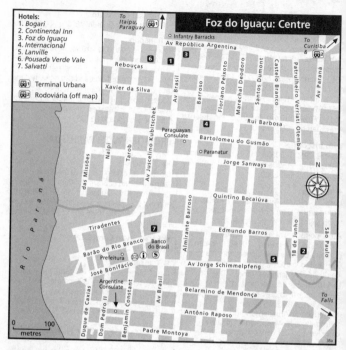

Hotels:
1. *Bogari*
2. *Continental Inn*
3. *Foz do Iguaçu*
4. *Internacional*
5. *Lanville*
6. *Pousada Verde Vale*
7. *Salvatti*

Terminal Urbana
Rodoviária (off map)

Foz do Iguaçu: Centre

usually only in Portuguese, will boggle your mind with stunning photography and amazing technical information. After the film, a coach will take you to the dam itself. As it crosses the top you get a stomach-churning view of the spillways and really begin to appreciate the scale of the project. There are several tours daily between 0800 and 1600 (closed between 1100 and 1400). The 'executive' bus and agency tours are an unnecessary expense. If it's sunny, go in the morning as the sun is behind the dam in the afternoon and you will get poor photographs.

The **Ecomuseu de Itaipu** (Avenida Tancredo Neves, Km 11, T 520-5065, Tuesday-Saturday 0900-1130, 1400-1700, Monday 1400-1700)and Iguaçu Environmental Education Centre are geared to educate about the preservation of the local culture and environment, or that part which isn't underwater (free with guide, recommended).

To the **artificial beaches on Lake Itaipu** The closest to Foz de Iguaçu are at Bairro de Três Lagoas, at Km 723 on BR 277, and in the municipality of Santa Terezinha do Itaipu, 34 km from Foz. The relaxing leisure parks have grassed areas with kiosks, barbecue sites and offer fishing as well as bathing, US$2.50. It is also possible to take boat trips on the lake.

To the **Parque das Aves** bird park, entrance US$8, at Rodovia das Cataratas Km 10.5, just before the falls, good reports; for guided tour T 523-1007.

Local information
● **Accommodation**

Hotels outside Foz do Iguaçu
L1 *Hotel das Cataratas*, T 523-2266, F 574-1688, directly overlooking the Falls, 32 km from Foz (40% discount for holders of the Brazil Air Pass), highly recommended, attractive colonial-style building with pleasant gardens (where a lot of wildlife can be seen at night and early morning) and pool. Check exchange rate if

…aying in dollars. Non-residents can eat here, US$27.50 midday and evening buffets; also …-la-carte dishes and dinner with show.

On road to Falls (Rodovia das Cataratas) are **L2** *Bourbon*, Km 2.5, T 523-1313, F 574-1110, …ll facilities, excellent buffet dinner, open to non-residents (US$12); **L3** *Colonial*, Km 16.5, T 574-1777, F 76-1960, near airport, pool, fine location; **A1** *Carimã*, Km 16, T 523-1818, F 574-3531, 3-star, very good value, air conditioning, pool, restaurant, bars, recommended; **A1** *Lanville Palace*, Jorge Schimmelpfeng 827, T 523-1511, F 523-1636, air conditioning, restaurant, bar, pool; **A3** *Panorama*, Km 12, T 23-1200, F 574-1490, good value, pool; many others.

Hotels in Foz do Iguaçu: in 1994, many street numbers were changed. Both old numbers (lower) and the new higher ones were still in use. We have altered numbers where known: bear changes in mind when looking for your hotel. If you know which hotel you wish to stay in (there are over 180), note that touts may say it no longer exists, or quote room rates below what is actually charged. There is a scam in which children will escort you to a cheap hotel, receiving commission for doing so. Your luggage is then stolen from the hotel. In high season (eg Christmas-New Year), you will not find a room under US$15. Many hotels offer excursions to the Falls.

L2 *Internacional*, Almirante Baroso 345, T 523-1414, F 574-5201, good.

A1 *Continental Inn*, Paraná 485, T/F 574-4122, good restaurant; **A1** *Salvatti*, Rio Branco 651, T 523-1121, F 574-3674, air conditioning, restaurant, cinema; **A2** *Rafahin*, Mal Deodoro 984, T 523-1213, F 523-2007, good restaurant, pool, well spoken of; **A2** *Suiça*, Felipe Wandscheer 3580, Swiss manager, helpful, pool; **A3** *Foz Presidente*, Rua Marechal Floriano 1851, T 523-2318, F 574-5155, shower, air conditioning, restaurant, pool, with breakfast, convenient for buses, recommended.

On Avenida Brasil: **A1** *Bogari Palace*, No 106, T 523-2243, F 523-1125, excellent restaurant, swimming pool; **A3** *Foz do Iguaçu*, No 97, T 574-4455, F 574-1775, good, expensive laundry, luggage store; **B** *City*, No 938, T 574-2074, fan, hot water; **C** *O Astro*, No 660, T 72-3584, OK, air conditioning; **C** *Dani Palace*, No 509, comfortable, good buffet breakfast; **D** *Ortega*, No 1140, T 574-1288, good breakfast.

In Rua Rebouças: **C** *Minas*, No 641, T 574-5208, basic, hot water, safe, no breakfast; **D** *German Pension*, No 1091, T 574-5603, recommended; **D** *Pietá*, No 84, T 574-5581, pool, good breakfast, car and guide, recommended; **D** *Piratini*, No 101, hot showers, shabby but recommended; **E** *Trento*, No 665, T 574-5111, air conditioning, noisy but recommended;

E *Pousada Verde Vale*, No 335, T 574-2925, youth hostel style, cramped but popular, buses to Falls stop outside.

Other mid range hotels: **B** *Estoril*, República Argentina 694, T 523-1233, F 523-2311, breakfast, pool, TV, recommended; **C** *Bastos*, Castelo Branco 831, T 574-5839, air conditioning, secure, helpful, recommended; **C** *Hotel Tarobá*, Tarobá 1048, T 574-3670/3890, helpful, good breakfast, recommended; **C** *Luz*, Almirante Barroso, T 573-1891, near Rodoviária, recommended; **C** *Patt's Hotel*, Marechal Floriano Peixoto, 1368, T 574-2507, good breakfast, air conditioning, TV, recommended; **C** *Pousada da Laura*, Naipi 671, T/F 572-3374, secure, Spanish, English, Italian and French spoken, excellent; **C** *San Remo*, Kubitschek e Xavier da Silva 467, T 572-2956, good breakfast, air conditioning, recommended.

D *Hospedaria Britos*, Santos Dumont e Xavier da Silva, shared shower, large breakfast, good value; **D** *Hospedaria Janice*, Santos Dumont 1222, very helpful; **D** *Piratini*, Rui Barbosa 237, T 523-3370, hot showers, good breakfast, safe, recommended; **D** *Pousada Evelina Navarrete*, Irlan Kalicheski 171, Vila Yolanda, T/F 574-3817, lots of tourist information, English, French and Spanish spoken, helpful, good breakfast and location, near Avenida das Cataratas on way to the Falls, warmly recommended; **D** *Pousada Pôr do Sol*, Santos Dumont 41, T 574-3122, family-run, helpful, recommended; **D** *Pousada Vitória*, Nereu Ramos 285, T 573-1239, good breakfast, clean, safe, near rodoviaria.

E *Holiday*, Xavier da Silva 1407, T 574-5948, good, breakfast; **E** *Maria Schneider*, Jorge Schimmelpfeng 483, T 574-2305, German spoken; **E** *Senhor do Bonfim*, Almirante Barroso 6, breakfast, fans, hot water, family atmosphere, not very secure, convenient for the Cataratas bus.

Youth hostel E pp *Paudimar*, Rodovia das Cataratas Km 11, Remanço Grande, near airport, T 574-5503, pool, soccer pitch, quiet, breakfast, out of town but arrange transport from terminal, highly recommended.

Camping (pretty cold and humid in winter). By National Park entrance *Camping Clube do Brasil*, 17 km from Foz, US$10 per person (half with International Camping Card), pool, clean; park vehicle or put tent away from trees in winter in case of heavy rain storms, no restaurants, food there not very good, closes at 2300. *Camping Ecológico*, Fazenda São João Batista (W Keller), T 574-1794, 8 km from Foz, turn left just before park entrance, basic, nice scenery, dormitory and space for tents. Camping not permitted by hotel and Falls. Sleeping in car inside the park also prohibited.

● **Places to eat**
Many open till midnight, most accept a variety of currencies. *Rafain*, Avenida das Cataratas, Km 6.5, with Paraguayan harp trio, good *alcatra* (meat), excellent buffet, but expensive; *Rafain Center*, Rebouças 600 block, next to *Minas Hotel*, a collection of food stalls for different tastes and budgets, with live music and dancing 2000 to 0200, lively, recommended; *Calamares*, No 686, all you can eat buffet US$5, closes 2300, recommended; *Santos Delavy*, Kubitschek 393, Argentine owner, cheap and friendly; *Ali Baba*, No 998, very good Arabic food; *Churrascaria Bufalo Branco*, Rebouças 530, all you can eat for US$17, good salad bar; *Churrascaria Cabeça de Boi*, Brasil 1325, large, live music, buffet US$9, also for coffee and pastries; *Cantina*, Rodrigues 720, buffet, all you can eat, recommended; *Clarks*, No 896, excellent food; *El Club Caxos*, No 249, cheap; *Scala*, Santos Dumont e Xavier da Silva, good atmosphere and value.

● **Airline office**
Varig, Brasil 821, T 523-2111; staff speak foreign languages; Vasp, T 574-2999.

● **Banks & money changers**
Rates are bad in Foz and it is very difficult to exchange on Sunday, but quite possible in Paraguay where US dollars can be obtained on credit cards. There are plenty of banks and travel agents on Avenida Brasil: **Banco do Brasil**, good rates for travellers' cheques (note that you cannot obtain US dollars in Brazil); **Bradesco**, No 1192, cash advance on Visa.

● **Electric current**
110 volts air conditioning.

● **Consulates**
Argentina, Bianchi 26, T 74-2877/2969, open 0800-1300; **Paraguay**, Bartolomeu de Gusmão 480.

● **Entertainment**
Discotheque Whiskadão with three different dance halls, Alm Barroso 763, reasonable, lively at weekends; *Oba! Oba!*, Avenida das Cataratas, live samba show after 2200; next door is *Chumiscana Rafain Cataratas*, with floor show and food, about US$25 eat all you can. There is a cinema on Barão do Rio Branco, US2.50, films over 1½ hours are cut.

● **Hospitals & medical services**
There is a free 24-hour clinic on Avenida Paraná, opposite Lions Club. Few buses: take taxi or walk (about 25 minutes). Ask for Sra Calça: friendly and helpful. Her son speaks English.

● **Post & telecommunications**
Post Office: Praça Getúlio Vargas 72, next to Tourist Office.

International phone: calls from the office of Rui Barbosa.

● **Shopping**
Kunda Livraria Universitária, Almirante Barroso, T 523-4606, for guides and maps of the area, books on the local wildlife, novels etc in several languages including French and English.

● **Sports**
Fishing: for *dourado* and *surubi* fishing contact Simon Williams at Cataratas late Club, General Meira, Km 5, T 523-2073.

● **Tour companies & travel agents**
Beware of overcharging for tours by touts at the bus terminal. There are many travel agents on Avenida Brasil. *Dicks Tours* is said to change up to US$100 per day, 10% charge, and has been recommended for its all-day tour to the Brazilian side of the Falls, Ciudad del Este and the Itaipú dam. Recommended guides, *Wilson Engel*, T 574-1367, friendly, flexible. Ruth Campo Silva, *STTC Turismo Ltda*, Hotel Bourbon, Rodovia das Cataratas, T 574-3557; *Chiderly Batismo Pequeno*, Almirante Barroso 505, T 574-3367.

● **Tourist offices**
Praça Getúlio Vargas 56; **Paranatur**, very helpful, Almirante Barroso 1300, T 574-2196; **Turifon**, Jorge Sanways 576, T 523-5222. Kiosk on Avenida Brasil, by Ponte de Amizade (helpful), book hotels. Airport tourist information is also good, open for all arriving flights, gives map and bus information. Helpful office, free map, at rodoviária, English spoken. A newspaper, *Triplice Fronteira*, carries street plans and other tourist informationThere is a help line number, 1516.

● **Transport**
Local Taxis: are only good value for short distances when you are carrying all your luggage.

Air Iguaçu international airport, 18 km south of town near the Falls. Money exchange on the 1st floor, small commission. Daily flights from Rio, São Paulo, Curitiba and other Brazilian cities. Taxis to town charge a fixed rate of US$20, rates posted on the walls at airport; Dois Irmãos town bus for US$0.50, first at 0530, does not permit large amounts of luggage (but backpacks OK). Many hotels run minibus services for a small charge.

Buses At bus terminals watch out for pickpockets who pose, with a coat over their arm, as taxi drivers. For transport to the Falls see above under Parque Nacional Foz do Iguaçu. Long distance terminal (*Rodoviária*), Avenida Costa e Silva, 4 km from centre on road to Curitiba; bus to centre, Anel Viario, US$0.35. Book departures as soon as possible. To **Curitiba**, Sulamericana,

9-11 hours, paved road, US$30; to Guaíra via Cascavel only, 5 hours, US$9.50; to **São Paulo**, 15 hours, Pluma US$39, *executivo* US$51; to **Campo Grande**, 15 hours by Maringá company (3 hours to Cascavel, and 12 from there to Campo Grande) 17 hours by Medianeira company direct, US$32.50, 1700, recommended; to **Brasília**, 26 hours, 1800, US$50; to **Rio** 22 hours, several daily, US$37 (*leito* 74).

To Argentina Buses to Puerto Iguazú run half-hourly from the Terminal Urbana, crossing the frontier bridge; 20 minutes journey, no stops for border formalities, 2 companies: Pluma and Tres Fronteiras, US$2, tickets not interchangeable between companies. **NB** Be sure you know when the last bus departs from Puerto Iguazú for Foz (usually 1900) and remember that in summer Argentina is an hour earlier than Brazil. Combined tickets to Puerto Iguazú and the Falls cost more than paying separately. To **Buenos Aires**, Pluma daily 1630, 18 hours, US$45. It is cheaper to go to **Posadas** via Paraguay. Taxi Foz-Argentina US$33, US$45 to *Hotel Internacional Iguazú*.

FRONTIER WITH PARAGUAY

The Ponte de Amizade/Puente de Amistad (Friendship Bridge) over the Río Paraná, 12 km north of Foz, leads straight into the heart of Ciudad del Este. Crossing is very informal but keep an eye on your luggage and make sure that you get necessary stamps – so great is the volume of traffic that it can be difficult to stop, especially with the traffic police moving you on. It is particularly busy on Wednesday and Saturday, with long queues of vehicles. Pedestrians from Brazil cross on the north side of the bridge allowing easier passage on the other side for those returning with bulky packages.

● **Immigration**
Paraguayan and Brazilian immigration formalities are dealt with at opposite ends of the bridge. There is a US$3 tourist charge to enter Paraguay. **NB** Remember to adjust your watch to local time.

● **Transport**
Buses (marked Cidade-Ponte) leave from the Terminal Urbana, Avenida Juscelino Kubitschek, for the Ponte de Amizade (Friendship Bridge), US$0.60.

Crossing by private vehicle: if only intending to visit the National Parks, this presents no problems.

(*Population* 83,000) founded as Ciudad Presidente Stroessner in 1957, the city grew rapidly during the construction of the Itaipú hydroelectric project. Described as the biggest shopping centre in Latin America, it attracts Brazilian and Argentine visitors in search of bargain prices for electrical goods, watches, perfumes etc. Dirty, noisy, unfriendly and brashly commercial, it is worth a visit just for the people-watching, but you should be careful with valuables and take particular care after dark.

Excursions

To the Paraguayan side of the **Itaipú** hydroelectric project (see above under Foz do Iguaçu). Buses run from Rodríguez y García, outside the terminal to the Visitors' Centre, open Monday-Saturday 0730-1200, 1330-1700, Sunday and holidays closed. Free conducted tours of the project include a film show (versions in several languages – ask) 45 minutes before bus tours which start at 0830, 0930, 1030, 1400, 1500, 1600, check times in advance. Take passport.

To the **Cascada del Monday** (Monday Falls), where the Río Monday drops into the Paraná gorge, 10 km south of Ciudad del Este. Return fare by taxi US$20. Worthwhile. There is good fishing below the falls.

Local information
● **Accommodation**
Generally expensive. **A3** *Convair*, Adrián Jara y García, T 500342, air conditioning, comfortable, cheaper rooms without bath; **A3** *Executive*, Adrián Jara y Curupayty, T 500942/3, with air conditioning, breakfast – restaurant recommended; **A3** *Residence de la Tour* at Paraná Country Club, 5 km from centre, T 60316, superb, Swiss-owned, excellent restaurant (US$12-16 per person), pool, gardens, beautiful view.

B *Catedral*, Calle A López 838, T 500378, includes breakfast, TV, air conditioning, several blocks from commercial area, large, modern with pool, restaurant; **B** *Gran Hotel Acaray*, 11 de Septiembre y Río Paraná, T/F 511471/5, with new extension, pool, casino, nightclub, restaurant; **B** *San Rafael*, Abay y Adrián Jara,

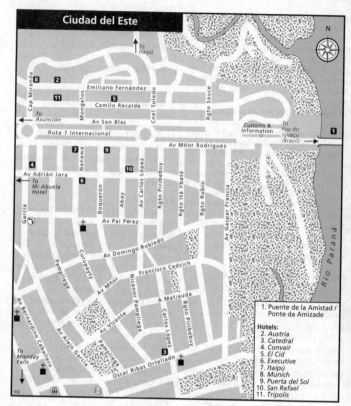

Ciudad del Este

1. Puente de la Amistad /
Ponte da Amizade

Hotels:
2. Austria
3. Catedral
4. Convair
5. El Cid
6. Executive
7. Itaipú
8. Munich
9. Puerta del Sol
10. San Rafael
11. Tripolis

T 68134, large rooms, with breakfast, German and English spoken.

C *Itaipú*, Rodríguez y Nanawa, T 500371, breakfast, air conditioning; **C** *Mi Abuela*, Adrián Jara 128, T 500348, with breakfast, fan, poor beds; **C** *Munich*, Fernández y Miranda, T 500347, with breakfast, air conditioning, garage, recommended; **C** *Puerta del Sol*, Rodríguez y Boquerón, T 500798, air conditioning, just off main street; **C-D** *El Cid*, Recalde 425, T 512221, breakfast, air conditioning, cheaper with fan.

D *Austria* (also known as *Viena*), Fernández 165, T 500883, above restaurant, with good breakfast and air conditioning, Austrian family, good views from upper floors, warmly recommended; **D** *Tripolis*, San Blas 331, T 512450, air conditioning, poor restaurant, unhelpful, unsafe.

● **Places to eat**

Coreío, San Blas 125, T 0448, good Korean food; *Osaka*, Adrián Jara and, 100m away, *New Tokyo*, Adrián Jara 202, both good, authentic Japanese; *Seoul*, Curupayty y Adrián Jara, good *parrillada*; *Hotel Austria/Viena*, good Austrian food, clean, good value. Cheaper ones along García and in market. Many restaurants close on Sunday.

● **Airline offices**

TAM, Edificio SABA, Monseñor Rodríguez.

● **Banks & money changers**

Banco Holandés Unido, cash on Mastercard, 5% commission; local banks (open Monday-Friday 0730-1100). Dollars can be changed into *reais* in town, but exchange may be better and easier in Foz do Iguaçu. Several *Casas de Cambio*: *Cambio Guaraní*, Monseñor Rodríguez, changes travellers' cheques for US$0.50, branch on Friendship Bridge has good rates for many currencies including dollars and *reais*; *Tupi Cambios*, Adrián Jara 351; *Cambios Chaco*, Adrián Jara y Curupayty. *Casa de cambio* rates are better than street rates. Money changers (not recommended) operate at the bus terminal but not at the Brazilian end of the Friendship Bridge.

● **Post & telecommunications**
International Phone: Antelco, Alejo García y Pai Pérez, near centre on road to bus terminal.

● **Shopping**
Prices are decidedly high for North American and European visitors. The leather market is well worth a visit, be sure to bargain. Don't buy perfume at tempting prices on the street, it's only coloured water. Make sure that shops which package your goods pack what you actually bought. Also watch the exchange rates if you're a short-term visitor from Argentina or Brazil.

● **Transport**
Air To Asunción, Arpa 3 flights Monday-Saturday, 1 on Sunday; also Lapsa/TAM daily en route to São Paulo.

Buses Terminal is on the southern outskirts. No 4 bus from centre, US$0.50 (taxi US$3.50).

Many buses (US$17.25 *rápido*, 4½ hours, at night only; US$9.50 *común*, 6 hours) to **Asunción**. Nuestra Señora and Rysa reported to run the best; to **Encarnación** (for Posadas and Argentina), along fully paved road, frequent, 4 hours, US$9 (cheaper than via Foz do Iguaçu).

To Brazil International bus from outside terminal to the long-distance terminal (*Rodoviária*) outside Foz. Local buses from the terminal run along Avenida Adrián Jara and go to the city terminal (*terminal urbana*) in Foz every 15 minutes, 0600-2000, US$1. Most buses do not wait at immigration, so disembark to get your exit stamp, walk across the bridge (10 minutes) and obtain your entry stamp; keep your ticket and continue to Foz on the next bus free. Paraguayan taxis cross freely to Brazil (US$18) but it is cheaper to walk across the bridge and then take a taxi, bargain hard. You can pay in either currency.

To Argentina Direct buses to Puerto Iguazú, frequent service by several companies from outside the terminal, US$3.50, you need to get Argentine and Paraguayan stamps (not Brazilian), bus does not wait so keep ticket for next bus.

The Lake District

THE LAKE ARGENTINE DISTRICT stretches along the the foot of the Andes from above 40° to below 50° in the area of the Parque Nacional Los Glaciares in Southern Patagonia. This section covers the northern lakes; for convenience the southern lakes are described under Patagonia. The lakes and the mountains provide opportunities for fishing, watersports, walking, climbing, skiing and other activities. The most important centre is the city of Bariloche. On the western side of the Andes, in Chile, there is also an area of attractive lakes: routes across the mountains to visit these are also described below.

GEOGRAPHY

This section covers the province of Neuquén and western parts of Río Negro and Chubut. Eastern areas of Neuquén are covered by the foothills of the Andes, rising steadily westwards. The Andes themselves are much lower than further north: most peaks range from 2,000m to 2,500m, though three volcanoes tower above this: Tromen (3,978m) Lanín (3,768m) and Tronador (3,478m).

In the north the western end of the lakes cut deeply into the mountains, their water lapping the forested skirts of some of the most spectacular snow-capped peaks in the world; their eastern ends are contained by the frontal moraines deposited by the ancient glaciers which gouged out these huge lakes. The water is a deep blue, sometimes lashed into white froth by the region's high winds.

A few rivers, notably the Ríos Hua Hum, Puelo and Futaleufú flow west into Chile, but most of the lakes drain into the Río Negro. This river, the most important in Argentina apart from those which form

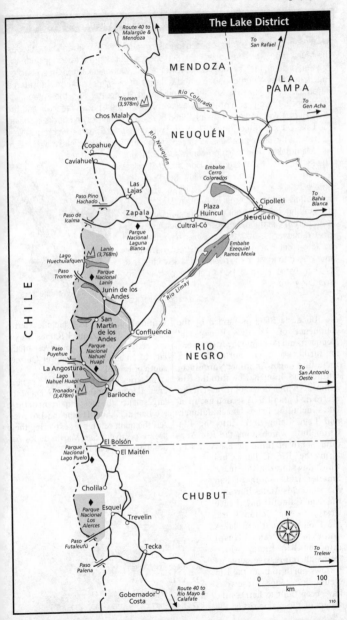

Fauna of the Southern beech forests

Although the southern beech forests extend across a wide range of latitudes, the fauna found in them varies little. Bird species found in the forests include the Austral Parakeet, the Chilean Flicker, the Magellanic Woodpecker, the Green-backed Firecrown (the only hummingbird found at these latitudes), the common Thorn-tailed Rayadito, the Austral Thrush, the Rufous-tailed Plantcutter and the Patagonian Sierra-finch. More typical of the Valdivian forest are the Chucao Tapaculo and the Huet-Huet. Lakes and rivers are inhabited by species of grebes and ducks including the Lake Duck and the Torrent Duck, as well as Kelp Gulls and cormorants. Near open areas the Black-faced Ibis, Fire-eyed Diucon and Austral Blackbird may be seen.

Mammals are harder to find. Native species include the Red fox and the Patagonian Hog-nosed Skunk as well as several endangered species: the Pudú (the smallest deer in the world), the Huillín (a species of river otter) and the Huemul or Andean deer.

Among species introduced are the Red Deer (most common in Neuquén) and Canadian Beavers, European rabbits and muskrats, all of which have flourished in Tierra del Fuego. Salmon and trout have been introduced to most of the rivers and lakes in the Lake District, Patagonia and Tierra del Fuego, mainly for sporting purposes.

Santiago de la Vega

Magellan Woodpeckers

---

the Río de la Plata, is formed by the confluence of the Ríos Limay and Neuquén, and flows into the Atlantic 637 km further west. The northern lakes, including Lagos Aluminé, Norquinco, Quillén and Tromen, flow into the Río Aluminé, which flows south, east of the Sierra de Catan Lil. A second group of lakes including Lagos Huechulafquen and Lago Lolog drain into the Río Chimehuin which joins the Río Aluminé south of Junín de los Andes to form the Río Collón Curá which flows into the Río Limay. Smaller lakes south of San Martín de los Andes flow into the Río Caleufú and thence west into the Collón Cura. Most of the southern lakes drain via Lago Nahuel Huapi into the Río Limay which forms an impressive gorge as it flows north to meet the Río Neuquén. Huge reservoirs have been built to harness the waters of the major rivers: the artificial lakes created include Cerros Colorados and Ezequiel Ramos Mexía, respectively west and southwest of the city of Neuquén, and Amutui Quimei, south of Esquel.

A series of National Parks has been created to protect the environment of the largest lakes: the most important of these are Lanín, Nahuel Huapi and Los Alerces: the main centres for exploring these are, respectively, San Martín de los Andes, Bariloche and Esquel.

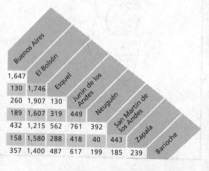

	Buenos Aires	El Bolsón	Esquel	Junín de los Andes	Neuquén	San Martín de los Andes	Zapala
El Bolsón	1,647						
Esquel	130	1,746					
Junín de los Andes	260	1,907	130				
Neuquén	189	1,607	319	449			
San Martín de los Andes	432	1,215	562	761	392		
Zapala	158	1,580	288	418	40	443	
Bariloche	357	1,400	487	617	199	185	239

The Monkey Puzzle Tree

The *Pehuen* (Araucaria araucana) is perhaps better known as the monkey puzzle tree; other names include the Chilean pine, umbrella tree or parasol tree. Very slow growing, it can grow to 40m high and some are believed to be 300 years old. Though its natural habitat is on both sides of the Andes between 37 and 39 south, it is much more widespread in Chile than Argentina and is the Chilean national tree. A true conifer, its is a descendent of the petrified pines found in the Bosques Petrificados. Its cones and its sharp leathery

Pehuén or monkey-puzzle tree

leaves were eaten by the Mapuche for centuries. Some isolated trees are still seen as sacred by the Mapuche who leave offerings to the tree's spirit. The characteristic cones can weigh up to 1 kg so take care sitting underneath!

Jane Norwich

CLIMATE

Annual rainfall varies in relation to the proximity of the Andes, from 200-400 mm in Eastern Neuquén to over 3,000 mm in some of the westernmost forest areas. Outside these westernmost areas rainfall mainly occurs between May and August. Summer temperatures range between 31°C and 13°C in Neuquén and between 21°C and 6°C in Esquel. Winter temperatures vary between 13°C and 0°C in Neuquén and between 6°C and -3°C in Esquel.

NB Off season, from mid-August to mid-November, many excursions, boat trips, etc, run on a limited schedule, if at all. Public transport is also limited.

FRONTIER CROSSINGS

There are eight crossing-points to Chile in this region, as follows:

From Zapala to Temuco via Paso Pino Hachado and Paso de Icalma.

From Junín de los Andes to Villarrica and Pucón via Paso Tromen.

From San Martín de los Andes to Panguipulli via Paso Hua Hum.

From Bariloche to Osorno via Paso Puyehue.

From Bariloche to Puerto Montt via Paso Pérez Rosales.

From Esquel to Chaitén via Paso Futaleufú and Paso Palena.

Further details of these are given in the text.

NEUQUEN PROVINCE

Bounded to the west by the Andes, the north by the Río Colorado and the south by the Río Limay, the province of Neuquén is the main gateway to the Lake District from Buenos Aires. It is reached by Route 22 which runs west from Bahía Blanca, crossing the Río Colorado at the town of **Río Colorado** and the Río Negro at **Choele Choel**.

Economy

Extensive irrigation has made Eastern Neuquén and the valley of the Río Negro a major dairy farming and fruit-growing region. About 75% of all Argentine fruit are grown in this area, about 60% of it for export. Apples are the principal crop but pears and table grapes are also grown and there are many wine *bodegas* nearby. The province is a major producer of petroleum and natural gas, meeting about 15% of Argentina's energy needs. Oil extraction is centred on Cultral-Có, the second-largest town in the province, and nearby Plaza Huincul. Marble and cement are mined further west around Zapala.

NEUQUEN

(*Population* 183,000; *Altitude* 265m; *Phone code* 099) Situated 538 km west of Bahía Blanca and 1,215 km west of Buenos Aires, Neuquén, lies at the extreme eastern tip of the province at the confluence of the Ríos Limay and Neuquén, which form the Río Negro. On the opposite side of the Río Neuquén and connected by bridge is Cipolletti (*population* 60,600) a prosperous centre of the Río Negro fruit-growing region. A pleasant provincial capital and industrial city, it was founded in 1904, just after the arrival of the railway; its origins are reflected in the central location of the railway station. The city's main industries are food processing, but it also benefits from serving the oilfields to the west with heavy equipment and construction materials. At the Parque Centenario is a *mirador* with good views of the city and the confluence of the rivers (be sure *not* to take the bus to Centenario industrial suburb).

Museums

Museo Histórico Dr Gregorio Alvarez, General San Martín 280. **Museo de Ciencias Naturales**, Avenida Argentina 1400, includes exhibitions of dinosaur fossils found in the region. **Museo Provincial Carlos Ameghino**, Yrigoyen 1047, modest but interesting.

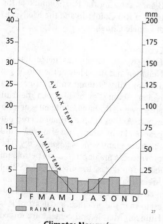

Climate: Neuquén

Excursions

To **Lago Pellegrini**, 36 km north, an artificial lake where watersports are held.

To **Embalse Cerro Colorado**, another artificial lake 40 km northwest, where there artificial and natural swimming pools (take bus marked 'Banda del Medio' from terminal). North of the lake is **Añelo**, where there is an archaeological museum.

Local festivals

All the towns in the valley celebrate the Fiesta Nacional de la Manzana in the second half of March.

Local information

NB Do not confuse the streets Félix San Martín and General San Martín.

● **Accommodation**

L3 *del Comahue*, Argentina 387, T 480112, 4-star, very good.

A2 *Res Arrayán*, Ruta 22, T 466128, with breakfast, parking, pool; **A3** *Apolo*, Avenida Olascoaga 361, T 422334, good, but overpriced; **A3** *Crystal*, Olascoaga 268, T 422414, adequate.

B *Hosp Neuquén*, Roca 109, T 422403, overpriced; **B** *Italia*, Justo 782, T 422234; **B** *Huemel*, Tierra del Fuego 335, T 422344.

Budget accommodation: **C** *Res Inglés*, Félix San Martín 534, T 422252; **C** *Res Belgrano*, Rivadavia 283, T 424311; **C** *Res Alcorta*, Alcorta 84, T 422652; **D** pp Montevideo 555.

Outside Neuquén: *ACA Cipolletti*, Ruta Nacional 22 y Avenida Luis Toschi, eastern outskirts, T 71827. **A1** *Hostal del Caminante*, 13 km west on Zapala road, T 466118, with pool and garden, popular.

● **Camping** Municipal site near river, free, local police warn that it's dangerous. Nearby is *Camping Balneario Biguá*.

● **Places to eat**

Las Tres Marías, Alberdi 126, excellent. Cheap places on Avenida Mitre opposite bus terminal.

● **Airline offices**

Austral, Santa Fe 54, T 422409; **Lapa**, Argentina 30, T 438555; **TAN**, 25 de Mayo 180, T 423076 (430096 at airport); **Kaiken**, Argentina 327, T 471333.

● **Banks & money changers**

Pullman, Alcorta 144, T 422438.

● **Consulates**

Chile, Rodriguez y La Rioja.

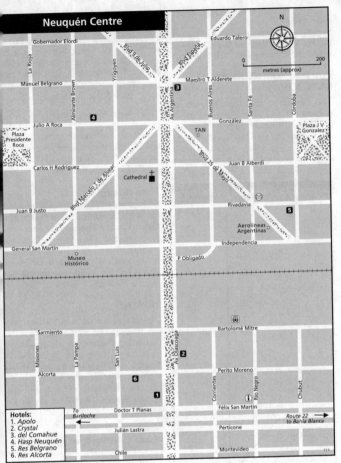

Neuquén Centre

Hotels:
1. Apolo
2. Crystal
3. del Comahue
4. Hasp Neuquén
5. Res Belgrano
6. Res Alcorta

To Bariloche ←

Route 22 →
to Bahía Blanca

● **Post & telecommunications**
Post Office: Rivadavia y Santa Fe.

● **Tourist offices**
Félix San Martín y Río Negro, T 424089, Monday-Friday 0730-2000, Saturday 0800-1500.

● **Transport**
Mechanic: Normando Toselli, Mitre 801 (Former South American superbike champion), for cars or motorbikes, highly recommended.

Air Airport 7 km west of centre. Taxi US$8. To Buenos Aires, Austral and Lapa; to Bahía Blanca, Lapa. The regional airline TAN flies to many Argentine cities including Bahía Blanca, Comodoro Rivadavia, Córdoba, Mendoza, Bariloche, San Martín de los Andes and, in Chile, Puerto Montt and Temuco. Kaiken flies to Comodoro Rivadavia, Esquel, Bariloche, Trelew, Ushuaia and Calafate and other destinations. Southern Winds to Córdoba, Rosario, Tucumán and Salta.

Buses Terminal at Mitre 147. La Estrella/El Cóndor, El Valle, TAC and Chevallier to **Buenos Aires** daily US$60, 18½ hours; to **San Rafael**, US$20; to **San Martín de los Andes** US$22, 4 hours; to **Zapala** daily, 7 hours; to **Mar del Plata**, US$40, 12 hours; to **Bariloche**, La Estrella or Chevallier (not El Valle as it stops too often), sit on left; to **Mendoza**, Andesmar, daily, US$46.

To Chile: services to **Temuco** via Zapala and Paso Pino Hachado, La Unión del Sud three times a week, Ruta Sur twice a week, US$30, 16 hours.

ROUTES FROM NEUQUÉN TO BARILOCHE

The most direct road from Neuquén to Bariloche (426 km) is by Route 237, which branches off Route 22 at a point 50 km east of Neuquén and runs southwest along the Embalse Ezequiel Ramos Mejía. Then it drops over an escarpment to cross the Río Collón Curá, where it joins Route 40

which follows the Río Limay valley to Confluencia (see page 358) and the Valle Encantado. This route is fast but misses Junín de los Andes and San Martín de los Andes. The most attractive route is to follow Route 237 (as above) to the Río Collón Curá, then take Route 40 (and later Route 234) northwest to Junín de los Andes.

NORTHERN NEUQUÉN

Route 22 runs west from Neuquén through the oil-producing zone which is centred on Plaza Huincul and **Cultral-Có** (*population* 33,500, Km 110).

From Neuquén to Bariloche

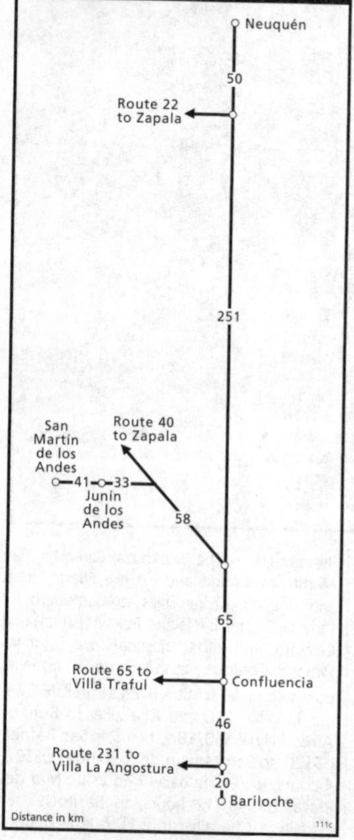

Neuquén
50
Route 22 to Zapala ←
251
San Martín de los Andes — Route 40 to Zapala
←41—33 Junín de los Andes
58
65
Route 65 to Villa Traful ← — Confluencia
46
Route 231 to Villa La Angostura ←
20
Bariloche

Distance in km

Plaza Huincul

(*Population* 11,000) Km 107, was the site of the first oil find in 1918. The **Museo Municipal Carmen Funes** includes the vertebrae of a dinosaur, believed to be the largest ever to have lived on Earth and estimated to have weighed 70 kilos each; a recovered tibia is 1.60m in length. **Accommodation** *Hostería Tunquelén*, T 63423.

ZAPALA

(*Population* 26,000; *Altitude* 1,012m; *Phone code* 0942) 185 km west of Neuquén, was founded as the western terminus of the railway line. Situated at the junction of Route 22 with Route 40, it is a convenient stopping point en route to Chile and a base for visiting the Parque Nacional Laguna Blanca. There is an airport and an ACA service station.

Museums

Museo Paleontológico Dr Juan Olsacher, Olascoaga 421, one of the best museums of its type in South America: among the collections of minerals, fossils, shells and rocks, is a complete crocodile jaw, believed to be 80 million-years-old, Monday-Friday 0900-1300, free, closed weekends.

Excursions

To **Lago Aluminé**, 107 km west, from where roads run to three smaller lakes **Lagos Pulmari**, **Ñorquinco** and **Pilhué**, the last two of which lie within the Parque Nacional Lanín (see below). North of Lago Aluminé are two small reserves,

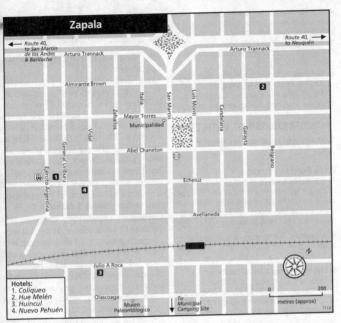

Zapala

Hotels:
1. Coliqueo
2. Hue Melén
3. Huincul
4. Nuevo Pehuén

Batea Mahuida and **Chany**, created to protect areas of *pehuén* trees. Accommodation is available at La Angostura on the northern side of Lago Aluminé and at Moquehué, further west.

- **Accommodation A3** *Hue Melén*, Brown 929, T 22391, good value, restaurant; **C** *Huincul*, Roca 313, T 21300, restaurant. Around bus terminal are: **B** *Coliqueo*, Etcheluz 159, T 21308, good; **B** *Nuevo Pehuén*, Vidal y Etcheluz, T 23135, recommended; **C** *Res Odetto Grill*, Ejército Argentino 455, OK. **Camping** Municipal site.

- **Banks & money changers** Banco de la Nación Argentina, good rates, efficient.

- **Buses** To Buenos Aires, TAC, daily, US$60; to Bahía Blanca 3 a day, Alto Valle, 15 hours, US$25; to San Martín de los Andes, El Petroleo, 5½ hours via Junín de los Andes, also TAC. to Bariloche direct buses about twice a week. Buses to Chile: Temuco all year, several companies including La Unión del Sud and Ruta Sur, US$22, 10-12 hours, as under Neuquén (see above), Igi-Llaimi Wednesday and Friday 0530, return 0330. Buy Chilean currency before leaving.

PARQUE NACIONAL LAGUNA BLANCA

35 km southwest of Zapala and covering 11,250 hectares at altitudes between 1,200m and 1,800m, is one of only two reserves in the Americas created to protect swans. The laguna, 1,700 hectares, is one of the most important nesting-areas of the black-necked swan in Argentina. Other bird-life includes the several duck species, among them the Andean ruddy duck, plovers, sandpipers, grebes and Chilean flamingos. The steep slopes of the Laguna are nesting sites for birds of prey such as the red-backed hawk and the peregrine falcon. The surrounding area, covered with scrub and bushes, provides a habitat for mountain cats, foxes and rodents. A rough track runs round the lake, suitable for 4WD vehicles only.

Climate Temperatures rise to 40°C in summer, but drop below 0°C in winter, when there are strong winds, drizzle and snow. Annual rainfall is around 200 mm. Spring is the best time to visit.

- **Access** Route 48, which runs across the park, branches off Route 40, 10 km south of Zapala. The park entrance is 10 km from this turning, and the lagoon lies 4-5 km beyond this. No public transport and little traffic makes hitchhiking difficult.

- **Services** *Guardaparque* post near southeast corner of the laguna. Small visitors centre and restaurant. Free camping. *Guardaparque's* office on Vidal, next to *Hotel Pehuén*, in Zapala.

FRONTIER CROSSINGS WITH CHILE

West of Zapala there are two frontier crossings:

Paso Pino Hachado

Paso Pino Hachado (1,864m) lies 105 km west of Zapala via Route 22. On the Chilean side *ripio* roads run northwest to Lonquimay, 77 km, and southwest to Melipeuco, 103 km; Temuco can be reached from both of these.

- **Argentine immigration & customs**
9 km east of the frontier, open 0700-1300, 1400-1900.

- **Chilean immigration & customs**
In Liucura, 22 km west of the frontier, open December-March 0800-2100, April-November 0800-1900. Very thorough searches and 2-3 hour delays reported.

- **Transport**
Buses from Zapala and Neuquén to Temuco use this crossing.

Paso de Icalma

Paso de Icalma (1,298m) lies 122 km west of Zapala and is reached by Route 13 (*ripio*). On the Chilean side this road continues to Melipeuco 53 km west and thence to Temuco.

- **Argentine immigration & customs**
Open 0700-1300, 1400-1900.

- **Chilean immigration & customs**
Open December-March 0800-2100, April-November 0800-1900.

NORTH OF ZAPALA

Route 22 continues northwest from Zapala to Las Lajas, Km 55, where two roads branch off. Route 40 runs north via Chos Malal and Malargüe to Mendoza. Unpaved from Chos Malal to Malargüe, this route to Mendoza is more scenic, but slower than main Neuquén-Mendoza route (Nos 151 and 143 via Santa Isabel and San Rafael). Route 21 goes northwest to Longcopue (handicrafts market on

Sundays), north of which Route 26 branches off northwest towards Caviahue and Copahue via the Hualcupen gorge.

The Reserva Provincial Copahue-Caviahue

90 km northwest of Las Lajas and covering 28,300 hectares, this park is situated on the slopes of the still-active Copahue volcano (2,953m) and protects the northernmost *pehuén* or monkey-puzzle trees in Argentina. The park includes the **Termas de Copahue** (*altitude* 1,980m; *phone code* 0948), a thermal resort, open December-April only, enclosed in a gigantic amphitheatre formed by mountain walls and considered to have some of the best thermal waters in South America.

Caviahue (*population* 400; *altitude* 1,600m) 18 km southeast, is a small winter sports resort, with 3 ski lifts, excellent for cross country skiing, snow-shoing and snowmobiling; cheaper than Bariloche. Horseriding and trekking are available in summer. Excursions can be made to Laguna Escondida, which offers great views of the volcano, lake and forests as well as ice-skating in winter. In summer you can also visit four waterfalls and climb the Copahue volcano, 4 hours; inside the crater is a lagoon. A bus service connects the two resorts.

- **Accommodation** In Copahue (*phone code* 0948): *Valle del Volcán*, T 95048, 3-star; *Termas*, T 95045, 3-star; *Pino Azul*, T 95071; **D** pp *Res Codihue*, T 95031, with poor breakfast; several others. In Caviahue: **B** *Lago Caviahue*, T 95074, very clean, with kitchens, restaurant, great views; *Farallon*, T 95062, with kitchens; *Caviahue Sky*, T 95064; **D** pp, *Caniche Lodge*, **E** pp in summer, kitchen facilities, run by Caniche and Gerard, ski instructors and guides. **Camping** 3 km out of town, summer only.

- **Buses** From Neuquén, El Petroleo and Centenario, both daily, 6 hours, US$22, via Zapala (US$13).

Chos Malal

(*Population* 8,600; *Altitude* 862m; *Phone code* 0948), 211 km north of Zapala, was founded as a fortress in 1879 and became a mining centre. The restored fortress houses the **Museo Histórico Olascoaga**, which contains artefacts of the 'Conquest of the Wilderness'.

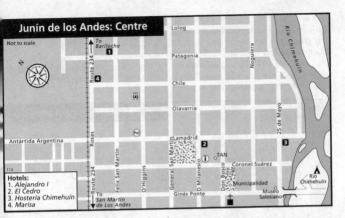

Junín de los Andes: Centre

Not to scale

To Bariloche

Lolog

Patagonia

Chile

Olavarría

Antártida Argentina

Lamadrid

TAN

Coronel Suárez

Río Chimehuín

Ginés Ponte

Municipalidad

Museo Salesiano

Hotels:
1. Alejandro I
2. El Cedro
3. Hostería Chimehuín
4. Marisa

● **Accommodation A3** *Chos Malal*, San Martín 89, T 21469, faded grandeur but clean; *Hostería El Torreón*, 25 de Mayo 137, T 21141; *Hosp Baal Bak*, 25 de Mayo 920, T 21495; *Hosp Lavalle*, T 21193.

Parque Provincial Tromen

Situated 37 km northeast of Chos Malal and covering 24,000 hectares, this park surrounds Lago Tromen, a nesting site for migratory birds. East of the lake is the **Tromen** volcano (3,978m).

● **Access** is by *ripio* road which runs north from Chos Malal along the west bank of the lake and then (unpaved) northeast to meet Route 40.

JUNIN DE LOS ANDES

(*Population* 7,350; *Altitude* 773m; *Phone code* 0944) lies on the Río Chimehuín, 199 km south of Zapala and 189 km north of Bariloche. Founded in 1883, it is known as the trout capital of Argentina. Less touristy than San Martín de los Andes, it is quieter and cheaper and offers a good base for visiting the northern part of Parque Nacional Lanín. There is a small **Museo Salesiano** in the centre at Ginés Ponte y Nogueira. Excursions can be made to **Lago Huechulafquen**, a very beautiful lake 15 km northwest with, at its western end, **Lago Paimún** where there is a campsite in the shadow of the Lanín volcano. **Bus** Koko, US$6 one way, check return journey with driver.

Local information
● **Accommodation**

A3 *Hostería Chimehuín*, Suárez y 25 de Mayo, T 91132, fishing hostelry, open all year; **B** *Alejandro I*, Route 234, on northern edge of town, T 91184, open fishing season only; **C** *Res Marisa*, Rosas 360, T 91175, cheapest; **C** *Res El Cedro*, Lamadrid 409, T 91182, gloomy; *Posada Pehuén*, Coronel Suárez 560, T 91237, good value, charming owners, Rosi and Oscar Marconi, recommended.

Campsite *Río Chimehuín*, T 91132, also municipal site, T 91296.

Estancia L3 *Estancia Huechahue* (reached from the Junín-Bariloche bus), T 91303, English run, comfortable, farmhouse accommodation, horseriding, fishing, river trips.

● **Places to eat**

Ruca Hueney, Milanesio 641, main plaza, good trout and pasta dishes, friendly service, recommended.

● **Tourist office**
On corner of main plaza.

● **Transport**
Air Between Junín and San Martín is Chapelco airport. Flights to **Buenos Aires**, Austral; to **Neuquén** and **Bariloche**, TAN (T 0972-27872).

FRONTIER WITH CHILE: PASO TROMEN

Paso Tromen, known in Chile as Paso Mamuil Malal, is situated 64 km northwest of Junín de los Andes, reached by a partially paved road which runs through Parque Nacional Lanín. 3 km east of the pass a turning leads to Lago Tromen. To the south of the Pass is the graceful cone of the Lanín volcano. This crossing is less developed than the Huahum and Puyehue routes further south; it is unsuitable for cycles and definitely not usable during heavy rain or snow (June to mid-November). Parts are narrow and steep.

● **Argentine immigration & customs**
at Puerto Tromen, 3 km east of the pass.

● **Buses**
Igi-Llaima, daily Junín de los Andes-Pucón US$26. Officially this only picks up passenger at the pass. Hitchhiking over the Pass is no difficult in summer.

Parque Nacional Lanín

N

CHILE

Lago Pilhué
Lago Rucuchoroi
○ Aluminé
Lago Hui Hui
Quillén ○
○ Rahue
0   15
km
Lago Quillén
Lago Tromen
Paso Tromen
Río Malleo
Río Aluminé
Mt Lanín (3,776m)
Lago Paimún
Lago Epulafquen
Lago Huechulafquen
Lago Currhué
○ Junín de los Andes
To Zapala
Lago Lolog
Lago Lacar
San Martín de los Andes
Lago Escondido
Lago de los Carmenes
Lago Meliquina
To Neuquén
Lago Hermoso
Lago Machónico
To Bariloche
To Confluencia & Bariloche

112a

Camping It is possible to camp in the area (though very windy), but take food as there are no shops at the pass. There is a CONAF campsite at Puesco, free, no facilities.

● **Chilean immigration & customs**
At Puesco, 8 km west of the pass, open December-March 0800-2100, April-November 0800-1900, US$2 per vehicle at other times.

● **Into Chile**
On the Chilean side the road continues through glorious scenery with the volcanoes of Villarrica and Quetrupillán to the south to Pucón, 135 km west, on Lago Villarrica.

PARQUE NACIONAL LANIN

One of the largest parks in Argentina, Lanín is dominated by the snow capped **Lanín Volcano** which lies in the north of the park on the Chilean frontier. Stretching along the frontier with Chile for some 200 km, the park covers 379,000 hectares and includes 24 glacial lakes, one of which (Lago Lacar) drains into the Pacific. The northern parts of the park are dominated by the *pehuén* tree, while further south there are large stretches of *roble*, *rauli* and *lenga* forest. These forests are denser further west where rainfall is heaviest.

The fauna is typical of Andean-Patagonian region, though it includes the rare and endangered *pudu*, as well as foxes, cougars and foxes. Another attraction are the large numbers of red deer, introduced into the park from Europe and Asia, which have degraded the vegetation and are hunted.

Climbing Lanín One of the world's most beautiful mountains, Lanín (3,768m) is geologically one of the youngest volcanoes of the Andes; it is now extinct. It is climbed from the Tromen pass, where there is a campsite (speak to the *guardaparque* at the border): a 4 hour hike leads to the *refugio* at 2,400m; from here it is 5 hours to the summit, not difficult but crampons and ice-axe are essential. Dr González, President of the Club Andino in Junín, can arrange guides and equipment hire. Limited *refugio* space.

● **Access** There are several entrances to the park, most of them reached from Route 23 which runs south from Lago Aluminé to Junín

de los Andes. Easiest access points are from Junín and San Martín de los Andes. Park entry US$3. Park Administration is in San Martín de los Andes.

● **Accommodation Near Lago Huechulafquen**: *Hostería Paimún*, T 91201, 3-star; *Refugio del Pescador*. **Camping** Sites throughout the park.

SAN MARTIN DE LOS ANDES

(*Population* 14,000; *Altitude* 642m; *Phone code* 0972), 40 km south of Junín and 158 km north of Bariloche, is a lovely but expensive little town at the eastern end of Lago Lacar. Founded in 1898, it is the best centre for exploring Parque Nacional Lanín. There are fine views over the town and lake from Mirador Bandurrias, 6 km west on the north shore of the lake. There is excellent skiing on Cerro Chapelco, 10 km south, and facilities for water skiing, windsurfing and sailing on Lago Lacar.

Excursions

On **Lago Lacar** the *ripio* road to the Chilean frontier at Paso Huahum runs along the northern shore and offers fine views. There is a daily boat service to Huahum at 0930, returns 1800, US$20 (T 27380).There is also a road along the southern shore to Quila Quina, 10 km west, where there are Indian engravings, a lovely waterfall and a guided nature trail. Quila Quina can also be reached by boat, 45 minutes one way, US$10 return.

To the **Cerro Chapelco** ski resort, which has 29 pistes, 11 lifts and a ski-school but no accommodation (daily lift passes US$37 high season, US$21 low season; weekly pass US$220 high season, US$126 low season). In summer a this is a good destination cyclists; take your bike up the hill on the lift, then down the paths back to the foot of the mountain.

The most popular trips by car are to **Lagos Lolog, Aluminé, Huechulafquen** and **Paimún** (bus from San Martín via Huechulafquen to Paimún, 0800, US$2, last return 1800, Empresa San Martín). Shorter excursions can be made on horseback or by launch.

Local information

The streets of San Martín might have been deliberately named to confuse the unwary traveller. Perito Moreno runs north-south crossing Mariano Moreno which runs east-west. Beware also Rudecindo Roca which is two blocks north of General Roca.

● Accommodation

Lots of accommodation, though it is expensive in season and single rooms are scarce. Motel **L2-L3** *El Sol de los Andes*, on Cerro Coronel Díaz above the town, T 27460, 5-star, shopping gallery, pool, sauna, nightclub, casino, regular bus service to centre of town.

L3-A1 range: *Alihuen Lodge*, Ruta 62, Km 5 (road to Lago Lolog), T 26588, F 26045, including breakfast, good restaurant, lovely location and grounds, very comfortable, highly recommended; *El Viejo Esquiador*, San Martín 1242, T 27690, recommended; *La Cheminée*, General Roca y Mariano Moreno, T 27617, with breakfast, very good, no restaurant; *La Masía* Obeid 811, T 27688, very good.

A2 *Turismo*, Mascardi 517, T 27592, recommended; *La Raclette*, Pérez 1170, T 27664, 3-star, charming, warm, excellent restaurant, recommended; *Posta del Cazador*, San Martín 175, T 27501, very highly recommended; **A3** *Hostería Hueney Ruca*, Obeid y Pérez, T 27499, with breakfast; **A3** *Hostería Los Pinos*, Brown 420, T 27207, **C** pp off season, German-run, with air conditioning, breakfast and heating, lovely garden; **A3** *Hostería Anay*, Cap Drury 841, T 27514, central, good value, recommended; **A3** *Hostería Las Lucarnas*,

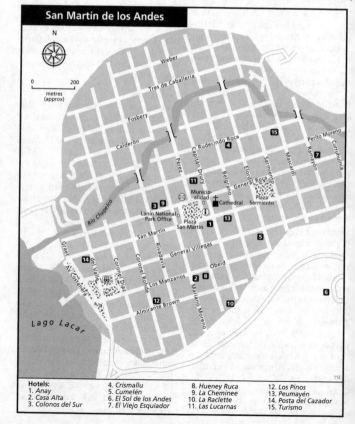

San Martín de los Andes

Hotels:
1. *Anay*
2. *Casa Alta*
3. *Colonos del Sur*
4. *Crismallu*
5. *Cumelén*
6. *El Sol de los Andes*
7. *El Viejo Esquiador*
8. *Hueney Ruca*
9. *La Cheminee*
10. *La Raclette*
11. *Las Lucarnas*
12. *Los Pinos*
13. *Peumayén*
14. *Posta del Cazador*
15. *Turismo*

Pérez 632, T 27085/27985, English and French spoken; **A3** *Res Peumayén*, San Martín 851, T 27232, with breakfast; **A3** *Villa Bibi*, Diaz 1186, T 27206, with breakfast, comfortable, recommended; **A3-B** *Curra-Huincla*, Rivadavia 686, T 27224, modern, recommended.

B *Casa Alta*, Obeid 659, T 27456, chalet in rose garden; **B** *Crismallu*, Rudecindo Roca 975, T 27283, F 27583, with breakfast, good value; **B** *Hostería Cumelén*, Elordi 931, T 27304 (or BsAs T 502-3467), hot water, breakfast, recommended; **B** *Colonos del Sur*, Rivadavia 686, T 27224, good value; **C** *Villalagos*, Villegas 717, without breakfast.

Budget accommodation: cheapest is **E** pp *Posta del Caminante*, Tres de Caballería 1164, summer only, good atmosphere, noisy; **E** pp *La Casa del Trabun*, Elordi 186, T 27755, sleeping bags essential, kitchen facilities. The following offer discounts to ISIC and youth card holders: **E** pp *Hosp Turístico Caritas*, Cap Drury 774, T 27313, run by church, floor space for sleeping bags in summer; *Albergue Universitario Técnico Forestal*, Pasaje de la Paz sin número, T 27618, youth hostel style, and *Hostería Los Pinos* (see above). Consult Tourist Office for other private addresses, but these are only supplied in high season.

Camping *ACA Camping*, Koessler 2176, T 27288, with hot water and laundering facilities, **F** pp, recommended. On southern shore of Lago Lacar: at Catritre, 6 km west; *Camping Quila Quina*, in Quila Quina, 27 km west, pleasant, with beaches.

● **Places to eat**
Try smoked venison, wild boar or trout, at *El Ciervo*, Villegas 724; *Piscis*, Villegas y Mariano Moreno, good *parrilla*; *Betty*, San Martín 1203, and *El Peñón*, Calderón, both good. *La Tasca*, Moreno 866, excellent trout and venison, home-baked bread, recommended; *Parrilla del Esquiador*, Belgrano 885, reasonable home-cooked food; *Mendieta*, San Martín 713, *parrilla*, popular; *Paprika*, Villegas 568, venison and trout, Hungarian, highly recommended; *Rancho Quitral*, Villegas 770, good food and service; *Jockey Club*, Villegas 657, also good; *Pizzería La Strada*, San Martín 721, good; *Fanfani*, Rodhe 786, has good pasta; *Pocha's*, Villegas y Belgrano, pizzas, friendly; *Tavola del Oso*, Pérez y Villegas, cheap, good; *Las Catalinas*, Villegas 745, excellent value.

● **Banks & money changers**
Banco de la Nación, San Martín 687, cash only; **American Express** San Martín 1141, T 28453; **Andino Internacional**, San Martín 876, 1st floor, only place to change travellers' cheques, commission 3%.

● **Laundry**
Laverap, Cap Drury 878, 0800-2200 daily and Villegas 986, cheaper, 0900-1300, 1600-2130 Monday-Friday, 0900-1300 Saturday.

● **Sports**
Fishing: for information on trout fishing, contact Logaine and David Denies at *Trails*, Pérez 662, San Martín.

Skiing: Cerro Chapelco is said to have some of the best slopes in Argentina. There are several chair-lifts of varying capacity and a ski-tow higher up. Bus from San Martín to slopes, US$7 return. Very good slopes and snow conditions. Lift pass US$20-35, ski hire US$13 a day from *Hostería Villa Lagos* or from lots of agencies in town. At the foot of the mountain are a restaurant and base lodge. There are three more restaurants on the mountain and a small café at the top.

● **Tour companies & travel agents**
Tiempo Patagónico, San Martín 950, T 27113, excursions and adventure tourism, 10% discount to ISIC and youth card holders; also *Pucará Viajes*, San Martín 943.

● **Tourist office**
Rosas y San Martín on main plaza, open 0800-2200, very helpful. **Parque Nacional Lanín** offfice on main plaza, helpful but maps poor.

● **Useful addresses**
Police station: at Belgrano 611.

● **Transport**
Local Car hire: Avis, San Martín 998, T 27704, F 28500 and at airport. **Localiza** at airport and Villegas 977, T 28876. **A1 Rent a Car** at airport. **Mechanic**: *Taller Fubol 5*, San Martín, recommended.

Air See under Junín de los Andes above.

Buses Terminal at Villegas y Juez del Valle, good toilet facilities. To **Buenos Aires**, US$60, daily, Chevallier and El Valle; to **Bariloche** via Confluencia, Ko Ko, 3 days a week, 0800, 4 hours, US$18, El Valle 4 a week; to **Bariloche** along the Seven Lakes Drive, daily 1445, US$18, Vía Bariloche (company); to **Villa La Angostura** via Seven Lakes, 3 days a week with La Petroule. See below on routes to Bariloche.

Buses to Chile Daily bus via Paso Huahum to Puerto Pirehueico, 0900, US$8, 2 hours. From mid-November to May there are also buses via Junín de los Andes and Paso Tromen to Pucón and Temuco, Empresa San Martín Monday, Wednesday and Friday, at 0700, returning from Temuco the following day at 0500; Igi-Llaimi Tuesday, Thursday and Saturday at 0600, returning next day at 0630, US$25, 7 hours, rough journey, sit on the left. Reduced service from June to mid-November. When Paso Tromen is closed buses go via Huahum and do not pass through Pucón en route to Temuco: in that case change to JAC bus in Villarrica for Pucón. When Paso Huahum is closed there are no buses.

FRONTIER WITH CHILE: PASO HUAHUM

This route is usually open all year round and is an alternative to the route via the Tromen Pass (see above). Paso Huahum (659m) is 47 km west of San Martín de los Andes along Route 48 (*ripio*) which runs along the north shore of Lago Lacar. For buses on this route see under San Martín.

● **Argentine immigration**
Open summer 0800-2100, winter 0900-2000.

● **Chilean immigration**
Open summer 0800-2100, winter 0800-2000.

● **Into Chile**
The road continues on the Chilean side to Puerto Pirehuico at the southern end of Lago Pirehueico, a long, narrow and deep lake, totally unspoilt except for some logging activity. At its northern end lies Puerto Fuy. Accommodation is available in in private houses in Puerto Pirehueico and Puerto Fuy. Ferries cross the lake between the two ports (Tuesday and Thursday 0700 out of season). Buses connect Puerto Pirehueico with Panguipulli, 3 daily, 3 hours, US$3, from where transport is available to other destinations in the Chilean Lake District.

FROM SAN MARTIN TO BARILOCHE

There are two routes from San Martín south to Bariloche:

THE DIRECT ROUTE

Route 63 turns southeast off Route 234 26 km south from San Martín and then runs along Lago Meliquina, Km 31-40. At Km 54 an unpaved track gives access to Lago Filohua-hum. At **Confluencia**, Km 93, the road meets Route 237, the paved Neuquén-Bariloche highway, which runs south, along the Río Limay through the **Valle Encantado**, where there are fantastic rock formations including *El Dedo de Dios* (The Finger of God) and *El Centinela del Valle* (The Sentinel of the Valley), before reaching Bariloche.

● **Accommodation At Confluencia**: *Hostería La Gruta de las Vírgenes*; also motel *El Rancho* just before Confluencia. ACA station.

THE SEVEN LAKES DRIVE

This very beautiful route (Route 234), though poor in parts, runs through the Lanín and Nahuel Huapi National Parks and is one of the most famous in the Argentine Lake District, offering views of the southern beach forests and the lakes. (National Park permit holders may camp freely along this route.) At Km 17 from a bridge you can see the **Arroyo Partido**: at this very point the rivulet splits, one stream flowing to the Pacific, the other to the Atlantic. The road passes **Lago**

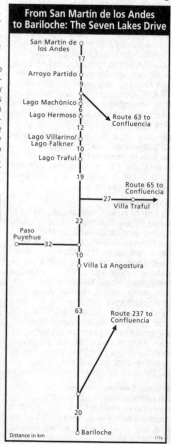

From San Martín de los Andes to Bariloche: The Seven Lakes Drive

San Martín de los Andes
17
Arroyo Partido
9
Lago Machónico
6
Lago Hermoso
12
Route 63 to Confluencia
Lago Villarino/ Lago Falkner
10
Lago Traful
19
Route 65 to Confluencia
27
Villa Traful
22
Paso Puyehue
32
10
Villa La Angostura
63
Route 237 to Confluencia
20
Bariloche
Distance in km

117a

Machónico at Km 30 and **Lago Hermoso** at Km 36. At Km 48 it runs between **Lago Villarino** and **Lago Falkner** before passing **Lago Traful** at Km 58.

Villa Traful

Beside Lago Traful; is reached by a turning at Km 77. Described as a 'camper's paradise', there are marvellous views, fishing (licence needed) excellent. All roads are dirt; drive carefully, avoiding wild cattle!

• **Accommodation At Lago Villarino**: *Hostería Lago Villarino*, good food, beautiful setting, camping. **At Villa Traful**: *Hostería Villa Traful*; *Hostería El Rincón del Pescador*.

At Km 80 the road runs along the north side of **Lago Correntoso** before turning south. At Km 99 Route 234 meets Route 231, the road between Bariloche and the Chilean frontier at Paso Puyehue (see below).

Villa La Angostura

(*Population* 3,000; *Phone code* 0944) Km 109, a picturesque town, lies 90 km northwest of Bariloche on Lago Nahuel Huapi. The port, 3 km south of town at the neck of the Quetrihué Peninsula, is spectacular in summer. 9 km north of town is **Cerro Bayo**, a small ski-resort with 21 pistes, 10 ski-lifts and ski-school. Ski-passes: daily US$26 high season, US$18 low; weekly US$156 high season, US$108 low.

• **Accommodation L2** *Hostería Las Balsas*, T 94308, small, exclusive, high standard, good location; **A3** *Correntoso*, T 94168, has a chalet next door, **B** for 2 bedrooms, shared use of kitchen and lounge, luxurious; *La Angostura*, T 94151. Cheaper are *La Cabañita* and *Don Pedro* in El Cruce, dirty, both **C**; **D-E** *Hostal Nahuel*, member of Red Argentina de Alojamiento para Jóvenes. Ask at the tourist office for lodgings in private houses, cheaper than hotels. **Camping** *El Cruce*, 500m from terminal, US$4 per person, dirty toilets; *ACA Osa Mayor* (2 km along Bariloche road, pleasant, open late December to mid-May), *Municipal Lago Correntoso* (Km 87 from Bariloche).

• **Tour companies & travel agents** *Turismo Cerro Bayo*, Arrayanes sin número, T 94401/94412, 10% discount for ISIC and youth card holders on ski packages, trekking, rafting, lake and adventure tours.

• **Tourist office** In bus terminal.

• **Buses** From **Bariloche** at 1900 daily, returning 0800, Transportes Mercedes, US$7. To **San**

Martín de los Andes, daily 1700. If going on to Osorno (Chile), you can arrange for the bus company to pick you up at La Angostura, US$11 to Osorno. There are also excursion buses from Bariloche (day trip, 8 hours).

FRONTIER WITH CHILE: PASO PUYEHUE

Paso Puyehue (1,280m) lies 125 km northwest of Bariloche and is reached by Route 231, a good paved highway which runs west from the main San Marín-Bariloche highway along the northern side of Lago Nahuel Huapi through Villa La Angostura. Although less scenic than the ferry journey across Lake Todos Los Santos and Laguna Verde this crossing is cheaper, more reliable and still a beautiful trip. **NB** This route is liable to closure after snow.

• **Argentine customs & immigration** Open winter 0900-2100, summer 0700-2200.

• **Into Chile** On the Chilean side the road is paved via Entre Lagos and Lago Puyehue to Osorno. Chilean immigration is at Anticura, 22 km west of the border Open second Saturday in October-second Saturday in March 0800-2100, otherwise 0800-1900. The Chilean frontier post

• **Accommodation In Anticura**: *Hostería y Canañas Anticura*; *Camping Catrue*.

• **Buses** For services from Bariloche to Osorno, Puerto Montt and Valdivia see under Bariloche.

• **Crossing by private vehicle** For vehicles entering Chile, formalities are quick (about 15 minutes), but includes the spraying of tyres and shoes have to be wiped on a mat (pay US$2 to 'Sanidad'). Passage will be much quicker if you already have Chilean pesos and don't have to change at the border. A circular trip from Bariloche can be done by going first via Puyehue to Puerto Montt, returning via Tromen Pass (see the Villarrica volcano, good road), then Junín and San Martín de los Andes.

PARQUE NACIONAL LOS ARRAYANES

This park, covering 1,000 hectares on the Quetrihué peninsula, within the Parque Nacional Nahuel Huapi, was created to protect 300-year-old specimens of the rare Arrayán tree.

• **Access** The park lies 15 km south of Villa La Angostura from where tour boats sail daily 1500 and 1600, US$12 return. See under Bariloche for tours by boat from Bariloche; out of season it is more difficult to visit as tour boats only sail if demand is sufficient.

PARQUE NACIONAL NAHUEL HUAPI

Covering some 750,000 hectares and stretching along the Chilean frontier for over 130 km, this is the oldest National Park in Argentina, created in 1934 but originating from a donation in 1903 by Francisco Perito Moreno of 7,500 hectares of land around Puerto Blest to the state. Extending across a mountainous environment, the park contains the most diverse and spectacular natural phenomena: lakes, rivers, glaciers, waterfalls, torrents, rapids, valleys, forest, bare mountains and snow-clad peaks. Among the peaks are: Tronador (3,478m), Catedral (2,388m), Falkner (2,350m), Cuyín Manzano (2,220m), López (2,076m), Otto (1,405m) and Campanario (1,405m).

There are several large lakes and dozens of smaller ones. The largest is **Lago Nahuel Huapi** (*altitude* 767m), 96 km long, not more than 12 km wide and covering over 60,000 hectares. Some 465m deep at its deepest spot around Puerto Blest, the lake is very irregular in shape; it has seven long arms or *brazos* reminiscent of the Norwegian fjords. There are many islands: the largest is **Isla Victoria**, on which stands the forest research station where new species of vegetation are acclimatized. The **Quetrihué peninsula** near Isla Victoria has been set aside as a separate park, the **Parque Nacional Los Arrayanes**. Trout and salmon have been introduced. The lake drains eastwards into the Río Limay which, below its junction with the Río Neuquén, becomes the Río Negro, Argentina's second largest river.

North of Lago Nahuel Huapi are other lakes: **Lago Correntoso**, separated from one of the northern *brazos* of Lago Nahuel Huapi by glacial morraine; **Lago Espejo** and **Lago Traful**. The three main lakes south of Lago Nahuel Huapi are **Lago Gutiérrez**, **Lago Mascardi** and **Lago Guillelmo**, can be reached by Route 258 from Bariloche to Esquel.

Vegetation varies with altitude but includes large expanses of southern beech forest and near the Chilean frontier, where rainfall is highest, there are areas of Valdivian rainforest. There are *coihues* (evergreen beeches) over 450 years old and *alerces* over 1,500 years old. Eastern parts of the park are more steppe-like with shrubs and bushes. Fauna include the *pudú*, the endangered *huemul* and river otter, as well as foxes, cougars and guanacos. Among the birds are Magellan woodpeckers and austral parakeets as well as large flocks of swans, geese and ducks. Best times to visit are August for skiing and February for walking, avoiding the busy months of July and January.

• **Sports Swimming**: in the larger lakes such as Nahuel Huapi and Huechulafquen is not recommended, for the water is cold. But swimming in smaller lakes such as Lolog, Lacar, Curruhué Chico, Hermoso, Meliquina, Espejo, Hess and Fonck is very pleasant and the water – especially where the bottom shelves to a shingly beach – can be positively warm.

• **Services** Park information centre in Bariloche. Visitors' Centre at Puerto Pañuelo; park entry US$5. Camping is permitted at specified sites but not along Lago Nahuel Huapi. Bariloche is the usual centre for visiting the park: details of accommodation, transport and tours are given in that section.

The Arrayán

🐛 (*Myerceugenella apiculata*). This myrtle-like tree, found on both sides of the Andes, grows near water in groves of 15-20 hectares which have been declared National Monuments. The twisted contorted trunks have pale orange bark which peels as the tree grows. It has pure white flowers in January and February and produces blue/black fruit in February/March. Its leaves have medicinal uses. Though it grows from Neuquén south to the Río Chubut, the two main arrayán forests in Argentina are on the Quetrihué peninsula (*Quetrihué* is myrtle in Mapuche) and Isla Victoria in Parque Nacional Nahuel Huapi and along the Río Arrayanes in the Parque Nacional Los Alerces.

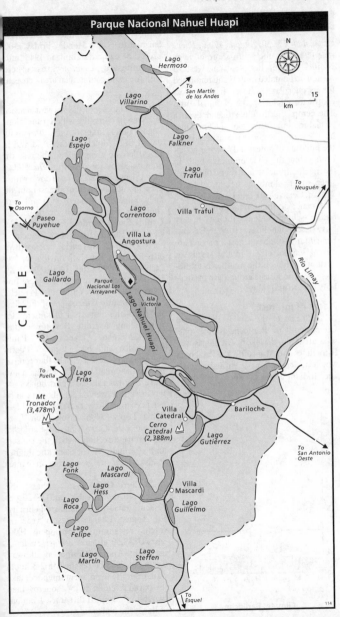

BARILOCHE

(*Population* 77,750; *Altitude* 770m; *Phone code* 0944), on the south shore of Lago Nahuel Huapi, lies 436 km west of Neuquén. Founded in 1903 and renowned for its chocolate industry, it is the best centre for exploring the National Park. The centre, beautifully-situated upon a glacial moraine at the foot of Cerro Otto, has been transformed in recent decades by the building of hotels and *hosterías* which overshadow the civic buildings built in 'Bariloche alpine' style. Around the centre steep streets climb the heights of Cerro Ventan, Cerro Negro and Cerro Carbón.

A major destination for groups of secondary school students, the city is very busy in school holidays (July; 15 December-10 January): best times for a visit are out of season, either in the spring or autumn, although the weather is unpredictable. The forests around are particularly beautiful in May.

Places of interest

At the heart of the city is the **Centro Cívico**, built in 'Bariloche Alpine style' separated from the lake by Avenida Rosas. It includes the **Museo de La Patagonia** which has collections of stuffed animals and Indian artefacts, open 1000-1200, 1400-1900 Tuesday-Friday, 1000-1300 Saturday US$3; the attached **Biblioteca Sarmiento** is open Monday-Friday, 1100-2200. The **cathedral**, built in 1946 (interior unfinished) lies six blocks east of here, with the main commercial area between.

Excursions

To **Llao-Llao**, a resort 24 km west, reached by Avendia Bustillo which runs along Lago Nahuel Huapi. (bus No 20, 45 minutes, US$2). Hotels on this road and in Llao-Llao are given below. The resort is dominated by the beautiful *Hotel Llao-Llao*, opened in 1937, burned down within a few months and rebuilt almost immediately. Superbly situated on a hill with chocolate box views, it overlooks the **Capilla San Eduardo**, like the hotel designed by Bustillo and Puerto Pañuelo.

To **Cerro Campanario**, reached by a chairlift from Km 17.7 on the road to Llao-Llao (0900-1200, 1400-1800 daily, US$10); from the summit there are fine views of Isla Victoria and Puerto Pañuelo.

The **Circuito Chico**, one of the 'classic' Bariloche tours, is a 61 km circular route along Avenida Bustillo around Lago Moreno Oeste, past Punto Panorámico and back through Puerto Pañuelo and Llao-Llao itself. Tour companies do the circuit and it can be driven in half a day (it can also be cycled, but beware bus drivers of Avenida Bustillo). It can be extended to a full day: Bariloche-Llao Llao-Bahía López-Colonia Suiza (on Lago Moreno Este)-Cerro Catedral-Bariloche; the reverse direction misses the sunsets and afternoon views from the higher roads, which are negotiable in winter (even when snow-covered).

To **Cerro Otto**, 5 km southeast, the nearest ski resort, cable car, US$20 per person; 0930-1800 January-February, July-August, 1000-1800 rest of year; revolving restaurant at top, opens 1000, entry US$3.50; also nice *confitería* belonging to Club Andino 20 minutes walk away. Cerro Otto can be reached in 2-3 hours walk from the town, recommended; take the paved Avenida de los Pioneros, then switch to the signed dirt track 1 km out of Bariloche (splendid views)

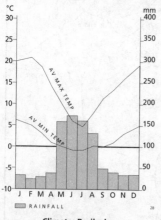

Climate: Bariloche

Alejandro Bustillo and the 'Estilo Bariloche'

Many of the public buildings of Bariloche owe their particular style to the architect Alejandro Bustillo and his colleague, Ernesto de Estrada. Though the so-called *Estilo Bariloche* (Bariloche style) of their designs drew its inspiration from the Alps, the materials employed were local: stone from Cerro Otto and timber from the forests.

Bustillo's opportunity came in 1935 when he won a public competition to design the Hotel Llao Llao, the first building to be commissioned by Parques Nacionales, the Argentine National Parks authority. In following years he designed many other buildings in the national park, among them the Cathedral and the National Park Intendancy in Bariloche, the Hotel on Isla Victoria (sadly destroyed by fire), the Capilla La Asunción in Villa La Angostura and the *refugio* on Cerro Catedral. The Centro Civico in Bariloche and a number of other buildings were the work of Estrada.

Admirers of Bustillo's work may like to look out for his buildings elsewhere in Argentina, among them the Banco de la Nación in the Plaza de Mayo in Buenos Aires and the monumental buildings which have come to symbolize Mar del Plata: the Casino, Hotel Provincial and Rambla.

• **Buses** Hourly service from Mitre y Villegas, 0930-1800 high season, reduced service low season, US$7 return.

To **Cerro Catedral** (2,300m), 21 km southwest, on the slopes of which is one of the major ski-resorts in Argentina. Divided into 2 sectors, Robles Catedral to the south and Alta Patagonia to the north, there are a total of 67 km of ski-slopes and 32 ski-lifts. In summer it is popular with walkers: red and yellow markers painted on the rock mark a trail from the summit which leads to *Refugio Frey* (well equipped, blankets, meals, US$5-8, bed US$5 per person) on the edge of a small mountain lake (allow 6 hours). A half-day excursion is possible taking a bus to Virgen de las Nieves on Cerro Catedral, walking 2 km to arrive at beautiful Lago Gutiérrez; walk along lake shore to the road from El Bolsón and walk back to Bariloche (about 4 hours).

• **Accommodation** *Catedral*, T 60044, 4-star; *Pire Hue*, T 60040, 4-star; 3 hosterías.

• **Services** Alta Patagonia: Lift passes, daily US$40 high season, US$22 low, weekly US$180 high season, US$99 low; hourly lessons US$60 high season, US$51 low; daily ski hire US$19 high season, US$16 low. Robles Catedral: lift passes, daily US$25 high season, US$18 low, weekly US$125 high season, US$80 low season.

• **Buses** Bus service with seasonal timetable every 10 minutes run by Mercedes bus company, Mitre 161, US$5 return. Coach tours from Bariloche to the foot of Cerro Catedral give time for less than 2 hours on top of the mountain.

Other excursions

The surrounding countryside offers beautiful walking, eg to Lago Escondido on a 3½ km trail off the Circuito Chico. A longer walk is to Cerro López (3 hours, with a *refugio* after 2); take Colonia Suiza bus (from Moreno y Rolando) and alight at Picada. Longer still is the hike to *refugio Italia* (same bus, but alight at SAC); details of this and 3-5 day continuations from Club Andino. One-day excursions can also be made to San Martín de los Andes along the Seven Lakes Drive (see above).

Boat excursions

To **Isla Huemul**, west of Bariloche in Lago Nahuel Huapi, from Puerto San Carlos, 30 minutes voyage, 2 hours on island, 5 sailings a day (reduced service off-season) US$16.

To **Isla Victoria**, half-day excursion (1300-1830) from Puerto Pañuelo (with transport from Bariloche). There is also a full-day excursion (0900-1830, or 1300 till 2000 in season) which includes the **Parque Nacional Los Arrayanes** on the Quetrihue peninsula further north, and Isla Victoria, picnic lunch advised. US$30. Book this trip through an agency, as the boat fare alone is US$21. These tours only visit part of Isla Victoria and you only spend 1 hour in the park which is often crowded. Some boats going to Arrayanes call first at Isla Victoria, early

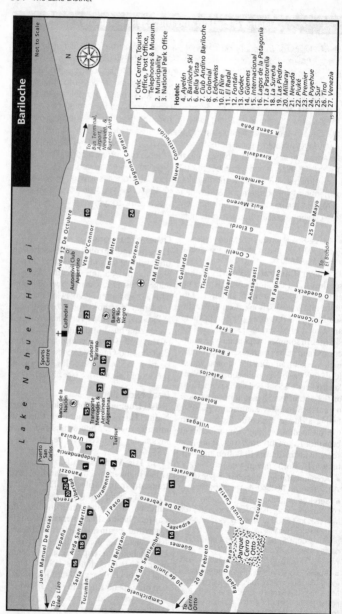

Bariloche

Not to Scale

1. Civic Centre, Tourist Office, Post Office, Telephones & Museum
2. Municipality
3. National Park Office

Hotels:
4. Ayelén
5. Bariloche Ski
6. Bella Vista
7. Club Andino Bariloche
8. Colonial
9. Edelweiss
10. El Nire
11. El Radal
12. Fontán
13. Godec
14. Guemes
15. Internacional
16. Lagos de la Patagonia
17. La Sureña
18. La Pastorella
19. Las Piedras
20. Millaray
21. Nevada
22. Piuké
23. Premier
24. Puyehue
25. Sur
26. Tirol
27. Venezia

enough to avoid boat-loads of tourists. (Turisur have four catamarans with a bar and cafeteria.) All boats are very crowded in season, but operators have to provide seating for all passengers.

To **Puerto Blest**, at the western end of Lago Nahuel Huapi, and **Lago Frías**, visiting native forest and rainforest, highly recommended. This trip is usually done as a 9-hour excursion, leaving at 0900 (afternoon departure also December-March), offered by *Turisur* and *Catedral*, US$35: bus to Puerto Pañuelo, boat to Puerto Blest, bus to Puerto Alegre and again by launch to Puerto Frías. A visit to the Cascada de los Cántaros is made (stay off the boat at the Cascada and walk around to Puerto Blest through beautiful forest, 1 hour, recommended). Alternatively take 0700 bus to Puerto Pañuelo, then 0800 boat to Puerto Blest, cheaper.

● **Accommodation B** *Puerto Blest*, half pension, good, book through *Catedral*.

Tours

There are numerous tours: most travel agencies charge the same price. It is best to buy tours on the spot rather than in advance, although they get very booked up in season. Tours offered include:

Whole-day trip to Lagos Gutiérrez, Mascardi, Hess, the Cascada Los Alerces and Cerro Tronador and the Black Glacier, leaving at 0800, US$29, interesting but too much time spent on the bus.

12-hour minibus excursions to San Martín de los Andes, US$34, via the Seven Lakes Drive and returning via Paso de Córdoba and the Valle Encantado but these involve 10 hours on the bus and few stops (taxi for this route US$30 per person).

There are also tours around the Circuito Chico (see above) US$13, half-day; to Cerro Catedral, half-day, US$13 plus ski-lift; to El Bolsón with a journey on *La Trochita*, full-day US45. For tours to Puella (Chile) see **The Lakes Route to Puerto Montt**, below).

If staying only 1-2 days in the area the best excursions are to Cerro Tronador the first day, and on the second to Cerro Catedral in the morning and Isla Victoria in the afternoon (possible only December-March when there are afternoon departures for the island).

Local information
● **Accommodation**

Hotel prices

L1	over US$200	**L2**	US$151-200
L3	US$101-150	**A1**	US$81-100
A2	US$61-80	**A3**	US$46-60
B	US$31-45	**C**	US$21-30
D	US$12-20	**E**	US$7-11
F	US$4-6	**G**	up to US$3

Unless otherwise stated, all hotels in range **D** and above have private bath. Assume friendliness and cleanliness in all cases.

The most complete listing with map is published by the Oficina Municipal de Turismo, who you are advised to consult if you arrive in the high season without a reservation. It also has a booking service at Florida 520 (Galería), room 116, Buenos Aires. Out of season, prices are reasonable, in all ranges, especially if you bargain; in season everything is very expensive. Most hotels outside the town include half-board, and those in the town include breakfast. Hotels with lake views normally charge US$3-4 extra per room per day, for the view in high season; the following selection gives lake-view high-season prices where applicable. The following specialise in school-trips in July and from 15 December to 15 January: Ayelén, Bariloche Ski, Interlaken, Millaray, Montana, Piedras and Pucón.

On the road to Llao Llao (Avenida Bustillo): **L2** *Apart-hotel Casablanca*, Km 23.5, T 48117, good, on a peninsula between Lagos Nahuel Huapi and Moreno; **L1** *Hotel Llao-Llao*, Km 25.5, deservedly famous, fine views, golf course, spa, water sports (reservations: Avenida Santa Fe 846, 6th floor, Buenos Aires, T/F 311-3432); **L1** *Tunquelen*, Km 25.5, 5-star, very good; **B** *La Caleta*, Km 1.9, bungalows sleeping 4, shower, open fire, excellent value, self-catering, recommended, T 25650; *Pájaro Azul*, Km 10.8, 4 rooms, friendly; **A1** *La Cascada*, Km 6, T 41046, 5-star, recommended.

In Bariloche: **L2** *Edelweiss*, Avenida San Martín 232, 5-star, T 26165, modern, excellent food, enclosed pool, highly recommended; **L2** *Lagos de la Patagonia*, San Martín 536, T 25846, 5-star, heated swimming pool.

A2 *Bella Vista*, Rolando 351, T 22435, large well-appointed rooms with lake view, 2 good restaurants; **A2** *Italia*, Tiscornia 892, new, good breakfast; **A3** *Bariloche Ski*, San Martín 352, 4-star, T 22913, Tx 18273, good; **A3** *Colonial*, Quaglia 281, T 26101, helpful, lake views; **A3** *Internacional*, Mitre 171, T 25938,

F 20072, reduction for ACA members; **A3** *La Pastorella*, Belgrano 127, T 24656, English and French-spoken, central, recommended; **A1** *Nevada*, Rolando 250, T 22778, heating, nice room; *Res Tirol*, Pasaje Libertad 175, T 26152, good, German spoken; **A3** *Ayelén*, Pasaje Libertad 157, T 23611, 3-star, comfortable, restaurant, recommended; **A3** *Millaray*, Libertad 195, T 21495, good, shower.

B *Aguas del Sur*, Moreno 353, T 22995/24329, including excellent 4-course meal and breakfast, helpful, recommended; **B** *Res La Sureña* 432, T 24875, San Martín, 500m west of Centro Cívico, helpful; **B** *Hostería Sur*, Beschtedt 101, T 22677; opposite is **B** *Res Piuké*, Beschtedt 136, T 23663, German, Italian spoken, recommended; **B** *Hostería El Ñire*, J O'Connor 94, T 23041, very pleasant, heated, German, English spoken, prefers longer-stay visitors, also apartments, recommended; **B** pp *Hostería El Radal*, 24 de Septiembre 46, T 22551, clean, comfortable, warm, English spoken, **D** pp in low season; **B** *Res Puyehue*, Elordi 243, T 22196, discount for SAH users.

C *Fontán*, Palacios 276, T 29431, pleasant, family-run, good beds; **C** *Res Premier*, Rolando 263, T 23681, hot showers, English and German spoken, small rooms, recommended; **C** *Venezia*, Morales 446, T 22407; **C** pp *Victoria*, Mitre 815, **D** pp without bath, poor beds; **C** *Hostería Güemes*, Güemes 715, T 24785, helpful, recommended; **C** *Las Piedras*, Palacios 235. **C/D** *Las Moiras*, Reconquista 72, family atmosphere, good.

D *Godec*, 24 de Septiembre 218, T 23085, run down, restaurant (reservations in Buenos Aires T 751-4335); **E** pp *Res No Me Olvides*, Avenida Los Pioneros Km 1, T 29140, 30 minutes walk from centre or Bus 50/51 to corner of Calle Videla then follow signs, nice house in quiet surroundings, use of kitchen, camping US$5 per person, highly recommended; **E** pp *Res Rosán*, Güemes 691, T 23109 (Sra Arco), repeatedly recommended, English and German spoken, cooking facilities, helpful, beautiful garden, camping US$5; **E** pp *El 1004*, San Martín 127, kitchen facilities, also floor space, English spoken; **E** pp *San Francisco*, Paso y 20 de Feb, good meals; **E** pp *La Bolsita del Deporte*, Palacios y Elflein, T/F 23529, dormitory, German, English spoken, sports equipment rented, recommended; **E** pp *Albergue Mochilero*, San Martín 82, T 31627, F 23187, dormitory, clean; **E** pp *Hosp Nevegal*, Rolando 615, very clean.

Family accommodation: the tourist office keeps a list. Among those recommended are: **E** pp *Sra Carlota Baumann*, Avenida de los Pioneros 860, T 29689, F 24502, follow 20 de Febrero uphill for 10-15 minutes, kitchen, bath, good breakfast, laundry service, English and German spoken **C-E** *Familia Dalfaro*, Rolando y Tiscorra (southwest corner), quiet; **E** *Pensión Venus*, Salta 571, heating, cooking facilities; **E** pp *Casa Diego*, Elflein 163, T 22556, in dormitory, without breakfast; **E** *Pire-Cuyen* Anasagasti 840, doubles only; **E** Frey 635, dormitory, cooking and laundry facilities, motorcycle parking; **E** Anasagasti 348; **E** pp *Sra Iris* Quaglia 526, with bath; **E** *Eloisa Lamuniere*, 24 de Septiembre 71, T 225614, with breakfast, homely, helpful, cooking facilities; **E** pp *Casa Nelly*, Beschtedt 658, T 22295, hot showers, kitchen, camping; **E** pp *Nogarre*, Elflein 58, comfortable, warm, eccentric owner; **D** pp *Lo de Giani*, Elflein, with breakfast; **E** pp *Hosp Nevegal*, Rolando 615, very clean; **E** *Mariana Pirker*, 24 de Septiembre 230, T 24873, two 3-bedded apartments with bath and kitchen. Apartments and chalets may also be rented, prices vary enormously according to the season: try Calle Ruiz 1870, T 26781 (ask for Teo), small but very good.

Youth hostels **E** pp *Albergue Patagonia Andina*, Morales 564, T 22783, small dormitories, kitchen facilities, information, recommended; *Alaska*, Avenida Bustillo, Km 7.5 (buses 10, 20, 21, get off at La Florida), T/F 61564, IYHA-affiliated, **D-E** pp, good atmosphere, poor beds, cooking and washing facilities, mountain bikes, pleasant location, English spoken, good information on local treks, book in advance in summer, recommended; all offer 10% discount to ISYC and youth card holders; **E** pp *Refugio Cordillera*, Avenida Bustillo, Km 18, T/F 48261, good kitchen.

Camping List of sites from Tourist Office. Several sites on Avenida Bustillo include: *Selva Negra*, Km 2.5, T 44013, US$8 per person, highly recommended; *Camping Km5*, Km 5; *El Yeti*, Km 5.6, recommended; *Petunia*, Km 14.9, well protected from winds by trees, hot showers, shop, recommended; *Camping Musical*, musicians' meeting point; shops and restaurants on most of these sites closed outside January-March.

● **Places to eat**
La Marmita, Mitre 329, small, cosy, excellent mixed fondues recommended; *El Viejo Munich*, Mitre 102, good meat and fish, recommended; *Caza Mayor*, Quaglia y Elflein, game and fish, good but expensive; *La Montaña*, Elflein 49, very good value; *Kandahar*, 20 de Febrero 698, T 24702, excellent, run by Argentine ski champion Marta Peirono de Barber; *Parrilla 1816*, Elflein 167, good meat, recommended; *Parrilla La Vizcacha*, Rolando 279,

good value, recommended; *Cantina Lotito*, Morales 362, very good *parrillada*, reasonably priced; *Lennon*, Moreno 48, small, good food, reasonably priced, English spoken; *La Jirafa*, Palacios 288, good food, good value; *Simoca*, Palacios 264, inexpensive Tucumán fare; *Familia Weiss*, Palacios 170 (with good delicatessen round corner on Mitre), excellent local specialities. Good pastries and hot chocolate at *Hola Nicolás*, Moreno y Urquiza (see the graffiti-graven tables). *La Rondine*, San Martín 536, Italian, luxurious, good (above *Hotel Panamericano*). *Jauja*, Quaglia 370, good local dishes; *La Andinita*, Mitre 56, recommended, pizzas, good value; *Cocodrilo*, Mitre y Urquiza, big choice of good pizzas, good value, take-away service; *Vegetariano*, Elflein y Morales, excellent fixed menu, good value, recommended; *Al Dente*, Mitre 370, vegetarian, cheap, good; *Pizzaiola*, Pagano 275, good pizzería; *La Nueva Estancia*, Elflein y Rolando, good meat and trout, occasional live entertainment; *La Alpina Confitería*, Moreno 98, open fire, reasonably priced, cheese fondue recommended, very popular; *Del Turista*, Mitre 231, chocolates, ice cream; *Algunas Frases*, Mitre 211, bar, open 24 hours. Many good delicatessen's with take-away food, including chicken, pizzas and cheeses, for picnics.

On Avenida Bustillo are: *La Glorieta*, Km 3.8, good; *Patacon Parrilla*, Km 7, excellent; *La Posta del Río*, Km 10, reasonable; *Ermitage*, tea rooms, Km 18.

● **Airline offices**

Aerolíneas Argentinas/Austral, Mitre 119 y Villegas, T 23161; **LADE**, Mitre 175; **Lapa**, Villegas 121, T 23714; **TAN**, Villegas 142, T 27889.

● **Banks & money changers**

There are several banks and exchange shops, which buy and sell virtually all European and South American currencies, besides US dollars; Saturday is a bad day. **Olano**, Quaglia 238, 2% commission on travellers' cheques; **Sudamerica**, Mitre 63; **American Express**, Mitre 387, T 25414, no exchange facilities, sends you to **Banco Nación**, Mitre y Villegas, to buy travellers' cheques, but does have emergency cash service. **Banco Integrado Departamental**, O'Connor y 12 de Octubre, for Thomas Cook travellers' cheques; **Banco Quilmes**, Mitre 300 block, cash advances on Visa. Beware forged Argentine banknotes. If everything closed try *Kiwanis* (boot rental), Mitre 210, 3% commission.

● **Consulates**

Chile, Rosas 180, friendly, helpful; **Germany**, Ruiz Moreno 45, T 25695; **Switzerland**, Quaglia 342, T 26111.

● **Entertainment**

Cinemas: *Arrayanes*, Moreno 39; *Cine Club*, Tuesday 2115 only, Biblioteca Sarmiento in the Centro Cívico.

● **Hospitals & medical centres**

Clinic: Cruz Azul, Capraro 1216.

● **Laundry**

Marva, San Martín 325, also Beschtedt 166; *Laverap*, Rolando 241; *Lavadero del Centro*, V A O'Connor 716.

● **Post & telecommunications**

Post Office: Centro Cívico (same building as tourist office). *Poste Restante* US$2.50 per letter.

Telecommunications: San Martín e Independencia and Elflein y Frey (3 minutes minimum charge); cheaper from *Hotel Bariloche*, San Martín 127. Outside the phone office is a telephone with links to several countries (eg UK, Chile, Japan).

Internet: Cybercafe, Galeria El Sol, Mitre 300 block.

● **Shopping**

The main commercial centre is on Mitre between the Centro Cívico and Beschtedt; there are lots of *galerías* here. The products of the local chocolate industry are excellent and are sold by several shops along Mitre. You can watch chocolates being made at *El Turista*, San Martín 252. One block away is *Mamushka*, excellent. Very good chocolate at *Estrella Alpina*, Villegas 216 or Albarracín 146, and *Benroth*, Beschtedt 569, and at *Abuela Goye*, Albarracín 157. Try 'Papas de Bariloche', the local chocolate speciality. Local wines, from the Alto Río Negro, are also good. Woollen goods are recommended. Handicraft shops all along San Martín. *Feria Artesanal Municipal*, Moreno y Rolando, recommended. *Burton Cerámica*, Avenida Bustillo 4100, T/F 41102, makes and sells 'Patagonian pottery'. Winter clothing at *Flying Patagonia*, Quaglia between B Mitre and VA O'Connor. *Feria Naturista*, Elflein 73, vegetarian and health foods; *Todo* supermarket, Moreno 319, good selection, cheap.

Bookshop: *Cultura*, Elflein 78, has a good range of technical books, some in English and German; *La Barca*, Mitre 131 and *Mileno*, Quaglia 262, local 19.

● **Sports**

Apart from sailing and boating, there are golf, mountaineering, walking, birdwatching, skiing, and fishing (for which you need a permit). Excellent trout fishing November-March; boat hire arranged with tackle shops. Racquet Club, Avenida Bustillo, Km 13.5, tennis and squash, snack bar.

Bicycles: may be hired beside the lake in high season (eg A Carlucci, Mitre 723, US$20 full day). *Dirty Bikes*, V A O'Connor 681, T/F 25616, for cycle hire and repairs. Mopeds from Vertigo Rental, San Martin 594.

Hiking: before going hiking, buy moisturizing creams for exposed skin areas and lips. Horseflies (*tábanos*) frequent the lake shores and lower areas in summer; lemon juice is good for keeping them away, but can cause skin irritation. Club Andino (see below) has sketch maps of hikes.

Horseriding: for horse trekking trips: Carol Jones, Casilla 1436 (or through Hans Schulz – see below under **Tourist agencies**), US$35 half-day, US$60 day trips, spectacular, highly recommended; *Cumbres Patagonia*, Villegas 222, US$40 for 3 hours, suitable for all levels of experience, enjoyable; *Tom Wesley*, Avenida Bustillo Km 15.5, T/F 48193. Or ask at Club Andino for Valerie, friendly, recommended.

Mountain climbing: best information from Club Andino Bariloche, 20 de Febrero 30, open 0900-1200, 1500-2000 Monday-Friday and Saturday 0900-1200. The Club arranges guides; ask for Sr Ricardo, the secretary, who organizes easy weekend climbs and walks. Its booklet 'Guía de Sendas y Picadas' gives details of climbs and it provides maps (1:150,000) and details of all campsites, hotels and mountain lodges. There is something in the area for every kind of mountaineer. National Park mountain guides are available but can be expensive. Book: *Excursiones, Andinismo y Refugios de Montaña en Bariloche*, by Tonek Arko, available in local shops, US$2, or from the author at Güemes 691. In treks to *refugios* remember to add costs of ski lifts, buses, food at *refugio* and lodging (in Club Andino *refugios*: US$6 per night, plus US$3 for cooking, or US$5 for breakfast, US$8 for dinner). Take a sleeping bag. Note that at higher levels, winter snow storms can begin as early as April, making climbing dangerous.

Skiing: there is good skiing on Cerro Otto and Cerro Catedral during the winter season (July to early October), supervised by the Club Andino Bariloche. It is best organized with a tour company, especially from Buenos Aires, through whom you can secure discounts as part of an inclusive deal. Skiing is cheaper at smaller resorts, such as Esquel, though more expensive at San Martín de los Andes. The only disadvantage at Bariloche is that the snow is unreliable except at the top. Ski hire US$9-16 a day, depending on quality, dearer at Cerro Catedral than in town. Ski clothes can also be rented by the day, at US$1-2 per item, from *Kiwanis* sport stores, Mitre 210, or *El Iglú*, Galería Arrayanes II, Rolando 244.

Swimming: the Lido swimming pool on the lake shore is beautifully sited but somewhat run down. See under **Parque Nacional Nahuel Huapi** for swimming in the lakes.

● **Tour companies & travel agents**
Tour buses pick you up from your hotel. Agencies charge same prices: details above under **Tours**. *Catedral Turismo*, Mitre 399, T 25443/5, F 26215, for trip to Puerto Montt via Lakes, US$90 one way, recommended, also local excursions (10% discount for ISIC and youth card holders); *Turisur*, Villegas 310, T 26109, organizes trips on lake and on land. *San Carlos Travel*, San Martín 127, local 19, F 26181/86, birdwatching and other specialist tours, recommended; *Limay Travel*, V A O'Connor 710, T/F 20268, English and German spoken; *Rafting Adventure*, San Martín 130, T 32928, for watersports; *Cumbres Patagonia*, Villegas 222, T 23283, F 31835, for rafting, horseriding, trekking, fishing, recommended; *Hans Schulz*, Casilla 1017, T 23835/26508 (speaks Spanish, German and English) arranges tours and guides, highly recommended; *Tacul Viajes*, San Martín 430, T 26321, English spoken, ISIC discount, recommended. Recommended guide *Daniel Feinstein*, T/F 42259, speaks fluent English, naturalist and mountaineer, very experienced in both Argentina and Chile. **NB** Check what the cost of your tour includes; funicular rides, chair lift and national park entry are usually charged as extras. Most agencies now sell excursions which include ride on 'la Trochita' from El Maitén.

● **Tourist offices**
Oficina Municipal de Turismo , in Centro Civico, open daily 0900-2100, Saturday 0900-1900. Has full list of city buses, and details of hikes and campsites in the area and is helpful in finding accommodation. The book, *Guía Busch, Turismo y Comercio*, is useful; there are two editions, one costs US$5, the other is free. **Parque Nacional Nahuel Huapi** office, San Martín 24, open 0800-2000, scanty information. Information also from Sociedad Profesional de Guías de Turismo, Casilla de Correo 51, 8400 SC de Bariloche.

NB Obtain maps and information about the district in Buenos Aires at the National Park Tourist Office at Santa Fe 690, or at the provincial offices (addresses given on page 122); it is hard to obtain these in the provinces themselves. Park wardens are also useful sources of information.

● **Useful addresses**
Immigration Office: Libertad 175.

● **Transport**
Local Car hire: Hertz, Avis (San Martín 130, T 31648, F 31649) and **A1 International**, at

airport and in town (latter at San Martín 235, T 22582, F 27494); no flat rates, unless reservation made outside Argentina. **Localiza**, at airport and San Martín 570, reliable, helpful, competitive, better kilometre allowance than others. **Guiñazú del Campo**, Libertad 118, good cars, English spoken; **Chapis Car**, Libertad 120, and **Carro's SACI**, Mitre 26, T 25907, out of season open Monday-Friday morning only; **Open**, Mitre 382, T/F 26325, are all much cheaper. To enter Chile a permit is necessary, US$50, allow 48 hours. **Mechanic**: *Auguen SA*, VA O'Connor 1068, fast, reasonable, highly recommended. **Taxis**: *Remise Bariloche*, T 30222; *Auto Jet*, España 11, T 22408. Some drivers speak English or German.

Air Aeropuerto L Candelaria, 15 km east of town. Taxi US$10; bus US$3 from AR office (timetable posted in office window). Many flights to **Buenos Aires**, with AR and Lapa (US$109). TAN and Kaiken fly to **Comodoro Rivadavia** and **Neuquén**; TAN also to **San Martín de los Andes** and, in summer only, to **Puerto Montt** (Chile). Kaiken also serves **Mendoza**, **Ushuaia**, **Calafate**, **Esquel** and **Trelew**. Southern Winds fly to **Córdoba**, **Rosario**, **Tucumán** and **Salta**.

Trains Station 3 km east of centre (booking office closed 1200-1500 weekdays, Saturday afternoon and all Sunday), reached by local buses 20 and 21 (US$0.75), taxi US$4-6. Information from the Tourist Office; tickets also available from *Hotel Pagano y Pamozzi*, three blocks from Centro Cívico. Train service to **Viedma** only, Tuesday/Friday 1800, 16 hours, US$41 pullman, U$28 first. Scenery only interesting between Bariloche and Jacobacci, 4½ hours.

Buses Terminal next to railway station, 3 km east of centre (buses 20, 70 and 71, US$1), taxi US$3. Left luggage US$1 per day. Bus company offices: Andesmar, Palacios 240, T 22140; La Estrella, Palacios 246; Mercedes, Mitre 161; TAC, Villegas 147, T26356; Chevallier, Moreno 107, T 23090; Tas Choapa, Moreno 138, T 26663; Cruz del Sur, San Martín 453, T 24163; Don Otto/Bus del Norte, San Martín 283; Ko-Ko, Moreno 107. To **Buenos Aires**, several companies daily, 22½ hours, US$60-69, Andesmar *coche cama* 21 hours, US$75; to **Mar del Plata**, Pampa, TAM, or El Rápido, US$60, 20 hours; to **Bahía Blanca**, TAC, US$55; to **La Plata**, 19 hours, US$80; to **Mendoza**, US$70, 22 hours, via Zapala, Buta Ranquil and San Rafael; to **Córdoba**, US$77; to **El Bolsón**, Charter and Empresa Vía Bariloche, 2 hours, US$10; to **Esquel**, Don Otto, Mercedes, Vía Bariloche, Andesmar; to **Puerto Madryn**, 24 hours via Esquel (7-hour wait), and Trelew, US$56; to **San Martín de los Andes**, Ko Ko, Monday-Saturday

1430, US$18, 4 hours; to **Junín de los Andes** US$19; to **Neuquén**, US$18 Transportes Mercedes and La Estrella, 1415, 6½ hours (a dull journey). No direct bus to **Río Gallegos**; you have to spend a night in Comodoro Rivadavia en route. Don Otto to Río Gallegos US$88.

Buses to Chile For Punta Arenas it may be cheaper to go via Puerto Montt. To **Santiago** (Chile), Tuesday, Friday and Sunday, 24 hours with tea and breakfast served en route. To **Puerto Montt** (7 hours), **Osorno** (6 hours) and **Valdivia** via Paso Puyehue, four bus companies, buses usually leave 0730-0800, there is at least one bus every day from Argentine side and fares range from US$18-20 (US$35 for a 1-day excursion including city tour and Termas de Puyehue). Companies include Bus del Norte, Mercedes, and Tas Choapa, recommended. Sit on left side for best views. You can buy a ticket to the Chilean border, then another to Puerto Montt, or pay in stages in Chile, but there is little advantage in doing this.

THE LAKES ROUTE TO CHILE

This popular route to Puerto Montt, involving ferries across Lago Nahuel Huapi, Lago Frías and Lago Todos Los Santos, is outstandingly beautiful whatever the season, though the mountains are often obscured by rain and heavy cloud. **NB** No cars are carried on the ferries on this route.

The route is as follows: from Bariloche to Puerto Pañuelo by bus, from Puerto Pañuelo to Puerto Blest by catamaran (2½ hours), from Puerto Blest to Lago Frías by bus, across the lake to Puerto Frías by boat (20 minutes), from Puerto Frías to Peulla by bus (1 hours) via the frontier at Paso Pérez Rosales (978m), from Puella to Petrohué by boat (2½ hours) across Lago Todos Los Santos, passing the Osorno volcano, then by bus to Puerto Montt via Puerto Varas. This journey is not recommended in wet or foggy weather (check weather forecast on Chilean TV, available in many hotels). It is also long, tiring and has been criticized as very commercialized.

● **Accommodation At Peulla**: **A1** *Hotel Peulla*, PO Box 487, Puerto Montt, T 253253 (includes dinner and breakfast, direct personal reservations A3, PO Box 487, Puerto Montt, cheaper out of season), beautiful setting by the lake and mountains, restaurant and bar, good but expensive meals, cold in winter, often full of

tour groups (tiny shop at back of hotel); **D** pp
Res Palomita, 50m west of Hotel, half board,
family-run, simple, comfortable but not spacious, separate shower, book ahead in season,
lunches; accommodation is also available with
local residents: Elmo and Ana Hernández Maldonado (only house with a balcony), **D** with
breakfast, use of kitchen, helpful, clean. **Camping** Opposite Conaf office, US$1.50. Ask the
commander of the military garrison at the beach
nearest the hotel if you can camp on the beach;
no facilities. Good campsite 1¾ hours walk east
of Puella, take food.

● **Transport** In theory this route can only be
followed by taking the package offered by Turismo Catedral: they own the exclusive rights,
using their own boats and bus from Puerto
Pañuelo to Puerto Frías and operating with
Andina del Sud on the Chilean side. The journey
can be done in one or two days: the one-day
crossing (operates 1 September-31 March) costs
US$104; this excursion does not permit return
to Bariloche next day. Lunch at Peulla is extra,
US$18, best take own food, buy ticket day in
advance, departs 0700. For the two-day crossing (operates all year round), there is an overnight stop in Peulla. Several tour companies sell
this tour, includes transport, board and lodging.
Book in advance during the high season. A
cheaper alternative is to buy the trip in sections
and take advantage of local bus services to
Puerto Pañuelo (0700). You can also walk the
29 km section from Puerto Frías to Puella, but
you will need to do this quickly to catch the boat.

FRONTIER WITH CHILE: PASO PEREZ ROSALES

● **Argentine immigration & customs**
At Puerto Frías, open all year.

● **Chilean immigration & customs**
At Peulla, open daily 0800-2100 summer, 0800-
2000 winter. There is an absolute ban in Chile
on importing any fresh food – meat, cheese,
fruit – from Argentina.

● **Exchange**
You are strongly advised to get rid of all your
Argentine pesos before leaving Argentina; it is
useful to have some Chilean pesos before you
cross into Chile from Bariloche. Chilean currency
can be bought at Peulla customs at a reasonable
rate.

INTO CHILE: PUERTO MONTT

(*Population* 110,000) situated 1,016 km
south of Santiago, was founded in 1853 as
part of the German colonization of the
area. Good views over the city and bay are
offered from outside the Intendencia Regional on Avenida X Region. The port is
used by fishing boats and coastal vessels
and is the departure point for vessels to
Puerto Chacabuco, Puerto Aisén, and
Punta Arenas. A paved road runs 55 km
southwest to Pargua, where there is a ferry
service to the island of Chiloé.

Places of interest

The **Iglesia de los Jesuitas** on Gallardo,
dating from 1872, has a fine blue-domed
ceiling; behind it on a hill is the **campanario** (clock tower). The little fishing
port of **Angelmó**, 2 km west, has become
a tourist centre with many seafood restaurants and handicraft shops (reached by
Costanera bus along Portales and by collective taxi Nos 2,3,20 from the centre,
US$0.30pp). The **Museo Regional Juan
Pablo II**, Portales 997 near bus terminal,
has displays on local history and a fine
collection of historic photos of the city;
also memorabilia of the Pope's visit. Open
daily 1030-1800, US$0.50.

Excursions

Puerto Montt is a popular centre for excursions to the Chilean Lake District. The
wooded **Isla Tenglo**, close to Puerto Montt
and reached by launch from Angelmó
(US$0.30), is a favourite place for picnics.
Magnificent view from the summit. The
island is famous for its *curantos*, a local
dish. **Chinquihue** (the name means "place
of skunks") west of Angelmó, has many
seafood restaurants, with oysters as a speciality. East of Puerto Montt, **Chamiza**, up
the Río Coihuin, has fine fishing. There is
a bathing beach with black sand (polluted)
at **Pelluco**, 4 km east of Puerto Montt
(accommodation including *cabañas*; several good seafood restaurants, including
Pazos, best *curanto* in Puerto Montt, recommended). **Isla Guar** may be visited by
boat from Angelmó harbour (1600, 2
hours); boat returns from the other end of
the island at 0730. The north shore is
rocky. Accommodation, if lucky, at the
church; best to camp.

West of Puerto Montt the Río Maullín,
which drains Lago Llanquihue, has some

attractive waterfalls and good fishing (salmon). The little fishing village of **Maullin**, founded in 1602 (**B** *Motel El Pangal*, 5 km away, T 244), at the mouth of the Río Maullin, is worth a visit. South-east of here, on the coast, is Carelmapu; 3 km away is an excellent beach, Playa Brava. **Calbuco**, centre of the fishing industry (*Restaurant San Rafael*, recommended) with good scenery, is on an island linked to the mainland by a causeway. It can be visited direct by boat or by road (the old coast road from Puerto Montt is very beautiful).

Local information

Detailed listings including accommodation and places to eat can be found in the *South American Handbook* and the *Chile Handbook*.

● Accommodation

Accommodation is expensive in season, much cheaper off season. Full listing available from Tourist Office.

Camping 'Wild' camping possible along the sea front. Several sites west of Puerto Montt: *Camping Municipal* at Chinquihue, 10 km west (bus service), open October-April, fully equipped. *Camping Anderson*, 11 km west, American run, hot showers, private beach, home-grown fruit, vegetables and milk products. *Camping Los Alamos*, T 256067, 13 km west, nice views, poor services, stray dogs, US$17 per site.

● Banks & money changers

Impossible on Sunday (but try *Hotel Pérez Rosales*). Exorbitantly high commission and low rates at Banco del Estado. For Visa try **Banco Concepción**, Pedro Montt y Urmaneta, good rates. **Banco Osorno**, Varas y Garrardo, good for Visa cash, but does not change travellers' cheques. Commission charges vary widely. Good rates at **Galería Cristal**, Varas 595, **El Libertador**, Urmeneta 529-A, local 3, and **Turismo Latinoamericano**, Urmeneta 531; *Travellers* travel agent in Angelmó (address below) has exchange facilities. **Fincard** (Access), Varas 437. **La Moneda de Oro** at the bus terminal exchanges Latin American currencies (Monday-Saturday 0930-1230, 1530-1800). Obtain Argentine pesos before leaving Chile.

● Consulates

Argentine, Cauquenes 94, 2nd floor, T 253996, quick visa service; **German**, Varas y Gallardo, 3rd floor, of 306, Tuesday/Wednesday 0930-1200; **Spanish**, Rancagua 113, T 252557; **Dutch**, Seminario 350, T 253428.

● Sports

Puerto Montt and the surrounding area provides great opportunities for sailing (there are two yacht clubs in Chinquihué), fishing, climbing, skiing, parachuting and numerous other sports.

● Tour companies & travel agents

Andina del Sud, very close to central tourist kiosk, Varas 437, T 257797, operate the Chilean part of the boat/bus trip via Lago Todos Los Santos between Puerto Montt and Bariloche as well as a range of other tours. *Travellers*, Avenida Angelmó 2456, T/F 258555, Casilla 854, close to 2nd port entrance, open Monday-Friday 0900-1330, 1500-1830, Saturday 0900-1400 for booking for Navimag ferry *Puerto Edén* south to Puerto Natales, as well as trips to Osorno volcano and other excursions, money exchange, flights. Also sells imported camping equipment and runs computerized tourist information service, book swap, English-run, recommended.

● Tourist offices

Sernatur (Chilean tourist authority) is in the Intendencia Regional, Avenida Décima Región 480 (3rd floor), Casilla 297, T 254580/256999, F 254580, Tx 270008. Open 0830-1300, 1330-1730 Monday-Friday. Also kiosk on Plaza de Armas run by the municipality, open till 1800 on Saturday. Telefónica del Sur and Sernatur operate a phone information service (INTTUR), dial 142 (cost is the same as a local call). Dial 149 for chemist/pharmacy information, 148 for the weather, 143 for the news, etc. **Automóvil Club de Chile**: Esmeralda 70, T 252968.

● Transport

Air El Tepual Airport, 13 km northwest of town. ETM bus from terminal 1½ hours before departure, US$2. To Santiago at least 2 daily flights by LanChile, Ladeco and National (cheaper). To Punta Arenas, LanChile, Ladeco and National (both cheaper) daily. National also flies to Concepción and Temuco. Flights to Bariloche, San Martín de los Andes and Neuquén, TAN, twice a week. Also flights to Coyhaique, Chaitén and Puerto Natales.

Trains New station under construction at Alerce, 10 km north of town. Old station at San Felipe 50, T 254908 functions only as ticket office (0830-1130, 1300-1700). Daily service in summer to **Santiago** departs from Puerto Varas, 1600, Rápido with 1930s German-built sleepers, 19 hours, book 3 days in advance, but 2 weeks in advance in high season

Buses Terminal on sea front at Portales y Lota, has telephones, restaurants, *casa de cambio* (left luggage, US$1 per item for 24 hours). There are services to all parts of the country.

SOUTH OF BARILOCHE

Route 258, the road from Bariloche to El Bolsón, is paved for about the first 45 km, after which it becomes narrow and steep with many south bends. It passes three beautiful lakes, Lagos Gutiérrez, Mascardi and Guillelmo. On the shore of Lago Gutiérrez, in a grotto, is the *Virgen de las Nieves* (Virgin of the Snows).

Villa Mascardi

Km 35, at the southern end of Lago Mascardi, is the starting point for a 2-day walk from **Pampa Linda** over Paso de los Nubes to Laguna Frías and Puerto Frías on the Chilean frontier. A *ripio* road with

South of Bariloche

		○ Bariloche
	35	
Pampa Linda ○——39——		○ Villa Mascardi
	42	
		○ Río Villegas
	53	
Parque Nacional Lago Puelo ○	16	○ El Bolsón
	35	
		○ Epuyén
	14	
Cholila	27	
To Parque Nacional Los Alerces	93	
		○ Esquel
	23	
To Parque Nacional Los Alerces		○ Trevelin

Distance in km

a one-way system (west only before 1400, east only after 1600) runs to Pampa Linda. Register at the Ranger station at Pampa Linda (entry US$5) and ask their advice about conditions. The route to Paso de los Nubes is not always well marked, and should only be attempted if there is no snow on the pass (normally passable only between December and February). Allow at least 6 hours to reach Puerto Frías from the pass. From Puerto Frías a 30 km road leads to Peulla in Chile.

Climbing Tronador

From Pampa Linda two other paths lead up Cerro Tronador (3,478m): one, 15 km long, leads to *Refugio Otto Meiling*, T 61861/22181 (2,000m), situated on the edge of the eastern glacier, another hour from the Refugio takes you to a view over Tronador and the lakes and mountains of Parque Nacional Nahuel Huapi; the other path leads to a *refugio* on the south side of the mountain.

● **Accommodation** *Tronador* on Lago Mascardi 24 km northwest of Villa Mascardi, luxury, beautiful setting, highly recommended, also **camping**, *La Querencia* and *Las Carpitas*; *Hostería Pampa Linda* T/F 0944-27049, restaurant, horseriding, excursions. There are campsites at the Ranger post in Pampa Linda and opposite the customs post in Puerto Frías.

● **Buses** Daily bus to Pampa Linda from *Club Andino* in Bariloche 0900, return departure 1700, US$20 return, summer only.

Río Villegas

Km 77, is a very beautiful village on the Río Villegas, just outside the gates of Parque Nacional Nahuel Huapi.

● **Accommodation D** *Hostería Río Villegas*, pleasant, friendly, restaurant.

EL BOLSON

(*Population* 8,000; *Altitude* 297m; *Phone code* 0944) Km 130, is an attractive small town situated in beautiful countryside, with many mountain walks and waterfalls (dry in summer) nearby. The town is famous for its local fruit preserves which can be bought at factories in town. Handicraft market Thursday and Saturday. It has good fishing and is fully developed as a tourist resort. Just west of the entre is the Balneario Municipal, pleasant river swimming.

Excursions

To **Cerro Piltriquitrón**, 9 km east, 6-7 hours walking round trip, great views, food and shelter at *refugio*; agencies arrange return transport. For the **Parque Nacional Lago Puelo**, see below.

Local festivals

Fiesta del Lúpulo (Hop Festival), end of February.

Local information
● Accommodation
Very difficult to find in the high season.

A3 *Cordillera*, San Martín 3210, T 92235, warm; *Motel La Posta*, T 92297, smart (Route 258).

B *Amancay*, San Martín 3217, welcoming.

C *Hostería Steiner*, San Martín 300, T 92224, pleasant, wood fire, lovely garden; **C** *Familia Sarakoumsky*, San Martín 3003, good; **C** *Salinas*, Rocas 641, T 92396, recommended.

D *Hosp Los Amigos*, Las Malvinas y Balcarce, 2 cabins or camping, hot water, cooking facilities, with breakfast, recommended (also has cabins and camping 6 km away on Río Azul, good hiking and swimming in river, owners will provide transport).

E *Campamento Ecológico*, Pagano y Costa del Río, T 92-954, bunks, US$5 camping, hot water, cooking facilities.

Youth hostel E pp *El Pueblito*, 3 km north in Luján, 1 km off Route 258, T 0847, cooking and laundry facilities, shop, open fire; 6 km from town is *La Casona de Odile*, small farm, home cooking, reservations only (Apartado 83, 8430 El Bolsón, Pca Río Negro, T/F 92753). 20 km north of El Bolsón, at Rinconada del Mallín Ahogado (daily bus from El Bolsón) is **A3** *Hostería María y Pancho Kramer*, warmly recommended, wholefood meals, hot shower, sauna, swimming pool, chess, volleyball, horseback and trekking excursions to lakes and mountains.

Camping *Del Sol*, Balneario Municipal, **F** pp, pleasant, friendly, cheap food. *La Chacra*, Route 288, 15 minutes walk from town, US$5 per person, hot showers, kiosk, restaurant. *Aldea Suiza*, 4 km north on Route 258, recommended, tennis courts, hot showers, good restaurant; *Nokan Cani*, 4 km south on road towards Lago Puelo, pleasant site near stream, picnic tables, toilets, hot showers, electricity, owner is an acupuncturist, recommended; *El Bolsón*, 1 km north of town, clean, recommended.

● Places to eat
Don Diego, San Martín 3217, good; *Ricar-Dos*, Roca y Moreno, good coffee (food less good); *Parrilla Achachay*, San Martín y Belgrano, basic, but reasonable value; *El Viejo Maitén*, Roca 359, good; *Amacuy*, San Mateo 3217, good; *Lustra*, Sarmiento 3212, good value; *Parrilla Las Brasas*, Sarmiento y P Hube, clean, good; *Jauja*, San Martín 2867, great pasta, very friendly, natural ice cream; *Café Bentler*, Güemes y Rivadavia, German run; *El Parador de Olaf*, at Las Golondrinas, Route 258, 6 km south, very good *parrilla* and Scandinavian specialities.

● Banks & money changers
Hotel Cordillera, or *Inmobiliaria Turneo* shop, cash only.

● Sports
Horseriding: Horacio Fernández, Loma del Medio, Apartado Postal 33, El Bolsón, CP 8430; trips of 1 or more days into the mountains, US$20 per day, plus US$15 for Horacio and his horse, highly recommended for all standards. Cross bridge over Río Azul, follow road to right, at power station turn left, follow path straight ahead and on hill is 'Cabalgatas' sign on left.

● Tour companies & travel agents
Turismo Translago, Perito Moreno 360, T 92523, 10% discount for ISIC and youth card holders on lake excursions to Chilean border and to Valle del Turbio, trekking to Lago Puelo and Cerro Platafoma. The local aeroclub (T 92412 or contact via *Hotel Cordillera*) offer spectacular flights over the Andes, US$100 per hour, max 3 passengers.

● Tourist offices
Office on main plaza, open 0900-2000. Sketch maps of the walks in the neighbourhood include roads that don't exist.

● Transport
Local Car hire: none; best bet is Esquel.

Buses Full-day tours from Bariloche are run by Don Otto and Mercedes, 11 hours, very crowded and difficult to get on in high season. Local buses to/from Bariloche, several companies, 3¼ hours; Empresa Charter offers 10% to ISIC and youth card holders between Bariloche and El Bolsón.

PARQUE NACIONAL LAGO PUELO

Situated 16 km southeast of El Bolsón on the Chilean frontier and covering 23,700 hectares, this park protects an area of southern beechforest around Lago Puelo which drains into Chile. Vegetation includes the rare arrayán as well as cypressses and *coihues* (evergreen beech). Fauna include huemuls, pudus and foxes. Canoes can be rented for US$3 per hour. Use *Fletes* (trucks) to get to more remote treks and campsites. The park is best visited between November and April. There is fishing for trout and salmon.

● **Services** Administration centre is 3 km north of the lake, good information. Entry free.

● **Access** is along an unpaved road south from El Bolsón via Villa Lago Puelo, 3 km north of the park, where there are a bank, shops and fuel.

● **Accommodation In Villa Lago Puelo:** *Hostería Enebros*, T 99054; *Hostería Lago Puelo*, T 99059; also *cabañas*. **In the park:** *Albergue El Turbio*, T 92523, horse and kayak hire, 10% discount for ISIC and youth card holders. **Camping** Two sites, one free, the other (charge US$5) has beautiful views across the lake to Tres Picos, expensive shop and café.

● **Transport** Regular buses from Avenida San Martín in El Bolsón. Turismo Translago in El Bolsón run excursions including half-day trip across the lake to Valle Río Turbio below Cerro Tres Picos, US$15; also to the Chilean border and Lago Interior.

SOUTH OF EL BOLSON

Route 258 continues southeast. At **Epuyén**, Km 165, a village famous for its hops and fruit, there are waterfalls; a side road runs west to Lago Epuyén.

● **Accommodation D** pp *Refugio del Lago*, T 0944-99025, with breakfast, also full and half pension; meals with fresh food; camping, tours, trekking, riding, recommended, French owned, Sophie and Jacques Dupont, Correo Epuyén, 9211 Chubut.

CHOLILA

Famous for the ranch where Butch Cassidy, the Sundance Kid and Etta Place lived between 1901 and 1905, Cholila lies 76 km south of El Bolsón on Route 71, which branches off Route 258 at Km 179. The ranch, 13 km north of town, can be visited. There are superb views of Lago Cholila, crowned by the Matterhorn-like mountains of Cerros Dos and Tres Picos. From Cholila Route 71 continues southwest into Parque Nacional Los Alerces (see below).

Excursions Good walk around Lago Mosquito: continue down the road from *El Trébol* past the lake then take a path to the left, following the river. Cross the river on the farm bridge and continue to the base of the hills to a second bridge. Follow the path to the lake and walk between the lake and the hills, crossing the exit river via a suspension bridge just past *El Trébol* – 6 hours (Nick Saunders and Sarah Jaggs London W1).

Local festivals Fiesta del Asado, 3rd week in January.

● **Accommodation C** pp *El Trébol*, T/F 98055, with breakfast, comfortable rooms with stoves, meals and half board also available, popular with fishing expeditions, reservations advised, bus stops in village 4 km away; *Hostería El Pedregoso*, at Lago Cholila, 8 km west; *Casa de Te*, Ruta 258 13 km north, with breakfast. **Camping F** pp *Autocamping Carlos Pelligrini*, next to El Trébol; free camping in El Morro park; *Camping El Abuelo*, 13 km south.

ESQUEL

(*Population* 23,000; *Altitude* 533m; *Phone code* 0945), 260 km south of Bariloche, is a modern town in a fertile valley. Originally an offshoot of the Welsh colony in the Chubut valley, nearly 650 km to the east, Esquel is known for its tulips, chocolate, jellies and jams. A centre for visiting the Parque Nacional Los Alerces, it is also famous for *La Trochita* (see below). There is a small musem, the **Museo Indigenista**

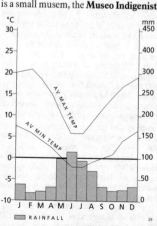

Climate: Esquel

Butch and Sundance

The tale of the most famous twosome in the history of the American West has been retold countless times and become the source of almost as many myths. Though the 1969 movie starring Paul Newman and Robert Redford showed them being gunned down by half the Bolivian army, rumours have persisted that, having faked their deaths, they returned to the United States. While painstaking research by Dan Buck and Ann Meadows discounts stories of their escape from Bolivia, the mystery continues: the exhumation in 1991 of the unmarked graves in Bolivia in which they were supposedly buried failed to provide conclusive evidence.

There is little mystery about the events which led the two outlaws along with Etta Place, Sundance's girlfriend, to move to Cholila between 1901 and 1905. Both Cassidy (real name Robert LeRoy Parker) and the Kid (born Harry Longabaugh) had pursued careers in which periods of legal employment had been mixed with distinctly illegal activity. In the late 1890s the two were part of a loosely-organized gang known as the Train Robbers' Syndicate, the Hole in the Wall Gang and the Wild Bunch, which operated out of Brown's Park, a high valley on the borders of Utah, Colorado and Wyoming. Gang members specialized in hold-ups on railway payrolls and banks. In 1900 they celebrated the wedding of one of their colleagues by having their photo taken. This was their big mistake: the photo was recognized by a Wells Fargo detective. With their faces decorating wanted posters across the land, Cassidy, Sundance and Etta left for Argentina in February 1901.

Using the names Santiago Ryan and Harry Place, the outlaws settled on government land near Cholila and applied to buy it. Pinkerton detectives soon tracked them down and informed the Argentine authorities. By 1905 it was time to move on before either the Pinkertons or the locals could make further moves. Needing money to start up elsewhere they raided banks in Río Gallegos and Villa Mercedes. The Río Gallegos job was particularly audacious: posing as ranching company agents, they opened a bank account with US$7,000, spent two weeks at one of the best hotels, socialized with the city's high society and then entered the bank to close their accounts and empty the safe before escaping to Chile. Shortly afterwards Etta returned to the United States and disappeared from the history books.

No longer welcome in Argentina, Butch and Sundance moved to Bolivia, finding work at the Concordia tin mine. Though scrupulously honest in their dealings with the mine, their occasional disappearances for a few days sometimes coincided with hold-ups. Lack of capital to settle as respectable ranchers was, however, to be their undoing. In 1908 near Tupiza in southern Bolivia they seized an Aramayo mining company payroll, gaining only a fraction of the loot they expected. With military patrols in pursuit and the Argentine and Chilean authorities alerted, they rode into the village of San Vicente but were recognised. Besieged, they did not, as in the film, run into the awaiting gunfire: with Sundance fatally wounded, Butch shot his partner and then committed suicide. Curiously their deaths were not widely reported in the United States until the 1930s. Ironically while wild stories of their deaths had circulated long before 1908, one of them featuring Butch face down in a Paris slum with a 'crooked knife fast between his shoulders', they were now reported as having secretly returned to the States: Butch was said to have become a businessman, a rancher, a trapper and a Hollywood movie extra, while Sundance had run guns in the Mexican Revolution, migrated to Europe, fought for the Arabs against the Turks in the First World War, sold mineral water, founded a religious cult and still found time to marry Etta.

(Adapted from *Digging Up Butch and Sundance* by Ann Meadows, London, 1996)

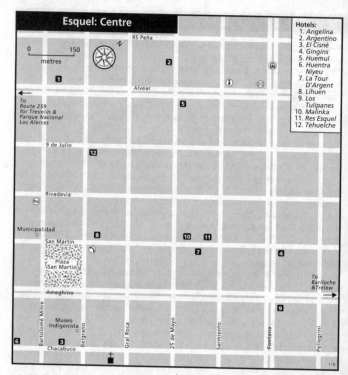

Esquel: Centre

0 150 metres

RS Peña

Alvear

To Route 259 for Trevelin & Parque Nacional Los Alerces

9 de Julio

Rivadavia

Municipalidad

San Martín

Plaza San Martín

Ameghino

Bartolomé Mitre
Museo Indigenista
Belgrano
Chacabuco
Gral Roca
25 de Mayo
Sarmiento
Fontana
Pellegrini

To Bariloche & Trelew

Hotels:
1. Angelina
2. Argentino
3. El Cisné
4. Gingins
5. Huemul
6. Huentra Niyeu
7. La Tour D'Argent
8. Lihuen
9. Los Tulipanes
10. Malinka
11. Res Esquel
12. Tehuelche

y de Ciencias Naturales, Belgrano y Chacabuco, daily except Tuesday 1600-2000. Some 15 km north is the ski-resort of La Hoya, which has 20 pistes and 9 ski-lifts. The surrounding area is good walking country: there are good walks to Laguna La Zeta, 5 km west, nice views, and to Cerro Nahuel Pan (2,440m), also good views.

Local information
● Accommodation
A2 *Tehuelche*, 9 de Julio 825, T 52421, heating, breakfast, English spoken, attentive; **A3** *Angelina*, Alvear 758, T 52763, good food, warm, run by Italian teacher, highly recommended.

B *La Tour D'Argent*, San Martín 1063, T 54612, with breakfast; **B** *Maika*, 25 de Mayo y San Martín, T/F 51466, without breakfast, *confitería*.

C *Hostería Los Tulipanes*, Fontana 365, T 52748, good rooms and service; **C** *Res*

Esquel, San Martín 1040, T 52534, helpful, heating, recommended; **C** *Hostal La Hoya*, Ameghino 2296, T 52473, on road to airport, 1 km (also **C** *Hostería La Hoya* at the Centro Deportivo de Ski at La Hoya itself); **C** *Res Lihuen*, San Martín 820, T/F 52589, without breakfast, English spoken, good value; **C** *Vascongada*, Mitre y 9 de Julio, T 52361, good cheap food; **C** *Huentru Niyeu* (no sign), Chacabuco 606, T 52576, quiet, modern, garage; **C** *Zacarias*, Roca 634, T 52270; **C** *Res Huemul*, Alvear y 25 de Mayo, T 52149, without breakfast, good *confitería*; **C** *Res Gingins*, Rivadavia 1243, T 52452, grubby; **C-D** Sra Helga Hammond, Antártida Argentina 522, German spoken.

Budget accommodation: **D** *Lago Verde*, Volta 1081, T 52251, doubles only, breakfast extra, modern, comfortable, highly recommended; **D** pp *Confitería Suiza*, Antártida Argentina 569, T 52727, rooms and apartments, German and English spoken; **D** *Res Argentino*, 25 de Mayo 862, T 52237, without breakfast, old fashioned, great bar, restaurant; **D** *Res El*

La Trochita (The Old Patagonian Express)

Esquel is the terminus of a 402 km branch-line from Ingeniero Jacobacci, a junction on the old Buenos Aires-Bariloche mainline, 194 km E of Bariloche. This narrow-guage line (0.75m wide) took 23 years to build, being finally opened in 1945. It was made famous outside Argentina by Paul Therroux who desribed it in his book *The Old Patagonian Express*. The 1922 Henschel and Baldwin steam locomotives (from Germany and USA respectively) are powered by fuel oil and use 100 litres of water every kilometre. Water has to be taken on at least every 40 km along the route. Most of the coaches are Belgian-built and also date from 1922. If you want to see the engines you need to go to El Maitén where the workshops are.

Until the Argentine government handed responsibility for railways over to the provincial governments in 1994, regular services ran the length of the line. Since then services have been maintained between Esquel and El Maitén by the provincial government of Chubut. For timetable see under **Esquel**.

In El Maitén there are two hotels, same owner, both overpriced: *Accomazzo*, with good restaurant; **A3** *La Vasconia*, near station, basic. On Thursday a bus for Esquel meets the train in El Maitén, check details first in Esquel.

Cisne, Chacabuco 778, with bath; **E** Mrs Megan Rowlands' guesthouse at Rivadavia 330, T 52578, Welsh spoken, recommended; **E** Sra Olga Daher, Sarmiento 269, quiet. Ask at tourist office for lodgings in private houses.

Youth hostel E *Lihuen*, San Martín 820, T/F 52589, open all year. Those with sleeping bags can go to the Salesian school and sleep in the school classrooms, December to March; get recommendation from tourist office

Camping *La Colina*, Darwin 1400, T 54962, on hill overlooking town, US$3 per person, hot showers, kitchen facilities, lounge with log fire, highly recommended; *La Rural*, Route 259, Km 1, on southwestern outskirts, full facilities; *El Hogar del Mochilero*, Roca 1028, US$3 per person, laundry facilities, free firewood, recommended; *Millalen*, Ameghino 2063, T 56164, good services. Free campsite at Laguna La Zeta.

● **Places to eat**
Jockey Club, Alvear 949, reasonably priced; *Ahla Wasahla*, Sarmiento y San Martín, good, cheap, friendly, closed Sunday; *Red Fox*, Sarmiento 795 y Alvear, a British-style pub with light, but expensive meals, open from 2200, closed Tuesday; *Don Chichino*, 9 de Julio 964, good, Italian; *Vascongada*, 9 de Julio y Mitre, trout specialities; *Parrilla La Estancia*, 25 de Mayo 541, quite good; *El Mesón*, Rivadavia 1034, reasonable, but slow service; *La Trochita*, Rivadavia 931, *parrilla*, good value; *Parrilla de María*, Rivadavia 1024, popular; *Pizzería Don Pipo*, Fontana 649, good pizzas and *empanadas*; *Atelier*, 25 de Mayo y San Martín, good coffee, cheap, open 24 hours; *Vestry*, Rivadavia 1065, Welsh tea room; great bar in the *Hotel Argentino*. Home made chocolate and the famous local mazard berry liquor is sold at the *Braese Store*, 9 de Julio 1540.

● **Airline offices**
Auala, Austral agents, Fontana y Ameghino, T 53614; **Kaiken**, Roca 687, T 53380; **LADE**, Alvear 1085, T 52124.

● **Banks & money changers**
Banco de la Nación Güemes y San Martín, accepts travellers' cheques, no commission on Mastercard, open 0730-1300; **Viajes Sol del Sur**, 9 de Julio 1086, accept travellers' cheques, open Monday-Friday, 1000-1300; **Viasur**, 9 de Julio 1027, Amex travellers' cheques only accepted.

● **Post & telecommunications**
Both opposite the bus terminal at Fontana y Alvear (open 0800-2000).

● **Laundry**
Laverap, Mitre 543; *Marva*, San Martín 941, US$10 per load; both open 0900-2100 Monday-Saturday.

● **Shopping**
Casa de Esquel (Robert Müller), 25 de Mayo 415, wide range of new and second hand books.

● **Sports**
Fishing: in the Arroyo Pescado, US$30 a day.

Skiing: La Hoya, 15 km north, has 7 ski-lifts and is cheaper than Bariloche. For skiing information ask at Club Andino Esquel; bus to La Hoya from Esquel, 3 a day, US$7 return, ski pass US$10-18 depending on season, gear hire US$7 a day.

● **Tour companies & travel agents**
Esquel Tours, Fontana 754, T 52704, and at airport, good for local tours to Lagos Menéndez and Cisnes. *Fairway Sports and Adventures*, Roca 687, T/F 53380, for trekking, canoeing, *estancias*, horseriding, knowledgeable guides, recommended.

● **Tourist office**
Alvear y Sarmiento, very friendly, can arrange lodgings in private homes. Closed Saturday and Sunday off-season.

● **Transport**
Local Car hire: Fiocaci, 9 de Julio 740, T 52299/52704; **Esquel Tours**, address above, very good US$60 per day. **Mechanic**: Claudio Peinados, Brown 660, T 53462, highly recommended.

Air Airport, 20 km east by paved road. US$14 by taxi; US$2.50 by bus; US$4 by Esquel Tours bus 1 hour before each LADE flight. To **Buenos Aires**, Austral, via San Martín de los Andes. Kaiken to Mendoza, Bariloche, Comodoro Rivadavia, Calafate, Ushuaia, Río Gallegos, Río Grande, Trelew and Neuquén.

Trains *La Trochita*: service to El Maitén, Thursday, US$15 one way, return Wednesday. There is also a *tren turístico* to Nahuel Pan, Monday, Wednesday, Saturday, US$15 return.

Buses Terminal at Alvear y Fontana, T 52233. Taxi rank at terminal. No direct buses to/from Buenos Aires so travel via Bariloche. To **Comodoro Rivadavia** (paved), Don Otto, 4 a week, US$25 (but usually arrives from Bariloche full in season) or Angel Giobbi, Tuesday, and Friday 0600, US$25, via Río Mayo; to **Bariloche**, US$16, Don Otto, Empresa Mercedes and other companies, 4 hours; to **El Bolsón**, 2 hours, US$10; to **Trelew**, US$32, 9 hours, leaves 0900 Tuesday, Thursday, Saturday, and 2200 Monday, Wednesday, Friday; to **Trevelin**, Codao, every hour 070-2100, US$1.

TREVELIN

(Population 4,000; *Altitude* 390m; *Phone code* 0945), another offshoot of the Welsh colony in the Chubut valley, lies 23 km southwest of Esquel. It has a Welsh chapel (built 1910, closed) and there are several tea rooms. 17 km southwest on the road to the frontier are the **Nant-y-fall** Falls, entrance US$0.50 per person including guide to all seven falls (1½-hour walk).

Museums

Museo Regional, in the old mill (1918) includes artefacts from the Welsh colony and, upstairs, a model of the Futaleufú hydro-electric dam (entry US$2).

Hogar de Mi Abuelo a private park and museum dedicated to John Evans, one of the first settlers, whose granddaughter acts as a guide, entry US$2.

● **Accommodation** *Hostería Estefanía*, Perito Moreno sin número, T 8148; *Hosp Trevelin*, San Martín 327, T 8102; *El Chalet*, San Martín y Brown, T 80159, cabins; *La Granja Trevelin*, 3 km north on road to Esquel, owned by Domingo Giacci, bungalows US$15 a day, camping, hot water and wc, macrobiotic meals and good Italian cooking, sells milk, cheese and onions; excellent horses for hire; *Granja La Colina*, 24 km south on road to Chile, T 80548, also camping, shop, cafetería, fishing, horseriding. **Camping** Municipal site near centre; *Aiken Leufu*, on route to the Futaleufú dam, T 51317, also *cabañas*, full services.

● **Places to eat** Grills at *Che Ferrada*, good mixed *parrillada* at *El Quincho*, and several tea rooms offering *té galés* and *torta negra*: eg *El Adobe* on Avenida Patagonia; *Nain Maggie*, Perito Moreno 179, recommended; *Owen See*, Molino Viejo 361; *La Cabaña*, 7 km out on the road from Trevelin to Lago Futalaufquén. There is a custom of giving a newly-married couple a *torta negra* (black cake) on their wedding day, to be eaten on their first anniversary.

● **Tourist office** Good office in central plaza.

PARQUE NACIONAL LOS ALERCES

Situated 60 km west of Esquel, this park covers 263,000 hectares, taking its name from the *alerces* (*Fitzroya cupressoides*), some of them over 1,000 years old, which it was established to protect. There are four large lakes and several smaller ones; the northern lakes, **Lagos Rivadavia** and **Menéndez**, drain into **Lago Futalaufquén** and from there into the southernmost **Lago Amutui Quimei**, an artificial lake which empties into the Río Futaleufú which flows into Chile.

The western side of the park, where rainfall is highest, has areas of Valdivian forest; the eastern side has similar natural attractions to those in the Nahuel Huapi and Lanín parks, including forests of *coihue*, *lenga* and *alerce*, but is much less developed for tourism. The most accessible part of the park is the east bank of Lago Futalaufquén, reached by Route 71 which runs through the park. The west side of the lake is untouched by tourism, by law. Here there is good walking eg to

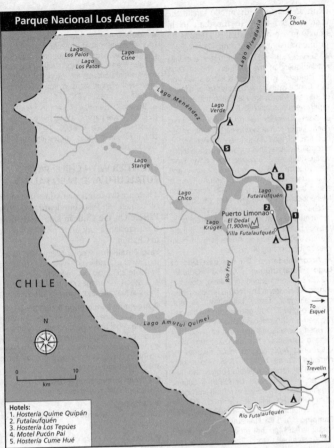

Parque Nacional Los Alerces

Hotels:
1. *Hostería Quime Quipán*
2. *Futalaufquén*
3. *Hostería Los Tepúes*
4. *Motel Pucón Pai*
5. *Hostería Cume Hué*

Cinco Saltos, and El Dedal (1,900m). The latter is a 6-hour hike from *Hotel Futalaufquén* up and back, with great views of the lakes and the cordillera from the top. There is also a 3-km nature trail looking across the Andes to Chile. A good information leaflet describing the flora and fauna encountered along the trail up to Cerro Dedal is available at the Visitors' Centre and the tourist office in Esquel has a pamphlet on all the walks in the Park. Lago Futalaufquén has some of the best fishing in this part of Argentina (season

15 November-Easter): local guides offer fishing trips on motor boats. A recommended journey for motorists is to spend the night at El Bolsón, enter the Los Alerces park via Cholila and drive right through it to Esquel, travelling the whole length of Lagos Rivadavia and Futalaufquén.

The southern part of the park can be reached from a separate entrance from Trevelin following the Río Futaleufú to reach the Futaleufú hydroelectric dam, behind which is Lago Amutui Quimei; the dam supplies power to the alumina plant at Puerto Madryn, 500 km to the east. Guided tours to the dam itself, hourly in season, small fee. There is no public transport to the dam.

● **Services** The park administration is at Villa Futalaufquén, at the southern end of Lago Futalaufquén, where there is also a small Visitors' Centre with displays on the flora and fauna of the park. Nearby are a service station and two expensive supermarkets.

● **Boats** Regular full day launch trip from Puerto Limonao (reached by early morning minibus) across Lago Futalaufquén (a sheer delight) through Río Arrayanes to windless Lago Verde where there are 2 campsites (see below). From here you can walk out to Lagos Rivadavia and Cholila (see above), 2 days minimum. There is also a boat service daily at 1400 across Lago Menéndez to its western side; the dock is reached by a 30-minute walk across the bridge between Lagos Futalaufquén and Verde; book the day before in Esquel, as it only sails if there are enough passengers. Arrive early to claim your space, crossing 90 minutes.

● **Accommodation** **On the east side of Lago Futalaufquén**: *Quime Quipán*, T 22272, recommended for fishing, closed in winter; **A2** *Hostería Los Tepúes*, simple, rustic, open all year, family bungalow for rent; **A2** *Pucón Pai*, T 3799, good restaurant, recommended for fishermen (holds a fishing festival to open the season); open out of season for large groups only; has campsite; next door **C** *Cabañas Tejas Negras*, good facilities for camping. *Cume Hué*, T 2858, also recommended for fishing. *Trevelin Lodge*, also specializes in fishing, run by O'Farrell Safaris, organizes tours, white-water rafting and horseriding. (Contact Telluride Flyfishers, PO Box 1634, Telluride, Colorado, T 800-828-7547.) **Camping** At Villa Futalaufquén and at Los Maitenes (US$4pp, hot showers, clean, closed May-September), store. There are also free campsites without facilities, registration essential. **On the west side**: **L2** *Hotel Futalaufquén* just north of Puerto Limonao, T 2648, recommended, especially rooms 2/3 and 4/5 which have balconies overlooking the lake, open all year (no heating in rooms); good walking near the hotel. **At Lago Krüger**: *Refugio Lago Krüger*, 10% discount to ISIC and youth card holders, camping and fishing also available. **At Lago Verde**: *Camping Agreste Lago Verde* US$3 per person, 10% discount to ISIC and youth card holders, very crowded in summer; also free campsite, nicely situated and with a small shop. **Near the Futaleufú dam**: *Autocamping Estancia La Paz*, T/F 0945-52478, full services, also cabañas,

activities including watersports, horseriding, fishing.

● **Tours** Agency tour booked in Esquel US$52, includes boat trip across Lago Menéndez and guided tour from the northwestern end of Lago Menéndez to Lago Cisne, 3 km. Other tours offered are less interesting because they only involve short stops in front of points of interest.

● **Buses** Transportes Esquel run from Esquel to Lago Verde passing along the east side of Lago Futalaufquén at 0800, 1400 and 1830 daily in season (it passes 3 hotels and drives into 2 camp sites).

FRONTIER WITH CHILE: PASO FUTALEUFU AND PASO PALENA

There are two frontier crossings just south of Esquel, at Paso Futaleufú and Paso Palena. On the Chilean side roads from these crossings link up to provide a route to Chaitén.

Paso Futaleufú Paso Futaleufú lies 70 km southwest of Esquel via Trevelin and is reached by Route 259 (*ripio* from Trevelin). The frontier is crossed by a bridge over the Río Futaleufú. This is an easy crossing: 1 hour for all formalities.

● **Argentine immigration & customs** on the Argentine side of the bridge. Travellers entering Argentina should note that Argentine border officials only give transit visas: you must legalize your stay within 10 days either by leaving the country or by renewing your entry stamp at an immigration office.

● **Chilean immigration & customs** In Futaleufú, 9 km west of the frontier.

● **Camping** *Camping Río Grande* on Argentine side of bridge.

● **Buses** From Esquel to Paso Futaleufú, Codao Monday, Friday, 0800, 1700, US$4.50, 2 hours, return departures 1100, 1900. On the Chilean side a minibus runs to Futaleufú, 10 km, US$3. Very little traffic for hitching.

● **Into Chile** The road continues on the Chilean side towards Chaitén. Outside Puerto Ramírez take the unsigned right turn to Chaitén (left goes to Palena).

FRONTIER WITH ARGENTINA: PASO PALENA

This crossing lies 111 km southeast of Esquel, reached by Route 17 from Trevelin which runs to Corcovado, 75 km east of

Not Butch and Sundance

In 1911 the North American bandits, William Wilson and Robert Evans, often confused with Butch Cassidy and the Sundance Kid, thanks to Bruce Chatwin's *In Patagonia*, were killed in Río Pico by the Argentine Frontier Police. Their bodies were buried near the old Hahn store, 4 km east of Río Pico on Route 19, 3 km up a very bad road. The grave is marked with an iron cross (1912 date on cross is incorrect).

Daniel Buck and Ann Meadows

Tecka (reached by *ripio* road). From Corcovado it is 22 km west to the frontier.

● **Argentine immigration & customs**
At the frontier, open daily 0900-1800. **NB** Only transit visas are issued (see above under Futaleufú crossing).

● **Chilean immigration**
At Palena, 8 km west of frontier.

● **Accommodation**
Several *pensiones* in Palena.

● **Buses**
From Esquel Sunday, Monday, Wednesday 1700, Friday 0900, return departures Monday, Tuesday, Thursday 0700, Friday 1700. On the Chilean side Expreso Yelcho bus runs to Chaitén twice a week, US$12, 5½ hours.

SOUTH OF ESQUEL

Route 40 continues (paved) south from Esquel. At **Tecka** (*population* 1,000; *phone code* 0945), Km 101, Route 62 (paved) branches off east and follows the valley of the Río Chubut to Trelew.

● **Accommodation** *Hotel Tecka; Res Josene.*

Río Pico

(*Population* 900; *Altitude* 350m) reached by a *ripio* road (65 km) which branches west off Route 40 at Km 171, is the site of an early 20th century German settlement). North of Río Pico, on the Chilean border, is Lago General Vintter, plus smaller lakes with good trout fishing (permits

from the *Municipalidad* in Gobernador Costa).

● **Accommodation** *Mi Residencial*, basic with restaurant; *Cabañas Laurín*, at Lago General Wintter.

Gobernador Costa

(*Population* 1,700; *Altitude* 640m; *Phone code* 0945) lies on the Río Genoa at Km 187. **Accommodation D** *Res Jair*, San Martín y Sarmiento, clean, friendly; **D** *Hotel Vega*. **Camping** Municipal site US$2.

South of Gobernador Costa

At Km 221, Route 40 (*ripio*) forks southwest through the town of **Alto Río Senguer** (*population* 1,700; *altitude* 697m; *phone code* 0945) while provincial Route 20 heads almost directly south for 81 km (ACA petrol station at isolated La Laurita), before turning east towards Sarmiento and Comodoro Rivadavia. At La Puerta del Diablo, in the valley of the lower Río Senguer, Route 20 intersects provincial Route 22, which joins with Route 40 at the town of Río Mayo (see page 404). This latter route is completely paved and preferable to Route 40 for long-distance motorists.

● **Accommodation** At Alto Río Senguer: *Bety Jay; Hosp Fogón Criollo.* **Camping** Good informal sites on the west side of the bridge across the Río Senguer.

Patagonia

THE VAST, windy, treeless plateau south of the Río Colorado: the Atlantic coast is rich in marine life, most easily seen around Puerto Madryn. The Chubut Valley, around Trelew, was the centre if Argentina's Welsh community. In the south of this region is the Parque Nacional los Glaciares, which offers journeys on lakes full of ice floes and to the Moreno glacier.

Although geographically Argentine Patagonia consists of the provinces of Neuquén, Río Negro, Chubut and Santa Cruz, this section describes only the latter two provinces and eastern parts of Río Negro: for Neuquén and western Río Negro see **The Lake District**.

GEOGRAPHY

Most of Argentine Patagonia is steppe, flat and dry land stretching west from the Atlantic coast and rising to over 1,000m in the foothills of the Andes. The mountain range is much lower than further north, with peaks between 2,000 and 2,500m and a few above 3,000m. Between the mountains are U-shaped glacial valleys, some filled by lakes. South of 45°C the Andes are covered by two large ice fields (*campos de hielo*) from the edges of which glaciers drop eastwards into the lakes and rivers of Argentine Patagonia and westwards into the fiords along the Chilean coast.

Several rivers flow eastwards from the Andean foothills. In the north are the Colorado, which marks the northern

Patagonia

boundary of Patagonia, and the Negro, which drains much of the Argentine Lake District. Further south is the Chubut, 500 km long, which takes the waters of the Southern Lake District; its major tributary, the Río Chico, receives the waters of the Río Senguer and drains Lagos Musters and Colhué Huapi, two large lakes near Colonia Sarmiento. The two main rivers of Santa Cruz province are the Río Deseado, which takes the waters of Lago Buenos Aires, and the Río Santa Cruz, which drains Lago Argentino and Lago Viedma, both of which are fed by the great

Southern Beeches

Seven species of Nothofagus are native to South America, some deciduous, some evergreen. They are found throughout the length of the country. The evergreen Nothofagus betuloides was used for canoes by the Yaghan indians who called it *shushci*. The Nothofagus antarctica prefers drier soils, grows to a height of 20m and was known to the Yaghan as *hanis*. Both of these trees were introduced to Europe in 1830. The Nothofagus nervosa has leaves like a hornbeam and is a quick growing tree with good autumn colour. Nothofagus dombeyi, which has shiny dark green evergreen leaves and is larger than Nothofagus betuloides, was not introduced into Europe until 1916. Nothofagus obliqua was introduced in 1902 and has toothed smooth leaves and is also known as the Roble beech. Nothofagus pumilo, well known for its vibrant red autumn colour, is found at higher elevations, and has the common name of *lenga*.

Jane Norwich

glaciers of the Parque Nacional Los Glaciares. Further south are two smaller rivers, the Ríos Coyle and Gallegos.

CLIMATE

There are marked differences between the seasons; spring and autumn are short, summer and winter are long. Temperature ranges are high, especially in western inland areas, though the highest absolute temperatures, rising to 45°C occur in the eastern parts of the valleys of the Río Negro and Río Colorado. Strong westerly winds are common especially in winter. Annual rainfall levels are high in the watershed of the Andes, but drop rapidly as you go east. Large parts of eastern Patagonia receive little rainfall.

FAUNA AND FLORA

Eastern and central areas, which receive little rainfall, are virtually desert, though, during a brief period in spring, after the melting of the snows, there is grass on the steppe. Further west, in the foothills of the Andes, the high rainfall supports a line of beech forests. Here there are two fine national parks, the Parque Nacional Los Glaciares, which attracts large numbers of visitors, and the little known Parque Nacional Perito Moreno.

The most impressive mammals on the steppe are the herds of guanacos. Other mammal species include the *maras* (Patagonian hare) and the Patagonian Piche (the southernmost armadillo in the world). Predators include red and grey foxes as well as the elusive puma.

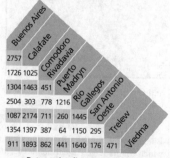

Buenos Aires	Calafate	Comodoro Rivadavia	Puerto Madryn	Río Gallegos	San Antonio Oeste	Trelew	Viedma
2757							
1726	1025						
1304	1463	451					
2504	303	778	1216				
1087	2174	711	260	1445			
1354	1397	387	64	1150	295		
911	1893	862	441	1640	176	471	

Patagonia: distance chart (km)

Lesser Rhea

Fauna of the Atlantic coast

One of the great attractions of the Atlantic coast is provided by the breeding seasons of bird species and marine mammals, mainly in spring and summer.

The most impressive birds are, perhaps, the Magellan Penguins, which nest in huge colonies on the Valdés Peninsula, at Cabo Dos Bahías, Ría Deseado, Cabo Vírgenes, Monte León and on the Isla de los Estados. Other sea-birds include four species of Cormorants, among them the beautiful Red-legged Cormorant (found only in Ría Deseado and Bahía San Julián in Santa Cruz), several species of gulls including the Kelp Gull and the Black-headed Gull, and terns including the South American Tern. Look out particularly for the

Southern Elephant Seal

Antartic Giant Petrel, the Black-browed Albatross, the Snowy Sheatbill and several species of oystercatcher.

Marine mammals include the Southern Elephant Seal, Southern Sea Lion, Southern Furry Seal, Southern Right Whale and Commerson's Dolphin. Breeding grounds and seasons of these are given in the table below. The Killer Whale is difficult to see, though the best place to spot them is in waters near colonies of Southern Sea lions in March and April.

Santiago de la Vega

Marine mammals and birds: breeding-grounds and seasons		
Species	**Breeding Grounds**	**Breeding Season**
Southern Elephant Seal	Valdés Peninsula	August-November
Southern Sea Lion	Valdés Peninsula	December-March
Southern Furry Seal	Santa Cruz	January-March
Southern Right Whale	Valdés Peninsula	June-December
Commerson's Dolphin	Ría Deseado and Bahía San Julián	December-March
Magellan Penguin	Valdés Peninsula, Cabo Dos Bahías, Ría Deseado, Cabo Vírgenes, Monte León, Isla de los Estados	Early September-late March

Along the Patagonian coast there are sea lion and penguin colonies; some protected waters are breeding grounds for the Commerson's dolphin and the grey dolphin. Elephant Seals and Southern Right whales breed along the coast of Valdés peninsula and the nearby gulfs.

Many bird species migrate northwards to avoid the harsh Patagonian winter. Bird species which may be seen include the Lesser Rhea, the Common Diuca-finch, the Austral Negrito (found mainly near water), the Patagonian Mockingbird, the Rufous-collared Sparrow (found

Mara or Patagonian Hare

Magellan Goose

nearly everywhere), the Patagonian Yellow-finch and the red-breasted Long-tailed Meadowlark. There are also mimetic species such as the Elegant-crested Tinamou, the lesser Seedsnipe and Burrowing Owl. The lakes are inhabited by ducks such as the Crested duck and the Red shoveller, as well as Chilean flamingoes and grebes, including the Silvery Grebe and the Hooded Grebe. Magellan Geese and Ashy-headed Geese can be found on grasslands and wetlands, though the Ruddly-headed Goose is an endangered species. Birds of prey include the Red-backed Hawk, the Black-breasted Buzzard-Eagle, the Peregrine Falcoln as well as the very common Crested Caracara. For further details of bird-species see *Aves de Argentina y Uruguay*, available, in English, from main bookshops in Buenos Aires as well as major tourist centres in Patagonia.

ECONOMY

Most of the land is devoted to sheep raising. The great sheep *estancias* are situated in the shelter provided by the canyons which intersect the land from east to west and in the depression which runs north from the Strait of Magellan to Lagos Argentino and Buenos Aires and beyond. Over-grazing has led to soil erosion. Wild dogs, pumas and red foxes are the sole predators of the sheep. Because of the high winds and insufficient rainfall there is

little arable farming except in the north in the valleys of the Colorado and Negro rivers. Some cattle are raised in both these valleys where irrigation permits the growing of alfalfa.

Patagonia is rich in extractive resources: the oil of Comodoro Rivadavia and Tierra del Fuego, the little exploited iron ore of Sierra Grande, the coal of Río Turbio, the hydro-electric capacity of El Chocón, plentiful deposits of minerals (particularly bauxite) and marine resources, but their exploitation has been slow.

The largest city in Argentine Patagonia is Comodoro Rivadavia, the only centre with a population over 100,000. Most of the towns are small ports, which used only to work during the wool-shipping season but have livened up since the local economy began to diversify. The high tidal range makes it impossible in most of them for ships to tie up at docks (except at Puerto Madryn, Puerto Deseado and Punta Quilla, near Santa Cruz.

ROADS

The main road south, Route 3 runs near the coast to Río Gallegos and then enters Chile and crosses the Magellan Straits to Tierra del Fuego by the car ferry at Primera Angostura: it has fairly regular traffic and adequate services. The alternative route,

Sheep farming in Patagonia

👣 As you travel around Patagonia you will probably see few sheep; they are hard at work grazing around the small streams which are usually hidden from the road. Some idea, however, of the importance of sheep to the rural economy is given by the way in which land values and incomes from *estancias* are calculated.

In many societies land is valued for status and security rather than its productivity. In Patagonia, however, with its vast expanses of unoccupied and poor quality land, the value of an *estancia* is calculated in terms of the area of land required to support one sheep: this ranges from 1 hectare in the *cordillera* to 2 hectares in the central *meseta* and three hectares on the *costa*. For the purpose of pricing land, one sheep is valued at US$60, a figure which has not changed for decades and which is well above the real market price of sheep. Thus a hectare of land which can support one sheep is valued at US$60.

In recent years many Patagonian *estancias* have looked to tourism as an additional (or even their major) source of income. Without such extra income, it is reckoned that the minimum viable size for an *estancia* is 5,000 sheep, which should produce an annual income of US$40,000. The calculations on which this is based are as follows. With raw wool priced at US$1.50 (the average sheep produces 4 kilos of wool a year) 5,000 sheep produce an income of US$30,000. Another US$10,000 can be earned through the sale of animals: about 10% of the flock is sold every year for an average price of US$20 per animal.

Not surprisingly the most popular breed of sheep is the one which works hardest converting the sparse grasslands into wool and meat. This is the Corriedale, originally from Scotland; it produces more wool than the Merino, but its wool is coarse, which, naturally, helps explain its low value. This, perhaps more than anything else, explains the economics of Patagonian *estancias*: sheep are grazed because the land is too poor for other uses.

Route 40, runs further west, zigzagging across the moors; it is lonely and is good in parts, poor in others (more details given below); there is hardly any traffic even between December and February, the tourist season. However, it is by far the more interesting road, with fine views of the Andes and plenty of wildlife; it also provides access to two national parks, the Parque Nacional Perito Moreno and the Parque Nacional Los Glaciares. Camping along this route is no problem, and there are good hotels at Perito Moreno and Calafate as well as more basic accommodation at Gobernador Gregores, Río Mayo and Río Turbio. Some of the best accommodation along Route 40 is in *estancias*.

Hitchhiking is generally difficult except on Route 3 in spring and summer; camping equipment is useful as long delays can be expected even in the tourist season.

DRIVING IN PATAGONIA

Many of the roads are gravelled (*ripio*). The price of a good windscreen protector varies according to make of car, but can be US$50 in Buenos Aires. For a VW Kombi they are hard to find at a reasonable price. More primitive versions can be bought for much less – eg US$5 in San Julián, and probably elsewhere – or made from wire mesh, wood and string. The best types are the grid-type, or inflatable plastic ones which are made for some standard-type vehicles, the only disadvantage being some loss of visibility.

Drivers should also look out for cattle grids (*guardaganados*) even on main highways. They are signed; cross them very slowly. Always carry plenty of fuel, as service stations may be as much as 300 km apart. Make sure you have plenty of warm clothing, and anti-freeze in your car. Fuel prices are very low throughout Patagonia, US$0.35 per litre, which is about half the price of the rest in the country.

SERVICES

In summer hotel prices are very high especially in Calafate. During Argentine summer holidays (January-February) getting a hotel room in Río Gallegos and Calafate can be very difficult. Note that ACA establishments, which charge the same prices all over Argentina, are a bargain in Patagonia, where all other accommodation is expensive. As very few hotels and restaurants have air conditioning o even fans, it can get uncomfortably hot ir January. Camping is increasingly popular travellers' cheques are hard to change throughout Patagonia. Many hotels are closed between early April and mid November and many bus services do not operate in this period.

HISTORY

The Portuguese Fernão Magalhães (Magellan), then in the service of Spain, was the first to visit the coast of Patagonia in 1519 The first European to traverse Patagonia from south to north was the English sailor,

'A little Wales beyond Wales'

The Welsh settlement in Patagonia dates from the arrival of 165 settlers in July 1865. Landing on the bay where Puerto Madryn now stands, they were forced by lack of water to walk south across the parched land to the Chubut valley, where they found flat cultivable land and settled. The first 10 years of the settlement were hard indeed and they were forced to rely on trade with the Tehuelches, supplies delivered by the British navy and support from the Argentine government which was eager to populate its territory.

The settlement was partly inspired by Michael D Jones, a non-conformist minister who provided much of the early finance and recruited settlers through the Welsh language press and through the chapels. Jones, whose aim was to create a 'little Wales beyond Wales' far from the intruding influence of the English, took particular care to recruit people with useful skills, particularly farmers and craftsmen. Between 1865 and 1915 the colony was reinforced by about 3,000 settlers from Wales and the United States. Finding that the land was barren unless irrigated, they began work on the network of irrigation channels which can still be seen. Early settlers were allocated 100 hectares of land, but by 1885 all irrigable land had been allocated and the settlement began to expand westwards along the valley.

The success of the colony was partly due to the creation of their own Cooperative Society, which sold their produce and bought necessities in Buenos Aires. By 1900 the Society, which also acted as a bank, had 14 branches. Early settlers were organised into chapel-based communities of 200-300 people, which were largely self-governing and which organised social and cultural activities as well as operating an insurance scheme. Relations with the Tehuelches were initially very poor; in the early days the settlers agreed to kill any approaching Tehuelche to prevent news of the colony spreading, but this was not done and gradually relations improved.

Though the colony prospered after 1880, it was badly weakened by the Great Depression of the 1930s in which the Cooperative Society collapsed and many farmers lost their savings. While the aim of creating a 'little Wales beyond Wales' succeeded in that the Welsh language was kept alive for four generations, it is now dying out. Nevertheless, it is interesting that this desert land gave the Welsh language one of its most enduring classics, *Dringo't Andes* ('Climbing the Andes'), written by one of the earliest women settlers.

Carder, who saved his life in a 1578 shipwreck in the Strait of Magellan, crossed the Strait, walked to the Río de la Plata and arrived in London 9 years later.

For several centuries European attempts to settle along the coast were deterred by isolation, lack of food and water and the harsh climate as well as the fierce resistance of the indigenous peoples, but these were almost entirely wiped out in the 'Campaign of the Wilderness' 1879-1883. Before this there had been a long established European colony at Carmen de Patagones; it shipped salt to Buenos Aires during the colonial period. There had also been a settlement of Welsh people in the Chubut Valley since 1865. After the Campaign of the Wilderness colonization was rapid, the Welsh, Scots and English taking a great part. Chilean sheep farmers from Punta Arenas moved north along the depression at the foot of the Andes, eastwards into Santa Cruz.

NORTHERN PATAGONIA

Two major rivers, the Ríos Colorado and Negro, empty into the Atlantic. The northernmost of these, the Río Colorado, is the northern limit of Patagonia.

CARMEN DE PATAGONES AND VIEDMA

These two towns lie opposite each other on the Río Negro, 30 km inland from the sea and some 250 km south of Bahía Blanca. They are connected by two bridges and a passenger ferry. The swimming is

recommended on the southern side, where the shore is shady. **Viedma** (*population* 40,000; *phone code* 0920), on the south bank, was founded as Mercedes de Patagonia in 1779, but was destroyed almost immediately by floods, after which **Carmen de Patagones** (*population* 16,000; *altitude* 44m; *phone code* 0920) was founded on higher ground on the north bank. Capital of Río Negro province, Viedma was destroyed again by floods in 1899.

Places of interest

Viedma To the west of the main square, Plaza Alsina, is the **Cathedral**, built by the Salesians in 1912. The former convent, next door, dating from 1887 is now a cultural centre housing the **Museo del Agua y del Suelo** and the **Museo Cardenal Cagliero**, which has ecclesiastical artefacts. Two blocks east, on the Plaza San Martín, are the French-style **Casa de Gobierno** (1926) and, opposite, the **Museo Gobernador Tello**, with displays on local history. The **Mercado Artesanal**, at Sarmiento 347, is worth a visit and there is an attractive treelined **Costanera** (riverside walk) with sailing clubs. Catamaran trips can be taken along the river.

Carmen de Patagones The town centre, just east of the river, lies around the Plaza 7 de Mayo. West of the plaza is the **Iglesia del Carmen**, built by the Salesians in 1880. Behind it is the **Torre del Fuerte**, the tower of the stone fortress built in 1780 against Indian attacks. The **Casa de la Tahona**, one block south of the Plaza, is a disused 18th century flour-mill, now housing the Casa de la Cultura. Another

The Battle of Carmen de Patagones

The church in Carmen de Patagones displays two Brazilian flags, seized in 1827 in one of the more unusual skirmishes of the early independence period. During the 1820s the Río Negro was used as a base by privateers who attacked shipping along the Brazilian coast. A Brazilian fleet of four ships entered the port to attack two privateers sheltering there. Fired on from above by guns on Punta Redondo, two Brazilian vessels foundered on the sandbanks of the Río Negro. The attackers landed 400 men to seize the guns but local forces, led by Captain Bynon, a Welshman, seized the Brazilian ships, preventing the attackers' escape. A total of 627 Brazilians were taken prisoner. A monument on Cerro Caballada, a hill east of the town, commemorates the 'victory'.

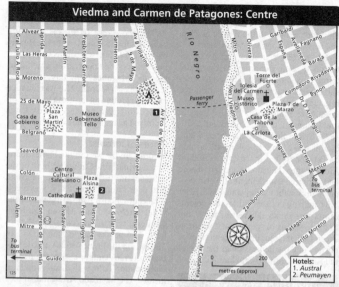

Viedma and Carmen de Patagones: Centre

late colonial building, **La Carlota**, stands one block east of La Tahona. Near the river bank at Viema y Baraja, is the **Museo Histórico Regional**, containing displays on the town's history. Open Monday-Friday 0900-1200, 1900-2100, Sunday 1900-2100. Nearby are the **Cuevas Maragatas**, the caves in which the first colonists lived.

Excursions

To **El Cóndor**, 30 km south, where there is a beautiful beach. The *Faro* (lighthouse) is the oldest in the country, dating from 1887. Facilities include hotel (open January-February), restaurants and shops, free camping on beach 2 km south. Three buses a day in summer. At **Playa Bonita**, 12 km further south, there is good fishing.

To **Punta Bermeja**, 60 km south, the site of a sealion colony covering 200 hectares and visited by some 2,500 sealions in summer. Daily bus in summer; hitching easy in summer.

Local information

Unless otherwise stated all services are in Viedma.

● **Accommodation**

B *Austral*, Villarino 292, T 22019, recommended, modern; *Viedma*, Zatti y Urquiza, T 25481; **C** *Peumayen*, Buenos Aires 334, T 25243; *Nigar*, Mitre 490, T 22833; *Res Río Mar*, Rivadavia y Santa Rosa, T 24188. **In Carmen de Patagones**: *Patagones*, Yrigoyen y Comodoro Rivadavia, T 61495; *Reggiani*, Bynnon 420, T 61389.

Camping: good municipal site near the river, US$14 per tent plus US$4 per person, all facilities including hot showers, but can be noisy at weekends.

● **Places to eat**

Restaurant Munich, Buenos Aires 150, open late.

● **Banks & money changers**

Travel agency at Namuncurá 78, , exchanges Amex cheques.

● **Tourist offices**

Belgrano 544, 9th floor.

● **Transport**

Air Aeropuerto Gobernador Castelo, 5 km south. To Buenos Aires and Bariloche, Austral (the city is also served by LADE).

Trains To Bariloche, Wednesday and Saturday, 16 hours, US$41 pullman, via San Antonio Oeste.

Buses Terminal at C A Zatti y Lavalle about 6

blocks from main plaza. To/from **Buenos Aires** US$45, La Estrellair conditioningóndor. To **San Antonio Oeste**, US$7.50.

SAN ANTONIO OESTE

(*Population* 11,000; *Phone code* 0934) is situated almost 180 km further west, on a peninsula in the Bahía San Antonio. **San Antonio Este**, a modern port on the eastern side, is the most important fruit exporting port in the country. The Bahía San Antonio is a nature reserve, protecting large numbers of migratory birds.

Excursions
To **Las Grutas** (*population* 750) 17 km south, a popular seaside resort, developed in the 1960s with good safe beach and seafood restaurants. The caves themselves are not really worth visiting. The whole resort closes down in mid-March and retires to Buenos Aires.

- **Accommodation** ACA has a *Unidad Turística*, T 97095, with 6-bed rooms, no restaurant. **C** *Tour du Golfe*, Bariloche y Sierra Grande, 3 bedrooms, cooking facilities. **Camping** Many good camping sites eg *La Entrada*, US$5 per tent, on edge of town above beach, *AMVI*, clean, near beach.

- **Buses** From San Antonio hourly US$1.30.

Local information
● **Accommodation**
B *Kandava*, Sarmiento 240, T 21430, hot water, good.

C *Golfo Azul*, simple; **C** *Iberia*, Sarmiento 241, without breakfast, small rooms, but recommended.

D *Betty*, Islas Malvinas 1410, T 22370

● **Transport**
Trains lines east to **Viedma** and west to **Bariloche**. Services: Wednesday and Saturday evening to Bariloche, Wednesday and Saturday 0600 to Viedma.

Buses North to **Bahía Blanca** and south to **Río Gallegos** and **Punta Arenas** by Transportes Patagónicos; to **Viedma** 0700 daily, US$7.50; to **Puerto Madryn** and **Trelew**, Don Otto, 0200 and 1530, 4 hours, US$20; to **Buenos Aires**, US$46 via Bahía Blanca, frequent.

ROUTES North From San Antonio Oeste a road runs north 91 km through bush country providing fodder for a few cattle, with a view to the west of the Salinas del Gualicho (salt flats), before joining Route 250 which

runs northwest to meet the Zapala-Bahía Blanca highway (Route 22) at Choele Choel, 178 km north of San Antonio Oeste (see page 166).

South Route 3 runs south to Puerto Madryn. At Km 123 is **Sierra Grande** (*population* 11,000; *altitude* 210m), a former iron ore mining town; the mines can be visited with local guides.

- **Accommodation** *La Posada*, Calle 2, No 170, T 81068; *La Terminal*, Calle 2, No 240, T 81250. **Camping** Behind ACA garage which has café, no facilities but free hot showers at YPF garage.

PUERTO MADRYN AND PENINSULA VALDÉS

PUERTO MADRYN

(*Population* about 50,000; *Phone code* 0965), some 250 km south of San Antonio Oeste is a port on a wide bay, Golfo Nuevo. The site of the first Welsh landing in 1865, the town was founded in 1886 and named after the Welsh home of the colonist, Jones Parry. The town has a giant alumina plant (visits, Monday 1430, arranged at the tourist office) and fish processing plants. A popular tourist centre, the town has a casino, while skin-diving and nature reserves are available both close to town and on the nearby Valdés peninsula.

Museums
Museo de Ciencias Naturales y Oceanográfico, Domecq García y J Menéndez, informative and worth a visit, open Tuesday-Saturday 1500-1830, entry US$2, ask to see video.
Museo de Arte Moderno, Roca 600, daily 1000-1800, US$1.

Excursions
To **Punta Loma**, a sealion reserve 15 km Southeast, open 0900-1200, 1430-1730; December and January are the best months. Information and video. Entry US$2. Taxis US$16. Sea-lions can even be seen in Puerto Madryn harbour. For the nature reserves on the **Peninsula Valdés**, see below.

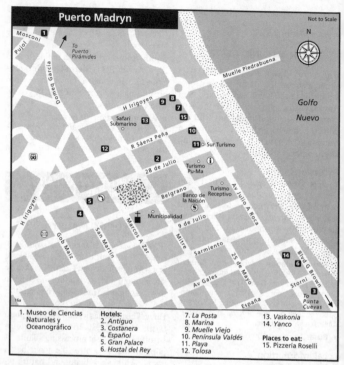

Puerto Madryn

Not to Scale

N

Moscom 1

To Puerto Pirámides

Muelle Piedrabuena

Golfo Nuevo

H Irigoyen 9 8

7

Safari Submarino 13 15

R Sáenz Peña 10

12 11 Sur Turismo

2 28 de Julio Turismo Pu-Ma

Belgrano Turismo Receptivo

Banco de la Nación

5 Municipalidad

4 9 de Julio

Sarmiento

14

Storni

3 To Punta Cuevas

España

1. Museo de Ciencias Naturales y Oceanográfico	**Hotels:** 2. Antiguo 3. Costanera 4. Español 5. Gran Palace 6. Hostal del Rey	7. La Posta 8. Marina 9. Muelle Viejo 10. Península Valdés 11. Playa 12. Tolosa	13. Vaskonia 14. Yanco **Places to eat:** 15. Pizzería Roselli

Local information
● Accommodation

Often full in summer, when prices rise; make bookings early. Many smaller places close out of season.

Hotel prices

L1	over US$200	**L2**	US$151-200
L3	US$101-150	**A1**	US$81-100
A2	US$61-80	**A3**	US$46-60
B	US$31-45	**C**	US$21-30
D	US$12-20	**E**	US$7-11
F	US$4-6	**G**	up to US$3

Unless otherwise stated, all hotels in range **D** and above have private bath. Assume friendliness and cleanliness in all cases.

A1 *Península Valdés*, Roca 155, T 71292 4-star, sea view, suites available, sauna, comfortable, recommended; **A2** *Playa*, Roca 187, T 50732, overpriced, small rooms, poor breakfast; **A2** *Bahía Nueva*, Roca 67, T/F 51677, with breakfast, bar, very comfortable; **A3** *Tolosa*, Sáenz Peña 250, T 71850, 3-star,

good breakfast; **A3** *Gran Madryn I*, Lugones 40, T 72205, 2-star, good; **A3** *La Posada de Madryn*, Matthews 2951, T 74087, quiet, English spoken, recommended; **A3** *Hostal del Rey*, Brown 681, T 71156, on beach, recommended, 2-star, breakfast extra, restaurant with fixed price menu; **A3** *Marina*, Roca 7, T 74044, heated, showers, warm, kitchen facilities.

B *Yanco*, Roca 626, T 71581, on beach, without breakfast, free nightly entertainment programme, has rooms for up to 6; **B** *Muelle Viejo*, Yrigoyen 38, T 71284, opposite pier, good restaurant, expensive breakfast, good, quiet; **B** *Gran Palace*, 28 de Julio 390, T 71009; **B** *Res Petit*, Alvear 845, T 51460, quiet, good; **B** *Res La Posta*, Roca 33, T 72422, good, heating, fan, cooking and laundry facilities.

C *Anclamar*, 25 de Mayo 875, T 51509, quiet, recommended; **C** *Antiguo/Central*, 28 de Julio 170, T 71742, good, basic, hot water; **C** *Costanera*, Brown 759, T 52800, good value; **C** pp *El Cid*, 25 de Mayo 865, with breakfast, parking; **C** *Español*, 28 de Julio y San Martín, basic, hot water, restaurant, parking, difficult to find; **C** *Hostería Hipocampo*, Vesta 33, helpful; **C** *Res J'os*, Bolívar 75, T 71433, pleasant; **C** *Res Manolo's*, Roca 763, T 72390, breakfast extra, small, quiet, kitchen facilities, homely; **C** *Vaskonia*, 25 de Mayo 43, T 72581, central, good value.

D *Aguas Mansas*, Hernández 51, T 53174, large rooms, kitchen; **D** pp *Hosp Santa Rita*, Gob Maiz 370, T 71050, kitchen facilites, heating, helpful.

Youth hostel/backpackers 25 de Mayo 1136, T 74426, **D** pp dormitory, **C** double room, laundry and kitchen facilities, bike rental, English and French spoken, tours.

Camping All closed out of season. At Punta Cuevas, 3.5 km south of town, is ACA site with evening hot showers, shop, café, good facilities and shady trees, US$12 per tent, free swimming pool in the rocks, which gets its water at high tide, very pleasant; many people camp on the beach. Two municipal sites: one at Ribera Sur, 1 km before ACA site on same road along beach (gives student discount). All facilities, very crowded, US$3 per person and US$2 per tent for first day. Also room with bunkbeds, **F** pp. Bus from town stops 100m before entrance. The other is north of town at Barrio Brown. Camping out can be interesting as you can watch foxes, armadillos, skunks and rheas roaming around in the evening.

● **Places to eat**
Las Aguilas, M A Zar y Sáenz Peña, recommended, large portions, good for seafood; *Don Jorge*, Sáenz Peña y Mitre, parrilla, recommended; *Cantina El Náutico*, Roca y Lugones, good food, especially fish; *París*, Muelle Piedrabuena, good and reasonably priced; *Pizzería Roselli*, Sáenz Peña y Roca, good, with vegetarian selections; *Quijote*, Belgrano 138, reasonable prices, very good; *Pequeño*, Roca 820, good value; *Barbarians*, 25 de Mayo y 28 de Julio, good coffee. For excellent Welsh afternoon teas, *La Goleta*, Roca 87, 1700-1900. Several local chocolate makers: try *Península* on Roca near *Turismo Receptivo*; *Café de la Ciudad*, 25 de Mayo y 28 de Julio, very popular.

● **Airline offices**
Aerolíneas Argentinas, 25 de Mayo 150, T 50110; **Lapa**, Belgrano 16, T 50893; **LADE** office at Roca 119, T 51256.

● **Banks & money changers**
Banks open Monday-Friday 0830-1330 (0800-1300 in summer). Banco de la Nación, 25 de Mayo y 9 de Julio, US$10 commission on travellers' cheques; **Banco Almafuerte**, 25 de Mayo y Sáenz Peña, 2% commission on travellers' cheques; **Banco del Sud**,Sáenz Peña, ATM

for Visa; **Banco Provincia Chubut**, 25 de Mayo, changes US$ cash, no commission, Mastercard and Amex ATM. There are no *casas de cambio*, but fair rates from travel agents (eg *Safari Submarino*, address below; go in the morning); **La Moneda**, Roca y 28 de Julio, will exchange large sums, not very good rates. High commission on changing travellers' cheques.

● **Entertainment**
Discos: *El Jardín*, Mitre y Sarmiento; *Salsa Discobar*, Brown y 3° Rotonda; *El Rancho*, Brown y 4° Rotonda, American music, small, entry US$10.

● **Laundry**
Laverap, 25 de Mayo 529, 0800-2000, recommended.

● **Post & telecommunications**
Post Office: Belgrano & A Maiz.
Telephone: Roca y 9 de Julio, also fax, 0700-2400; phone and fax at kiosk at Roca 733.

● **Sports**
Puerto Madryn is a diving centre. Tours, including for those who have never dived before, are organized by several agencies: *Safari Submarino*, Mitre 80, T/F 74110, only one open all year; *Ocean Divers*, Brown entre 1 y 2 Rotundas; *Abismo*, Roca 516, prices include equipment, US$50 beginners, US$40 experts (less with own equipment) courses on video, photography and underwater communication; PADI instruction US$200. No courses in January-February.

● **Tour companies & travel agents**
Several agencies do tours to the Valdés Peninsula, all are for 12 hours, see below. Prices are fixed by law, but some agencies run larger buses than others. Note that return distances of some tour destinations are high: Peninsula Valdés 380 km, Punta Tombo 400 km, Ameghino Dam 400 km. The last two are better from Trelew as they often involve 'sight-seeing' in the Chubut valley and a lot of time is spent travelling. The largest agency is *Sur Turismo*, Roca 175, T 73585, ISIC discount; *Safari Submarino*, Mitre 80, Tito Botazzi, small groups, very good, plenty of time at sites (10% reduction to SAH owners) see also under Puerto Pirámides. Other agencies include: *Receptivo*, Roca 303 y Belgrano, T 51048, Amex agent, weekend and off-season tours, recommended; *Pu-Ma*, 28 de Julio 48, T 71482, small groups, recommended; *Mar y Valle*, Roca y Belgrano, T 72872, recommended; *South Patagonia*, 25 de Mayo 226, small groups; *Coyun Co*, Roca 171, T 51845. *Franca del Sur*, Reconquista 378, T 50710, small groups, Spanish only, recommended; *Aquatours*, Muelle Piedrabuena, T 51954, recommended.

● Tourist offices
Roca 223, T 73029, Monday-Friday 0700-1300, 1500-2100, Saturday/Sunday 0800-1300, 1700-2100 but only Monday-Friday in winter; helpful, has notice board for messages, list of current hotel rates and interesting video on the region.

● Transport
Local Car hire: very expensive (US$150 per day). **Fiorasi,** on Sarmiento; **Localiza,** Belgrano 196, T 71660; **Coyun-Co,** Roca 171; **Renta Car Patagonia,** Roca 295. **Cycle hire:** *XT,* Roca 700 block; many other agencies. **Taxis:** outside bus terminal and on main plaza.

Air Airport 7 km north of Trelew. Buses to Trelew stop at entrance to airport if asked. Direct services, Puma, US$5, leaves 1½ hours before flights and picks up arriving passengers. Taxi US$45.

Buses Terminal at Yrigoyen y San Martín in old railway station. To **Buenos Aires,** 18 hours, daily, Don Otto (US$57), La Puntual (US$50), long delays, QueBus (daily except Wednesday); to **Río Gallegos,** about 20 hours, Don Otto, 1745 daily US$49, also Andesmar US$58; to **Comodoro Rivadavia,** Don Otto, Andesmar, US$26; to **Bahía Blanca** and Viedma, 12 hours, US$36; to **Mar del Plata,** change at Bahía Blanca; to **Bariloche,** Andesmar daily US$56; to **Córdoba,** US$72, 1900, Tus Tur; to **Caleta Oliva,** US$20, 0700; to **Mendoza,** US$68; Andesmar to **Neuquén,** US$31; to **Santiago** (Chile) via Neuquén, Andesmar, US$89; to **Trelew,** joint service by 28 de Julio and Mar y Valle, approximately every 30 minutes, US$4.50, 1 hour. Take own food and drink on long trips, regardless of what refreshments you are promised when booking.

Hitching For hitching north, try on the industrial estate road, or take a Trelew bus to the main highway then walk 3 km to the service station/truck stop. With luck it is possible to get to Bahía Blanca in 1 day.

PENINSULA VALDÉS

The Peninsula Valdés is connected to the mainland by a narrow isthmus, the Istmo Carlos Ameghino, which separates the Golfo San José to the north from the Golfo Nuevo to the south. In the heart of the peninsula are large saltflats, one of which, Salina Grande, is 42m below sea level. Though the peninsula is private property, it is a nature reserve: its coastline is one of the main centres of marine life in Argentina. The beach along the entire coast is out of bounds; this is strictly enforced. There is an interesting Visitor' Centre at the entrance to the reserve on the isthmus, some 79 km east of Puerto Madryn: a conservation officer is stationed here; entry US$5 (US$3 with ISIC card).

The main marine wildlife colonies are as follows:

Isla de los Pájaros, in the Golfo San José near the entrace. Its seabirds can only be viewed through fixed telescopes (at 400m distance), except for recognized ornithologists who can get permission to visit.

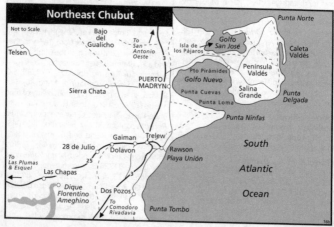

Northeast Chubut

Not to Scale

Telsen · Bajo del Gualicho · To San Antonio Oeste · Isla de los Pájaros · Golfo San José · Punta Norte · Caleta Valdés

Sierra Chata · PUERTO MADRYN · Pto Pirámides · Golfo Nuevo · Península Valdés · Punta Cuevas · Punta Loma · Salina Grande · Punta Delgada

Gaiman · Trelew · Punta Ninfas

28 de Julio · Dolavon · Rawson · Playa Unión

To Las Plumas & Esquel · Las Chapas · Dique Florentino Ameghino · Dos Pozos · To Comodoro Rivadavia · Punta Tombo

South Atlantic Ocean

Punta Norte, at the northern end of the peninsula, where there are elephant seals (breeding season late September/early October but during the first half of August the bull-seals arrive to claim their territory; best seen at low tide) and sea lions.

Caleta Valdés, 45 km south of Punta Norte, where there are colonies of Magallanic penguins and elephant seals which can be seen at close quarters.

Punta Delgada, at the southern end of the peninsula, where elephant seals and other wildlife can be seen, but not penguins.

● **Access** The peninsula is easily reached if you have your own transport, in fact the best way to see the wildlife is by car. See above for car hire; taking a taxi is worth considering if you can get a group together (taxi US$30 per person for the day). Hitching is very difficult,

Penguins

Distinctive for their dark upper and white underparts, penguins are flightless but highly aquatic birds. Their wings have been reduced to short hard flippers which can propel them up to 40 km per hour when they porpoise through the water (leaping quickly over the surface to take breath). Their feet are webbed with strongly developed claws. They are essentially marine mammals; they come ashore only to breed and/or moult. On land they are clumsy birds which walk with a distinctive slow waddle; when on snow or ice they can move much faster by tobogganing using their feet and flippers.

Magellan Penguins

There are 17 species, recognised in six genera, found throughout the southern hemisphere from the Galapagos Islands to Antarctica. Fossil evidence from Antarctica indicates that early penguins included a species which stood almost 8m high. Seven species breed in the Southern Ocean; these have particularly adapted feathers and a layer of blubber for insulation. The sexes are alike; they breed in large rookeries near the sea, or, in the case of Emperor Penguins, on pack-ice. Most species, except the larger ones, lay two eggs and both sexes share incubation. The chicks are fed by regurgitation of partly digested food from the parents. Penguins east krill, fish, squid, and smaller organisms, which they capture by diving, for some species, to great depths. They are preyed upon at sea by Leopard seals and Killer whales; on land skuas, fulmars and mammals such as dogs take their eggs and chicks and sometimes seize the occasional adult.

The Magellan Penguin (*Spheniscus magellanicus*) is a medium sized (75 cm high) temperate penguin with conspicuous black and white bands on the face, neck and upper breast. Its range covers southern South America but vagrants have been found on South Georgia. In Argentina there are large rookeries on Peninsula Valdés and at Punta Tombo, Cabo Dos Bahías, Ría Deseado, Cabo Virgenes, Monte Leon and on the Isla de los Estados. Occasionally a vagrant of another species can be found at these sites. Magellan penguins excavate burrows, up to a metre long, where they nest. The young are paler and greyer blue with only a single indistinct breast-band and dirty grey cheeks. During summer parades of adults may be seen going to sea and returning with food for the chicks.

R K Headland

even at weekends in season. Peninsula roads are all gravel except the road from Puerto Madryn to Puerto Pirámides.

Puerto Pirámides (*population* 100), 90 km east of Puerto Madryn, is the centre for visits to the peninsula. It is from here that whale-watching boat trips depart; sailings are controlled by the Prefectura, according to weather and sea conditions.

● **Accommodation** At Puerto Pirámides: **A2** *ACA Motel*, T 72057, poor restaurant, camping; there is also an ACA service station (open daily) with good café and shop; **A3** *Res El Libanés*, T 95007; **C** *Español*, basic but pleasant; **B** *Cabañas El Cristal*, T 95033, 4 bed cabañas, recommended. **Camping** Municipal site by the black sand beach, US$5 per person (free out of season), hot showers in evening only, dirty, busy, get there early to secure a place. Do not camp on the beach: people have been swept away by the incoming tide. At Punta Delgada: **A2** pp *Faro*, T 71910, full board, comfortable, excellent food, recommended (reservations at *Hotel Península Valdés* in Puerto Madryn).

● **Places to eat** At Puerto Pirámides: *Posada del Mar*, T 95016, restaurant; **A3** pp *Paradise Pub*, T 95030, helpful, recommended, good value food and beer, good atmosphere. Reasonably priced restaurant at Punta Norte for meals and snacks. Restaurant at Punta Delgada.

● **Shopping** In summer there are several well-stocked shops, but if staying take sun and wind protection and drinking water. There is a shop that sells original Patagonian Indian work.

● **Tour companies & travel agents** Tours: excursions are organized by tourist agencies in Puerto Madryn (addresses above). Full-day tours take in Puerto Pirámides (with whale-watching in season), plus some, but not necessarily all, of the other wildlife viewing points. Prices are US$25-30 per person plus the entry to the National Park; boat trip to see whales US$20 extra. On all excursions take drink with you, food too if you don't want to eat in the expensive restaurants (binoculars are also a good idea). Most tour companies stay 50-60 minutes on location. Tito Bottazzi, T 95050, recommended, can also be contacted via *Safari Submarino* in Puerto Madryn. *Hydro Sports* rents scuba equipment and boats, has a small restaurant, and organizes land and sea wildlife tours (ask for Mariano). Off season tours run when demand is sufficient, usually on Thursday and Sunday, departing at 0955 and returning at 1730. To avoid disappointment check all excursion dates and opening times in advance if possible. Tours do not run after wet weather in the low season.

● **Tourist offices** There is a small tourist office on the edge of Puerto Pirámides, useful information for hikes and driving tours.

● **Buses** Empresa 28 de Julio from Puerto Madryn, Thursday, Sunday at 1000 returns 1800, US$6.50 each way.

THE CHUBUT VALLEY

The Río Chubut, 820 km long and one of the most important rivers in Patagonia, rises in the eastern foothills of the Andes and flows into the Atlantic at Bahía Engaño. The river has been dammed upstream from Trelew to form the Embalse Florentino Ameghino, which irrigates the lower valley and provides electricity. A paved road (Route 25) runs west through

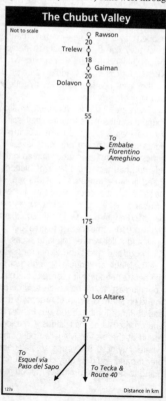

The Chubut Valley

Not to scale

Rawson
20
Trelew
18
Gaiman
20
Dolavon

55

To Embalse Florentino Ameghino

175

Los Altares
57

To Esquel via Paso del Sapo

To Tecka & Route 40

127a   Distance in km

he valley to Esquel (see page 374) and Trevelin.

RAWSON

(*Population* 19,000; *Phone code* 0965) the capital of Chubut Province, lies on the Río Chubut 7 km inland from its mouth. Founded in 1865, the first Welsh settlement in the valley, it is a town of official buildings. There are two small musuems: the **Museo de la Ciudad**, above the cinema on Jardín de las Americas, containing a collection of historical objects and old photos; and the **Museo Regional Don Bosco**, Don Bosco y Sarmiento, with a varied collection including artefacts from Welsh settlement. There is a small port, Puerto Rawson, 5 km down river; nearby is Playa Unión, a beach with casino and many restaurants.

● **Accommodation A3** *Provincial*, Mitre 551, T/F 81400, renovated, comfortable, restaurant; **C** *Res Sampedrano*, Belgrano 744.

● **Places to eat** *La Plaza*, M Moreno y B Vacchina; *Petit Café*, Belgrano y Costa; *Don Ignacio*, 25 de Mayo 251, basic, friendly.

● **Tourist office** 9 de Julio 280.

● **Buses** Terminal, Antárdida near 25 de Mayo, but buses to Trelew and La Unión are best caught from the plaza. To Trelew US$2; to Playa Unión US$1, 20 minutes.

TRELEW

(*Population* 61,000; *Phone code* 0965) pronounced 'TrelAYoo', and situated some 20 km west of Rawson, is the largest town in the valley. Founded in 1884 and named in honour of Lewis Jones, an early settler, it has lost its Welsh look.

Places of interest

The **Capilla Tabernacle** on Belgrano between San Martín and 25 de Mayo is a red brick chapel dating from 1889. Nearby is another brick building from the same period, the Asociación San David. On the road to Rawson, 3 km south is **Chapel Moriah**, the oldest standing Welsh chapel. Built in 1880, it has a simple interior and a cemetery with the graves of many original settlers.

Museums

The **Museo Paleontológico Egidio Feruglio**, 9 de Julio 655, Monday-Friday 0830-1230 1330-2000, Saturday 0900-1200, 1400-2100, Sunday/holidays 1400-2100, US$5 (ask for leaflet in English), organizes excursions to the Parque Paleontológico Bryn-Gwyn, traces the history of dinosaurs with models made from moulds of dinosaur bones (not all from Patagonia). Note the dinosaur eggs filled with quartz.

Museo Regional, Fontana y 9 de Julio, 0700-1300, 1400-2000, US$2, displays on indigenous societies, on failed Spanish attempts at settlement and on Welsh colonization; interesting.

Excursions

To **Playa Isla Escondida**, 50 km south, where there is a lovely rock and sand beach with bird and wildlife, secluded camping, no facilities.

To the **Embalse Florentino Ameghino**, an oasis of cool green trees west along the Chubut valley, recommended for a change of landscape, and to the towns of the Chubut valley, see below.

To the **Reserva Natural Punta Tombo**, a wildlife reserve covering 210 hectares, the largest breeding ground for Magellanic penguins in Patagonia: over 180,000 couples nest here every year. The wildlife is very varied: guanacos and rheas are visible on the way to the colony, where scavenger birds like chimangos, skuas and kelp gulls can be seen.

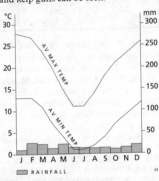

Climate: Trelew

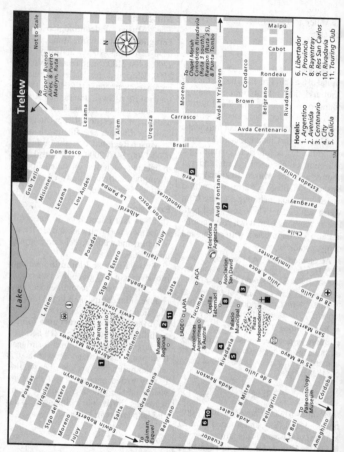

Trelew

Not to Scale

To Airport, Buenos Aires, & Puerto Madryn, Ruta 3

To Chapel Moriah Comodoro Rivadavia (Ruta 3 south), Rawson (Ruta 5), & Punta Tombo

Hotels:
1. Argentino
2. Avenida
3. Centenario
4. City
5. Galicia
6. Libertador
7. Provincia
8. Rayentray
9. Res San Carlos
10. Rivadavia
11. Touring Club

Lake

Punta Tombo should be visited between September and March; in January-February the young take to the water while the Reserve closes from late March. Check with the Tourist Office in Trelew that visits are permitted: when they are it is a fantastic experience. Best time to visit is early morning.

● **Access** There are two routes to the reserve: one is by a well marked road which branches off Route 3, west of Dos Pozos (not shown on ACA map): driving time 1¾ hours. The other is by a turning which branches off Route 1, a *ripio* road between Trelew and Camarones. Park en-

trance US$5. Trelew and Puerto Madryn travel agencies run tours, spending 30 minutes at the site. You can share a taxi from Trelew (US$30 per person).

Local holidays

28 July (Founding of Chubut); 13 December (Petroleum Day).

Local information
● **Accommodation**

L3 *Rayentray*, San Martín y Belgrano, T 34702, pool, expensive but excellent restaurant, helpful, comfortable.

A2 *Centenario*, San Martín 150, T 30042,

21524, expensive restaurant, Punta Tombo travel agency; **A3** *Libertador*, Rivadavia 31, 35132, T 20220, without breakfast, good rooms, poor restaurant, quiet, good value; **A3** *Touring Club*, Fontana 240, T 33998, excellent, with breakfast.

B *Galicia*, 9 de Julio y Rivadavia, T 33803, 24273, very warm, without bath; **B** *City*, Rivadavia 254, T 33951/2; **B** *Res San Carlos*, Sarmiento 758, T 31538, recommended; **B** *Res Rivadavia*, Rivadavia 55, T 34472, F 23591, helpful, recommended, also cheaper rooms, **D** pp.

Near bus terminal: C *Res Argentino*, Abraham Matthews 186, T 36134, quiet, good; **D** *Hostal Avenida*, Lewis Jones 49, T 34172, without bath, old fashioned, basic but quiet.

Camping Raul G Lerma, Rucahue 964, T 30208, offers free camping space in garden and local information, speaks English (taxi US$5 or ask at Estrella del Sur Turismo). Also at the Municipal Sports Centre, south of town on the road to Rawson, just over the bridge over Río Chubut, US$12, dirty, run-down, beware of mosquitoes; take Rawson bus, No 7 or 25. Public swimming pool.

● **Places to eat**
Eulogia Fuentes, Don Bosco 23, good pasta; *El Quijote*, 25 de Mayo 90, good seafood; *Sugar*, 25 de Mayo 247, good *minutas*; *El Mesón*, Rivadavia 588, seafood; *El Marfil*, Italia 42, good, cheap; *La Primera*, Rivadavia y Pasaje Mendoza, excellent *rotisería* and meat, expensive *tenedor libre*; *El Galeón*, San Martín 118, seafood specialities, good; *Cabildo Star*, Roca 76, excellent and cheap pizzas; *Napoli*, Rivadavia y 9 de Julio, old fashioned *confitería*; *Capítulo II*, Roca 393, *tenedor libre*, good and cheap; *La Casa de Juan*, Moreno 360, cosy, good pizzas; *Las Empanadas de Isidro*, Bell 220; *Café Vittorio*, Belgrano 341, good service; café at *Hotel Touring Club*, popular, good coffee.

● **Airline offices**
Austral and *Aerolíneas Argentinas*, 25 de Mayo 33, T 20170; *LADE*, Fontana 227, T 35925; *Lapa*, Fontana 285, T 23438; *TAN*, T 34550.

● **Banks & money changers**
Banco de la Nación, 25 de Mayo y Fontana, accepts Amex and Thomas Cook travellers' cheques; *Lloyds Bank* (BLSA), 9 de Julio y Belgrano, does not change travellers' cheques, cash advance on Visa but high charge for call to verify card; *Banco Provincia del Chubut*, Rivadavia y 25 de Mayo; *Banco del Sud*, 9 de Julio 370, cash advance on Visa, high commission; *Banco Almafuerte*, 9 de Julio 270; *Cambio* at *Caja de Ahorro y Seguro*, San Martín y Fontana. Banks change currencies before midday only.

● **Post & telecommunications**
Post Office: 25 de Mayo y Mitre.

Telephone: *Telefónica Fontana*, Fontana 418; *Telefónica Argentina*, Roca near Fontana; *Los Alerces*, Pellegrini 321, for fax.

● **Shopping**
Chocolates Patagónicos, Belgrano y Pasaje Mendoza, for local chocolate. *Camping Sur*, Pellegrini 389 for camping equipment.

● **Tour companies & travel agents**
Agencies run tours to Punta Tombo US$30, Chubut Valley half-day US$15, Florentino Ameghino US$30. Tours to Península Valdés are best done from Puerto Madryn. *Sur Turismo*, Belgrano 326-330, organizes good excursions, T 34550; *Estrella del Sur Turismo*, San Martín 129, T 31282, English spoken, recommended; *Nievemar*, Italia 20, T 34114; *Punta Tombo Turismo*, San Martín 150, T 20358; and others.

● **Tourist offices**
On ground floor of bus terminal, at airport and in Municipalidad, entrance on San Martín. Free maps, hotel prices and self-guided city tour.

● **Transport**
Local Car hire: expensive (cheaper to take a tour to Punta Tombo and Península Valdés). Avis, Localiza and Renta Car Patagonia desks are staffed only at flight arrival times and cars are snapped up quickly. *Localiza*, Urquiza 310, T 35344; *Avis*, Paraguay 105, T/F 34634; *Rent A Car*, San Martín 125, T 20898.

Air Airport 5 km east of centre; taxis about US$8. Local buses to/from Puerto Madryn stop at the airport entrance if asked, turning is 10 minutes' walk, US$4.50; Aerolíneas Argentinas runs special bus service to connect with its flights. Lapa and Aerolíneas Argentinas have flights to/from **Buenos Aires**, **Río Gallegos** and **Ushuaia**. Aerolíneas Argentinas also to **Río Grande**; Lapa (and TAN) also to **Comodoro Rivadavia**. Kaiken flies to **Comodoro Rivadavia**, **Ushuaia**, **Río Grande**, **Río Gallegos**, **Esquel**, **Neuquén** (also TAN), **Bariloche** and several other cities; also to **El Calafate** daily, 2 hours 50 minutes, 0830, US$127 one way with overflight of Perito Moreno Glacier.

Buses Terminal north of centre on east side of Plaza Centenario. To **Buenos Aires**, 4 daily, 21½ hours US$60; to **Bahía Blanca**, US$32 daily with Don Otto, 0600, several a week with La Puntual, 0600; to **Mar del Plata**, changing at Bahía Blanca, US$35 with La Puntual; to **Esquel**, US$32, 8-12 hours, Mar y Valle and Empresa Chubut; to **Bariloche** daily; to **Rawson** every 15 minutes; frequent buses to **Gaiman**, US$1.15; hourly to **Puerto Madryn**, US$3.50 with 28 de Julio and Mar y Valle; to **Comodoro Rivadavia** daily at 2000, and Sunday,

Wednesday, Thursday and Friday at 1035, US$26, 4 hours; to Río Gallegos, daily, TAC, 6 hours, US$55.

Hitching south: take the Rawson bus to the flyover 5 km out of town; there is a junction north of town for Puerto Madryn traffic.

WEST OF TRELEW

Route 25 runs west along the northern edge of the irrigated floodplain of the Río Chubut, past Gaiman and Dolavon, before continuing through attractive scenery to Esquel and Trevelin.

GAIMAN

(*Population* 4,400; *Altitude* 25m; *Phone code* 0965) 18 km west of Trelew, is a pretty town of well-built brick houses. On the south side of the river there are two chapels, the **Capilla Bethel** (1913) and, next to it, an older building dating from 1880. **El Desafío**, two blocks west of the plaza, is a private theme-park, 16 years work by Sr Joaquín Alonso. Made entirely of rubbish (drinks cans, bottles, piping and wire), it is a labyrinth of coloured plastic, glass and aluminium with mottos at every turn, US$5, tickets valid 2 months.
Museums Museo Histórico, 28 de Julio y Sarmiento, in the old railway station, displays artefacts from the period of Welsh settlement; the curator Mrs Roberts is 'full of stories'. US$1 (open in summer, Monday-Saturday 1600-2000; in winter, Tuesday-Saturday 1500-1900)

Welsh chapels in the Chubut

One of the main remnants of the Welsh influence in this area are the 15 chapels which scatter the lower Chubut. The largest, in Gaiman, holds about 450 people, a large congregation for what was then a very small town. The Salón San David in Trelew was intended as a replica of the church in the town of St David's in South Wales. Almost all are of brick though one, Capilla Salem, 5 km south of Gaiman, was built of wood covered entirely with corrugated zinc.

Camping site east of centre on river bank no facilities.

Local festivals Every October Gaiman hosts the annual Eisteddfod (Welsh festival of arts).

• **Places to eat** Welsh teas are served from about 1500 (US$10-12) by several **Tea Rooms** including *Casa de Té Gaiman*, Yrigoyen 738, excellent; *Plas y Coed*, Miguel D Jones 123 ,oldest, excellent tea 'and good food for a week', Marta Rees speaks English and is very knowledgeable about the area, highly recommended; *Ty Gwyn*, 9 de Julio 111, recommended; *Ty Nain*, Yrigoyen 283, frequented by tour buses, display of historical items; *Ty Te Caerdydd*, Finca 202, 2 km from town, very good, and *Eima*, Tello 571. Most facilities are closed out of season.

DOLAVON

(*Population* 2,000; *Altitude* 27m; *Phone code* 0965) Km 38, a small town founded in 1919, is the most westerly Welsh settlement in the valley. The main street runs parallel to the irrigation canal built by the settlers; there is a chapel over the canal. The old flour mill at Maipú 61, dates from 1930 and can be visited: key kept in the Municipalidad, Roca 188 (next to Banco Provincial del Chubut).. Some Trelew-Gaiman buses continue to Dolavan; check at Trelew bus terminal.

• **Accommodation** Motel on outskirts. **Camping** Municipal site near two blocks north of the river, good facilities, free.

WEST OF DOLAVON

At Km 113 a road branches south to the **Embalse Florentino Ameghino**. This reservoir stretches along some 80 km of the Chubut valley, covers 7,000 hectares and irrigates 20,000 hectares in the lower Chubut valley. Black-necked swans can be seen and there are watersports facilities and campsites.

Route 25 continues west, crossing the Río Chubut at Las Plumas (Km 184) before running alongside it: there are towering rock formations in varied colours. At **Los Altares**, Km 288, there is an ACA Motel. At **Tecka**, Km 508 (see page 381), where it meets Route 40, the Esquel-Gobernador Costa road. At Km 345 a *ripio* road branches north from

Valley of the Martyrs

West of Las Plumas, Route 25 runs through the Valle de los Martires, named after three Welsh settlers, captured here in 1884 by the Indians and killed, while prospecting for gold. A fourth, John Evans, escaped thanks to the speed of his horse. Evans later settled in Trevelin, where there is a grave to the horse to which he owed his life.

Route 25 providing an alternative route to Esquel via **Paso del Sapo**; this road, 170 km long, joins Route 40 some 30 km south of Esquel.

CENTRAL PATAGONIA

CAMARONES

(*Population* 800; *Altitude* 23m; *Phone code* 097) Situated 275 km south of Trelew and 300 km north of Comodoro Rivadavia, Camarones is a fishing port on Bahía Camarones, reached by a 72 km paved road branching off Route 3.

● **Accommodation B** *Kau I Keu Kenk*, Sarmiento y Roca, good food, recommended, owner runs trips to penguin colony; 2 others, **C**, the one by the power station is not recommended. Campsite.

● **Buses** Don Otto from Trelew, Monday and Friday, 2½ hours, returns to Trelew same day 1600.

Reserva Natural Cabo Dos Bahías

This reserve, 35 km southeast at the southern end of the bay and reached by a dirt road, covers 160 hectares and protects a penguin colony of some 12,000 couples; there are also sea lions and guanacos. Entry US$5, open all year. Ask the park ranger in Camarones for a lift on Monday or Friday. Hitchhiking is difficult, but possible at weekends. No taxis available (private cars charge US$50-60, ask at *Busca Vida*).

COMODORO RIVADAVIA

(*Population* 158,000; *Phone code* 0967) the largest city in the province of Chubut, is 387 km south of Trelew. Founded in 1901 as a port for the agricultural communities around Colonia Sarmiento, early development was limited by lack of water. Early settlers included Boer immigrants fleeing British rule in southern Africa. **Rada Tilly** (*population* 3,000), 12 km south, is a resort with a good beach and restaurants. Sealions can be seen at low tide. (**Buses** Expreso Rada Tilly every 30 minutes). Excursions may be made to **Sarmiento** and the **Bosques Petrificados** (see below).

Museums

Museo del Petroleo, 3 km north in Gral Mosconi, with exhibits on exploration and production. Open Tuesday-Friday 1400-2000, Saturday/Sunday 1430-2030 (bus No 6 from San Martín y Abasolo).

Museo Paleontológico, in Astra, 16 km north, open Saturday/Sunday only 1400-2000.

Local holidays

28 July (Founding of Chubut); 13 December (Petroleum Day).

Local information

● **Accommodation**

A3 *Austral*, Rivadavia 190, T 32200, noise from traffic but otherwise comfortable, reasonable restaurant; **A3** *Comodoro*, 9 de Julio 770, T 32300, overpriced, restaurant, nightclubs, car

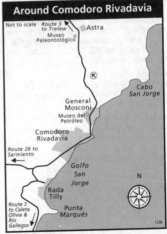

Around Comodoro Rivadavia

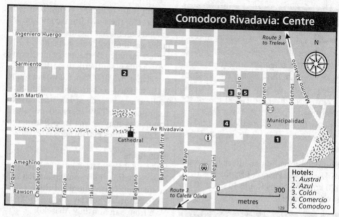

Comodoro Rivadavia: Centre

Hotels:
1. Austral
2. Azul
3. Colón
4. Comercio
5. Comodoro

Route 3 to Trelew

Route 3 to Caleta Olivia

0   300
metres

rental; **A3** *Res Azul*, Sarmiento 724, T 24874, comfortable, spotless, recommended.

C *Colón*, San Martín 341, T 22283, run down, but not much else; **C** *Comercio*, Rivadavia 341, T 22341, old fashioned, dirty, near bus terminal, hot showers; **C** *Hosp Belgrano*, Belgrano 546, T 24313, hot water; **C** *Hosp Praga*, España y Sarmiento, shower; **C** *Rada Tilly*, Piedrabuena, in Rada Tilly, T 51032, modern; *Motel Astra*, southern access of Route 3, T 25394.

Camping Municipal site at Rada Tilly, hot and cold water. There is another, free, campsite at north end of beach, cold water only (watch out for clayslides when it rains).

● **Places to eat**
La Rastra, Rivadavia 384, very good for *churrasco*, but not much else; *Pizzería El Nazareño*, San Martín y España, good. *Bom-Bife*, España 832, good food, inexpensive. Several *rotiserías*, much cheaper, on 400 block of Rivadavia, in municipal market.

● **Airline offices**
Austral, 9 de Julio 870, T 40050; Lapa, Rivadavia 396, T 471685; LADE, Rivadavia 396, T 472400; TAN, T 23855.

● **Banks & money changers**
Lloyds Bank, Rivadavia 276, October-March 0700-1300; April-September 1200-1800; no exchange transactions after 1000 in summer, 6% commission on travellers' cheques, pays US$ cash on travellers' cheques but minimum US$300; the Banco de la Nación, San Martín 108, has the best rates on US$ but does not change travellers' cheques. Amex agent is *Orbe Turismo Show*, San Martín 488, T 29699, 5% commission for US$, does not change travellers' cheques. Several travel agencies also change

money including Roqueta Travel, Rivadavia y Pellegrini, Ceferino, 9 de Julio 852, and CRD Travel, Moreno 844 (travellers' cheques accepted).

● **Consulates**
Belgium, Rivadavia 283; Chile, Sarmiento 936; Italy, Belgrano 1053.

● **Post & telecommunications**
Post Office: San Martín y Moreno.

● **Shopping**
From here southward, prices begin to rise very rapidly, so stock up before reaching Río Gallegos (although bear in mind you are not allowed to take food into Chile).

● **Tour companies & travel agents**
Puelche EVT, Rivadavia 527; Richard Pentreath, Mitre 952; San Gabriel and Atlas at San Martín 488 and 263, respectively; Monitur, 9 de Julio 948.

● **Tourist offices**
Rivadavia y Pellegrini.

● **Transport**
Local VW dealer: Comercial Automotor, Rivadavia 380, recommended. VW concession: Avenida Irigoyen in Barrio Industrial, also recommended. Car rental: Patagonia Car Sur, T 967-26768; Avis, 9 de Julio 687, T/F 496382.

Air Airport, 9 km north. Bus No 6 to airport from bus terminal, hourly (45 minutes), US$0.40. Taxi to airport, US$7. To Buenos Aires, Lapa, Dinar and Austral. All major cities south of Córdoba and Mendoza are served by Austral, Lapa, TAN, Kaiken and Andesmar. LADE flies once a week (Wednesday) to Perito Moreno, Gobernador Gregores, Calafate, Río Gallegos, Río Grande, Ushuaia, and on Monday

Oil

👣 Since the first discoveries of oil in the region, Comodoro Rivadavia's prosperity and growth have fluctuated with the prospects of the oil industry. The first major oil find in Argentina occurred just north of the town while drilling for water in 1907. Although in 1910 the government established an agency to drill for oil elsewhere in the region, international oil companies only became interested in Argentina after the First World War. Between 1919 and 1923 over 30 oil companies were registered in the country, most of them with capital from Europe or the United States. In 1922, in response to this, President Hipólito Yrigoyen created Yacimientos Petroleros Fiscales, destined to become the most important company in oil exploration and extraction. Much of its success is usually attributed to its first director, Col Enrique Mosconi, who is remembered by the name given to the neighbourhood of Comodoro Rivadavia where the 1907 find occurred.

Today most of Argentina's oil production occurs in Patagonia, about 33% of it from wells in south and west of the Comodoro Rivadavia. A 1,770-km pipeline carries natural gas to Buenos Aires, and there is a petrochemical plant.

to Puerto Deseado, San Julián, Gob Gregores, Calafate, Río Turbio, Río Gallegos, Santa Cruz; once a week to Bariloche via Trelew and Viedma, or Trelew and Esquel, or via Esquel, El Maitén and El Bolsón; other services to Neuquén via the Lake District and to Trelew.

Buses Terminal conveniently located in centre; has luggage store, good *confitería* upstairs, lousy toilets, *remise* taxi booth, some kiosks. Services to **Buenos Aires** daily at 1200 and 2115, 32 hours, US$108 (same fare on Costera Criolla; also daily with La Estrellair conditioningóndor at 1335); to **Bariloche**, US$55 (Don Otto at 2150, Sunday, Tuesday, Thursday, stops at Sarmiento midnight, Esquel at 0600 and for 30 minutes at El Bolsón at 0900, arrives 0600 at Bariloche); to **Esquel** (paved road) direct, Friday 1230, 10 hours, via Río Mayo, Monday, Thursday, 0100, 15½ hours, to Río Mayo Tuesday, Thursday, Sunday, 1700 and 1900, 5½ hours. In summer buses heading south usually arrive full; to **Río Gallegos**, Don Otto 2345 daily, and Transportes Patagónica 2200 daily, 11 hours, US$30; to **Puerto Madryn** and **Trelew**, US$26, at 1200; to **Caleta Olivia**, La Unión, hourly, US$3.50; to **Sarmiento**, US$7, 2½ hours at 0700, 1300, 1900; to **Mendoza**, daily at 0130, 20 hours; to **Córdoba**, Tuesday, Friday, Sunday, 1200, 33 hours.

Buses to Chile To Coyhaique, Angel Giobbi, US$30, 12 hours, twice a week (Monday and Thursday) 0100, June-September and 3 a week (Monday, Wednesday, Friday), 0100, October-May (weather permitting), also Turibus, Tuesday and Saturday 0800.

Hitchhiking: there is a truck stop at Astra, 20 km north on Route 3, where you can contact drivers whether heading north or south. Hitch out of the centre or take any bus going north. Expensive truckdrivers' restaurants along the road; buy food in supermarkets.

FROM COMODORO RIVADAVIA TO CHILE

Route 26 runs west, amid oil wells, from Comodoro Rivadavia towards the Chilean frontier and the Chilean towns of Coyhaique and Puerto Aisén.

SARMIENTO

(*Population* 7,000; *Altitude* 270m; *Phone code* 097), 156 km west of Comodoro Rivadavia, lies on the Río Senguer just south of two great lakes, **Lago Musters** and **Lago Colhué Huapi**, both of which offer good fishing in summer. Founded in 1897 and formally known as Colonia Sarmiento, its early settlers were Welsh, Lithuanians and Boers. On the north side of the plaza is the **Museo Desiderio Torres**, with displays of Indian artefacts, open Monday-Friday 0900-1400, Saturday/Sunday 1000-1400 summer, Monday-Friday 1330-1930 winter.

Excursions

To two areas of **petrified forest**: the **Bosque Petrificado José Ormachea**, 32 km south along a gravel road, entry US$5, and the **Bosque Petrificado Víctor**

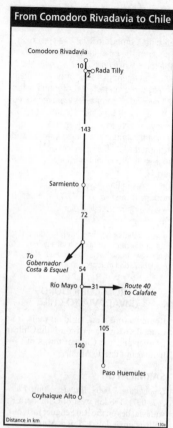

From Comodoro Rivadavia to Chile

Comodoro Rivadavia

10 ○ Rada Tilly
2

143

Sarmiento ○

72

To
Gobernador
Costa & Esquel
54

Río Mayo ○—31—→ Route 40
to Calafate

105

140

Paso Huemules

Coyhaique Alto ○

Distance in km
130a

Szlapelis, some 40 km further southwest along the same road (follow signposts, road from Sarmiento in good condition). These forests, 60 million years old, of fallen araucaria trees nearly 3m round and 15-20m long, are a remarkable sight. There are rangers at both sites. The forests should be visited in summer: winters are very cold. Taxi from Sarmiento US$39 (3 passengers), including 1 hour wait, for each extra hour US$9. Hitching is difficult, even in summer. Contact Sr Valero, the park ranger, for guided tours, ask at *Hotel Colón* (see also the *Monumento Natural Bosques Petrificados* below, page 410).

● **Accommodation** B *Hostería Los Lagos* Roca y Alberdi, T 93046, good, heating, restaurant; **E** *Colón*, P Moreno 645, restaurant cheap; **B** *Lago Musters*, P Moreno y Coronel, T 93097; *San Martín*, San Martín y P Moreno, cheap, good restaurant; **D** *Ismar*, Patagonia 248, restaurant. In December-March you may be permitted to sleep in the Agricultural School (take sleeping bag) on the road to petrified forest, opposite the ACA petrol station. **Camping** Municipal site near Río Senguer, 2 km north of centre on Route 23, basic, no shower, US$3 for tent, US$1 per person.

● **Tourist office** In the Municipalidad.

● **Buses** Overnight services to **Esquel** on Sunday, Tuesday and Thursday, take food for journey as cafés are expensive; to **Comodoro Rivadavia**, 0700, 1300, 1900; to **Chile**, Giobbi buses leave at 0200.

WEST AND SOUTH OF SARMIENTO

Route 20 continues west and then northwest along the valley of the Río Senguer, before joining Route 40 which runs north to Esquel, 448 km, at the southern edge of the Lake District (see page 374). Hitching along this road is very difficult, even in summer. Route 22, branching off 72 km west of Sarmiento runs southwest, 54 km, to meet route 40 at Río Mayo.

RIO MAYO

(*Population* 2,600; *Altitude* 270m; *Phone code* 097; fuel) is little more than a route centre, though each November it is the site of the *Fiesta Nacional de la Esquila* (the National Sheep-shearing Competition). The area is so windy that windmills have been built to generate electricity. The small **Museo F Escalada** is just off the plaza. If travelling south buy food here as it gets more expensive.

● **Accommodation** C *Covadonga*, San Martín 575, T 20014, very good; C *Hotel Pingüino*; C *A'Ayones*, T 20044, modern, heating; **D** pp *San Martín*, San Martín y Perito Moreno, T 20066, comedor; *Res Aka Ta*, San Martín 400, T 20054. **Camping** Free site on northern outskirts near river.

● **Buses** Giobbi buses from Comodoro Rivadavia to Coyhaique, Chile, pass through Río Mayo at 0600 on Monday, Wednesday and Friday (Monday and Thursday, June-September), US$14, 6 hours, but seats are scarce. To Esquel, Giobbi, 0600.

FRONTIER WITH CHILE

There are two crossings west of Río Mayo.

Coyhaique Alto

Reached by a 133 km road (87 km *ripio*, then dirt) which branches off Route 40 about 7 km north of Río Mayo. On the Chilean side this road continues to Coyhaique, 50 km west of the frontier. See above under Comodoro Rivadavia for bus services on this route.

● **Chilean immigration**

At Coyhaique Alto, 6 km west of the frontier, open May-August 0800-2100, September-April 0700-2300.

Paso Huemules

Reached by a road which branches off Route 40, some 31 km south of Río Mayo and runs west 105 km via **Lago Blanco** (fuel), where there is a small *estancia* community, 30 km from the frontier. No hotel, but police are friendly and may permit camping at the police post; wild but beautiful place (this route is reported as better than that via Coyhaique Alto). This road continues from **Balmaceda** on the Chilean side of the frontier to Coyhaique.

● **Chilean immigration**

open May-July 0800-2100, September-April 0700-2100.

ROUTE 40 FROM RIO MAYO TO CALAFATE

This stretch of Route 40 crosses one of the most uninhabited parts of Patagonia. Road conditions vary, depending on how recently each stretch was repaired. It is paved as far as Perito Moreno; south of there it is *ripio*, though it improves considerably after Las Horquetas. There is no public transport and very few other vehicles even in mid summer. Hitching along this road is virtually impossible. Super' grade fuel is available in most places: it is important to carry extra, especially between Bajo Caracoles and Tres Lagos since the only source of fuel between them involves a 72-km detour to Gobernador Gregores (see page 408).

PERITO MORENO

(*Population* 3,000; *Altitude* 400m; *Phone*

code 0963), 137 km south of Río Mayo, lies near the source of the Río Deseado. Southwest of the centre is the Laguna El Cisne, where varied birdlife can be seen including flamingos and black-necked swans. (Do not confuse this town with the famous glacier of the same name near El Calafate, nor with Parque Nacional Perito Moreno.) The second largest lake in South America, **Lago Buenos Aires**, lies 25 km west, extending into Chile as Lago General Carrera and draining westwards into the Río Baker, one of the biggest rivers in Chile.

South of Perito Moreno is the crater of **Cerro Volcán**; after passing the Gendarmería on your right, take the first left

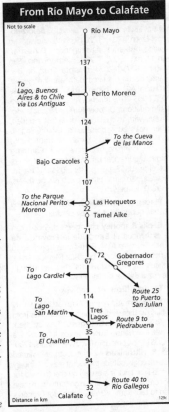

From Río Mayo to Calafate

Not to scale

Río Mayo

137

Perito Moreno — To Lago, Buenos Aires & to Chile via Los Antiguas

124

To the Cueva de las Manos →

Bajo Caracoles

3

107

To the Parque Nacional Perito Moreno ← Las Horquetas

22

Tamel Aike

71

72 → Gobernador Gregores

67

To Lago Cardiel ←

Route 25 to Puerto San Julián

114

To Lago San Martín ←

Tres Lagos

Route 9 to Piedrabuena

35

To El Chaltén ←

94

Route 40 to Río Gallegos

32

Calafate

Distance in km

129c

Patagonian Estancias

👣 *Estancias* offer some of the best accommodation along Route 40 as well as a variety of activities. The architecture of Patagonian *estancias* is adpated to the climate and surroundings and is usually less luxurious than that of *estancias* on the pampas. Due to the climate most *estancias* receive guests only between October and April. Estancias in Santa Cruz province, including those along Route 40, maintain an information office in Buenos Aires which also arranges reservations (see under **Buenos Aires, Tourist offices**). Even in season booking ahead is advisable because of the long distances involved.

Chita van der Sande, *Flyer Viajes y Turismo*

(dirt road) at the 3-road junction with Route 40. It is 12 km to the path to the crater – ask permission at the Estancia to continue. (Hitching may be possible in summer.) For the **Cueva de las Manos**, see below.

- **Accommodation** C *Argentino*, San Martín 1386, dirty, no showers; C *Belgrano*, San Martín 1001, T 2019, with shower, no heating, restaurant, recommended; D *Austral*, San Martín 1327, T 2042; *Americano*, San Martín 1327, T 2074; C *Santa Cruz*, on Belgrano, heating, shared bath and hot water. **Estancia**, A2 pp *Telken*, 30 km south on Route 40, T 0963-2079 (Buenos Aires 797-7216), accommodation October-April, discounts for families with two children, breakfast included, other meals extra, horseriding, fishing, English and Dutch spoken, transport from Perito Moreno, camping, recommended. **Camping** Parque Laguna near Laguna El Cisne, sheltered, but dirty, US$2 per person, US$1 extra for showers, also cabañas, sleep 6, basic, no sheets, clean, D per person.

- **Places to eat** *Pipach III*, next to *Hotel Austral*, good pizzas and *empanadas*.

- **Banks & money changers** US$ cash can be exchanged at Banco de la Provincia de Santa Cruz. No ATM. Better rates from Plácido Treffinger, San Martín opposite Municipalidad. Difficult to change travellers' cheques, though the *Hotel Belgrano* may do so.

- **Tourist offices** At camp site.

- **Transport Air** Airport 7 km east of town, try to hitch as there is only one taxi; LADE flies from Perito Moreno to **Río Gallegos** on Tuesday, check in well in advance. **Buses** To Los Antiguos, 2 a day, US$3; to Comodoro Rivadavia, 6 hours, 1730, US$18. **Hitchhikers** To the south are warned that, especially outside the tourist season (January to mid-February), it is usually quicker to head for the coast at Caleta Olivia and go south from there than to take Route 40 via Gobernador Gregores and Piedrabuena.

FRONTIER WITH CHILE

Though there are two crossings west of Perito Moreno, the easiest and most commonly used is via Los Antiguos.

Los Antiguos

(*Population* 1,500; *Altitude* 326m; *Phone code* 0963), 67 west of Perito Moreno and 2 km east of the frontier, is reached by Route 43 which runs along the southern edge of Lago Buenos Aires. Enjoying a favourable microclimate, it is a fruit-growing area with an annual cherry festival in early January. Salmon fishing is also available. (Fuel.)

- **Accommodation** B *Argentino*, comfortable, restaurant. **Camping** outstanding municipal site, hot showers, 2 km from centre, US$2.50 per person. At Km 29 A3 *Hostería La Serena* offers accommodation in *cabinas*, 10% reduction to *South American Handbook* readers, good restaurant and organizes trips in both the Chilean and Argentine Lake Districts, open October-June; further details from Geraldine des Cressonières, Estancia La Serena, Casilla 87, 9040 Perito Moreno, Santa Cruz. Nearby is Los Chilcas where Indian remains can be found (trout fishing).

- **Buses** To Comodoro Rivadavia, US$20, Co-op Sportsman, from near *Hotel Argentino*, 1630 daily, 7 hours, via Perito Moreno and Caleta Olivia, and Empresa La Unión, 0700, 1300 from bar *El Triunfo*. To Chile Transportes VH buses cross the border by new bridge to Chile Chico, 8 km west, US$3, 45 minutes. If hitching to Chile Chico look for lift on Argentine side of frontier to avoid problems returning to Los Antiguos if you can't get a lift.

North of Lago Buenos Aires

The other route is via the roads which go around the north side of Lago Buenos

Route 40

🥾 "To see the real Patagonia, with its immense desert-like plains and mountains, rent a car and travel along Route 40 between Perito Moreno and Calafate. The road has been improved in recent years so you so not need four-wheel drive (in summer); the only bad bit is a 5 km section north of Tres Lagos, where there are big stones on the road, but drive slowly if you are not used to gravel. This region is the most isolated in Patagonia; because of low wool prices a lot of *estancias* have been abandoned and most of the hotels marked on the maps have been closed. The landscape is of mesetas, mountains and valleys, mostly covered with yellow grass; in the evening light you have the impression of endless, shimmering golden plains and hills. Stay overnight at *estancias* in the middle of nature and allow yourself at least ten days, with excursions off the road to the Cueva de las Manos, Lago Posadas, Parque Nacional Perito Moreno and Chaltén."

Friederike Dónngies, Stuttgart, Germany

Aires to Puerto Ibáñez. At the roundabout, north edge of town, go straight, on the biggest road; at the police checkpoint, turn right onto a small road. Follow this 75 km and then turn left along north side of Lago Buenos Aires.

AROUND BAJO CARACOLES

Bajo Caracoles

(*Population* 100; *Altitude* 450m; *Phone code* 097), Km 264, is a tiny, forlorn pit stop, with its expensive grocery store and is the nearest stepping off point for visiting the **Cueva de las Manos** (see below). West of Bajo Caracoles, 72 km along Route 39 are **Lago Posadas** and **Lago Pueyrredón**, two beautiful lakes with contrasting blue and turquoise waters and separated by a narrow isthmus. Guanacos and rheas can be seen and there are sites of archaeological interest.

● **Accommodation Bajo Caracoles**: **C** *Hotel Bajo Caracoles*, T 34963. decent, meals. **At Lago Posadas**: *Hostería Lagos del Furioso*, open November-April, comfortable, horse-riding, trekking and excursions in vehicles offered. *Lago Posadas*, cabañas, meals.

The Cueva de las Manos

situated 47 km northeast of Bajo Caracoles in the canyon of the Río Pinturas, contains outstanding examples of prehistoric cave paintings, the oldest of which are estimated to be 10,000 years old. In the cave's four galleries are over 800 paintings of human hands, all but 31 of which are of left hands, as well as images of guanacos and cameloids. Painted in red, orange, black, white and green, they are interesting even for those not interested in rock art. The canyon itself, 270m deep and 480m wide, is worth seeing: its rock walls are hues of red and green and are especially beautiful in the evening light. A ranger lives at the site; he looks after the caves and is helpful with information.

● **Accommodation** *Estancia Los Toldos*, 7 km off Route 40, 15 km from caves. Camping is permitted at the caves but very windy. If it is not busy the ranger may let you sleep inside the park building.

● **Access** is via an unpaved road which branches east off Route 40 3 km north of Bajo Caracoles. Entrance US$3. No public transport goes anywhere near the caves.

● **Tours**, from Perito Moreno, US$200 for groups of up to 10; ask at tourist office. Hector Yerio, T 32127, takes up to 7 people in a pickup, US$100, 2 hours journey, 5 hours at site. A cheaper alternative is to ask at the only hotel in Bajo Caracoles. No transport at all off season.

FRONTIER WITH CHILE: PASO ROBALLOS

Paso Roballos is 99 km northwest of Bajo Caracoles via (unpaved) Route 41, which runs past Lago Ghio and Lago Columna. On the Chilean side this road continues to Cochrane, Km 177. Though passable in summer, it is often flooded in spring. No public transport. If hitching, allow a week.

FROM BAJO CARACOLES TO CALAFATE

There is no food between Bajo Caracoles and Tres Lagos; water can be obtained from streams and *estancias* about every 25 km, except between Río Chico and Lago Cardiel (90 km). South of Bajo Caracoles Route 40 crosses the Pampa del Asador and then, near **Las Horquetas**, Km 371, swings southeast to follow the Río Chico. At **Tamel Aike**, Km 393, there is a police station and water but little else. At Km 464 Route 25 branches off to San Julian via **Gobernador Gregores** (*population* 1,000; *altitude* 370m; *phone code* 0962) 72 km southeast (where there is fuel and a good mechanic), while Route 40 continues southwest towards Tres Lagos. At Km 531 a road heads west to **Lago Cardiel**, a very saline lake with no outlet (good salmon fishing). **Tres Lagos** (*population* 300) Km 645, is a solitary village (supermarket, fuel) at the junction with Route 288. A road also turns off northwest to **Lago San Martín**, which straddles the frontier (the Chilean part is Lago O'Higgins).

- **Accommodation At Las Horquetas**: *Hotel Las Horquetas*. **At Gobernador Gregores**: *San Francisco*, T 91039. Also municipal campsite. **At Tres Lagos**: **E** pp *Restaurant Ahoniken*. Municipal campsite, dirty showers, US$3 per person. Camping also at *Estancia La Lucila*, 52 km north of Tres Lagos off Route 40, basic, US$3, home made bread and jam.

- **Estancias A2** pp *La Angostura*, also horseriding, trekking, fishing, recommended. **At Lago San Martín: A3** pp *Estancia La Maipú*, T 0966-22613, F 903-4967, the Leyenda family offer accommodation, meals, horse riding, trekking and boat excursions on the lake, "real atmosphere of a sheep farming *estancia*" (Santiago de la Vega), recommended.

From Tres Lagos Route 40 (in poor condition) runs west towards **Lago Viedma**. At Km 680 a road runs west to the Fitz Roy sector of Parque Nacional Los Glaciares (see below). At Km 701 there is a bridge over Río La Leona. Nearby is a hotel which has a bar/café. From here it is 73 km further to Route 11, the main (paved) highway from Río Gallegos to Calafate.

PARQUE NACIONAL PERITO MORENO

Situated southwest of Bajo Caracoles on the Chilean frontier, this is one of the wildest and most remote parks in Argentina. Extending over 115,000 hectares at altitudes above 800m, the park includes eight large lakes, seven of which drain into Chile, while the eighth, Lago Burmeister, empties into the Río Chico which flows towards the Atlantic. There are also numerous smaller lakes and ponds. Outside the park, but towering over it to the north is **Cerro San Lorenzo** (3,706), the highest peak in southern Patagonia. Between the lakes are other peaks, permanently snow-covered, the highest of which is Cerro Herros (2,770m). The Sierra Colorada, its rocks a mass of differing colours runs across the northeast of the park: erosion of these coloured rocks has given the lakes differing colours. At the foot of Cerro Casa de Piedra are a network of caves which contain cave paintings, accessible only with a guide. Ammonite fossils can be found in many parts of the park.

Lower parts of the park are steppe, covered with dense *coiron* grasses and shrubs. Higher up are areas of southern beech forest especially *lenga* and *coihue*. Wildlife includes guanacos, foxes and one of the most important surviving populations of the rare huemul. Birds include flamingos, ñandus, steamer ducks, grebes, black-necked swans, Patagonian woodpeckers, eagles and condors. The lakes and rivers are unusual for Argentina in that only native species of fish are found.

The most accessible part of the park is around Lago Belgrano, 12 km from the entrance. Several good hikes are possible from here: to the peninsula of Lago Belgrano, 8 km, where there are fine views of Cerro Herros; to the Río Lacteo, 20 km; to Lago Burmeister, via Cerro Casa de Piedra, 16 km. You should inform rangers before setting out on a hike.

- **Access** is via an unpaved road, 75 km, which branches off Route 40 near Las Horquetas. Ranger post near Lago Belgrano. Rangers have maps and information. Entrance US$5.

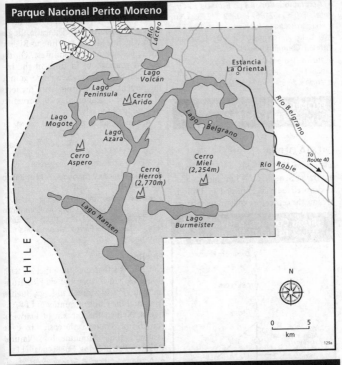

Parque Nacional Perito Moreno

Francisco Moreno, 'El Perito'

Travellers to Patagonia will find it hard to miss the name of Francisco Pascasio Moreno (1852-1919). Commemorated by a national park, a town and a world famous glacier, Moreno, a naturalist and geographer, travelled ceaselessly in Patagonia, exploring areas previously unknown to the authorities in Buenos Aires. At the age of 20 he paid his first visit to Patagonia, travelling up the Río Negro to Lago Nahuel Huapi, along the Río Chubut and then up the Río Santa Cruz to reach the giant lake which he named 'Lago Argentino'. Expeditions such as this were dangerous: apart from the physical hardships encountered, relations between whites and Indians were frequently poor. On a later expedition, Moreno was seized as a hostage but escaped on a raft which carried him for eight days down the Río Limay to safety.

His fame established, Moreno was elected to congress and was appointed Director of the Museo de Ciencias Naturales in La Plata. In 1901 he became an expert (*perito*) adviser to the Argentine team in the negotiations to draw the frontier with Chile. His reward was a grant of lands near Bariloche, which he handed over to the state to manage, an act which can be seen as the initial step in the creation of the national parks system. Fittingly his remains are buried in a mausoleum on Isla Centinela in Lago Nahuel Huapi.

• **Accommodation A3** pp *Estancia La Oriental*, T 0962-52196, F 0962-52235, 1 km from Lago Belgrano, full board, clean, horseriding, trekking, camping site **D** pp, recommended. **Camping** free, no facilities.

• **Buses** There is no public transport into the park but it may be possible to arrange a lift with *estancia* workers from *Hotel Las Horquetas*.

FROM COMODORO RIVADAVIA TO RIO GALLEGOS

CALETA OLIVIA

(*Population* 28,000; *Phone code* 097), lies on the Bahía San Jorge, 74 km south of Comodoro Rivadavia. Founded in 1901, it became the centre for exporting wool from

the *estancias* of Santa Cruz. Since the discovery of oil in 1944, it has become an important oil town: Pico Truncado, the gas field which feeds the pipeline to Buenos Aires, is some 50 km southwest. On the central roundabout in front of the bus terminal is *El Gorosito*, a huge granite monument of an oil driller with the tools of his trade. Local holiday 20 November (founding of the city).

• **Accommodation B** pp *Robert*, San Martín 2151, T 61452, 3-star; **A3** *Grand*, Mosconi y Chubut, T 61393, 2-star; **B** *Capri*, Hernández 1145, T 61132. Municipal campsite with hot showers near beach, US$3 per person.

• **Banks & money changers** ATM at Banco del Chubut, on San Martín.

• **Buses** To Río Gallegos, Pingüino, US$27, 2230, TAC US$32, 12 hours; to Comodoro Rivadavia, many buses, 1 hour, US$4; to Calafate, 5 hours; to Perito Moreno and Los Antiguos, 5 hours, 2 daily.

Fitz Roy

Km 144, is situated at the junction with Route 43, which runs west via Pico Truncado and Perito Moreno to Lago Buenos Aires and the Chilean frontier at Los Antiguos. Named the captain of Darwin's ship, *Beagle*, Fitzroy is the easiest base for visiting the **Monumento Natural Bosques Petrificados**. Fuel is available.

• **Accommodation B** *Fitzroy*, good, cheap food, camping sometimes possible.

MONUMENTO NATURAL BOSQUES PETRIFICADOS

extending over 10,000 hectares, in a bizarre landscape surrounding the Laguna Grande, contains much older petrified trees than the forests further north around Sarmiento. The trunks, mainly of *araucaria* trees, are up to 35m long and 1.5m in diameter. There is a small visitors' centre and a well documented 1 km nature walk. Open 1000-2000, no charge but donations accepted; please do not remove 'souvenirs'.

• **Camping** Site at *Estancia la Paloma*, 25 km east of the entrance.

• **Access** Two access roads branch off from Route 3 south of Fitzroy: at Km 22 provincial route 93 (dirt) runs southwest for 70 km where it joins the other road, provincial route 49 (*ripio*)

From Comodoro Rivadavia to Río Galleggos

Not to scale

- Comodoro Rivadavia
- 74
- Caleta Olivia
- 70
- Fitzroy
- 10
- To Monumento Nacional Bosques Petrificados — 15
- 62 — 126 — Puerto Deseado
- 178
- Puerto San Julián
- 146
- Luis Piedrabuena
- 9 — 27 — Santa Cruz
- 201
- To Calafate
- Distance in km — Río Gallegos — 129d

which turns off at Km 86 and runs west 48 km to the entrance.

PUERTO DESEADO

(*Population* 7,100; *Phone code* 0967; airport), lies on the northern shore of the estuary of the Río Deseado which drains Lago Buenos Aires. It is reached by Route 281 which branches off Route 3, 10 km south of Fitzroy. Founded in 1884, it is the most important fishing port in Patagonia and a centre for visiting a number of nature reserves along this part of the coast. Outside the former railway station is the **Vagón Histórico**, a carriage now used as the tourist office.

Museums
Museo Regional Patagónico, in the Colegio Salesiano, Colón y Almirante Brown.

Excursions
To the **Reserva Natural Ría Deseado**. The submerged estuary (*ría*) of the Río Deseado, 42 km long, is an important nature reserve. Extending over some 10,000 hectares, it protects a colony of Magellanic penguins, the nesting areas of 4 species of cormorants including the unique red legged cormorant, and breeding grounds of Commerson's dolphin, which, with its black and white pattern, is considered one of the most beautiful in the world.

To the **Gruta de Lourdes**, 24 km west, a huge cave which attracts pilgrims to see the Virgen de Lourdes. Further south along the same road is the **Cañadon del Puerto**, a *mirador* offering fine views over the estuary.

To **Cabo Blanco**, a nature reserve 88 km north, the site of the largest fur seal colony in Patagonia; breeding season December-January. The lighthouse (1916) is one of the oldest along this coast.

To the **Reserva Natural Bahía Laura**, an uninhabited bay 155 km south along *ripio* and dirt roads, where there are black-necked cormorants, ducks and other seabirds.

To **Isla Pinguinos**, an offshore island, where there is a colony of Magallanic penguins, as well as cormorants and steamer ducks.

Local holidays
31 January (San Juan Bosco); 9 October (Coat of Arms day).

A railway carriage with a history

Built in 1898, the *Vagon Histórico*, now operating as a tourist office, has a grimly appropriate name: in 1921 it was the headquarters of Col Hector Benigno Varela, a cavalry officer despatched by Argentine President Hipolito Yrigoyen to end a strike by shepherds in an episode little known outside Patagonia until the publication of Bruce Chatwin's *In Patagonia*.

Although the strike of 1920-1921 began as a protest movement in Río Gallegos led by anarchists, it spread rapidly across the sparsely populated countryside. Living in barracks on *estancias* and employed by owners who, whether British or Argentine, lived elsewhere, the shepherds, mostly Chileans, were badly hit by wage cuts which followed the collapse of world wool prices at the end of the First World War. The isolation of Patagonia made it impossible for *estancia* owners to bring in workers from elsewhere to break the strike. Facing armed groups riding across Patagonia to enforce the strike, the owners appealed for government help.

Under pressure from the army and ultra right-wing groups who used the fact that most of the shepherds were Chileans to claim that the strike was really a Chilean plot to seize the territory, Yrigoyen ordered Varela to pacify Santa Cruz at all costs. Varela seems to have had no qualms about obeying his orders: offering the strikers an amnesty in return for surrender, he had many of them shot. The final showdown came at the *Estancia La Anita*, near Calafate, one of the largest in the province: some 300 men surrendered of whom 120 were shot after being forced to dig a mass-grave.

Local information
● Accommodation
A3 *Los Acantilados*, Pueyrredón y España, T 70167, beautifully located, ACA discount, poor breakfast; **A3** *Colón*, Almirante Brown 450, T 70304; **A3** *Isla Schaffers*, San Martín y Moreno, T 72246, modern, central; *Oneto*, Fernández y Oneto, T 70455; *Res Sur*, Ameghino 1640, T 70522; *Res Alvares*, Pueyrredón 367, T 70053; *Hosp Los Olmos*, Gob Gregores 849, T 70077; *Albergue Municipal*, Colón y Belgrano, T 70260, dormitory style.

Estancia *La Madrugada*, accommodation, excursions to sea lion colony and cormorant nesting area, English spoken, highly recommended, T 34963 or in Puerto Deseado: Almirante Zar 570, T 70204, F 72298.

Camping Municipal site, Avenida Costanera, dirty.

● Places to eat
El Viejo Marino, Pueyrredón 224, considered best by locals; *La Casa de Don Ernesto*, San Martín 1245, seafood and *parrilla*; *El Pinguino*, Piedrabuena 958, *parrilla*.

● Tour companies & travel agents
Gipsy Tours, T 72155, F 72142, run by Ricardo Pérez, excursions by boat to Río Deseado reserve, 2 hours, US$25.

● Tourist office
San Martín y Almirante Brown, in the *vagón histórico*, T 70220.

PUERTO SAN JULIAN

(*Population* 5,300; *Phone code* 0962), lies on Bahía San Julian 268 km south of Fitzroy and is the best place for breaking the 834 km run from Comodoro Rivadavia to Río Gallegos. Founded in 1901 on a peninsula overlooking a fine natural harbour, the town grew up to serve the sheep *estancias* of this part of Santa Cruz: north of town the ruins of the *Frigorífico Swift*, a meat-packing plant opened in 1910, can be seen. Today it is an important fishing port. Clay grinding can be seen at Molienda Santa Cruz and ceramics are made at the Escuela de Cerámica. There is a good handicraft centre at Moreno y San Martín. Just north of the town is Punta Caldera, a popular summer beach. The first mass in Argentina was held here after Magellan had executed a member of his crew. Francis Drake also put in here to behead Thomas Doughty, after amiably dining with him.

Museums
Museo Regional, at the southern end of San Martín, mainly archaeology.

Museo de Arte Marino, 9 de Julio y Mitre, Monday-Friday 0900-1400, local paintings.

Excursions
To the **Reserva San Julian**, on the shores of Bahía San Julian. Covering 10,400 hectares, this reserve includes the islands, Banco Cormorán and Banco Justicia, where there is a colony of Magallanic penguins and where there are nesting areas for these species of cormorants and other birds. Boat hire US$10.

To **Cabo Curiosa**, 15 km north, where there are fine beaches.

To the ruins of **Florida Blanca**, a colony 10 km west, founded in 1870 by Antonio Viedma.

To the **Estancia La María**, 150 km west, which offers transport, accommodation meals and trekking. The estancia covers one of the main archaeological areas of Patagonia, including a huge canyon with 25 caves with paintings of human hands, guanacos etc 4,000-12,000 years old, less visited than the Cueva de las Manos. Contact Fernando Behm, Saavedra 1168, T 2328, F 2269.

Local information
● Accommodation
A3 *Municipal*, 25 de Mayo 917, T 2300/1, very nice, well-run, good value, no restaurant; **A3** *Bahía*, San Martín 1075, T 3144, modern, comfortable, good value, recommended; **A3** *Res Sada*, San Martín 1112, T 2013, good rooms, poor breakfast, on busy main road. **B** *Colón*, San Martín 301, older. **C** *Aguila*, San Martín 500 block, sleazy, cheapest in town.

Camping Good municipal site on the waterfront at Avenida Costanera entre Rivadavia y Roca, US$5 per site plus US$3 per person, repeatedly recommended, all facilities.

● Places to eat
Sportsman, Mitre y 25 de Mayo, excellent value; *Rural*, Ameghino y Vieytes, good, but not before 2100; a number of others. Also bars and tearooms.

● Banks & money changers
Banco de la Nación, Mitre y Belgrano, and Banco de la Provincia de Santa Cruz, San Martín y Moreno.

● **Post & telecommunications**
Post Office: Belgrano y San Martín.

● **Hospitals & medical services**
Hospital: Avenida Costanera entre Roca y Magallanes.

Pharmacy: *Del Pueblo* on San Martín 570.

● **Tourist offices**
San Martín 581, T 2871.

● **Transport**
Air Weekly services (Monday) with LADE to Santa Cruz, Río Gallegos, Puerto Deseado, Gob Gregores, Comodoro Rivadavia, Calafate/Lago Argentino and Río Turbio.

Buses To **Buenos Aires**, Transportadora Patagónica, Pingüino; to **Río Gallegos**, Pingüino, 6 hours, US$14; Transportes Staller goes weekly (Saturday) to **Lago Posadas** stopping in Gobernador Gregores, *Hotel Las Horquetas*, Bajo Caracoles and Río Blanco.

Hitching Walk 5 km to petrol station on Ruta 3.

ROUTES Route 521 (*ripio*) runs inland northwest from San Julián to Route 40. The

only settlement along this road is **Gobernador Gregores** (see above) 215 km west of San Julián.

PIEDRABUENA

(*Population* 3,300; *Phone code* 0962), 146 km south of San Julián, lies on the Río Santa Cruz which drains Lago Argentino and is one of the most important rivers in Patagonia. Known officially as Comandante Luís Piedrabuena, the town is named after the first Argentine citizen to settle in Patagonia (1859), who lived on Isla Pavón, an island in the river; a small museum marks the spot and there is a campsite.

Excursions To **Santa Cruz** (*population* 3,000; airport), 36 km east on the estuary of the Río Santa Cruz. Founded in 1878, Santa Cruz was capital of Santa Cruz province until 1904. There is a small museum,

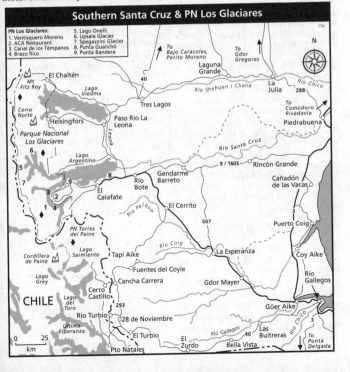

Southern Santa Cruz & PN Los Glaciares

PN Los Glaciares:
1. Ventisquero Moreno
2. ACA Restaurant
3. Canal de los Témpanos
4. Brazo Rico
5. Lago Onelli
6. Upsala Glacier
7. Spegazzini Glacier
8. Punta Gualichó
9. Punta Bandera

the **Museo Regional de História** at Avenida Piedrabuena y Moreno. Southeast of town, near the mouth of the Río Santa Cruz is **Punta Quilla**, a major deep water port.

To **Monte León**, a provincial nature reserve 56 km south of Piedrabuena, which includes the Isla Monte León, an important breeding area for cormorants and terns, where there is also a penguin colony and sea lions. There are impressive rock formations and wide isolated beaches at low tide. It is reached by a 22 km dirt road which branches off Route 3 36 km south of Piedrabuena.

● **Accommodation At Piedrabuena:** **A3** *ACA Motel*, T 7145, simple, functional but good, warm and nice food; **A3** *Hostería El Alamo*, Lavalle 08, T 7249, quiet, breakfast extra, recommended; *Andalucia*, Belgrano 170, restaurant (good pasta); **C** *Res Internacional*, Ibáñez 99, T 7197, recommended; **C** pp *Hotel Vani*. **Camping** Sites north of town on Route 3; also on Isla Pavón. **At Santa Cruz:** **A3** *Hostal de la Ría*, 25 de Mayo 645, T 8038; *Hostería Turística*; *Anel Aike*, both **C**; *Posada de Pinky*, Balestra y 25 de Mayo. **Camping** free muncipal site.

ROUTES Inland Provincial Route 9 (1603 on some maps, unpaved, no petrol) branches off Route 3 43 km south of Piedrabuena and runs west to Calafate along the edge of a plateau with occasional panoramic views across the valley of the Río Santa Cruz below. Then at about Km 170 it drops down into the valley itself to follow the river into the hills and to Lago Argentino. Route 288 runs direct from Piedrabuena to Tres Lagos on Route 40, thence west and south to Lagos Viedma and Argentino. Most traffic to El Calafate goes via Río Gallegos.

RIO GALLEGOS

(*Population* 75,000; *Altitude* 16m; *Phone code* 0966), 235 km south of Piedrabuena, lies on the estuary of the Río Gallegos, 18 km from its mouth. Founded in 1885, it is capital of Santa Cruz province and has a large military base. It grew rapidly after 1945 as the port for transporting coal from the mines of El Turbio and as a centre for trade in wool and meat from the *estancias* of the province. There is a deep-water port

at Punta Loyola at the mouth of the estuary. It is drab, but has a good shopping centre on the main street, Avenida Roca. The small Plaza San Martín, 1 block from the post office is well tended, with flower beds and statues; outside the post office is a balcony, preserved from a demolished house, commemorating the meeting of Presidents Errázuriz and Roca to end Chile and Argentina's 1883 Magellan Strait dispute.

Museums
Museo Provincial Mario Echevarría Baleta, Ramón y Cajal 51, has collections of local history, flora, fauna, rock samples (open 0800-1900, weekends 1500-2000); **Museo de los Pioneros**, Alberdi y Elcano in the former house of a Arthur Fenton, a British physician who was one of the early pioneers, free, open 1300-2000. **Museo de la Ciudad**, Avenida Los Immigrantes, open air display of agricultural and railway machinery.

Excursions
To **Laguna Azul**, 62 km south near the Monte Aymond frontier crossing, a lagoon in the crater of an extinct volcano, reached by Route 3.

To **Cabo Vírgenes**, 134 km south, where there is a provincial nature reserve protecting the second largest colony of

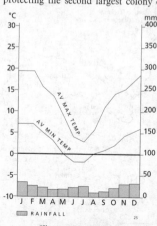

Climate: Río Gallegos

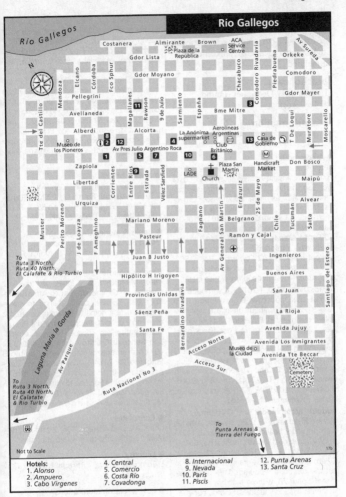

Río Gallegos

Hotels:

1. Alonso	4. Central	8. Internacional	12. Punta Arenas
2. Ampuero	5. Comercio	9. Nevada	13. Santa Cruz
3. Cabo Vírgenes	6. Costa Río	10. Paris	
	7. Covadonga	11. Piscis	

Magellanic penguins in Patagonia, entry US$3. The Navy allows visitors to climb up Cabo Vírgenes lighthouse for a superb view. Branch off Route 3 onto Route 1 (unpaved), 15 km south of Río Gallegos, from where it is 119 km. You can hitch from this junction with oil workers going to the lighthouse at the cape. Take a taxi to be at the turn off by 0700. Take drinking water. It is possible to arrange return with

day trippers from Río Gallegos, or ask at the lighthouse or naval station. South of Cabo Vírgenes are the ruins of *Nombre de Jesús*, one of the two settlements founded by Pedro Sarmiento de Gamboa in 1584; the other was south of Punta Arenas in Chile (see under **Chilean Patagonia**).

To several **estancias** including **Hill Station**, 63 km north of Río Gallegos and **Monte Dinero**, T 0966-26900, 13 km north of Cabo Virgenes, where the Fenton family offers accommodation **L3** pp, food and excursions to penguins, horseriding, English spoken, expensive, excellent, recommended.

Local holidays

31 January; 19 December (Foundation of Río Gallegos).

Local information

NB Do not confuse the street Comodoro Rivadavia with (nearby) Bernardino Rivadavia.

● **Accommodation**

Accommodation is hard to find because of the number of transient workers in town. **A1** *Costa Río*, San Martín 673, new, comfortable, discounts for ACA members; **A3** *Alonso*, Corrientes 33, T 22414, F 21237, without breakfast, good beds; **A3** *Santa Cruz*, Roca 701, T 20601, with heating, good coffee bar, breakfast; **A3** *Punta Arenas*, Sphur 55, T 22742, in new wing, very comfortable, also **B** in old wing, without breakfast; **A2** *Comercio*, Roca 1302, T/F 22172, with breakfast, good beds, comfortable, restaurant with good fixed-price menu.

B *París*, Roca 1040, T 20111, **C** without bath, old fashioned, poor beds; **B** *Covadonga*, Roca 1214, T 20190, without breakfast, comfortable, recommended; **B** *Nevada*, Zapiola y Entre Ríos, T 25990, English spoken, good beds, parking; **D** pp *Piscis* (no sign), Avellaneda y Magallanes, T/F 20329, owned by army officers' club, without breakfast, good beds, excellent value, recommended; **B** *Cabo Virgenes*, Comodoro Rivadavia 252, T 22141, recommended; **B** *Oviedo*, Libertad 746, T 20118, comfortable, kitchen facilities, recommended.

Budget accommodation: **C** *Colonial*, Urquiza y Rivadavia, T 22329, cheaper without bath, hot water, heating; **C** *Central*, Roca 1127, central, quiet, cold shower, no heating; **C** *Ampuero*, Sphur 18, T 22189, poor beds, smelly; **C** *Pensión Belgrano*, Belgrano 123, dirty, basic but friendly, good restaurant; **D** *Res Internacional*, Sphur 78, without bath, with heating, kitchen and laundry facilities, helpful, but insecure; **D** pp *Res Betty*, Alberdi 458, meals, recommended. **Private house**: Barrio Codepro II, Casa 71, T 23789, **E** pp, recommended.

Camping *Camping ATSA* Route 3, behind YPF station and west of bus terminal, US$3 per person plus US$1 for tent. Also try the YPF service station. Another site at Guer Aike, 30 km away.

● **Places to eat**

Plenty and good, some specializing in seafood. Evening meals are hard to find before 2000.

Restaurant Díaz, Roca 1173, cheap; *Bifería La Vasca*, Roca 1084, snack bar, good value, young crowd, rock music, open till 0300; *El Horneo*, bar of *Club Español*, Roca 862, good meals, cosy, reasonably priced; *Jardín*, Roca 1315, good, cheap, popular; *Club Británico*, Roca 935, good, reasonably priced; *El Palenque*, Corrientes 73, *parrilla*, recommended; *Sociedad Italiana*, Magallanes 69, good; *Café Carrera*, Fagnano y Roca, good but expensive breakfast; *Cosa Nostra*, 9 de Julio 230, fresh pasta, good, reasonably priced; *El Herreo*, Roca 1450, good; *Monaco*, Roca y San Martín, good café; *Le Croissant*, Zapiola y Estrada, good bakery.

● **Airline offices**

Aerolíneas Argentinas, San Martín 545, T 20181; **Austral**, Roca 917, T 22038; **Dinar**, San Martín 695; **LADE**, Fagnano 53, T 22316; **Lapa**, Estrada 71, T 28382; **TAN**, T 25259.

● **Banks & money changers**

Lloyds Bank, Sarmiento 47, open 1000-1600, cash advance on Visa and Mastercard, high commission. Many banks on Roca including **Banco de Santa Cruz**, Roca y Errázuriz, fair rates, Mastercard, best rates for travellers' cheques, no commission. **Banco Almafuerte**, Roca 990, changes cash. Change travellers' cheques here if going to Calafate, where it is even more difficult. **Banco Tierra del Fuego**, changes travellers' cheques without commission; **Banco de Crédito Argentino**, Roca 936, quick cash advance on Visa upstairs. **Cambio El Pingüino**, Zapiola 469, may also change European and South American currencies, 7% commission; **Cambio Sur**, San Martín y Roca, often has good rates. ATMs at *La Caja*, Roca y San Martín, and at *La Anónima* supermarket.

● **Consulates**

Chile, Mariano Moreno 136, Monday-Friday, 0900-1300; tourist cards issued at border.

● **Laundry**

El Tumbaíto Alberdi y Rawson; *Laverap*, Corrientes 277.

● **Post & telecommunications**

Post Office: Roca 893, *poste restante* service unreliable, and at the airport.

Telephones: Roca 613.

● **Shopping**

Artesanías Koekén, San Martín 336, leatherwork, woollen goods, local produce; *Artesanías Santacruceñas*, Roca 658; *Tia* department store, Roca 740, good supermarket section; **Supermarket** *La Anónima*, Roca y España. Most places take a 2-3-hour lunch break.

● **Sports**
Fishing: the southern fishing zone including the Ríos Gallegos, Grande, Fuego, Ewan, San Pablo and Lago Fagnano, near Ushuaia. It is famous for runs of sea trout. See **Fishing** in **Where to go**, page 18.

● **Tour companies & travel agents**
Interlagos, *Pingüino* and *Quebek* at bus terminal and airport offer tours to Calafate and Perito Moreno glacier, US$70, without accommodation.

● **Tourist offices**
Provincial office, Roca 1551, Monday-Friday, 0900-2000, Saturday/Sunday (summer only) 1000-2000, helpful, English spoken, has list of *estancias*. They will phone round hotels for you. Municipal office in former carriage, Roca y San Martín, Monday-Friday 1000-1800, Saturday/Sunday (summer only) 1000-1300, 1700-2000. Also at airport 0830-1830 daily and bus terminal.

● **Transport**
Local Car rental: Localiza, Sarmiento 237, T 24417; **Eduardo Riestra**, San Martín 1508, T 21321. Essential to book rental in advance in season. **Car parts and repairs**: *Turbisur*, Corrientes 177, cheapest; *Repuestos Sarmiento*, on Sarmiento, owner very friendly and helpful. **Motorcycle mechanic**: Juan Carlos Topcic, Costa Rica 25, friendly and helpful. **Taxis**: Radio taxi, V Sarsfield y Roca, T 22369. Hiring a taxi for group excursions may be no more expensive than taking a tour bus. *A1*, Entre Ríos 350, T 22453, for taxis and car rental, not cheap.

Air Airport 6 km west of town. Bus No 1 to Barrio Consejo Agraria takes you most of the way there. Taxi (*remise*) to/from town US$6; hitching from car park is easy. You can spend the night at the airport prior to early morning flights. In summer make your bookings in advance. Aerolíneas Argentinas's Buenos Aires-Auckland-Sydney flight (twice a week) stops at Río Gallegos, but the return journey does not. To/from **Buenos Aires**: Aerolíneas Argentinas (direct or via Trelew), Austral (via Bahía Blanca and Comodoro Rivadavia), Lapa (via Trelew or Comodoro Rivadavia), Dinar (via Comodoro Rivadavia). Several flights to **Ushuaia** and **Río Grande**, direct (Aerolíneas Argentinas, always booked, but standby seats available), Austral, Kaiken or Lapa. Kaiken also to **Comodoro Rivadavia**, **Calafate**, **Punta Arenas** and many southern Argentine destinations. LADE to **Río Turbio** and Calafate, twice a week, to Ushuaia and **Comodoro Rivadavia** once a week.
  NB Flights may leave early, sometimes up to 40 minutes. LADE flights should be booked as far in advance as possible.

Both Pingüino and Interlagos can arrange packages to Calafate including accommodation and trip to Moreno glacier from their offices at the airport.

Buses Terminal at corner of Route 3 and Avenida Parque, 3 km from centre (crowded, no left luggage, *confitería*, few toilets, kiosks); taxi to centre US$3, bus US$1 (Nos 1 and 12 from posted stops on Roca).
  To **Calafate** via airport, 4-5 hours, US$20-25, Pingüino and Quebek, sometimes with double-deckers offering great views, very crowded in season; turn up with ticket 30 minutes before departure: in winter both companies operate 3 times a week; Pingüino offers 2-night excursion to Calafate, sold at airport only, US$93 in single room, credit cards accepted.
  Pingüino daily at 2100 to **Caleta Olivia**, US$30, 11 hours. To **Trelew** and **Puerto Madryn** daily (18 hours), US$55. To **Comodoro Rivadavia**, Pingüino, Don Otto and TAC, 10 hours, US$30. For **Bariloche**, take this bus to Comodoro Rivadavia, then the 2150 Don Otto bus to Bariloche (fare to Bariloche US$88). Andesmar to **Mendoza**, leaves Friday 1300, arrives 0900 Sunday, via Comodoro Rivadavia, Puerto Madryn and Neuquén.
  To **Buenos Aires**, 36 hours, Pingüino, Don Otto, TAC, US$70-100. To **Río Turbio**, 4 hours Pingüino, US$14 (hitching practically impossible); also Ezquerra, US$19. No buses to/from Río Grande. To **El Chaltén**, Burmeister (San Martín 470, T 20293) Monday, Wednesday, Friday 1500, US$40.

To Chile By Bus: to **Puerto Natales**, Pingüino, Tuesday-Saturday, 7½ hours, US$18. To **Punta Arenas**, Pingüino, US$20 daily. **By car**: make sure your car papers are in order (go first to Tourist Office for necessary documents, then to the customs office at the port, at the end of San Martín, very uncomplicated).

Hitchhiking To Buenos Aires is possible in about 5-7 days; appearance important; hitching to Tierra del Fuego possible from service station on Ruta 3 at edge of town, trucks stop here for customs check, be there before 0700. To Calafate, from police control outside town.

ROUTES Argentina's longest road, Route 40, ends at Río Gallegos, or, more precisely, Punta Loyola; it runs from Bolivia for over 4,667 km. Its last section has been rerouted south of Lago Argentino to follow the Chilean border and go through Río Turbio. The original route, via La Esperanza, forms the main part of the Río Gallegos-El Calafate route (see below). This road (323 km, all paved) is worth while for the number of animals and birds which can be seen; however, it is flat and subject to strong winds.

FRONTIER CROSSING: MONTE AYMOND

This crossing, 68 km south of Río Gallegos and reached by Route 3, provides the only direct route from Río Gallegos to Tierra del Fuego. For bus passengers the border crossing is very easy; similarly for car drivers if papers are in order. On the Chilean side the road continues to Punta Delgada, Km 30, and Kimiri Aike, where a road turns off for the crossing to Tierra del Fuego via the Primera Angostura (see under **Tierra del Fuego**).

CALAFATE AND THE PARQUE NACIONAL LOS GLACIARES

EL CALAFATE

(*Population* 3,000; *Altitude* 225m; *Phone code* 0902) 312 km northwest of Río Gallegos, this little town is situated on the southern shore of Lago Argentino, one of the largest lakes in the country. Founded in 1927, it is a modern town which has grown rapidly as a tourist centre for the **Parque Nacional los Glaciares**, which is 50 km further west.

Places of interest

From the Centro Cívico, visit Capilla Santa Teresita in Plaza San Martín. Walk to the top of the hill for the views of the silhouette of the southern end of the Andes, Bahía Redonda and Isla Solitaria on Lago Argentino. Just west of the town centre is Bahía Redonda, a shallow part of the lake, in winter when it freezes, ice-skating and skiing are possible. At the eastern edge of Bahía Redonda is **Laguna Nimes**, a bird reserve where there are flamingos, black necked swans and ducks, recommended. There is scope for good hill-walking to the south of the town, while Cerro Elefante, west of Calafate on the road to the Moreno glacier, is good for rock climbing.

Excursions

For excursions to the Moreno glacier, Upsala Glacier and Fitz Roy, see below. Travel by road to the most interesting spots is limited and may require expensive taxis. Tours can be arranged at travel agencies, or with taxi drivers at the airport who await arrivals.

To **Punta Gualichó**, on the shores of Lago Argentino 15 km east of town, where there are painted caves (badly deteriorated), several agencies run tours, 2 hours, US$16); 12 km east of Calafate on the edge of the lake there are fascinating geological formations caused by erosion.

To **El Galpón**, 21 km west, an *estancia* offering evening visits (from 1730) which feature walks through a bird sanctuary

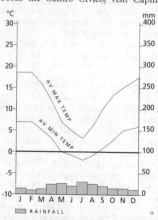

Climate: Calafate

The Calafate

(*Berberis buxifolia*). Whoever eats the fruits of the Calafate will return to Patagonia or so the story goes: whether they do or not, they are likely to have purple stained lips and fingers! This spiny, shiny leaved, hardy shrub grows to 2m in height and has single bright yellow/orange flowers dotted along its arching branches in Spring. The deep purple grape-like edible berries are also found singly or in pairs. Also known as the Magellan barberry, its wood is used for making red dye.

Jane Norwich

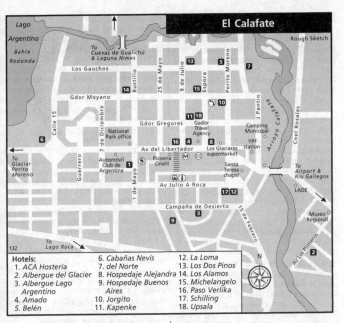

El Calafate

Rough Sketch

Hotels:
1. ACA Hostería
2. Albergue del Glacier
3. Albergue Lago Argentino
4. Amado
5. Belén
6. Cabañas Nevis
7. del Norte
8. Hospedaje Alejandra
9. Hospedaje Buenos Aires
10. Jorgito
11. Kapenke
12. La Loma
13. Los Dos Pinos
14. Los Alamos
15. Michelangelo
16. Paso Verlika
17. Schilling
18. Upsala

where 43 species of birds have been identified, displays of sheep shearing and a barbecue as well as horseriding (visits at other times on request), transport arranged, English spoken; in Calafate T/F 91793; Buenos Aires, Paseo Colón 221, 7th floor, T 343-8185, F 334-2669.

To **Lago Roca**, 40 km south, where there is trout and salmon fishing, climbing, walking, and branding of cattle in summer. Good camping in wooded area, restaurant.

Local festivals

People flock to the rural show on 15 February (Lago Argentino Day) and camp out with much revelry; dances and *asados*. There are also barbecues and rodeo etc on Día de la Tradición, 10 November.

Local information

Calafate is very popular in January-February, when booking all transport in advance is recommended and accommodation can be difficult to find. Many hotels are open only from October to April/May. Credit cards are not popular, apart from hotels, and high commissions are charged.

● **Accommodation**

L2 *Los Alamos*, Moyano y Bustillo, T 91144, F 91186, best, comfortable, very good food and service, extensive gardens, recommended; **L3** *Frai Toluca*, Calle 6 No 1016, T/F 91773/91593 (Buenos Aires T/F 523-3232) good views, comfortable, restaurant; **L3** *Hostería Kau-Yatún*, 25 de Mayo (10 blocks from town centre), T 91059, F 91260, many facilities, old *estancia* house, comfortable, restaurant and barbecues, horse-riding tours with guides; **L3** *El Mirador del Lago*, Libertador 2047, T/F 91213, good accommodation, acceptable restaurant (wines not recommended), better not to take half-board.

A1 *Kalken*, V Feilberg 119, T 91073, F 91036, with breakfast, spacious; **A2** *Michelangelo*, Espora y Gob Moyano, T 91045, F 91058, with breakfast, modern, reasonable, good restaurant, accepts travellers' cheques (poor rates); **A2** *El Quijote*, Gob Gregores 1191, T 91017, F 91103, recommended; **A3** *ACA Hostería El Calafate*, 1° de Mayo, T 91004, F 91027, modern, good view, open all year; **A3** *Hostería Schilling*, Paradelo 141, T 91453, with breakfast, nice rooms, poor beds; **A2-3** *La Loma*, Roca 849, T 91016 (Buenos Aires: Callao 433, 8a 'P', T/F 371-9123), with breakfast, modern (poor beds) highly recommended, multilingual, restaurant, tea room, spacious rooms, attractive gardens, also cheaper rooms, **D** pp, without bath.

B *Amado*, Libertador 1072, T 91134, without breakfast, restaurant, good; **B** *Upsala*, Espora 139, T 91166 F91075, with breakfast, good beds, recommended; **B** *Cabañas Del Sol*, Libertador 1956, T 91439 (**D** in low season), good meals, highly recommended; **B** *Hosp del Norte*, Los Gauchos 813, T 91117, open all year, kitchen facilities, comfortable, owner organizes tours, highly recommended; **B** *Paso Verlika*, Libertador 1108, T 91009, F 91279, with breakfast; **B** *Kapenke*, 9 de Julio 112, T 91093, includes breakfast, good beds, recommended; **B** *Las Cabañitas*, V Feilberg 218, T 91118, cabins, hot water, kitchen and laundry facilities, helpful, recommended; **B** *Los Lagos*, 25 de Mayo 220, T 91170, very comfortable, good value, recommended; **B** *Hosp Cerro Cristal*, Gob Gregores 989, T 91088, helpful, recommended; **C** pp *Cabañas Nevis*, about 1 km from town towards glacier, Libertador 1696, T 91180, for 4 or 8, lake view, full board good value.

Budget accommodation: **D** pp *Albergue & Hostal del Glaciar*, Los Pioneros, 200m off Avenida Libertador, T/F 91243 (reservations in Buenos Aires T 448-69416 off season only), discount for ISIC or IYHA members, open 1 October-31 March, good kitchen facilities and lounge, English German and Italian spoken, also rooms with bath (**B**) and sleeping bag space (**E** pp), restaurant with good value fixed menu, repeatedly recommended, tour agency Patagonia Backpackers, runs tours to Moreno glacier (US$32, repeatedly recommended) and elsewhere, free shuttle service from bus terminal, *poste restante*; **E** pp *Lago Azul*, Perito Moreno 83, T 91419, only 2 double rooms, highly recommended; **C** *Hosp Belén*, Los Gauchos 300 y Perito Moreno, T 91028, warm, hot water, cooking facilities, family welcome, highly recommended; **E** pp *Hosp Jorgito*, Gob Moyano 943, T 91323, without bath, basic, cooking facilities, heating, breakfast extra, often full, also camping, recommended; **E** pp *Hosp Los Dos Pinos*, 9 de Julio 358, T 91271, dormitory accommodation, cooking and laundry facilities, also cabins **C**, and camping **F** pp, arranges tours to glacier, popular; **E** pp *Hosp Buenos Aires*, Buenos Aires 296, 200m from terminal, T 91147, kitchen facilities, helpful, good hot showers, luggage store; **E** pp *Hosp Alejandra*, Espora 60, T 91328, without bath, good value, recommended; and airport, Navimag agents, book in advance in summer. **E** pp *Albergue Lago Argentino*, Campaña del Desierto 1050, T 91423, near bus terminal, dormitory accommodation, limited bathrooms, kitchen facilities, English spoken, helpful. Some private houses

offer accommodation: these include Enrique Barragán, Barrio Bahía Redonda, Casa 10, T 91325, **E**, recommended; **F** pp *Apartamentos Lago Viedma*, Paralelo 158, T 91159, F 91158, hostel, 4 bunks to a room, cooking facilities. **F** pp *La Cueva de Jorge Lemos*, Gob Moyano 839, behind YPF station, bunk beds, bathroom, showers, kitchen facilities, popular and cheap. If in difficulty, ask at tourist office from which caravans, tents (sleep 4) and 4-berth *cabañas* may be hired, showers extra.

In the Parque Nacional los Glaciares: 40 km west of Calafate on the road to the Moreno glacier: **L3** *Los Notros*, T/F 91437, half-board, spacious, rooms with glacier views, recommended (in Buenos Aires: Talcahuano 1457, 7th floor, T 825-4243, F 815-7645). In the far south of the park on the shores of Brazo Sur: **A3** pp *Estancia Nibepo Aike*, T/F 0966-20180, horseriding, expeditions, fishing, boat tours to glacier, recommended. On the southern shore of Lago Viedma: **L3** pp *Estancia Helsingfors*, T/F 0966-20719 (San Martín 516, Río Gallegos, or Buenos Aires T/F 824-6623/3634), with breakfast, all other meals available, many treks, boat trips and flights over glaciers available, also riding, sheep-shearing, recommended; **E** pp *La Leona*, T 91418, 106 km north of Calafate near east end of Lago Viedma, without bath, camping. For accommodation in El Chaltén in the northern part of the park see below.

Camping Municipal campsite behind YPF service station, T 91344/91440, reservations off season 91829 US$4 per person, hot water, security, parillada, open 1 October-30 April. Three campsites in the Park en route to the glacier: *Río Mitre*, near the park entrance, 52 km from Calafate, 26 km east of the glacier, US$3 per person; *Bahía Escondida*, 7 km east of the glacier, toilets and hot showers, free but no water; site at Arroyo Correntoso, 10 km east of the glacier, no facilities but nice location and lots of firewood. Take food to all three. Another campsite is *Camping Río Bote*, 35 km, on road to Río Gallegos.

● **Places to eat**
Excellent restaurant at *Hotel Los Alamos*; *Pizzería Onelli*, Libertador 1197, reasonable, stays open out of season; *Pizzería Casablanca*, Libertador 25 de Mayo, good breakfasts; *Michelangelo*, Espora y Gob Moyano, very expensive but magnificent steaks, recommended; *Paso Verlika*, Libertador 1108, small, 2 courses with wine US$16, credit cards 10% extra, good value; *Don Raul*, Libertador 1472, cosy, *tenedor libre*; *Mi Viejo*, Libertador 1111, *parrilla*; *El Rancho*, 9 de Julio y Gob Moyano, large, cheap and good pizzas, popular, free video shows of the glacier, highly recommended; *La Loma* (address

above), friendly, home food. Tea rooms: *Maktub*, Libertador 905, excellent pastries, pricey; *Bar Don Diego de la Noche*, Libertador 1603, lamb and seafood, live music, good atmosphere.

● **Airline office**
Sur Turismo, 25 de Mayo 23, T 91266/91854, Kaiken agents.

● **Banks & money changers**
Take cash as there are no *Casas de Cambio*, and high commission is charged on travellers' cheques. **Banco de la Provincia de Santa Cruz**, Libertador, ATM, 3% commission on travellers' cheques, 20%! commission on Visa and Mastercard advances. Travel agencies such as Interlagos change notes; **YPF garage** and **Chocolate El Calafate** and some other shops give good rates for cash; *Albergue del Glaciar*, 5% commission on travellers' cheques; **El Pingüino** bus company, 6% commission; the **Scorpio** snack bar on Libertador is reported to give best rates; try also Dos Glaciares supermarket.

● **Laundry**
El Lavadero, Libertador 1474, US$8 a load.

● **Post & telecommunications**
Post Office: on Libertador; postal rates much lower from Puerto Natales (Chile) and delivery times much quicker.

Telephones: run by Cooperativa Telefónica de Calafate, office on Espora, 0700-0100. Fax US$6.50 per page, cheaper from Puerto Natales. All services expensive, collect call impossible.

● **Shopping**
Los Glaciares Supermarket, Libertador y Perito Moreno, accepts US$ cash and Visa. There is a *ferretería* selling white gas by the litre for camping (this is the only place for white gas). Wider selection of food for camping here than in Puerto Natales.

● **Tour companies & travel agents**
Many agencies, most of them along Libertador, including *Interlagos*, No 1175, T 91179, F 91241; *Los Glaciares*, No 920, T 91158, F 91159, recommended, good value; *Hielo y Aventura*, No 935, T 91053; *Upland Goose*, Roca 1004, Local 2, T 91446, recommended; *El Pingüino*, in terminal, T 91273; *Aventrek*, Gob Moyano 839, Aptdo Postal Esp No 7 (9405), El Calafate, Telex Cab pública 86905, run by Jorge Lemos, recommended. Several hotels also organize tours by minibus including *Hosp del Norte* and *Albergue del Glaciar*. Most agencies charge the same rates for excursions: to the Moreno Glacier US$25 for a trip leaving 0830, returning 1800, without lunch, 3 hours at glacier; to Lago Roca, at 0930 return 1700, US$25; to Cerro Fitz Roy, at 0600 return 1900, US$50, Gualichó caves, 2 hours, US$16 (see **Excursions**, above). Several

agencies offer walking excursions on the Perito Moreno glacier, usually finishing with champagne or whisky with ice chipped from the glacier; these include *Hielo y Aventura*, 1½ hours, US$65 January-February and Holy Week, US$50 other times between 15 October and March 15, plus US$15 for transport to the glacier, book ahead. Mountain bikes can be hired from Sr Daniel Alvarez, also recommended as source of information, at the Mercado Artesanal on Libertador.

● **Tourist offices**
Tourist office in bus terminal. Hotel prices detailed on large chart at tourist office; has a list of taxis but undertakes no arrangements. Helpful staff. October-April 0700-2200 daily. For information on the Parque Nacional los Glaciares, park office at Libertador 1302, T 91005, Monday-Friday 0800-1500.

● **Transport**
Air Lago Argentino airport, 1 km east of town, with an all-weather runway (though flights may be suspended in severe weather). Kaiken from Río Gallegos, Río Grande, Ushuaia, Bariloche, Esquel, Trelew, Comodoro Rivadavia, Mendoza and Neuquén; LADE twice a week to Río Turbio, US$20, 3 a week in summer to connect with buses to Puerto Natales and Torres del Paine. LADE once a week to Perito Moreno (Thursday high season, Friday low season, US$42; LADE also to Río Gallegos and Comodoro Rivadavia. Air fares can be cheaper than buses.

Buses Terminal on Roca, 1 block from Libertador. Journey to **Ushuaia** requires four changes, and ferry, total cost US$43. To **Río Gallegos**, Interlagos Turismo daily at 0800 (summer) or 0915 Tuesday, Thursday, Saturday (winter); also Quebek (0900) and El Pingüino daily at 0600 and 1630 (Wednesday, Friday, Saturday, in winter) 4½ hours, US$20-25, all via Río Gallegos airport. Passengers on this bus wishing to go to Chile get off at Güer Aike to catch Pingüino's Gallegos-Río Turbio bus 50 minutes later, arriving at 1700. To **Río Turbio**, Cootra daily, Pingüino 4 times a week, 7 hours, US$27, Quebek, 2 a day, US$24, 4 hours. To **Puerto Madryn**, Quebek US$48, 18 hours. Taxi to Río Gallegos, 4 hours, US$200 irrespective of number of passengers, up to 5 people.

Direct services to Chile: COOTRA to **Puerto Natales** via Río Turbio, several times a week, US$25, 7 hours (recommended to book in advance). Travel agencies including *Albergue del Glaciar* run regular services in summer, on demand in winter, up to US$60, 5 hours. These connect at Cerro Castillo with buses from Puerto Natales to Torres del Paine (**NB** Argentine pesos cannot be exchanged in Torres del Paine.)

PARQUE NACIONAL LOS GLACIARES

This park, the second-largest in Argentina, extends along the Chilean frontier for over 170 km and covers more than 660,000 hectares. Some 40% of the park is covered by the *hielos continentales*, giant ice fields which straddle the frontier. Of the 47 major glaciers which flow from the icefields, 13 run east descending into the park to feed two great lakes: Lago Argentino and, further north, Lago Viedma, both of which are heavily silted by glacial deposits. The Río La Leona, flowing south from Lago Viedma, links the two lakes. There are also about 190 smaller glaciers not connected to the ice fields.

East of the ice fields are areas of southern beech forest, especially *lenga*, ñire and *guindo* (evergreen beech). Further east are areas of Patagonian steppe, with shrub vegetation including the *notro* (firebush) and the *calafate*. Among over 100 bird species are the patagonian woodpecker, the austral parakeet, the green-backed firecrown as well as black-necked swans, Andean ruddy ducks and torrent ducks. Guanacos, grey foxes, skunks and rheas can be seen on the steppe while the rare *huemul* inhabits the forest.

Climate

Generally cold, depending on altitude and season. Rainfall ranges from 2,000 mm in the far west to 400 mm in the east, falling mainly between March and late May. The best time to visit is between October and March. Many facilities are closed off-season. Lighting fires is prohibited throughout the park.

Two sectors of the park are popular with travellers: the southern area around Lago Argentino and the northern area around Mount Fitz Roy. Access to the central sector, north of Lago Argentino and south of Lago Viedma, is difficult and there are few tourist facilities though *estancias* such as *Helsingfors* and *La Cristina* offer accommodation and excursions.

LAGO ARGENTINO

The source of the Río Santa Cruz, one of the most important rivers in Patagonia,

The Advance of the Moreno Glacier

The Moreno Glacier is frequently said to be in retreat as a result of global warming. Though the glacier no longer blocks Brazo Rico on a three yearly cycle as it last did in 1988, such statements must be treated with caution.

Glaciers are usually described by glaciologists as advancing, retreating or stable. This can cause confusion since even a retreating glacier will continue moving slowly forward; its frontage or snout retreats because it melts or breaks up at a faster rate than its forward movement. Though the Moreno glacier no longer behaves as it did until 1988, it is considered by glaciologists to be stable: its rates of forward movement and break-up are in a rough equilibrium.

One of the most puzzling things about glaciers is the way they change their behaviour. As far as is known, the Moreno glacier did not block Brazo Rico until 1917; according to early scientific studies its snout was 750m away from the Magallanes Peninsula in 1900, a distance that had dropped to 350m by 1908. In 1917 the small dam formed by the ice broke after a few weeks; the next time the glacier blocked the fiord was in 1934-5. Between this date and 1988 the glacier moved forward more vigorously: in 1939 when it reached the Magallanes Peninsula again, the water in Brazo Rico rose 9m and flooded coastal areas, leading to attempts by the Argentine navy to bomb it from the air. These failed but the waters eventually broke through. After 1939 the glacier reached the Peninsula about every three years until 1988. Its changed behaviour since then **may** be related to global warming, but perhaps we also need to know why the glacier started advancing so vigorously in the first place.

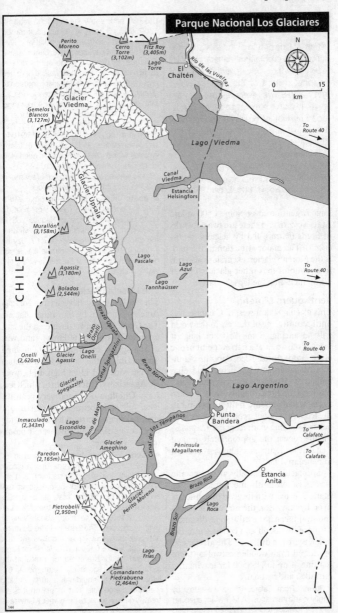

Parque Nacional Los Glaciares

Beware: flying ice

🐾 "One or two of the tourists who ignore the prohibition signs and walk down to the rocks overlooking the channel in front of the glacier always get washed away every season. They all think it won't happen to them, but it does: 60m of ice break off and hits the water just in front of them. But it isn't the water that kills them; its the chunks of flying ice."

Carlos Dupáez, Superintendent, Parque Nacional Los Glaciares, interviewed in the *Buenos Aires Herald*, 1 November 1997.

Lago Argentino covers some 1,400 sq km. At its western end there are two networks of fiords (*brazos*), fed by glaciers (*ventisqueros*). The major attraction in the park is the Moreno glacier; excursions also run to a group of four other glaciers further north, including the Upsala glacier.

Ventisquero Moreno

This glacier, 80 km west of Calafate, was until recently one of the few in the world still advancing. Some 250 km long, it reaches the water at a narrow point in one of the fiords, Brazo Rico, opposite Peninsula Magallanes: 5 km across and 60m high, it used to advance across Brazo Rico, blocking the fiord roughly every 3 years; as the water pressure built up behind it, the ice would break, reopening the channel and sending giant icebergs (*témpanos*) rushing down the appropriately named Canal de los Témpanos. This last occurred in February 1988.

Spectacular especially at sunset, the glacier is constantly moving and never silent. The ice, with its vivid blue hues, is riven by cravasses; the noise as it cracks and strains can be heard at some distance. As pieces break off and collapse into the water, there is a dull roar. The glacier can be viewed from wooden catwalks (there is a fine of up to US$500 for leaving the catwalks) and by boat.

● **Tours** From Calafate there are buses by Pingüino and Interlagos, US$10. Many agencies also run minibus tours, US$25-28 return (plus US$3.50 park entry) leaving 0800 returnin 1800, giving 3 hours at glacier, book throug any agency in Calafate, return ticket valid if yo come back next day (student discount available *Albergue del Glaciar* trips go out by differer route passing the *Estancia Anita* and have bee repeatedly recommended. Walking tours on th glacier are offered by several agencies in Cala fate (see above). Taxis, US$80 for 4 passenge round trip. Out of season, trips to the glacier a difficult to arrange, but you can gather a par and hire a taxi (remise taxis T 91745/91044 take warm clothes, and food and drink. (camp ing near ranger post, very popular, good view of glacier, showers at confiteria, US$2). As rangers where you can camp out of season, n facilities except a decrepit toilet block.

● **Boats** Trips on the lake are organized b *Hielo y Aventura*, T 91053, with large boats fc up to 60 passengers: 'Safari Náutico', US$2 per person, 1 hour offering the best views c the glacier; or 'Minitrekking', US$67, day tri including 2½ hours' walk on the glacier, rec ommended, but not for the fainthearted, tak your own lunch.

The Upsala Glacier

The fiords at the northwestern end of Lag Argentino are fed by four other glaciers The **Upsala** glacier is considered the larg est in South America, 60 km long and, wit a frontage 4 km wide and 60m high **Spegazzini**, further south, has a frontag 1½ km wide and 130m high. In betwee are **Agassiz** and **Onelli**, both of which feed **Lago Onelli**, a quiet and very beautifu lake, full of icebergs of every size an sculpted shape, surrounded by beech for ests on one side and ice-covered moun tains on the other.

● **Tours** Tour boats from Punta Bandera, 5 km west of Calafate, visit the Upsala glacie Lago Onelli and glacier (restaurant) and the Spegazzini glacier. (check before going tha access to the face of the Upsala glacier is possi ble), daily service in season on the catamara Serac, US$90, or the motor boat Nunata (slightly cheaper). The price includes bus fare and park entry fees – pay in dollars and tak food. Bus departs 0730 from Calafate for Punta Bandera. 1 hour is allowed for a meal at the restaurant near Lago Onelli. Return bus to Ca lafate at 1930; a tiring day, it is often cold and wet, but memorable. Out of season it is ex tremely difficult to get to the glacier. Many trave agencies make reservations.

Peaks in the Fitz Roy Range

FITZ ROY AND EL CHALTEN

In the far north of the park, 230 km north
of Calafate at the western end of Lago
Viedma is **Cerro Fitz Roy** (3,405m), part
of a granite massif which also includes the
peaks of Cerro Torre (3,128m), Poincenot
(3,076m), Egger (2,673m), Guillaumet
(2,503m), Saint-Exupery (2,600m), Aguja
Bífida (2,394m) and Cordón Adela
(2,938m). Clearly visible from a distance,
Fitz Roy towers above the nearby peaks,
its sides normally too steep for snow to
settle. Named after the captain of the *Beagle* who saw it from afar in 1833 (its Tehuelche name was El Chaltén), it was first
climbed by a French expedition in 1952.

The area around the base of the massif
offers fine walking opportunities (see below) and there are stupendous views:
"anyone within 500 miles would be a fool
to miss them" (Julian and Cordelia
Thomas). Occasionally at sunrise the
mountains are briefly lit up bright red for
a few seconds: this phenomenon is known
as the *amanecer de fuego* ('sunrise of fire').

Hiking Trails around the base of the
Fitzroy massif are: 1) Northwest from El
Chaltén via a good campsite at Lago Ca-
pri, wonderful views, to Campamento
Río Blanco, and, nearby Campamento
Poincenot, 2-3 hours, from where a path
leads up to Lago de los Tres (blue) and
Lago Sucia (green), 2-3 hours return from
the camps. 2). From Campamento Río
Blanco a trail runs north along the Río
Blanco and west along the Río Eléctrico
via Piedra del Fraile (4 hours) to Lago
Eléctrico. At Piedra del Fraile, just out-
side the park, there are cabanas (**E** pp

with hot showers) and campsite, US$5
per person, plus expensive shop; from
here a path leads south up Cerro Eléctrico
Oeste (1,882m) towards the north face of
Fitz Roy, 2 hours, tough but spectacular
views. This route passes through private
property: the owner allows you to walk
through only. 3) West from El Chaltén
along the Río Fitz Roy to Laguna Torre,
beautifully situated at Cerro Torre and
fed by Glaciar Torre, 3 hours. 4) Southwest from El Chaltén along a badly
marked path to Laguna Toro (6 hours),
the southern entrance to the icefields. Do
not stray from the paths. A map is essential, even on short walks.

El Chaltén

(Phone code 0962), 230 km northwest of
Calafate, is a small village at the foot of
Fitz Roy, founded in 1985 for military
reasons (to settle the area and preempt
Chilean territorial claims). Growing rapidly as a centre for trekking (information
from National Park office) and climbing,
it also offers cross-country skiing opportunities in winter. The *Día de la Tradición*
(10 November) is celebrated with gaucho
events, riding and barbecue (US$5).

● **Accommodation   A3** *Fitz Roy Inn*,
T 93062 or Calafate 91368, with breakfast,
restaurant, also **D** pp in shared cabins; opposite
is **D** pp *Albergue Patagonia*, T 61564/93019,
dormitory accommodation, kitchen and laundry
facilities, TV and video, book exchange, accepts
travellers' cheques, comfortable, recommended; **A3** *Posada Lago del Desierto*,
T 93010, good beds, *comedor*, Italian spoken,
camping US$5 per person; **D** pp *Albergue
Rancho Grande*, T 93005, small dormitories,
good bathrooms, laundry and kitchen facilities,

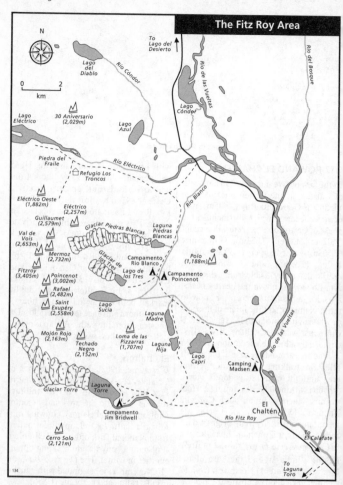

The Fitz Roy Area

N

0   2
km

To Lago del Desierto

Río Cóndor

Río de las Vueltas

Río del Bosque

Lago del Diablo

30 Aniversario (2,029m)

Lago Azul

Lago Cóndor

Piedra del Fraile

Río Eléctrico

Refugio Los Troncos

Eléctrico Oeste (1,882m)

Eléctrico (2,257m)

Río Blanco

Guillaumet (2,579m)

Glaciar Piedras Blancas

Laguna Piedras Blancas

Val de Vois (2,653m)

Mermoz (2,732m)

Glaciar de los Tres

Campamento Río Blanco

Polo (1,188m)

Fitzroy (3,405m)

Poincenot (3,002m)

Lago de los Tres

Campamento Poincenot

Rafael (2,482m)

Saint Exupéry (2,558m)

Lago Sucia

Laguna Madre

Mojón Rojo (2,163m)

Techado Negro (2,152m)

Loma de las Pizarras (1,707m)

Laguna Hija

Río de las Vueltas

Glaciar Torre

Laguna Torre

Lago Capri

Camping Madsen

El Chaltén

Campamento Jim Bridwell

Río Fitz Roy

Cerro Solo (2,121m)

To El Calafate

To Laguna Toro

134

English, Italian, French, German spoken, highly recommended, reservations in Chaltén Travel, Calafate, T 91833; **B** pp *Estancia La Quinta*, 3 km from Chaltén, half-board, no heating, prepares lunch for trekkers, recommended; **L3** *La Aldea*, T 93040, 5 bed apartments; **D** pp *Casa de Piedra*, T 93015, in shared cabins, also **A1** 4 bed cabins; **D** pp *Cabaña de Miguel*, shared cabins; **D** pp *Cabañas Cerro Torre*, T 93061, built for the Herzog film "El Grito de la Piedra", cabins sleep 4/6, kitchenette; **E** pp *Albergue Los Ñires*, T 93009, small dormitories, also

camping US$5 per person; **E** pp *Despensa 2 de Abril*, one room, cheapest. **Camping** *Camping Madsen* (free); *Ruca Mahuida*, T 93018, very helpful, US$6 per person, showers, stores gear, recommended; two free campsites. A stove is essential for camping as firewood is scarce and lighting fires is prohibited in the National Park. Take plenty of warm clothes and a good sleeping bag. It is possible to rent equipment in El Chaltén, ask at park entrance. Equipment and cycles for hire at artesania shop on road to camping Madsen, past Albergue

Patagonia. All campsites in National Park free, no toilets, please bury your waste. Hot showers available at Albergue Patagonia and Confiteria La Senyera, US$2.

● **Places to eat** *La Senyera del Torre*, excellent bread, recommended; *Josh Aike*, excellent *confitería*, homemade food, beautiful building, recommended; *The Wall Pub*, breakfasts and meals, interesting, shows videos of ascents of Fitz Roy and Cerro Torre.

● **Shopping** There are several small shops selling food, gas and batteries (*Dispensa 2 de Abril* is said to be cheapest) but buy supplies in Calafate (cheaper and more choice). Sra Isolina bakes the best bread. Fuel is available.

● **Sports Climbing**: base camp for climbing Fitz Roy is Campamento Río Blanco (see above). Most of the peaks in the Fitzroy massif are for very experienced climbers as is the *Campo de Hielo Continental* (Ice Fields) which mark the frontier with Chile (no access from Chile). Ask Sr Guerra about hiring animals to carry equipment. 'Fitz Roy Expediciones, in Chaltén, T 93017/F 91364, owned by experienced guide Alberto del Castillo, organize adventure excursions including on the *Campo de Hielo Continental*, 8 hours, US$75 including equipment, highly recommended, English and Italian spoken. For the icefields guides are essential; necessary gear is double boots, crampons, pickaxe, ropes, winter clothing; the type of terrain is ice and rock. The best time is mid-February to end-March; November-December is very windy; January is fair; winter is extremely cold. Permits for climbing are available at the national park information office.

● **Trekking** The park information centre provides photocopied maps of treks but the best is one published by Zagier and Urruty, 1992, US$10 (Casilla 94, Sucursal 19, 1419 Buenos Aires, F 572-5766) and is available in shops in Calafate and Chaltén. For trekking by horseback with guides: Rodolfo Guerra, T 93020; *El Relincho*, T 93007; *Albergue Los Ñires*, T 93009. Prices: Laguna Capri US$20; Laguna Torre, US$25, Río Blanco US$30, Piedra del Fraile US$30, Laguna Toro US$30.

● **Transport Local Mechanic**: ask for Julio Bahamonde or Hugo Masias. **Buses** Daily services in summer from **Calafate**, 4 hours, US$25 one way, are run by Chaltén Travel 0800 return departure 1800, Caltur, 0700, return departure 1700, and Los Glaciares, 0800, return departure 1800. Best to book return before departure during high season. From **Río Gallegos**, Burmeister, Monday, Wednesday, Friday 1500, US$40, return departures same days. Day trips from Calafate involve too much travelling and too little time to see the area.

Some agencies offer excursions eg return travel by regular bus and 1 night accommodation US$79. Off season, travel is difficult: little transport for hitching. Agencies charge US$200 one way for up to 8 people, US$300 return.

The Lago del Desierto

37 km north of El Chaltén and surrounded by forests, this lake is reached by an unpaved road which leads along the Río de las Vueltas via Laguna Condor, where flamingos can be seen. A path runs along the east side of the lake to its northern tip, from where a trail leads west along the valley of the Río Diablo to Laguna Diablo. There is a campsite at the southern end of the lake and *refugios* at its northern end and at Laguna Diablo. Excursions from El Chaltén by *Chaltén Travel* daily in summer; daily boat trips on the lake on *La Mariana II*, 1030, 1330, 1630, 2 hours, US$30 (details and booking, *Hotel El Quijote*, Calafate).

FROM CALAFATE TO CHILE

There are two alternative routes, the longest but easiest of which is via the main Calafate-Río Gallegos road as far as La Esperanza, Km 161, where Provincial Route 7, newly paved, branches off west along the valley of the Río Coyle. The alternative is to take Route 40 (*ripio*) which branches off at El Cerrito, Km 91 and runs 70 km southwest to join Route 7 at a point 78 km west of La Esperanza; this shorter route is closed in winter. From here the road continues to the border crossing at Cancha Carrera (see below) and then runs south towards Río Turbio. Guanacos and condors can be seen at intervals along this route and on clear days there are fantastic views of Torres del Paine to the west. For public transport on this route see under Calafate.

● **Accommodation At La Esperanza**: **D** pp *Restaurant La Esperanza*, bunk beds, with bath; also *cabañas* at the YPF service station, **A3**, sleep 6; campsite. **At Fuentes del Coyle**, 92 km west of La Esperanza, there is a small but acceptable bar/*confitería* with 2-3 rooms for travellers and a Hotel, **D** pp, cold, dirty.

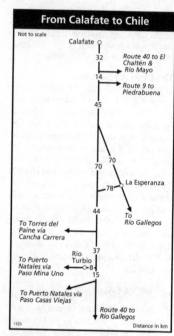

From Calafate to Chile

Not to scale

Calafate

Route 40 to El Chaltén & Río Mayo — 32

Route 9 to Piedrabuena — 14

45

70 — 70

La Esperanza — 78

44 — To Río Gallegos

To Torres del Paine via Cancha Carrera

Río Turbio

To Puerto Natales via Paso Mina Uno — 8 — 37

15

To Puerto Natales via Paso Casas Viejas

Route 40 to Río Gallegos

132b   Distance in km

Argentina's largest coalfield. Little visited by travellers, it is a good centre for trekking and horse riding. Visits can be made to **Mina Uno**, the first mine to the south of the town, and to the present mining and industrial area, on the eastern outskirts where there is a museum, the **Museo del Carbón**, open Monday-Friday 0700-1200. About 4 km south of town is **Valdelén**, a ski resort, situated just inside the frontier on the slopes of Sierra La Dorotea.

● **Accommodation** Hotels almost always full: **A3** Hostería Capipe, at Dufour, 9 km west, T 21240; **A3** Gato Negro, T 21226, also dormitory accommodation **E** pp; **E** pp Hostería La Frontera, an albergue at Valdelén; Hostería Municipal at Mina Uno.

● **Places to eat** Restaurant El Ringo, near bus terminal, will shelter you from the wind.

● **Sports** Skiing: Valdelén, with 6 pistes, is ideal for beginners. There is also scope for cross-country skiing nearby. Season runs from early June to late September, the pistes enjoying electric lighting to extend the short winter afternoons.

● **Tourist office** In the Municipalidad.

● **Transport Air** Airport 15 km southeast near 28 de Noviembre; taxi US$10 per person. LADE flights to Río Gallegos. **Buses** To Puerto Natales, 2 companies, US$4, regular. To Calafate, Pingüino and Quebek, 6 hours, US$27. Pingüino runs daily at 0600 (plus 1300 Tuesday, Thursday, Saturday, 6 hours) in summer or 1300 Wednesday, Thursday, Saturday in winter to Río Gallegos, but LADE flights are cheaper.

FRONTIER WITH CHILE: PASO CACHA CARRERA

Situated 129 km west of La Esperanza and 42 km north of Río Turbio, this is the most convenient crossing for Parque Nacional Torres del Paine. Open November-April only. On the Chilean side the road continues to Cerro Castillo, 7 km west of the frontier, where it meets the road from Puerto Natales, 65 km south, to Parque Nacional Torres del Paine.

● **Argentine customs & immigration**
At Cancha Carrera, 2 km east of the frontier, fast and friendly.

● **Chilean customs & immigration**
at Cerro Castillo, open 0830-1200, 1400-2000.

● **Accommodation**
Two hospedajes in Cerro Castillo.

RIO TURBIO

(*Population* 8,000; *Phone code* 0902), 257 km west of Río Gallegos to which it is linked by railway line (no passengers) and only 30 km northeast of the Chilean town of Puerto Natales, is the site of

FRONTIER WITH CHILE
Paso Mina Uno

5 km south of Río Turbio and 25 km north of Puerto Natales, this crossing is open all year, daytime only. On the Chilean side the road runs south to join the main Puerto Natales-Punta Arenas road.

● **Argentine immigration**
Open 0800-2200.

Paso Casas Viejas

This crossing, 33 km south of Río Turbio is reached by Route 40 via 28 de Noviembre. On the Chilean side this runs east to join the main Puerto Natales-Punta Arenas road, 3 km west of the frontier.

● **Argentine immigration**
Open all year 0800-2200.

● **Chilean immigration**
Open all year 0800-2000.

Chilean Patagonia

THIS SECTION covers the Chilean part of southern Patagonia. Punta Arenas and Puerto Natales are the two main towns, the latter being the gateway to the Torres del Paine and Balmaceda national parks. In summer this is a region for climbing, hiking and boat trips.

GEOGRAPHY

The coastline of Chilean Patagonia is indented by fjords and offshore are numberous islands, few of which are inhabited. The remnants of the Andes stretch along the coast, seldom rising above 1,500m. Mountains above this altitude include the Cordillera del Paine (several peaks over 2,600m) and Cerro Balmaceda (2,035m). Vegetation varies from thick rainforest on the wet west coast to grassland further east.

This area is sparsely populated: although it covers 17.5% of Chilean territory, its population is around 165,000, under 1% of the Chilean total. This population is overwhelmingly urban: over 150,000 live in towns, most of them in Punta Arenas, the main settlement.

LOCAL ECONOMY

Sheep farming is still important to the local economy; much of the meat is exported to Islamic countries, whereas locally produced beef is mainly sold domestically. Potatoes are an important

Guanaco

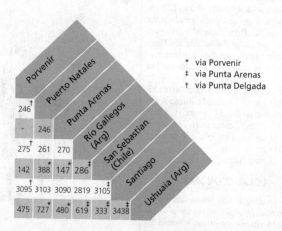

Chilean Patagonia: distance chart (km)

crop, but owing to the climate most other vegetables are grown under cover. Fishing is a traditional activity, though changing with the growth of salmon farming. Forestry has grown in importance and become controversial as a result of the use of native forests for woodchips for export to Japan, Taiwan and Brazil. Although oil production has declined as reserves have been depleted, large quantities of natural gas are now produced. About 33% of Chilean coal comes from large open cast coal mines on the Brunswick Peninsula, northwest of Punta Arenas; most of it is shipped to the thermal power stations of northern Chile. Tourism is growing rapidly, making an increasingly important contribution to the local economy.

CLIMATE

Strong, cold, piercing winds blow, particularly during the spring, when they may exceed 100 km an hour. These bring heavy rain to coastal areas, over 4,000 mm a year on the offshore islands. Further east the winds are much drier; annual rainfall at Punta Dungeness at the east end of the Straits of Magellan is only 250 mm. Along the coast temperatures are moderated by the sea: summer temperatures are more variable, though seldom rising above 15°C. In winter snow covers the country, except those parts near the sea, making many roads more or less impassable, except on horseback. The winds parch the ground and prevent the growth of crops, except in sheltered spots and greenhouses. When travelling in this region, protection against the sun's ultraviolet rays is essential.

HISTORY

Although southern Patagonia was inhabited from the end of the ice ages, the first Europeans did not visit until the 16th century. In 1519 Hernando de Magallanes, a Portuguese sailor serving the Spanish crown, sailed through the Straits that bear his name. The strategic importance of the Straits, connecting Europe with the Pacific, was quickly recognized: soon Spanish naval and merchant ships were using the route, as were others such as Francis Drake on his world voyage (1578). However the route became less important after 1616 when the Dutch sailors Jacob le Marie and Cornelius van Schouten discovered a quicker route round Cape Horn.

Although at independence Chile claimed the far southern territories, little was done to carry out this claim until 1843 when, concerned at British activities in the area and at rumours of French plans to start a colony, President Bulnes ordered the preparation of a secret mission. The expedition established Fuerte Bulnes on a rocky point; the fort was abandoned in 1848 in favour of the new settlement of Punta Arenas.

PUNTA ARENAS

(*Population* 110,000; *Phone code* 061), the most southerly city in Chile, and capital of XII Región, 2,140 km south of Santiago, lies on the eastern shore of the Brunswick Peninsula facing the Straits of Magellan at almost equal distance from the Pacific and Atlantic oceans. It is a centre for the local sheep farming and fishing industries and exports wool, skins, and frozen meat. It is also the home of La Polar, the most southerly brewery in the world. Although it has expanded rapidly, particularly in recent

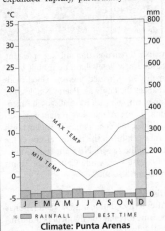

Climate: Punta Arenas

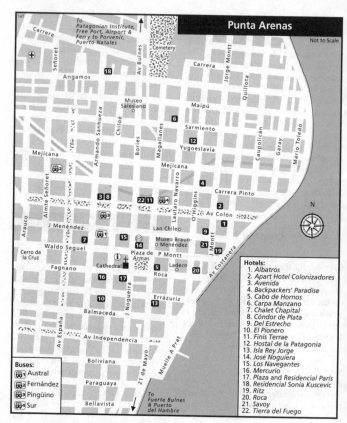

Punta Arenas

Not to Scale

To Patagonian Institute, Free Port, Airport & Ferry to Porvenir, Puerto Natales

To Fuerte Bulnes & Puerto del Hambre

Hotels:
1. *Albatros*
2. *Apart Hotel Colonizadores*
3. *Avenida*
4. *Backpackers' Paradise*
5. *Cabo de Hornos*
6. *Carpa Manzano*
7. *Chalet Chapital*
8. *Cóndor de Plata*
9. *Del Estrecho*
10. *El Pionero*
11. *Finis Terrae*
12. *Hostal de la Patagonia*
13. *Isla Rey Jorge*
14. *José Noguiera*
15. *Los Navegantes*
16. *Mercurio*
17. *Plaza and Residencial París*
18. *Residencial Sonia Kuscevic*
19. *Ritz*
20. *Roca*
21. *Savoy*
22. *Tierra del Fuego*

Buses:
1. Austral
2. Fernández
3. Pingüino
4. Sur

years, it remains tranquil and pleasant. Several new hotels have been built in response to increased tourism. Good roads connect the city with Puerto Natales, 247 km north, and with Río Gallegos in Argentina. Punta Arenas has certain free-port facilities; the Zona Franca is 3½ km north of the centre, on the righthand side of the road to the airport. **NB** Calle Pedro Montt runs east-west, while Calle Jorge Montt runs north-south.

History

After its foundation in 1848, Punta Arenas became a penal colony modelled on Australia. In 1867 it was opened to foreign settlers and given free port status. From the 1880s it prospered as a refuelling and provisioning centre for steam ships and whaling vessels. It also became a centre for the new sheep estancias since it afforded the best harbour facilities. The city's importance was reduced overnight by the opening of the Panama Canal in 1914.

Places of interest

Around the **Plaza Muñoz Gamero** are a number of former mansions of the great sheep ranching families of the late 19th century. See the **Palacio Sara Braun**, which dates from 1895. In the centre of the plaza is a statue of Magellan with a

La Anónima

The centre of Punta Arenas bears witness to the influence of the people who benefitted most from the Chilean government's distribution of lands in the area after 1881: José Menéndez, whose San Gregorio Estancia covered 90,000 hectares, his neighbours Sara and Mauricio Braun at the Pecket Harbour Estancia, their associate Juan Blanchard, and José Noguiera, who married Sara Braun. After Noguiera's death in 1893, his holdings were merged into Braun & Blanchard, which became the largest commercial landowner in Chile; their factory at Puerto Bories, north of Puerto Natales, processed and exported meat from all over southern Argentina and Chile.

Further opportunities came the way of Menéndez and Braun & Blanchard after 1899. Following the meeting between the Argentine and Chilean Presidents in Punta Arenas, the Argentine government allowed Chilean entrepreneurs to invest in Argentine Tierra del Fuego. José Menéndez founded two *estancias* in the Río Grande area, which were named after himself and after his wife, Maria Behety, while Braun & Blanchard established the *Estancia Sara*, near San Sebastian.

Although the two companies were linked by marriage in 1895 when Mauricio Braun married José Menéndez's daughter Josefina, rivalry between them was intense until both were hit by an economic crisis in 1907. In the following year they merged their holdings into the *Sociedad Anónima Importadora y Exportadora de la Patagonia*, usually known simply as *La Anónima*, and in 1910 they moved their headquarters to Buenos Aires. In the following years the company extended its influence over southern Argentina; apart from its extensive landholdings, it established a chain of general stores in 45 cities and towns, built slaughter houses, meat-processing plants and port facilities, and operated shipping services, newspapers and radio stations. Its continued existence can be seen in Argentina in the form of the supermarket chain known simply as *La Anónima*.

mermaid and two Fuegian Indians at his feet. According to local wisdom those who rub the big toe of one of the Indians will return to Punta Arenas. Just north of the plaza on Calle Magallanes are the **Palacio Braun Menéndez** (see below) and the **Teatro Cervantes** (now a cinema): the interiors of both are worth a visit. Further north, at Avenida Bulnes 929, is the **Cemetery**, even more fantastic than the one at Castro (Chiloé), with a **statue of Indiecito**, the little Indian (now also an object of reverence, bedecked with flowers, the left knee well-rubbed, northwest side of the cemetery), cypress avenues, and many memorials to pioneer families and victims of shipping disasters (open 0800-1800 daily).

East of the Plaza Muñoz Gamero on Calle Fagnano is the **Mirador Cerro de La Cruz** offering a view over the city. Nearby on Waldo Seguel are two reminders of the British influence: the **British School** and **St James' Church** next door. The **Parque María Behety**, south of town along 21 de Mayo, features a scale model of Fuerte Bulnes and a campsite, popular for Sunday picnics.

Museums

Museo Regional Salesiano Mayorino Borgatello, in the Colegio Salesiano, Avenida Bulnes 374, entrance next to church, covering history of the indigenous peoples, sections on local animal and bird life, and other interesting aspects of life in Patagonia and Tierra del Fuego, excellent. Tuesday-Saturday 1000-1200 and 1500-1800, Sunday 1500-1800, hours change frequently (entry US$1.25).

Museo de Historia Regional Braun Menéndez, Magallanes 949, off Plaza de Armas, T 244216, located in the former mansion of Mauricio Braun, built in 1905, recommended. Part is set out as room-by-room regional history, the rest of the house is furnished (guided tours in Spanish only). Closed Monday, otherwise open 1100-1600 (summer) and 1100-1300 (winter, entry US$1), free booklet in English.

The **Instituto de la Patagonia**, Avenida Bulnes Km 4 north (opposite the University), T 244216, houses the **Museo del Recuerdo**, an open-air museum with artefacts used by the early settlers, pioneer homes, a naval museum and botanical gardens. Outdoor exhibits open Monday-Friday 0800-1800, indoor pavilions: 0830-1115, 1500-1800.

Naval and Maritime Museum, Pedro Montt 981, open Monday-Friday 0930-1230, 1500-1800, Saturday 1000-1300, 1500-1800.

Excursions

The **Reserva Forestal Magallanes**, 7 km west of town and known locally as the Parque Japonés, extends over 13,500 hectares and rises to 600m. Follow Independencia right through town and up the hill; 3 km from the edge of town is the turnoff for Río de las Minas to the right. The entrance to the reserve is 2 km beyond, there you will find a self-guided nature trail, 1 km, free leaflet. The road continues through the woods for 14 km, passing by several small campgrounds. From the top end of the road a short path leads to a lookout over the Garganta del Diablo (Devil's Throat), a gorge formed by the Río de las Minas, with views over Punta Arenas and Tierra del Fuego. From here a slippery path leads down to the Río de las Minas valley and thence back to Punta Arenas. Administration at Conaf in Punta Arenas. *Turismo Pali Aike* offers tours to the park, US$3.75 per person.

Local information
● **Accommodation**
Most hotels include breakfast in the room price. Hotel prices are substantially lower during winter months (April-September).

Hotel prices

L1	over US$200	L2	US$151-200
L3	US$101-150	A1	US$81-100
A2	US$61-80	A3	US$46-60
B	US$31-45	C	US$21-30
D	US$12-20	E	US$7-11
F	US$4-6		up to US$3

Unless otherwise stated, all hotels in range **D** and above have private bath. Assume friendliness and cleanliness in all cases.

L2 *Hotel José Nogueira*, Plaza de Armas, Bories 959 y P Montt, in former Palacio Sara Braun, T 248840, F 248832, beautiful loggia, good food, lovely atmosphere, recommended; **L3** *Cabo de Hornos*, Plaza Muñoz Gamero 1025, T/F 242134, recommended; **L3** *Finis Terrae*, Colón 766, T 228200, F 248124, modern, some rooms small but all very nice, safe in room, rooftop café/bar with lovely views, parking; **L3** *Isla Rey Jorge*, 21 de Mayo 1243, T 222681, F 248220, modern, pleasant, pub downstairs; **L3** *Los Navegantes*, José Menéndez 647, T 244677, F 247545; **L3** *Tierra del Fuego*, Colón 716, F 226200, good breakfast, parking, recommended, *Café 1900* downstairs.

A2 *Hostería Yaganes*, Camino Antiguo Norte Km 7.5, T 211600, F 211400, cabins on the shores of the Straits of Magellan, nice setting; **A1-A2** *Apart Hotel Colonizadores*, Colón 1106, T 243578, F 244499, clean, fully furnished apartments (2 bedrooms **A1**, 1 bedroom **A2**) discounts for long stay; **A3** *Hostal de la Patagonia*, O'Higgins 478, T 241079, with bath (**B** without), good breakfast, excellent; **A3** *Colonizadores*, 21 de Mayo 1690, T 244144, F 226587, with bath; **A3** *Hostal Carpa Manzano*, Lautaro Navarro 336, T/F 248864, recommended; **A3** *Cóndor de Plata*, Colón 556, T 247987, F 241149, very good; **A3** *Mercurio*, Fagnano 595, T/F 242300, bath, TV and phone, good restaurant and service, recommended; **A3** *Plaza*, Nogueira 1116, 2nd floor, T 241300, F 248613 (**B** without bath), pleasant, good breakfast.

B *Savoy*, Menéndez 1073, T 241951, F 247979, pleasant rooms but some lack windows, good place to eat; **B** *Ritz*, Pedro Montt 1102, T 224422, old, clean and cosy, recommended; **B** *Hotel El Pionero*, Chiloé 1210, T 248851, F 248263, with bath; **C** *Res Central*, No 1 España 247, T 222315, No 2 Sanhueza 185, T 222845, with bath (**D** without), comfortable; **B** *Chalet Chapital*, Sanhueza 974, T 242237, F 225698 (cheaper without bath), good, comfortable, doubles only, welcoming; **B** *Hostal de la Avenida*, Colón 534, T 247532, good breakfast, friendly, safe, recommended; **B** *Hostal Del Estrecho*, Menéndez 1048, T/F 241011, with breakfast and bath.

Albatros, Colón 1195, T 223131, without bath, good; **C** *Res Sonia Kuscevic*, Pasaje Darvin 175 (Angamos Altura 550), T 248543, popular, IYHA accepted, with bath, breakfast, hot water, heating, parking.

D *Casa Dinka*, Caupolicán 169, T 226056, with breakfast, use of kitchen, noisy, very popular; **D** pp *Res Roca*, Roca 1038, T 243903, without bath, clean; **D** pp *Res Rubio*, España 640, T 226458, with bath, helpful. Accommodation available in many private houses, usually **E** pp, ask at tourist office; **D** *Hosp Lodging*, Sanhueza 933, T 221035, good value, clean, heating, modern; **D** Sra Carolina Ramírez, Paraguaya 150, T 247687, nice and friendly, hot water, safe motorcycle parking, meals, recommended.

E pp Caupolicán 99, T 222436, with breakfast, clean; **E** pp *Casa Deportista*, O'Higgins 1205, T 225205, T 243438, cheap meals, cooking facilities, dormitory style, noisy; **E** pp *Casa Roxas*, Angamos 971, very good, clean, with bath; **E** pp *Hostal Paradiso*, Angamos 1073, T 224212, with breakfast, parking, use of kitchen, recommended; **E** pp *Backpackers' Paradise*, Carrera Pinto 839, T 222554, F 226863, hot water, popular, large dormitories, cooking facilities, internet bathroom facilities, good meeting place, luggage store, recommended; **E** pp Sra Lenka, José Miguel Carrera 1270, heating, clean, use of kitchen, recommended; **E** Nena's, Boliviana 366, T 242411, friendly, with breakfast, highly recommended; **E** pp, España y Boliviana, T 247422, without bath, clean, friendly, use of kitchen; **E** Sanhueza 750, homely, recommended.

F pp *Alojamiento Prat*, Sargento Aldea 0520, clean, recommended; **F** pp Sanhueza 712, T 225127, basic, use of kitchen; **F** pp Bellavista 577, dormitory accommodation, kitchen, hot showers, clean.

Camping In Reserva Forestal Magallanes (no public transport, see **Excursions** above). *Camping Pudú*, 10.5 km north on Route 9, **G** pp, pleasant, good facilities.

● **Places to eat**
Main hotels: good value set lunches and dinners at *Cabo de Hornos*, excellent restaurants at *Los Navegantes* and *José Nogueira*.

Many places closed on Sunday. *El Mercado*, Mejicana 617, open 24 hours, reasonably-priced set lunch, expensive à la carte; *Centro Español*, Plaza Muñoz Gamero 771, above Teatro Cervantes, large helpings, limited selection, reasonably priced; *El Mesón del Calvo*, Jorge Montt 687, excellent, seafood, lamb, small portions, pricey, recommended; seafood at *Sotitos*, O'Higgins 1138, good service and cuisine, excellent, recommended; *La Mama*,

Sanhueza 700 block, little Argentine-style pasta house, recommended; *Lucerna*, Bories 624, excellent meat, reasonably priced, good; *Dino's Pizza*, Bories 557, cheap, good, big pizzas; *Café Garogha*, Bories 817, open Sunday afternoon, busy at night, smoky; *Bianco's Pizza*, Bulnes 1306, excellent pizzas, recommended; *El Quijote*, Lautaro Navarro 1087, good sandwiches, highly recommended; *Asturias*, Lautaro Navarro 967, good food and atmosphere; *Venus*, Pedro Montt 1046, good food, service and atmosphere, reasonable prices; *La Casa de Juan*, O'Higgins 1021, Spanish food; *El Estribo*, Carrera Pinto 762, good grill, also fish; *Yaganes*, Camino Antiguo Norte Km 7.5, beautiful setting, weekend buffet; *Golden Dragon*, Colón 529, Chinese, good, expensive; *La Terraza*, 21 de Mayo 1288, sandwiches, *empanadas* and beer, cheap and good; *La Taberna del Club de la Unión*, Plaza Muñoz Gamero y Seguel, for drinks. For economic set lunches several along Chiloé: *Restaurant de Turismo Punta Arenas*, No 1280, good, friendly, recommended; *Los Años 60 The Mitchel*, No 1231, also serves beer and 26 varieties of sandwiches, open 24 hours; *Parrilla Apocalipsis*, Chiloé y Balmaceda; *Carioca*, Menéndez 600 y Chiloé, *parrilla*, snacks and beer, very friendly; *Lomit's*, Menéndez 722, cheap snacks and drinks, open when the others are closed; *Kiosco Roca* (no sign), Roca 875, early morning coffee. Cheap fish meals available at stalls in the *Cocinerías*, Lautaro Navarro south of the port entrance. Excellent *empanadas*, bread and pastries at *Pancal*, 21 de Mayo 1280; also at *La Espiga*, Errázuriz 632; excellent pastries at *Casa del Pastel*, Carrera Pinto y O'Higgins. Lobster has become more expensive because of a law allowing only lobster pots. *Centolla* (king crab) is caught illegally by some fishermen using dolphin, porpoise and penguin as live bait. There are seasonal bans on *centolla* fishing to protect dwindling stocks, do not purchase *centolla* out of season. At times *centolla* fishing is banned because the crabs can be infected with a disease which is fatal to humans. If this ban refers to the *marea roja* (red tide), it does not affect crabs, only bivalve shellfish. Mussels should not be picked along the shore owing to pollution and the *marea roja*.

● **Airline offices**
LanChile, Lautaro Navarro 999, T 241232, F 222366; Ladeco, Lautaro Navarro 1155, T/F 241100/223340. National, Bories 701, T 221634. Aerovías DAP, O'Higgins 899, T 223340, F 221693, open 0900-1230, 1430-1930; Kaiken, Magallanes 974, T 242134 ext 106, F 241321.

● **Banks & money changers**

Banks open Monday-Friday 0830-1400. *Casas de cambio* open Monday-Friday 0900-1230, 1500-1900, Saturday 0900-1230; outside business hours try *Buses Sur*, Colón y Magallanes, kiosk at *Garogha Café*, Bories 817 and the major hotels (lower rates). **Fincard** (Mastercard), Pedro Montt 837, T 247864, Monday-Friday 0900-1400, 1530-1730. **Banco Concepción**, Magallanes y Menéndez, for Visa. **Banco O'Higgins**, Plaza de Armas, changes travellers' cheques, no commission. Argentine pesos can be bought at *casas de cambio*. Good rates at *Cambio Gasic*, Roca 915, Oficina 8, T 242396, German spoken; *La Hermandad*, Lautaro Navarro 1099, T 243991, excellent rates, US$ cash for Amex travellers' cheques; *Sur Cambios*, Lautaro Navarro 1001, T 225656 accepts travellers' cheques. *Kiosco Redondito*, Mejicana 613 in the shopping centre, T 247369.

● **Consulates**

Argentine, 21 de Mayo 1878, T 261912, open 1000-1400, visas take 24 hours, US$25; **Brazilian**, Arauco 769, T 241093; **Belgian**, Roca 817, Oficina 61, T 241472; **British**, Roca 924, T 247020; **Danish**, Colón 819, Depto 301, T 221488; **Dutch**, Sarmiento 780, T 248100; **Finnish**, Independencia 660, T 247385; **German**, Pasaje Korner 1046, T 241082, Casilla 229; **Italian**, 21 de Mayo 1569, T 242497; **Norwegian**, Independencia 830, T 242171; **Spanish**, J Menéndez 910, T 243566; **Swedish**, Errazúriz 891, T 224107.

● **Entertainment**

Discotheques: discos in the city centre often have a young crowd: *Gallery*, J Menéndez 750, T 247555; *Yordi*, Pedro Montt 937; *Borssalino*, Bories 587. On the outskirts of town, to the south: *Club Boulevard*, Km 5.5, T 265807; *Torreones*, Km 5.5, T 261985; *Salsoteca*, Km 5. To the north: *Drive-In Los Brujos*, Km 7.5, T 212600; *Salsoteca*, Km 6.

Nightlife: *The Queen's Club*, 21 de Mayo 1455. Lots of *Whiskerías*: *Sexywoman*, Avenida España, and *Tentación*, Avenida Colón, recommended.

● **Hospitals & medical services**

Dentists: *Dr Hugo Vera Cárcamo*, España 1518, T 227510, recommended; *Rosemary Robertson Stipicic*, 21 de Mayo 1380, T 22931, speaks English.

Hospitals: *Hospital Regional Lautaro Navarro*, Angamos 180, T 244040, public hospital, for emergency room ask for *La Posta*; *Clínica Magallanes*, Bulnes 01448, T 211527, private clinic, medical staff is the same as in the hospital but fancier surroundings and more expensive.

● **Laundry**

Lavasol, the only self-service, O'Higgins 969, T 243067, Monday-Saturday 0900-2030, Sunday (summer only) 1000-1800, US$6 per machine, wash and dry, good but busy; *Lavaseco Josseau*, Carrera Pinto 766, T 228413; *Lavandería Limpec*, 21 de Mayo 1261, T 241669.

● **Post & telecommunications**

Note that postal and telecommunication charges are much lower than in Argentina.

Post Office: Bories 911 y J Menéndez, Monday-Friday 0830-1930, Saturday 0900-1400.

Telecommunications: for international and national calls and faxes (shop around as prices vary): *CTC*, Nogueira 1106, Plaza de Armas, daily 0800-2200, *CTC*, Roca 886, local 23, daily 0900-2030; *Entel*, Lautaro Navarro 957, Monday-Friday 0830-2200, Saturday-Sunday 0900-2200; *Telex-Chile/Chile-Sat*, Bories 911 and Errázuriz 856, daily 0830-2200, also offers telex and telegram service. *VTR*, Bories 801, closed Saturday afternoon and Sunday. For international calls and faxes at any hour *Hotel Cabo de Hornos*, credit cards accepted, open to non-residents.

● **Shopping**

For leather goods and sheepskin try the Zona Franca; quality of other goods is low and prices little better than elsewhere in Chile; Monday-Saturday 1030-1230, 1500-2000 (bus E or A from Plaza de Armas; many colectivo taxis; taxi US$3). Handicrafts at *Pingüi*, Bories 404, *Artesanía Ramas*, Independencia 799, *Chile Típico*, Carrera Pinto 1015, *Indoamérica*, Colón y Magallanes and outdoor stalls at the bottom of Independencia, by the port entrance.

Supermarkets: *Listo*, 21 de Mayo 1133; *Cofrima*, Lautaro Navarro 1293 y Balmaceda, *Cofrima 2*, España 01375; *Marisol*, Zenteno 0164.

Cameras: wide range of cameras but limited range of film, from Zona Franca. *Foto Arno*, Bories 893, for Kodak products. *Foto Sánchez*, Bories 768, for Fuji film and *Fotocentro*, Bories 789, for Agfa: all have same day print-processing service.

Chocolate: hand made chocolate from *Chocolatería Tres Arroyos*, Bories 448, T 241522 and *Chocolatería Regional Norweisser*, José Miguel Carrera 663, both good.

● **Sports**

Golf: 9-hole golf course 5 km south of town on road to Fuerte Bulnes.

Skiing: Cerro Mirador, only 9 km west from Punta Arenas in the Reserva Nacional Magallanes, the most southerly ski resort in the world and one of the few places where you can ski with a sea view. Transtur buses 0900 and 1400 from in front of *Hotel Cabo de Hornos*, US$3, return, taxi US$7. Daily lift-ticket, US$7; equipment rental, US$6 per adult. Mid-way lodge with food, drink and equipment. Season June to September, weather permitting. Contact the Club Andino, T 241479, about cross-country skiing facilities. Also skiing at Tres Morros.

● **Tour companies & travel agents**
Turismo Lazo, Angamos 1366, T/F 223771, wide range of tours, highly recommended; *Turismo Aventour*, J Nogueira 1255, T 241197, F 243354, English spoken, helpful, good, specializes in fishing trips, organize tours to Tierra del Fuego. *Turismo Comapa*, Independencia 840, T 241437, F 247514, tours to Torres del Paine, Tierra del Fuego and Isla Magdalena, also trips to the Falklands/Malvinas, charter boats to Cape Horn; *Turismo Runner*, Lautaro Navarro 1065, T 247050, F 241042, adventure tours; *Arka Patagonia*, Carrera Pinto 946, T 248167, F 241504, all types of tours, rafting, fishing, etc; *Turismo Pehoé*, Avenida Colón 782, T 244506, F 248052, organizes tours and hotels, enquire here about catamaran services; *Turismo Aonikenk*, Magallanes 619, T 228332, recommended; *Turismo Pali Aike*, Lautaro Navarro 1129, T 223301; *El Conquistador*, Menéndez 556, T 222896, recommended; *Turismo Viento Sur*, Fagnano 565, T/F 225167, for camping equipment; *Turismo Patagonia*, Bories 655 local 2, T 248474, F 247182, specializes in fishing trips; and others. Most organize tours to Torres del Paine, Fuerte Bulnes and *pingüineras* on Otway sound: shop around as prices vary; Sr Mateo Quesada, Chiloé 1375, T 222662, offers local tours in his car, up to 4 passengers.

In-Tur is an association of companies which aims to promote tourism in Chilean Patagonia. The members are *Arka Patagonia*, *Turismo Aventour*, *Turismo Pehoé*, *Turismo Runner*, *Aerovías DAP* and *Hostería Las Torres* (in the Parque Nacional Torres del Paine). The head office is at Errázuriz 840, 2nd floor, Punta Arenas, T/F 229049, which can be contacted for information. See **Bus services**, below, for In-Tur's SIB bus to Torres del Paine.

● **Tourist offices**
Sernatur, Waldo Seguel 689, Casilla 106-D, T 241330, at the corner with Plaza Muñoz Gamero, 0830-1745, closed Saturday and Sunday, helpful, English spoken. Kiosk on Colón between Bories and Magallanes Monday-Friday 0900-1300, 1500-1900, Saturday 0900-1200, 1430-1730, Sunday (in the summer only) 1000-1230. Turistel Guide available from kiosk belonging to *Café Garogha* at Bories 831. **Conaf**, Menéndez 1147, 2nd floor, T 223841, open Monday-Friday.

● **Transport**
NB All transport is heavily booked from Christmas through to March: advance booking strongly advised.

Local Car hire: Hertz, Colón 798 and Carrera Pinto 770, T 248742, F 244729; **Australmag**, Colón 900, T 242174, F 226916; **Autómovil Club**, O'Higgins 931, T 243675, F 243097, and at airport; **Budget**, O'Higgins 964, T 241696; **Internacional**, Sarmiento 790-B, T 228323, F 226334, recommended; **Willemsen**, Lautaro Navarro 1038, T 247787, F 241083, highly recommended; **Lubac**, Magallanes 970, T/F 242023/247060; **Todoauto**, España 0480, T 212492, F 212627. **NB** You need a hire company's authorization to take a car into Argentina. **Car repair**: *Automotores del Sur*, O'Higgins 850, T 224153. **Taxis**: ordinary taxis have yellow roofs. Collective taxis (all black) run on fixed routes, US$0.25 for anywhere on route. Reliable service from *Radio Taxi Austral*, T 247710/244409.

Air Carlos Ibáñez de Campo Airport, 15 km north of town. Bus service by Austral Bus, between the airport and Plaza Muñoz Gamero scheduled to meet flights, US$2.50. LanChile, DAP and Ladeco have their own bus services from town, US$2.50; taxi US$10. The airport restaurant is good. To Santiago, LanChile, Ladeco, DAP and National daily US$220, via Puerto Montt (sit on right for views), some National flights also stop in Concepción. When no tickets are available, go to the airport and get on the standby waiting list. To Porvenir, Aerovías DAP daily at 0815 and 1730, return 0830 and 1750 (US$20), plus other irregular flights, with Twin-Otter and Cessna aircraft. (Heavily booked with long waiting list so make sure you have your return reservation confirmed.) Military (FACh) flights approximately twice a month to Puerto Montt US$30, information and tickets from airforce base at the airport, Spanish essential, T 213559; need to book well in advance. It is very difficult to get space during the summer as all armed forces personnel and their families have priority over civilians.

Services to Argentina: to Ushuaia, Aerovías DAP twice a week, also Kaiken in summer (schedules change frequently). To Río Grande, Kaiken 5 a week. Reserve well in advance from mid-December to February.

Buses Company offices: Pingüino and Fernández, Sanhueza 745, T 242313, F 225984; **Ghisoni**, Lautaro Navarro 975, T 223205; **Pacheco**, Colón 900, T 242174; **Bus Sur**, Colón y Magallanes, T 244464; **Austral Bus**, Menéndez 565, T 247139, T/F 241708; **Los Carlos**, Plaza Muñoz Gamero 1039,

T 241321; **Turbus**, Errázuriz 932, T/F 225315; **Gesell**, José Menéndez 556, T 222896. Bus timetables are printed daily in *La Prensa Austral*.

Bus services: buses leave from company offices. To **Puerto Natales**, 3½ hours, Fernández, Austral Bus, and Bus Sur, several every day, last departure 1800, US$6. *In-Tur* (see **Tour companies**, above) runs a twice daily circuit Punta Arenas-Puerto Natales-Torres del Paine in minibuses with snack, English-speaking guide and includes National Park entry; service runs mid-October to mid-April. Turbus, Ghisoni and Austral have services through Argentina to **Osorno, Puerto Montt** and **Castro**. Fares: to Puerto Montt or Osorno US$60-75 (cheaper off season) 36 hours; to Castro US$ 67-83; Turbus continues to **Santiago**, US$95 (cheaper in winter), 46 hours.

Buses to Argentina To **Río Gallegos**, Pingüino daily 1200, return 1300; Ghisoni, daily except Friday, 1000; Mansilla Friday 1000, US$22, Magallanes Mayor, Tuesday 1000. Fares US$20-22, officially 5 hours, but can take up to 8, depending on customs, 15 minutes on Chilean side, up to 3 hours on Argentine side, including 30 minutes lunch at Km 160. All customs formalities now undertaken at the border, but ask before departure if this has changed (taxi to Río Gallegos US$130). To **Río Grande**, Hector Pacheco, Monday, Wednesday, Friday 0730 via Punta Delgada, return Tuesday, Thursday and Saturday, 0730, 10 hours, US$27, heavily booked. To **Ushuaia** via Punta Delgada, Los Carlos, Tuesday and Saturday, 0700, return Monday and Friday, 0300, 14 hours, US$48, book any return at same time. Alternatively, Tecni Austral runs daily from Río Grande to Ushuaia at 0730 and 1800, 4 hours, US$20.

Ferries For services to Porvenir (Tierra del Fuego), see page 454.

Shipping Offices Navimag, Colón 521, T 244400, F 242003; **Comapa** (Compañía Marítima de Punta Arenas), Independencia 830, T 244400, F 247514.

Shipping Services For Navimag services to Puerto Montt see under Puerto Natales. Visits to the beautiful fjords and glaciers of western Tierra del Fuego are highly recommended. Comapa runs a once a fortnight 22-hour, 320-km round trip to the fjord d'Agostino, 30 km long, where many glaciers come down to the sea. The luxury cruiser, *Terra Australis*, sails from Punta Arenas on Saturday via Ushuaia and Puerto Williams; details from Comapa. Advance booking (advisable) from Cruceros Australis SA, Miraflores 178, 12th floor, Santiago, T 696-3211, F 331871. Government supply ships are recommended for the young and hardy, but take sleeping bag and extra food, and travel pills. For transport on navy supply

ships to Puerto Williams, enquire at Tercera Zona Naval, Lautaro Navarro 1150, or ask the captain direct, but be prepared to be frustrated by irregular sailings and inaccurate information. All tickets on ships must be booked in advance January-February.

● **To the Falkland Islands/Islas Malvinas**
Punta Arenas is now the main South American link with the islands. Aerovías DAP (address above) fly the following schedule: depart Santiago Wednesday 1300, arrive Punta Arenas 1600, depart 1700, arrive Mount Pleasant, Falklands/Malvinas 1815; depart Mount Pleasant Thursday 1530, arrive Punta Arenas 1700, depart 1800, arrive Santiago 2100, all year. Book well in advance.

● **To Puerto Williams**
For details of sea and air service, see page 437.

● **To Antarctica**
Other than asking in agencies for possible berths on cruise ships, the only possibility is with the Chilean Navy. The Navy itself does not encourage passengers, so you must approach the captain of the vessel direct. Spanish is essential.

● **Overland to Argentina**
From Punta Arenas there are 3 routes to Calafate and Río Gallegos: 1) Northeast via Route 255 and Punta Delgada to the frontier at Kimiri Aike and then along Argentine Route 3 to Río Gallegos. 2) North along Route 9, turning 9 km before Puerto Natales for Dorotea (good road) and then northeast via La Esperanza (fuel, basic accommodation). 3) Via Puerto Natales and Cerro Castillo on the road to Torres del Paine joining the road to La Esperanza at Paso Cancha Carrera.

LONGER EXCURSIONS

Fuerte Bulnes

56 km south, is a replica of the wooden fort erected in 1843 by the crew of the Chilean vessel *Ancud*. Nearby is Puerto Hambre. Tours by several agencies, US$12. At the intersection of the roads to Puerto del Hambre and Fuerte Bulnes, 51 km south of Punta Arenas, is a small marker with a plaque of the Centro Geográfico de Chile, ie the midway point between Arica and the South Pole.

Reserva Forestal Laguna Parrillar

53 km south, covering 18,814 hectares, has older forest than the Magallanes Reserve and sphagnum bogs. There is a 3-hour walk to the tree-line along poorly-marked paths. (No public transport, radio taxi US$60.)

Local wildlife

🐋 'A good place to photograph rheas (ñandúes) is a few kilometres north of the checkpoint at Kon Aiken, near the turnoff for Otway. Antarctic cormorants can be seen sitting on offshore rocks from the road to Fuerte Bulnes. The local skunk (chingüe) is apparently very docile and rarely sprays. Also look out for foxes and the Great Horned Owl.' Arthur Shapiro (Dept of Zoology, Univ of California, Davis).

Otway Sound

60 km north of Punta Arenas, is the site of a small colony of Magellanic penguins which can be visited (November-March only). Patience is required to see the penguins since they nest in burrows underground (tread carefully on the soft ground so as not to damage the nests); in the late afternoon they can be seen by the beach where screens have been built to facilitate viewing. Rheas and skunks can also be seen. Tours by several agencies, US$12, entry US$4; taxi US$35 return.

Isla Magdalena

A small island 25 km northeast, this is the location of the **Monumento Natural Los Pingüinos**, a colony of 150,000 penguins. Deserted apart from the breeding season (November-January), the island is administered by Conaf. Magdalena is one of a group of three islands (the others are Marta and Isabel), visited by Drake, whose men killed 3,000 penguins for food. It can be visited by boat with Comapa (address above): Tuesday, Thursday, Saturday, 0800 (December-February), 2 hours each way, with 2 hours on the island, returns 1400, coffee and biscuits served, US$60, recommended.

NORTH FROM PUNTA ARENAS

From Punta Arenas a gravel road runs north to Puerto Natales; beside it, the southbound lane is paved. Fuel is available in Villa Tehuelches, 100 km from Punta Arenas.

• **Accommodation** Along this road are several hotels, including **B** *Hostal Río Penitente*, Km 138, T 331694, in an old *estancia*, recommended; **C** *Hotel Rubens*, Km 183, T 226916, popular for fishing; *Hostería Llanuras de Diana*, Km 215, T 248742, F 244729 (Punta Arenas), T 411540 (Puerto Natales) hidden from road, highly recommended; **C** *Hostería Río Verde*, Km 90, east off the highway on Seno Skyring, T 311122, F 241008, private bath, heating.

PUERTO NATALES

(*Population* 15,000; *Phone code* 061) is 247 km north of Punta Arenas and close to the Argentine border at Río Turbio. It stands on the *Seno Ultima Esperanza* (Last Hope Sound) amid spectacular scenery and is the jumping-off place for the magnificent Balmaceda and Torres del Paine national parks. Very quiet in the winter it is packed with tourists in the summer. Puerto Bories, 6 km north, was the site of the biggest meatpacking factory in Patagonia; though much of the old plant was destroyed by fire, the administration buildings and housing can be visited.

Museums

Museo de Agostini, in the Colegio Salesiano at Padre Rossa 1456, 1 room, Tierra del Fuego fauna, free.

Museo Histórico Municipal, Bulnes 285, Tuesday-Sunday 1500-1800.

Excursions

A recommended walk is up to **Cerro Dorotea** which dominates the town, with superb views of the whole Ultima Esperanza Sound. Take any bus going east and alight at the jeep track for summit (Km 9.5).

The **Monumento Natural Cueva Milodón** (50m wide, 200m deep, 30m high), 25 km north, contains a plastic model of the prehistoric ground-sloth whose bones were found there in 1895. Evidence has also been found here of occupation by early Patagonian humans some 11,000 years ago. There are fine views over Seno Ultima Esperanza. (Free camping once US$4 entrance fee has been paid.)

• **Transport** Buses J and B regular service US$7.50; taxi US$15 return or check if you can

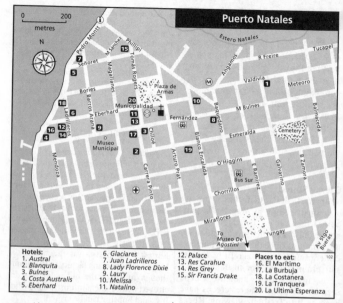

Puerto Natales

Hotels:
1. Austral
2. Blanquita
3. Bulnes
4. Costa Australis
5. Eberhard
6. Glaciares
7. Juan Ladrilleros
8. Lady Florence Dixie
9. Laury
10. Melissa
11. Natalino
12. Palace
13. Res Carahue
14. Res Grey
15. Sir Francis Drake

Places to eat:
16. El Marítimo
17. La Burbuja
18. La Costanera
19. La Tranquera
20. La Ultima Esperanza

get a ride with a tour; both Adventur and Fernández tour buses to Torres del Paine stop at the cave.

Local information

● Accommodation

In season cheaper accommodation fills up quickly after the arrival of the *Puerto Edén* from Puerto Montt. Most prices include breakfast.

L3 *Costa Australis*, Pedro Montt 262, T 412000, F 411881, new in 1994, modern, good views, popular cafetería; **L3** *Eberhard*, Pedro Montt 58, T 411208, F 411209, excellent views, restaurant.

A1 *Palace*, Ladrilleros 209, T 411134, good food, overpriced; **A2** *Glaciares*, Eberhard 104, T 412189, F 411452, new, snack bar; **A2** *Juan Ladrilleros*, Pedro Montt 161, modern, with bath, good restaurant, clean, T 411652, F 412109, recommended; **A2** *Hostal Sir Francis Drake*, Phillipi 383, T/F 411553, good views, snack bar, recommended; **A3** *Hostal Lady Florence Dixie*, Bulnes 659, T 411158, F 411943, modern, friendly, recommended; *Martín Guisinde*, Carlos Bories 278, T 412770, F 412820, phone, TV, tourist information, parking, pub, restaurant, new.

B *Blanquita*, Carrera Pinto 409, quiet, recommended; **B** *Hostal Melissa*, Blanco Encalada 258, T 411944, private bath; **B** *Natalino*,

Eberhard 371, T 411968, clean and very friendly (tours to Milodón Cave arranged), **C** without bath, parking.

C *Bulnes*, Calle Bulnes 407, T 411307, with breakfast, good, stores luggage; **C** *Hostal Puerto Natales*, Eberhard 250, T 411098, private bath; **C** *Hostal Los Antiguos*, Ladrilleros 195 y Bulnes, T/F 411488, shared bath, pleasant; **C** *Res Carahue*, Bulnes 370, T 411339, with breakfast, laundry facilities, nice.

D pp *Lago Sarmiento*, Bulnes 90, T 411542, hot water, some rooms with heating, very friendly, good dinners; **D** *Res Centro*, Magallanes 258A, T 411996, private bath; **D** *Res Sutherland*, Barros Arana 155, with and without bath, welcoming, clean, kitchen facilities.

E pp *Hosp La Chila*, Carrera Pinto 442, use of kitchen, welcoming, luggage store, bakes bread, recommended; **E** pp *María José*, Magallanes 646, cooking facilities, helpful; **E** pp *Hostal Famatina*, Ladrilleros 370, T 412067, clean, friendly; **E** pp *Hosp Gamma/Milodón*, El Roble 650, T 411420, cooking and laundry facilities, evening meals, tours; **E** pp *Los Inmigrantes*, Carrera Pinto 480, good breakfast, clean, kitchen facilities, luggage store, recommended; **E** pp *Res El Mundial*, Bories 315, T 412476, large breakfast, use of kitchen, good value meals, luggage stored, recommended;

E pp *Tierra del Fuego*, Bulnes 29, clean, family of Juan Osorno, will store luggage, good; **E** pp *Casa de familia Bustamante*, Bulnes 317, T 411061, clean, good breakfast, helpful, luggage store, recommended; **E** pp *Casa de familia Elsa Millán*, O'Higgins 657, good breakfast, homemade bread, dormitory-style, popular, hot water, warm, friendly, cooking facilities, recommended; **E** pp *Casa de familia Dickson*, Bulnes 307, T 411218, good breakfast, clean, helpful, cooking and laundry facilities, recommended; **E** pp *Pensión Ritz*, Carrera Pinto 439, full pensión available, friendly; **E** pp *Res Temuco*, Ramírez 310, T 411120, friendly, reasonable, good food, clean; **E** pp *Hosp Laury*, Bulnes 222, with breakfast, cooking and laundry facilities, clean, warm, friendly; **E** pp *Bories*, Bories 206, hostel type, use of kitchen, sleeping bag necessary, good meeting place, friendly; **E** pp *Casa Cecilia*, Tomás Rogers 60, T/F 411797, backpackers' annexe **F** pp, clean, cooking and laundry facilities, only one bathroom, English, French and German spoken, rents camping equipment, information on Torres del Paine, organizes tours, highly recommended; **E** pp *Patagonia Adventure*, Tomás Rogers 179, T 411028, dormitory style, and private rooms, friendly, clean, use of kitchen, breakfast, English spoken, camping equipment for hire, book exchange, recommended; **E** pp Sra Bruna Mardones, Pasaje Don Bosco 41 (off Philippi), friendly, meals on request; **E** pp *Casa de familia Alicia*, M Rodríguez 283, with breakfast, clean, spacious, luggage stored, helpful, recommended; **E** pp *Don Bosco*, Padre Rossa 1430, good meals, use of kitchen, helpful, recommended, motorcycle parking, luggage store; **E-F** pp Sra Teresa Ruiz, Esmeralda 463, good value, warm, cheap meals, quiet, friendly, recommended, tours to Torres del Paine arranged; **F** pp *Res Lago Pingo*, Bulnes 808, T 411026, basic, breakfast extra, hot water, laundry, use of kitchen, will store luggage; similar at O'Higgins 70, 431 and Perito 443; **F** pp private house at Magallanes 1, friendly, cheap meals.

North of Puerto Natales are: **L3-A2** *Cisne de Cuello Negro*, a former guest house for meat buyers at the disused meat packing plant, T 411498 (Avenida Colón 782, Punta Arenas, T 244506, F 248052), friendly, clean, reasonable, excellent cooking, recommended, 5 km from town at Km 275 near Puerto Bories; **A2** *Patagonia Inn*, Km 26 north, reservations Hotel Cabo de Hornos, T/F 242134, Punta Arenas, private bath, restaurant; **C** *Hotel 3 Pasos*, 40 km north, T 228113, simple, beautiful. In Villa Cerro Castillo, 63 km north: **B** *Hostería El Pionero*, T/F 411646, with bath, country house ambience, good service. For accommodation in

the Torres del Paine area, see below. **NB** Hotels in the countryside open only in summer months: dates vary.

● **Places to eat**

Don Alvarito, Blanco Encalada 915, hospitable; *El Marítimo*, Pedro Montt 214, seafood and salmon, good views, popular, slow service; *Mari Loli*, Baquedano 615, excellent food, good value; *La Ultima Esperanza*, Eberhard 354, recommended for salmon, seafood, enormous portions, not cheap but worth the experience; *La Costanera*, Bories y Ladrilleros, good food, superb views; *Andrés*, Ladrilleros 381, excellent, good service; *La Burbuja*, Bulnes 371, huge portions, reasonably priced; *Tierra del Fuego*, Bulnes 29, cheap, good, slow service; *Café Josmar*, Yungay 743, only café open every day, packed lunches sold for boat trips; *Melissa*, Blanco Encalada, good coffee and cakes; *Centro Español*, Magallanes 247, reasonable; *La Frontera*, Bulnes 819, set meals and à la carte, good value; *La Tranquera*, Bulnes y Blanco Encalada, popular. Cheap meals at Club Deportivo Natales, Eberhard 332. *Cristal*, Bulnes 439, good sandwiches and salmon; *Tío Cacho*, Phillipi 553, pizzas and sandwiches; *Delicatessen Pollo Loco*, Baquedano 330, T 411393, good, does packed lunches, recommended. Best coffee in town in the cafetería of the *Hotel Costa Australis*.

● **Banks & money changers**

Poor rates for travellers' cheques, which cannot be changed into US$ cash. Banco O'Higgins, Bulnes 633, Mastercard, ATM. Casas de cambio on Blanco Encalada 226 (Andes Patagónicos) and 266 (Enio América) where Argentine pesos can be changed. *Cambio Stop*, Baquedano 380, good for cash (also arranges tours). Another two at Bulnes 683 and 1087 (good rates; also Argentine pesos); others on Prat. Shop around as some offer very poor rates.

● **Language schools**

Natalis English Centre, Bulnes 1231, T 411193, F 411300, one to one tuition US$4 per hour, good.

● **Entertainment**

Discos: *El Cielo*, Esmeralda y Ramírez; *Milodón*, Blanco Encalada.

● **Laundry**

Lavandería Papaguayo, Bulnes 518; *Tienda Milodón*, Bulnes, cheap; *Liberty*, Bulnes 513, or try Sra María Carcamo (at Teresa Ruiz's *Hospedaje* at 1000-1200, 1800-2200), good service, more expensive.

● **Post & telecommunications**

Post Office: Eberhard 417, open Monday-Friday 0830-1230, 1430-1745, Saturday 0900-1230.

Telephones: CTC, Blanco Encalada 23 y Bulnes, phones and fax.

● **Shopping**
Shoe repairs: *París*, Miraflores between Blanco Encalada and Baquedano.

Supermarket: *El Favorito*, Bulnes 1008, 24-hour supermarket Bulnes 300 block; markets good; food prices variable so shop around; cheaper in Punta Arenas.

● **Sports**
Camping equipment: *Patagonia Adventures*, see **Hotels** above; *Casa Cecilia*, Tomás Rogers 54, German, French and English spoken, imported gear, also for sale, recommended; *Patagonia Adventures*, Tomás Rogers 179. Check all equipment and prices carefully. Average charges, per day: tent US$6, sleeping bag US$3-5, mat US$1.50, raincoat US$0.60, also cooking gear, US$1-2. (**NB** Deposits required: tent US$200, sleeping bag US$100.) Camping gas is widely available in hardware stores, eg at Baquedano y O'Higgins and at Baquedano y Esmeralda.

Fishing: tackle for hire at *Andes Patagónicos*, Blanco Encalada 226, T 411594, US$3.50 per day for rod, reel and spinners; if you prefer fishing with floats, hooks, split shot, etc, take your own. Other companies up to 5 times as expensive.

● **Tour companies & travel agents**
Turis Ann, Tomás Rogers 255, T/F 411141, very helpful, accommodation arranged, tours, equipment hire; *San Cayetano*, Eberhard 145, T 411112; *Michay*, Baquedano 388, T 411149/411957 (Pedro Fueyo recommended); *Andescape*, Pedro Montt 308, next to harbour, T 412592; *Knudsen Tours*, Encalada 284, T 411531, recommended; *Onas*, Bulnes 453, T 412707 (Casilla 78); *Servitur*, Pratt 353, T 411028; *Turismo Zalej*, Bulnes 459, recommended, T 412260, F 411355. Patricio Canales, Eberhard 49, recommended as a good guide; *Turismo Cabo de Hornos*, Pedro Montt 380; *Turismo Tzonka*, Carrera Pinto 626, T 411214. Reports of the reliability of agencies, especially for their trips to Torres del Paine National Park, are very mixed. It is better to book tours direct with agents in Puerto Natales than through agents in Punta Arenas.

Several agencies offer tours to the Perito Moreno glacier in Argentina, 1 day, US$70 without food or park entry fee. The agencies are reluctant to let tourists leave the tour in Calafate and continue into Argentina.

● **Tourist offices**
Offices in kiosk on waterfront, Avenida Pedro Montt y Phillipi; maps for US$1 from Eberhard 547. **Conaf**: Carrera Pinto 566.

● **Transport**
Local Bicycle hire: *Onas*, Bulnes 453, US$1 a day; also try *Hotel Eberhard*. **Bicycle repair**: *El Rey de la Bicicleta*, Arauco 779, good helpful. **Car hire**: Andes Patagónicos, Blanc Encalada 226, T 411594, helpful, US$85 pe day including insurance and 350 km free; To doauto, Bulnes 20, T 412837. US$110 per da for high clearance vehicle, others US$80 per day or US$85 with driver. Hire agents can arrang permission to drive into Argentina, but this i expensive and takes 24 hours to arrange. Me chanic: Carlos González, Ladrilleros entre Borie y Eberhard, recommended.

Air Alta from Puerto Montt, fine views, 3 hours US$50, a recommended alternative to the ferry

Buses To Punta Arenas, several daily, 3½ hours, US$6. Bus Fernández, Eberhard 555 T 411111, Bus Sur, Baquedano 534, T 41132! and Austral Bus, Baquedano y Valdivia, T 411415. Book in advance. To Coyhaique vi Calafate, Urbina Tours, 4 days, US$120 (November-March). Out of season the only service to rest of Chile: Austral Bus, Tuesday to Puert Montt, US$150, book days in advance.

To Argentina: to Río Gallegos direct, Bus Sur, US$22, Tuesday and Thursday 1830 and El Pingüino, Wednesday and Sunday 1200, US20; hourly to Río Turbio, Lagoper, Baquedano y Valdivia, and other companies, US$3, 2 hours (depending on Customs – change bus at border). To Calafate, Río Turbio bus from Onas, Bulnes 453, 0630, US$17.50, otherwise travel agencies run several times a week depending on demand, 7 hours, US$50, shop around, reserve 1 day ahead.

Shipping Navimag: Pedro Montt 262 Local B, Terminal Marítimo, T/F 411421.

Navimag's *Puerto Edén* sails to **Puerto Montt** every 8 days, taking 4 days and 3 nights to cover the 1,460 km along the Chilean coast past innumerable islands and across the rough seas of the Golfo de Peñas; the fare ranges from US$160 per person economy (including meals) to US$660 per person in various classes of cabin (also including meals); 10% discount on international student cards in cabin class only. Payment by credit card or foreign currency generally not accepted. Economy class accommodation is basic, in 24-berth dormitories and there is limited additional space for economy class passengers when weather is bad. Apart from videos, entertainment on board is limited. Economy class and cabin passengers eat in separate areas. Some report good food, others terrible. Standards of service and comfort vary, depending on the number of passengers and weather conditions. Take seasickness tablets.

Another Navimag vessel, the *Amadeus*, carries cargo between Puerto Natales, Puerto Chacabuco and Puerto Montt, with a few passenger, same price as cheaper cabins on the *Puerto Edén*, no fixed timetable.

Booking: economy class can only be booked, with payment, through Navimag offices in Puerto Natales and Puerto Montt. Economy tickets are frequently sold just before departure. Cabin class can be booked in advance through *Travellers* travel agency in Puerto Montt (see under **Puerto Montt**), through Navimag offices in Puerto Montt, Puerto Natales and Punta Arenas, or through Cruceros Austalis (Navimag parent company) in Santiago. All of these have their own ticket allocation: once this is used up, they have to contact other offices to request spare tickets. Book well in advance for departures between mid-December and mid-March although the voyage north is less heavily booked than from Puerto Montt to Puerto Natales. It is well worth going to the port on the day of departure if you have no ticket. Note that departures are frequently delayed – or even advanced.

FRONTIER WITH ARGENTINA

There are three crossing points:

1) PASO CASAS VIEJAS

16 km east of Puerto Natales. On the Argentine side the road continues to a junction, with alternatives south to Río Turbio and north to La Esperanza and Río Gallegos.

● **Chilean immigration**
Open all year 0800-2000.

2) VILLA DOROTEA

16 km northeast of Puerto Natales. On the Argentine side this joins the Río Turbio-La Esperanza road.

● **Chilean immigration**
Open all year daytime only.

3) CERRO CASTILLO

65 km north of Puerto Natales on the road to Torres del Paine. On the Argentine side, Paso Cancha Carrera (14 km), the road leads to La Esperanza and Río Gallegos.

● **Chilean immigration**
Open 0830-1200, 1400-2000, November-March or April only.

● **Accommodation**
2 *hospedajes* in Cerro Castillo.

PARQUE NACIONAL BERNARDO O'HIGGINS

Usually referred to as the **Parque Nacional Monte Balmaceda**, this park lies at the north end of Ultima Esperanza Sound and can be reached by sea only. Two boats *21 de Mayo* and *Alberto de Agostini* sail daily from Puerto Natales in summer and on Sunday only in winter (minimum 10 passengers), when weather conditions may be better with less cloud and rain, US$38. After a 3-hour journey up the Sound, the boat passes the Balmaceda Glacier which drops from the eastern slopes of Monte Balmaceda (2,035m). The glacier is retreating; in 1986 its foot was at sea level. The boat docks 1 hour further north at Puerto Toro, from where it is a 1-km walk to the base of Serrano Glacier on the north slope of Monte Balmaceda. On the trip dolphins, sea-lions (in season), black-necked swans, flightless steamer ducks and cormorants can be seen.

Bookings through *Andes Patagónicos* (address above) or other agencies, expensive lunch extra, take own food, drinks available on board. Take warm clothes, hat and gloves. This trip can also be combined with a visit to Torres del Paine. You have to pay full fare on the boat and you need a permit from Conaf. The 35 km walk from Puerto Toro along the Río Serrano to the Torres del Paine administration centre is hard going with no clear path; it is not an authorized route and the *guardaparques* in Torres del Paine discourage its use.

PARQUE NACIONAL TORRES DEL PAINE

Situated 145 km northwest of Puerto Natales and covering 181,414 hectares, this national park is a 'must' for its wildlife and spectacular scenery. In the centre of the park is a granite *massif* from which rise the *Torres* (Towers) and *Cuernos* (Horns) of Paine, oddly shaped peaks of over 2,600m. The valleys are filled by beautiful lakes at 50m to 200m above sea level. There are 15 peaks above 2,000m, of which the highest is Cerro Paine Grande (3,050m). On the

Torres del Paine

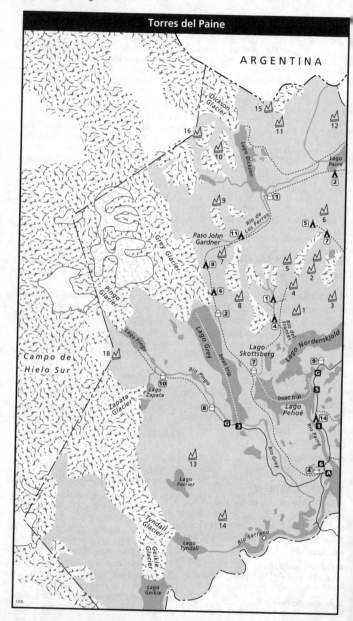

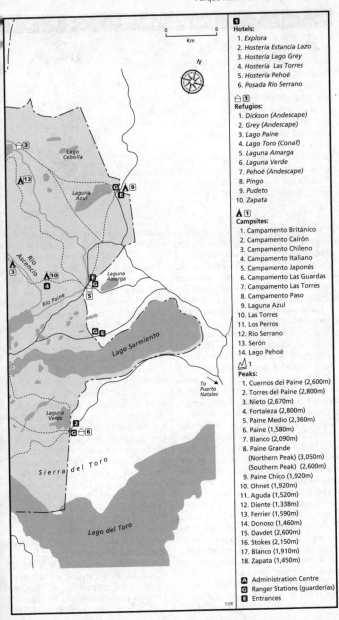

103R

Look under your feet

Few of the 50,000 people a year who visit Torres del Paine look closely at what they are treading on; a blanket of orchids, orange and yellow slipper plants (*Calceolaria*), Lathyrus (mauve sweet pea like flowers) and mauve Oxalis. In spring the hill slopes are a blaze of embothrium, with its brilliant red flowers, pernettya with its copious ruby-like fruits and calafate (*Berberis buxifolia*), a low shrub with bright yellow single flowers and delicious red/mauve berries. In damper shady areas are clumps of tiny 3 cm high Gunnera magellanica as well as the copihue (*Lapageria rosea*), the Chilean national flower.

Jane Norwich

Calceolaria

west edge of the Park is the enormous *Campo de Hielo Sur* icecap; 4 main glaciers (*ventisqueros*), Grey, Dickson Zapata and Tyndall, branch off this and drop to the lakes formed by their meltwater. Two other glaciers, the *Francés* and *Los Perros* descend on the west side of the central *massif*.

The scenery in the Park is superb, with constantly changing views of fantastic peaks, ice-fields, vividly coloured lakes of turquoise, ultramarine and grey and quiet green valleys. The Park enjoys a micro-climate especially favourable to wildlife and plants: there are 105 species of birds including 18 species of waterfowl and 11 birds of prey. Particularly noteworthy are condors, black-necked swans, rheas, kelp geese, ibis, flamingoes and austral parrots. There are also 25 species of mammals including *guanaco*, hares, foxes, *huemules* (a species of deer), pumas and skunks. Over 200 species of plants have been identified. The Park is open all year round, although snow may prevent access in the winter: warmest time is December-March, although it can be wet and windy. It is also more crowded at this time. October-November can be very nice with lots of spring flowers. In winter there can be good, stable conditions and well-equipped hikers can do some good walking.

Torres del Paine has become increasingly popular with foreigners and Chileans alike: in 1996 it received 51,000 visitors, most during the summer. Despite the best efforts to manage this large influx of visitors rationally, their impact is starting to show. Litter has become a problem especially around the *refugios* and camping areas. Please take all your rubbish out of the Park and remember that toilet paper is also garbage.

The Park is administered by Conaf: the Administration Centre is in the south of the Park at the north end of Lago del Toro (open 0830-2000 in summer, 0830-1230, 1400-1830 off season). The Centre provides a good slide show at 2000 on Saturday and Sunday and there are also excellent exhibitions on fauna and flora (in Spanish), but no maps or written information to take away. For information (in Spanish) on weather conditions phone the Administration Centre (T 691931). There are six ranger stations (*guarderías*) staffed by rangers (*guardaparques*) who give help and advice and will also store luggage (except at Laguna Amarga where they have no room). Rangers keep a check on the whereabouts of all visitors: you are required to register and show your passport when entering the park. You are also requested to register at a ranger station before setting off on any hike. There are entrances at Laguna Amarga, Lago Sarmiento and Laguna Azul. Entry for foreigners: US$12 (proceeds are shared between all 35 Chilean National Parks) climbing fees US$800. Allow a week to 10 days to see the park properly.

Warning It is vital not to underestimate the unpredictability of the weather (which can change in a few minutes), nor the arduousness of some of the stretches on the long hikes. Rain and snowfall are heavier the further west you go, and bad weather sweeps off the *Campo de Hielo Sur* without warning. It is essential to be properly equipped against cold, wind and rain. The only means of rescue are on horseback or by boat; the nearest helicopter is in Punta Arenas and high winds usually prevent its operation in the park.

Hikes

There are about 250 km of well-marked trails. Visitors must keep to the trails: cross-country trekking is not permitted. **NB** The times indicated should be treated with caution: allow for personal fitness and weather conditions.

El Circuito The most popular hike is a circuit round the Torres and Cuernos del Paine: usually it is done either anticlockwise starting from the Laguna Amarga *guardería* or clockwise from the administration centre. From Laguna Amarga the route is north along the west side of the Río Paine to Lago Paine, before turning west to follow the Río Paine to the south end of Lago Dickson. From here the path runs along the wooded valley of the Río de los Perros before climbing steeply to Paso John Gardner (1,241m, the highest point on the route), then dropping to follow the Grey Glacier southeast to Lago Grey, continuing to Lago Pehoé and the Administration Centre. There are superb views, particularly from the top of Paso John Gardner.

Although some people complete the route more quickly, it normally takes 5-6 days. Lone walkers are not allowed on this route and camping gear must be carried. The circuit is often closed in winter because of snow. The longest lap is 30 km, between Refugio Laguna Amarga and Refugio Dickson (10 hours in good weather), but the most difficult section is the very steep slippery slope between Paso John Gardner (1,241m) and *Campamento Paso*. Although most people go anti-clockwise round the circuit, some advise doing it clockwise so that you climb to Paso John Gardner with the wind behind. The major rivers are crossed by footbridges, but these are occasionally washed away.

The Valley of the Río del Francés From *Refugio Pehoé* this route leads north across undulating country along the west edge of Lago Skottberg to *Campamento Italiano* and then follows the valley of the Río del Francés which climbs between (to the west) Cerro Paine Grande and the Ventisquero del Francés and (to the east) the Cuernos del Paine to *Campamento Británico*. Allow 2½ hours from Refugio Pehoé to *Campamento Italiano*, 2½ hours further to *Campamento Británico*. The views from the *mirador* above *Campamento Británico* are superb.

To Lago Pingo From *Guardería Grey* (18 km west by road from the Administration Centre) follow the Río Pingo, via *Refugio Pingo* and *Refugio Zapata* (4 hours), with views south over Ventisquero Zapata (plenty of wildlife, icebergs in the lake) to reach the lake (5 hours from *Guardería Grey*). Ventisquero Pingo can be seen 3 km away over the lake.

To the base of the Torres del Paine From *Refugio Laguna Amarga* the route follows the road west to *Hostería Las Torres* before climbing along the west side of the Río Ascensio via *Campamento Chileno* to *Campamento Las Torres*, close to the base of the Torres and near a small lake. Allow 1½ hours to *Hostería Las Torres*, then 2 hours to *Campamento Chileno*, 2 hours further to *Campamento Torres* where there is a lake: the path is well-marked, but the last 30 minutes is up the morraine; to see the torres lit by sunrise (spectacular but you must have good weather), it's well worth humping camping gear up to *Campamento Torres* and spending the night. 1 hour beyond *Campamento Torres* is the good site at *Campamento Japonés*.

To Laguna Verde From the administation centre follow the road north 2 km, before taking the path east over the Sierra del Toro and then along the south side of Laguna Verde to the *Guardería Laguna Verde*. Allow 4 hours. This is one of the easiest walks in the park and may be a good first hike.

To Laguna Azul and Lago Paine This route runs north from Laguna Amarga to the west tip of Laguna Azul, from where it continues across the sheltered Río Paine valley past Laguna Cebolla to the *Refugio Lago Paine* at the west end of the lake. Allow 8½ hours.

Equipment

A strong, streamlined, waterproof tent is preferable to the free *refugios* and is essential if doing the complete circuit. Also essential are protective clothing against wind and rain, strong waterproof footwear, compass, good sleeping bag, sleeping mat, camping stove and cooking equipment. In summer take shorts and sun-screen also. Equipment is checked at the entrance. Take your own food: the small shops at the Andescape *refugios* (see below) and at the *Posada Río Serrano* are expensive and have a limited selection. Note that rats and mice have become a major problem around camping sites and the free *refugios*. Do not leave food in your pack (which will be chewed through): the safest solution is to hang food in a bag on wire. Maps (US$3), are obtainable at Conaf offices in Punta Arenas or Puerto Natales. Most maps are unreliable but the one produced by Sociedad Turística Kaonikén, US$5, has been recommended as more accurate than the Conaf map (available at *Nandú Artesanía* at port end of Bulnes).

Park information

● **Accommodation**

Hotels: L1 *Hotel Explora*, new, luxurious and comfortable, at Salto Chico on edge of Lago Pehoé, T 411247, offering spectacular views, pool, gym, tours (reservations: Avenida Américo Vespucci 80, 7th floor, Santiago, T 228-8081, F 208-5479); **L3** *Hostería Pehoé*, T 411390, 60 rooms, private facilities, cheaper off season, 5 km south of Pehoé ranger station, 11 km north of park administration, on an island with spectacular view across the Lake to Cerro Paine Grande and Cuernos del Paine, good meals (reservations: *Turismo Pehoé* in Punta Arenas or

Antonio Bellet 77, office 605, T 235-0252, F 236-0917, Santiago); **L3** *Hostería Las Torres* head office Lautaro Navarro 1125, Punta Arenas, T/F 222641, new, modern conveniences, separate restaurant, English spoken at reception, horse-riding, transport from Laguna Amarga ranger station, recommended; **L3** *Hostería Lago Grey*, T/F 227528, or Punta Arenas T/F 241042/248167, good food, new, on edge of Lago Grey (reservations through *Arka Patagonia* or *Turismo Runner* in Punta Arenas); **A1** *Hostería Estancia Lazo*, on the east edge of the park, 8 cabins beautifully situated on Laguna Verde with spectacular views, very friendly, comfortable, excellent food, very highly recommended (reservations: *Operatur Patagónia SA*, Avenida Colón 568, T/F 61-221130/240056, Punta Arenas); **A2** pp *Posada Río Serrano*, an old *estancia*, some rooms with bath, some with shared facilities, breakfast extra, near park administration, with expensive but good restaurant and a shop (reservations advisable: run by *Turismo Río Serrano*, Prat 258, Puerto Natales, T 410684).

Refugios: F pp *Refugio Lago Toro*, near administration centre, run by Conaf, hot showers, cooking facilities, good meeting place, sleeping bag and mattress essential, no camping, open summer only – in the winter months another more basic (free) *refugio* is open near administration centre. The following are run by Andescape (addresses under Puerto Natales and Santiago): *Refugio Lago Pehoé*, on the northeast arm of Lago Pehoé; *Refugio Grey*, on the eastern shore of Lago Grey; *Refugio Lago Dickson*; all **D** pp, modern, closed in winter until 10 September, clean, with dormitory accommodation (sheets not provided), hot showers (US$2 for non-residents), cooking and laundry facilities, meals served, kiosk with basic food and other supplies, rental of camping equipment, campsite (US$3 per person). **D** pp *Refugio Las Torres*, is owned by *Hostería Las Torres*, meals served.

In addition there are 6 free *refugios*: *Zapata*, *Pingo*, *Laguna Verde*, *Laguna Amarga*, *Lago Paine* and *Pudeto*. Most have cooking areas (wood stove or fireplace) but *Laguna Verde* and *Pingo* do not. These are now in very poor condition and are very crowded in summer (rangers know how many people are on each route and can give you an idea of how busy refugios will be).

Camping In addition to sites at the Andescape *refugios* there are the following sites: *Camping Serón* and *Camping Las Torres* (at *Hostería Las Torres*) both run by Estancia Cerro Paine, US$4, hot showers; *Camping Los Perros*, run by Andescape, US$3 per person, shop and hot showers; *Camping Lago Pehoé* and *Camping Serrano*, both run by Turismo Río Serrano (address above), US$20 per site at former (maximum 6 persons, hot showers) and US$15 per site at latter (max 6 persons, cold showers, more basic); *Camping Laguna Azul*, hot showers, **D** per site. Free camping is permitted in seven other locations in the park: these sites are known as *campamentos*. Fires may only be lit at organized *camping* sites, not a *campamentos*. The *guardaparques* expect people to have a stove if camping. (**NB** These restrictions should be observed as forest fires are a serious hazard.) Beware mice, which eat through tents. Equipment hire in Puerto Natales (see above).

● **Boat trips**
From *Hostería Grey* at the south end of Lago Grey to the Grey Glacier, minimum 8 passengers, US$25 including refreshments, 2-3 hours, a stunning trip. From *Refugio Lago Pehoé* to *Refugio Pudeto*, US$12 one way daily, from Pudeto 1030, 1600, from Pehoé 1200, 1530, 1 hour, in high season reserve in advance at the *refugios* at either end or at *Turismo Tzonka* in Puerto Natales. Off-season, radio for the boat from *Refugio Pehoé*.

● **Transport**
Local Car hire: hiring a pick-up from **Budget** in Punta Arenas is an economical proposition for a group (up to 9 people): US$415 for 4 days. If driving yourself, the road from Pto Natales is being improved and, in the Park, the roads are narrow, bendy with blind corners, use your horn a lot; it takes about 3½ hours from Pto Natales to the administration, 3 hours to Laguna Amarga. Petrol available at Río Serrano, but fill up in case. **Horse hire**: Baquedano Zamora, Blanco Encalada 226, Puerto Natales, T 411592.

Buses San Cayetano, Servitur and JB Buses (addresses above) run daily bus services to the park from Puerto Natales leaving between 0630 and 0800, returning between 1300 and 1500, 3½ hours journey, US$8.75 one way, US$12.50 open return (return tickets are not interchangeable between different companies, buy single ticket), from early November to mid-April. See also under Punta Arenas **Buses** for the daily In-Tur minibus service from Punta Arenas. Buses pass *Guardería Laguna Amarga* at 1030, *Guardería Pehoé* at 1130, arriving at Admin at 1230, leave Admin at 1400 (in high season the buses fill quickly so it is best to board at the Administration). All buses wait at *Refugio Pudeto* until the 1430 boat from *Refugio Lago Pehoé* arrives. Travel between two points within the park (eg Pudeto-Laguna Amarga) US$1.25. At other times services by travel agencies are dependent on demand: arrange return date with driver and try to arrange your return date to coincide with other groups to keep costs down. Luis Díaz has been recommended, about US$12 per person, minimum 3 persons. A new road to the Park from Puerto Natales has been built to the southern entrance, at Lago Toro, although in March 1996, a bridge over the Río Serrano was still missing.

To go from Torres del Paine to Calafate (Argentina) either return to Pto Natales and go to Río Turbio for bus to La Esperanza, or take a bus or hitch from the park to Villa Cerro Castillo border point (106 km south of the administration), cross to Paso Cancha de Carreras and try to link with the Río Turbio-La Esperanza-Río Gallegos bus schedule, or hitch. (See Accommodation **North of Puerto Natales**, above.)

Tours Several agencies in Puerto Natales including *Servitur, Scott Tours* and *Luis Díaz* offer 1-day tours by minibus, US$37.50 (some travellers report that these are a waste of time as you need to stay overnight to appreciate the park). José Torres of *Sastrería Arbiter* in Calle Bulnes 731 (T 411637) recommended as guide. *Enap* weekend tours in summer cost US$45 including accommodation and meals. *Buses Fernández* offer 2-day tours, US$132 and 3-day tours (which includes trip to the Balmaceda Glacier) US$177. Before booking a tour check carefully on details and get them in writing: increasingly mixed reports of tours. Many companies who claim to visit the Grey Glacier only visit Lago Grey (you see the Glacier in the distance). Taxi costs US$80 per day, run by *Zalej* (Arturo Prat 260), but may be cheaper if you catch him when he's going to the Park anyway. After mid-March there is little public transport (ask *San Cayetano*) and trucks are irregular.

Onas Turismo (address under Puerto Natales **Tour companies**) runs trips from the Park down the Río Serrano in dinghies to the Serrano glacier and from there, on the *21 de Mayo* or *Alberto de Agostini* tour boats to Puerto Natales, US$90 per person all inclusive. Book in advance.

Tierra del Fuego

THE LARGEST ISLAND at the extreme south of South America, Tierra del Fuego is divided between Argentina (east side) and Chile (west): both of these are covered in this section as well as the Chilean island of Isla Navarino, south of Tierra del Fuego. The south has beautiful lakes, woods and mountain scenery, and there is much birdlife to see. Boat trips can be made on the Beagle Channel; there is skiing in winter. March-April is a good time to visit because of the beautiful autumn colours.

GEOGRAPHY

Tierra del Fuego is separated from the South American mainland by the Magellan Strait to the north; to the east is Atlantic Ocean; the Beagle Channel to the south separates it from the southern islands; a complex network of straits including the Whiteside, Gabriel, Magdalena and Cockburn channels divide it from the islands situated to the west.

The north of Tierra del Fuego is steppe but further south the island is crossed from east to west by the continuation of the Andes; in the Argentine sector these rise to around 1,500m but in the Chilean part in the far southwest there are peaks of well over 2,000m. The main rivers drain into the Beagle Channel and into Lago Fagnano, the largest lake on the island, which flows west to the sea via the Río Azopardo. There are a number of other lakes including Lagos Yehuin and Chapelmuth, just north of Lago Fagnano, and Lagos Blanco, Chico and Lynch in Chilean territory.

The northern and southern parts of the island have contrasting vegetation: the steppe is covered with grassland,

Fuschia Magallanica

As its name suggests this beautiful arching shrub was first identified along the coast of the Magellan Straits during the voyage of HMS *Beagle*, but it can be found in many areas of the country. It has long slender flowers with a scarlet calyx and violet petals. Its dark green leaves are found in whorls of three.

Jane Norwich

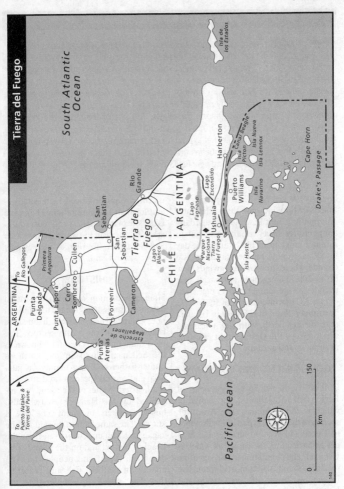

while further south subantarctic forests grow on hills up to about 600m. Poorly-drained low-lying areas in the south are covered with spagnum moss. Native fauna include guanacos and red foxes; musk rats, beaver and rabbits have been imported. In summer wild geese and ducks can be seen and some 150 other bird species have been identified; the Bahía San Sebastian is an important area for migratory birds. Trout and salmon inhabit nearly all the lakes and rivers.

CLIMATE

The island's climate is cold sub-Antarctic, though extremes of temperature are moderated by the sea and there are significant differences between north and south of the island. In Ushuaia southwesterly winds prevail, ranging in force from 15 km per

The fate of the Patagonians

Though widespread contact between the indigenous populations of Tierra del Fuego and white settlers was delayed until the end of the 19th century, immigration, once it began, led to their extinction within a generation. The granting by the Chilean and Argentine governments of large land concessions to sheep-farmers ended the nomadic life-style of the Onas. The Yaganes (or Yámanas) and the Alacalufes were killed by diseases and alcohol introduced by the whalers and sealers who began to work along the coasts. The fate of the Onas, though, was particularly tragic. Many were hunted down and slaughtered by gunmen employed by the ranchers, the gunmen being paid for each pair of ears which they presented. Although the Salesian missionaries attempted to save them by moving them to missions on Dawson Island and near Río Grande, few survived the change of lifestyle for long.

hour to 100 km per hour. September to March are the windy months, while winter is normally calmer. In winter average daily temperatures hover around zero but in summer range from 13°C during the day to 5°C at night. Further north in Río Grande, where strong westerly winds blow up to 200 km per hour almost all year round, average temperatures range from -3°C to 2°C in winter and from 5°C to 15°C in summer. Rainfall is higher in Ushuaia than further north, with slight seasonal variations; in Río Grande most rain falls in summer and autumn.

GOVERNMENT AND ECONOMY

Chilean Tierra del Fuego forms part of Region XII (Magallanes), the capital of which is Punta Arenas. The Argentine section of the island is part of the Province of Tierra del Fuego, Antartida y Las Islas del Atlántico Sur, the capital of which is Ushuaia. The population of the Argentine sector is around 70,000, most of whom live in the two towns of Río Grande and Ushuaia. Chilean Tierra del Fuego has a population of some 7,000, the majority of whom live in Porvenir.

For many years the main economic activity of the northern part of the island was sheepfarming, but Argentine government tax incentives to companies in the 1970s led to the establishment of new industries in Río Grande and Ushuaia and a rapid growth in the population of both cities; the subsequent withdrawal of

incentives has produced increasing un-employment and emigration. The island is the site of the smallest and most south-erly oil refinery in the world in Argentine San Sebastian. Tourism is increasingly important in Ushuaia.

HISTORY

Human habitation of Tierra del Fuego dates back some 10,000 years; four indige-nous groups, all now extinct, inhabited the island until the early 20th century. The most numerous, the Onas (also known as the Selk'nam), lived in the north as hunter-gatherers living mainly on gua-naco and several species of rodents. The southeastern corner of the island was in-habited by the Haus or Hausch, also hunter-gatherers, of whom very little is known. The same cannot be said for the Yaganes or Yámanas, who lived along the Beagle Channel and on the islands fur-ther south. A seafaring people who lived mainly on seafood, fish and seabirds, they were physically smaller than the Onas, but with a strongly developed up-per body for rowing long distances. The fourth group, the Alacaluf, lived in the west of Tierra del Fuego as well as on the islands along the Chilean coast, surviving in these inhospitable conditions by fishing and hunting seals.

The first Europeans to visit the island were members of an expedition led by the Portuguese Fernão Magalhães, who, in 1520, sailed through the channel that

Thomas and Lucas Bridges

🐾 An orphan from Bristol, Bridges was so named because he was found as a child under a bridge with the letter T on his clothing. Bridges arrived in Tierra del Fuego in 1871 with his wife, young daughter and his adoptive father, Rev Despard, an early Christian missionary; he remained when Despard left after a massacre of Christians by the Indians. Until his death in 1898 Bridges lived near the shores of the Beagle Channel, first at Ushuaia and then Harberton, devoting his life to his work with the Yámanas (Yaghanes) and compiling a dictionary of their language. Of his six children the most famous was Lucas (1874-1949), who, after spending his early life among the Yámanas and Onas and learning their languages, became an outspoken defender of their rights and an opponent of the early sheepfarmers. His memoirs, *The Uttermost Part of the Earth* (1947), trace the tragic fate of the native population with whom he grew up.

bears his name. As a result of the extreme dangers of such a voyage and the failure of Sarmiento de Gamboa's attempt to found settlements along the Straits in 1584, the indigenous population were left undisturbed until after South American independence.

Though Fitz Roy and Darwin visited in 1832, European settlement only occurred much later in the 19th century. In 1851 the South American Missionary Society, an Anglican society with missions on the Falkland Islands/Islas Malvinas sent seven missionaries to Picton Island

Gold fever

🐾 The Tierra del Fuego Gold Rush is closely linked to the name of Julio Popper who settled in San Sebastián in 1887 where he founded the El Paramó mine. Popper died young in 1893, by which time his company had extracted 600 kilos of gold from El Paramó and from along the Beagle Channel. After his death gold mining became a much larger scale business until, in 1909, the gold suddenly ran out. Despite its short life the gold rush had lasting consequences: among the prospectors from North America and Europe who arrived hoping to get rich, the largest group were Croats from Dalmatia, then part of the Austrian Empire; many of their descendents still live in the area.

to establish a mission, but they were driven off by the Yaganes and the first successful mission was only established 18 years later, at Ushuaia.

The work of the missionaries was, however, disturbed by two developments, the discovery of gold and the growth of sheep-farming. As in southern Patagonia, the settlement of the frontier disputes between Argentina and Chile was followed by a desire by both governments to settle the area by allocating large expanses of land for sheepfarming. The main beneficiaries of this policy on Tierra del Fuego were the Menéndez and Braun families, already established in Punta Arenas.

COMMUNICATIONS

Note that flights to and from the island are heavily booked in summer, especially in January and that bus and ferry services are subject to cancellation due to weather conditions.

ROUTES TO TIERRA DEL FUEGO

There are no road/ferry crossings between the Argentine mainland and Argentine Tierra del Fuego: you have to go through Chilean territory. It is not always possible to cross the Chilean part in one day because of the irregularity of the ferry.

There are two routes:

Via Punta Delgada

The easternmost crossing, across the Primera Angostura (First Narrows), is 127

Shipwrecked in the Magellan Straits

The Estrecho de Magallanes, 534 km long, was and still is a treacherous passage and over the centuries it has claimed a long succession of victims. The hostile conditions which can prevail are perhaps best summed up in the words of Sir John Narborough: 'horrible like the ruins of a world destroyed by terrific earthquakes.'

From the Atlantic end the first navigational problem facing sailors is simply the difficulty of entering the Straits in the face of the fierce westerly gales which prevail, numerous sailing vessels having been forced back out to sea to wallow for weeks on end. Once in the straits the dangers are far from over: many ships have fallen victim to the notorious Williwaws, winds with the ferocity of tornados which spring up from nowhere, or the vicious Pamperos, which blow off the land with enough force to capsize a vessel.

Though in 1520 Magellan succeeded in passing through the straits which bear his name, few others managed to do so in the years which followed: of 17 ships which attempted the passage in the early 16th century only one, the Victoria, succeeded in reaching the Pacific and returning to Europe. Twelve were lost near the eastern entrance and four returned in failure. The great attraction which drove these early navigators was the lure of a short route between Europe and the spices of the East. Once it was clear that there was no short route it was still a useful way for Europeans to reach the rich Pacific ports of Peru and Chile without disembarking and crossing Mexico or Panama on foot or by mule.

Although by the 19th century the replacement of sail by steam and the development of advanced navigation techniques lessened the dangers, losses continued: in 1869, for instance, the *Santiago*, an iron paddle steamer built in Glasgow and owned by the Pacific Mail line, went down off Isla Desolación at the western end with a cargo of gold and silver; there are no records of any salvage operation having taken place. While the opening of the Panama Canal in 1914 provided an alternative route between the Atlantic and Pacific Oceans, increases in ships' size mean that the Straits are still a busy shipping route, though today the cargo is more commonly oil than gold and silver. Casualties still occur, with, of course, the added risk of environmental disaster from oil spillage.

Nigel Pickford

km south of Río Gallegos, 59 km south of the frontier at Monte Aymond. From **Punta Espora** on Tierra del Fuego, the road runs a further 128 km south through Cerro Sombrero to the frontier at San Sebastian (see below).

● **Ferry** There are several crossings a day; schedules vary with the tides. Fares: foot passengers US$1, cycles free, cars US$14, one way. The ferry takes about 4 trucks and 20 cars; before 1000 most space is taken by trucks. There is no bus service to or from this crossing. If hitching, this route is preferable as there is more traffic.

● **Accommodation In Punta Delgada**: **E** pp *Hotel El Faro*; **C** *Hostería Tehuelche*, T 061-694433 at Kamiri Aike 17 km from port, with restaurant.

Via Punta Arenas

The alternative ferry crossing is between Punta Arenas and Porvenir. The road from Río Gallegos continues southwest from Punta Delgada 103 km to the intersection with the Punta Arenas-Puerto Natales road, 54 km north of Punta Arenas. From Porvenir, on Tierra del Fuego, a 225-km road runs east to Río Grande via the frontier at San Sebastián

● **Hitching** The best way to hitch from Río Gallegos to Punta Arenas is to take any lorry as far as the turn-off for Punta Delgada ferry. Then there is plenty of Chilean traffic from Punta Delgada to Punta Arenas.

● **Ferry** From Tres Puentes, 5 km north of Punta Arenas (bus A or E from Avenida Magallanes,

US$1; taxi US$3) the *Melinka* sails at 0900 daily (0930 Sunday) in season, less frequently off season, depending on tides, 2½ hours crossing (can be rough and cold). Fares: foot passengers US$6, cycles US$5, vehicles US$30. Reservations essential especially in summer, obtainable from Agencia Broom, Bulnes 05075, Punta Arenas, T 218100, F 212126. Timetable subject to change: check in advance. Return from Porvenir same day at 1400 (1630 Sunday). The ferry company accepts no responsibility for damage to vehicles on the crossing.

TRANSPORT ON TIERRA DEL FUEGO

Throughout Tierra del Fuego the main roads are narrow and gravelled. The exceptions are San Sebastián (Argentina)-Ushuaia, which is paved, and the road for about 50 km out of Porvenir (Chile), which is being widened. Fuel is available in Porvenir, Cerro Sombrero and Cullen (Chile), and Río Grande, Ushuaia and San Sebastian (Argentina).

CHILEAN TIERRA DEL FUEGO

PORVENIR

(*Population* 4,500; *Phone code* 061), founded in 1894 as a port serving the sheep *estancias* of the island, is is the only town in Chilean Tierra del Fuego. There is a small museum, the **Museo Fernando Cordero Rusque**, Samuel Valdivieso 402, mainly Indian culture.

● **Accommodation A2** *Los Flamencos*, Teniente Merino, T 580049, best; **C** *Central*, Philippi 298, T 580077, hot water; **C** *Rosas*, Phillippi, T 580088, with bath, hot water, heating, restaurant and bar, recommended; **E** pp *Res Colón*, Damián Riobó 198, T 580108, also full board; **C** *España*, Santos Mardones y Croacia, good restaurant with fixed price lunch; *Res Los Cisnes*, Soto Salas 702, T 580227; **E** pp *Res* at Santos Mardones 366 (**D** with full board), clean, friendly, heaters in rooms, hot water, good; **E** pp *Res Cameron*, Croacia, for shared room, 'friendly folk', good meals, **D** full board, sleep on dining-room floor for US$1; there is a hotel at the Transportes Senkovic office, Croacia y Almeyda; many good **D** *pensiones*, with full board, but they are often fully occupied by construction workers. **Other hotels on Chilean Tierra del Fuego**: at Cerro Sombrero, 46 km south of Primera Angostura: **E** pp *Hosteria*

Tunkelen, recommended; **F** *Pensión del Señor Alarcón*, good, friendly. *Posada Las Flores*, Km 127 on the road to San Sebastián, reservations via *Hostal de la Patagonia* in Punta Arenas. For accommodation at San Sebastián see below.

● **Places to eat** *Club Croacia* does wholesome and reasonable lunch (about US$5), also *Restaurante Puerto Montt*, Croacia 1169, for seafood, recommended. Many lobster fishing camps where fishermen will prepare lobster on the spot.

● **Banks & money changers** At *Estrella del Sur* shop, Santos Mardones.

● **Transport Air** From Punta Arenas – weather and bookings permitting, Aerovías DAP, Oficina Foretic, T 80089, Porvenir, fly daily except Sunday at 0815 and 1730, return at 1000 and 1930, US$20. Heavily booked so make sure you have your return reservation confirmed. **Buses** To Río Grande, Tuesday and Saturday 1400, Gesell, US$20 heavily booked, buy ticket in advance, or phone. **Hitchhiking** Police may help with lifts on trucks from Porvenir to Río Grande; elsewhere in Chilean territory hitching is difficult as there is so little traffic. **Ferries** Terminal at Bahía Chilota, 7 km west, see above for details. From bus terminal to ferry, taxi US$6, bus (if running) US$1.50.

Cameron

Cameron lies 149 km southeast of Porvenir on the opposite side of Bahía Inútil; from here a road runs southeast to Estancia Vicuña. Before Vicuña is a scenic fishing-ground; beyond Vicuña a horse trail leads across the Darwin Range to Yendegaia. From there you will have to retrace your steps as it seems impossible to get permission to cross the unmanned border to Ushuaia or to get a Chilean exit stamp.

● **Buses** To Cameron from Porvenir, from Calle Manuel Señor, Monday and Friday, 1700, US$10.

FRONTIER BETWEEN CHILE AND ARGENTINA: SAN SEBASTIAN

The only legal frontier crossing between the Chilean and Argentine parts of Tierra del Fuego is at San Sebastian, 142 km east of Porvenir. There are two settlements called San Sebastián, one on each side of the frontier but they are 14 km apart; taxis are not allowed to cross. **NB** Argentine time is 1 hour ahead of Chilean time, March-October.

● **Entering Argentina**
Make sure you get an entry stamp for as long as you require.

● **Entering Chile**
No fruit, vegetables, dairy produce or meat permitted.

● **Accommodation**
In Chilean San Sebastian: **E** pp *Hostería de la Frontera*, in the annex which is 1 km away from the more expensive main building. In Argentine San Sebastian: **A3** *ACA* motel (service station open 0700-2300)

● **Hitching**
Hitching south of San Sebastián is relatively easy: border police will sometimes arrange lifts to Ushuaia or Río Grande.

ARGENTINE TIERRA DEL FUEGO

RIO GRANDE

(*Population* 35,000; *Phone code* 0964), 87 km south of San Sebastian and 374 km south of Río Gallegos, is situated on the southern edge of the Bahía San Sebastian, an important area in summer for migratory birds. The largest settlement in Tierra del Fuego, it is a sprawling modern town in windy, dust-laden sheep-grazing and oil-bearing plains. The *frigorífico* (frozen meat) plant and sheep-shearing shed are among the largest in South America. There is a small museum, the **Museo de Ciencias Naturales y História**, at El Cano 225, open Tuesday-Friday 0900-1700, Saturday/Sunday 1500-2000.

Excursions
To the Salesian Mission of **La Candelaria**, 11 km north along Route 3, where there is a historical museum housing a collection Indian artefacts and; there is also a natural history section. Monday-Saturday 1000-1230, 1500-1900, Sunday 1500-1900, US$1.50. Afternoon teas, US$3. Nearby is the first parish church of Río Grande.

To **Estancia María Behety**, 18 km southwest where horses can be hired. To the **Refugio Dicky**, a private bird sanctuary covering 1,900 hectares on Bahía San Sebastian.

Local festivals
Trout Festival, 3rd Sunday in February; Snow Festival, 3rd Sunday in July; Woodsman Festival, 1st week of December.

Local information
● **Accommodation**
Accommodation can be difficult to find if arriving at night.

A2 *Atlántida*, Belgrano 582, T/F 31914, said to be best, without breakfast, restaurant, parking; **A2** *Posada de los Sauces*, El Cano 839, T/F 30868/32895, with breakfast, good beds, comfortable, good restaurant, bar, recommended; **A3** *Los Yaganes ACA*, Belgrano 319, T 30823, F 33897, comfortable, good expensive restaurant; **A3** *Federico Ibarra*, Rosales y Fagnano, T 32485, with breakfast, good beds, large rooms, excellent restaurant; **A3** *Isla del Mar*, Güemes 963, T/F 22883, next to bus terminal, with breakfast.

Budget accommodation: **B** *Res Rawson*, Estrada 750, T 25503, F 30352, cable TV, clean, poor beds; **B** *Villa*, San Martín 277, T 22312, without breakfast, very warm; **B** *Hosp Noal*, Rafael Obligado 557, lots of bread and coffee for breakfast, cosy, recommended; **C** *Hostería Antares*, Echeverría 49, T 21853; **C** *Avenida*, Belgrano 1001, T 22561. No campsite. The gymnasium has free hot showers for men, as has the ACA garage on the seafront.

● **Places to eat**
Don Rico, Belgrano y Perito Moreno, in ultra-modern building in centre, interesting, closed Monday; *La Nueva Colonial*, Rosales 640, pizzeria, friendly; *Club de Pesca*, El Cano; *Rotisería CAI*, on Moreno, cheap, fixed price, popular with locals.

The Salesian Missions

Founded in 1893 by José Fagnano, La Candelaria was one of three missions set up by the Salesians to try to protect the Onas of Tierra del Fuego from the gold prospectors and *estancieros* (sheepfarmers). The first was established in Punta Arenas in 1886, the second, on Isla Dawson two years later. The latter quickly attracted over 1,000 Onas, shipped there by the *estancieros*. It was finally closed in 1920, by which time the anthropologist Martín Gusinde, counted only 276 surviving Onas, most of them on an *estancia* owned by the Bridges family.

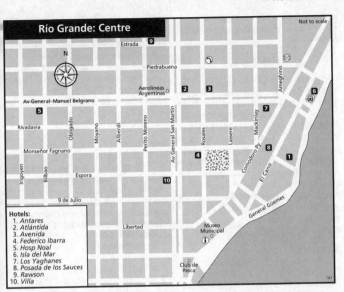

Río Grande: Centre

Not to scale

Estrada **9**

Piedrabuena

Aerolíneas Argentinas **2** **3**

Av General Manuel Belgrano

5

Rivadavia

Monseñor Fagnano

Espora

9 de Julio

Libertad

Ameghino

6

7

8 **1**

El Cano

General Güemes

Museo Municipal

Club de Pesca

Hotels:
1. Antares
2. Atlántida
3. Avenida
4. Federico Ibarra
5. Hosp Noal
6. Isla del Mar
7. Los Yaghanes
8. Posada de los Sauces
9. Rawson
10. Villa

● **Airline offices**
Aerolíneas Argentinas, San Martín 607, T 22711; **Lapa**, 9 de Julio 747, T 32620; **LADE**, Laserre 425, T 22968; **Kaiken**, Perito Moreno 937, T 30665; **DAP**, 9 de Julio 597, T 30249; **TAN**, Moyano 516, T 22885.

● **Banks & money changers**
Banco de la Nación Argentina, San Martín 200; **Banco del Sud**, Rosales 241, cash advance on Visa; **Superkiosko**, Piedrabuena y Rosales, cash only. Exchange is difficult: if coming from Chile, buy Argentine pesos there.

● **Laundry**
El Lavadero, P Moreno y 9 de Julio.

● **Post & telecommunications**
Post Office: Piedrabuena y Ameghino.

● **Shopping**
La Nueva Piedmontesa, Belgrano y Laserre, 24-hour food store; *Tía* supermarket, San Martín y Piedrabuena, good selection. Food is cheaper than in Ushuaia.

● **Tour companies & travel agents**
Yaganes, San Martín 641, friendly and helpful.

● **Tourist offices**
Tourist information at the Municipalidad, on Elano, Monday-Friday.

● **Transport**
Local Car hire: Rent-a-Car, Belgrano y Ameghino, T 22657. **Avis**, El Cano 799,

T/F 22571 and airport; **Localiza**, at airport, T 30482. **Mechanic**: and VW dealer *Viaval SRL*, Perito Moreno 927.

Air Airport 4 km west of town. Bus US$0.50. Taxi US$5. To **Buenos Aires** Aerolíneas Argentinas, daily, 3½ hours direct. Austral daily (except Sunday) and Lapa daily (except Saturday) via Bahía Blanca, Comodoro Rivadavia and Río Gallegos. To **Ushuaia**, Aerolíneas Argentinas and Kaiken, daily. LADE also to **Río Gallegos**, 1 hour (book early in summer, 1 a week, Thursday), continuing to **Comodoro Rivadavia** via Calafate, Gob Gregores and Perito Moreno. Kaiken flies to **Calafate** daily except Sunday; also to **Punta Arenas**, **Río Gallegos**, **Bariloche**, **Trelew** and many other southern destinations.

Buses All buses leave from terminal, El Cano y Güemes. To **Porvenir**, Chile, 5 hours, Gesell, Wednesday, Sunday, 0800, meticulous passport and luggage control at San Sebastián; to **Punta Arenas**, Chile, via Punta Delgada, 10 hours, Pacheco, Tuesday, Thursday, Saturday 0730, US$30, Los Carlos, Monday, Friday, 0700, US$30; To **Ushuaia**, Tecni Austral, 4 hours, daily 0730 and 1800, US$21 and Los Carlos, Tuesday, Saturday 1700, sit on right for better views, US$20, stopping at *Hostería El Kaiken*, Lago Fagnano (recommended for the view). No buses to Río Gallegos.

Hitching Very difficult to hitch to Porvenir or north into Argentina (try the truck stop opposite the bus terminal or the police post 7 km out of town). Hitching to Ushuaia is relatively easy in summer.

USHUAIA

(*Population* 30,000; *Phone code* 0901), the most southerly town in Argentina and one of the most expensive, is 234 km southwest of Río Grande by a new road via Paso Garibaldi. Founded in 1884 it is the provincial capital. Situated on the northern shore of the Beagle Channel, its streets climb steeply towards snow covered Cerro Martial to the north. There are fine views over the green waters of the Beagle Channel and the snow-clad peaks. The mainstays of the local economy are fishing and tourism. Ushuaia and its environs are worth a 2-3 day visit.

Museums

The **Presidio** or old prison, Yaganes y Gob Paz, at the back of the Naval Base, houses the **Museo Marítimo**, with models and artefacts from seafaring days, the **Museo Antártico** and, in the cells, the **Museo Penitenciario**, which details the history of the prison. Open daily 1000-1200, 1600-2300, US$5, students US$3.

Museo Territorial, Maipú y Rivadavia, T 21863, open Monday-Friday 0900-1300, 1630-1930, US$3, small but interesting display of early photos and artefacts of the local Indian tribes, the missionaries and first settlers, as well as natural history section. Known as the 'museum at the end of the world' (you can get a stamp in your passport). Highly recommended. The building also contains an excellent library with helpful staff and a post office, open afternoons when the main one is closed.

Excursions

To **Cerro Martial**, offering fine views down the Beagle Channel and to the north, about 7 km behind the town; to reach the chairlift (*Aerosilla*, US$5) follow Magallanes out of town, allow 1½ hours. Pasarela and Kaupen run minibus services, several departures daily in summer, US$5 return. There is skiing on the glacier in winter.

To **Harberton**, (T 22742), 85 km east of Ushuaia, the oldest *estancia* on the island. Run by descendents of its founder, the British missionary Thomas Bridges, it offers guided walks through protected forest and refreshments are sold in the *Manacatush confitería*. Camping is possible.

● **Access** is from a dirt road which branches off Route 3, 40 km east of Ushuaia and runs past Lago Victoria, then 25 km through forest before the open country around Harberton.

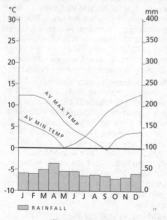

°C / mm / RAINFALL
Climate: Ushuaia

Fauna of the Beagle Channel

Many bird-species can be viewed from the shore or on a boat-trip along the Channel. These include the Black-browed Albatross (whose long wings enable it to glide effectively over large distances), the Antarctic Giant Petrel, the Southern Fulmar, the Great Glebe, the Kelp Goose (the male of which is an unmistakeable white), Imperial and Rock Cormorants, Steamer ducks, Kelp gulls, the South American tern, the Black Oystercatcher, the Snowy Sheatbill and the Antarctic Skua. The shores of the Beagle Channel are also breeding grounds for several sea mammals, including the Southern Sea Lion and the Southern Fur Seal.

Santiago de la Vega

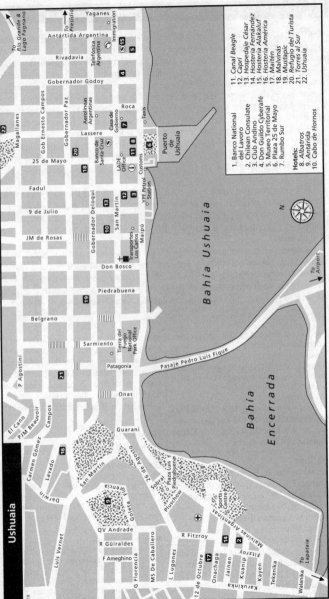

1. Banco National del Lavoro
2. Chilean Consulate
3. Club Andino
4. Don Guildo Cyberafé
5. Museo Territorial
6. Plaza 25 de Mayo
7. Rumbo Sur

11. Canal Beagle
12. Capri
13. Hospedaje César
14. Hosteria Fernández
15. Hosteria Alakaluf
16. Hosteria América
17. Maitén
18. Malvinás
19. Mustapic
20. Refugio del Turista
21. Torres al Sur
22. Ushuaia

Hotels:
8. Albatros
9. Antárida
10. Cabo de Hornos

Estancia Harberton

In a land of extremes and superlatives, Harberton still stands out as special. The oldest *estancia* on Tierra del Fuego and the oldest house on the island, it was built in 1886 on a narrow peninsula overlooking the Beagle channel. Its founder, the missionary Thomas Bridges, was given the land by President Roca for his work among the local Indians and for his help in rescuing the victims of the numerous shipwrecks in the channel. Harberton is named after the Devonshire village where his wife Mary was born. The farmhouse was prefabricated by her carpenter father and then assembled on a spot chosen by the Yamana Indians as the most sheltered. The English connection is still evident in the neat garden of lawns, shrubs and trees between the jetty and the farmhouse. Behind the buildings is a large vegetable garden, a real rarity on the island. Visitors will notice that there is much more wildlife around the *estancia* than in the Tierra del Fuego National Park, probably owing to the remoteness of Harberton.

Still operating as a working farm, mainly with cattle and sheep, Harberton is run by Thomas Goodall, great-grandson of the founder. Visitors receive a conducted tour of the farm buildings and immediate surroundings: though there are guides, Thomas in his dungarees and horn-rimmed glasses, and his wife, Natalie, are usually also on hand.

Natalie is an internationally recognized expert on whales and dolphins, which accounts for the whale jawbone arch over the garden entrance. There is also a "house of bones" where dolphin, whale and seal carcasses are cleaned and labelled for research, and entire skeletons displayed. Harberton is well worth the visit, particularly by sea as the voyage up the Beagle Channel is equally memorable.

Philip Horton

Some parts of the road are bad; tiring driving, 5 hours there and back.

• **Tours** are offered by agencies in Ushuaia. By land these cost US$30 plus US$6 entrance; take your own food if not wishing to buy meals at the Estancia. For excursions to Harberton by boat see below.

Other excursions include: to the **Parque Nacional Tierra del Fuego** (see below); to the **Río Olivia** falls; to **Lagos Fagnano** and **Escondido**.

Sea Trips

Excursions can be booked through most agencies. The main trips are: to the sealion colony at Isla de los Lobos, 2 hours on the *Ana B*, US$35, 4 hours on the *Tres Marías*, US$40; to Lapataia Bay and Isla de los Lobos, 5 hours on the *Ezequiel MB*, US$35; to Isla de los Lobos and Estancia Harberton, 6 hours on the *Luciano Beta*, US$75, Tuesday, Thursday, Saturday; to Isla de los Lobos and the Isla Martillo Penguin colony, 4 hours on the *Luciano Beta*, US$60. Some tour agencies imply

that their excursions to Harberton go to the *estancia* though in fact they only go to the bay; others go by inflatable launch from main boat to shore. Check thoroughly in advance. Food and drink on all boats is expensive, best to take your own. Note that the Beagle Channel can be very rough.

Local festivals

12 October: Founding of Ushuaia.

Local information

NB Prices double on 12 December and accommodation may occasionally be hard to find December-March – the tourist office will help with rooms in private homes and with campsites. Accommodation, food and drink are all expensive.

● **Accommodation**

On the road to the Martial Glacier overlooking the city are: **L2 Las Hayas**, Km 3, T 30710, F 30719, colourful large rooms, pool, and **L1 del Glacier**, Km 3.5, T 30640, F 30636, modern, casino, pool rooms, shuttle to/from Hotel Albatros; **L3 Tolkeyen**, at Estancia Río

Hotel prices

L1	over US$200	**L2**	US$151-200
L3	US$101-150	**A1**	US$81-100
A2	US$61-80	**A3**	US$46-60
B	US$31-45	**C**	US$21-30
D	US$12-20	**E**	US$7-11
F	US$4-6	**G**	up to US$3

Unless otherwise stated, all hotels in range **D** and above have private bath. Assume friendliness and cleanliness in all cases.

Pipo 5 km from town, T 22637, with recommended restaurant (see below); **L3** *Albatros*, Lasserre y Maipú, T 30003, F 30666, modern, includes breakfast, good views; **L3** *Ushuaia*, Laserre 933, 1 km north of town, T 30671, F 24217, with breakfast, restaurant, sauna.

A1 *Las Lengas*, Florencia 1722, T 23366, F 24599, superb setting, heating, good dining room; **A2** *Canal Beagle*, Maipú y 25 de Mayo, T 21117, F 21120, restaurant; **A2** *Malvinas*, Deloqui 615, T 22626, F 24482, without breakfast, pleasant, helpful, central heating, recommended; **A2** *Cabo de Hornos*, San Martín y Rosas, T 22187, F 22313, comfortable, often full, good value, restaurant not open to non-residents; **A2** *César*, San Martín 753, T 21460, F 32721, comfortable, includes breakfast, recommended; **A3** *Fernández*, Onachaga y Fitzroy, T 21192, with breakfast, good beds, overpriced; **A3** *Posada Fin del Mundo*, Valdez 281, T 22530, family atmosphere, recommended; **B** *Mustapic*, Piedrabuena 238, T/F 23557, multi-lingual owner, breakfast extra, poor beds, great views.

B *Maitén*, 12 de Octubre 140, T 22745, F 22733, good value, 1 km from centre, no singles, 10% discount for ISIC and youth card holders; **B** *Hostería América*, Gob Paz 1665, T 23358, F 31362, without breakfast, modern; **B** *Capri*, San Martín 720, T 21833, without breakfast; **B** *Hostería Alakaluf*, San Martín 146, T 36705, without breakfast, quiet, recommended.

Budget accommodation: **D** pp *Hosp Torres al Sur*, Gob Paz 1437, T 30745, dormitories, heating, good atmosphere, kitchen facilities, highly recommended; **D** pp *Alojamiento Internacional*, Deloqui 395, 1st floor, T 23483/23622, with bath, kitchen facilities, good meeting place, recommended; **E** pp *Casa Azul*, Las Primulas 283, Barrio Ecológico, T 34769, floor space; **D** pp *Refugio del Turista*, 25 de Mayo 237, small dormitories with kitchen facilities; **E** pp *Casa del Turista*, Belgrano 236, T 21884, large kitchen, helpful.

Accommodation in private homes: **A3** *Julio Linares*, Deloqui 1522, T 23594, **B** without bath; **A3** *Miguel Zapruscky*, Deloqui 271, T 21316, **B** without bath, parking, TV, kitchen, English spoken, recommended; **E** pp *Silvia Casalaga*, Gob Paz 1380, T 23202, dormitories, comfortable, heating, breakfast extra, no sign, recommended; **B** *María Navarrete*, 25 de Mayo 440, T 23068, without bath or breakfast, cooking facilities; **B** *Familia Cárdenas*, 25 de Mayo 345, T 21954, without bath or breakfast, quiet; **B** *Zulema Saltzmann*, Roca 392 y Campos; **D** pp *Hosp Turístico*, Magallanes 196, good views; **E** pp *Posada de los Angeles*, Gob Paz 1410, basement, good kitchen; **D** pp *Adrienne Grinberg*, Bouchard y Rivadavia, T 23148, with breakfast, warm, English, French spoken. List of private accommodation available from the tourist office. Many people offer rooms in private houses at the airport. There is no youth hostel. Hostel for sporting groups only at Haruwen Sports Complex.

At Lago Escondido: **B** *Hostería Petrel*, 54 km from Ushuaia after a challenging climb through Garibaldi Pass, on the road to Río Grande (bus departs 0900, returns 1500, US$17 return, minimum 4 people), T 33569, trout fishing possible, boat rides, friendly staff.

At Lago Fagnano: **B** *Hostería El Kaiken*, 100 km north of Ushuaia on a promontory, T 92208, also **C** cheaper rooms and bungalows, nice site. Facilities at *Kaiken* and *Petrel* are open all year round. These inns are recommended for peace and quiet.

Camping None in town. West of Ushuaia are: *Ushuaia Rugby Club Camping* (Km 4) US$15 per tent, restaurant and good facilities; *Ushuaia Camping Municipal* (Km 8) US$15 per tent, toilets, cold showers. East of town on Route 3 are: *Camping del Solar del Bosque* (Km 14) US$5 per person, hot showers; *Camping Río Tristen*, in the Haruwen Winter Sports complex (Km 36), T/F 24058, US$5 per tent, electricity, bar, restaurant. Inside the Parque Nacional Tierra del Fuego (entry fee US$5) is *Camping Lago Roca*, 18 km from Ushuaia, at Lapataia, by forested shore of Lago Roca, with good facilities, dirty, showers (US$3), noisy, reached by bus January-February, small shop, cafeteria. There are also four free sites with no facilities: *Camping Río Pipo*, 10 km from Ushuaia; *Ensenada Camping* 14 km from Ushuaia; *Camping Las Bandurrias* and *Camping Laguna Verde*, both 21 km from Ushuaia. Hot showers, free, at YPF on main road

● **Places to eat**
Barcleit 1912, Fadul 148, cordon bleu cooking at reasonable prices; *Kaupé*, Roca 470, English spoken, excellent food and wine, recommended, expensive. Best place to eat lamb is at *Tolkeyen*, Estancia Río Pipo, 5 km from town,

meal US$15, taxi US$7; *Barcito Ideal*, San Martín 393, good, cheap, *tenedor libre* US$14, very popular with travellers; *Los Amigos*, San Martín 130, quick service, some cheap dishes; *Moustacchio*, San Martín 298, good fish, good *tenedor libre*; *Volver*, Maipú 37, interesting decor, sea view, good food and service, not cheap; *Quick*, San Martín 130, clean, good service, recommended, 10% discount for ISIC card holders; also *Split*, Piedrabuena 238, pizzería, offers same discount, cheap; *Mi Viejo*, Campos 758, *tenedor libre*, good value; *Café de la Esquina*, San Martín y 25 de Mayo, recommended; *Don Guido Cybercafe*, Godoy 45, surf the net for US$10 per hour, also offers mailbox facilities for e-mail, 0800-2400; *Turco*, San Martín 1460, cheapest in town, friendly; *Der Garten*, *confitería*, San Martín 638, in Galería shopping arcade. *Bidu Bar*, San Martín 898, good music, lunches, good meeting place; excellent homemade chocolate sold at a shop at San Martín 785. *Helados Massera*, San Martín 270-72, good. The coffee bar at the airport is very expensive. Ask around for currently available *centolla* (king crab) and *cholga* (giant mussels).

● **Airline offices**
LADE, San Martín 552, T 21123, airport T 21700; Aerolíneas Argentinas, Roca 116, T 21218, airport 21265; Lapa, 25 de Mayo 64, T 32112, F 30532; Kaiken and Alta, San Martín 884, T 32963, or at airport, T 22620/23049; DAP, San Martín 626, T 31373; Lan Chile, Gob Godoy 169, T 31110.

● **Banks & money changers**
Banks open 1000-1500 (in summer). Useful to have credit cards here as difficult to change travellers' cheques and very high commission (up to 10%), but *Banco del Sud*, Maipú 600 block, only place for changing travellers' cheques (downstairs). *Banco de la Nación Argentina*, Rivadavia y San Martín, only bank which accepts Chilean pesos. Cash advance on Mastercard at *Banco de Tierra del Fuego*, San Martín 1044, accepts Amex travellers' cheques. *Casas de Cambio* include *Gredi Sol*, 25 de Mayo 50 Tourist agencies and the *Hotel Albatros* give poor rates. *Listus* record shop, San Martín 973, sweet shop next door, or *Caminante* travel agency for better rates for cash.

● **Consulates**
Chile, Malvinas Argentinas y Jainen, Casilla 21, T 21279; Finland, Paz y Deloqui; Germany, Rosas 516; Italy, Yaganes 75.

● **Entertainment**
A popular spot at night is the disco *Siglo* at 9 de Julio y Maipú; other discos are *Barny's*, Antártida Argentina just off San Martín and

Garage, San Martín 20; *El Ñaupe*, Gob Paz y Fadul, bar with live music.

● **Laundry**
Rosas 139, between San Martín and Deloqui, open weekdays 0900-2100, US$8.

● **Post & telecommunications**
Post Office: San Martín y Godoy, Monday-Friday 0900-1300 and 1700-2000, Saturday 0830-1200.

Telephones: San Martín 1541.

● **Shopping**
Good boots at *Stella Maris*, San Martín 443. Bookshop at San Martín y 9 de Julio (Lapataia Arcade). Film is cheaper in Chile. Supermarkets: *Surty Sur*, San Martín y Onas (clean toilets), good stock, Visa accepted, climbing and trekking clothing at European prices, and *Sucoop*, Paz 1600. Most things are more expensive than elsewhere but some cheap imported goods, eg electrical equipment and cigarettes.

● **Sports**
Sports Centre on Malvinas Argentinas on west side of town (close to seafront). Ice skating rink at Ushuaia gymnasium in winter (when lagoon is frozen). Beachcombing can produce whale bones.

Fishing: trout. Season 1 November-31 March, licences US$20 per week, US$10 per day. Contact Asociación de Caza y Pesca at Maipú y 9 de Julio, which has a small museum. Fishermen may be interested in visiting the fish hatchery 7 km east of Ushuaia, visiting hours daily 1400-1700. There are brook, rainbow and brown trout and land-locked salmon. Take No 1 bus east-bound on Maipú to the end of the line and continue 2½ km on foot to the hatchery. Birdwatchers will also find this ride rewarding. Fishing excursions to Lago Fagnano are organized by *Yishka*, Gob Godoy 115, T 31535, F 31230.

Skiing, hiking, climbing: contact Club Andino, Fadul 5. **Skiing**: a downhill ski run (beginner standard) on Cerro Martial. There is another ski run, Wallner, 3 km from Ushuaia, open June-August, has lights for night-skiing and is run by Club Andino. The area is excellent for cross country skiing; *Caminante* organizes excursions 'off road'. 20 km north east of Ushuaia is Valle Tierra Mayor, a large flat valley with high standard facilities for cross country skiing, snow shoeing and snowmobiling; ski-school, rentals and a cafetería; bus in the morning and 1400 from *Antartur*, San Martín 638. The Haruwen Winter Sports complex is 36 km east on Route 3 (Km 36).

● **Tour companies & travel agents**
All agencies charge the same fees for excursions: Tierra del Fuego National Park, 4 hours, US$19;

Lago Escondido, 5 hours, US$25; Lagos Escondido and Fagnano, 8 hours, US$30. With 3 or 4 people it is often little more expensive to hire a *remise* taxi. The two largest agencies are: *Rumbo Sur*, San Martín 342, T 30699, runs a range of tours on water and on land and offers a 2-day package to Calafate, US$150 including transport and hotel, good value, also organizes bus to ski slope, very helpful; and *Tolkeyen*, 12 de Octubre 150, T 22237, recommended. Others include *Antartur*, San Martín 638, T 23240; *All Patagonia*, 25 de Mayo 31, Oficina A, T 24432, F 30707, Amex agent. Recommended guide: Domingo Galussio, Intervú 15, Casa 211, 9410 Ushuaia, bilingual, not cheap (US$120), recommended.

● **Tourist offices**
San Martín 660, T/F (0901) 24550, 'best in Argentina', literature in English, German and Dutch, helpful, English spoken. Large chart of hotels and prices and information on travel and staying at Estancia Harberton. Has noticeboard for messages. Open Monday-Friday 0830-2030, Saturday and Sunday 0900-2000. **National Park Office**, San Martín 1395, has small map but not much information. The **ACA** office on Maipú also has maps and information.

● **Transport**
Car hire: Tagle, San Martín y Belgrano, T 22744, good; **Río Grande**, El Cano 799, T 22571; **Localiza**, in *Hotel Albatros* and at airport, recommended, T 30663; **Avis**, San Martín 1195, T 22744, F 24082 and airport.

Air New airport 4 km from town, taxi, US$5 (no bus). Services are more frequent in high season; in winter weather often impedes flights. In the summer tourist season it is sometimes difficult to get a flight out: it may be worth trying Río Grande. Aerolíneas Argentinas (AR) and Lapa to Buenos Aires via Río Gallegos and/or Trelew, all year round, 5 hours. To **Río Grande**, Kaiken, US$36, LADE, US$14. Kaiken's services to/from Ushuaia are as for Río Grande. To **Río Gallegos**, LADE twice a week US$39, also Kaiken, Lapa, Aerolíneas Argentinas and Austral US$50-63. LADE to **Comodoro Rivadavia** via Río Grande, Río Gallegos, and Calafate (US$55), Gobernador Gregores and Perito Moreno on Wednesday (to Calafate only in summer). To **Punta Arenas**, DAP twice a week, US$91; Lan Chile US$95; Alta Monday-Friday US$89. To **Puerto Natales**, Alta, Sunday-Friday, US$125.
   At the airport ask around for a pilot willing to take you on a 30-minute flight around Ushuaia, US$38 per person (best to go in afternoon when wind has dropped). Alternatively ask about flights at the tourist office in town. Aerial excursions over the Beagle Channel with local flying club, hangar at airport, 3-5 seater planes,

30 minutes: Lago Fagnano, Lapataia and Ushuaia Bay.

Trains A Decauville gauge train for tourists runs along the shore of the Beagle Channel between the Fin del Mundo station, west of Ushuaia and the boundary of the Tierra del Fuego National Park, 4.5 km, 3 departures daily, US$26 (tourist), US$30 (first class), plus US$5 park entrance and US$3 for bus to the station. Run by Ferrocarril Austral Fueguino with new locomotives and carriages, it uses track first laid by prisoners to carry wood to Ushuaia; tickets from Tranex kiosk in the port, T 30709. Sit on left outbound.

Buses To **Río Grande** 4 hours, Los Carlos, Monday-Friday 0300, US$20 and Tecni Austral, daily 0730, 1800, US$21; to **Punta Arenas**, Los Carlos, Monday and Friday, 0300, 14 hours, US$58, a comfortable and interesting ride via Punta Delgada. Bus company offices: Los Carlos, *Ticatur Turismo*, San Martín 880, T 22337; Tecni Austral, 25 de Mayo 50, T 23396/23304.

Hitching Trucks leave Ushuaia for the refinery at San Sebastián Monday-Friday; a good place to hitch from is the police control on Route 3.

To Puerto Williams (Chile) No regular sailings. Yachts based at the Club Náutico carry charter passengers in summer, returning the same day; enquire at the Club, most possibilities in December because boats visit Antarctica in January. Luxury cruises around Cape Horn via Puerto Williams are operated by the Chilean company, *Tierra Austral*, 7/8 days, US$1,260.

To Antarctica: most tourist vessels to Antarctica call at Ushuaia and, space permitting, take on passengers. Enquire at *Rumbo Sur* or other agencies. All agencies charge similar price, US$2,200pp for 8/9 day trip, though prices may be lower for late availability, which are posted in window of *Rumbo Sur*.

PARQUE NACIONAL TIERRA DEL FUEGO

Covering 63,000 hectares of mountains, lakes, rivers and deep valleys, the park stretches west to the Chilean frontier and north to Lago Fagnano, though large areas have been closed to tourists to protect the environment. The lower parts are forested; tree species include lenga, ñire and coihue. Fauna include several species of geese including kelp geese, ducks among them the beautiful torrent duck, Magellanic woodpeckers and austral parakeets. Introduced species like rabbits, beavers and muskrats, have done serious environmental damage. Near the Chilean frontier beaver dams can

Parque Nacional Tierra del Fuego

0   10
km

N

Sierra de Beauvoir

Lago Fagnano

CHILE

Sierra de Vinciguerra

Lago Alto

Sierra de Valdivieso

Río Pipo

Cascada del Río Pipo

Cerro Martial

Route 3 to Río Grande

Ushuaia

Lago Roca

Camping Lago Roca

Camping Río Pipo

Cerro Cóndor

Laguna Negra

Bahía Lapataia

Canal Beagle

There are several beautiful walks: the most popular ones are an interpreted trail along Lapataia Bay, good for birdwatching; a 5 km walk along Lago Roca to the Chilean frontier at Hito XXIV; and a 2½ km climb to Cerro Pampa Alta which offers fine views. Good climbing on Cerro Cóndor, recommended. There are no recognized crossing points to Chile. In winter the temperature drops to as low as -12°C, in summer it goes up to 25°C. Even in the summer the climate can often be cold, damp and unpredictable. The *Club Andino* in Ushuaia has a booklet explaining routes in the park (in Spanish) and poor map.

● **Access** The park entrance is 12 km west of Ushuaia. Park administration is at **Lapataia Bay**. Entry US$5. In summer buses and minibuses, US$5, to the park are run by several companies: *Pasarela*, Fadul 5, T 21735, leaving from Maipú y Fadul; *Kaupen*, T 34015, leaving from Maipú y 25 de Mayo; and *Eben-Ezer*, T 31133, leaving from San Martín y 25 de Mayo. Timetables vary with demand, tourist office has details. *Caminante* also runs a 1 day excursion to the Park, including trek, canoeing, *asado* lunch, US$70 inclusive (small groups, book early). Ask at the tourist office about cycling tours in the park, US$65 full day, also 'Eco Treks' available and cultural events. It is possible to hitchhike, as far as Lapataia.

● **Accommodation** See above for **Camping** possibilities.

ISLA NAVARINO (CHILE)

Situated on the southern shore of the Beagle Channel, Isla Navarino is totally unspoilt and beautiful, with a chain of rugged snowy peaks, magnificent woods and many animals, including large numbers of beaver which were introduced to

be seen and with much luck and patience the beavers themselves. Stand still and down-wind of them: their sense of smell and hearing are good, but not their eyesight.

Isla de Los Estados

"This long (75 km) and guarded island lies east of Tierra del Fuego. Except for the caretakers of the lighthouse and an occasional scientist few people ever set foot on this cloud-shrouded reserve of Fuegian flora and fauna that no longer exist on the main island. During the 18th and 19th centuries large numbers of ships were wrecked or lost in the treacherous waters surrounding this island. Much gold, silver and relics await salvage." Robert T Cook

Further information and tours from *Rumbo Sur*, San Martín 342, Ushuaia

the island and have done a lot of damage. The only settlement on the island is **Puerto Williams** (*population* 1,500; *phone code* 061), a Chilean naval base. Situated about 50 km east of Ushuaia at 54° 55' 41" south, 67° 37' 58" west, this is the most southerly place in the world with a permanent population. It is small, friendly and remote (it suffered a serious fire in 1994). The **'Museo del fin del Mundo'** ('End of the World Museum') is full of information about vanished Indian tribes, local wildlife, and voyages including Charles Darwin and Fitzroy of the *Beagle*, a 'must'. Open 1000-1300, 1500-1800 (Monday-Thursday); 1500-1800 (Saturday-Sunday), Friday closed (subject to change). Admission US$1.

Excursions

Sights include beaver dams, cascades, the Villa Ukika, 2 km east of town, the place where the last descendants of the Yaghan people live, and the local *media luna* where rodeos are held. For superb views, climb Cerro Bandera (3-4 hours round trip, steep, take warm clothes).

Local information
● **Accommodation**
A3 *Hostería Walla*, on the edge of Lauta bay, T 223571, 2 km out of town (splendid walks), very hospitable, good food. **D** pp *Pensión Temuco*, Piloto Pardo 224, also half board, comfortable, hospitable, good food, hot showers, recommended; you can also stay at private houses. **E** pp *Res Onashaga* (run by Señor Ortiz – everyone knows him), cold, run down, good meals, helpful, full board available.

Camping You can camp near the *Hostería*; collect drinking water from the kitchen. No equipment rental on island; buy food in Punta Arenas.

● **Airline offices**
Aerovías DAP, LanChile, Ladeco in the centre of town.

● **Post & telecommunications**
Post Office: closes 1900.

Telephone: CTC, Monday-Saturday 0930-2230, Sunday 1000-1300, 1600-2200). Telex.

● **Tourist offices**
Near the museum (Closed in winter). Ask for details on hiking. Maps available.

● **Transport**
Air From Punta Arenas, DAP on Monday and Friday 1400, Wednesday 0830, return Monday and Friday 1800, Wednesday 1000, US$64 single. Book well in advance; 20 seater aircraft and long waiting lists (be persistent). The flight is beautiful, with superb views of Tierra del Fuego, the Cordillera Darwin, the Beagle Channel, and the islands stretching south to Cape Horn. Also army flights available (they are cheaper), but the ticket has to be bought through DAP. Aeropetrel will charter a plane to Cape Horn (US$2,600 for 8-10 people).

Boats No regular sailings to/from Ushuaia (see above). From Punta Arenas, the *Ñandú* or *Ultragas* leaves on a fixed schedule every 10 days, about midnight, arrives 1700 each way, reclining chairs, no food, US$45 one way. Enquire at the office, Independencia 865, next to service station. The *Navarino* sails from Punta Arenas in 3rd week of every month, 12 passengers, US$150 per person one way; contact the owner, Carlos Aguilera, 21 de Mayo 1460, Punta Arenas, T 228066, F 248848 or via Turismo Pehoé. A small cargo vessel, the *Beaulieu*, sails from Punta Arenas once a month and carries a few passengers, US$300 return, 6 days. Navy and port authorities may deny any knowledge, but everyone else in Puerto Williams knows when a boat is due.

Boat trips: ask at the yacht club on the off chance of hitching a ride on a private yacht. Luxury cruises around Cape Horn are run by Tierra Austral for US$800, 6 days. Captain Ben Garrett offers adventure sailing in his schooner *Victory*, from special trips to Ushuaia to cruises in the canals, Cape Horn, glaciers, Puerto Montt, Antarctica in December and January. Write to Victory Cruises, Puerto Williams (slow mail service); Fax No 1, Cable 3, Puerto Williams; phone (call collect) asking for Punta Arenas (Annex No 1 Puerto Williams) and leave message with the Puerto Williams operator.

Information for travellers

BEFORE TRAVELLING

ENTRY REQUIREMENTS

● **Documents**

Check visa requirements in advance. Passports are not required by citizens of neighbouring countries who hold identity cards issued by their own Governments. No visa is necessary for US citizens, British citizens and nationals of other Western European countries, Canada, Bolivia, Brazil, Chile, Panama, Paraguay, Uruguay, Mexico, El Salvador, Nicaragua, Honduras, Costa Rica, Colombia, Ecuador, Peru, Haiti, Barbados, Jamaica, Hong Kong, Malaysia, Israel, Hungary, Poland, Turkey, Croatia, Yugoslavia, Slovenia and Japan, who may stay for 3 months, a period which can be renewed for another 3 (fee US$100) months at the National Directorate of Migration. For all others, including Australians, New Zealanders and South Africans, there are three forms of visa, all of which cost US$30: a business visa (valid 1 year), a transit visa (for engineers, students, artists, valid up to 15 days) and a tourist visa. (Australians applying for a visa in London must have a return ticket.) Tourist visas are multiple entry and are valid for 12 months but you may only stay for 3 months at at time. If leaving Argentina on a short trip, check on re-entry that border officials look at the correct expiry date on your visa, otherwise they will give only 30 days. Renewing a visa is difficult and can only be done for 30-day periods. It is illegal not to have identification handy: visitors should carry passports at all times. Backpackers are particular targets for thorough searches – just stay calm. When crossing land frontiers, remember that though the migration and customs officials are generally friendly, helpful and efficient, the police at the control posts a little further into Argentina tend to be extremely bureaucratic.

At land borders, 90 days permission to stay is usually given without proof of transportation out of Argentina. If you need a 90-day extension for your stay in Argentina, get a new stamp at the first opportunity. Do not be put off by immigration officials in provincial cities who say that the stamp is not necessary, or too complicated to obtain. You can also leave the country, at Iguazú or to Uruguay, and 90 further days will be given on return. Without a valid stamp you will be fined US$40 on leaving.

At Argentine/Uruguayan borders one immigration official will stamp passports for both countries. Under Mercosur regulations (1992), borders between Argentina, Uruguay, Paraguay and Brazil are open 24 hours a day. Argentine immigration and customs officials wear civilian dress. The border patrol, *gendarmería*, in green combat fatigues, operate some borders.

NB Latin Americans, especially officials, are very document-minded. You should always carry your passport in a safe place about your person, or if not going far, leave it in the hotel safe. If you are staying for several weeks, it is worth while registering at your Embassy or Consulate. Then, if your passport is stolen, the process of replacing it is simplified and speeded up. Keeping photocopies of essential documents, including your flight ticket, and some additional passport-sized photographs, is recommended.

It is your responsibility to ensure that your passport is stamped in and out when you cross frontiers. The absence of entry and exit stamps can cause serious difficulties: seek out the proper migration offices if the stamping process is not carried out as you cross. Do not lose your entry card; replacing one causes a lot of trouble, and possibly expense. Citizens of countries which oblige visitors to have a visa can expect more delays and problems at border crossings.

● **Membership cards**

Membership cards of European and US motoring organizations are useful for discounts off hotel charges, car rentals, maps, towing charges, etc. Business people should carry a good supply of visiting cards, which are essential for good business relations in Latin America. Identity, membership or business cards in Spanish (or a translation) and an official letter of introduction in Spanish are also useful.

If you are in full-time education you will be entitled to an International Student Identity Card (ISIC), which is distributed by student travel offices and travel agencies in 77 countries and which ISIC gives you special prices on all forms of transport (air, sea, rail etc), and access to a variety of other concessions and services. If you need to find the location of your nearest ISIC office contact: The ISIC Association, Box 9048, 1000 Copenhagen, Denmark T (+45) 33 93 93 03. All student cards must carry a photograph if they are to be of any use for discounts.

● **Tourist information**

The address of the national tourist office in Buenos Aires is Santa Fe 883. Addresses of tourist offices around the country are given in the text. For a list of Argentine tourist offices overseas see under **Useful addresses**, page 493.

MONEY

● **Cost of living**

In 1998, Argentina was very expensive for the foreign visitor. Budget travellers should allow US$35-40 a day minimum, though less if camping. High costs can be expected for items such as slide film and clothing, as well as basics, although you can save money by preparing your own food. Imported electronic goods are relatively cheap.

● **Currency**

The peso, which is at par with the dollar, is divided into 100 centavos. Peso notes in circulation: 2, 5, 10, 20, 50 and 100. Coins in circulation: 5, 10, 25 and 50 centavos and 1 peso.

NB The provinces of Córdoba, Salta, Jujuy and Catamarca and issue *bonos* (bonds) which circulate at face value alongside the national currency. Tucumán issues *cheques predatos*. Two warnings: they are not accepted outside the province of issue and even inside province of issue they are not accepted for some transactions, eg trains, long distance buses. Also,

they bear redemption dates, after which they are valueless. Try always to use cash in these provinces and pay the exact amount; change may be given in *bonos*.

Most major towns have exchange shops (*casas de cambio*). Exchange rates are quoted in major newspapers daily. The three main ways of keeping in funds while travelling are with US dollars cash, US dollar travellers' cheques, or plastic.

● **Cash**

It is best to take US$ cash rather than sterling and other currencies. Dollars are widely accepted especially in cities and tourist destinations, but take only utterly unblemished notes, as dirty or torn notes are usually refused, and always carry some some small denomination notes. Though the risk of loss is greater than with travellers' cheques, better rates and lower commissions can usually be obtained for them. If you are travelling on the cheap watch weekends and public holidays carefully and never run out of local currency, especially away from major cities.

● **Travellers' cheques**

These are convenient but they attract thieves (though refunds can of course be arranged). Denominations of US$50 and US$100 are preferable to larger values, but it is a good idea to take some US$20 cheques. Travellers' cheques are generally difficult to change, especially in smaller towns and at weekends. They are often scrutinized very closely: any variation between signatures can lead to their being refused. Passport is essential and you may have to show proof of purchase. Transactions can take a long time and many forms. Because of fraud there are periodic crackdowns on particular types of travellers' cheque; take more than one type to avoid being stuck without funds. There is a 3% tax and banks generally charge about 4% commission; commissions can be as high as 10% (higher in Calafate). Commission can be avoided if you go to a branch of the issuing bank, especially if changing small amounts. Hotels will normally change travellers' cheques for their guests (often at a rather poor rate).

American Express, Visa or Thomas Cook US$ travellers' cheques are better known by hotels and other establishments than Citibank or Bank of America travellers' cheques. American Express travellers' cheques, which can be changed at the American Express bank in Buenos Aires, are hard to change in northern Argentina. Citibank travellers' cheques have been recommended; no commission is charged at their own branches around the country. Thomas Cook Mastercard travellers' cheque refund assistance point, 25 de Mayo 195, 6th floor, Buenos Aires, T 343-8371.

● **Plastic**

American Express, Diners Club, Visa and Mastercard cards are all widely accepted in the major cities and provincial capitals, though less so outside these. There is a 10% surcharge on credit card transactions in many establishments; many hotels offer reductions for cash. Credit cards are readily accepted in all main towns, even in the south, but outside main towns their use is limited. Many service stations accept credit cards (ACA stations only take cards from members; YPF accepts Visa). All shops, hotels and places showing Argencard (head office, H Yrigoyen 878, Buenos Aires, T 331-2088) signs will accept Eurocard and Access, but you must state that these cards are affiliated to Mastercard. Argencard will not permit cash advances on these cards in outlying regions, and is itself very slow in advancing cash. Lloyds Bank, in many cities, handles Mastercard. Emergency cash from Amex is available only in Buenos Aires and Bariloche.

Make sure you know the correct procedure if your cards are lost or stolen. For security, insist that imprints are made in your presence and that any imprints incorrectly completed should be torn into tiny pieces. Also destroy the carbon papers after the form is completed (signatures can be copied from them).

NB In many countries, you can get at least US$500 in Amex travellers' cheques on the American Express card (US$1,000 on the gold card). You can also obtain cash at American Express via personal cheques, eg Eurocheque.

It is straightfoward to obtain a cash advance against a credit card and, in the text, we give the names of banks which do this. **Automatic Telling Machines** (ATMs), known as *Cajeros Automáticos*, are available in Buenos Aires and a few other major cities.

There are two international ATM acceptance systems, Plus and Cirrus. Many issuers of debit and credit cards are linked to one, or both (eg Visa is Plus, Mastercard is Cirrus). Visa can be used at Banelco ATMs. Cirrus card can be used at ATMs with Link sign, eg Banco Nacional de Lavoro. Look for the relevant symbol on an ATM and draw cash using your PIN. Frequently, the rates of exchange on ATM withdrawals are the best available. Find out before you leave what ATM coverage there is in the countries you will visit and what international 'functionality' your card has. Check if your bank or credit card company imposes handling charges. Obviously you must ensure that the account to which your debit card refers contains sufficient funds. With a credit card, obtain a credit limit sufficient for your needs, or pay money in to put the account in credit. If travelling for a long time, consider a direct debit to clear your account regularly. Do not rely on one card, in case of loss. If you do lose a card, immediately contact the 24-hour helpline of the issuer in your home country (keep this number in a safe place). (With thanks to Nigel Baker, Debit Card Manager, Natwest Bank plc, London.)

● **Transfers**

Money can be transferred between banks. A recommended method is, before leaving, to find out which local bank is correspondent to your bank at home, then when you need funds, telex your own bank and ask them to telex the money to the local bank (confirming by fax). Give exact information to your bank of the routing number of the receiving bank. Allow 2-3 days; cash is usually paid in pesos and is be subject to tax. For Western Union, T (1) 322-7774. If staying for a long time in Argentina and especially Buenos Aires, it may be a good idea to transfer money into a local bank, opening an account in pesos or dollars. Paperwork is not complicated and your money is safe and gaining interest. Check with your bank before leaving.

● **Value-added tax**

VAT is not levied on most medicines and some foodstuffs but on all other products and services at 21%.

WHAT TO TAKE

Everybody has his/her own list but items most often mentioned include air cushions for slatted seats, inflatable travel pillow for neck support, strong shoes, a small first-aid kit and handbook, fully waterproof top clothing, waterproof treatment for leather footwear, wax earplugs (which are almost impossible to find outside large cities) and airline-type eye mask to help you sleep in noisy and poorly curtained hotel rooms, sandals (rubber-thong Japanese-type or other – can be worn in showers to avoid athlete's foot), a polyethylene sheet 2 x 1m to cover possibly infested beds and shelter your luggage, polyethylene bags of varying sizes (up to heavy duty rubbish bag size) with ties, a toilet bag you can tie round your waist; if you use an electric shaver, take a rechargeable type, a sheet sleeping-bag and pillow-case or separate pillow-case – in some cheap hotels they are not changed often in cheap hotels; a 1½-2m piece of 100% cotton can be used as a towel, a bedsheet, beach towel, makeshift curtain and wrap; a mosquito net (or a hammock with a fitted net), a straw hat which can be rolled or flattened and reconstituted after 15 minutes soaking in water, a clothes line, a nailbrush (useful for scrubbing dirt off clothes as well as off yourself), a vacuum flask, a water bottle, a small dual-voltage immersion heater, a small dual-voltage (or battery-driven) electric fan, a light nylon waterproof shopping bag, a universal bath- and basin-plug of the flanged type that will fit any waste-pipe (or improvise one from a sheet of thick rubber), string, velcro, electrical insulating tape, large penknife preferably with tin and bottle openers, scissors and corkscrew – the famous Swiss Army range has been repeatedly recommended (for knife sharpening, go to a butcher's shop), alarm clock or watch, candle, torch (flashlight) – especially one that will clip on to a pocket or belt, pocket mirror, pocket calculator, an adaptor and flex to enable you to take power from an electric-light socket (the Edison screw type is the most commonly used), a padlock (combination lock is best) for the doors of the cheapest and most casual hotels (or for tent zip if camping), spare chain-lengths and padlock for securing luggage to bed or bus/train seat. Remember not to throw away spent batteries containing mercury or cadmium; take them home to be disposed of, or recycled properly.

Useful medicaments are given in the 'Health' section (see page 500); to these might be added some lip salve with sun protection, and pre-moistened wipes (such as "Wet Ones"). Always carry toilet paper. Dental floss can be used for backpack repairs, in addition to its original purpose. **Never** carry firearms. Their possession could land you in serious trouble.

Contact lens wearers will find a wide selection of products for the care of lenses, sold in a chemist/pharmacy, rather than an optician's.

Lastly, a good principle is to take half the clothes, and twice the money, that you think you will need.

GETTING THERE

BY AIR
● From Europe
British Airways (non-stop, 3 times a week) and Aerolíneas Argentinas (via Madrid) each fly from London. Aerolíneas Argentinas also fly to the following European destinations (with other carriers in parentheses): Frankfurt (once a week, Lufthansa); Madrid (6 a week, Iberia, daily); Paris (4 a week, Air France); Rome (4 a week, also Alitalia); Zurich (2, Swiss Air). KLM flies 3 times a week from Amsterdam. Aeroflot flies from Moscow once a week.

● From North America
Aerolíneas Argentinas fly from Los Angeles. Other carriers as follows: from Los Angeles (Lan Chile, United); from Miami (American, United); from New York (American, United); from Dallas, American, daily via Miami; from Chicago, American and United. Canadian Air International fly 5 times a week from Toronto; Aerolíneas Argentinas fly twice a week from Toronto, once from Montreal. **NB** Aerolíneas

Argentinas is part of Continental's frequent flier programme.

● From Australasia and South Africa
Aerolíneas Argentinas fly from Sydney, Australia, via Auckland, New Zealand, 3 times a week. On the outward flight from Argentina, Aerolíneas stop at Río Gallegos, but it is difficult to board there in high season. Malaysia Airlines and South African Airways both fly 5 times a week from Johannesburg and Cape Town.

● From Latin America
Aerolíneas Argentinas (AR) and Mercosur daily from Asunción; Aerolíneas Argentinas and Avianca from Bogotá; Aerolíneas Argentinas from Caracas; Aerolíneas Argentinas from La Paz via Santa Cruz, and LAB direct from Santa Cruz; from Lima, Aerolíneas Argentinas (3), Lan Chile, AeroPerú (en route from Cancún) from Montevideo (apart from those given in the Buenos Aires section), AR, Pluna, United and Iberia; frequent flights also to Punta del Este, with many more in holiday season; Ecuatoriana from Guayaquil and Quito (5 a week); from Santiago, Chile, daily with Aerolíneas Argentinas and Lan Chile and other Latin American, European and North American carriers on various days. Mexicana and Lan Chile fly from Mexico City.

From Brazil, Aerolíneas Argentinas, Varig and Vasp fly daily from Rio de Janeiro and São Paulo; Transbrasil also fly from São Paulo and some European airlines stop over there; Varig stops over in Porto Alegre. Varig flies daily from Brasília; Transbrasil from Manaus, São Paulo and Porto Alegre. Transbrasil, Varig and Vasp from Curitiba and Florianópolis. Vasp flies daily from Recife and Salvador. See below for the for the Mercosur Air Pass.

● General tips
Airlines will only allow a certain weight of luggage without a surcharge; this is normally 30 kilos for first class and 20 kilos for business and economy classes, but these limits are often not strictly enforced when it is known that the plane is not going to be full. On some flights from the UK special outbound concessions are offered (by Iberia, Air France, Avianca) of a 2-piece allowance up to 32 kilos, but you may need to request this. Passengers seeking a larger baggage allowance can route via USA, but with certain exceptions, the fares are slightly higher using this route. On the other hand, weight limits for internal flights are often lower; best to enquire beforehand.

● Prices and discounts
1 It is generally cheaper to fly to Latin American destinations from London rather than a point in continental Europe; travellers starting their journey in continental Europe should make local enquiries about charters and agencies offering

the best deals. Fares vary from airline to airline, destination to destination and according to time of year. Check with an agency for the best deal for when you wish to travel.

2 Most airlines offer discounted fares of one sort or another on scheduled flights. These are not offered by the airlines direct to the public, but through agencies who specialize in this type of fare.

The very busy seasons are 7 December – 15 January and 10 July – 10 September. If you intend travelling during those times, book as far ahead as possible. Between February-May and September-November special offers may be available.

3 Other fares fall into three groups, and are all on scheduled services:

• **Excursion (return) fares** with restricted validity eg 5-90 days. Carriers are introducing flexibility into these tickets, permitting a change of dates on payment of a fee.

• **Yearly fares** These may be bought on a one-way or return basis. Some airlines require a specified return date, changeable upon payment of a fee. To leave the return completely open is possible for an extra fee. You must fix the route (some of the cheapest flexible fares now have 6 months validity).

• **Student (or Under 26) fares** Some airlines are flexible on the age limit, others strict. One way and returns available, or 'Open Jaws' (see below). Do not assume that student tickets are the cheapest; though they are often very flexible, they are usually more expensive than Excursion or Yearly fares. On the other hand, there is a wider range of cheap one-way student fares originating in Latin America than can be bought outside the continent. **NB** If you foresee returning home at a busy time (eg Christmas-beginning of January, August), a booking is advisable on any type of one-return ticket.

4 For people intending to travel a linear route and return from a different point from that which they entered, there are 'Open Jaws' fares, which are available on student, yearly, or excursion fares.

5 Many of these fares require a change of plane at an intermediate point, and a stopover may be permitted, or even obligatory, depending on schedules. Simply because a flight stops at a given airport it does not mean you can break your journey there – the airline must have traffic rights to pick up or set down passengers between points A and B before it will be permitted. This is where dealing with a specialized agency (like Journey Latin America!) will really pay dividends. There are dozens of agencies that offer the simple returns to Rio or Lima at roughly the same (discounted) fare but on multi-stop itineraries, the specialized agencies can often save clients hundreds of pounds.

6 Although it's a little more complicated, it's possible to sell tickets in London for travel originating in Latin America at substantially cheaper fares than those available locally. This is useful for the traveller who doesn't know where he will end up, or who plans to travel for more than a year. Because of high local taxes (see paragraph 7) a one-way ticket from Latin America is more expensive than a one-way in the other direction, so it's always best to buy a return (but see **Student fares**, above). Taxes are calculated as a percentage of the full IATA fare; on a discounted fare the tax can therefore make up as much as 30-50% of the price.

7 If you buy discounted air tickets *always* check the reservation with the airline concerned to make sure the flight still exists. Also remember that IATA airlines' schedules change in March and October each year, so if you're going to be away a long time it's best to leave return flight coupons open (but see **NB** under **Student fares**, above).

In addition, check whether you are entitled to any refund or re-issued ticket if you lose, or have stolen, a discounted air ticket. Some

airlines require the repurchase of a ticket before you can apply for a refund, which will not be given until after the validity of the original ticket has expired. The Iberia group and Air France, for example, operate this costly system. Travel insurance in some cases covers lost tickets.

8 Note that some South American carriers change departure times of short-haul or domestic flights at short notice and, in some instances, schedules shown in the computers of transatlantic carriers differ from those actually flown by smaller, local carriers. If you book, and reconfirm, both your transatlantic and onward sectors through your transatlantic carrier you may find that your travel plans have been based on out of date information. The surest solution is to reconfirm your outward flight in an office of the onward carrier itself.

We advise people who travel the cheap way in Latin America to pay for all transport as they go along, and not in advance. This advice does not apply to people on a tight schedule: paying as you go along may save money, but it is likely to waste your time somewhat. The one exception to this general principle is in transatlantic flights; here money is saved by booking as far as possible in one operation. International air tickets are very expensive if purchased in Latin America. If buying airline tickets routed through the USA, check that US taxes are included in the price.

● **Airpasses**

The Mercosur Airpass which applies to Brazil, Argentina, Uruguay, Paraguay and Chile (1998), using 9 local carriers, is available to any passenger with a return ticket to a Mercosur country. It must be bought in conjunction with an international flight; minimum stay is 7 days, maximum 30, at least 2 countries must be visited. Maximum number of coupons is eight. Fares are calculated on a mileage basis and range from US$225 to US$870. See below for the Aerolíneas Argentinas 'Visit Argentina' airpass.

BY LAND

There are many entry points from the neighbouring states: Bolivia, Brazil, Chile, Paraguay and Uruguay. Details of these and of transport are given in the text. There are no passenger rail services into Argentina.

The Amerbuspass covers the whole of Latin America, from Mexico City to Ushuaia, and entitles the holder to 15-20% discounts on tickets with participating operators; bookable in all Latin American capitals, Europe, Asia, Africa, Oceania, it is valid for 9,999 miles, up to 180 days. Unlimited stopovers, travel with either a confirmed or open itinerary. Contact TISA Internacional, B Irigoyen 1370, Oficina 25/26, 1138 Buenos Aires, Argentina, T 307-1956, F 300-5591, PO Box 40 Suc 1 (B), 1401 Buenos Aires.

BY SEA

Voyages on passenger-carrying cargo vessels between South America and Europe, the USA, or elsewhere, are listed here: the Grimaldi Line sails from Tilbury to Brazil (Vitória, Santos, Paranaguá, Rio) and Buenos Aires via Hamburg, Amsterdam and Antwerp, Le Havre, round trip about 51 days, US$3,040-5,400, also from Genoa to Paranaguá, Santos and Rio for US$1,100-1,400 (round trip or south-bound only, no north-bound only passages).

A number of German container ships sail the year round to the east coast of South America: Felixstowe, Hamburg, Antwerp, Bilbao or Algeciras, Santos, Buenos Aires, Montevideo, Rio Grande do Sul, Itajaí, Santos, Rio de Janeiro, Rotterdam, Felixstowe (about 45 days, £3,100-3,500 per person round trip). There are also German sailings from Genoa or Livorno (Italy), or Spain to the east coast of South America.

Polish Ocean Line's services include Gdynia to Buenos Aires, Montevideo and Santos (2-2½ months, £2,700 per person double, £2,900 single.

From the USA, Ivaran Lines serve East Coast USA, Brazilian ports, Montevideo and Buenos Aires; the *Americana* container ship carries 80 passengers in luxury accommodation (New Orleans, Houston, Puerto Cabello, La Guaira, Rio, Santos, Buenos Aires, Montevideo, Rio Grande

do Sul, Itajaí, Paranaguá, Santos, Salvador, Fortaleza, Bridgetown, San Juan, Veracruz, Tampico, New Orleans, £6,645-11,340 per person round trip, fares depend on season, one-way north or south possible. Ivaran also have the *San Antonio*, carrying 12 passengers on the route Port Elizabeth (New Jersey), Baltimore, Norfolk, Savannah, Miami, Puerto Cabello, La Guaira, Rio, Santos, Buenos Aires, Montevideo, Rio Grande do Sul, Itajaí, Santos, Rio (possibly Salvador and Fortaleza), Port Elizabeth; 44-day round trip £4,085-4,825 per person, one-way subject to availability.

Enquiries regarding passages should be made through agencies in your own country, or through John Alton of Strand Cruise and Travel Centre, Charing Cross Shopping Concourse, The Strand, London WC2N 4HZ, T 0171-836 6363, F 0171-497 0078. Strand Cruise and Travel are booking agents for all the above. Elsewhere in Europe, contact Wagner Frachtschiffreisen, Stadlerstrasse 48, CH-8404, Winterthur, Switzerland, T (052) 242-1442, F 242-1487. In the USA, contact Freighter World Cruises, 180 South Lake Ave, Pasadena, CA 91101, T (818) 449-3106, or Traveltips Cruise and Freighter Travel Association, 163-07 Depot Road, PO Box 188, Flushing, NY 11358, T (800) 872-8584. Do not try to get a passage on a non-passenger carrying cargo ship to South America from a European port; it is not possible.

CUSTOMS

No duties are charged on clothing, personal effects, toilet necessities, etc. Cameras, typewriters, binoculars, radios and other things which a tourist normally carries are duty-free if they have been used and only one of each article is carried. This is also true of scientific and professional instruments for the personal use of the traveller. Travellers may only bring in new personal goods up to a value of US$200 (US$100 from neighbouring countries); the amount of duty and tax payable amounts to 50% of the item's cost. There are red and green divisions at airport customs. Baggage claim tags are inspected at the exit from the customs inspection area.

2 litres of alcoholic drinks, 400 cigarettes and 50 cigars are also allowed in duty-free; for tourists originating from neighbouring countries the respective quantities allowed are 1 litre, 200, 20 and 2 kilos. You can buy duty-free goods *on arrival* at Ezeiza airport.

If having packages sent to Argentina, do not use the green customs label unless the contents are of real value and you expect to pay duty. For such things as books or samples use the white label if available.

ON ARRIVAL

● Airport information

Do not send unaccompanied luggage to Argentina; it can take up to 3 days of form-filling to retrieve it from the airport. Paying overweight though expensive, saves time.

● Airport tax

US$15 for all international flights, except to Montevideo from Aeroparque, which is subject to US$5 tax; US$3-6, payable only in pesos also for internal flights (US$1.75 in Ushuaia). When in transit from one international flight to another, you may be obliged to pass through immigration and customs, have your passport stamped and be made to pay an airport tax on departure. There is a 5% tax on the purchase of air tickets. Airport tax can be prepaid.

● Appearance

There is a natural prejudice in all countries against travellers who ignore personal hygiene and have a generally dirty and unkempt appearance. Most Argentines, if they can afford it, devote great care to their clothes and appearance; it is appreciated if visitors do likewise. How you dress is mostly how people will judge you. Buying clothing locally can help you to look less like a tourist. It may be advantageous to carry a letter from someone in an official position testifying to one's good character, on official-looking notepaper.

Shorts are worn in Buenos Aires and residential suburbs in spring, summer and autumn, but their use is not common outside the capital. Bermuda-type shorts are very fashionable, as are jogging suits. In general, dress tends to be formal (unless casual wear is specified on an invitation) in Buenos Aires and for evening outings to shows, etc. The general standard of dress among Argentines is very high: collar and tie, with jacket, are very much the standard for men, and women 'should always err on the side of elegance' – David Mackintosh. Men wearing earrings can expect comments, even hostility, in the provinces.

A medium weight shawl with some wool content is recommended for women: it can double as pillow, light blanket, bathrobe or sunscreen as required.

● Courtesy

Remember that politeness – even a little ceremoniousness – is much appreciated. In this connection professional or business cards are useful. Men should always remove any headgear and say "con permiso" when entering offices, and be prepared to shake hands (this is much commoner in Latin America than in Europe or North America); always say "Buenos días" (until midday) or "Buenas tardes" and wait for a reply before proceeding further. Always remember that the traveller from abroad has enjoyed greater advantages in life than most Argentine minor officials, and should be friendly and courteous in consequence. Never be impatient; do not criticize situations in public: the officials may know more English than you think and they can certainly interpret gestures and facial expressions. Be judicious about discussing politics with strangers. Politeness can be a liability, however, in some situations; most Latin Americans are disorderly queuers. In commercial transactions (buying a meal, goods in a shop, etc) politeness should be accompanied by firmness, and always ask the price first.

Politeness should also be extended to street traders; saying "No, gracias" with a smile is better than an arrogant dismissal. Whether you give money to beggars is a personal matter, but your decision should be influenced by whether a person is begging out of need or trying to cash in on the tourist trade. In the former case, local people giving may provide an indication. Giving money to children is a separate issue, upon which most agree: don't do it. There are occasions where giving food in a restaurant may be appropriate, but first inform yourself of local practice.

Moira Chubb, from New Zealand, suggests that if you are a guest and are offered food that arouses your suspicions, the only courteous way out is to feign an allergy or a stomach ailment. If worried about the purity of ice for drinks, ask for a beer.

Be careful when asking directions. Women probably know more about the neighbourhood; men about more distant locations. Policemen are often helpful. However people may sometimes give you the wrong answer rather than admit they do not know.

● **Hours of business**

Banks, government offices, insurance offices and business houses are not open on Saturday. **Government Offices**: 1230-1930 in the winter and 0730-1300 in summer. **Banks**: generally 1000-1600 but time varies according to the city, and sometimes according to the season. (See under names of cities in text.) **Post Offices**: stamps on sale during working days 0800-2000 but 0800-1400 on Saturday. **Shops** are open from about 0900 to 1900, though many close at midday on Saturday. Outside the main cities many close for the daily afternoon siesta, re-opening at about 1700. 24-hour opening is allowed except on Monday; this applies mainly to restaurants, foodshops, barbers, newspaper shops, art, book and record stores.

Dance halls open at 2300 but don't fill up till after midnight; nightclubs open after midnight. In city centres, cafés and restaurants are busy till after midnight and many evening events, such as lectures, may not start before 2200.

● **Official time**

3 hours behind GMT.

● **Photography**

Always ask permission before photographing people. Film is expensive in Argentina and cheaper in Chile (in the Punta Arenas Tax Free Zones) and Paraguay (always check the expiry date). Pre-paid Kodak slide film cannot be developed anywhere in South America; it is also very hard to find. Kodachrome is almost impossible to buy. Some travellers (but not all) have advised against mailing exposed films home; either take them with you, or have them developed, but not printed, once you have checked the laboratory's quality. Note that postal authorities may use less sensitive equipment for X-ray screening than the airports do. Modern controlled X-ray machines are supposed to be safe for any speed of film, but it is worth trying to avoid X-ray as the doses are cumulative. Many airport officials will allow film to be passed outside X-ray arches; they may also hand-check a suitcase with a large quantity of film if asked politely.

Dan Buck and Anne Meadows add that developing black and white film is a problem. Often it is shoddily machine-processed and the negatives are ruined. Ask the store if you can see an example of their laboratory's work and if they hand-develop.

Jeremy Till and Sarah Wigglesworth suggest that exposed film can be protected in humid areas by putting it in a balloon and tying a knot. Similarly keeping your camera in a plastic bag may reduce the effects of humidity.

● **Police**

Whereas in Europe and North America we are accustomed to law enforcement on a systematic basis, enforcement in Latin America is often achieved by periodic campaigns. The most typical is a round-up of criminals in the cities just before Christmas. In December, therefore, you may well be asked for identification at any time, and if you cannot produce it, you will be jailed. If a visitor is jailed his/her friends should provide food every day. This is especially important for people on a diet, such as diabetics. In the event of a vehicle accident in which anyone is injured, all drivers involved are automatically detained until blame has been established, and this does not usually take less than 2 weeks.

Never offer a bribe unless you are fully conversant with the customs of the country. Wait until the official makes the suggestion, or offer money in some form which is apparently not bribery, eg "In our country we have a system of on-the-spot fines (*multas de inmediato*). Is there a similar system here?" Do not assume that an official who accepts a bribe is prepared to do anything else that is illegal. You bribe him to persuade him to do his job, or to persuade him not to do it, or to do it more quickly, or more slowly. You do not bribe him to do something which is against the law. The mere suggestion would make him very upset. If an official suggests that a bribe must be paid before you can proceed on your way, be patient (assuming you have the time) and he may relent.

● **Safety**

Argentina is one of the safest countries in South America. In provincial towns, main places of interest, on day time buses and in ordinary restaurants the visitor should be quite safe. Nevertheless, in Buenos Aires and other large cities (particularly in crowded places, eg bus stations, markets), crime exists, most of which is opportunistic. If you are aware of the dangers, act confidently and use your common sense you will lessen many of the risks.

General tips The following tips, all endorsed by travellers, are meant to forewarn, but not alarm, you. They mainly apply to major cities. Keep all documents secure; hide your main cash supply in different places or under your clothes: extra pockets sewn inside shirts and trousers, pockets closed with a zip or safety pin, money-belts (best worn below the waist rather than outside or at it or around the neck), neck or leg pouches, a thin chain for attaching a purse to your bag or under your clothes and elasticated support bandages for keeping money and cheques above the elbow or below the knee have been repeatedly recommended (the last by John Hatt in *The Tropical Traveller*). Keep cameras in bags (preferably with a chain or wire in the strap to defeat the slasher) or briefcases; take spare spectacles (eyeglasses); don't wear wrist-watches or jewellery. If you wear a shoulder-bag in a market, carry it in front of you. Backpacks are vulnerable to slashers: a good idea is to cover the pack with a sack (a plastic one will also keep out rain and dust) with maybe a layer of wire netting between, or make an inner frame of chicken wire. Use a pack which is lockable at its base.

In Buenos Aires and other major cities beware of the common trick of spraying mustard, ketchup or some other substance on you and then getting an accomplice to clean you off (and remove your wallet). If you are sprayed, walk straight on. Ignore also strangers' remarks like "what's that on your shoulder?" or "have you seen that dirt on your shoe?" Furthermore, don't bend over to pick up money or other items in the street. These are all ruses intended to distract their attention and make you easy for an accomplice to steal from. If someone follows you when you're in the street, let him catch up with you and "give him the eye". While you should take local advice about being out at night, do not assume that daytime is safer than nighttime. If walking after dark in dangerous parts of big cities, walk in the road, not on the pavement/sidewalk.

Be wary of "plainclothes policemen"; insist on seeing identification and on going to the police station by main roads. Do not hand over your identification (or money – which he should not need to see anyway) until you are at the station. On no account take them directly back to your lodgings. Be even more suspicious if he seeks confirmation of his status from a passer-by. If someone tries to bribe you, insist on a receipt. If attacked, remember your assailants may well be armed, and try not to resist.

It is best, if you can trust your hotel, to leave any valuables you don't need in safe-deposit there, when sightseeing locally. Always keep an inventory of what you have deposited. If you don't trust the hotel, lock everything in your pack and secure that in your room (some people take eyelet-screws for padlocking cupboards or drawers). If you lose valuables, always report to the police and note details of the report – for insurance purposes.

When you have all your luggage with you at a bus or railway station, be especially careful: don't get into arguments with any locals if you can help it, and lock all the items together with a chain or cable if you are waiting for some time. Take a taxi between airport/bus station/railway station and hotel, if you can possibly afford it. Keep your bags with you in the taxi and pay only when you and your luggage are safely out of the vehicle. Make sure the taxi has inner door handles, in case a quick exit is needed. Avoid night buses; never arrive at night; and watch your belongings being stowed inside. Major bus lines often issue a luggage ticket when bags are stored in the bus' hold. When getting on a bus, keep your ticket handy; someone sitting in your seat may be a distraction for an accomplice to rob you while you are sorting out the problem. Finally, never accept food, drink, sweets or cigarettes from unknown fellow-travellers on buses or trains. They may be drugged, and you would wake up hours later without your belongings. In this connection, never accept a bar drink from an opened bottle (unless you can see that that bottle is in general use): always have it uncapped in front of you.

Rape This can happen anywhere in the world. If you are the victim of a sexual assault, you are advised in the first instance to contact a doctor (this can be your home doctor if you prefer). You will need tests to determine whether you have contracted any sexually-transmitted diseases; you may also need advice on post-coital contraception. You should also contact your embassy, where consular staff are very willing to help in cases of assault.

Drugs Users of drugs, even of soft ones, without medical prescription should be particularly careful, as some countries impose heavy penalties – up to 10 years' imprisonment – for even the simple possession of such substances. In this connection, the planting of drugs on travellers, by traffickers or the police, is not unknown. If offered drugs on the street, make no response at all and keep walking. Note that people who roll their own cigarettes are often suspected of carrying drugs and subjected to intensive searches. Advisable to stick to commercial brands of cigarettes – but better still not to smoke at all.

Travelling alone Many points of security, dress and language have been covered already. First time exposure to countries where sections of the population live in extreme poverty or squalor and may even be starving can cause odd psychological reactions in visitors. So can the exceptional curiosity extended to visitors, especially women. Simply be prepared for this and try not to over-react. These additional hints have mainly been supplied by women, but most apply to any single traveller. When you set out, err on the side of caution until your instincts have adjusted to the customs of a new culture. If, as a single woman, you can befriend a local woman, you will learn much more about the country you are visiting. Unless actively avoiding foreigners like yourself, there is a very definite "gringo trail" which you can join, or follow, if seeking company. This can be helpful when looking for safe accommodation, especially if arriving after dark (which is best avoided). Remember that for a single woman a taxi at night can be as dangerous as wandering around on her own. At borders dress as smartly as possible. Travelling by train is a good way to meet locals, but buses are much easier for a person alone; on major routes your seat is often reserved and your luggage can usually be locked in the hold. It is easier for men to take the friendliness of locals at face value; women may be subject to much unwanted attention. To help minimize this, do not wear suggestive clothing and, advises Alex Rossi of Jawa Timur, Indonesia, do not flirt. By wearing a wedding ring, carrying a photograph of your "husband" and "children", and saying that your "husband" is close at hand, you may dissuade an aspiring suitor. If politeness fails, do not feel bad about showing offence and departing. When accepting a social invitation, make sure that someone knows the address and the time you left. Ask if you can bring a friend (even if you do not intend to do so). A good rule is always to act with confidence, as though you know where you are going, even if you do not. Someone who looks lost is more likely to attract unwanted attention. Do not disclose to strangers where you are staying. (Much of this information was supplied by Alex Rossi, and by Deirdre Mortell of Carrigaline, Co Cork, Ireland).

● **Shopping**

Best buys Local leather goods in Buenos Aires, eg coats (leather or suede), handbags and shoes. **NB** Leather from the *carpincho* is from the capybara and should not be purchased. A gourd for drinking *yerba mate* and the silver *bombilla* which goes with it, perhaps a pair of *gaucho* trousers, the *bombachas*. Ponchos (red and black for men, all colours for women). Articles of onyx, specially in Salta. Silver handicrafts. Knitted woollens, especially in Bariloche and Mar del Plata.

If British travellers have no space in their luggage, they might like to remember Tumi, the Latin American Craft Centre, who specialize in Mexican and Andean products and who produce cultural and educational videos for schools: at 23/2A Chalk Farm Road, London NW1 8AG (F 0171-485 4152), 8/9 New Bond Street Place, Bath BA1 1BH (T 01225 462367, F 01225 444870), 1/2 Little Clarendon Street, Oxford OX1 2HJ (T/F 01865-512307), 82 Park Street, Bristol BS1 5LA (T/F 0117 929 0391). Tumi (Music) Ltd specializes in different rhythms of Latin America. See *Arts and Crafts of South America*, by Lucy Davies and Mo Fini, published by Tumi (1994), for a fine introduction to the subject. There are similar shops in the USA.

● **Voltage**

220 volts (and 110 too in some hotels), 50 cycles, AC, European Continental-type plugs in old buildings, Australian 3-pin flat-type in the new. Adaptors can be purchased locally for either type (ie from new 3-pin to old 2-pin and vice-versa).

● **Weights and measures**

The metric system is used.

● **Working in Argentina**

The main opportunities for English-speakers is teaching English. Most teaching posts are in the Buenos Aires area. Further details of opportunities in English teaching are given in the Buenos Aires section. It is possible to get jobs in some countries of South America, *Jobs Abroad* will arrange work permits, visas and immigration, send 2 x 25p stamps for information to Worldwide House, Broad Street, Port Ramsgate, Kent, CT11 8NQ.

WHERE TO STAY

● **Hotels**

There are often great seasonal variations in hotel prices especially in resorts. In the beach and inland resorts where there are many good hotels and *pensiones* names are not always given in the text. *Residenciales* and *hospedajes* are usually cheaper than hotels; in many cities they are found near bus terminals. Good value hotels can also be found near truckers'

Hotel prices

Our hotel price ranges, including taxes and service charges but without meals unless stated, are as follows:

L1	Over US$200	**L2**	US$151-200	**L3**	US$101-150
A1	US$81-100	**A2**	US$61-80	**A3**	US$46-60
B	US$31-45	**C**	US$21-30	**D**	US$12-20
E	US$7-11	**F**	US$4-6	**G**	Up to US$3

NB Prices are for double rooms, except in **F** and **G** ranges where the price is almost always per person.

stops/service stations; they are usually secure. Note that in the text "with bath" usually means "with shower and toilet", not "with bath tub". Remember, cheaper hotels don't always supply soap, towels and toilet paper. Useful tips: book even cheap hotels in advance by registered mail, if you receive no reply don't worry. In any class, hotel rooms facing the street may be noisy, especially in big cities, but interior rooms may not have windows; always ask for the best, quietest room. To avoid price hikes for gringos, ask if there is a cheaper room or a discount.

NB The electric showers used in innumerable hotels should be checked for obvious flaws in the wiring; try not to touch the rose while it is producing hot water.

● **Cockroaches**

These are unpleasant, but not dangerous. Take some insecticide powder if staying in cheap hotels; Baygon (Bayer) has been recommended. Stuff toilet paper in any holes in walls that you may suspect of being parts of cockroach runs.

● **Toilets**

Many hotels, restaurants and bars have inadequate water supplies. In most places used toilet paper should **not** be flushed down the pan, but placed in the receptacle provided. This applies even in quite expensive hotels. Failing to observe this custom will block the pan or drain, a considerable health risk. It is quite common for people to stand on the toilet seat (facing the wall – easier to balance).

● **Camping**

Organized campsites are referred to in the text immediately below hotel lists, under each town. Camping is very popular in Argentina (except in Buenos Aires) and there are sites with services, both municipal, free, and paying private campsites in most tourist centres. Most are very noisy and many are closed off-season. In Patagonia strong winds can make camping very difficult. Prices have increased in recent years, though the quality of service is variable. Campers should always make sure they carry insect repellent. Camping is allowed at the side of major highways and

in all national parks (except at Iguazú Falls) Many ACA and YPF service stations have a site where one can camp (usually free) and in general service station owners are very friendly to campers, but ask first. Service stations usually have hot showers. A list of camping sites is available from ACA (labelled for members, but should be easily available) and from the national tourist information office in Buenos Aires, which has a free booklet, *1ra Guía Argentina de Campamentos*; see also Autoclub magazine. ACA campsites offer discounts to members, and to holders of the International Driving Licence; European automobile clubs' members are allowed to use ACA sites.

'Wild' camping is possible in deserted area. Obey the following rules for "wild" camping: (1) arrive in daylight and pitch your tent as it gets dark; (2) ask permission to camp from the parish priest, or the fire chief, or the police, or a farmer regarding his own property; (3) never ask a group of people – especially young people; (4) never camp on a beach (because of sandflies and thieves). If you can't get information from anyone, camp in a spot where you can't be seen from the nearest inhabited place, or road, and make sure no one saw you go there. As Béatrice Völkle of Gampelen, Switzerland, adds, camping wild may be preferable to those organized sites which are treated as discotheques, with only the afternoon reserved for sleeping.

If taking a cooker, the most frequent recommendation is a multifuel stove (eg MSR International, Coleman Peak 1), which will burn unleaded petrol or, if that is not available, kerosene, *benzina blanca*, etc. Alcohol-burning stoves are simple, reliable, but slow and you have to carry a lot of fuel: for a methylated spirit-burning stove, the following fuels apply, *alcohol desnaturalizado*, *alcohol metílico*, *alcohol puro (de caña)* or *alcohol para quemar*. Ask for 95%, but 70% will suffice. Fuel can usually be found in chemists/pharmacies. Gas cylinders and bottles are usually exchangeable, but if not can be recharged; specify whether you use butane or propane. Gas canisters are not always available.

Regular (blue bottle) Camping Gaz International is available in Buenos Aires, at an electrical

Food and drink **479**

goods store on Avenida 9 de Julio, near Teatro Colón, and *Suntime*, Lima 225, Guatemala 5908 (Palermo), Juramento 2452 (Belgrano) and *América Pesca*, Alfredo Pollini Alvear 1461. White gas (*bencina blanca*) is readily available in hardware shops (*ferreterías*). *Camping Center*, Acoyte 1622, Buenos Aires, T 855-0619, rents camping, fishing and backpacking equipment, 5% discount for ISIC holders.

● **Youth Hostels**

The Danmark Organization, Junín 1616, 3rd floor, Buenos Aires, T (54-1) 803-3700, has a network of clean, cheap youth hostels throughout Argentina (no age limit, but card needed): in Bariloche, El Bolsón, Pinamar, Calafate and the Tigre Delta. See also under Buenos Aires. There are few other youth hostels (many open only January to March), but some towns offer free accommodation to young travellers in the holiday season, on floors of schools or church halls; some fire stations will let you sleep on the floor for free (sometimes men only).

FOOD AND DRINK

● **Food**

For information on Argentine cuisine see the article under **Horizons**.

Lunch is usually eaten between 1300 and 1430 and the evening meal after 2200. Many restaurants serve a set price meal at lunchtime; often this is very good value. Eating out in the evening is usually much more expensive with no set price options. In major cities some large modern supermarkets have self-service cafeterias, which offer good quality food at good prices.

Vegetables (other than chips) are not included in menu prices, but in cheaper restaurants outside Buenos Aires you can sometimes ask for a salad instead of chips and fill up on bread if you are hungry. In cheaper restaurants you will usually be offered corn oil with a salad, but it is always worth asking whether olive oil is available.

Vegetarians should be able to list all the foods they cannot eat; saying "Soy vegetariano/a" (I'm a vegetarian) or "no como carne" (I don't eat meat) is often not enough.

● **Drink**

Argentine wines are very good. The ordinary *vinos de la casa*, or *comunes* are wholesome and relatively cheap; reds better than the whites. See the introductory article under **Horizons** for more details. The local beers, mainly lager-type, are quite acceptable. In restaurants wines have become more expensive (up to US$20 per bottle for a good quality wine). Hard liquor is relatively cheap, except for imported whisky. *Clericó* is a white-wine *sangria* drunk in summer. It is best not to drink the tap water; in the main cities it is often heavily chlorinated. It is usual to drink soda or mineral water at restaurants, and many Argentines mix it with their cheaper wine, with ice, as a refreshing drink in summer.

GETTING AROUND

AIR TRANSPORT

Internal air services are run by Aerolíneas Argentinas, Austral and Lapa (reliable turbo-prop and Boeing 737 services, cheaper than main airlines) as well as an expanding group of regional airlines including TAN (Transporte Aéreo Neuquén) in the south (book tickets through Austral), Dinar (based in Salta, serving the capital, Mar del Plata and the north, cheap fares), Kaiken (serving Patagonia, Córdoba, Mendoza), LAER (Entre Ríos, Mesopotamia), Andesmar and Southern Winds (both in the north and west) and the army airline LADE (in Patagonia), which provides a good extended schedule with new Fokker F-28 jets. The naval air passenger service, Aeronaval, carries paying civilian passengers, one third cheaper than LADE. No firm schedule though; 2 flights a week between Ushuaia, Río Grande and Río Gallegos; once a week between Ushuaia and Buenos Aires. **NB** LADE's computer reservation system is linked to Aerolíneas Argentinas, so flight connections are possible between these airlines. LADE will not accept IATA MCOs.

Deregulation and privatization has permitted the introduction of discounts by the major carriers. Ask at a travel agency. (Even though sometimes offices in various towns may tell you the flights are full, it is usually worth a try out at the airport.). Some airlines operate during the high season, or are air taxis on a semi-regular schedule. Aerolíneas Argentinas and Austral offer discounted, *banda negativa* fares on a limited number of seats on many flights, but reserve well in advance. Lapa and Dinar maintain low fares as long as a flight is not fully booked.

All airlines operate standby systems, at half regular price, buy ticket 2-3 hours before flight. It is only worth doing this off season. *Plan familiar* tickets allow couples to travel with a 25% discount for the spouse. Children under 3 travel free. LADE also operates discount spouse (65%) and children (35%) tickets. If travelling by Aerolíneas Argentinas or Austral a long linear distance, eg Río Gallegos-Buenos Aires, but wishing to stop en route, it is cheaper to buy the long flight and pay extra (about US$2) for stopovers. **NB** All local flights are fully booked way in advance for travel in December. Don't lose your baggage ticket; you won't be able to collect your bags without it. Some travellers have recommended checking in 2 hours before flight to avoid being 'bumped off' from overbooking. There is a US$3 airport tax on internal flights and a 5% tax on airline tickets.

Timetables are given in *Guía Argentina de Tráfico Aéreo* and *Guía Internacional de Tráfico*. It is unwise to set up too tight a schedule because of delays which may be caused by bad weather. Flights between Buenos Aires and Río Gallegos are often fully booked 2 to 3 weeks ahead, and there may be similar difficulties on the routes to Bariloche and Iguazú. If you are 'wait-listed' they cannot ensure a seat. Reconfirmation at least 24 hours ahead of a flight is important and it is essential to make it at the point of departure. Extra charges are made for reconfirming LADE flights but they are not high. It can be difficult to obtain cash refunds for internal airline tickets if you change your plans: better to change your ticket for a different one.

● **Visit Argentina fare**

Aerolíneas Argentinas sells a Visit Argentina ticket: 4 flight coupons costing US$450, with US$120 for each extra coupon up to a maximum of 8. It is valid for 30 days and must be purchased outside Argentina and in conjunction with an international flight ticket. Note that for children under 2 years Visit Argentina fare is 10% while normally very young children travel free. Austral sell similar tickets (known as Jetpaq) and they are interchangeable (but cannot be used on Inter Austral, its subsidiary). Routing must be booked when the coupons are issued: one change of date and of destination is free (but subsequent changes cost US$50). One stop only is permitted per town; this includes making a connection (as many flights radiate from Buenos Aires, journeys to and from the capital count as legs on the airpass, so a 4-coupon pass might not get you very far). If you start your journey outside Buenos Aires on a Sunday, when Aerolíneas Argentinas offices are closed, you may have difficulty getting vouchers issued at the airport. If you wish to visit Tierra del Fuego and Calafate it is better fly on the Visit Argentina pass to Río Grande or Ushuaia and travel around by bus or LADE from there than to stop off in Río Gallegos, fly to Ushuaia and thence back to Buenos Aires, which will use 3 coupons.

LAND TRANSPORT

● **Trains**

On 10 March 1994, the government withdrew its funding for Ferrocarriles Argentinos, handing responsibility for all services to the provinces through which the lines run. Few provinces accepted the responsibility, because of lack of resources. As a result trains now run on only 22,000 of the original 42,000 km of track and most of its is used only by freight services. Surviving passenger services are run either by provincial governments or by the private sector.

There are few passenger services outside the Buenos Aires area.

● **Buses**

Fares are charged at about US$4.50 per 100 km. Sleeper services from the capital to Mendoza, Córdoba and Bariloche cost US$7 per 100 km. There are also 'ómnibus truchos' (fake buses) which do not start or end services at bus stations and which have less reliable equipment or time-keeping; they charge less than US$4 per 100 km (ask at travel agents or hotels). Bus companies may give a 20% student discount if you show an international student card; a YHA card is also useful. The same discount may also be given to foreign, as well as Argentine, teachers and university professors but you must carry documentary proof of your employment. It can be difficult to get reductions between Dec and March. Express buses between cities are dearer than the *comunes*, but well worth the extra money for the fewer stops. When buying tickets at a bus office, don't assume you've been automatically allotted a seat: make sure you have one. Buses have strong air conditioning, even more so in summer; take a sweater for night journeys. Note that luggage is handled by *maleteros*, who expect payment (theoretically US$1, but in practice you can offer less) though many Argentines refuse to pay.

● **Motoring**

Most main roads are paved, if rather narrow (road maps are a good indication of quality), and roadside services are good. Road surface conditions vary once one leaves main towns: on the dirt and gravel roads a guard for the windscreen is essential. Most main roads now have private tolls, ranging from US$2 to US$10; tolls are spaced about every 100 km. Secondary roads (which have not been privatized) are generally in poor condition. Sometimes you may not be allowed to reach a border if you do not intend to cross it, stopping eg 20 km from the border.

All motorists are required to carry two warning triangles, a fire-extinguisher, a rigid tow bar, a first aid kit, full car documentation together with international driving licence (for non-residents, but see **Car hire** below), and the handbrake must be fully operative. Safety belts must be worn if fitted. Although few checks are made in most of the country, with the notable exceptions of roads into Rosario and Buenos Aires, checks have been reported on cars entering the country. **NB** Police checks around Buenos Aires can be very officious, even to the point of charges being invented and huge 'fines' demanded. You may not export fuel from Argentina, so use up fuel in spare jerry cans while you are in the country. Always fill up when you can in less developed areas like Chaco and Formosa and in parts of Patagonia as filling stations are infrequent. Diesel fuel 'gas-oil' prices are US$0.27 per litre. Octane rating for gasoline ('*nafta*') is as follows: regular gasoline 83 (US$0.65 per litre); super 93 (US$0.78 per litre). Unleaded fuel is not widely available but its use is increasing (it is called Ultra SP and costs a little more than super). ACA sells petrol vouchers (*vales de nafta*) for use in ACA stations. Shell and Esso stations are slightly more expensive.

To obtain documents for a resident (holder of resident visa, staying at least 6 months in the country) to take a car out of Argentina, you can go to ACA in Buenos Aires, which may take up to 4 working days, or you can ask for a list of other ACA offices that can undertake the work; take forms with you from Buenos Aires, and papers may be ready in 24 hours. You will need at least one passport-size photo, which you can have taken at ACA at a fair cost. If the car is not your own (or is hired), you require a special form signed by the owner and witnessed by a notary public. **NB** Non-residents may buy a car in Argentina but are in no circumstances allowed to take it out of the country; it must be resold in Argentina, preferably in the province where it was purchased. Non-residents who take cars into Argentina are not allowed to sell them and will encounter problems trying to leave the country without the vehicle. Third party insurance is obligatory; best obtained from the ACA, for members only.

Automóvil Club Argentino (ACA), Avenida Libertador General San Martín 1850, 1st floor, touring department on 3rd floor, 1425 Buenos Aires, T 802-6061/9, open 1000-1800 (take colectivo 130 from LN Alem and Corrientes down Alem, Libertador and F Alcorta, alight opposite ACA and walk one block through park; to return take the 130 from corner of Libertador on left as you leave building), office on Florida above Harrod's, 2nd floor, has a travel document service, complete car service facilities, insurance facilities, road information, road charts (*hojas de ruta*-about US$2.35 each to members, if available) and maps (dated with the code letters in the bottom corner – road map of whole country, with service stations and *hosterías* shown, US$4 to members, US$9.50 to non-members, and of each province), a hotel list, camping information, and a tourist guide book sold at a discount to its members and members of other recognized, foreign automobile clubs upon presentation of a membership card. (YPF, the state oil agency, also produces good maps for sale.) **NB** Members of other recognized automobile clubs are advised to check if their club has reciprocity with ACA, thus allowing use of ACA facilities and benefit from lower prices for their rooms and meals at ACA *hosterías*. The Club has service stations, some with parking garages, all over the country. If you are not a member of ACA you will not get any help when

in trouble. ACA membership, US$20 per month, permits you to pay with Eurocard (Argencard) for fuel at their Service stations, gives 20% discount on hotel rooms and maps, and discounts at associated hotels, and 10% discount on meals.

ACA accommodation comes in 4 basic types: *Motel*, *Hostería*, *Hotel*, and *Unidad Turística*, and they also organize campsites. A *motel* may have as few as 3 rooms, and only 1 night's stay is permitted. *Hosterías* have very attractive buildings and are very friendly. *Hotels* are smarter and more impersonal. All have meal facilities of some kind. Anyone can get in touch with the organization to find out about accommodation or road conditions. **NB** ACA is facing competition from others providing cheaper towing services, and better service stations, so *hosterías* and service stations are closing.

Touring Club Argentino, Esmeralda 605 and Tucumán 781, 3rd floor, T 392-6742, has similar travel services but no service stations.

The machine What kind of motoring you do will depend on what kind of car you set out with. Four-wheel drive is not necessary, but it does give you greater flexibility in mountain terrain and unmade roads off the beaten track. In Patagonia, main roads are gravel rather than paved: perfectly passable without four-wheel drive, just rough and dusty. Consider fitting wire guards for headlamps, and for windscreens too, if you don't mind peering out through a grill like a caged chimpanzee. Wherever you travel you should expect from time to time to find roads that are badly maintained, damaged or closed during the wet season, and delays because of floods, landslides and huge potholes. Don't plan your schedules too tightly.

Diesel cars are much cheaper to run than petrol ones, and the fuel is easily available. Most towns can supply a mechanic of sorts, and probably parts for Bosch fuel injection equipment. Watch the mechanics like a hawk, since there's always a brisk market in spares, and some of yours may be highly desirable. That apart, they enjoy a challenge, and can fix most things, eventually.

For prolonged motoring over 3,000m, you may need to fit high altitude jets on your carburettors. Some fuel injection engines need adjusting too, and ignition settings may have to be changed: check the manufacturer's recommendations. The electronic ignition and fuel metering systems on modern emission controlled cars are allergic to humidity, heat and dust, and cannot be repaired by bush mechanics. The most easily maintained petrol engined cars, then, are the types manufactured in Latin American countries, ie pre-emission control models such as the VW Kombi with carburettors and conventional (non-electronic) ignition. Older model American cars, especially Ford or GM pickups, are easily maintained, but high fuel consumption offsets this advantage. Argentina is very expensive for maintenance of any make of car.)

Preparation Preparing the car for the journey is largely a matter of common sense: obviously any part that is not in first class condition should be replaced. It's well worth installing extra heavy-duty shock-absorbers (such as Spax or Koni) before starting out, because a long trip on rough roads in a heavily laden car will give heavy wear. Fit tubes on "tubeless" tyres, since air plugs for tubeless tyres are hard to find, and if you bend the rim on a pothole, the tyre will not hold air. Take spare tubes, and an extra spare tyre. Also take spare plugs, fan-belts, radiator hoses and headlamp bulbs; even though local equivalents can easily be found in cities, it is wise to take spares for those occasions late at night or in remote areas when you might need them. You can also change the fanbelt after a stretch of long, hot driving to prevent wear (eg after 15,000 km per 10,000 miles). If your vehicle has more than one fanbelt, always replace them all at the same time (make sure you have the necessary tools if doing it yourself). If your car has sophisticated electrics, spare "black boxes" for the ignition and fuel injection are advisable, plus a spare voltage regulator or the appropriate diodes for the alternator, and elements for the fuel, air and oil filters if these are not a common type. (Some drivers take a spare alternator of the correct amperage, especially if the regulator is incorporated into the alternator.) Dirty fuel is a frequent problem, so be prepared to change filters more often than you would at home: in a diesel car you will need to check the sediment bowl often, too. An extra in-line fuel filter is a good idea if feasible (although harder to find, metal canister type is preferable to plastic), and for travel on dusty roads an oil bath air filter is best for a diesel car. It is wise to carry a spade, jumper cables, tow rope and an air pump. Fit tow hooks to both sides of the vehicle frame. A 12 volt neon light for camping and repairs will be invaluable. Spare fuel containers should be steel and not plastic, and a siphon pipe is essential for those places where fuel is sold out of the drum. Take a 10 litre water container for self and vehicle.

Security Apart from the mechanical aspects, spare no ingenuity in making your car secure. Your model should be the Brink's armoured van: anything less secure can be broken into by the determined and skilled thief. Use heavy chain and padlocks to chain doors shut, fit security catches on windows, remove interior window winders (so that a hand reaching in from a forced vent cannot open the window). All these will help, but none is foolproof. Anything on the outside – wing mirrors, spot lamps, motifs etc – is likely to be stolen too. So are wheels if not secured by locking nuts. Try never to leave the car unattended except in a locked garage or guarded parking space. Remove all belongings and leave the empty glove compartment open when the car is unattended. Also lock the clutch or accelerator to the steering wheel with a heavy, obvious chain or lock. Street children will generally protect your car fiercely in exchange for a tip. Be sure to note down key numbers and carry spares of the most important ones (but don't keep all spares inside the vehicle).

Documents In general, motorists in South America seem to fare better with a *libreta* or *carnet de passages* than without it.

The *libreta*, a 10-page book of three-part passes for customs, costs about US$350, but is more for those who are not members of automobile clubs; about a third of the cost is refundable. The *carnet de passages* is issued only in the country where the vehicle is registered (in the UK it costs £65 for 25 pages, £55 for 10 pages, valid 12 months, either bank indemnity or insurance indemnity, half of the premium refundable value of the vehicle and countries to be visited required), available from the RAC or the AA. In the USA the AAA does not issue the *carnet*, although the HQ in Washington DC may give advice. It is available from the Canadian Automobile Association (1775 Courtwood Crescent, Ottawa, K2C 3JZ, T 613-226-7631, F 613-225-7383) for Canadian and US citizens, cost C$400; full details obtainable from the CAA. For this information thanks go to Paul Gowen, RAC Touring Information Manager, Binka Le Breton and other motorists.

Land entry procedures are simple though time-consuming, as the car has to be checked by customs, police and agriculture officials. All you need is the registration document in the name of the driver, or, in the case of a car registered in someone else's name, a notarized letter of authorization. Officially you are required to give a written undertaking that the car will be exported after a given period, either of the *carnets*, or the *libreta* (in practice, nothing is asked for beyond the title document, except at remote border crossings which may demand a *libreta*). Of course, you should be very careful to keep **all** the papers you are given when you enter, to produce when you leave. If the car is stolen or written off you will be required to pay very high import duty on its value.

Taking a car in by sea or air is much more complicated and expensive: generally you will have to hire an agent to clear it through customs, expensive and slow. Insurance for the vehicle against accident, damage or theft is best arranged in the country of origin, but it is getting increasingly difficult to find agencies who offer this service. If anyone is hurt, do not pick them up (you may become liable). Seek assistance from the nearest police station or hospital if you are able to do so.

Journey's End When you finally reach your destination, what happens to the car? Shipping it back is one alternative: there are also frequent sailings from Montevideo and Buenos Aires to most destinations. Selling it is now legal – if not simple. Legalizing the permanent import of a temporarily imported car costs about 30% of its street value. If you leave it to the buyer to "take care of" obtaining the correct documentation, you should not expect to receive a very favourable price. Dealers are adept at taking advantage of the fact that they can wait, and you cannot, so be prepared for "on – off – on again" dealing.

Car hire The main international car hire companies operate in Argentina, but they tend to be very expensive, reflecting the high costs and accident rates. Hotels and tourist agencies will tell you where to find cheaper rates, but you will need to check that you have such basics as spare wheel, toolkit and functioning lights etc. You'll probably have more fun if you drive yourself, although it's always possible to hire a car with driver. If you plan to do a lot of driving and will have time at the end to dispose of it, investigate the possibility of buying a second hand car locally: since hiring is so expensive it may well work out cheaper and will probably do you just as well.

To rent a small car (for 4 plus luggage) costs from US$40 to US$110 a day, not including mileage, fuel, insurance and tax (20%); highest prices are in Patagonia. Discounts are available for several days', or weekly rental. Minimum age for renting is 25 (private arrangements may be possible). A credit card is useful. You must ensure that the renting agency gives you ownership papers of the vehicle, which have to be shown at police and military checks. At tourist centres such as Salta, Posadas, Bariloche or Mendoza it may be more economical to hire a taxi with driver, which includes the guide, the fuel, the insurance and the mechanic. Avis offers a good and efficient service with the possibility of complete insurance and unlimited mileage for rentals of 7 days or more, but you should prebook from abroad; no one-way fee if returned to another Avis office, but the car may not be taken out of the country. Localiza, a Brazilian company, accepts drivers aged at least 21 (according to Brazilian rules, but higher insurance). They also offer 4WD vehicles, though only from Buenos Aires. Taking a rented car out of Argentina is difficult with any company. Other companies are given in the text.

If you do not have an international driver's licence, you can get a 3-month licence from Dirección de Transportes de la Municipalidad, Avenida Roca 5225, Buenos Aires, T 602-6925, Monday-Friday 0800-1300; bring documentation from home.

Car Hire Insurance Check exactly what the hirer's insurance policy covers. In many cases it will only protect you against minor bumps and scrapes, not major accidents, nor "natural" damage (eg flooding). Ask if extra cover is available. Also find out, if using a credit card, whether the card automatically includes insurance. Beware of being billed for scratches which were on the vehicle before you hired it.

Shipping a vehicle You can ship a vehicle from Europe to Argentina. Recommended as good value are Polish Ocean Lines, 10 Lutego, Gdynia, Poland. *Carnet* is necessary; POL agent deals with customs. Departure dates are not scheduled in advance. Vehicles can also be shipped from the USA. Anything left inside the car while it is being shipped will be stolen. As long as your vehicle is not over 2.28m high, it can go in a container, but permission must be obtained for any belongings to remain in the car, and separate insurance for effects purchased. If the car is going ro-ro (drive on), it should be empty of all belongings, unless they are thoroughly secured.

Two books containing much practical information on South American motoring conditions and requirements are *Driving to Heaven*, by Derek Stansfield (available from the author, Ropley, Broad Oak, Sturminster Newton, Dorset DT10 2HG, T/F 01258-472534, £8.85 plus postage, if outside the UK), and the more recent *Central and South America by Road*, Pam Ascanio (Bradt Publications 1996, see also **Maps and Guide Books**, below).

● **Motorcycling**

People are generally very amicable to motorcyclists and you can make many friends by returning friendship to those who show an interest in you.

The Machine It should be off road capable: for example the BMW R80/100/GS for its rugged and simple design and reliable shaft drive, but a Kawasaki KLR 650s, Honda Transalp/Dominator, or the ubiquitous Yamaha XT600 Tenere would also be suitable. A road bike can go most places an off road bike can go at the cost of greater effort.

Preparations Many roads in Argentina are rough. Fit heavy duty front fork springs and the best quality rebuildable shock absorber you can afford (Ohlins, White Power). Fit lockable luggage such as Krausers (reinforce luggage frames) or make some detachable aluminium panniers. Fit a tank bag and tank panniers for better weight distribution. A large capacity fuel tank (Acerbis), +300 mile/480 km range is essential if going off the beaten track. A washable air filter is a good idea (K&N), also fuel filters, fueltap rubber seals and smaller jets for high altitude Andean motoring. A good set of trails-type tyres as well as a high mudguard are useful. Get to know the bike before you go, ask the dealers in your country what goes wrong with it and arrange a link whereby you can get parts flown out to you. If riding a chain driven bike, a fully enclosed chaincase is useful. A hefty bash plate/sump guard is invaluable.

Spares Reduce service intervals by half if driving in severe conditions. A spare rear tyre is useful but you can buy modern tyres in most cities. Take oil filters, fork and shock seals, tubes, a good manual, spare cables (taped into position), a plug cap and spare plug lead. A spare electronic ignition is a good idea, try and buy a second hand one and make arrangements to have parts sent out to you. A first class tool kit is a must and if riding a bike with a chain then a spare set of sprockets and an 'o' ring chain should be carried. Spare brake and clutch levers should also be taken as these break easily in a fall. Parts are few and far between, but mechanics are skilled at making do and can usually repair things. Castrol oil can be bought everywhere and relied upon.

Take a puncture repair kit and tyre levers. Find out about any weak spots on the bike and improve them. Get the book for international dealer coverage from your manufacturer, but don't rely on it. They frequently have few or no parts for modern, large machinery.

Clothes and Equipment A tough waterproof jacket, comfortable strong boots, gloves and a helmet with which you can use glass goggles (Halcyon) which will not scratch and wear out like a plastic visor. The best quality tent and camping gear that you can afford and a petrol stove which runs on bike fuel is helpful.

Security Not a problem. Try not to leave a fully laden bike on its own. An Abus D or chain will keep the bike secure. A cheap alarm gives you peace of mind if you leave the bike outside a hotel at night. Most hotels will allow you to bring the bike inside. Look for hotels that have a courtyard or more secure parking and never leave luggage on the bike overnight or whilst unattended.

Documents Passport, International Driving Licence, bike registration document are necessary. Riders fare much better with a *carnet de passages* than without it.

● **Cycling**
At first glance a bicycle may not appear to be the most obvious vehicle for a major journey, but given ample time and reasonable energy it most certainly is the best. It can be ridden, carried by almost every form of transport from an aeroplane to a canoe, and can even be lifted across one's shoulders over short distances. Cyclists can be the envy of travellers using more

orthodox transport, since they can travel at their own pace, explore more remote regions and meet people who are not normally in contact with tourists.

Choosing a bicycle The choice of bicycle depends on the type and length of expedition being undertaken and on the terrain and road surfaces likely to be encountered. Unless you are planning a journey almost exclusively on paved roads – when a high quality touring bike such as a Dawes Super Galaxy would probably suffice – a mountain bike is strongly recommended. The good quality ones (and the cast iron rule is **never** to skimp on quality) are incredibly tough and rugged, with low gear ratios for difficult terrain, wide tyres with plenty of tread for good road-holding, cantilever brakes, and a low centre of gravity for improved stability. Although touring bikes, and to a lesser extent mountain bikes, and spares are available in the larger cities, remember that locally manufactured goods are shoddy and rarely last. Buy everything you possibly can before you leave home.

Bicycle equipment A small but comprehensive tool kit (to include chain rivet and crank removers, a spoke key and possibly a block remover), a spare tyre and inner tubes, a puncture repair kit with plenty of extra patches and glue, a set of brake blocks, brake and gear cables and all types of nuts and bolts, at least 12 spokes (best taped to the chain stay), a light oil for the chain (eg Finish-Line Teflon Dry-Lube), tube of waterproof grease, a pump secured by a pump lock, a Blackburn parking block (a most invaluable accessory, cheap and virtually weightless), a cyclometer, a loud bell, and a secure lock and chain. *Richard's Bicycle Book* makes useful reading for even the most mechanically minded.

Luggage and equipment Strong and waterproof front and back panniers are a must. When packed these are likely to be heavy and should be carried on the strongest racks available. Poor quality racks have ruined many a journey for they take incredible strain on unpaved roads. A top bag cum rucksack (eg Carradice) makes a good addition for use on and off the bike. A Cannondale front bag is good for maps, camera, compass, altimeter, notebook and small tape-recorder. (Other recommended panniers are Ortlieb – front and back – which is waterpoof and almost "sandproof", Mac-Pac, Madden and Karimoor.) "Gaffa" tape is excellent for protecting vulnerable parts of panniers and for carrying out all manner of repairs.

All equipment and clothes should be packed in plastic bags to give extra protection against dust and rain. (Also protect all documents, etc carried close to the body from sweat.) Always take the minimum clothing. It's better to buy extra items en route when you find you need them. Naturally the choice will depend on whether you are planning a journey through tropical lowlands, deserts, high mountains or a combination, and whether rain is to be expected. Generally it is best to carry several layers of thin light clothes than fewer heavy, bulky ones. Always keep one set of dry clothes, including long trousers, to put on at the end of the day. The incredibly light, strong, waterproof and wind resistant goretex jacket and over-trousers are invaluable. Training shoes can be used for both cycling and walking.

Useful tips Wind, not hills is the enemy of the cyclist. Try to make the best use of the times of day when there is little; mornings tend to be best but there is no steadfast rule. In parts of Patagonia there can be gusting winds of 80 kph around the clock at some times of year, whereas in other areas there can be none. Take care to avoid dehydration, by drinking regularly. In hot, dry areas with limited supplies of water, be sure to carry an ample supply. For food, carry the staples (sugar, salt, dried milk, tea, coffee, porridge oats, raisins, dried soups, etc) and supplemented these with whatever local foods can be found in the markets. Give your bicycle a thorough daily check for loose nuts or bolts or bearings. See that all parts run smoothly. A good chain should last 2,000 miles, 3,200 km or more but be sure to keep it as clean as possible – an old toothbrush is good for this – and to oil it lightly from time to time. Always camp out of sight of a road. Remember that thieves are attracted to towns and cities, so when sight-seeing, try to leave your bicycle with someone such as a café owner or a priest. However, don't take unnecessary risks; always see that your bicycle is secure (most hotels will allow bikes to be kept in rooms). In more remote regions dogs can be vicious; carry a stick or some small stones to frighten them off. Most towns have a bicycle shop of some description, but it is best to do your own repairs and adjustments whenever possible. In an emergency it is amazing how one can improvise with wire, string, dental floss, nuts and bolts, odd pieces of tin or "Gaffa" tape!

Most cyclists agree that the main danger comes from other traffic, especially on major roads. A rearview mirror has been frequently recommended to forewarn you of vehicles which are too close behind. You also need to watch out for oncoming, overtaking vehicles, unstable loads on trucks, protruding loads etc. Make yourself conspicuous by wearing bright clothing and a helmet.

The Expedition Advisory Centre, administered by the Royal Geographical Society, 1, Kensington Gore, London SW7 2AR has published a useful monograph entitled *Bicycle Expeditions*, by Paul Vickers. Published in March 1990, it is available direct from the Centre, price £6.50 (postage extra if outside the UK). (In the UK there is also the Cyclist's Touring Club, CTC, Cotterell House, 69 Meadrow, Godalming, Surrey, GU7 3HS, T 01483-417217, e-mail cycling@ctc. org.uk, for touring, and technical information.)

● **Motorhomes**

Casa Import Trailer, Avenida Juan de Garay 331, T 361-5674, sells articles for motorhomes. *Casa Car*, Humberto Primo 236, T 30-0051, rents motorhomes. *Rancho Móvil*, Luis Viale 2821, T 59-9470, is club for motorhome owners; all in Buenos Aires. Porta-Potti toilets are widely sold in Argentina, sometimes under a different name.

● **Hitchhiking**

Argentina seems to be getting increasingly difficult for this. Ask at petrol stations. Traffic can be sparse, especially at distances from the main towns, and in Patagonia, which is popular with Argentine hitchhikers. It may be useful to carry a letter from your Consulate. Though they tend to be more reserved in manner than most Latin Americans, Argentines are generally friendly and helpful, especially to foreigners (display your flag, but not the Union Jack).

● **Internal checkpoints**

There are checkpoints to prevent food, vegetable and meat products entering Patagonia, the Western provinces of Mendoza and San Juan, and the Northwestern provinces of Catamarca, Tucumán, Salta and Jujuy. All vehicles and passengers entering these areas are searched and prohibited products are confiscated.

● **Trekking and Hiking**

Hiking and backpacking should not be approached casually. Even if you only plan to be out a couple of hours you should have comfortable, safe footwear (which can cope with the wet) and a daypack to carry your sweater and waterproof (which must be more than shower-proof). At high altitudes the difference in temperature between sun and shade is remarkable. The longer trips mentioned in this book require basic backpacking equipment. Essential items are: backpack with frame, sleeping bag, closed cell foam mat for insulation, stove, tent or tarpaulin, dried food (not tins), water bottle, compass. Some but not all of these things are available locally.

When planning treks in the Andes you should be aware of the effects and dangers of acute mountain sickness, and cerebral and pulmonary oedema (see **Health** section). These can be avoided by spending a few days acclimatizing to the altitude before starting your walk, and by climbing slowly. Otherwise there are fewer dangers than in most cities. Hikers have little to fear from the animal kingdom apart from insects (although it's best to avoid actually stepping on a snake), and robbery and assault are very rare. You are much more of a threat to the environment than vice versa. Leave no evidence of your passing; don't litter and don't give gratuitous presents of sweets or money to rural people. Respect their system of reciprocity; if they give you hospitality or food, then is the time to reciprocate with presents.

For trekking in mountain areas, where the weather can deteriorate rapidly, trekkers should consider taking the following equipment (list supplied by Andrew Dobbie of Swansea, who adds that it "is in no way finite"): **Clothing**: warm hat (wool or man-made fibre), thermal underwear, T-shirts/shirts, trousers (quick-drying and preferably windproof, never jeans), warm (wool or fleece) jumper/jacket (preferably two), gloves, waterproof jacket and over trousers (preferably Gore-Tex), shorts, walking boots and socks, change of footwear or flip-flops. **Camping Gear**: tent (capable of withstanding high winds), sleeping mat (closed cell – Karrimat – or inflatable – Thermarest), sleeping bag (3-season minimum rating), sleeping bag liner, stove and spare parts, fuel, matches and lighter, cooking and eating utensils, pan scrubber, survival bag. **Food**: very much personal preference but at least 2 days more supplies than you plan to use; tea, coffee, sugar, dried milk; porridge, dried fruit, honey; soup, pasta, rice, soya (TVP); fresh fruit and vegetables; bread, cheese, crackers; biscuits, chocolate; salt, pepper, other herbs and spices, cooking oil. **Miscellaneous**: map and compass, torch and spare batteries, pen and notebook, Swiss army knife, sunglasses, sun cream, lip salve and insect repellent, first aid kit, water bottle, toiletries and towel.

COMMUNICATIONS

● **Language**

Spanish, with variant words and pronunciation. English comes second; French and Italian (especially in Patagonia) may be useful.

The chief variant pronunciations are the replacement of the 'll' and 'y' sounds by a soft 'j' sound, as in 'azure' (though note that this is not done in Mendoza), the omission of the 'd' sound in words ending in '-ado' (generally considered uncultured), the omission of final 's' sounds, the pronunciation of 's' before a consonant as a Scottish or German 'ch', and the substitution in the north and west of the normal rolled 'r' sound by a hybrid 'rj'. In grammar the Spanish 'tú' is replaced by 'vos' and the second person singular conjugation of verbs has the accent on the last syllable eg *vos tenés, podés*, etc. In the north and northwest, though, the Spanish is more akin to that spoken in the rest of Latin America.

● **Postal services**

Letters from Argentina take 10-14 days to get to the UK and the USA. Rates for letters up to 20 grams: US$0.75 Mercosur, US$1 rest of Latin America, US$1.25 rest of world (add US$2 for *certificado*); up to 150 grams, US$1.50, US$2.25, US$3 respectively.

Small parcels only of 1 kilos at post offices; larger parcels from Encomiendas Internacionales, Centro Postal Internacional, Avenida Antártida Argentina, near Retiro Station, Buenos Aires, and in main provincial cities, about US$40 for 5 kilos. Larger parcels must first be examined, before final packing, by Customs, then wrapped (up to 2 kilos, brown paper; over 2 kilos must be sewn in linen cloth), then sealed by Customs, then taken to Encomiendas Internacionales for posting. Cheap packing service available. Open 1100-1700 on weekdays. Used clothes have to be fumigated before they will be accepted. Having parcels sent to Argentina incurs a customs tax of US$5.75 per package. *Poste restante* is available in every town's main post office, fee US$1.

● **Telephone services**

Two private companies operate telephone services, Telecom in the north and Telefónica Argentina in the south. Buenos Aires Federal District and the country as a whole are split roughly in two halves. For the user there is no difference and the two companies' phone cards are interchangeable. For domestic calls public phones operate on *cospeles* (tokens) which can be purchased at news stands (different tokens for local and inland calls). Domestic phone calls are priced at 3 rates: normal 0800-1000, 1300-2200, Saturday 0800-1300; peak 1000-1300 Monday-Friday; night rate 2200-0800, Saturday 1300-0800 and all day Sunday and holidays. Peak is most expensive; night rate is cheapest and at this time also international calls are reduced by 20%. International call rates per minute (DDI) are: Uruguay US$0.82; USA, Canada, Brazil, Chile, Paraguay, Bolivia US$1.13 (0.85 each subsequent min); France, Germany, UK, Spain, Italy US$1.90 (1.43); Japan, Australia, New Zealand US$4.66 (3.50); operator-connected calls more expensive. In main cities there are also privately-run 'Centros de Llamadas', offering a good telephone and fax service. International public phones display the DDI sign (Discado Directo Internacional); DDN (Discado Directo Nacional) is for phone calls within Argentina. Provide yourself with enough tokens or phone cards in Buenos Aires because, in the regions, phone booths exist, but the tokens and cards are not on sale (few phone booths in Patagonia). Most telephone company offices in principal cities have a phone for USA Direct; if they do not, they can direct you to one. BT Chargecard can be used to the UK via the operator. There is frequently a high mark-up on calls made from hotels. No reverse-charge calls to South Africa. It is now easy to call reverse charge to Australia. Operator speaks English. Fax: American Express in Buenos Aires allows card holders to receive faxes at US$1 per sheet and to send them at US$8 per sheet (to Europe). Telefónica and Telecom send faxes abroad for US$1.23 per page, plus cost of the call, and US$1.82 per page to receive. (You get charged for sending the fax even if it does not get through.) Communications on the internet are difficult. Some Centros de Llamadas have compatible equipment but static on the lines makes data transmission difficult and you are charged regardless.

MEDIA

● **Newspapers**
Buenos Aires dailies: *La Nación*, *La Prensa*, *Clarín*, *La Razón*. Evening paper: *Crónica*. English language daily: *Buenos Aires Herald* (which includes *The Guardian Weekly* free on Sunday). Magazines: *Noticias*, *Gente*, *Redacción*, *Mercado*, *El Gráfico* (sports). The daily, *Página Doce*, is very popular among students and intellectuals. *La Maga* is a weekly cultural review, Wednesday, US$5. German-language weekly, *Argentinisches Tageblatt*, available everywhere, very informative. There is a weekly international edition of *La Nación*, priced in Europe at US$1.30. Write for further information to: La Nación, Edición Internacional, Bouchard 557, 1106 Buenos Aires.

● **Radio**
English language radio broadcasts can be heard daily on short wave: 0100-0130 on 6060 KHz 49m, 0230-0300 on 11710 KHz 25m, 0430-0500 and 2230-2300 on 15345 KHz 19m; Radiodifusión Argentina al Exterior, Casilla de Correo 555, 1000, Buenos Aires. This is a government station and broadcasts also in Japanese, Arabic, German, French, Italian and Portuguese. Broadcasts by foreign radio stations (including the BBC) are receivable on short wave.

HOLIDAYS AND FESTIVALS

The main holiday period, generally to be avoided by business visitors, is January-March, though some areas, such as Tierra del Fuego, begin to fill up in November/December. Winter school holidays, in which travelling and hotels may be difficult, are the middle 2 weeks of July. No work may be done on the national holidays (1 January, Good Friday, 1 May, 25 May, 10 June, 20 June, 9 July, 17 August, 12 October and 25 December) except where specifically established by law. There are no bus services on 25 and 31 December. On Holy Thursday and 8 December employers are left free to decide whether their employees should work, but banks and public offices are closed. Banks are also closed on 31 December. There are gaucho parades throughout Argentina, with traditional music, on the days leading up to the Día de la Tradición, 10 November. On 30 December (not 31 because so many offices in centre are closed) there is a ticker-tape tradition in downtown Buenos Aires: it snows paper and the crowds stuff passing cars and buses with long streamers.

Rounding up

ACKNOWLEDGEMENTS

Many people in Argentina and in Britain assisted in the preparation of this book. Though their written contributions are acknowledged elsewhere, special thanks are due to Federico and Marlú Kirbus and their colleague Santiago de la Vega for their hospitality, constant support and generosity. Brad Krupsaw and Gilda Bona also provided invaluable support and practical help on Buenos Aires while Herbert S Levi provided regular insights from his trips around the country. Among the many others whom the editor wishes to thanked for their kindness and hospitality during his research visits in August/September 1995, August/September 1996 and January 1997 are: Stella Barrera Oro (Mendoza), Miriam Colla (Rosario), Danny Feldman and family (*Albergue del Glaciar*, Calafate), Federico Helfer (*Castillo Villa la Fontana*, Sierras de Córdoba), Jorge Herbst (*Herbst Rent a Car*, Mendoza), Javier Manceira (*Chaltén Travel*, Calafate), Daniel Oviedo and family (Merlo), the *Residencial Savigliano*, Mendoza, and René Boretto (Director of Tourism, Fray Bentos Uruguay). Thanks must also be offered to the staff of tourist information and national parks information

offices in Buenos Aires and throughout the country; particular mention is due to the offices in Calafate, Mendoza, Ushuaia and Malargüe.

Thanks are also due to the specialist contributors mentioned at the beginning of the book. Additional material was written by Bob Headland (penguins), Naomi Peirce (Iguazú and Ciudad del Este), Nigel Pickford (shipwrecks) and Peter Pyne (history). Henry Stobart advised on *Pachamama* and Theo Schulte on the *Graf Spee*.

Ben Box was as usual, a constant source of encouragement, support and ideas.

Thanks are also due to all those travellers and correspondents who contributed to the 1998 edition of the *South American Handbook*.

FURTHER READING

MAPS AND GUIDE BOOKS

Federico Kirbus has probably written the widest range of books for travellers in Argentina. These include his excellent *Guía Ilustrada de las Regiones Turísticas Argentinas*, 4 volumes, Northwest, Northeast, Centre, South, with about 300 black and white photos, colour pictures and colour plates on flora and fauna (El Ateneo, 1995, US$18-21 each). Among his other works are the highly informative *Guía de Aventuras y Turismo de la Argentina* (with comprehensive English index – 1989), obtainable at El Ateneo, or from the author at Casilla de Correo 5210, 1000, Buenos Aires; *La Argentina, país de Maravillas*, Manrique Zago ediciones (1993), a beautiful book of photographs with text in Spanish and English; *Patagonia* (with Jorge Schulte) and *Ruta Cuarenta*, both fine photographic records with text (both Capuz Varela, 1996); *Las Mil Maravillas de la Argentina* (1989) which focusses on archaeological and geological sites; *La Primera De Las Tres Buenos Aires* (1990) which examines the first founding of the capital city; *Arqueológia Argentina* (El Ateneo, 1994) and *El Fascinante Tren a Las Nubes* (El Ateneo, 1993) which recounts the building of many of the most famous railway lines in South America.

Other books include the excellent *Guía Pirelli*, edited by Diego Bigongiari (Planeta, 1995, US$20 including map) highly recommended for cultural, historical and nature information; The former state oil company Yacimientos Petroliferos Argentinos has published a six volume guide, US$10 each, recommended for its extensive town maps but not for its lack of regional maps. Written, understandably, with the motorist in mind, it has good background sections on history, geology and natural history. Backpackers will find *Backpacking in Chile and Argentina*, by Tim Burford, published by Bradt (UK) and Globe Pequot (USA), 4th edition 1998, useful. The Fundación Vida Silvestre (conservation organization and bookshop), Defensa 245/251, has information and books on Argentine Flora and fauna. Birdwatchers should consult the field guide to Argentine birds: *Guía para la identificación de las aves de Argentina y Uruguay* by T Narosky and D Yzurieta, with drawings and colour. Available in USA: *Birds of Isla Grande* (Tierra del Fuego) by Philip S Humphrey, and *A Guide to the Birds of South America*, by Rodolphe Meyer de Schauensee. For fishing try *Argentine Trout Fishing: A Fly Fisherman's Guide to Patagonia* by William C Leitch.

Several series of road maps are available including those of the Automóvil Club Argentino (ACA) and the *Automapas* published by Línea Azul. The former are available from ACA offices around the country, though usually they will only stock local maps. These are half-price to ACA members and to members of national motoring associations with reciprocity. Topographical maps are issued by the Instituto Geográfico Militar, Cabildo 301, Casilla 1426, Buenos Aires, one block from Ministro Carranza *Subte* station (Line D), or take bus 152 from Retiro. 1:500,000 sheets cost US$3 each and are 'years old'; better coverage of 1:100,000 and 1:250,000, but no general physical maps of the whole country or city plans. Helpful staff, sales office accessible from street, no passport required, map series indices on counter, open Monday-Friday, 0800-1300.

HISTORY

Most general histories of Latin America has extensive sections on Argentina. Among those which can be recommended is Edwin Williamson, *The Penguin History of Latin America* (Penguin, 1992). Though heavy going, perhaps the best single volume history of Argentina is David Rock, *Argentina 1516-1987* (I B Taurus, 1987); more accessible for the modern period is Eduardo Crawley, *A House Divided: Argentina 1880-1980* (Hurst 1984); cultural, social and political aspects of the 1930s are dealt with in M Falcoff and R H Dolkart, *Prologue to Peron: Argentina in Depression and War* (University of California Press, 1975); on Perón: R Crassweller, *Perón and the Enigmas of Argentina* (Norton, 1987), offers a fine portrait of its subject, but is poor on the historical context; an alternative is Joseph Page, *Perón: A Biography* (1983); on Evita see Marysa Navarro, *Evita* (1980); on the military dictatorship of 1976-1983 and the Dirty War: M E Anderson, *Dossier Secreto* (Westview, 1993), argues that the 'threat' of guerrilla insurgency was deliberately exaggerated by the armed forces themselves; Andrew Graham-Youll, *A State of Fear* (Eland, 1986), is a chilling first-hand account by a 'Buenos Aires Herald' journalist. The South Atlantic conflict of 1982 has produced a flood of books: a good introduction which examines the Argentine background is *The Land Which Lost Its Heroes*, by Jimmy Burns, a 'Financial Times' journalist who was in Buenos Aires at the time (I B Taurus, 1987).

On other aspects of Argentine history: *Nuestros Paisanos Los Indios* by Carlos Martínez Sarasola is an excellent compendium on the history and present of Argentine Indian communities, recommended. The British connection with Argentina is examined in Andrew Graham-Youll, *The Forgotten Colony* (1981) and in Alastair Hennessy and John King (ed) *The Land That England Lost* (I B Taurus, 1992). On the Welsh community of Patagonia see Glyn Williams, *The Desert and the Dream: The History of Welsh Colonisation of the Chubut* (University of Wales Press, 1975). In *The Afro-Argentines of Buenos Aires 1800-1900* (University of Wisconsin Press, 1980) G R Andrews explores a forgotten aspect of the city's history. Nigel Pickford's *The Atlas of Shipwreck and Treasure* (Dorling Kindersley, 1994), offers further details of shipwrecks off the Argentine coast. On Che Guevara see *Che Guevara: A Revolutionary Life* (Bantam, 1997).

CINEMA

J King, *Magical Reels: A History of Cinema in Latin America* (London and New York, 1990); Tim Barnard and Peter Rist, eds, *South American Cinema: A Critical Filmography, 1915-1994* (New York and London, 1996); Tim Barnard, *Argentine Cinema* (Toronto, 1986); Michael Chanan (ed) *Twenty five Years of the New Latin American Cinema* (London, 1983); Julianne Burton, ed, *The Social Documentary in Latin America* (Pittsburgh, 1990) and Zuzana M Pick, *The New Latin American Cinema: A Continental Project* (Austin, 1993).

LITERATURE

Gerald Martin, *Journeys Through the Labyrinth* (London and New York, 1989); J King, ed, *Modern Latin American Fiction: A Survey* (London, 1987); J King, *Sur: an Analysis of the Argentine Literary Journal and its Role in the Development of a Culture* (Cambridge, 1985); Nicolas Shumway, *The Invention of Argentina* (Berkeley, 1991); Beatriz Sarlo, *Jorge Luis Borges: A Writer on the Edge* (London and New York, 1993); S Boldy, *The Novels of Julio Cortázar* (Cambridge, 1977), Leslie Bethell, ed, *The Cambridge History of Latin America, Volume X* (Cambridge, 1995); Verity Smith, ed, *The Encyclopaedia of Latin American Literature* (London 1997). S Collier, *The Life, Music and Times of Carlos Gardel* (University of Pittsberg Press, 1986).

TRAVEL LITERATURE

Early writing on Argentina includes *At Home with the Patagonians*, by George Musters, a history of 19th century life of Patagonian Indians, John Murray (London 1871/1973); R B Cunninghame Graham, *A Vanished Arcadia* (Century, 1988), a somewhat romantic view of the Jesuit missions, first published 1901; Lucas Bridges, *Uttermost Part of the Earth* (Century, 1987) is the classic account of growing up among the indigenous peoples of Tierra del Fuego, first published 1948. Among the works of W H Hudson are: *Far Away and Long Ago* (Everyman, 1985) and *Idle Days in Patagonia* (Everyman, 1984), both of which deal with his early life in the countryside.

The most famous recent travel book on Argentina is probably Bruce Chatwin, *In Patagonia* (Picador), a wonderful mixture of fact and fantasy; John Pilkington, *An Englishman in Patagonia* (Century, 1991) offers a critical commentary on Chatwin. *The Motorcycle Diaries* by Che Guevara (Verso, 1995) offer an illuminating, and at times humorous, account of the young Che's trip through Argentina and Chile in 1952. Also worth reading is Eric Shipton, *Tierra del Fuego: The Fatal Lodestone* (Charles Knight, 1973).

The Latin American Travel Advisor is a quarterly news bulletin with up-to-date detailed and reliable information on countries throughout South and Central America. The publication focuses on public safety, health, weather and natural phenomena, travel costs, economics and politics in each country. Annual airmail subscriptions cost US$39, a single current issue US$15, electronically transmitted information (fax or e-mail), US$10 per country. Payment by US$ cheque, MasterCard or VISA (no money orders, credit card payments by mail or fax with card number, expiry date, cardholder's name and signature). Free sample available. Contact PO Box 17-17-908, Quito, Ecuador, international F 593-2-562-566, USA and Canada toll free F (888) 215-9511, e-mail LATA@pi.pro.ec, World Wide Web http://www.amerispan.com/latc/.

Information on travel and language schools is available from AmeriSpan Unlimited, one of several language school brokers in the USA, PO Box 40007, Philadelphia, PA 19106-0007, T (USA and Canada) 800-879-6640, worldwide 215-751-1100, F 215-751-1986, e-mail: info@amerispan.com, website: http://www.amerispan.com. See also the website http://www.planeta.com of Ron Mader's *El Planeta Platica: Eco Travels in Latin America*.

Useful addresses

EMBASSIES AND CONSULATES

Australia
100 Miller Street, Suite 6, Level 30, North Sydney, New South Wales 2060, T 2922-7272, F 2 923-1798.

Belgium
225 Avenue Louise B.3, 1050 Brussels, T 2 647-7812, F 2 467-9319.

Canada
90 Sparks Street, Suite 620, Ottawa KIP 5B4, T 613 236-2351, F 613 235-2659.

France
Rue Cimarosa 75116 Paris, T 1 4553-3300, F 1 4553-44633.

Germany
Wiesenhuettenplatz 26, 8th Floor, 6000 Frankfurt, T 496 923-1050, F 496 923-6842.

Netherlands
Herengracht 94 1015 BS, Amsterdam, T 2 023-2723/6242, F 2 062-67344.

New Zealand
11 Floor, Harbour View Building, 52 Quay Street, PO Box 2320, Auckland, T 9 39-1757, F 9 373-5386.

Spain
Paseo de la Castellana 53, Madrid 1, Madrid, T 1 442-4500, F 1 442-3559.

United Kingdom
27 Three Kings Yard, London W1Y 1FL, T 0171 318-1340, F 0171 318-1349.

United States
12 West 56th Street, New York 10019, T 212 603-0400, F 212 397-3523.

TOURIST INFORMATION

Brazil
Ruben Eduardo Ali, Argentine Embassy, Avenida Paulista 2319, São Paulo, F (5511) 881-4063.

Germany
Eduardo Piva, Penthouse 1, Suite F, Building AmeriFirst, Adenauerallee 52, 5300 Bonn, T 228-222011.

Italy
Luis Ruzzi, Via B Ammamati 6, Rome, T 963-60-1485.

United States
López Lecube, 12 West 56 Street, New York, NY10019, T 603-0400.

SPECIALIST TOUR COMPANIES

Journey Latin America
14-16 Devonshire Road, Chiswick, London, W4 2HD, T 0181-747 8315, and 28-30 Barton Arcade, 51-63 Deansgate, Manchester, M3 2BH, T 0161 832 1441. Long established company running escorted tours throughout the region. They also offer a wide range of flight options.

Trailfinders
194 Kensington High Street, London, W8 7RG, T 0171-938 3939.

South American Experience
47 Causton Street, Pimlico, London, SW1P 4AT, T 0171-976 5511, F 0171-976 6908. Small efficient company offering range of escorted tours, flights, hotel bookings and other services.

Last Frontiers
Swan House, High Street, Long Crendon, Buckinghamshire, HP18 9AF, T 01844 208405, e-mail: travelinfo@lastfrontiers.co.uk, web: http://www.lastfrontiers.co.uk.

Passage to South America
Fovant Mews, 12 Noyna Road, London, SW17 7PH, T 0181 767 8989.

STA Travel
Priory House, 6 Wrights Lane, London, W8 6TA, T 0171-361 6166.

Encounter Overland
267 Old Brompton Road, London, SW5 9JA, T 0171 370 6845.

Hayes & Jarvis
152 King Street, London, W6 0QU, T 0181 222 7844.

Cox & Kings Travel
St James Court, 45 Buckingham Gate, London, T 0171-873 5001.

Ladatco Tours
2220 Coral Way, Miami, Florida 33145, USA, T USA (305) 854-8422, F (USA) (305) 285-0504, e-mail: tailor@ladatco.com, website: www.ladatco.com.

Austral Tours
20 Upper Tachbrook Street, London SW1, T 0171-233 5384, F 0171-233 5385, e-mail: 100532.255@compuserve.com.

Useful words and phrases

NO AMOUNT of dictionaries, phrase books or word lists will provide the same enjoyment as being able to communicate directly with the people of the country you are visiting. Learning Spanish is an important part of the preparation for any trip to Argentina and you are encouraged to make an effort to grasp the basics before you go. As you travel you will pick up more of the language and the more you know, the more you will benefit from your stay. The following section is designed to be a simple point of departure.

General pronunciation

The stress in a Spanish word conforms to one of three rules: 1) if the word ends in a vowel, or in **n** or **s**, the accent falls on the penultimate syllable (*ventana, ventanas*); 2) if the word ends in a consonant other than **n** or **s**, the accent falls on the last syllable (*hablar*); 3) if the word is to be stressed on a syllable contrary to either of the above rules, the acute accent on the relevant vowel indicates where the stress is to be placed (*pantalón, metáfora*). Note that adverbs such as *cuando*, 'when', take an accent when used interrogatively: *¿cuándo?*, 'when?'

Vowels

a not quite as short as in English 'cat'

e as in English 'pay', but shorter in a syllable ending in a consonant

i as in English 'seek'

o as in English 'shop', but more like 'pope' when the vowel ends a syllable

u as in English 'food'; after 'q' and in 'gue', 'gui', **u** is unpronounced; in 'güe' and 'güi' it is pronounced

y when a vowel, pronounced like 'i'; when a semiconsonant or consonant, it is pronounced like English 'yes'

ai, ay as in English 'ride'

ei, ey as in English 'they'

oi, oy as in English 'toy'

Unless listed below **consonants** can be pronounced in Spanish as they are in English.

b, v their sound is interchangeable and is a cross between the English 'b' and 'v', except at the beginning of a word or after 'm' or 'n' when it is like English 'b'

c like English 'k', except before 'e' or 'i' when it is as the 's' in English 'sip'

g before 'e' and 'i' it is the same as **j**

h when on its own, never pronounced

j as the 'ch' in the Scottish 'loch'

ll as the 'g' in English 'beige'; sometimes as the 'lli' in 'million'

ñ as the 'ni' in English 'onion'

rr trilled much more strongly than in English

x depending on its location, pronounced as in English 'fox', or 'sip', or like 'gs'

z as the 's' in English 'sip'

GREETINGS, COURTESIES

hello
hola

good morning
buenos días

good afternoon/evening/night
buenas tardes/noches

goodbye
adiós/chao

see you later
hasta luego

how are you?
¿cómo está?/¿cómo estás?

pleased to meet you
mucho gusto/encantado/encantada

please
por favor

thank you (very much)
(muchas) gracias

yes
sí

no
no

excuse me/I beg your pardon
con permiso

I do not understand
no entiendo

please speak slowly
hable despacio por favor

what is your name
¿cómo se llama?

Go away!
¡Váyase!

BASIC QUESTIONS

where is_?
¿dónde está_?

how much does it cost?
¿cuánto cuesta?

how much is it?
¿cuánto es?

when?
¿cuándo?

when does the bus leave?
¿a qué hora sale el autobus?
– arrive?
– llega –

why?
¿por qué?

what for?
¿para qué?

what time is it?
¿qué hora es?

how do I get to_?
¿cómo llegar a_?

is this the way to the church?
¿la iglesia está por aquí?

BASICS

bathroom/toilet
el baño

police (policeman)
la policía (el policía)

hotel
el hotel (la pensión,el residencial, el alojamiento)

restaurant
el restaurante

post office
el correo

telephone office
el centro de llamadas

supermarket
el supermercado

bank
el banco

exchange house
la casa de cambio

exchange rate
la tasa de cambio

notes/coins
los billetes/las monedas

travellers' cheques
los travelers/los cheques de viajero

cash
el efectivo

breakfast
el desayuno

lunch
el almuerzo

dinner/supper
la cena

meal
la comida

drink
la bebida

mineral water
el agua mineral

soft fizzy drink
la gaseosa/cola
beer
la cerveza
without sugar
sin azúcar
without meat
sin carne

GETTING AROUND

on the left/right
a la izquierda/derecha
straight on
derecho
second street on the left
la segunda calle a la izquierda
to walk
caminar
bus station
la terminal (terrestre)
train station
la estación (de tren/ferrocarril)
bus
el bus/el autobus/la flota/el colectivo/
el micro etc
train
el tren
airport
el aeropuerto
aeroplane/airplane
el avión
first/second class
primera/segunda clase
ticket
el boleto
ticket office
la taquilla
bus stop
la parada

ACCOMMODATION

room
el cuarto/la habitación
single/double
sencillo/doble
with two beds
con dos camas
with double bed
con cama matrimonial
with private bathroom
con baño

hot/cold water
agua caliente/fría
noisy
ruidoso
to make up/clean
limpiar
sheets
las sábanas
blankets
las mantas
pillows
las almohadas
clean/dirty towels
toallas limpias/sucias
toilet paper
el papel higiénico

HEALTH

Chemist
farmacia
(for) pain
(para) dolor
stomach
el estómago
head
la cabeza
fever/sweat
la fiebre/el sudor
diarrhoea
la diarrea
blood
la sangre
altitude sickness
el soroche
doctor
el médico
condoms
los preservativos
contraceptive (pill)
anticonceptivo (la píldora anticonceptiva)
period/towels
la regla/las toallas
contact lenses
las lentes de contacto
aspirin
la aspirina

TIME

at one o'clock
a la una
at half past two/ two thirty
a las dos y media

at a quarter to three
  a cuarto para las tres/
  a las tres menos quince
it's one o'clock
  es la una
it's seven o'clock
  son las siete
it's twenty past six/
six twenty
  son las seis y veinte
it's five to nine
  son cinco para las nueve/
  son las nueve menos cinco
in ten minutes
  en diez minutos
five hours
  cinco horas
does it take long?
  ¿tarda mucho?
Monday lunes
Tuesday martes
Wednesday miercoles
Thursday jueves
Friday viernes
Saturday sábado
Sunday domingo
January enero
February febrero
March marzo
April abril
May mayo
June junio
July julio
August agosto
September septiembre
October octubre
November noviembre
December diciembre

NUMBERS

one uno/una
two dos
three tres
four cuatro
five cinco
six seis
seven siete
eight ocho
nine nueve
ten diez
eleven once
twelve doce

thirteen trece
fourteen catorce
fifteen quince
sixteen dieciseis
seventeen diecisiete
eighteen dieciocho
nineteen diecinueve
twenty veinte
twenty one, two veintiuno, veintidos
etc
thirty treinta
forty cuarenta
fifty cincuenta
sixty sesenta
seventy setenta
eighty ochenta
ninety noventa
hundred cien or ciento
thousand mil

KEY VERBS

To Go
  ir

I go '*voy*'; you go (familiar singular) '*vas*';
he, she, it goes, you (unfamiliar singular)
go '*va*'; we go '*vamos*'; they, you (plural) go
'*van*'.

To Have (possess)
  tener

tengo; tienes; tiene; tenemos; tienen (also
used as To Be, as in 'I am hungry' '*tengo
hambre*')
(**NB** haber also means to have, but is used
with other verbs, as in 'he has gone' '*ha ido*'.
he; has; ha; hemos; han.
'*Hay*' means 'there is'; perhaps more common is '*No hay*' meaning 'there isn't any')

To Be (in a permanent state)
  ser

soy (profesor – I am a teacher); eres; es;
somos; son

To Be (positional or temporary state)
  estar

estoy (en Londres – I am in London); estás;
está (contenta – she is happy); estamos;
están.

*This section has been compiled on the basis of
glossaries compiled by André de Mendonça
and David Gilmour of South American Experience, London, and the Latin American
Travel Advisor, Number 9, March 1996.*

Health in Latin America

WITH the following advice and precautions you should keep as healthy as you do at home. Most visitors return home having experienced no problems at all apart from some travellers' diarrhoea. In Latin America the health risks, especially in the lowland tropical areas, are different from those encountered in Europe or the USA. It also depends on where and how you travel. There are clear health differences between the countries of Latin America and in risks for the business traveller, who stays in international class hotels in large cities, the backpacker trekking from country to country and the tourist who heads for the beach. There is huge variation in climate, vegetation and wildlife from the deserts of Chile to the rain forests of Amazonia and from the icy remoteness of Andean peaks, to the teeming capital cities. There are no hard and fast rules to follow; you will often have to make your own judgment on the healthiness or otherwise of your surroundings. There are English (or other foreign language) speaking doctors in most major cities who have particular experience in dealing with locally-occurring diseases. Your Embassy representative will often be able to give you the name of local reputable doctors and most of the better hotels have a doctor on standby. If you do fall ill and cannot find a recommended doctor, try the Outpatient Department of a hospital – private hospitals are usually less crowded and offer a more acceptable standard of care to foreigners.

BEFORE TRAVELLING

Take out medical insurance. Make sure it covers all eventualities especially evacuation to your home country by a medically equipped plane, if necessary. You should have a dental check up, obtain a spare glasses prescription, a spare oral contraceptive prescription (or enough pills to last) and, if you suffer from a chronic illness (such as diabetes, high blood pressure, ear or sinus troubles, cardio-pulmonary disease or nervous disorder) arrange for a check up with your doctor, who can at the same time provide you with a letter explaining the details of your disability in English and if possible Spanish and/or Portuguese. Check the current practice in countries you are visiting for malaria prophylaxis (prevention). If you are on regular medication, make sure you have enough to cover the period of your travel.

Children

More preparation is probably necessary for babies and children than for an adult and perhaps a little more care should be taken when travelling to remote areas where health services are primitive. This is because children can be become more rapidly ill than adults (on the other hand they often recover more quickly). Diarrhoea and vomiting are the most common problems, so take the usual precautions, but more intensively. Breastfeeding is best and most convenient for babies, but powdered milk is generally available and so are baby foods in most countries. Papaya, bananas and avocados are all nutritious and can be cleanly prepared. The treatment of diarrhoea is the same for adults, except that it should start earlier and be continued with more persistence. Children get dehydrated very quickly in hot countries and can become drowsy and uncooperative unless cajoled to drink water or juice plus salts. Upper respiratory infections, such as colds, catarrh and middle ear infections are also common and if your child suffers from these normally take some antibiotics against the possibility. Outer ear infections after swimming are also common and antibiotic eardrops will help. Wet wipes are always useful and sometimes difficult to find in South America, as, in some places are disposable nappies.

MEDICINES AND WHAT TO TAKE

There is very little control on the sale of drugs and medicines in South America. You can buy any and every drug in pharmacies without a prescription. Be wary of this because pharmacists can be poorly trained and might sell you drugs that are unsuitable, dangerous or old. Many drugs and medicines are manufactured under licence from American or European companies, so the trade names may be familiar to you. This means you do not have to carry a whole chest of medicines with you, but remember that the shelf life of some items, especially vaccines and antibiotics, is markedly reduced in hot conditions. Buy your supplies at the better outlets where there are refrigerators, even though they are more expensive and check the expiry date of all preparations you buy. Immigration officials occasionally confiscate scheduled drugs (Lomotil is an example) if they are not accompanied by a doctor's prescription.

Self-medication may be forced on you by circumstances so the following text contains the names of drugs and medicines which you may find useful in an emergency or in out-of-the-way places. You may like to take some of the following items with you from home:

Sunglasses
ones designed for intense sunlight

Earplugs
for sleeping on aeroplanes and in noisy hotels

Suntan cream
with a high protection factor

Insect repellent
containing DET for preference

Mosquito net
lightweight, permethrin-impregnated for choice

Tablets
for travel sickness

Tampons

can be expensive in some countries in Latin America

Condoms

Contraceptives

Water sterilising tablets

Antimalarial tablets

Anti-infective ointment eg Cetrimide

Dusting powder
for feet etc containing fungicide

Antacid tablets
for indigestion

Sachets of rehydration salts
plus anti-diarrhoea preparations

Painkillers
such as Paracetamol or Aspirin

Antibiotics
for diarrhoea etc

First Aid kit
Small pack containing a few sterile syringes and needles and disposable gloves. The risk of catching hepatitis etc from a dirty needle used for injection is now negligible in Latin America, but some may be reassured by carrying their own supplies – available from camping shops and airport shops.

Vaccination and immunisations

Smallpox vaccination is no longer required anywhere in the world. Neither is cholera vaccination recognized as necessary for international travel by the World Health Organisation – it is not very effective either. Nevertheless, some immigration officials are demanding proof of vaccination against cholera in Latin America and in some countries outside Latin America, following the outbreak of the disease which originated in Peru in 1990-91 and subsequently affected most surrounding countries. Although very unlikely to affect visitors to Latin America, the cholera epidemic continues making its greatest impact in poor areas where water supplies are polluted and food hygiene practices are insanitary.

Vaccination against the following diseases are recommended:

Yellow Fever This is a live vaccination not to be given to children under 9 months of age or persons allergic to eggs. Immunity lasts for 10 years, an International Certificate of Yellow Fever Vaccination will be given and should be kept because it is sometimes asked for. Yellow fever is very rare in Latin America, but the vaccination is practically without side effects and almost totally protective.

Typhoid A disease spread by the insanitary preparation of food. A number of new vaccines against this condition are now available; the older TAB and monovalent typhoid vaccines are being phased out. The newer, eg Typhim Vi, cause less side effects, but are more expensive. For those who do not like injections, there are now oral vaccines.

Poliomyelitis Despite its decline in the world this remains a serious disease if caught and is easy to protect against. There are live oral vaccines and in some countries injected vaccines. Whichever one you choose it is a good idea to have booster every 3-5 years if visiting developing countries regularly.

Tetanus One dose should be given with a booster at 6 weeks and another at 6 months and ten yearly boosters thereafter are recommended. Children should already be properly protected against diphtheria, poliomyelitis and pertussis (whooping cough), measles and HIB all of which can be more serious infections in Latin America than at home. Measles, mumps and rubella vaccine is also given to children throughout the world, but those teenage girls who have not had rubella (german measles) should be tested and vaccinated. Hepatitis B vaccination for babies is now routine in some countries. Consult your doctor for advice on tuberculosis inoculation: the disease is still widespread in Latin America.

Infectious Hepatitis Is less of a problem for travellers than it used to be because of the development of two extremely effective vaccines against the A and B form of the disease. It remains common, however, in Latin America. A combined hepatitis A & B vaccine is now licensed and will be available in 1997 – one jab covers both diseases.

Other vaccinations:

Might be considered in the case of epidemics eg meningitis. There is an effective vaccination against rabies which should be considered by all travellers, especially those going through remote areas or if there is a particular occupational risk, eg for zoologists or veterinarians.

FURTHER INFORMATION

Further information on health risks abroad, vaccinations etc may be available from a local travel clinic. If you wish to take specific drugs with you such as antibiotics these are best prescribed by your own doctor. Beware, however, that not all doctors can be experts on the health problems of remote countries. More detailed or more up-to-date information than local doctors can provide are available from various sources. In the UK there are hospital departments specialising in tropical diseases in London, Liverpool, Birmingham and Glasgow and the Malaria Reference Laboratory at the London School of Hygiene and Tropical Medicine provides free advice about malaria, T 0891 600350. In the USA the local Public Health Services can give such information and information is available centrally from the Centre for Disease Control (CDC) in Atlanta, T (404) 3324559.

There are additional computerized databases which can be accessed for destination-specific up-to-the-minute information. In the UK there is MASTA (Medical Advisory Service to Travellers Abroad), T 0171 631 4408, F 0171 436 5389, Tx 8953473 and Travax (Glasgow, T 0141 946 7120, ext 247). Other information on medical problems overseas can be obtained from the book by Dawood, Richard (Editor) (1992) *Travellers' Health: How to stay healthy abroad*, Oxford University Press 1992, £7.99. We strongly recommend this revised and updated edition, especially to the intrepid traveller heading for the more out of the way places. General advice is also available in the UK in *Health Information for Overseas Travel* published by the Department of Health and available from HMSO, and *International Travel and Health* published by WHO, Geneva.

STAYING HEALTHY

INTESTINAL UPSETS

The thought of catching a stomach bug worries visitors to Latin America but there have been great improvements in food hygiene and most such infections are preventable. Travellers' diarrhoea and vomiting is due, most of the time, to food poisoning, usually passed on by the insanitary habits of food handlers. As a general rule the cleaner your surroundings and the smarter the restaurant, the less likely you are to suffer.

Foods to avoid: uncooked, undercooked, partially cooked or reheated meat, fish, eggs, raw vegetables and salads, especially when they have been left out exposed to flies. Stick to fresh food that has been cooked from raw just before eating and make sure you peel fruit yourself. Wash and dry your hands before eating – disposable wet-wipe tissues are useful for this.

Shellfish eaten raw are risky and at certain times of the year some fish and shellfish concentrate toxins from their environment and cause various kinds of food poisoning. The local authorities notify the public not to eat these foods. Do not ignore the warning. Heat treated milk (UHT) pasteurized or sterilized is becoming more available in Latin America as is pasteurized cheese. On the whole matured or processed cheeses are safer than the fresh varieties and fresh unpasteurized milk from whatever animal can be a source of food poisoning germs, tuberculosis and brucellosis. This applies equally to icecream, yoghurt and cheese made from unpasteurized milk, so avoid these homemade products – the factory made ones are probably safer.

Tap water is rarely safe outside the major cities, especially in the rainy season. Stream water, if you are in the countryside, is often contaminated by communities living surprisingly high in the mountains. Filtered or bottled water is usually available and safe, although you must make sure that somebody is not filling bottles from the tap and hammering on a new crown cap. If your hotel has a central hot water supply this water is safe to drink after cooling. Ice for drinks should be made from boiled water, but rarely is so stand your glass on the ice cubes, rather than putting them in the drink. The better hotels have water purifying systems.

TRAVELLERS' DIARRHOEA

This is usually caused by eating food which has been contaminated by food poisoning germs. Drinking water is rarely the culprit. Sea water or river water is more likely to be contaminated by sewage and so swimming in such dilute effluent can also be a cause.

Infection with various organisms can give rise to travellers' diarrhoea. They may be viruses, bacteria, eg Escherichia coli (probably the most common cause worldwide), protozoal (such as amoebas and giardia), salmonella and cholera. The diarrhoea may come on suddenly or rather slowly. It may or may not be accompanied by vomiting or by severe abdominal pain and the passage of blood or mucus when it is called dysentery.

How do you know which type you have caught and how to treat it?

If you can time the onset of the diarrhoea to the minute ('acute') then it is probably due to a virus or a bacterium and/or the onset of dysentery. The treatment in addition to rehydration is Ciprofloxacin 500 mg every 12 hours; the drug is now widely available and there are many similar ones.

If the diarrhoea comes on slowly or intermittently ('sub-acute') then it is more likely to be protozoal, ie caused by an amoeba or giardia. Antibiotics such a Ciprofloxacin will have little effect. These cases are best treated by a doctor as is any outbreak of diarrhoea continuing for more than 3 days. Sometimes blood is passed in ameobic dysentery and for this you should certainly seek medical help. If this is not available then the best treatment is probably Tinidazole

(Fasigyn) one tablet four times a day for 3 days. If there are severe stomach cramps, the following drugs may help but are not very useful in the management of acute diarrhoea: Loperamide (Imodium) and Diphenoxylate with Atropine (Lomotil). They should not be given to children.

Any kind of diarrhoea, whether or not accompanied by vomiting, responds well to the replacement of water and salts, taken as frequent small sips, of some kind of rehydration solution. There are proprietary preparations consisting of sachets of powder which you dissolve in boiled water or you can make your own by adding half a teaspoonful of salt (3.5 gms) and four tablespoonsful of sugar (40 gms) to a litre of boiled water.

Thus the linchpins of treatment for diarrhoea are rest, fluid and salt replacement, antibiotics such as Ciprofloxacin for the bacterial types and special diagnostic tests and medical treatment for the amoeba and giardia infections. Salmonella infections and cholera, although rare, can be devastating diseases and it would be wise to get to a hospital as soon as possible if these were suspected.

Fasting, peculiar diets and the consumption of large quantities of yoghurt have not been found useful in calming travellers' diarrhoea or in rehabilitating inflamed bowels. Oral rehydration has on the other hand, especially in children, been a life saving technique and should always be practised, whatever other treatment you use. As there is some evidence that alcohol and milk might prolong diarrhoea they should be avoided during and immediately after an attack.

Diarrhoea occurring day after day for long periods of time (chronic diarrhoea) is notoriously resistent to amateur attempts at treatment and again warrants proper diagnostic tests (most towns with reasonable sized hospitals have laboratories for stool samples). There are ways of preventing travellers' diarrhoea for short periods of time by taking antibiotics, but this is not a foolproof technique and should not be used other than in exceptional circumstances. Doxycycline is possibly the best drug. Some preventatives such as Enterovioform can have serious side effects if taken for long periods.

Paradoxically constipation is also common, probably induced by dietary change, inadequate fluid intake in hot places and long bus journeys. Simple laxatives are useful in the short-term and bulky foods such as maize, beans and plenty of fruit are also useful.

HIGH ALTITUDE

Spending time at high altitude in South America, especially in the tropics, is usually a pleasure – it is not so hot, there are no insects and the air is clear and spring like. Travelling to high altitudes, however, can cause medical problems, all of which can be prevented if care is taken.

On reaching heights above about 3,000m, heart pounding and shortness of breath, especially on exertion are a normal response to the lack of oxygen in the air. A condition called acute mountain sickness (Soroche in South America) can also affect visitors. It is more likely to affect those who ascend rapidly, eg by plane and those who over-exert themselves (teenagers for example). Soroche takes a few hours or days to come on and presents with a bad headache, extreme tiredness, sometimes dizziness, loss of appetite and frequently nausea and vomiting. Insomnia is common and is often associated with a suffocating feeling when lying in bed. Keen observers may note their breathing tends to wax and wane at night and their face tends to be puffy in the mornings – this is all part of the syndrome. Anyone can get this condition and past experience is not always a good guide: the author, having spent years in Peru travelling constantly between sea level and very high altitude never suffered symptoms, then was severely affected whilst climbing Kilimanjaro in Tanzania.

The treatment of acute mountain sickness is simple – rest, painkillers (preferably not aspirin based) for the headache and anti-sickness pills for vomiting. Oxygen is actually not much help, except at very high altitude. Various local panaceas – Coramina glucosada, Effortil, Micoren are popular in Latin America and mate de coca (an infusion of coca leaves widely available and perfectly legal) will alleviate some of the symptoms.

To prevent the condition: on arrival at places over 3,000m have a few hours rest in a chair and avoid alcohol, cigarettes and heavy food. If the symptoms are severe and prolonged, it is best to descend to a lower altitude and to reascend slowly or in stages. If this is impossible because of shortage of time or if you are going so high that acute mountain sickness is very likely, then the drug Acetazolamide (Diamox) can be used as a preventative and continued during the ascent. There is good evidence of the value of this drug in the prevention of soroche, but some people do experience peculiar side effects. The usual dose is 500 mg of the slow release preparation each night, starting the night before ascending above 3,000m.

Watch out for **sunburn** at high altitude. The ultraviolet rays are extremely powerful. The air is also excessively dry at high altitude and you might find that your skin dries out and the inside of your nose becomes crusted. Use a moisturiser for the skin and some vaseline wiped into the nostrils. Some people find contact lenses irritate because of the dry air. It is unwise to ascend to high altitude if you are pregnant, especially in the first 3 months, or if you have a history of heart, lung or blood disease, including sickle cell.

A more unusual condition can affect mountaineers who ascend rapidly to high altitude – acute pulmonary oedema. Residents at altitude sometimes experience this when returning to the mountains from time spent at the coast. This condition is often preceded by acute mountain sickness and comes on quite rapidly with severe breathlessness, noisy breathing, cough, blueness of the lips and frothing at the mouth. Anybody who develops this must be brought down as soon as possible, given oxygen and taken to hospital.

A rapid descent from high places will make sinus problems and middle ear

Water purification

There are a number of ways of purifying water in order to make it safe to drink. Dirty water should first be strained through a filter bag (camping shops) and then boiled or treated. Bringing water to a rolling boil at sea level is sufficient to make the water safe for drinking, but at higher altitudes you have to boil the water for longer to ensure that all the microbes are killed.

There are sterilising methods that can be used and there are proprietary preparations containing chlorine (eg Puritabs) or iodine (eg Pota Aqua) compounds. Chlorine compounds generally do not kill protozoa (eg giardia).

There are a number of water filters now on the market available in personal and expedition size. They work either on mechanical or chemical principles, or may do both. Make sure you take the spare parts or spare chemicals with you and do not believe *everything* the manufacturers say.

infections worse and might make your teeth ache. Lastly, don't fly to altitude within 24 hours of Scuba diving. You might suffer from 'the bends'.

HEAT AND COLD

Full acclimatization to high temperatures takes about 2 weeks. During this period it is normal to feel a bit apathetic, especially if the relative humidity is high. Drink plenty of water (up to 15 litres a day are required when working physically hard in the tropics), use salt on your food and avoid extreme exertion. Tepid showers are more cooling than hot or cold ones. Large hats do not cool you down, but do prevent sunburn. Remember that, especially in the highlands, there can be a large and sudden drop in temperature between sun and shade and between night and day, so dress accordingly. Warm jackets or woollens are essential after dark at high altitude. Loose cotton is still the best material when the weather is hot.

INSECTS

These are mostly more of a nuisance than a serious hazard and if you try, you can prevent yourself entirely from being bitten. Some, such as mosquitos are, of course, carriers of potentially serious diseases, so it is sensible to avoid being bitten as much as possible. Sleep off the ground and use a mosquito net or some kind of insecticide. Preparations containing Pyrethrum or synthetic pyrethroids are safe. They are available as aerosols or pumps

and the best way to use these is to spray the room thoroughly in all areas (follow the instructions rather than the insects) and then shut the door for a while, re-entering when the smell has dispersed. Mosquito coils release insecticide as they burn slowly. They are widely available and useful out of doors. Tablets of insecticide which are placed on a heated mat plugged into a wall socket are probably the most effective. They fill the room with insecticidal fumes in the same way as aerosols or coils.

You can also use insect repellents, most of which are effective against a wide range of pests. The most common and effective is diethyl metatoluamide (DET). DET liquid is best for arms and face (care around eyes and with spectacles – DET dissolves plastic). Aerosol spray is good for clothes and ankles and liquid DET can be dissolved in water and used to impregnate cotton clothes and mosquito nets. Some repellents now contain DET and Permethrin, insecticide. Impregnated wrist and ankle bands can also be useful.

If you are bitten or stung, itching may be relieved by cool baths, antihistamine tablets (care with alcohol or driving) or mild corticosteroid creams, eg hydrocortisone (great care: never use if any hint of infection). Careful scratching of all your bites once a day can be surprisingly effective. Calamine lotion and cream have limited effectiveness and antihistamine creams are not recommended – they can cause allergies themselves.

Bites which become infected should be treated with a local antiseptic or antibiotic cream such as Cetrimide, as should any infected sores or scratches.

When living rough, skin infestations with body lice (crabs) and scabies are easy to pick up. Use whatever local commercial preparation is recommended for lice and scabies.

Crotamiton cream (Eurax) alleviates itching and also kills a number of skin parasites. Malathion lotion 5% (Prioderm) kills lice effectively, but avoid the use of the toxic agricultural preparation of Malathion, more often used to commit suicide.

TICKS

They attach themselves usually to the lower parts of the body often after walking in areas where cattle have grazed. They take a while to attach themselves strongly, but swell up as they start to suck blood. The important thing is to remove them gently, so that they do not leave their head parts in your skin because this can cause a nasty allergic reaction some days later. Do not use petrol, vaseline, lighted cigarettes etc to remove the tick, but, with a pair of tweezers remove the beast gently by gripping it at the attached (head) end and rock it out in very much the same way that a tooth is extracted. Certain tropical flies which lay their eggs under the skin of sheep and cattle also occasionally do the same thing to humans with the unpleasant result that a maggot grows under the skin and pops up as a boil or pimple. The best way to remove these is to cover the boil with oil, vaseline or nail varnish so as to stop the maggot breathing, then to squeeze it out gently the next day.

SUNBURN

The burning power of the tropical sun, especially at high altitude, is phenomenal.

Always wear a wide brimmed hat and use some form of suncream lotion on untanned skin. Normal temperate zone suntan lotions (protection factor up to seven) are not much good; you need to use the types designed specifically for the tropics or for mountaineers or skiers with protection factors up to fifteen or above. These are often not available in Latin America. Glare from the sun can cause conjunctivitis, so wear sunglasses especially on tropical beaches, where high protection factor sunscreen should also be used.

PRICKLY HEAT

A very common intensely itchy rash is avoided by frequent washing and by wearing loose clothing. Cured by allowing skin to dry off through use of powder and spending two nights in an airconditioned hotel!

ATHLETES FOOT

This and other fungal skin infections are best treated with Tolnaftate or Clotrimazole.

OTHER RISKS AND MORE SERIOUS DISEASES

Remember that rabies is endemic throughout Latin America, so avoid dogs that are behaving strangely and cover your toes at night from the vampire bats, which also carry the disease. If you are bitten by a domestic or wild animal, do not leave things to chance: scrub the wound with soap and water and/or disinfectant, try to have the animal captured (within limits) or at least determine its ownership, where possible, and seek medical assistance at once. The course of treatment depends on whether you have already been satisfactorily vaccinated against rabies. If you have (this is worthwile if you are spending lengths of time in developing countries) then some further doses of vaccine are all that is required. Human diploid vaccine is the best, but expensive: other, older kinds of vaccine, such as that derived from duck embryos may be the only types available. These are effective, much cheaper and interchangeable generally with the human derived types. If not already vaccinated then anti rabies serum (immunoglobulin) may be required in addition. It is important to finish the course of treatment whether the animal survives or not.

AIDS

In South America AIDS is increasing but is not wholly confined to the well known high risk sections of the population, ie homosexual men, intravenous drug abusers and children of infected mothers. Heterosexual transmission is now the dominant mode and so the main risk to travellers is from casual sex. The same precautions should be taken as with any sexually transmitted disease. The Aids virus (HIV) can be passed by unsterilized needles which have been previously used to inject an HIV positive patient, but the risk of this is negligible. It would, however, be sensible to check that needles have been properly sterilized or disposable needles have been used. If you wish to take your own disposable needles, be prepared to explain what they are for. The risk of receiving a blood transfusion with blood infected with the HIV virus is greater than from dirty needles because of the amount of fluid exchanged. Supplies of blood for transfusion should now be screened for HIV in all reputable hospitals, so again the risk is very small indeed. Catching the AIDS virus does not always produce an illness in itself (although it may do). The only way to be sure if you feel you have been put at risk is to have a blood test for HIV antibodies on your return to a place where there are reliable laboratory facilities. The test does not become positive for some weeks.

MALARIA

In South America malaria is theoretically confined to coastal and jungle zones, but is now on the increase again. Mosquitos do not thrive above 2,500m, so you are safe at altitude. There are different varieties of malaria, some resistant to the normal drugs. Make local enquiries if you intend to visit possibly infected zones and use a prophylactic regime. Start taking the tablets a few days before exposure and continue to take them for 6 weeks after leaving the malarial zone. Remember to give the drugs to babies and children also. Opinion varies on the precise drugs and dosage to be used for protection. All the drugs may have some side effects and it is important to balance the risk of catching the disease against the albeit rare side effects. The increasing complexity of the subject is such that as the malarial parasite becomes immune to the new generation of drugs it has made concentration on the physical prevention from being bitten by mosquitos more important. This involves the use of long sleeved shirts or blouses and long trousers, repellents and nets. Clothes are now available impregnated with the insecticide Permethrin or Deltamethrin or it is possible to impregnate the clothes yourself. Wide meshed nets impregnated with Permethrin are also available, are lighter to carry and less claustrophobic to sleep in.

Prophylaxis and treatment

If your itinerary takes you into a malarial area, seek expert advice before you go on a suitable prophylactic regime. This is especially true for pregnant women who are particularly prone to catch malaria. You can still catch the disease even when sticking to a proper regime, although it is unlikely. If you do develop symptoms (high fever, shivering, headache, sometimes diarrhoea), seek medical advice immediately. If this is not possible and there is a great likelihood of malaria, the treatment is:

Chloroquine, a single dose of four tablets (600 mg) followed by two tablets (300 mg) in 6 hours and 300 mg each day following.

Falciparum type of malaria or type in doubt: take local advice. Various combinations of drugs are being used such as Quinine, Tetracycline or Halofantrine. If falciparum type malaria is definitely diagnosed, it is wise to get to a good hospital as treatment can be complex and the illness very serious.

INFECTIOUS HEPATITIS (JAUNDICE)

The main symptoms are pains in the stomach, lack of appetite, lassitude and yellowness of the eyes and skin. Medically speaking there are two main types. The less serious, but more common is Hepatitis A for which the best protection is the careful preparation of food, the avoidance of contaminated drinking water and scrupulous attention to toilet hygiene. The other, more serious, version is Hepatitis B which is acquired usually as a sexually transmitted disease or by blood transfusions. It can less commonly be transmitted by injections with unclean needles and possibly by insect bites. The symptoms are the same as for Hepatitis A. The incubation period is much longer (up to 6 months compared with 6 weeks) and there are more likely to be complications.

Hepatitis A can be protected against with gamma globulin. It should be obtained from a reputable source and is certainly useful for travellers who intend to live rough. You should have a shot before leaving and have it repeated every 6 months. The dose of gamma globulin depends on the concentration of the particular preparation used, so the manufacturer's advice should be taken. The injection should be given as close as possible to your departure and as the dose depends on the likely time you are to spend in potentially affected areas, the manufacturer's instructions should be followed. Gamma globulin has really been superseded now by a proper vaccination against Hepatitis A (Havrix) which gives immunity lasting up to 10 years. After that boosters are required. Havrix monodose is now widely available as is Junior Havrix. The vaccination has negligible side effects and is extremely effective. Gamma globulin injections can be a bit painful, but it is much cheaper than Havrix and may be more available in some places.

Hepatitis B can be effectively prevented by a specific vaccine (Engerix) – three shots over 6 months before travelling. If you have had jaundice in the past it would be worthwhile having a blood test to see if you are immune to either of these two types, because this might avoid the necessity and costs of vaccination or gamma globulin. There are other kinds of viral hepatitis (C, E etc) which are fairly similar to A and B, but vaccines are not available as yet.

TYPHUS

Can still occur carried by ticks. There is usually a reaction at the site of the bite and a fever. Seek medical advice.

INTESTINAL WORMS

These are common and the more serious ones such as hookworm can be contracted from walking barefoot on infested earth or beaches.

Various other tropical diseases can be caught in jungle areas, usually transmitted by biting insects. They are often related to African diseases and were probably introduced by the slave labour trade. Onchocerciasis (river blindness) carried by black flies is found in parts of Mexico and Venezuela. Leishmaniasis (Espundia) is carried by sandflies and causes a sore that will not heal or a severe nasal infection. Wearing long trousers and a long sleeved shirt in infected areas protects against these flies. DET is also effective. Epidemics of meningitis occur from time-to-time. Be careful about swimming in piranha or caribe infested rivers. It is a good idea not to swim naked: the Candiru fish can follow urine currents and become lodged in body orifices. Swimwear offers some protection.

LEPTOSPIROSIS

Various forms of leptospirosis occur throughout Latin America, transmitted by a bacterium which is excreted in rodent urine. Fresh water and moist soil harbour the organisms which enter the body through cuts and scratches. If you suffer from any form of prolonged fever consult a doctor.

SNAKE BITE

This is a very rare event indeed for travellers. If you are unlucky (or careless) enough to be bitten by a venomous snake, spider, scorpion or sea creature, try to identify the creature, but do not put yourself in further danger. Snake bites in particular are very frightening, but in fact rarely poisonous – even venomous snakes bite without injecting venom. What you might expect if bitten are: fright, swelling, pain and bruising around the bite and soreness of the regional lymph glands, perhaps nausea, vomiting and a fever. Signs of serious poisoning would be the following symptoms: numbness and tingling of the face, muscular spasms, convulsions, shortness of breath and bleeding. Victims should be got to a hospital or a doctor without delay. Commercial snake bite and scorpion kits are available, but usually only useful for the specific type of snake or scorpion for which they are designed. Most serum has to be given intravenously so it is not much good equipping yourself with it unless you are used to making injections into veins. It is best to rely on local practice in these cases, because the particular creatures will be known about locally and appropriate treatment can be given.

Treatment of snake bite Reassure and comfort the victim frequently. Immobilize the limb by a bandage or a splint or by getting the person to lie still. Do not slash the bite area and try to suck out the poison because this sort of heroism does more harm than good. If you know how to use a tourniquet in these circumstances, you will not need this advice. If you are not experienced do not apply a tourniquet.

Precautions

Avoid walking in snake territory in bare feet or sandals – wear proper shoes or boots. If you encounter a snake stay put until it slithers away, and do not investigate a wounded snake. Spiders and scorpions may be found in the more basic hotels, especially in the Andean countries. If stung, rest and take plenty of fluids and call a doctor. The best precaution is to keep beds away from the walls and look inside your shoes and under the toilet seat every morning. Certain tropical sea fish when trodden upon inject venom into bathers' feet. This can be exceptionally painful. Wear plastic shoes when you go bathing if such creatures are reported. The pain can be relieved by immersing the foot in extremely hot water for as long as the pain persists.

DENGUE FEVER

This is increasing worldwide including in South and Central American countries and the Caribbean. It can be completely prevented by avoiding mosquito bites in the same way as malaria. No vaccine is available. Dengue is an unpleasant and painful disease, presenting with a high temperature and body pains, but at least visitors are spared the more serious forms (haemorrhagic types) which are more of a problem for local people who have been exposed to the disease more than once. There is no specific treatment for dengue – just pain killers and rest.

CHAGAS' DISEASE (SOUTH AMERICAN TRYPANOSOMIASIS)

This is a chronic disease, almost endemic in rural parts of Argentina, and difficult to treat. It is, however, very rarely caught by travellers. It is transmitted by the simultaneous biting and excreting of the Reduvid bug, also known as the Vinchuca or Barbeiro. Somewhat resembling a small cockroach, this nocturnal bug lives in poor adobe houses with dirt floors often frequented by opossums. If you cannot avoid such accommodation, sleep off the floor with a candle lit, use a mosquito net, keep as much of your skin covered as possible, use DET repellent or a spray insecticide. If you are bitten overnight (the bites are painless) do not scratch them, but wash thoroughly with soap and water.

DANGEROUS ANIMALS

Apart from mosquitos the most dangerous animals are men, be they bandits or behind steering wheels. Think carefully about violent confrontations and wear a seat belt if you are lucky enough to have one available to you.

WHEN YOU RETURN HOME

Remember to take your antimalarial tablets for 6 weeks after leaving the malarial area. If you have had attacks of diarrhoea it is worth having a stool specimen tested in case you have picked up amoebas. If you have been living rough, blood tests may be worthwhile to detect worms and other parasites. If you have been exposed to bilharzia (schistosomiasis) by swimming in lakes etc, check by means of a blood test when you get home, but leave it for 6 weeks because the test is slow to become positive. Report any untoward symptoms to your doctor and tell the doctor exactly where you have been and, if you know, what the likelihood of disease is to which you were exposed.

The above information has been compiled for us by Dr David Snashall, who is presently Senior Lecturer in Occupational Health at the United Medical Schools of Guy's and St Thomas' Hospitals in London and Chief Medical Adviser to the British Foreign and Commonwealth Office. He has travelled extensively in Central and South America, worked in Peru and in East Africa and keeps in close touch with developments in preventative and tropical medicine.

Travelling with Children

PEOPLE CONTEMPLATING overland travel in South America with children should remember that a lot of time can be spent waiting for buses, trains, and especially for aeroplanes. On bus journeys, if the children are good at amusing themselves, or can readily sleep while travelling, the problems can be considerably lessened. If your child is of an early reading age, take reading material with you as it is difficult, and expensive to find. A bag of, say 30 pieces, of Duplo or Lego can keep young children occupied for hours. Travel on trains, while not as fast or at times as comfortable as buses, allows more scope for moving about. Some trains provide tables between seats, so that games can be played. Beware of doors left open for ventilation especially if air-conditioning is not working.

Food

Food can be a problem if the children are not adaptable. It is easier to take biscuits, drinks, bread etc with you on longer trips than to rely on meal stops where the food may not be to taste. Avocados are safe, easy to eat and nutritious; they can be fed to babies as young as 6 months and most older children like them. A small immersion heater and jug for making hot drinks is invaluable, but remember that electric current varies. Try and get a dual-voltage one (110v and 220v).

Fares

On all long-distance buses you pay for each seat, and there are no half-fares if the children occupy a seat each. For shorter trips it is cheaper, if less comfortable, to seat small children on your knee. Often there are spare seats which children can occupy after tickets have been collected. In city and local excursion buses, small children generally do not pay a fare, but are not entitled to a seat when paying customers are standing. On sightseeing tours you should *always* bargain for a family rate – often children can go free. (In trains, reductions for children are general, but not universal.)

All civil airlines charge half for children under 12, but some military services don't have half-fares, or have younger age limits. Children's fares on Lloyd Aéreo Boliviano are considerably more than half, and there is only a 7 kilos baggage allowance. (LAB also checks children's ages on passports.) Note that a child travelling free on a long excursion is not always covered by the operator's travel insurance; it is advisable to pay a small premium to arrange cover.

Hotels

In all hotels, try to negotiate family rates. If charges are per person, always insist that two children will occupy one bed only, therefore counting as one tariff. If rates are per bed, the same applies. In either case you can almost always get a reduced rate at cheaper hotels. Occasionally when travelling with a child you will be refused a room in a hotel that is "unsuitable". On river boat trips, unless you have very large hammocks, it may be more comfortable and cost effective to hire a 2-berth cabin for 2 adults and a child. (In restaurants, you can normally buy children's helpings, or divide one full-size helping between two children.)

Travel with children can bring you into closer contact with Latin American families and, generally, presents no special problems – in fact the path is often smoother for family groups. Officials tend to be more amenable where children are concerned and they are pleased if your child knows a little Spanish or Portuguese. Moreover, even thieves and pickpockets seem to have some of the traditional respect for families, and may leave you alone because of it!

Insurance tips

Insurance companies have tightened up considerably over recent years and it is now almost impossible to claim successfully if you have not followed procedures closely. The problem is that these often involve dealing with the country's red tape which can lead to some inconvenience at best and to some quite long delays at worst. There is no substitute for suitable precautions against petty crime.

The level of insurance that you carry is often dictated by the sums of medical insurance which you carry. It is inevitably the highest if you go through the USA. Also don't forget to obtain sports extensions if you are going to go diving, rafting, climbing etc. Most policies do not cover very high levels of baggage/cash. Don't forget to check whether you can claim on your household insurance. They often have worldwide all risks extensions. Most policies exclude manual work whilst away although working in bars or restaurants is usually alright.

Here are our tips: they apply to most types of policies but always check the details of your own policy before you leave.

1. Take the policy with you (a photocopy will do but make sure it is a complete one).
2. Do not travel against medical advice. It will invalidate the medical insurance part of the cover.
3. There is a 24 hour medical emergency service helpline associated with your insurance. You need to contact them if you require in-patient hospital treatment or you need to return home early. The telephone number is printed on the policy. Make sure you note the time of the call, the person you were talking to and get a reference number. Even better get a receipt from the telephone company showing the number you called. Should you need to be airlifted home, this is always arranged through the insurance company's representative and the hospital authorities. Ironically this can lead to quite intense discussions which you will not be aware of: the local hospital is often quite keen to keep you!
4. If you have to cancel your trip for whatever reason, contact your travel agent, tour operator or airline without delay.
5. If your property is damage by an airline, report it immediately and always within 3 days and get a "property irregularity report" from them.
6. Claims for baggage left unattended are very rarely settled unless they were left in a securely locked hotel room, apartment etc; locked in the boot of a car and there is evidence of a forced entry; cash is carried on your person or is in a locked safe or security box.
7. All loss must be reported to the police and/or hotel authorities within 24 hours of discovery and a written report obtained.
8. If medical attention is received for injury or sickness, a medical certificate showing its nature must be obtained, although some companies waive this if only out-patient treatment is required. Keep all receipts in a safe place as they will be needed to substantiate the claim.
9. Check your policy carefully to see if there is a date before which claims must be submitted. This is often within 30 days of returning home. It is now usual for companies to want your policy document, proof that you actually travelled (airline ticket or travel agent's confirmation of booking), receipts and written reports (in the event of loss). **NB** photocopies are not accepted.

TEMPERATURE CONVERSION TABLE

°C	°F	°C	°F
1	34	26	79
2	36	27	81
3	38	28	82
4	39	29	84
5	41	30	86
6	43	31	88
7	45	32	90
8	46	33	92
9	48	34	93
10	50	35	95
11	52	36	97
12	54	37	99
13	56	38	100
14	57	39	102
15	59	40	104
16	61	41	106
17	63	42	108
18	64	43	109
19	66	44	111
20	68	45	113
21	70	46	115
22	72	47	117
23	74	48	118
24	75	49	120
25	77	50	122

The formula for converting °C to °F is:
$$(°C \times 9 \div 5) + 32 = °F$$

and for converting to °C is:
$$(°F - 32) \times 5 \div 9 = °C$$

WEIGHTS AND MEASURES

Metric

Weight
1 Kilogram (Kg) = 2.205 pounds
1 metric ton = 1.102 short tons

Length
1 millimetre (mm)= 0.03937 inch
1 metre = 3.281 feet
1 kilometre (km) = 0.621 mile

Area
1 heactare = 2.471 acres
1 square km = 0.386 sq mile

Capacity
1 litre = 0.220 imperial gallon
       = 0.264 US gallon

Volume
1 cubic metre (m³) = 35.31 cubic feet
                  = 1.31 cubic yards

British and US

Weight
1 pound (lb) = 454 grams
1 short ton (2,000lbs) = 0.907 m ton
1 long ton (2,240lbs) = 1.016 m tons

Length
1 inch = 25.417 millimetres
1 foot (ft) = 0.305 metre
1 mile = 1.609 kilometres

Area
1 acre = 0.405 hectare
1 sq mile = 2.590 sq kilometre

Capacity
1 imperial gallon = 4.546 litres
1 US gallon = 3.785 litres

Volume
1 cubic foot (cu ft) = 0.028 m³
1 cubic yard (cu yd) = 0.765 m³

NB 5 imperial gallons are approximately equal to 6 US gallons

Tinted boxes

Illustrations

Writing to us

Many people write to us - with corrections, new information, or simply comments. If you want to let us know something, we would be delighted to hear from you. Please give us as precise information as possible, quoting the edition and page number of the Handbook you are using and send as early in the year as you can. Your help will be greatly appreciated, especially by other travellers. In return we will send you details about our special guidebook offer.

For hotels and restaurants, please let us know:

- each establishment's name, address, phone and fax number
- number of rooms, whether a/c or air-cooled, attached (clean?) bathroom
- location - how far from the station or bus stand, or distance (walking time) from a prominent landmark
- if it's not already on one of our maps, can you place it?
- your comments - either good or bad - as to why it is distinctive
- tariff cards
- local transport used

For places of interest:

- location
- entry, camera charge
- access - by whatever means of transport is most appropriate, eg time of main buses or trains to and from the site, journey time, fare
- facilities - nearby drinks stalls, restaurants, for the disabled
- any problems, eg steep climb, wildlife, unofficial guides
- opening hours
- site guides

Advertisers

Index

Maps

ROUTE MAPS

Map Symbols

Administration

International Border	
State / Province Border	
Cease Fire Line	
Neighbouring country	
Neighbouring state	
State Capitals	□
Other Towns	o

Roads and travel

Main Roads (National Highways)	
Other Roads	
Jeepable Roads, Tracks	
Railways with station	

Water features

River	Amazon
Lakes, Reservoirs, Tanks	
Seasonal Marshlands	
Sand Banks, Beaches	
Ocean	
Waterfall	
Ferry	

Topographical features

Contours (approx), Rock Outcrops	
Mountains	
Mountain Pass	
Gorge	
Escarpment	
Palm trees	

Cities and towns

Built Up Areas	
One Way Street	→
National Parks, Gardens, Stadiums	
Fortified Walls	▲ ▲ ▲
Airport	⊗
Banks	⑤
Bus Stations (named in key)	🚌 🚌1 🚌2
Hospitals	⊕
Market	Ⓜ
Police station	Pol
Post Office	⊗
Telegraphic Office	◯
Tourist Office	①
Key Numbers	1 2 3 4 5
Bridges	
Cathedral, church	†
Guided routes	....

National parks, trekking areas

National Parks and Bird Sanctuaries	♦
Hide	⇑
Camp site	Å
Refuge	⌂
Motorable track	- - - - - -
Walking track	....

Other symbols

Archaeological Sites	⚬⚬⚬
Places of Interest	o
Viewing point	✿